THE NEWS SORORITY

Also by Sheila Weller

Girls Like Us: Carole King, Joni Mitchell, Carly Simon—
and the Journey of a Generation

Dancing at Ciro's: A Family's Love, Loss,
and Scandal on the Sunset Strip

Saint of Circumstance: The Alex Kelly Rape Case:
Growing Up Rich and Out of Control

Marrying the Hangman: A True Story of Privilege,
Marriage, and Murder

Raging Heart: The Intimate Story of the
Tragic Marriage of O. J. and Nicole Simpson

Hansel & Gretel in Beverly Hills

THE
NEWS SORORITY

Diane Sawyer, Katie Couric, Christiane Amanpour—
and the (Ongoing, Imperfect, Complicated)
Triumph of Women in TV News

SHEILA WELLER

PENGUIN PRESS | *New York* | 2014

PENGUIN PRESS
Published by the Penguin Group
Penguin Group (USA) LLC
375 Hudson Street
New York, New York 10014

USA · Canada · UK · Ireland · Australia
New Zealand · India · South Africa · China

penguin.com
A Penguin Random House Company

First published by Penguin Press, a member of Penguin Group (USA) LLC, 2014

Copyright © 2014 by Sheila Weller

Photograph credits appear on page 483.

LIBRARY OF CONGRESS CATALOGING-IN-PUBLICATION DATA
Weller, Sheila.
The news sorority : Diane Sawyer, Katie Couric, Christiane Amanpour—and the
(ongoing, imperfect, complicated) triumph of women in TV news / Sheila Weller.
        p.   cm.
Includes bibliographical references and index.
ISBN 978-1-59420-427-2
1. Women television journalists—United States—Biography.   2. Women television news anchors—
United States—Biography.   3. Sawyer, Diane. Couric, Katie. Amanpour, Christiane.   I. Title.
PN4872.W42   2014
070.1'950922—dc23
[B]   2014009725

Printed in the United States of America
1   3   5   7   9   10   8   6   4   2

Designed by Marysarah Quinn

TWENTY-SECOND TEASERS
An Arc of a Story in Eight Sound Bites

"In the early 1950s, the possibility of a woman being a major TV news
reporter was never discussed because it was never a possibility. A
woman being a TV news *anchor*? Out of the question."

SANDY SOCOLOW, *Walter Cronkite's producer*

"In the late 1950s and early '60s, I refused to send women reporters to
Vietnam, even though they wanted to go. I thought I was protecting
them."

AV WESTIN, *CBS News and ABC News producer*

"Audiences are less prepared to receive news from a woman's voice."

REUVEN FRANK, *NBC News president, 1970*

"The most successful women in this business are the ones who have no
shame, who are pushy—and at the same time reserve a little
'feminine.' The guys are a lot easier to figure out—they're what they
appear, they're aggressive, they're snakes, whatever. But the women
have to be all things to all people. Trot out the sexiness when they need
it. Trot out the cattiness when they need *that*. They're much more
interesting. And you don't have this career without being a little off-
kilter. People who want to succeed in the public spotlight, night after
night—'Look at me! I'm significant! But I'm also fun and human!' If

there's a spectrum from Asperger's to normalcy, well, somewhere in the middle is network TV anchor."

NETWORK EXECUTIVE PRODUCER

"These three are formidable, *formidable* women. They take no prisoners."

CONNIE CHUNG, highly successful network news reporter
and former CBS News coanchor

"Isn't it fascinating? Everybody said women have a short shelf life, but these three are all outlasting the guys."

DON BROWNE, former executive vice president, NBC News

"Don't cry. They're fuckers. And we can have a good time. Honest!"

Note scribbled in 1973 by CBS News assistant (now longtime 60 Minutes star)
Lesley Stahl to fellow assistant (now longtime CBS executive producer)
Susan Zirinsky, during a difficult moment during Watergate. It's still in Zirinsky's wallet.

"Martha Gellhorn, [the] great, great, great war correspondent, . . . said, 'In all my reporting life I have thrown small pebbles into a very large pond, and I have no way of knowing whether any pebble caused the slightest ripple. I don't need to worry about that. My responsibility was the effort.'"

CHRISTIANE AMANPOUR

CONTENTS

PART ONE

UP-FRONTS

INTRODUCTION

The News You Give Begins with the News You've Lived

Diane, Christiane, Katie: 1969, 1997, 2000

I. Pushing Past Grief: Diane, 1969

Twenty-three-year-old Diane Sawyer (she used her real first name, Lila, ironically, only in affectionate letters) was working as the first ever full-time female news reporter in her hometown of Louisville, Kentucky—on WLKY, Channel 32—in mid-September 1969. She had been on the job for two years, and she—a Wellesley graduate and former beauty queen—was itching to leave for a bigger opportunity, in the nation's capital. Still, Diane's years at WLKY had not been uneventful.

Louisville in the late 1960s had a roiling temper. Some of its residents were hell-bent on overturning the recent federally mandated civil rights advances. When black demonstrators peacefully marched through the streets to protest the stubbornly still segregated neighborhoods, angry whites rushed them, bearing swastikas, hurling bottles. On top of that, the country had just passed through a nightmare of a year, and Diane Sawyer of WLKY had reported on all of it.

Diane and her colleague Bob Winlock—who rejected being "the black reporter" as much as she disliked being "the female reporter"—witnessed painful backlash against advances they had both been a part of. Diane was kept off the riot-scene beat by her gallant bosses—at least one front-line reporter had gotten beaten—but the city's racial anguish was on clear display everywhere, including during the emotionally fraught press conferences she covered for the station.

Violence became commonplace. Early in her tenure at WLKY, Martin Luther King Jr. had been spat upon by a little white girl who couldn't have been more than seven. During another visit, the civil rights leader's skull had barely evaded a rock hurled through his car window (he later held the rock high and pronounced it a "foundation" of his struggle there). Then, of course, came Dr. King's murder—close by, in Memphis—and that of Bobby Kennedy, in Los Angeles, during that surreally violent patch of spring to summer 1968. "Diane was disconsolate" at both assassinations, the station's general manager, Ed Shadburne, says. Still, she dutifully went out to get person-on-the-street responses. That was being a reporter: Tuck in the pain and do your job. You were a witness.

But that was the ironic thing. Diane had *already* been a witness—indeed, a participant—in some amazing ground-level integration gains almost a full decade earlier. Her junior high and high school, Seneca, had integrated startlingly early, in 1957, well before the city's neighborhoods, restaurants, restrooms, and theaters had stopped barring blacks or roping them off in dingy "Coloreds" quarters. By a fluke of the school's newness and geography, the 1957–1963 Seneca kids ("a third white, a third Jewish, a third black," the alums today like to proudly exaggerate) and their teachers were on their own, improvising a racial amity.

In 1958, when Diane was in the eighth grade (four years before James Meredith's federally assisted singular integration of the University of Mississippi), white boys in ducktails and low-slung jeans had written GO HOME, NIGGER! on the walls when the first black students bravely but nervously entered, and some of the kids were beaten. But by the time her class reached eleventh grade, in 1961, the students were protesting restaurant segregation together. When the boys' basketball team traveled to racist Kentucky towns for away games, the white players refused to go into the coffee shops that didn't allow their black teammates; they *all* ate in their bus. Now, in 1969, the still resonating killings of Martin Luther King and Bobby Kennedy seemed like a Molotov cocktail hurled against those fragile, cherished Seneca High advances.

. . .

DIANE'S FAMILY WAS her stable haven during a period of violence, regression, and sadness. Even as a working reporter four months shy of twenty-four, she was still living at home with her parents.

The elder Sawyers had come to their security and respectability the hard way. Erbon Powers Sawyer and Jean Dunagan Sawyer had grown up during the Depression in dire poverty in the Appalachian Mountains of Kentucky, just north of the Tennessee border. Diane's father was one of nine siblings. Diane's mother, whose parents had the folksy names of Foxie and Norma Belle, was one of four daughters. The Dunagan children teetered on the brink of starvation. "There were sometimes only pennies and a few potatoes in winter—there were bruises, *real* bruises in that life" of theirs, Diane has said. Erbon and Jean had limited themselves to two children. Diane's two-year-older sister, Linda, was the vivacious, prettier girl; Diane was the adoring little sister—circumspect, awkwardly tall, her poor eyesight requiring thick glasses.

The Sawyer family was comfortable but not seriously prosperous. The bar was *very* high in Louisville, a city of century-old debutante balls and Kentucky Derby Winners' Circle families of six generations of gentry who patronized the exclusive fox-hunting clubs in Lexington. Diane's father had made it up from a tiny junior college all the way through law school, and by 1969 he had long been the Jefferson County judge—Judge "Tom" Sawyer his jaunty sobriquet. Jean Sawyer—"Mrs. Sawyer" to decades of students—officiated at the blackboard at Hite Elementary. She was known as the best third-grade teacher in the city.

The Sawyer family was deeply Methodist. Diane had attended Methodist Youth Association camp, and, as busy as she now was as a reporter, she still made it to practice two evenings a week to blend her gifted soprano, on classic hymns, with a mélange of other voices in the St. David's Church–based choir called the Motet Singers. When Diane was growing up, the Sawyers had hosted home Bible meetings on Sunday and sometimes Wednesday nights at their home, while their family church, St. Mark's, was under construction. "Purpose" was a word heard in many sermons. The ideal—to live a life *"of purpose"*—was also fortified by Judge Sawyer.

"Diane's father was the one who really put the idea of 'purpose' in her life; he was her moral compass," says her close friend ABC producer Mark Robertson, on the basis of what she has told him. "She always says, 'Those are *real lives* at stake!'" of her responsibility to the people whose stories she is telling on television. *"That* came from her father."

Judge Sawyer was a serious man—a thoughtful intellectual. Diane's love of D. H. Lawrence and e. e. cummings seems to have derived from his respect for literature. Diane was very close to him, a closeness amplified by the serendipitous fact that she was the spitting image of his sister Lila, after whom she'd been named. She'd even tried law school for one semester, mainly, friends say, because law was what *he* did.

Judge Sawyer was paternal in an old-fashioned way. Just after Diane had been hired at WLKY, he had pointedly dropped in one day, unannounced, on the station's general manager to make good and sure that this man who'd hired his daughter did *not* have any designs on her. He was a fierce Republican—Diane's eventual, abiding loyalty to Richard Nixon, incomprehensible to so many, owes much to his strong party affiliation. Yet the judge was not stern; he had a palpable sense of compassion. The judge's "love for his family, intellectual curiosity, and evenhandedness were as perfect as a person's could be," says Diane's high school English teacher and confidante, Alice Chumbley Lora. Finally, Judge Sawyer had given Diane the yardstick by which she chose her profession. "Answer three questions," he said one day. "One: What are you passionate about? Two: What can you have adventure doing? Three: What can you do to make a difference?" Four decades later she would recount those unforgettably impactful words to a young ABC News female protégée.

Diane's mother was perhaps an even greater influence. Jean Sawyer was not an intellectual ("I never saw Mrs. Sawyer reading a book," one friend says), but she was a seizer of life, an ambitious perfectionist—and Diane was awed by this. "Growing up, I didn't have distant idols, I had *proximate* ones," Diane once made clear.

Jean Sawyer had a tremendous hold on her daughters. "Diane's mother was a very, *very* aggressive woman. She was a force of nature," says Greg Haynes, a Louisville friend whom Diane dated in college. "She pushed her daughters into all these beauty contests." And lessons: Diane took piano, ballet, tap, voice, classical guitar, and fencing, sacrificing her social life for the palette of activities her mother lined up. "Mrs. Sawyer was a 1950s version of the Tiger Mom," says one who knew the family: pushing her daughters, using criticism to make sure they did their best. Every opportunity Jean Sawyer hadn't had, she made sure her daughters did have. "Mrs. Sawyer was *very* ambitious for her daughters," Haynes says. "She was extremely devoted to their achievement." Sometimes it seemed that was *all* she cared about. It was as if so much insecurity had suffused Jean's and Erbon's youths, the opposite would now be fiercely willed. A pristine security, unmarred by lack of opportunity—and certainly unmarred by tragedy—would be obtained for the Sawyer girls, come hell or high water.

And then, on September 23, 1969, that plan—that dream—fell apart in an instant.

Diane's father had risen early that morning and gotten into his car to drive to work. The route was familiar enough to be rote; he had driven it innumerable times. Somehow, this morning, something went very wrong very fast. Minutes from his home, while ascending an overpass above the interstate highway, his car suddenly veered and shot off the unshielded bridge abutment, over the overpass. Did the judge fall asleep at the wheel? Did a tire blow out? Whatever the cause, rumors would circulate, all unconfirmed, that the fatal plunge was a suicide.

Louisville in 1969 was a small town when tragedies happened, so it was not surprising that the first newsperson who heard of the accident happened to be a member of Diane's Motet Singers: Bob McDonald, a reporter at radio station WKLO. He was announcing the morning news when the bulletin came in that the judge's car had plummeted and he'd been taken to General Hospital, where Diane and Jean were now rushing. Judge Sawyer's death was announced on WKLO; then Jim Smith, Diane's WLKY assignment editor, assumed the grim task of filming the removal of his junior colleague's father's destroyed vehicle for airing on the very newscast, that evening, to which Diane normally would have contributed.

WLKY's news director, Ken Rowland, rushed to the Sawyer house to pay a condolence call. The women were "in shock more than anything," he recalls, like "any other family who's just lost someone in a tragic accident that there's no real explanation for." Diane's friend Greg Haynes hurried to the funeral home. "Diane was very distraught," he says. "She was devastated."

At Judge Sawyer's funeral service the Motet Singers performed one of his favorite songs, "The Battle Hymn of the Republic." The judge had been a navy officer in World War II and he was a border-Southern postwar Republican—which meant: *anti*-Dixiecrat. He'd stood up for some ideals that were regionally unpopular. Choir member Celia McDonald remembers, "The family"—Jean, Linda, Diane—"was just *crushed*" as they sat in their pews through the service.

For Jean Sawyer and her daughters, this grievous loss was also perhaps a grim reminder: For all the effort taken in thwarting them, storms of awful luck, like Depression winter winds, could still destructively whoosh out of nowhere in a heartbeat. Diane's good friend ABC executive Phyllis McGrady views this moment as a turning point: "They lost their husband and father, these three real Southern women: charming, delightful, perfect manners yet unbelievably determined." From this point on, Jean taught her daughters "they didn't have to find a man to lead them through this world," Mark Robertson says Diane told him. This was not your typical midcentury Southern mother-to-daughter lesson—proper young women in the region at the time were supposed to marry upon graduation from college—and it was one that Diane took to heart, with good result. She would become enormously successful as a single woman and would not marry until she was forty-two. In the wake of her father's death, Diane's determination leapt into overdrive. She surprised everyone by returning to the WLKY newsroom sooner than expected. Jim Smith recalls, "She was not out that long. She was determined to go on and do her job and we respected her for that." Work emerged as an ennobling, distracting, consoling—and *healing*—device.

Dogged dedication would become Diane's defining characteristic, at once a key to her remarkable success and a challenge for her colleagues. Even now, long past the years of earning her due, Diane barely sleeps, is known to e-mail staffers in the middle of the night, and works (says a male producer whom she fired) "harder than ten people." That dedication would guide her journey—and an eventful journey, artfully navigated, it would be.

When this high-achieving Louisville girl had gone on to Wellesley College, she'd encountered Northeastern elitism (a little discomfiting at first) but had absorbed its useful value system, and had won distinction as a singing star. Then she utilized her instinctive ownership of the brand-new ideas about women and ambition during her two years at WLKY. Next—after her father's death—she would blend personal independence with a political conservatism unshared by most of the emerging journalists of her generation, and she would work loyally, for eight years, for the most disgraced president in recent history. In that crucible—playing defense against an aggressive and triumphant press corps—she would sharpen her intellectual fighting skills. After that, she would meld her daunting work ethic with a deft humility in the service of proving herself to highly skeptical colleagues at her first major national news job. From then on she would soar, becoming, over the decades, a star in every TV news format, minting a compelling persona that was at once glamorous and serious—and winding up in the pinnacle position as a 6:30 anchor.

Throughout, she has been impelled by that Methodist-sermon word—her father's word, *purpose*. It's a simple word, employed by a complex woman. Nicknamed the Golden Sphinx, Diane incites awe for being an unsurpassable player of the chess game of career machinations. But while her seductive charm and elegant indirectness are legendary, so is her generosity. Not everyone who has worked with Diane trusts her, though nearly all of them respect her.

She witnessed fickle loss in her family and fickle cruelty in her community: mysteries that make a person seek answers to troubling questions. She was "never not sophisticated," even as a poodle-skirt-wearing small-city girl, says her hometown friend Greg Haynes, and she married one of America's most sophisticated men. Her curiosity, both about the painful mesh of agency and fate and about the world's wide swath of arts and politics, is, she has said, why she keeps working. "Diane is the most curious person I've ever worked with," Jon Banner, her original executive producer at *World News*, declares. And it is becoming more and more a curiosity of "purpose." Her parents' vanquished early hardship, her father's death, the racial strife in Louisville: Those imprints would impel her to investigate social injustice and the deprivation—and stamina—of vulnerable children, resulting in award-winning specials that would become her mature career's proudest achievements. The more years that passed from her days in Kentucky churches, the more notches carved on her belt of urbanity and accomplishment, the more she circled home.

Not too many years ago, a friend of Diane's heard that a close relative of his had died in a car crash like the one in which Erbon Sawyer perished. The friend was distraught. Diane was tough with him, but it was a hopeful toughness. "Look at me!" she ordered. "You can turn your pain into purpose!" She even repeated the exhortation, word for word. The friend, who didn't know about Diane's own swift return to work after she'd been devastated by her father's 1969 death, was so struck by her mysterious adamance—and her passionate use of that folksy homily—that he muses now, "I don't know where she got that. . . ."

II. PUSHING PAST DANGER

It was September 27, 1997, and Christiane Amanpour was walking toward a building in Kabul, Afghanistan, that was supposed to be a women's hospital. She was led there by the Red Cross and the European Union, whose members were increasingly concerned that the aid they were giving to support Afghani women was in fact being siphoned off for nefarious purposes. Afghanistan's new Islamist government—the group that was now in control of the lower two-thirds of the country—had a sonorous name barely known to most Americans at the time: the Taliban.

But if American viewers didn't know the Taliban, they did know thirty-nine-year-old Christiane Amanpour, particularly through her reporting several years earlier, from the grievously embattled little country of Bosnia. She'd cut a distinctive image on CNN for half a dozen years now. In a TV landscape of neatly coiffed and perfectly made-up, often blond, suit-jacketed stateside female CNN anchors and only male war reporters, there she was, in "that ratty old parka that she wore three winters in a row," as her friend and Bosnia colleague Emma Daly affectionately recalls it. Her thick black hair was as mussed as one would expect for someone standing not far from exploding mortar shells; her black eyes were intense; her approachably attractive face was bare. "Most men on TV wore more makeup than she did," says a man who worked with her. American audiences were used to that deep, emphatic, English-accented voice of hers. It was an arresting voice—"posh and exotic" as her early CNN friend Sparkle Hayter describes it; "a voice," her confidant and colleague Pierre Bairin says, "that could command an army." She had reported the intentional rapes of women and the targeted killing of children, the constant shelling, the unique awfulness of a war launched against civilians in the middle of a European city, Sarajevo. She had reported the ethnic cleansing of eight thousand Muslim Bozniak boys and men during what came to be known as the Srebrenica Massacre, and she had pushed and pushed CNN into *staying on* the story and on subsequent stories she'd reported on atrocities, mostly with child victims, in Rwanda, Ghana, and Uganda.

Her impassioned reportage had implicitly exhorted American viewers to attend to global strife, during a time when celebrity crime came to dominate the news. This was the 1990s, the era of the Tonya Harding case, the O. J. Simpson case, and the JonBenét Ramsey case. For Christiane, global news was personal. Her family had been forced out of Iran with the 1979 Islamic Revolution, and with an exile's perspective she made it her mission to find stories of injustice and tell them in a way that would make Americans care.

The Pentagon had started tracking her country-hopping on a map; she anticipated hot spots *for* them. A jaunty rhyme had been bandied about: "Where there's a war, there's Amanpour." And a concept had been coined: the Amanpour Factor, meaning if *she* was there, the international community had better respond with humanitarian aid or else they'd be embarrassed. The formula, she found, did not always work. In Rwanda, the genocide coverage had failed to inflame the American public with the sympathy and foreign aid it deserved. She was determined to not see another atrocity neglected, as Rwanda had been, and it was this she had in mind as she covered this new story: Afghanistan's Taliban.

Walking to the building along with Christiane were a dozen or so European Union and Red Cross officials and two of her CNN colleagues, cameraman Mark Phillips and producer Nic Robertson. Nic had been Christiane's reporting partner when she went into Iraq toward the end of the first Gulf War. She had met Mark in 1993, while covering Bosnia.

Christiane was never incautious or impetuous; she was the opposite of the thrill seeker that war reporters are stereotyped to be. Still, despite her realism about danger, she was unusually calm and steady when danger did strike. Mark had worked with her a lot in Bosnia and he had never seen her genuinely frightened. "She had no overbearing emotion—everything she did was measured," he says. Did this come from being the responsible— even venerated—oldest of four sisters? Or was it a result of her unusual upbringing? Amanpour had been raised in stable, affluent Iran before her world came crashing down. After the Revolution, she had scrambled to relocate, living first in England with her family and then in the United States at college, where, among a glamorous and privileged clique, she managed to display an enviable aplomb. Her traumatic, globe-trotting years would instill an unusual resilience, which came in handy while she battled her way on air as a young, foreign reporter, and proved critical once she entered the high-stakes field of war reporting. It was in Bosnia that Christiane became valued for her on-air coverage. Bosnia had made Christiane a cruasader and a member of the conflict-reportage community that she would come to consider a real family. Bosnia had given her her calling, and now she was continuing with it, as she approached the Kabul hospital for women.

Except: This was *not* a hospital.

Once they walked past the facade, they realized that "the building was a half-constructed shell," Mark Phillips says. He and Christiane and

Nic "saw *no* women in distress." In fact, they didn't see a single woman, in distress or otherwise. Three so-called security guards boxed them in—blocked Mark, Christiane, and Nic from moving farther and from retreating—and one of them shouted to a farther-off sentry, "The foreigners are here!" Christiane, Nic, Mark, and the EU and Red Cross personnel who accompanied them were surrounded. In five or ten minutes Taliban militiamen careened through the streets to the site, jostling up and down in the open backs of their flatbed trucks. They stormed the building shell, shouting wildly, pumping aloft their Kalashnikov automatic rifles—AK-47s. One of the men, sighting Mark's running camera, grabbed it from him, then struck Mark on the head with his rifle—once, then a second time. Christiane stood to the side, watching silently. "Christiane and I had been in these situations before. If you got involved you were going to get whacked," Mark says.

Fear now rippled wordlessly through the group of Westerners: All of this furious machismo was hip-shot; there was no order or logic to any of it. It was one thing when fundamentalist or fascist regimes had rules; they were at least consistent, and you were forewarned. But here, as Emma Bonino, the European commissioner for humanitarian affairs, who was one of the besieged, recalled, *"No one* was in charge." This was "a situation of random terror." Christiane and the others were now loudly declared "under arrest." The official charge was photography, which was now apparently illegal (especially photographs of women, though there were none in the hospital). More realistically, the militiamen were protecting themselves from being exposed for extorting the Red Cross funds.

Christiane, Mark, and Nic were pushed by the Taliban into the Red Cross van that had delivered them there. The Red Cross workers tried to stop them. The Taliban threatened to shoot the Red Cross workers.

The van driver, rifle to his back, was ordered to drive the detainees to a large field, where they were herded out by the Taliban and forced to sit in formation in the sun.

One of the armed men walked up to Christiane and stared at her and spat out the words—in Dhahri, a language close enough to her native Farsi for her to know it—*"You're Iranian!"* It wasn't her celebrity that made him ascertain this. "Christiane has a certain look—they just *knew*," Mark believes.

As an Iranian and a foreign woman, Christiane was a double target for the Afghan Arab members of the Taliban, who were particularly vehement and who, as a result of complex recent history in the Muslim world, hated Iranians. The man looked at her, ran his finger across his own neck, gesturing *I am going to kill you.* He walked slowly around the group, staring at her, circling while Christiane averted his gaze. She stayed astonishingly cool, but he did not relent. "I'd been with Christiane for years, and I had never seen her nervous," Mark says. "*Now* she was. She was *very* nervous."

The fear of losing her life was particularly pointed at this moment. For years—all through her twenties and thirties—Christiane had concentrated on her work. She believed she might never marry or have children and she was pretty okay with that. To be sure, she'd had lots of romances during these years—with journalists, photographers, dashing men, heroic men, single men, and, if rumors are to be believed, at least one married man. She'd been the subject of a roman à clef in which she'd been a droll, swaggering femme fatale. Then she met Jamie Rubin, Secretary of State Madeleine Albright's spokesman. They immediately clicked. Considered one of Washington's most handsome bachelors, he was besotted right away. Though Christiane and Jamie were often in different parts of the globe between their patches of time together, the intensity of the romance was such that, when they *were* together, even their cynical journalist friends were moved to render over-the-top appraisals. "If you walk between them, you could get burned," said *Washington Post* columnist Richard Cohen. "It's a zoning violation."

And now, two months after falling in love, here she was: being threatened with death in a field in Kabul.

The Afghan Arab's threats escalated from gestures to words. He walked around her and said, "Iranian! I'm gonna kill you! I'm gonna slit your throat!"

Mark and Nic both felt very afraid for her—and helpless. In the past, they had defended her, even if she didn't need it. What could they do now?

Two of the detainees managed, sometime over the next few hours, to call the Taliban foreign ministry. When that agency declined to help, someone in the group placed a stealthy SOS call to EU headquarters. Two and a half hours into their ordeal, three male wire service reporters from the AP and Reuters strode into the compound. The Taliban came to understand that holding a group of EU and Red Cross workers hostage would get them unwanted media coverage and would promptly end their funding. After their hours of bravado, the Taliban caved on a dime. The captives were released. Mark was given back his camera—miraculously, almost hilariously, it was still running! The militiaman who'd confiscated it had never thought to turn it off.

Back at the UN safe house, "Christiane was relieved that the long ordeal was over and her antagonist was gone. But she was very calm," says Mark. Once she realized she was safe, it was back to the job. *They had gotten footage!* Mark had observed this kind of recovery from Christiane before.

"Nothing fazed her," he says. "She does not have a roller-coaster personality. It was just Christiane." Once again, she had survived a near-death experience and kept her wits about her.

FOR THE NEXT TEN YEARS, Christiane—soon married to Jamie and soon after that a mother—would report from a staggering number of conflict zones around the world, probably more than any other war reporter in history and almost certainly more than any other woman with a young child, a conundrum that she, a devoted parent, continually tried to reconcile. She worked outside the day-to-day in-house TV news establishment and was a singular, sometimes intimidating, presence—"a combination of bullishness, charm, manners, and a strong moral code," as her friend the English novelist Bella Pollen puts it.

She also dared fly in the face of the assumption that a female professional had to be self-effacing. "I have spent ten years in just about every war zone there was," she said, accepting the Edward R. Murrow Award in September 2000. "I have made my living bearing witness to some of the most horrific events of the end of our century. . . . I'm so identified with war and disaster that wherever I go, people say, jokingly, that they shudder when they see me. U.S. soldiers . . . joke that they track my movements in order to know where they will be employed next. I calculated that I have spent more time at the front than most military units."

It was when, in 2009, she took a job *inside* the system that she struggled. After seventeen years in the field, she had more than earned the right to an anchor post, and to a relief from the dangers and the family stress of nonstop travel. Like ex–war reporters before her—Edward R. Murrow, Walter Cronkite, and Peter Jennings among them—she was ready for a prestigious desk job. But Christiane would find that years of experience and momentous accomplishments didn't make it less hard for foreign-accented women—and assertive, no-nonsense women—to succeed in traditional high-status posts.

Every bit as ironic as being threatened with death right after you've just fallen in love is the fact that you can excel at the most dangerous, public policy affecting investigatives and yet fail at the safe and the chatty. Her response to challenge, however, carries echoes of Diane Sawyer's earnest exhortation to "Turn your pain into purpose!" Christiane knew struggle, and she had never run from it before—not as a young exile, or as a scrappy minor-beat reporter, or as the world's leading conflict journalist. "Never be afraid of failure or loss," she has counseled firmly. Instead, "*Use* it." Just like she did.

III: PUSHING PAST TRAGEDY

It was around ten p.m. on a weekday night in the spring of 2000, and Katie Couric was sitting in the greenroom of *The Tonight Show*, a plastic bib encircling her neck, her light brown hair about to be hot-combed, a makeup artist doing a touch-up. She would be going on Jay Leno's show as a guest in a half hour. Improvised humor was one of the strong suits of the *Today* show host who, now at forty-three, had been the undisputed queen of what the TV industry simply calls "Morning" for nine years. She'd virtually grabbed that title the minute she ascended the seat as a chipmunk-cheeked, pregnant thirty-four-year-old from out of nowhere in 1991.

Morning—seven to nine a.m. on the three networks—is one of the most surprisingly hard to expertly master genres of television. The host is required to be an emotional quick-change artist, segueing from serious news to cooking segments to human interest pieces to celebrity interviews and back again in crisp, tiny, majority-live time parcels. The tone is intimate yet professional, funny but never tasteless; the image projected must be relatable to the diverse viewership that becomes possessive of the morning stars and sees them as presumed family members.

Morning is also the networks' cash cow; and while, right now, Katie was actually beginning to tire of the format, she was never more in her glory, never more in her prime. Her *Today* position had fed her love of attention, had gratified the tremendous ambition she'd had to be a TV news star—an ambition she'd nurtured since childhood. It had made her a famous, wealthy woman, and, perhaps most important now, it had served as her bully pulpit to launch an audacious public health campaign in honor of her late husband, Jay Monahan. She had recently done something that would have been unthinkable from anyone *but* her—she'd had a colonoscopy on live TV, to acquaint viewers with the little-understood, much-avoided procedure that might have saved her forty-two-year-old husband's life and could so easily save others.

Hanging out with Katie in the greenroom was her good friend and colleague Lisa Paulsen. Tall, blond, and, like Katie, high-spirited, Lisa was the president and CEO of the Entertainment Industry Foundation, a major philanthropy. Lisa and Katie were laughing and joking while Katie was getting her makeup done. As much as the two enjoyed gossiping and talking shoes-to-die-for (Katie was an almost in-your-face "girlfriend girl"; she had a posse of friends, many from college, with whom she regularly lunched), Katie and Lisa had become close through a serious mission a year ago: raising money for cancer awareness, prevention, treatment, and research.

It was good that Katie was in an easy mood tonight, Lisa thought. All of Katie's friends were protective of her; they knew that Jay's death two years earlier had not stopped hurting. Katie and Jay had been having marital problems just before his out-of-the-blue diagnosis, and though the instant perspective that came with his direly advanced illness had swept those problems away, Katie was still almost certainly racked with the regret and guilt that had intensified her grief. *Would we have fought if we'd known this was coming?* the healthy survivor in such a situation often thinks.

It was an inconceivable loss. Jay, despite their period of conflict, had been the love of her life and her steady complement and reality test (sometimes her disapproving, behavior-correcting reality test) when fame became disorienting. What's more, she was now the single parent to two daughters, ages six and two at the time of his death. This was no small thing. Katie had had an uncommonly normal childhood. She was raised in surburan Virginia, the youngest of four children in a happy nuclear family—working dad, stay-at-home mom—that was rare even during the decade, the 1960s, that represented the last moment that template was the norm. She'd always had a smart aleck's provoking wit, and over the years it could be ascribed to different sources: initially to youngest-kid-in-the-family indulgence and attention lust. Then as she came to understand challenge, first as the only sister not accepted into an elite university, her humor acquired an edge. This sharpened when she began her career in news and found herself in the role of the perennially underestimated striver at one television station after another. Fantastically ambitious—and wily—Katie alone believed in the depths of her seriousness and talent. Her drive and pluck became her way of proving herself, and it carried her to *Today*, where she would defy all expectations.

When Jay died, everything changed. His death meant that "my first four decades of life"—those ridiculously lucky years!—"seemed to be getting some kind of psychic payback" from the redistributive hand of fate.

Now Katie's irony—the sting in her appraisals, the woundedness under those barbed jokes—had a deeper resonance. People could call her "perky" all they wanted—she knew she was substantial. She had gone through more tragedy than her sunny persona suggested. In a sense, Katie had a secret self: Let them think her breezy and trivial; the more she went through, the less the clueless stereotypers could touch her.

Not that Katie had time—or cause—for bitterness in the spring of 2000. She was too busy being a single mother; an aggressive, consummate professional on her seven to nine a.m. show; and a passionate cancer activist. And she knew that her lot as a widow with children was enormously eased by the outsized resources she commanded.

Not only did Katie have money and public respect to help her through this period, she had family—*close* family. During the months of Jay's deepening illness, a particular source of help was her ten-year-older sister, Emily. Katie had always felt about Emily the way any youngest, irrepressible, mischievous sister feels about her oldest, most sensible, and empathic one: She idolized Emily, measured herself against Emily (sometimes insecurely), and she relied on her.

Emily's and Katie's paths had developed increasingly satisfying symmetries. While Emily became a journalist specializing in legal issues, Katie was a University of Virginia student in the midseventies, trying out that same profession by writing for the college newspaper. When Emily published her first book, *The Trial Lawyers*, in 1988, Katie was doing her own breakthrough investigative story at a Miami TV station: sleeping on the street as a homeless woman. Then, the same year—1991—that Katie started at *Today*, Emily was elected to the Virginia state senate. Oldest and youngest sister were mutually proud of each other, and the legislation Emily sponsored—she was a fierce advocate for heightened educational standards and for specialized medical research and treatment—addressed issues that Katie was passionate about in her coverage. Whenever Emily got up to New York, Katie and Emily could be seen strolling around Katie's neighborhood, arm in arm, with "smiles on their faces, listening intently to each other," as Katie's NBC colleague Barbara Harrison observed.

But it was when Jay got sick—so rapidly and suddenly—that Katie leaned on Emily the hardest. Not only did Katie call Emily and Emily's second husband, cardiologist George Beller, frequently for medical advice, comfort, and support, but Emily wasted no time introducing and pushing through legislation making Virginia the first state in the nation to require insurance carriers to cover screening for colorectal cancer.

The most exciting family news had come half a year ago: Emily called to tell Katie that the Virginia Democratic Party had tapped her to be their nominee for lieutenant governor. Katie was ecstatic. There was even talk that Emily Couric could, after her probable term of lieutenant governor was over, run to become the state's first female governor.

Just as the makeup artist was finishing Katie's touch-up in *The Tonight Show* greenroom, Katie's cell phone sounded.

Lisa looked at the number displayed and saw that it was Katie's sister Emily.

Katie put the phone to her ear. It was clear pretty quickly that this was no ordinary call. "Katie stood up," Lisa recalls. "She was silent, as if her breath was taken away. She started shaking her head." She looked grave and incredulous.

After Katie snapped closed her cell phone, Lisa asked, "What *happened?*"

Katie took a breath and said, "Emily was just diagnosed with pancreatic cancer."

Pancreatic cancer is one of the most insidious forms of the disease. Two years after Jay, it was almost too much to believe this could be happening, again, to a person she loved.

Katie said, "I can't believe this." She and Lisa were both stunned.

Katie gathered what were surely her careening thoughts—shock, heartsickness, disbelief, anger—as the countdown to her appearance on *The Tonight Show* stage began. Then, about ten minutes after hearing the news from Emily, she walked onto the stage. That night and in the ensuing months and years—during which Emily died and Katie's brother Johnny's wife died and both of Lisa's parents died, one by one by one by one—"Katie and I cried a lot. We cry a lot about all the cancers," Lisa says.

These traumas would not merely deepen her as an interviewer, especially of people in crisis; they would have the unbidden auxiliary effect of steeling her from the intense criticism that would come not long afterward when, in September 2006, she became the first solo female anchor of a six thirty p.m. network newscast. Her appointment had been an experiment on the part of CBS, part of a large-scale reimagining of the evening news and what it could be. Although marked by highs such as the presidential game-changing interview with Sarah Palin, the experience of anchoring the *CBS Evening News*, from 2006 to 2011, was an infelicitous whirlwind for Katie, and it ended in what has been called a "mutual decision" for her to leave CBS. Katie was sensitive to the criticism she elicited. "I feel like a human piñata, but . . . no candy is going to spill out," she quipped, while the media had a field day over her plummeting, then recovering, then static approval index. "This may not be a lot of fun, but it goes with the territory, unfortunately, of being successful and female," she said. Having lost the anchorship, she skipped gamely over to a new format—Daytime—and another highly compensated and anticipated new show. The result, in 2013: another failure.

Katie is nothing if not resilient, and her weatheredness shows in her interview style: probing and compassionate, but also vigilant, dukes up, ever wry. She has warned people, "Before you gag at the absolute adorableness of it all"—her happy family-of-origin story—they should know: There was payback. She has said: "To paraphrase that L'Oreal commercial, 'Don't hate me because I'm happy.' *Trust me.* I've been to the other side."

She has transformed her heartbreak into activism. Katie Couric's work on the front lines of the colon cancer war is virtually unmatched by any other public figure. Just as there was an Amanpour Factor, there was a Couric Effect, a scientifically quantified rise in lifesaving colonoscopies because of her campaign to acquaint viewers with and demystify the procedure. And through her intensive work through five organizations and fund-raising and research projects that she established or joined and energized and remains closely involved in, she has made a $320 million impact. "This"—cancer fighting—"is the most important thing she does," says Kathleen Lobb, her old UVA friend and now the senior vice president of Stand Up to Cancer, which Katie and Lisa Paulsen launched as an Entertainment Industry Foundation initiative. "Even if you're not thick-skinned, when you've been through experiences like she has, you have a pretty good ability to see through to what's really important." On a recent anniversary of Jay's death, at a fund-raiser, Katie said words to the effect of, "When my obituary is written—and I hope it won't be for a very long time—I would want it to be said that I helped in the fight against cancer." Kathleen remembers, "She always says that, outside of raising her daughters, fighting cancer is her most important accomplishment."

Katie Couric is the ultimate trooper. You don't become the master of live, upbeat TV and *not* know how to deliver, even under duress, even under shock, even under sadness. Toward the end of her tenure at *Today*, the crew used to marvel, half admiringly, half with annoyance, at how late—how dangerously near seven a.m.—she would stride into the studio and *still* make it onto the couch with none of the viewers having any idea how close she'd cut it. She was *that* good at the form of live and upbeat, enough so that she could be cheeky and take shortcuts.

But as well as being that good at the *form* of it, she was also that good at the *responsibility* of it, and this involved discipline. No matter what personal news was thrown in your face moments before a slotted, unchangeable appearance on a major live broadcast, you could not *not* show up and you could not be off-tone. After Katie got that call from Emily that night in the *Tonight Show* greenroom, she pulled herself together, and none of Jay Leno's viewers had any idea of the profoundly worrisome news she'd just heard from her sister.

It was after she left the stage that she broke down. And after she broke down, she got to work to help Emily, just as she had helped Jay. Her energy—her need to prove herself, her desire to get ahead—had seemed disconcerting, and even excessive, to some who had watched Katie's climb to the top. But now those traits were useful and helpful and a marker of resilience: the same kind of resilience that had made Katie Couric, against dismissive predictions, a major TV news star.

DIANE SAWYER, Christiane Amanpour, and Katie Couric have succeeded as television news broadcasters as no other women have. They have each brought a unique persona to their broadcasts—Sawyer: circumspection, elegance, and personal restraint; Amanpour: an outsider's muckraking zeal, a fearlessness, and a passionate commitment to help America understand international pain; Couric: an everywoman's touch, a sly wit, an appealing relish for besting those who would dismiss her, and a willingness to experiment and throw out old models. They have each wielded a fierce—and necessary—ambition and a faith in herself that was able to conquer adversity and defy expectations. In the wake of tragedy, Diane would transform herself from a mannered daughter of the South into a hard-nosed, singularly driven newswoman, her forty-five-year-long career spanning every form of TV news, from beat reporting, to groundbreaking TV newsmagazine work at *Primetime* and *60 Minutes*, to high-stakes Morning, to her current position as the sole female anchor in the prized six-thirty evening news chair. As for Christiane, she felled the conventional wisdom that her appearance, accent, affect, and national origin would keep her from getting on American television, and she persevered to bravely bring heart and soul to the world's most devastating crises, becoming her era's best-known and most respected TV foreign correspondent. Katie used her disarming girl-next-door relatability and her ferocious single-mindedness to reach unequalled success (and achieve new gender parity) in Morning, only to exit her cushiony position to become the seemingly odd choice as the first major-network solo female news anchor—and the one who also dared to try to change that format's ossified paradigm.

The three women are united by their strength of character, which they honed during these respective episodes: a father's shocking death, a threat to one's own life, a second loved one's serious cancer. Their resilience—and their practiced comprehension of the limits of safety—resonated when they became the News Sorority: the rare women, in a field that is overwhelmingly male, who would tell the world's stories.

Collectively, these women have been our guides and our proxy witnesses to just about every tragedy, scandal, war, controversial personality of good or ill, election, crisis, major social or cultural trend, titillating celebrity dustup, headline-generating act of everyday heroism, or egregious practice of inequity and oppression that has transpired over the last three or more decades. Because they have entered our lives so consistently, for so many years and so intimately—looking us in the eye through screens in our living rooms, kitchens, and bedrooms, sometimes during times of national pain and terror, when we are most vulnerably in need of information—we feel that we know them. But do we? Do we know what it took for them to climb, against a pushback that prevails to this day, to that peculiarly thin perch as a narrator of our world who also happens to be female?

Diane, Katie, and Christiane have shed great light on many *other* people's stories.

Here are their own stories, from the beginning.

PART TWO

MORNING

CHAPTER ONE

Louisville Idealist Becomes Nixon Loyalist

Diane: 1945 to 1978

LILA DIANE SAWYER was born on December 22, 1945, in Glasgow, Kentucky, deep in the south of the state, where both of her parents had grown up. Her sister, Linda, preceded her by two years, born during World War II, when Erbon Powers Sawyer was away with the navy, so Jean Dunagan Sawyer's already substantial strength, toughened by her Depression childhood of poverty, was tested all the more by the experience of being alone with her infant. Still, Jean was surrounded by her bevy of sisters—Anna Jo, Wanda, and Maxine—who were all so close that they talked to one another on the phone every day of their lives. The feistiness of the ever present Dunagan women would come to impress young Diane immeasurably. Jean and her sisters were "amazing," she has said. "Every place you would look there would be these women—taking chances, not for a minute thinking there was anything they couldn't do."

Diane, born after the war ended, was a little girl when her father, a graduate of Lindsey Wilson Junior College, attended the Jefferson School of Law (now the University of Louisville's law school); the family moved to the cosmopolitan capital Louisville, in the far north of the state, bordering Ohio. Diane dropped the "Lila," perhaps thinking it was too homespun; indeed, Linda and Diane (along with Susan and Carol) were favored girls' names in the early to mid-1940s.

Lawyer Tom Sawyer became Judge Tom Sawyer; the family bought a two-story brick house on Lowe Road and Jean began teaching at Hite Elementary. Diane was in her mother's third-grade class, and, despite Mrs. Sawyer's commanding style, the kids were typical rapscallions. Diane was gamey enough to perennially tease the boy, Stewart Robensen, who by virtue of alphabetical seating always sat in front of her. "She'd torment me by unbuttoning the little buttons on my back collar and sometimes she'd scribble things on my neck," Robensen recalls. She played Cinderella's evil stepsister in the class play. Marc Fleischaker, one of a pair of twins from one of the affluent Jewish families in the school district, fashioned himself Diane's third-grade "boyfriend." Years later, in their high school senior yearbooks, Diane would write in Marc's: "Goodness! After all these passionate expostulations by all your friends (female gender!), fond memories of the boy who used to chase me and try to kiss me on the playground in 3rd grade." This quality—blushing maiden flirtation with a self-parodying edge—would eventually come to figure in her TV persona.

Outgoing Linda was shy Diane's idol and protector. It's not clear what Diane needed protection from as a secure little girl with doting parents, but she would later say that "Linda [was] a saint. I'm not kidding. I've never known anybody like her in my life. She only worries about me— this has been true since I've been little. She would take me with her, let me tag along, from the time I was tiny."

By the middle of elementary school, however, both Sawyer girls were constantly going to performance classes; their distinction and perfection was their mother's mission. Still, for all her rabid ambition for her daughters, and abiding conservatism (Jean was a lifelong Republican), and "indomitable" affect (Diane has always used this adjective on her mother, noting that this steely role model of hers never came to the breakfast table less than perfectly groomed and dressed for the day), Jean Sawyer also modeled originality and open-mindedness for her daughters. She practiced yoga—hardly typical of a Kentucky mother in the 1950s. She was sure that there was Native American blood, as well as German and Scottish, in the Dunagan bloodlines; she had the family's genealogy traced and she was gratified when her hunch was confirmed.

Louisville's racial landscape during the 1950s was as turbulent as anywhere in the South. In 1954, a white couple, the Bradens, activist progressives, were charged with sedition for helping a black family, the Wades, buy a home in a "non-Colored" area. The Bradens were convicted of that crime, and Carl Braden served jail time before the conviction was reversed. Housing integration would be Louisville's bane, from Diane's girlhood through her early work as a reporter, but that turmoil was unsurprising—it was sadly par for the course in the South during the McCarthy era of the Eisenhower years.

All national news that was funneled into the Sawyer household's black-and-white television set during Diane's girlhood had a nonurban overlay. It came through the voices of Douglas Edwards on CBS or, on NBC, the popular duo of Huntley and Brinkley. Though they broadcast from New York, all three were men of rural American origin—Edwards an Oklahoman, Brinkley a North Carolinian, Huntley from Montana. Edwards was old-school formal; the widely popular Huntley and Brinkley played off each other, with Brinkley's wit balancing Huntley's solemnity. Still, as popular as Brinkley was, Huntley's baritone trumped Brinkley's higher voice; Huntley was the main anchor of the duo during a time that high-pitched voices were considered unacceptable.

FROM THE OUTSIDE, the new school that Diane entered in seventh grade in 1958, Seneca High, seemed normal for its time and place—the students had to stand and recite the Lord's Prayer every morning; Frankie Avalon and Pat Boone were the radio favorites, while Elvis was deemed unappealingly "greaser," even though he hailed from the state next door. Girls wore cinch-belted skirts and circle pins, and if a girl wore shorts on a hot day, she had to be separated from the boys on the school bus. But Seneca drew from an unusual geographic swath: from a largely Jewish neighborhood as well as a white Protestant one. In addition, a group of African American students also entered. This was an almost unheard-of mixture, but principal Kenneth Farmer resolutely insisted that everything be peaceful. The "GO HOME, NIGGER!" signs were scrubbed from the walls. The hate mail was kept from the students. "Seneca was a school that everyone was watching, all across the country, because integration was going on there," says one of its black students, Diane's classmate David Cosby, who became one of the high school's basketball stars. Seneca would boast two all-American basketball players—Wes Unseld and Mike Redd—during Diane's years there, both of them black, and that integrated, game-winning basketball team, the Seneca Redskins (later Redhawks), helped to make what could have been a very bumpy process of integration less so.

The injustice was sharp at first, though many of the white kids were too naive or privileged to immediately notice: "'Coloreds Not Served Here' were signs at the Greyhound station and at the restaurants—I remember seeing them as a kid and as a teenager," George Unseld, Wes's younger brother and also a Seneca basketball star, recalled, before his 2010 death. And the irony was sharp: Here were the black kids winning the basketball games, yet they were legally unable to enter the after-game hangout—the coach brought their food back to the car. "It was really hard for me, scoring forty points in the basketball game, and then when we went to Frisch's and the white kids went inside, *I* had to sit in the car. That's hard for a sixteen-year-old," says David Cosby. It didn't take long for the white players to rise to the challenge: All for one and one for all—if *they* can't eat in a restaurant, then *we* won't, whether in Louisville or farther out in some of the more provincial counties, where the sight of a mixed team of basketball players eating together in a bus could be potentially dangerous. It was an improvised, ground-level, teenage protest against segregation that preceded its counterparts in the deeper South. (And it was helped along by some of the Jewish students' *own* earlier protests—they didn't want to read the New Testament in class, for example—which had made the school more open-minded than others.) By Diane's senior year the basketball team was a third black, a third white Christian, a third Jewish.

As an idealistic, thoughtful—and Christian—girl, Diane was sympathetic. In fact, David Cosby says, sometimes in 1961 he and Diane talked about how unfair it was that they couldn't date. "Yes, Diane and I talked about doing it [dating]." (Diane has affirmed this publicly.) "We teased each other about it in school—in the hallway, in the cafeteria. We laughed about it—I was a handsome guy and she was an attractive girl. I was the basketball star and she was doing everything she was doing," including cheerleading at his games. "But what could we have done and both be alive right now? We knew that, publicly, black and white kids couldn't date. We were ahead of our times."

In fact, Diane Sawyer of Seneca High basically did *not* date—perhaps that is why she could so easily joke about it. She was always busy at voice or dance lessons, or at rehearsals. She sang *My Fair Lady*'s "Wouldn't It Be Loverly" on a local TV variety show. She traveled during the summer, on exchange programs, going to South America, living briefly on the German-Swiss border (and learning almost fluent German). These were programs her mother determinedly found for her. Besides, she was somewhat hard to categorize. At five foot nine, she was tall for her age—somewhat gawky—and with her late December birthday, she was young for her grade. Tall *and* young *and* smart *and* always otherwise occupied after school and on school breaks: It somehow put her off-limits. Diane "was harder to get to know for a lot of people," say Marc Fleischaker. Her friends were older. "I think there weren't but a handful of guys who would have had the confidence to ask her out," says Greg Haynes. "She was too beautiful for us fragile-ego'd guys," says another classmate, Tom Hampton. She appeared aloof, even though that wasn't necessarily the case. "She wasn't terribly confident in social situations," explains one female classmate. Her rectitude and extracurricular activities gave her a seeming diffidence, an "apartness," as some students noticed.

When as a sophomore she first walked into the class of the young, brand-new English teacher, Miss Chumbley, the teacher felt almost sorry for Diane. "Diane did not have that apple-pie beauty queen look that her sister, Linda, had. She wore black horn-rimmed glasses with very thick lenses—looks were not paramount to her. I thought, 'Oh, it must be very difficult to have a sister as beautiful as Linda!'" says Alice Chumbley Lora.

If her mother gave her the message that she should hold out for *more*—more opportunity, more distinction—there seemed a part of her that felt that, too—in a subtle way, as in a kind of gentle, high-minded alienation from convention. "I think Diane felt like an outsider, and I felt like one, too, and that's why we were friends," recalls classmate Sallie Schulten Haynes, Greg Haynes's wife. The two girls indulged in "deep conversation. We talked about our philosophy of life and what was meaningful," Sallie says. "We had this little group," Diane has said. "We were Unitarian, Jewish, Methodist. We used to get together and read Thoreau and Emerson, and we'd sit by this squalid little creek every day at lunch and imagine ourselves as philosophers. We called ourselves the New Transcendentalists. Oh, I was earnest—so, so earnest!"

But if she was self-important, it was in a harmless way, without snobbery. "I don't think Diane cared about status," says Sallie Haynes. "*I* did, but she didn't." In their "Old Louisville" of private schools with exclusive fraternities and sororities, their ethnically mixed, meritocratic public high school was "looked down on by some of the kids in the other schools. We were 'less desirable,'" says Sallie. "Diane was not alienated, she was not insecure; she just knew there was more out there than what everybody was caught up with," not only in terms of social class but also with gender expectations. "I consciously tried to appear 'not smart.' Diane didn't."

Diane came to Miss Chumbley and said she wanted to start a debate team. Once the team was started, she was one of only two girls in the field of nine debaters. Diane liked to debate *both* sides of a topic—her desire for evenhandedness, for logical argument, was something that struck Miss Chumbley. Over the last two of Diane's high school years, Diane began to confide in Miss Chumbley—there was a similarity, both women sensed. They were highly attractive, ladylike, questing young Southern women. Alice, who was then in her early twenties, had been Miss Kentucky in the Miss America pageant just before coming to Seneca, but she was pushing past cultural expectations; she would soon go to Duke for a PhD in English. Diane's sister, Linda, had been Miss Kentucky in the Miss America pageant and now she was at Wellesley. Both of these women were models for Diane, combining beauty and charm with intellectual ambition.

One day toward the end of her junior year, Diane came into Miss Chumbley's homeroom in tears. She had not been invited to the junior prom! Everyone else had been. Actually, she had been worse than not invited; she'd been *dis*invited. Her classmate Jim Crunkelton had invited her, but she was his second choice. "I asked a girl to go; she said yes but then she changed her mind, so I asked Diane," Crunkelton explains. "Then the mothers got involved and they thought it was wrong for that first girl to break her date with me." So that first girl *re*accepted Jim's invitation and Diane was disinvited.

Miss Chumbley told Diane, "'Why don't you ask your dad? Everybody loves your dad! And he's such a good dancer!' Of course, that brought more tears—no girl wants to bring her father to the prom." The Monday after prom weekend Diane walked into Miss Chumbley's homeroom with a look of quiet triumph: When all the other girls were getting dressed, she had gone by herself with a book to the creek—the "squalid little creek"—and read the poems of Wallace Stevens. She was proud of this thumbing of convention, this use of literature to best the world of wrist corsages and spaghetti-strapped taffeta gowns. Miss Chumbley was proud of her, too.

But that whole thing was kind of a fluke—in fact, Diane had won the crown of homecoming queen in her junior year. George Unseld, the new Seneca Redskins basketball team captain, presented her with a bouquet of roses at the homecoming game, and Diane moved her cheek toward him—Queen getting a kiss from Captain had always been a tradition, at least in the old days of segregated schools. But George didn't kiss her. "A lot of guys asked me about it. 'She's the best-looking woman in the school and you *didn't* kiss her!' I got this from both black and white guys," Unseld said, before his death. "Diane asked me why I didn't do it—she'd expected me to." Unseld told her about his mother's lingering worries because of the murder, seven years earlier, of Emmett Till, and she understood. In a separate situation, not more than a year earlier, Miss Chumbley, as a faculty chaperone, had accompanied two black star Seneca players to a game at a college to which they were applying for admission; her own friends—educated white women—called her afterward and exclaimed, "Alice! You're going to ruin your reputation!" Alice was angry, and surprised. Years later, Alice Chumbley Lora and Diane agreed that these lines from the Sara Teasdale poem "The Long Hill" captured their, and their Seneca peers', naive, improvised groping toward integration before they could fully comprehend the obstacles they were facing down:

> I must have passed the crest a while ago
> And now I'm going down
> Strange to have crossed the crest and not to know.

Indeed, they didn't "know" that they had passed a "crest" ahead of the time for their region. "I think the white kids at Seneca got educated from" it all, George Unseld said. "When we got there as freshmen we had problems. Some of the kids even fought us." But by Unseld's senior year, the Seneca kids protested Louisville's theater segregation together: When the black kids couldn't sit with the white kids, they *all* turned around and walked out. By the time of Unseld's senior prom, in 1962, the Jewish kids and the black kids even "banded together," Unseld said, in choosing the music: "It wasn't so much that we *had* to have doo-wop. We just didn't want country western."

AT THE BEGINNING of her senior year (1962–1963), Diane had been recruited to be a possible contestant as Miss Kentucky in the America's Junior Miss contest. Linda had been the runner-up two years earlier (aside from her run as Miss Kentucky in the far more prestigious Miss America competition). The scholarship money had helped pay for Linda's tuition at Wellesley, where Diane would soon be accepted. Conflicted about whether or not to enter America's Junior Miss, Diane consulted Miss Chumbley, as she often did. Miss Chumbley counseled Diane against entering. Still, if she won, the scholarship money would be crucial to her being able to accept Wellesley.

Diane entered the pageant.

Actually, despite its cutesy name, America's Junior Miss was a competition that focused more on spiritual qualities than did many other pageants. Its charismatic den mother and mistress of ceremonies, Catherine Marshall, was the daughter, widow, and mother of Presbyterian ministers, and, after her first husband's death, she married Leonard LeSourd, Pastor Norman Vincent Peale's publishing partner. Peale's pulpit was Manhattan's Marble Collegiate Church; there he preached the enormously popular "Power of Positive Thinking"—in sermons, and also through books, national radio broadcasts, and his and LeSourd's magazine, *Guideposts.*

The Christian self-help/help-others doctrine that undergirded the pageant was precisely the one that Diane had grown up with, and in Catherine Marshall there were uncanny echoes of Diane's mother. Like Jean Dunagan Sawyer, Catherine Marshall was an Appalachia-bred woman, a schoolteacher, a survivor of adversity—she'd had tuberculosis as a child— a successful, self-made woman who was a best-selling author of inspirational books. She was a woman who forcefully preached to her contestants the secular gospel that Jean Sawyer drummed into her daughters: No excuses! Be the best you can be! Push yourself! Diane was blown away by Catherine's backstage pep talks at the Mobile, Alabama, pageant theater. Meeting her "was a seismic wake-up call," Diane would later recall. Catherine "seemed almost disappointed at how we, the contestants, expressed our ambitions. She challenged us to take whatever each of us had to start thinking beyond our limited horizons. She dared us to dream big. She hated . . . waste of human capacity. She wanted to shake us up. 'There's so much more you can do!' She could see the way the world could be and the way your life could be. I had never met a person who lived and worked her faith like that." Catherine Marshall's impassioned mentoring of the contestants was like Diane's thoughtful father's "three questions," and it was like her aggressive, perfectionistic mother's impelling her to take all those performance lessons—and her insistence, after Judge Sawyer died, that she not rely on a man. Diane's homily-like exhortations to her friends today—"When it's the hardest, do something for somebody else; it will make you feel better," she has told at least one friend—seem to have come from an amalgam of her mother, her father, and Catherine Marshall, who left a deep impression on her.

For her talent presentation at Junior Miss, Diane, representing Kentucky, read a poem she had written about the Civil War, and, having honed her self-avowed interest in evenhandedness through work with Miss Chumbley, she sang songs from both sides of that conflict. Catherine Marshall was very taken with Diane. "Mom said Diane was the one who seemed to strike the deepest chord, who had a deeper vision" than the other contestants, recalls the late Marshall's stepson Chet LeSourd. The judges must have agreed; they selected her.

When Diane was crowned America's Junior Miss—flanked by the runners-up (now her "princesses")—she threw her head back in a thrilled laugh. She was handed a bouquet of long-stemmed roses, and in her white bouffant-skirted dress—her chin-length blond hair framing her face in the tight, neat curls of the time—she seemed the very picture of ladylike WASP graciousness that had dominated the country's imagery since the Eisenhower years.

But that female meme was now on its last legs.

The night she was crowned was also the night the Seneca Redskins won the state basketball championship. Her pageant win—untelevised, in another state—was dwarfed by the school's excitement at its triumph. Here was its racially integrated team hoisting the state banner! As much as Diane had contributed to the quiet gains that were now Seneca's legacy, being the blond beauty queen in an all-white-girls contest in 1963 was being on the wrong side of history.

THE PERSPECTIVE WAS AUGURING. Shortly after parading down the runway, bouquet in arms, Diane found the elation of her win dissipating. It was embarrassing to wear her crown and sash to official America's Junior Miss events. (She even had to wear them on airplanes *to* the events.) The inspiration of Marshall's persona and words and the significance of the event didn't translate beyond the South, beyond the world she was leaving—the sensibility that the *country* was leaving.

She felt she got her main comeuppance when she arrived at Wellesley in the fall of 1963. She'd been voted Seneca High's "Most Likely to Succeed"—"the dreariest possible thing to be," she would later say. She had been a sophisticate at Seneca, and many of her friends there could, and did, travel with minimal bumps to higher-barred environs—several boys to Harvard, including Barry Cooper, who took her to the senior prom, and Lee Goldstein, who was her debate team partner.

It was perhaps harder for a female to make the transition from Louisville to an elite Eastern college. There were more cultural and stylistic obstacles. Traveling from the South to a New England campus in September 1963 meant entering a world of Northeastern girls in Lord & Taylor A-line coats and Pappagallo flats who'd been going to world-class museums and Broadway plays since they were five; of devotees of the esoteric whose long, straight hair had never touched a brush roller and who unpacked Kahlil Gibran's *The Prophet* and Joan Baez albums from their hatbox-round suitcases; of debutantes whose parents had grown up not scrambling for sustenance on small farms, as Diane's had, but owning large ones.

So, at first, Diane acutely felt her Southernness. "When the other girls were getting packages of Kron chocolates, I was sent turnips and tomatoes from home, beautifully wrapped," she has said, with a mix of pride and self-deprecation. She came to perceive her America's Junior Miss crown as an embarrassment—a provincial's gauche trophy—and today her Wellesley classmates recall the mixed reactions to it. "It was one of those things—if you're jealous, you mock it, but secretly everybody wanted to be her," recalls Aviva Bobb, now a retired California Superior Court judge. "Yes, there were people who were disdainful of the beauty queen thing and the 'graciousness' aura and they were not impressed with her," concedes Judi Lempert Green, who became a Michigan psychologist. But "those were the days before beauty contests were ripped apart as body shows like they are today," says Beth Johnson, also a psychologist, based in New Mexico. "We knew America's Junior Miss was about talent and intelligence. I think Diane was respected."

Although it was considered second only to Radcliffe in rigor (though Smithies might beg to differ), Wellesley in 1963 put a premium on decorum and tradition. Arriving first-year students were given a class called Fundamentals, a sort of charm school offering instruction on how to enter and exit a car so their derrieres wouldn't protrude and how to erase an unseemly—New Jersey, for example—accent. The girls had mandatory "posture"-revealing photographs taken in the nude. Graduates of inclusive public schools found themselves going backward. At Wellesley, unlike Seneca, there was a quota for Jews (applicants were asked to state their religion), and minority girls were bunched together—"the Jewish girls rooming with the Jewish girls, the Asians with the Asians," recalls Aviva Bobb.

Formal tea was served in dorm living rooms. Grace was said before dinner, a meal at which slacks were banned. Bible class was mandatory. If you had a gentleman caller in your room during the two-hour visiting period on Sunday afternoon, three feet had to be touching the floor at all times. (Dorm mothers checked.) There was no TV, just radio; and if liquor was found in your room during weekly inspection, you were suspended. Most of these rules were tossed in 1968. "I wish I had stayed at Wellesley at least one more year, without those constraints," pines Diane's classmate Leesa Campbell, slightly more than tongue in cheek.

The late Nora Ephron (Wellesley '62), who would later become Diane's friend by way of Mike Nichols, criticized the college's early 1960s shoehorning of deeply intelligent girls into an anachronistic mold that would soon be jettisoned. As one of Ephron's classmates expressed at a reunion, Wellesley "was a dress rehearsal for a life we never had."

Even more than Ephron's 1959–1962 stretch, Diane's 1963–1967 years at Wellesley were marked by a sharp cultural turnabout. The year Diane entered, only two Wellesley women—a student and a professor—attended Martin Luther King's March on Washington, according to Judi Lempert Green. But by 1968, a year after Diane graduated, Green says the climate had changed so significantly that student body president Hillary Rodham "led busloads of women" to the 1969 Mobilization for Peace in the nation's capital. Moreover, during Diane's sophomore year, 1964, Betty Friedan's freshly published *The Feminine Mystique* "was being read all over campus," recalls Diane's classmate Beth Johnson. The slow boil of the women's movement—no turning back—had begun.

Many a woman who entered a top college in 1963 faced a forked road: Half of her friends married their college beaux (many divorcing them later) and planned to become teachers while supporting their husbands through law or med school; the other half veered off into heady new zones, from radical politics to psychedelic drugs and communes. The more indelible revolution—involving new ideas about women and serious careers, women and ambition, women and singleness—wouldn't occur for a few more years, so it was the slightly younger women who most naturally caught that wave as it rolled in. Diane Sawyer, who'd come to Wellesley insecure about her provincialism, would actually prove to be ahead of her times, quickly making a "male" career her goal, not marrying until she was forty-two, forgoing motherhood without regret or apology.

One of Diane's best friends at Wellesley was Marie Fox, now an artist living in Los Angeles. The two met their first year because Linda Sawyer was assigned to be Marie's Wellesley "big sister." If Diane was circumspect about entering Wellesley, Linda was confident and jubilant enough to have snuck a bottle of scotch into her desk drawer—Linda's opening the door and brandishing it was a giddily rebellious *"Wa-hoo!"* that Marie remembers. Marie and Diane had height in common—Marie is six feet tall. "Diane was *very* funny—very witty, very playful. And caring. She'd write you a poem to thank you for something. She was persistent, hardworking, and ladylike—a Southern thing—but not in a formal way."

One late November day during their first year, the campus was sharply disrupted, as were campuses all over the country. Aviva Bobb remembers "walking out of my dorm around noon and there were a swarm of people in the quadrangle and people walking out of their dorms and rushing out of classes, and they started to mix in a crowd." As word spread, "there was this incredible grief and sadness." Marie Fox was "in German class, when a school official somberly walked in and delivered the news, which stunned us all." President John F. Kennedy had been assassinated in Dallas. Diane was one of the shocked mourners of this signal tragedy of her generation. The bringer of this news—Diane and her classmates watched the footage again and again—was CBS's Walter Cronkite. The anchor's dignified grief—the way he briefly took off his glasses and paused, tear in eye, as he announced the president's death in a manner that perfectly combined personal pain and the necessity to do one's job—seemed to represent the best of America. The gesture would make him the most beloved and respected TV newsman in the country, a prototype of avuncular authority (indeed, he would be called "America's Uncle") that would serve as a high bar for more than forty years, even after he'd been replaced by Dan Rather. Another aspect of him, his presumed modesty, was so legendary that Kurt Vonnegut called him "the reluctant bigshot." But in truth Cronkite was not so avuncular or so humble. "He was a tough, *tough* guy. And demanding," says Sandy Socolow, who produced Cronkite's show from the beginning and who has been a venerable—and opinionated— witness to the history of women in TV news over all these decades. "You don't get to be Walter Cronkite unless you have an ego as big as an elephant." "He was called the eight-hundred-pound gorilla," explains veteran producer Joe Peyronnin, for the way Cronkite *im*modestly threw his weight around but was not thought of any less for doing so. ("But if a woman throws her weight around," Peyronnin says, "she's a 'diva.'") As she sat in front of a Wellesley TV screen mourning the president's assassination with her classmates, Diane Sawyer could probably never imagine that, in her mature career, the pervasive "avuncular" and "modest" conventional wisdom about Cronkite—the worship of the man—would complicate things in a then far-off future when women, including Diane herself, would fill national anchor roles.

Marie and Diane roomed together during sophomore year in one of the new dorms, Freeman Hall. Diane was an English major and Marie was an art major. A small dose of activism was creeping its way into Wellesley, and Diane briefly caught the bug—or, at least, faked it in order to fit in—marching in a protest against compulsory Bible class. But later she would confess that she'd felt guilty about doing so because, in fact, and perhaps unsurprisingly, "I *loved* Bible class!"

Diane's at-the-time conservatism—as well as the fraught, absolutist bifurcations that marked student politics during the early 1960s—was highlighted during a disastrous blind date she had toward the end of her America's Junior Miss reign, in Palm Springs, with a very incompatible young man named Martin Snapp. Martin's brother was highly placed in the National Junior Chamber of Commerce, and it was his job to find escorts for Diane and her princesses for a Jaycees event, so he fixed Diane up with his brother, a very smart but not conventionally handsome Yale undergraduate and Beverly Hills native. Martin Snapp was enamored of student protestors, such as those who'd recently organized the Free Speech Movement at Berkeley. "I thought those students were heroes; Diane thought they were traitors," he remembers keenly. "Diane and I spent the whole night arguing about politics—her judgments on protestors were very harsh," says Martin. "I thought she was a snob, a Junior League type, and she probably thought I was a dirty [beatnik]—she clearly didn't like me. I found her rigid and uptight. Her princesses were a lot hipper than she was. I wish I'd had a date with one of them."

Still, Diane's self-image—and Wellesley's image of her—was hardly as rigid as that striking impression would suggest. At that still cloistered woman's college with its hint of social conservatism, Diane and her roommate Marie fancied themselves quixotic—rather literally: They hung a poster of Don Quixote and Sancho Panza on their wall. "One day, to soothe our sense of boredom—'This room is so mundane!' we said—we decided to turn the poster upside down," Marie recalls. "Then we turned the *furniture* upside down. It was one of those 'We have to rebel!' moments."

Diane also joined the Wellesley jazz and blues singing group, the Blue Notes, which her sister Linda led. "We dressed in white blouses and 'Wellesley blue' knee-length skirts," recalls Marie, who was also a member of the twenty-girl group. The Blue Notes' repertoire was pegged to their name, covering blues standards like "Mood Indigo," "Basin Street," "Little Girl Blue," "Blues in the Night," and "When Sunny Gets Blue." They performed at top-tier schools: MIT, Harvard, Cornell, Dartmouth, Yale, and Bowdoin. Diane was renowned for what Marie recalls as "her killer soprano." They produced an LP, *You Ain't Been Blue*, whose title and theme contrasted the album cover photos of fresh-faced white girls who could have stepped out of the pages of *Mademoiselle* magazine.

In interviews, Diane has always portrayed her Wellesley self as dorky and wallflowerish. "I went to my first mixer my first year, and I heard some guy say to his date, 'That can't be her. She's nothing special,'" she has said. "I slinked out of the room and never went to a mixer again. I became very self-conscious. I only dated four or five times in college." Still, if this is true rather than a combination of diplomatic modesty, a then self-conscious state of mind, and some objective reality, at least two desirable young Ivy League men certainly were among this handful of dates. A very tall Missouri boy who'd been such a high school basketball sensation he'd been offered multiple college scholarships was one suitor. He drove all the way in from Princeton, where he was a senior when Diane was a sophomore, to take her out. "I went downstairs and there he was, waiting for her: standing there in all his wonderful height," Marie recalls. He was Bill Bradley, later to be a Rhodes scholar, Hall of Fame basketball player, Democratic senator from New Jersey, and, briefly, in 2000, presidential candidate.

Diane also dated Jamie Niven, the son of the British actor David Niven and "a big, hail-fellow, Swiss-boarding-school-educated Harvard hotshot," as a classmate describes Niven, who is now a vice president of Sotheby's. By this point, Diane's reputation as an unapproachable Wellesley beauty had spread to Harvard, but when Jamie Niven returned to his room after the date, he arrogantly told his Harvard buddies he didn't know what the "big deal" was about her.

And she kept up with Greg Haynes, her counterpart at Seneca High— he'd also been voted Most Likely to Succeed. She wrote Greg funny letters; he wrote her back, opening with, "Dear Lila." She visited him at the highly social Davidson College in North Carolina, with her minimal weekend wardrobe crammed into a bag "the size of a purse," he remembers having marveled. He saw her indifference to clothes—a hint of her extreme indifference to domesticity in the years to come—as a sign of "confidence."

The girl who'd sung the *My Fair Lady* song at the Louisville TV show used that talent to make her mark at Wellesley. It was as cowriter, chairperson, and lead of the junior play, *One Knight Stand*, that Diane Sawyer gained distinction—so much so that her friends like Greg Haynes expected her to go into the performance arts. Diane spent part of the summer of 1966 on Cape Cod with other classmates creating the play. Diane starred as Tupelora, so named because Tupelo Point was the spot along the campus's Lake Waban where Wellesley girls received marriage proposals from beaux on bended knee. And just like the unisex plays in Shakespeare's London, a Wellesley girl portrayed the knight in shining armor, Veritas (Harvard's motto). "It was a spoof on getting engaged and a spoof on the looming sexual revolution," Beth Johnson says. "Everybody loved Diane in it—and they loved the girl who played the knight, who was about five inches shorter than Diane," making for a very humorous "romance."

The next year, *Time* magazine pressed a nose to the Seven Sisters' glass and did a schematic breakdown: Radcliffe was "breathless brilliance," Barnard "corpuscular," Mount Holyoke "country sweet," Wellesley "wholesome and well-adjusted." The grooming grounds of well-heeled women were being romanticized just as their relevance was collapsing.

Diane spent her senior year in a single room next to Marie Fox's in Severance Hall, one of the beautiful Gothic-style buildings on campus, completed her work for her English major, and made plans for what to do next. Many small-city Wellesley girls were going to big cities; others were staying in the hospitably heady climes of leafy Massachusetts. But for Diane, who was close both to her family and to her church, home beckoned.

After graduation, she returned to Louisville and decided to cover her bases—possibly influenced by her father's distinction, she would go to law school at night. But what she really wanted to be was a TV news reporter. That calling meant putting her performance skills into practice with her other skills. Alice Chumbley Lora says today, "Looking back, I can see how that career choice involved aggression, curiosity, performance, willingness to work—all traits she combined into her final career."

WLKY was the CBS affiliate in town, and she applied for a job in their news division shortly after returning home in early summer 1967. There were no openings in news. Indeed, there were only two women on the local TV stations in Louisville at the time, and both of them—Julie Shaw at WAVE and Phyllis Knight at WHAS—were women's talk show hosts; neither was a newscaster. Not only that, Ken Rowland, WLKY's anchor and news director, was "a little skeptical of beauty queens," he says. Still,

Ed Shadburne, the station's general manager, had received Diane's application and knew her name, both from her term as America's Junior Miss and as Judge Sawyer's daughter. He pressed the dubious Ken Rowland to meet her anyway—even though there wasn't a job in news, there *was* an opening in weather.

Rowland took Diane to lunch at the restaurant in Stouffer's Hotel. "Just by the questions she asked, just by her curiosity about the world in general," he ended up thinking, "'I'm in the company of a very, very smart young woman.'" Rowland asked her if she'd like the job of weather woman, and she said, "No. I'm not interested in that job. I want to be a member of your *news* staff."

But being on the news staff was impossible, so Diane agreed to the weather job to get her foot in the door.

It was a wacky door to set one's foot into. Before the days of modern, localized meteorology, a station's weatherperson just called the National Weather Service a half hour before broadcast and then stood in front of a map and talked. Thus, novelty was called for. Diane's gimmick: She snuck bits of poetry—Auden, Baudelaire—into her disquisitions about imminent thunderstorms and patches of sunshine and the movement of high- and low-pressure fronts. She was known as the Weather Maiden. Half of the time she had difficulty seeing the board because of her very poor eyesight—her Coke-bottle glasses were a no-no on TV—and sometimes she made mistakes. "But if she got a forecast wrong she was delightful about it the next day," making fun of her error to the viewers, says Bob Taylor, WLKY's operations manager, who was in charge of hiring her. "She had no background" in weather *or* TV broadcasting—"no experience. But she had a confidence, a delivery." They loved Diane in the weather department at WLKY. A former weatherwoman had taken herself very seriously, and Diane, says one who worked with her, "was a one-hundred-eighty-degree turnabout" from that predecessor, as well as a hit with the viewers. Still, her fellow Seneca High high achievers, like Marc Fleischaker, who'd graduated from Penn, wondered what she was doing back in her hometown, in the house she grew up in, being a *weather* girl!

Weather, of course, was exactly where Diane *didn't* want to be. She wanted the big stories—like the riots that occurred when SNCC leader Stokely Carmichael was rumored to be coming to Louisville. "She constantly badgered me: 'Look, if you've got a news story and you don't have anybody to cover it on the weekend, would you let me go and do it?'" Ken Rowland recounts. "And I said yes." Rowland got a sense of her work ethic. After a day on weather, if he needed her to cover a fire, she was up for it. If there was a suspicious hospital death on a weekend, she could do that, too. She quit night law school.

Finally, after eight months, in March 1968, there was an opening in news. Weather didn't want to let Diane go and refused to trade her, but Rowland was tickled that he'd sneakily advised Diane not to sign a contract when she originally took the job. Sans contract, she could skip over to the news department. She did so in a heartbeat. Thus Diane Sawyer became the first full-time female TV news reporter in Louisville—just in time to help cover two country-shaking news stories: the assassinations of Martin Luther King Jr. and Bobby Kennedy.

AT JUST THIS MOMENT, women a generation older than Diane were finally opening the doors—a crack—as network anchors. Only four pioneers—Nancy Hanschman Dickerson, Marya McLaughlin, Lisa Howard, and Marlene Sanders—had put any real dents in the aircraft-metal ceiling of network news during the 1960s. That formidable ceiling had been pierced once—long before, in 1948—but since then had resisted much battering.

The reason that TV news's ceiling might be called "aircraft metal" is because service during World War II had been its hallowed and glamorous breeding ground. There were the dashing, risk-taking Murrow's Boys, newsman Edward R. Murrow's team that included Charles Collingwood, Eric Sevareid, and Howard K. Smith; and then there was feisty, independent Walter Cronkite filing copy for UPI. It was a guys' club up and down, long excused from the male-chauvinism rap because of the drama, heroism—the sheer élan—of being a war correspondent.

Even the way the first woman scored a moment on TV news has the

romantic sheen of a swing dance. Frances Buss was a young would-be actress working as a substitute receptionist at CBS TV in Grand Central
Terminal in early December 1941. Television was the brand-new novelty
medium that had yet to gain the authority of radio, which itself had only
recently leapt over newspapers and wire services by giving Americans
World War II news in real time. When Frances heard, through a friend
who had a radio, that the Japanese had attacked a big American naval
base somewhere in the South Pacific, "I quickly took the train from the
suburbs to the TV station," Frances Buss Buch recounted shortly before
her death, at ninety-two, in January 2010. Everyone there was panicked,
not just because of the attack on Pearl Harbor, but because "we—our
newscaster Bob Hubbell and the small crew—we didn't have maps! We
didn't have atlases! Hawaii wasn't a state yet, of course, and nobody at the
station knew where this naval base, Pearl Harbor, *was*." But Frances took
the phone call that came in with the geographic information and, with
her decent drawing skills, sketched a map and held it up to the CBS cameras to illustrate the world-shaking news. After honing her skills working
on some navy training films, in 1945 Buch became the first female director of an American TV show, a quiz show.

But the first serious pound on that metal ceiling came in 1948, by way
of forty-year-old Pauline Frederick. Frederick was essentially the founding mother of the women-in-TV-news cause. By the late forties she'd become that rarest thing: a female news gatherer for ABC TV, having paid
her dues as a print and then radio reporter. Pauline was the "exception—
she was 'above' women! She was *so* serious!" says Beryl Pfizer, mocking
her own midcentury self as the awed secretary for the *Arthur Godfrey
Show*. (Pfizer went on to be a *Today* show girl—a "tea pourer"—just before pioneer Barbara Walters got and transformed that job.)

Frederick was put on the air in desperation. She happened to be the
only reporter available the day a particularly important story came
through from the brand-new United Nations in 1947. The following year,
Frederick became the first ever female TV news commentator in the
United States.

Frederick, at ABC, was like CBS's Alice Weel, "who had gotten in the door during World War II only because there were no men around," says Walter Cronkite's longtime producer Sandy Socolow. "Any female who could write a sentence was hired" to scribble copy for anchor Douglas Edwards—"we just needed a body." Weel was "a freak," Socolow stresses, the only woman in the TV newsroom. "And God bless her, I loved her, but she was kind of sloppy. She wasn't particularly well groomed. Everyone at CBS was a white male who had previous experience in hard news somewhere else, and I assume NBC was the same." (ABC was a minor third network back then.) But Alice Weel—who the CBS men could reassuringly dismiss as ill-groomed, just as the ABC men reassuringly dismissed Pauline Frederick as dour—was merely a writer, behind the scenes. By contrast, Pauline Frederick got *on the air* as the first female anchor on a midday NBC New York affiliate—squeezed in between soap operas, but on the air nonetheless. Much of Frederick's airtime longevity was owed to an accident of the larynx: She had a very low, male-like voice.

Veteran network news producer Richard Wald remembers well what he calls the "*Father Knows Best* sexism" of early TV news, "when we didn't let anybody else in our tree house." Frederick never stopped fighting against this attitude. "Pauline *pushed*. Pauline was a feminist" well before the Second Wave feminism of Friedan and Steinem began. For over a decade Pauline Frederick had made the unpopular argument that women could be broadcasters.

Frederick's fortitude laid the groundwork for four younger "sisters"— born between 1926 and 1931, essentially a full generation older than Diane Sawyer—to make their own advances in the early to mid-sixties, when the *Mad Men* days were in full swing. This quartet was not just more feminine than the faux-masculine "sloppy" Alice and humorless Pauline; they were frankly sexy, and they rolled their eyes at their ghettoization. Nancy Hanschman Dickerson—who had dated John F. Kennedy when he was a senator from Massachusetts—had turned down a women's-page editorship at a Washington, D.C., paper "because," she'd scoffed, "it seemed outlandish to try to change the world by writing shopping and food columns." She became CBS's first female behind-the-scenes reporter in 1960, and went on to NBC, becoming, along the way, a well-married woman who threw A-list parties in twist-era Georgetown. Marya McLaughlin—who for thirty years had a romance with Senator Eugene McCarthy—became CBS's first on-camera reporter in the spring of 1965. McLaughlin once fielded a request to "cover cooking" with: "Oh, *now* I understand. If a 707 crashed this afternoon, you want me to take my camera crew to the pilot's house and . . . ask [his widow] what she would have cooked for dinner."

McLaughlin's ascent to the air prompted a trend piece in the *New York Times*. The article was written by a freelancer named Gloria and commissioned by another Gloria, the Food-Fashion-Furnishings editor. It was headlined "Nylons in the Newsroom." As the breezy title makes clear, 1965 was a hinge year—the exact middle of the decade—when one female paradigm was exaggerated in a last-gasp way as another was rumbling in its egg. The article's editor was Gloria Emerson, who went on to become, after lobbying the paper furiously for the posting, an award-winning Vietnam War correspondent. The freelance writer was Gloria Steinem.

ABC's Lisa Howard, the third pathfinder, was too idiosyncratic to succumb to constraints. The actress-turned-broadcaster became so close to Fidel Castro that she helped open negotiations with Castro for the Kennedy administration. Beset by depression, Howard killed herself in 1965.

Marlene Sanders, the only one of the four pioneers still alive, started as a secretary and became, in October 1964, the first woman to anchor a network news TV show that was more than five minutes long between soap operas. But, like Frederick's breakthrough sixteen years earlier, that was by default: As an ABC press release took pains to explain, Sanders would be "a temporary female replacement . . . for an indispensable Ron Cochran," who'd lost his voice one day. Sanders, a Midwestern-bred straight shooter who became friends with Betty Friedan early on and has retained a feminist's gimlet eye on women in TV news (and who happens to be the mother of journalist and TV legal pundit Jeffrey Toobin), earned the spot through the same random attribute that had aided Frederick: "My voice was low." Lest the novelty of her appointment be missed, Sanders's eventual afternoon straight-news broadcast was called *News with a Woman's Touch*.

So this was the state of isolated gains—fleeting anchor slots grabbed by default, accidents of timing, or flukes of voice timbre, all undercut by network apologies—that Diane Sawyer, at a local station in a small city, was braving in 1968.

Some parts of Diane's early time in news could have been fodder for a period sitcom about a gal reporter at a provincial TV station: The time she'd borrowed Ken Rowland's car, opened the trunk to store her big Bell & Howell camera . . . and found a cache of girly magazines that the city's chief of police had confiscated during a magazine-stand public-decency raid—and had then mock-grilled Rowland: "What kind of literature have you been reading?" Or the mistake of going off to cover the Ringling Brothers Circus in a miniskirt—only to realize that a miniskirt was the last thing you want to be televised in while straddling an elephant. There were politicians' wives to sip tea with and Lions Club meetings to cover. And, yes, WLKY was, even its own staff quipped, "the fourth of the city's three TV stations."

But the lowliness had advantages. At the bare-bones station that was struggling to stay alive, Diane carried her own camera (or parts thereof)—in those days, shooting in sound required heavy equipment, "a huge tripod, and you had to put lights on two different ends of the room to shoot a subject," says Rowland. One night Diane, Rowland, and assignment editor Jim Smith were hauling equipment to cover a public meeting, "and there must have been half a dozen men who saw her, this beautiful blond, carrying all this equipment, and they all said, 'May I help you?'" She had to keep saying, "No, thank you, I can handle it," over and over again. "And she did, and you would never know it from her face but I knew she was furious. *Furious!* I was biting my tongue to keep from laughing." Kidding aside, "Diane wanted to be one of the boys. She didn't want any special favors." ("I know where Diane was coming from," says Ginny Vicario. In 1974, a full six years after Diane was shooing off these chivalrous men, Vicario became the first female news camera operator ever hired by a network. "You could *not* accept help," Vicario says of the late sixties and early seventies. "You could *not* accept 'chivalry.' If you did, the man would turn around and say he'd *had* to help you.")

Being at a small-staffed station also meant doing her own on-site reporting *and* in-studio editing *and* on-air reporting. On the night of a local election, "it was a quarter to ten and Democratic headquarters was mobbed." In order to escape the room to get back to the station to edit her report for her narration on the eleven p.m. broadcast, "Diane took [a teenage intern] by the hand and said, 'Follow me,' and they got down on their hands and knees and they *crawled* out," Ken Rowland recalls.

WLKY's reporters and producers were affected by community events on a personal level. News directors' houses were egged when reporters, including Diane, covered the open housing marches and reported on the violence. "Communist! Communist!" callers yelled into Ken Rowland's home phone. The worst violence in Louisville took place when a young black boy was killed by police who thought he'd robbed a store. It turned out he'd been unarmed and was running out of fear, not guilt. Protests and riots broke out all over the city and suburbs; though Rowland would not send Diane out into riots, she covered the daily press conferences, and when the dead boy's mother begged for calm and forgiveness, Diane's eyes were as misty as many members of the public's. During one of the city's civil rights battles, a handsome, extremely self-assured national and international reporter visited Louisville to see things close up. Rowland spent the day taking the young news VIP and his crew to relevant locations. "When we got back to the newsroom, he saw Diane at her desk and he poked me and said, 'Introduce me.'" Rowland did, but "Diane was very cool about it; she didn't seem to be impressed." Whether she felt hit upon and didn't like it or whether she got a whiff of this fellow's eventually storied arrogance and was defending her small, scrappy station from the subtle condescension of a privileged interloper, he seemed to have gotten her coolness. "And," Ken Rowland says, "I think that's the first time that ever happened to Peter Jennings."

SOON THE WORLD beyond Louisville beckoned. Washington, D.C., was the closest major market, and Diane had a connection there. The Washington, D.C., head of CBS News—Bill Small—had run a TV station in

Louisville until 1962 and he knew of Diane's family. "But I didn't know she existed until I read her résumé and saw that she worked for the Louisville station," Small says. She came to Washington in 1969 looking for work at the worst time possible—during a job freeze—which was a shame because "she was smart as hell," he soon discovered.

Small asked Diane to write a five-minute newscast, go into the studio, and tape it. "She did all of that with flying colors: She wrote fast, she wrote well, and her presentation was excellent. I said, 'If you'll be patient, these job freezes don't last forever.'" He called the CBS local news director, Jim Snyder, and said, "'This young woman strikes me as having terrific talent. I can't hire her right now. Can I send her to you?' But Snyder said, 'We're in the same boat.'" Diane returned to Louisville. However, Small never stopped following Diane, or regretting his initial inability to hire her. Later, he would be a key champion at a crucial juncture.

Then came her father's tragic death on the bridge that morning in late September. Perhaps to cleave to his memory as a distinguished Republican elected official, and to honor the contacts he had to bequeath to her, Diane sought a job with the Nixon White House. She called a senator who had been a close friend of her father's, who called Lamar Alexander, then the chairman of the Republican Party. Soon, Diane was officially applying for a job with Ron Ziegler, President Nixon's press secretary. Ziegler hailed from Kentucky (Alexander was from adjacent Tennessee) and knew Judge Sawyer's reputation. As for taking a job in politics and government, "I felt that the journalist's perspective was home for me," Diane has said, referring to the satisfaction she'd felt during her year and a half as full-time news reporter, "but I really wanted to know something about making decisions, about taking responsibility."

Bearing a recommendation from one of Kentucky's senators, who had known her father, Diane was granted an interview with Ziegler's deputy, Gerry Warren. "None of us knew Diane. Before I could even talk to her, she sat on the podium while I was giving a briefing; it showed me an ease, a sense of self," Warren remembers. "She was young and very wholesome and very fresh—fresh in the sense of eager to learn—but also quite refined. She was self-assured, but in a way that wasn't arrogant." Diane now cut a stylish, even glamorous figure. Long gone was the crimped beauty queen hairdo and the prim smile. Her blond hair was now several inches past shoulder length and lightly flipped up, slightly teased at the crown. She started wearing fashionable large sunglasses, big bracelets, and patterned miniskirts that showcased her long legs. Although Richard Nixon and his lieutenants (several sporting military buzz cuts) represented retrograde uptightness, this period of Diane's life, oddly enough, presents her at her most sultry looking. Aside from her attractiveness, "she was eager to work—she was not afraid of work," Gerry Warren says, immediately perceiving a quality that would last throughout her career. "We just happened to have an opening and she moved in. It was clear that she was not going to be a secretary. She was going to help us on substantive issues."

As excited as she was to take the White House job, "Diane was concerned about leaving her mother home in Louisville," says Jim Smith, her immediate boss at WLKY. "She mentioned, kidding around after a newscast, "'Gee, I wish somebody could find someone for my mother to meet.' So we did find someone, Dr. Ray Hayes," an occasional guest on a WLKY afternoon show. An introduction was made. Dr. Hayes, the medical director of the state mental hospital in Louisville, was a recent widower, his wife having committed suicide. The dramatically sudden loss of spouses is something Ray Hayes and Jean Sawyer had in common. The two began seeing each other. They eventually married, and remained together until Dr. Hayes's death in 2004. Diane would become close to her stepfather over the years—according to friends' accounts, she liked him very much.

Relieved that her mother was not alone, Diane left for Washington, D.C., in 1970.

WHAT A TIME to go to work at the Nixon White House! The counterculture was in ascent; so many of Diane's peers were going left, yet she was heading right. The Republican Party in Kentucky was different back then, explains one of Diane's Seneca classmates. "We didn't have the right wing we have today, not the ones who are as fanatical about Jesus. There were no Pat Robertsons. Those people didn't exist, or if they did, they were a small minority." Besides, two other Seneca '63 students—Greg Haynes and his wife, Sallie Schulten Haynes—were going to work for Nixon, too. So from a local standpoint, it wasn't necessarily out of sync. Still, Diane's time with Nixon would be the most controversial eight years on her résumé—and she has ruefully laughed that, over her long career, she's been simultaneously criticized for being a flaming liberal *and* an unconscionable conservative.

Nixon had won the 1968 election against Hubert Humphrey in a very divided America. Humphrey represented old-style liberal values. Nixon was representing law and order. And after a tumultuous two years of assassinations and riots, and the theatrics-for-the-sake-of-it at the 1968 Democratic Convention in Chicago, law and order, for older Americans, was an attractive position. Diane *herself* seemed to have a divided political and social philosophy. She had lived a personal, day-to-day version of the civil rights struggle, but she was a daughter of Republicans, and on the matter of protests against the Vietnam War—which were never popular even among the relatively liberal reporter class in Kentucky—she was likely agnostic, and, at least six years earlier, toward the end of her America's Junior Miss reign, she had, according to Martin Snapp, virtually condemned the student protests.

The odd thing about Nixon, though, was that his personal affect included a woundedness that belied his reputation as a tough guy (and, later, as a criminal), and people who worked with him saw this. "I don't think there's any question of Nixon's vulnerability," says John Dean, Nixon's chief counsel in the early 1970s. "As Kissinger once said, 'If somebody would have loved the man, he'd have been a different person.' Nixon was an unusual person to be in the political business. He was not a people person. He couldn't do small talk. When you took anybody to the Oval Office, you had to give some words for him to start a conversation, like, 'I understand you just won the Philadelphia bowling contest.'

"He was a complex man—fascinatingly complex, a different person to different people," Dean continues. "In my relationship with him, he didn't swear—he was high-minded. But [Chief of Staff H. R.] Haldeman and

[Special Counsel Charles] Colson seemed to bring out the worst in him. With Kissinger, he was constantly showing off, trying to convince Henry how tough he was."

The Nixon White House "was not a boys' club," John Dean insists, even as he contradicts himself to note that "there were women all over the place—extremely attractive women. I was a bachelor in those days. The White House was a lovely place to work." Those women mainly ran the social and communications offices, though Dean did hire a female attorney ("Haldeman thought I was crazy"). Still, there were whiffs of feminism from unexpected quarters: First Lady Pat Nixon, the president's younger daughter, Julie Nixon, and even Martha Mitchell—the later-thought "hysterical" wife of Attorney General John Mitchell—were pushing Nixon to nominate a female Supreme Court justice, a landmark that would not come for another ten years. Nixon was willing to consider it. He brought the idea up to Chief Justice Warren Burger, but Burger, Dean recalls, "threatened to resign if Nixon put a woman on the court." Burger's threat caused Nixon to back down, with somewhat absurd reasoning. "Those chambers are small," the president said. "It would be like putting a woman into a space capsule with men." Even then, though, he didn't quite give up. "'You know, John,'" Dean recalls the president telling John Mitchell, "'we don't have any women in the cabinet.' Mitchell barked his response: 'Keep 'em in the kitchen or the bedroom!'"

This was the self-contradictory, challenging atmosphere toward women that twenty-five-year-old Diane Sawyer was entering. She handled it deftly, parlaying her intellect, her work ethic, and her charm. "She brought an intellectual spark to the press office and creativity that was invaluable," Ron Ziegler, who died in 2003, told a reporter in 1989. In fact, the spark may have been more than intellectual. A journalist who covered Nixon says that some people thought that Diane was having some kind of relationship with (the married) Ziegler. "Diane was ferociously ambitious, though she hid it well," that journalist adds. Gerry Warren says: "She was just so capable. She just stepped into situations. I would tell her what I needed to prepare Ron for his briefing, and she would get the answers for us."

Diane's job unexpectedly intensified within a year. In early 1971, a huge cache of decades' worth of secret government reports, known as the Pentagon Papers, were leaked by RAND Corporation analyst Daniel Ellsberg to the *New York Times*. These documents revealed, as the *Times* put it, "that the Lyndon Baines Johnson Administration had systematically lied . . . to the public [and] Congress, about a subject of transcendent national interest and significance": the Vietnam War, which Nixon was continuing to wage, despite a well-advanced antiwar movement. It was at this moment, says John Dean, "that the dark side of Richard Nixon surfaced."

A series of explosive developments ensued: The *Washington Post* also published the incendiary documents about the prior administration's highly questionable and falsified grounds for the war; the Nixon White House went after the *Times* and the *Post*, and lost; the antiwar movement gained even more momentum; and a sensational, bungled break-in into Daniel Ellsberg's psychiatrist's office in Beverly Hills was discovered, auguring darker, more desperate dirty tricks on the part of the administration. Were some of the days dramatic for Ron Ziegler, Gerry Warren, and Diane Sawyer in their efforts to manage the press? "They were *all* dramatic," Warren responds, with a grim laugh. "We were working pretty hard in those days, our heads down. We had a small staff and Diane really played a big role." Diane "worked like a Trojan" during this time, her Seneca High friend Greg Haynes could see. Haynes was working at the old Executive Office Building, which shared a parking lot with the White House. "When I'd drive in very early every morning, her car was already there."

IN FEBRUARY 1972, Diane accompanied Nixon on his historic trip to China, the first visit by an American president since Mao's Cultural Revolution, thawing relations that had been frozen for twenty-five years. Av Westin, then executive producer of ABC's coverage of the trip, met the "bright and with-it assistant to Ron Ziegler" in Beijing and appreciated Diane's help in tipping him off about each day's events, enabling "a geometric increase in the amount of coverage" by not having to spread his reporters and cameramen out everywhere. Diane's attractiveness clearly did not hurt. Her old WLKY boss Ed Shadburne remembers seeing the televised images of Nixon's key meeting with the Chinese premier "and Diane was sitting at the right-hand side of Chou En-lai and you could tell by the animated way he was talking to her he was totally enthralled with her." Bill Small, who'd sorely regretted not having a job for Diane, was along on the trip, too. He remembers an embarrassing moment that Diane handled deftly: The press was "gathered in a hotel lobby," about to leave. "The Chinese at that time were unbelievably honest—if you left a pen in your room, they came running after you. Diane had apparently discarded some underwear. A man came running out, "Miss Sawyer! Miss Sawyer!"—earnestly waving a pair of panties. "She stuffed them into her purse before anyone could see."

The only female TV reporter on the trip was Barbara Walters, then the cohost to Frank McGee on *Today.* "The fact that I was there at all was a minor miracle," she wrote in her 2008 autobiography, *Audition.* "The networks sent their heavyweight, politically experienced superstars"—Walter Cronkite, Dan Rather, Eric Sevareid, Harry Reasoner, John Chancellor, Ted Koppel. "My inclusion," at NBC executive Richard Wald's insistence, "ruffled a lot of feathers." Bill Small observed Walters's intense preparation on the flight over. "Thirteen hours, and she never once took her head out of the research," he remembers. The trip to China was the first time the two women met. Diane—who was "in the president's entourage," Barbara was quick to note—seemed to Barbara like "a very pretty, young blond with whom I would have a nodding acquaintance but no real contact." Later they would be ABC colleagues and—as Walters's wary, even icy appraisal hints at—intense rivals.

Despite her by then estimable success and popularity, Barbara Walters was suffering daily humiliation at *Today,* where Frank McGee insisted he get the first four questions with every interview subject. Walters put up with second-class citizenship throughout all three years—1971 to 1974— she cohosted the show. "Barbara was a pioneer—she took all the sexist [slings and arrows]," says former TV executive Paul Friedman, generally a great skeptic about using the *s*-word and a man who likes her tremendously. (Friedman, a TV news veteran, was Peter Jennings's producer at ABC *World News Tonight*, and went on to produce for Diane in her mature career—as well as for Katie Couric. But he can be strikingly non–politically correct about women in TV news.) It's hard to find a male producer who doesn't agree with Friedman about her.

Barbara Walters had been the canary in the coal mine for women in television. First a press agent, then *Today* lead writer, and the one *Today* "tea pourer" who made the leap to cohost in 1971, Barbara would pave the way for women anchors/interviewers in all three TV formats: morning, evening, and newsmagazine. "Prior to Barbara, the women on the *Today* show were all decorations," having to hide their brainpower, says Richard Wald. "We didn't show that sort of stuff": smart women. "But Barbara was different. Even when she was just beginning on the *Today* show, she worked harder than anybody else, and she had more imagination about what would work on television than the people around her. Barbara built the system of letting girls in the tree house."

Still, while Walters was opening that tree house for future female anchors, many less-well-placed women at NBC had a tougher road—and were paying a price. "The 1970 NBC Women's Revolt," as it's called, was a legendary battle, recalls *Today* veteran Beryl Pfizer. Pfizer witnessed the inciting incident. "One morning around ten, I heard a slight disturbance outside my door. A producer yelled, to researcher Marilyn Schultz, 'Hey, Schultzie, we need coffee!' Schultzie yelled back, 'I am *not* your waitress!' He yelled back: '*Damn it*, Schultzie! I said: We need coffee! *Go get it!*'" Schultzie refused again—and an underdog's class-action suit was born.

"Schultzie was brave! She was a true revolutionary!" Pfizer says. The women's movement was still slightly under the radar, although Betty Friedan's National Organization for Women (NOW) had been launched and that year would stage its Women's Strike for Equality. Marilyn Schultz and a few other midlevel women at NBC who instigated the demand for equitable treatment and pay were risking their careers. "The management of NBC was just horrible," Marlene Sanders says. "Secretaries' and newswomen's careers were ended by that lawsuit—they were regarded as troublemakers. And Barbara Walters wouldn't help," Sanders contends. Walters would later help the cause of women in TV, but she declined "to be involved in the suit in the very early seventies, when it mattered," Sanders says, with her usual candor and a feminism that's never lost its bite. Perhaps back then the only recently ascendant Walters didn't feel she could afford to help the cause of female colleagues lower in the hierarchy. Or perhaps such narrow self-interest was an inevitable part of getting ahead when the deck was stacked against you.

FOUR MONTHS AFTER THE TRIP to China, the Nixon administration spun criminally out of control. On June 17 came the break-in at the Democratic National Committee headquarters at the Watergate office complex. Diane's boss, Ron Ziegler, tried to brush it off as a "third-rate burglary attempt." Arrests were made, and a name in the address books of two of the burglars tied the perpetrators to E. Howard Hunt, of the president's Special Investigations Unit, otherwise known as the White House Plumbers. A month and a half later, a sizable payment from the Nixon reelection campaign was traced to one of the burglars; then *more* money was traced. A month after that, it was revealed that John Mitchell oversaw a secret bank account for intelligence gathering activities against the Democratic Party.

In stunning, weekly, drip-by-drip increments, it became clear that the break-in was part of an enormous, complex campaign of sabotage and spying by the reelection committee. Still, despite these falling dominoes, the president vigorously campaigned against Democratic presidential nominee George McGovern, with the support of entertainers respected by Diane's generation. James Taylor, Carole King, Carly Simon, and Barbra Streisand were involved in a concert supporting McGovern. To many of that generation, anyone who supported Richard Nixon, even apart from this deepening scandal—including Diane—was highly suspect, and such peers were considered to be contemptibly, almost unbelievably, on the wrong side of this early battle of the yet unnamed culture wars.

Despite the revelations of Watergate, Nixon won the presidency in 1972 by a near landslide. The McGovern/McCarthy wing had pulled the Democratic Party too far left for middle America's taste. Even a likely lawbreaker was deemed preferable to a possible coddler of hippies and radicals.

In early February 1973 the Senate voted unanimously to set up a special committee to investigate Watergate. The unraveling quickened in March 1973, when one of the Watergate burglars admitted perjury. John Dean, Nixon's counsel, secretly began to cooperate with the prosecution, breaking the story wide open and paving the way for indictments and imprisonments (including his own brief one). But he also warned Nixon, in private talks, that Watergate was "a cancer on the presidency" and that hush money supplied to the Watergate burglars was "the most troublesome post-thing because" H. R. Haldeman, John Ehrlichman, John Mitchell, and Dean himself were involved in that aspect, which constituted "obstruction of justice." Dean says today that he cooperated with authorities in part as a warning to others. "It was very hard to convince people that a disaster was imminent. One of my theories was that by blowing it up and going to the prosecutors, my colleagues would follow me and Nixon would survive. That didn't happen. Instead, Nixon got more mired."

Haldeman, Ehrlichman, and Dean—Nixon's closest advisers—were out of the White House by the end of April, the first two forcibly resigning and Dean being fired. "As things disintegrated, more doors were closed and the circle got smaller," Dean says. He adds, significantly, "This is the key period when Diane gets closer to Nixon." With a shrinking team of loyalists, aides farther out moved closer in to do damage control.

The Senate Watergate televised hearings took place from mid-May to early August. The public was riveted. A full 85 percent of Americans with TV sets watched at least some of the proceedings.

During it all, Diane knew that her junior position offered her a prime perch for witnessing the psychology of powerful people in crisis. "I was able to listen, because no one was really interested in what I had to say," she's said. "To be in the White House at that time, learning about human nature, as you can when you aren't in the center of the action, was such an education." She also drew an inspirational lesson from the crisis. She has said that she "learned," from watching Nixon, how to "get up in the morning when—for whatever reasons, self-inflicted or otherwise—your vision of yourself has been shattered" and you are facing a "cataclysm."

IRONICALLY, JUST AS Diane was becoming key in protecting the ever more embattled—and ever less innocent-seeming—Richard Nixon, a quartet of young female reporters were fighting to unearth the truth about Watergate from the very bureau—Bill Small's CBS newsroom in D.C.—that Diane had applied for a job with four years earlier. While Watergate made rock stars of Bob Woodward and Carl Bernstein, who were breaking the biggest stories, Lesley Stahl, Connie Chung, Susan Zirinsky, and Marcy McGinnis had, with less fanfare, eagerly invaded the CBS newsroom and were pushing *against* Diane's team, and having the time of their lives doing so.

Their hirings had come about as a form of corporate damage control. In 1971, CBS president Dick Salant was—half forcibly, but effectively—turned into a de facto feminist. This was a full year before Congress enacted Title IX, in June 1972, extending the Civil Rights Act of 1964 to cover gender as well as race. Title IX meant companies could be sued for discrimination if they didn't meet "certain minimum percentages" of women staffers, and, adds former network executive Paul Friedman, cynically, "That's a powerful incentive—being afraid of being sued. Most of the men who made it happen for the women [in TV news] were doing it out of fear."

Salant jumped the gun on Title IX because he saw the backlash after CBS chairman William Paley issued a memo decreeing that CBS women could no longer wear slacks to work—a peculiarly old-fashioned edict that incensed the women at the network. As the first "consciousness-raising groups" were being set up on Central Park West and Upper East Side living rooms, as Betty Friedan's NOW was protesting gender-segregated newspaper employment ads and the long-established practice of denying women mortgages and even department store credit, as *Ms.* magazine was about to be launched, the order for women to wear skirts to work could not have been more ill-timed.

The female staff at *Newsweek* magazine had already begun to organize. Their complaint was that women—including the soon-to-be disgusted and defecting Nora Ephron and Ellen Goodman—were stuck being "researcher"; they couldn't advance to "writer." Now the women of CBS joined the fray. In a parallel complaint to those of the (eventually triumphant) *Newsweek* and the (ill-fated) NBC women, the CBS crew, led in part by the soon-to-be-prominent Sylvia Chase, protested that they had been hired as secretaries at the same time that their male counterparts had been hired as copyboys, yet now the men were producers and reporters and they, like the *Newsweek* women, were stuck as researchers.

Spurred by William Paley's ham-handed memo, Dick Salant decided to head off the outcry. "Salant said we could not hire anyone unless it was a female—that was an absolute dictum," Sandy Socolow says. "If we were desperate for a particular male, we had to go to him and make a case." The new female hires "were dogged reporters," says Bill Small, and each came via a different path. Stahl was the oldest—thirty when she was hired. She'd worked for NBC in London and was back at a station in her hometown of Boston when Socolow, who had a family connection to her, urged her to send an audition tape. Hurriedly she complied, with a laughable offering: She was dressed as a pilgrim re-creating the first Thanksgiving. "I said, 'Salant will fire me if I give him this. Send me another one,'" Socolow says. Lesley did—and she was hired.

Connie Chung, the twenty-five-year-old American-raised daughter of a Chinese diplomat, was a young local Washington, D.C., TV reporter. One day she burst into the restaurant—Provençal—that happened to be the CBS honchos' favorite lunch hangout, and aggressively questioned its owner and patrons about the unsanitary conditions that had earned the restaurant a health code violation. Impressed by her ballsiness, Bill Small gave her his card. "Connie called twenty minutes after I got back to the office. I hired her, and she became one of the most terrific reporters we've ever seen."

"Lesley and I were like Thelma and Louise," says Connie. "We were so hungry, we were indefatigable—we were cub reporter *killers.* The men didn't know what hit them. Lesley was amazing. She jumped into Watergate and developed sources and was able to break all sorts of stories." Bill Small: "Lesley went out to interview John Dean. He wouldn't open his door. Lesley lifts up the slot where you put the letters in and says, 'I just want to ask you a few questions.' She did the whole interview through the mail slot." Connie: "We staked out Ehrlichman, Haldeman, Dean. They'd say, 'Send Connie out! Send Lesley out! *They'll* get 'em.'"

One day Connie was phoning in a scoop from a phone booth when two "old stuffed shirts" from a rival network, knowing she had coveted information, shoved into the tight space to forcibly eavesdrop. Seated in the booth, eye level to the men's waists, Connie needed to one-up their bullying and to clear them out. "So I unzipped both of their flies." Stunned, they exited.

"Lesley and I didn't have desks" for their first months at CBS, Connie says. They'd troll the newsroom with their brimming notebooks and they'd cadge typewriters. "Later, they gave us kiddies' desks." They'd peck out their copy "while juggling our typewriters on the desks' slanted tops."

Susan Zirinsky, the third hire, was an American University undergrad who'd been desultorily licking envelopes for New York congressman Ed Koch amid highly manicured volunteers who, unlike her, were looking not for careers but for husbands. So she felt like "Alice falling down the rabbit hole" when she found her way to CBS and came upon the other young female reporters pecking away on kindergarten desks—"the *tiniest* desks! Way in the back where the secretaries sat," Zirinsky says. Then she realized, "Holy shit! That's Lesley Stahl! That's Connie Chung!"

Pint-size Zirinsky—"Z," as she is called, then and now—was quickly revealed as a dynamo. ("She fought a lot—you don't screw around with Susan Zirinsky," Av Westin says.) "I was staking out John Mitchell at the Jefferson Hotel, looking for Deep Throat in every parking garage every weekend, calling in all the firings—*bing! bing! bing!*—in the Saturday Night Massacre to Cronkite. It was like good sex! You got thrown a question at six twenty-five from someone going live in five minutes. You were on the phone with Capitol Hill and the White House. (I wasn't high up enough to talk to Diane; I got some kid.) It was like being on *Jeopardy!* every single night."

Marcy McGinnis, as tiny and young and avid as Susan Zirinsky, was a mere stenographer in the CBS office, "literally taking down the Watergate hearings, minute by minute, in shorthand, for the producers. Z and I were two little munchkins running around: the researcher and the secretary," Marcy says. "We became friends"—just as Lesley and Connie had—"because we were so alike: tiny, there's-nothing-we-wouldn't-do go-getters."

All four women are now legends. Marcy McGinniss became the first female senior vice president of CBS News and is now senior vice president of newsgathering at Al Jazeera America. Susan Zirinsky, a decades-long senior executive producer at the network (and the inspiration for Holly Hunter's character in the movie *Broadcast News*); Connie Chung, the second ever female cohost of a six-thirty p.m. news show; and Lesley Stahl, a longtime *60 Minutes* star. All would later interact with Diane as Diane turned, improbably, from loyal Nixon protector to grunt TV news reporter and then to TV news star and then to *major* TV news star, showing herself to be as aggressive and indefatigable as they were.

While Diane was on the other side of the Watergate fence from these emerging women, in the midst of the crisis she began a romance with a new young White House staffer, Frank Gannon. Three years older than she, Gannon was a "really smart guy with a wonderfully ironic sense of humor," says one who knew him. A product of Queens, New York, and a Catholic tradition-minded enough to collect sacramental objects, he'd attended Georgetown University's School of Foreign Service, the London School of Economics, and Oxford. He had recently returned to the United States as a White House Fellow. He was as loyal to Nixon as Diane was.

The small knot of remaining Nixon staffers, including Diane and Gannon and Gerry Warren, believed the president was innocent: that he had never known about, much less sanctioned, the sabotage or the cover-up. They *willed* themselves into believing this. Warren, who went on to become editor of the *San Diego Union-Tribune* and then to become an Episcopal lay cleric, puts what we now call "being in denial" in these understandable words: "You cannot be loyal and think your boss is involved—it just isn't human."

But the truth was growing undeniable. The most dramatic day of the saga was October 20, 1973—the Saturday Night Massacre—during legal maneuverings over the release of Nixon tapes to independent prosecutor Archibald Cox. Nixon fired Cox in an effort to avoid complying with the subpoena. Attorney General Elliot Richardson and Deputy Attorney General William Ruckelshaus resigned, rather than carry out Nixon's order. Less than a month later, a federal district judge ruled that the dismissal of Cox had been illegal. A record number of telegrams—seventy-one thousand—from citizens flooded the Washington office of Western Union, many calling for Nixon's impeachment.

"We continued to be loyal," Gerry Warren says. In his and Diane's beleaguered situation, they stonewalled the press. "There was only one message to give and we weren't giving that: 'What about the tapes?'" (Secret, unheard tapes existed, detailing the planning stages of the operation.) Reporters pummeled them: "'What about John Dean's testimony?' 'What about this meeting?' '*That* meeting?'" Warren's and Sawyer's desperate effort to change the subject to non-Watergate issues—to talk about *anything* else—"was like a tree falling in the forest. The atmosphere in the press room was *not* pleasant—that's the best way I can put it." Warren stresses: "Diane was a brick throughout the whole thing. She was strong—very, very strong." She had learned about strength by coming back to work at WLKY soon after her father died. Working nonstop through this very different emotional adversity was more of the same: an act of service that became an act of healing.

As 1973 turned to 1974, Watergate deepened. In February, the House of Representatives voted nearly unanimously—410 to 4—to investigate Nixon for possible impeachment. In March, a grand jury indicted Haldeman, Ehrlichman, Mitchell, Colson, and three others for obstruction, and named Nixon as an unindicted coconspirator. The clamor grew loud for the release of transcripts of Nixon's tape-recorded conversations with his aides—transcripts that would reveal, in Senator Howard Baker's famous formulation, what the president knew and when he knew it.

"It was a siege mentality. It was a *siege!*" says Gerry Warren of these months. Ron Ziegler was now assistant to the president, Warren was de facto press secretary, and Diane was Warren's deputy. Diane and Warren worked "twelve, sometimes fourteen, sixteen hours a day—we'd order up meals from the White House mess hall. Someone calls from *Newsweek* Saturday night: 'What about this?' We crash and try to find the answers and get them in the newspapers. I worked with Diane every day. I saw the passion she brought to her work. She was loyal; that's quintessential Diane."

"Bruising, nerve-deadening torment" is how Diane has recalled this period. Thoroughness was her armor—and her weapon. "I read all the newspapers and all the testimony and all the lawyers' briefs. I became a kind of walking computer. Even the lawyers would call me occasionally, because I seemed to have everything on file." Such stressful crisis research was, of course, the best kind of preparation for the intensely competitive, time-pressured TV reporting that would come in her future.

Finally, in late April 1974, edited transcripts of the tapes were issued, revealing Nixon's contempt for the country's institutions, which not only the media but even hitherto loyalists found disturbing. In late July, Nixon was ordered by the Supreme Court to hand over the tapes themselves.

The hard-core defenders bit the bullet. And then it came, on August 5: the "smoking-gun tape," which had been recorded a few days after the 1972 break-in. On it, Nixon and Haldeman could be heard discussing the obstruction of justice and the cover-up. It was clear: Nixon knew everything. "Good. Good deal. Play it tough," the president had told Haldeman.

Diane and Gerry Warren heard the tape before the public did. Warren looked over at Diane and "I saw the sorrow that hit her. It was like a sledgehammer to the stomach." "When it was clear what had happened"— that Nixon had in fact been guilty—"it was too late to be mad," Diane has said. "It was over." She seems to have felt more despondency and regret than anger. "What a considerable presidency it would have been without Watergate . . . ," she later reflected.

Diane would see Pat Nixon walking around the White House compound from time to time, and Julie and Tricia would come to visit their father a lot—Diane got to know them. One day, right after the sledgehammer-to-the-stomach moment, Diane and the others noticed Nixon's secretary, Rose Mary Woods, leave her office to go to a private room to talk to the assembled Nixon women: Pat, Tricia, Julie. There was a buzz among the staff—what was this about? It soon became clear that the president had dispatched his secretary to tell his wife and daughters that he had made the decision to resign. Nixon could not face telling them himself. All the other close-in staffers—the men—"thought it was so strange and removed and formal," Diane has said of this moment. Only Diane understood. "Of course it wasn't" removed and formal, this choice of his, she would say, much later, to writer Kevin Sessums, in 2011. It wasn't about formality at all—"It was about pain." Diane's sympathy for Nixon remained oddly pure; it's hard to know where it came from, except that, despite the extreme wrongdoing, his vulnerability was the paramount thing she saw in him. "He also had a courtly feeling about women," she continued, which was why he had his secretary tell them—this was perhaps more dignified, more deferential, less hurtfully self-revealing. "He felt he was responsible for having manners of a certain kind."

Just before his official resignation, Nixon made a speech to his staff in the East Room that appealed to his staff's religiosity, a quality that Diane and Warren shared. "It was very poignant. He said something that has been imprinted on my mind ever since," Warren says. "'Don't hate. The one you hate will always win.'" Pastor Owen or Catherine Marshall could not have said it better.

On August 8, 1974, Richard Nixon announced his resignation, effective at noon the next day. He thus became the only American president ever to give up the office. The next day, with an oddly triumphal salute at the top of the stairs to the helicopter, he bade farewell to America and, in disgrace, flew to San Clemente.

Diane was exhausted, emotionally and physically. She only recently disclosed what she did in the immediate aftermath of Nixon's resignation. "I went away by myself to Tahiti for a month, moving from island to island." It is not clear whether Frank Gannon was with her or not. "I kept trying to get further and further away. Talk about a metaphor. I ended up on an island with no hotels, sleeping in the living room of a small house. . . . I didn't know what was next."

But she must have known, because what she did next was this: She flew out to San Clemente, to help Nixon research and write his memoirs. Gannon did, too, and they would continue to be a couple for the next four years. Thus, during the exact time that TV networks were eager to hire young women—talented young women in communications, just like Diane—she was going into hiding with the most despised politician in America. Aside from being unimaginable to those who hated Nixon, Diane's decision was imponderable to her old friends at WLKY. "This could ruin her!" they thought. It was even imponderable to Nixon's loyalists and staff. Bruce Whelihan had been Gerry Warren's deputy, and he had considered himself lucky for ducking the postresignation service in San Clemente. That Diane had volunteered to go stunned Whelihan. "I was shaking my head that she was there."

So why *did* she go? She has described her decision thusly: "His world had collapsed. He had been decimated. We were beyond moralizing. It was a human consideration. Here was a man whose dreams were shattered. If I didn't come through for him at a time when he needed me, I couldn't live with myself." So there, again, was the issue of responsibility. Her service to him was like a marriage, for better or for worse. "I had a sense of duty," she said, as recently as 2011. "I felt: You don't get to choose just being there in the celebrated times and then get to walk away when someone is living in defeat." She also felt, "No matter how they got [to that defeat] . . . and how bruising [Watergate] was for American politics," to not have continued with Nixon after his resignation? "I just don't think that's the person I can be."

ONE THING BEING at San Clemente did was give Diane the opportunity to learn big-story research and writing. Diane was "really key in putting together Nixon's autobiography; she oversaw the whole project," says a man who visited her there. She did much of the research on Watergate herself: She read the transcripts of every single newscast devoted to the scandal, interviewed Ehrlichman and Haldeman in prison, and created a comprehensive flowchart. She then presented her findings to Nixon (with a bit of held breath), and took his dictation on the subject. Nixon was fitful and testy in recounting the ordeal, but Diane prodded him the way any reporter would prod any truculent head of state. "She had no illusions about Nixon" or his guilt by then, says one who knew her then. Still, Nixon *the man* somehow remained not merely sympathetic but also charismatic to her.

During her time at San Clemente, she saw a scenario repeat itself. As she would later describe it: "Everybody talks about his awkwardness with social talk. Not only is he not awkward [but] when he gets into substance, he weaves magic in a room. . . . It used to be one of the rare amusements at San Clemente to see people come in who held no brief for him, who were firmly defended by their political and personal preconceptions, and watch how long it took for their mouths to drop open. It usually took somewhere between three and four minutes, *and then they were captive.* And it happened over and over again."

One of Diane's jobs at San Clemente was reading the mail. When Nixon was stricken with serious phlebitis, a small pile of letters arrived from supporters wishing him a speedy recovery. A larger pile carried a nastier message. Diane herself coined a term for these—"She called them 'Get Well, Motherfucker' letters," says a person she confided in. But while this person and other insiders laughed at her tough élan, she desperately didn't want it getting out to the public that she'd used the word "motherfucker," and she pleaded with a writer to that effect.

It wasn't that the word "motherfucker" would have offended Nixon, her boss. That isn't what bothered her. There was, after all, someone who captured her loyalty even more, far more, than did the former president.

What bothered her was that her use of the word "motherfucker" would have upset her mother.

CHAPTER TWO

The Secret Princess Becomes the Exile in Atlanta

Christiane: 1958 to 1983

CHRISTIANE MARIA AMANPOUR was born on January 12, 1958, in London, England, the first of four children of Patricia Hill Amanpour and Mohammed Amanpour. The couple and their baby soon moved to Tehran, Iran, where Mohammed resumed his work as an airline executive. Another daughter, Fiona, followed a year and a half later. Elizabeth—Lizzy—was born nine years after Fiona, and Leila two years after that. Four daughters! Christiane was the eldest, the leader—"like a second mother to Lizzy and me," Leila says.

Christiane's parents had met the way destined lovers meet in movies. Patricia Hill, a beautiful, restless, adventurous brunette, was the daughter of upper-middle-class Britons who'd moved to Paris because of Patricia's father's work in the insurance industry there. When she was eighteen, and her father's business associate needed his Mercedes driven from Paris to Istanbul to Tehran, she hounded her father to let her do the driving—she wanted to see an exotic part of the world. After the long and arduous delivery of the vehicle, Patricia Hill, through random circumstance, met Mohammed Amanpour in that then lively capital of the ancient Persian empire. "He fell head-over-heels in love with her. It was a grand romance," says Lizzy Amanpour. "He gate-crashed all these high-society Iranian parties" to which Patricia, the lovely English newcomer, was invited, "just to see her," just to try to win her heart.

Mohammed Amanpour was roughly twice Patricia Hill's age. He was fond of cognac and backgammon and caviar—a charming, outgoing bon vivant in a country that had been proudly, though forcibly, modernized two decades earlier, back in 1936, when the then current shah's father, Reza Shah, had banned the wearing of the veil by women. When Mohammed proposed marriage, Patricia said yes, but she had a condition: Their children had to be raised Catholic. Patricia, a convert to Catholicism, was devout. Not being a particularly religious Muslim—and besotted by his young bride-to-be—Mohammed agreed to the terms. After all, it was possible to practice Catholicism in cosmopolitan Iran. The couple married in Paris, Christiane was born in London, and family life proceeded happily in Iran.

Christiane has said that she was "very shy" as a child and "also very curious—some people would say I was nosy. I always wanted to be around the grown-ups and listen to what they were saying." She was an athletic girl: She started horseback riding at five, and she has said that she believes that the nervy grit that would characterize her throughout her career was born during those years of "falling off a very, very fast horse a *lot*. I was literally picked up and put back on the horse by the scruff of my neck. My riding teacher gave me no choice." Christiane won trophies racing her Arabian stallion. She also swam competitively, and she and Fiona learned to ski almost as soon as they could walk.

The Amanpour family lived in great comfort in North Tehran. "It was still in the city," says Lizzy, "but the mountains were so close you could see them out our windows. We were very lucky—it was leafy, with streams running down the side of the street." Theirs was a handsome brick house. There were servants (the family's nanny was a beloved household member who, after the Revolution, they helped support for many years). There was a pool; there were gardens and horses. A walled outdoor patio was shaded by trees, and when the Amanpours gave parties—which, indeed, they did—lamps were hung from the branches. Christiane's parents were complements. "Our mom had a sense of humanity and religion, and our dad a sense of fun—he was very gregarious and jokey," says Lizzy. Mohammed immediately coined affectionate nicknames for his two older daughters and they stuck all their lives: Christiane became Kissy, and Fiona became Fuffles. Four decades after his firstborn darling girl bounced on his lap—when she was now the most famous female TV war reporter in the world—as part of a CNN special report on the changes in life in Iran from her childhood through the Revolution and into the post-Revolution years, father and daughter were televised coming upon each other at the burned-out shell of their once lovely family home. Father greeted daughter poignantly: "Hello, Kissy."

THE IRAN THAT Christiane lived in daily for eleven years was just about as outwardly modern as it would ever be. Women drove, were educated, were employed. The chador—the face-framing head scarf that covered a woman's hair for religious reasons—was worn by women in the provinces (some could wear the stricter, lower-face-covering veil if they wished), but most urban women chose not to; those who did often wore a bright-colored one. "You could see the Western influence in the number of restaurants that were open in Tehran and how men and women would go there together and would mix in the cinemas," says scholar, author, and human rights activist Haleh Esfandiari, who was a young woman there at the time. "You could go to opera and art exhibits in Tehran. You could listen to Nat King Cole and Charles Aznavour records. The Westernization was *palpable.*"

Something else was palpable: the *glamour* of Iran. The monarch, the dashing Shah, Reza Pahlavi, was ostentatiously regal, even decadent. He flew to Hollywood nightclubs and sat in banquettes with Howard Hughes and gifted cigarette girls with full-length mink coats for entertaining his bodyguards. The Shah's second wife, Princess Soraya, was a striking beauty who greatly resembled Ava Gardner: sculpted nose, high cheekbones, sensually lidded eyes and all. At their 1951 wedding (to which President Truman, Queen Elizabeth, and Joseph Stalin all sent gifts), Soraya's frothy, feather-edged couture wedding gown—which was spread out a good twenty feet from waist to hem when she was seated—was over-the-top magnificent for any corner of the globe in any decade. But the Shah was ultimately compelled to divorce Soraya; she did not bear him any children, and her tragic infertility was a grand soap opera that was commented upon in international newspapers and even in American movie magazines.

A year after Christiane was born, the Shah married his third wife, an upper-class part-Azerbaijani beauty named Farah Diba. Farah Diba's wedding gown was designed by the new darling at the house of Dior, Yves Saint-Laurent. Eight years later, when Christiane was nine, the Shah decided to make a grand statement. He had himself crowned King of Kings (or Shahanshah) of Iran, and Empress Farah became Queen. At the 1967 coronation, which drew media attention from all over the world, the new queen wore a full-length royal robe and a fantastically jeweled crown. Standing next to her was the Shahanshah in medal-bedecked military finery, his gleaming gold crown taller than the length of his face. This revival of Persian majesty was meant to inspire awe and pride in the country's children, and it would soon be evident that it probably *did* have this effect on Christiane. Besides, the Amanpours already traveled in high circles; they knew Persian aristocracy. The Amanpours were in social contact with Queen Farah Diba and other members of the Pahlavi family, and one of young Christiane's closest friends, Ayshe Farman-Farmaian, was in fact a princess—a descendant of the Qajar dynasty, which had ruled Persia from 1795 until 1925, when it was overthrown by the Pahlavis. Even as a teenager, Ayshe was a dazzling beauty—tall and lean with wild black hair and a sense of privilege worn lightly and confidently. She represented all the glamour that being Iranian—being Persian—could be, and there were aspects of her that matched Christiane's sense of self.

However dazzling a picture it took of itself for the Western world, Iran was now, quietly, on a collision course with itself. "There was Westernization but not freedom," says Haleh Esfandiari. The intellectuals were being surveilled. "Everybody was concerned and worried about SAVAK," the Shah's secret police, whose pervasiveness sparked anxiety among the media class during the years of Christiane's childhood. "If you worked in an office, in publishing—if you were a professional—you *never* talked in front of strangers, and there was a sense of self-censorship." Esfandiari was an editor on the foreign news desk of a daily paper in the 1960s. "And I was very much aware of what not to write, what not to say." Most alarming were the disappearances. Esfandiari "would see colleagues picked up" off the street by SAVAK, "just disappearing" as if into thin air.

Young Christiane seemed to have a high-minded imagination, and she bonded with literature in a way that mirrored her current life and somehow inspired her future. She especially savored Louisa May Alcott's classic novel *Little Women*, possibly seeing her bonds with her sisters reflected in the four sisters of that novel. She loved Rudyard Kipling's "If—," the classic poem that defines character and humility in the British colonial era. "Christiane was a very strong character. I looked up to her *so* much," says her youngest sister, Leila. Being so very much older than the youngest two, she seemed "the trailblazer, the toughest personality, the most charismatic—very driven and *so* tough," says Lizzy. "I really think Christiane's personality doesn't necessarily come from our parents—you wouldn't say she's a chip off of anyone's block." In the view of Diana Bellew, a friend of Christiane's who has known the family for almost forty years, "*All* the Amanpour sisters are strong, and *all* that strength came straight from their mother." Patricia was not a career woman—she was a homemaker and a "lovely, elegant, sweet woman, a serene, sometimes even saintly" presence. But there was also a tensile integrity to Patricia; *this* is the strength, Diana says, that came down to the girls.

Christiane and Fiona were so close in age that they shared friends. But the two were polar opposites. Christiane was serious, Fiona flighty. "Fiona was a lot more outgoing and gregarious; Christiane was always very, very focused," says Lizzy. Eventually, when they became teenagers, Fiona had the boyfriends—and dashing ones: rock singers, jockeys. Fiona had a bit of a wacky streak. Christiane, by contrast, was more self-contained and skeptical, introverted, not seeking out boyfriends, and she served as a steadying force on her slightly younger sister. "Christiane," Diana Bellew says, "does not have a wacky bone in her body."

Young Christiane may have been comparatively staid and serious, but it may come as a surprise that she was, in her way, *starstruck*. She was romantic in both the high and the charmingly common ways. "She was obsessed with Liza Minnelli and Elizabeth Taylor," says Leila. "And with lots of movie stars. Growing up, she had these huge scrapbooks of famous people." She'd buy fan magazines and newspapers and cut out the images and paste them neatly onto the thick pages. She also loved romantic black-and-white movies of the grand 1930s—watching Fred Astaire and Ginger Rogers glide across a dance floor was thrilling to her, and she could name all her favorite films. She read about Jackie Kennedy, and she and Fiona adored American popular music—the Eagles especially. In the brand-new global culture of the early 1970s the black-haired, black-eyed daughters of ancient Persia mentally transported themselves to Laurel Canyon, where fair-haired Texas and Michigan boys affecting a Death Valley desperado vibe they didn't really have were minting the lucrative California sound.

When Christiane was eleven, she was sent to convent boarding school at the Holy Cross Convent in Buckinghamshire, England. She later liked to say that the nuns there whipped her about the legs for minor infractions and she was proud she hadn't cried. But if this is not an exaggeration, then by the time she got to her next boarding school—six years later, at age sixteen—she had somehow turned into another young woman entirely: a skillfully ingratiating girl whom the nuns and the headmistresses point-edly favored, says Diana Bellew, who met her then and there.

In fact, it was perhaps there at New Hall School, the Convent of the Holy Sepulchre, near Chelmsford, England, that lesser-known elements of Christiane Amanpour—the emotional intelligence, the emotional*ism*, the secret sense of grandeur, all of which would be hidden under her idealistic principles, her workmanlike appearance, her blunt talk, and her bravery, but which would power her career—first flowered, first manifested them-selves.

NEW HALL IS A FORTRESSLIKE school for Catholic girls, founded in 1642 and situated in a sprawling isolated complex of old stone castles. Some of the buildings date back to 1062, and one of them was inherited by Anne Boleyn's father and acquired by Henry VIII in 1518. All of English history whispers through the school's winding halls. In 1974, the school was used to having a decent number of international students in atten-dance, but "most of us were country girls," says Gig Moses, one of the sixteen-year-old sixth formers who crossed themselves daily in chapel and were instructed almost exclusively by women—primarily nuns. "New Hall was very strict. No boys! We were locked up," says Diana Bellew.

Virtually all the girls at New Hall—Diana, Gig, and the rest—had been there from age eleven; rarely were there transfer students. "Then into our midst one day," Gig recalls, "came this . . . *exotic bird* . . . with striking features and long black hair! She was mad about Hollywood film stars and Fred and Ginger movies, and always had glorious coffee table books about them." It is hard to overestimate the impact this glamorous girl had on the dull student body, Gig says. "She seemed from another world."

Christiane's grand entrance to New Hall included an artfully lobbed fiction: She said she was a Persian princess. Her family indeed knew the Shah, she knew Queen Farah Diba, and, of course, one of her close friends *was* a princess. So appropriating a genuinely royal biography wasn't that far a stretch. Perhaps it was also a testing of the waters—or a sense of budding inner distinction searching for an outlet and stumbling onto a suitably teenaged one. Whatever the reason, Christiane said she was a princess.

She did it cleverly, telling just one girl she quickly intuited was very indiscreet. She swore that girl not to tell. So, of course, that girl *did* tell—and the girls she told then told *more* girls. It spread all over New Hall that a Persian princess was in their midst. All eyes were on her, this girl with the black hair fluffed into Farrah Fawcett layers. During chapel, she was "the best reader of the gospel—and was *loved* by the nuns," says Diana Bellew, adding that the savvy "princess" "always got on well with the people she needed to get on well with."

Though she was "warm and enthusiastic," Gig Moses says, and drew other girls to her—she became popular immediately—Christiane at New Hall exuded a natural sense of privilege that exempted her from cer-tain dreary efforts. As athletic as she'd been in Tehran, she was now "def-initely not keen on waving a lacrosse stick or venturing onto a netball court in the middle of winter," says Gig. "She got away with all kinds of mischief—she got away with murder," says Diana.

Diana was assigned to be her roommate—that is how they met. "I couldn't *stand* her!" Diana says. "She complained so much, just because she missed her old school." The adjustment was so bothersome to Christiane that "she was angry and moaning all the time about it," and she intentionally chose and wore "horrible clothes," Diana says, as a form of rebellion. "After a month, I cried to the nuns, 'I can't live with that girl! She's *awful*—she's always moaning about everything being a nightmare.'" But Diana's tears were useless. The nuns insisted that she endure rooming with Christiane. Christiane had become "friends with the headmistress. Those nuns who were in charge absolutely adored her. She really got along with these older women."

So Diana resigned herself and began to observe her new roommate in perplexed admiration. Christiane had the temerity to rail against how cold it was in science lab to "the terrible old drunk Irish woman" who brooked no guff in the chemistry class she taught. To underscore her point, Christiane returned to class after a weekend in London wearing gloves—*fur* gloves from Harrods, purchased by her maternal grandmother, whom she and her friends sometimes later irreverently referred to as Granny with the Checkbook. That cheeky elitism infuriated the chemistry teacher, but it rather tickled the headmistress, who had taken a great liking to the brazen, posh Persian girl. Diana had to admire Christiane's nerve and pizzazz.

And so Diana and Christiane became friends, and then best friends—lifelong friends, it would turn out. "She *was* something," Diana finally realized. "Even at sixteen and seventeen, you could *see* it"—especially on weekends, when Christiane ditched the ugly clothes and wore "fabulous platform shoes and really great jeans." "Oh, the platform shoes!" remembers Gig Moses of those days when they'd all three visit the boutique Biba on High Street in Kensington on weekends. The sixth- and then seventh-form girls were quite full of themselves in that wonderful young English era of "T. Rex, Queen, Rod Stewart, David Bowie, and the world seeing Arthur Ashe win at Wimbledon!" Christiane and Gig were very competitive, as house captain and vice captain—class leaders—and after Christiane's spoiled-acting homesickness for her last school had long passed, the two girls would slide along Aloysius Corridor, the school's long main hall, after it was freshly scrubbed and slick enough to skate on in their Idlers (popular brown leather loafers), "full of gumption for the daily routine of housework after breakfast," Gig recalls.

Despite the trendy hairdo and the Liza Minnelli fixation and other fripperies, Christiane was "not a girly girl," says Diana, and she had a distinct fearlessness. "She was never scared to ask questions—any question, ever. I would think, 'I'm stupid if I ask.' But she had no shame, no embarrassment—she would want to get to the bottom of things." Diana had a boyfriend who was big man on campus at "a very posh Catholic boys' school. He was a real prize, and I was actually completely terrified of him. I didn't know the things he knew, like art history. But Christiane had no fear of him—*none.* And she didn't know any more about art history than I did." Yet she stood her ground and argued with him. One thing Christiane could not do was learn to drive—at least not drive well. She had many lessons with the patient New Hall instructor but, according to Diana, she failed her driving test many times before finally passing it.

WHILE CHRISTIANE WAS ENJOYING those years at New Hall, the native country she came home to in the summer and on holidays was radically changing. Starting around 1973, "the regime of the Shah became more and more autocratic," says Iranian-born Shaul Bakhash, one of the world's leading scholars on Iranian history. Bakhash recalls that "even modicums of freedoms tightened. The Shah became far less tolerant of dissent—he imposed a single party . . . where in the past there had been elections, and there was pressure on people in civil service and the universities to join in, and people resented it." Most alarmingly, torture had become widespread, especially for those militating against the government. Trade unions were suppressed, and there were suddenly "mindless" measures involving "constant interference in details of people's private lives," such as outlawing the cutting down of trees—you could theoretically be punished for cutting down a tree in your own backyard. The 1973–1974 explosion of oil prices (which "quadrupled overnight") spurred the intensive modernization process that the Shah had started in 1963. "Had I not seen it with my own eyes," Bakhash says, "I would not believe you could dislocate an economy in such a short period of time."

Iranians felt the country was losing its identity. "Suddenly you had Korean truck drivers, Filipino maids, and American military advisers. There were forty thousand to fifty thousand foreigners in a country of thirty-six million, but the impact was huge. It wasn't just a fear of the clergy, the threat of this quote-unquote 'Westernization.' Even my friends"—intellectuals—"said, 'We're losing our identity.'" There was "a *deadening* effect on society, on political discourse, and certainly on intellectual discourse. And it was far worse, of course, for the traditional people in rural areas." Suddenly, in the early to mid-1970s, in conservative areas like Isfahan—"there were bars, and women wearing shorts. Suddenly you injected into a provincial town large numbers of Americans who had their own style of living. It was shocking."

At the same time, something else was happening, something that might seem contradictory but would actually dovetail with the rural conservatives' disapproval of the Shah's changes: For the first time, Iranian students from traditional, lower-middle-class families were getting college scholarships to America, and the experience of witnessing freedom turned them very antimonarchy, very anti-Shah. Being in the States created in them a desire for a more open society. "Why don't we have these things at *home?*" they wondered angrily. Meanwhile, the Shah's suppression of political parties and trade unions was making it so that "nothing was left *but* religion," Bakhash says. "Where could people gather *but* mosques?"

A further complication, he adds, was "the unusual factor of an extraordinarily charismatic opposition leader in the person of Ruhollah Khomeini," a cleric "who had a powerful way with words" and who, during that same early to mid-1970s period "had the good luck to be abroad." Which meant two things: "He was free to speak out against the Shah, and he was not tainted by association with the government." A tinderbox was close at hand.

.   .   .

AS CHRISTIANE EDGED toward high school graduation, being a journalist was the last thing on her young mind. She planned to be a doctor
and therefore devoted her time to studying science. "She didn't study very
hard, but it wasn't her fault," Diana Bellew says. "New Hall was a traditional girls' school and the science teaching was atrocious. She didn't stand
a chance with the quality of instruction in biology and chemistry there."
It would take a serendipitous decision, coupled with a tumultuous, historic
international event, to awaken in Christiane a passion for a career that, in
retrospect, seems to have fit her as perfectly as those expensive Harrods
gloves.

Following their graduation ceremony, New Hall's 1976 class was given
a "leaving dinner." The girls all wore long, debutante-style gowns; their
parents joined them. (Mohammed Amanpour even charmed one of the
nuns into fetching him a manly whiskey instead of the bottom-shelf
sherry that was being served.)

What to do next? No cherished college admission letter was tacked
on Christiane's wall. "She didn't get the grades she would have expected,
and this was the first time this had happened," says her sister Lizzy. Her
poor marks in science ruled out acceptance into a pre-med program. She
worked as a salesgirl in Fenwick's department store. Fiona—the "flighty,
hippie" sister (as Lizzy describes her)—was also in London. This would
prove providential.

Fiona enrolled in a journalism class, which her parents paid for. Fiona
began her studies—but then she got distracted. She fell in love with a
member of the white reggae group G.T. Moore and the Rhythm Guitar-
ists "and she went off with the band," recalls Lizzy. Ever the practical one,
"Christiane tried to get a refund from our sister's class for our parents,"
says Lizzy, "but the school said no. The only way she wouldn't waste all
our parents' money was to take the course herself." Duty to her family,
compensation for her madcap sister: *This* is what brought Christiane to
journalism.

It was a revelation. Christiane "was excited about the class. It gave her direction. She realized this was something she was *meant* to do," Lizzy says. Journalism loomed into focus—just like that.

Meanwhile, Christiane's newly gleaned enthusiasm seemed to be bumping up against fate—dramatic and unhappy fate. In Iran, protests against the Shah began in October 1977, for the diverse reasons historian Shaul Bakhash mentioned: the Shah's rapid modernization program, his quashing of political dissent and trade unions, the sharp economic disloca- tion, the jarring Western "impiety" of the oil-working foreigners, the fear and punishment meted out by SAVAK—the "deadening" effect it all had on the citizenry. By December 1978, the outcry had turned explosive, shocking the world. Early in the month, two million people flooded Teh- ran's Shahyad Square. Then, days later, six to nine million people—a stunning 10 percent of the population—marched throughout Iran, put- ting the protesters on a par, numerically, with those who fomented the French and Russian Revolutions.

Bakhash, who was in Tehran during those heated months, describes this incendiary chain of events as the desperate flailing of the population. "The fact that people came out into the streets in support of Khomeini didn't mean" they wanted an Islamic culture, he contends. "The majority of the demonstrators did not want to go back to that. No! Iranians read into the growing protest movement what they wanted to see. Khomeini, in opposition"—and exile—"had preached a form of Islam that would bring about social justice and economic and political freedom. Many thought that once the Shah was overthrown, a secular government [would come in its place]. You'd be astonished at the kind of people that supported the Revolution—very wealthy, upper middle classes, the Westernized as well as the masses."

The Shah and his wife, Empress Farah, fled on January 16, 1979. "SHAH LEAVES IRAN FOR INDEFINITE STAY; CROWDS EXULT, MANY EXPECT LONG EXILE," blared the front-page headline of the *New York Times*, adding that "tears appeared to be welling in the ruler's eyes" as he arrived in Egypt, courtesy of the largesse of Anwar Sadat.

Khomeini returned, triumphant, from exile, on February 1, to an over- whelming throng of supporters.. A month later, the new Ayatollah decreed:

"Do not use this term, 'democratic.' That is the Western style." The anti-Shah secularists' and intellectuals' dreams were dashed. Their idealism had been misplaced. Islamic fundamentalism became the law of the land.

Christiane traveled back and forth between Tehran and London during these tumultuous months. Her younger sisters, who lived at home full-time, recall the jarring, even frightening developments. Says Lizzy, "I remember trucks going by at night firing shots." And during the daytime: "Armed men on the roof of my school and revolutionaries in the street, and power cuts—we had gas lamps around the house because there was not much electricity. Dad was not able to go out to his tennis club, because everybody was affected by the curfew. So he taught me and Leila how to play backgammon. I remember Mom, who used to wear T-shirts in summer, coming home *shocked*—a man in the street spat on her arm for wearing short sleeves! We knew the atmosphere was changing."

Leila remembers how the family fled. "We left home with a couple of suitcases" to return to England in December 1979. "We left the house with all the furniture and all our possessions behind. We were due back in August 1980, but we never came back—our dad was advised not to go back." There was at least one brief trip back: Christiane has remembered being in the living room of the house with her father sometime in 1980. She described it vividly during a tour of the now ruined house in 1999 for the CNN special: "My father was standing over there"—she pointed to a corner of what had once been a comfortable living room—"and he said, 'Life as we know it is going to come to an end.'"

Life as we know it is going to come to an end. . . . The Revolution had come, their house was being taken over, they had to flee. "My life changed," Christiane said of that moment. "My political consciousness began."

Perhaps self-protectively, but also with the hard nugget of a pain and idealism that was destined to grow into work that was tough and humanitarian at once, Christiane's instinct to "use" the tragedy leapt to the fore. She has, intentionally, put it in a jarringly utilitarian way: "My first 'big break' was the Iranian Revolution." Then: "History completely turned over my country and put me in a place where I had to figure out what to do with my life. I *knew* what I wanted to do with my life: *I wanted to be a foreign correspondent.* Having grown up in a nice, privileged, comfortable environment, suddenly I couldn't depend on anything anymore, not [even] my parents. . . . Overnight we were strangers in our own homeland. We watched in horror as our friends and family members were arrested, jailed, tortured, and some even executed. My world and worldview turned upside down."

Lizzy says, "We lived a fairly nomadic life for a year in England. We stayed in people's houses, and every three months we would move. We really struggled." Ultimately, the family found a small flat. Three of the four Amanpour sisters, separately, make the identical, blunt, sad remark. Leila: "For all intents and purposes, we lost everything." Lizzy: "We lost everything." Finally, Christiane: "We lost home, possessions, and people—*everything.*"

Patricia Amanpour "just got on with it" as best she could in their new "tiny apartment," Diana Bellew recalls. While the more sybaritic Mohammed "tried to get his hands on caviar," anesthetizing his deep sense of shock and loss with exaggerations of cosmopolitan trivialities, Patricia reacted the opposite way. "She became very devout. I think she went to Mass every day."

As for Christiane, she later recalled, "I quickly decided to turn loss and failure into my driving force." This was similar to the spot lesson Diane Sawyer forced herself to learn when her father suddenly died, and to Katie Couric's fairly immediate resolve to help others escape the tragedies of the cancer deaths of her husband and sister. A family tragedy could be an excuse for contemplative retreat—or it could be an emergency window to an adrenalized perspective unobtainable otherwise, and a crisis stimulus to a sense of vocation. In Christiane's case, that vocation seemed waiting to claim her.

BY NOW SHE WAS A DOUBLE EXILE. Pushed by her family, she went to America to study, entering the University of Rhode Island in 1979. "Our family members, especially our mom's aunt Gladys, clubbed together [money] to help her get there," says Lizzy. Not only was tuition challenging for the fresh exiles, whose finances were often held up in their now radicalized country, but Christiane "didn't really have the sorts of grades" to get into a top-ranked school. "She had to really work hard when she got to America." But even if London represented solace and was reassuringly familiar, *America*, all the Amanpours seemed to know, was the future. In fact, in 1979 and 1980, whole American cities—Beverly Hills was one— seemed to turn half Iranian overnight.

"I loved every hard-won step along the way—I loved being at the University of Rhode Island, where I learned so much about American values and culture," Christiane has said. She declared journalism her major and by now knew she wanted to be a foreign correspondent. Her role models were Martha Gellhorn, the dashing journalist of the Spanish civil War, the Normandy landing, the Vietnam War, and the Six Day War (and one-time wife of Ernest Hemingway), and Oriana Fallaci, the outspoken Italian correspondent who covered myriad conflict zones and who, in 1968, was viciously attacked by forces in Mexico. Christiane took classes in "all the things I didn't learn growing up in Iran and England: American literature, political philosophy, political science."

Perhaps even more important to her personal growth was URI's proximity to Brown University, just an hour away, where several of her friends were attending classes, including her girlhood friend Ayshe Farman-Farmaian and a friend from London, Christa D'Souza. Chic and social, Ayshe and Christa were standouts, even on a campus full of many wealthy, self-assured students. Christiane may have been enrolled at URI, but socially, intellectually, and emotionally, she belonged to the Brown community; she even chose to live closer to Brown than to her own university. Brown in 1979 was a bit off the radar compared with other Ivy League colleges, but it was a glamour school, attracting the children of wealthy and sophisticated families, and it was an intellectually daring and precocious place: It had recently instituted a new curriculum that allowed students, unfettered by department requirements and even grades, to map out their own educations to a remarkably high degree.

Midway through her first semester at URI, on November 4, a group of young Islamists—furious that the Shah had received asylum in the

United States for cancer treatment and that the Shah's army had been shooting protestors on the street for months beforehand—invaded the American embassy in Tehran and seized fifty-two diplomats and embassy workers. Even Iranian nonfundamentalists—even liberals—saw this as what Shaul Bakhash, who was present that day, calls "an incredibly galvanizing moment in the history of the country. Iran had had a long history of nineteenth- and twentieth-century domination by two great powers, Britain and Russia. Breaking that hold was important. So America became the new imperial power, and, I think, the ability to stand up to this great power and impose your will on it was more important than hatred." This perspective was hard for Americans to grasp, and the diplomats and embassy workers were held hostage for 444 days. Christiane was "slightly miffed," she said two decades later, when, at URI, "to the tune of 'Barbara Ann,' fellow students would sing, *'Bomb bomb bomb bomb! Bomb bomb Iran!'*" Her beloved homeland—bombed? Surely there had to be an understanding of that part of the world deeper than this wounded cravenness of her fellow students. There was a whole other perspective available, and ultimately, if she succeeded at what she now longed to do, she could provide it.

Still, she kept quiet about the offensive anti-Iran sentiment. People who met her socially, especially at Brown, took her as more British than anything else.

When Christiane flew back to England for vacations during that first exciting year abroad, her family laughed at her enthusiastic new Americanness. Leila says, "I remember her accent starting to change, and we would laugh about her new expressions. She'd say, 'Hang a left' and 'Hang a right' and *'Gross!'* We thought that was quite sweet and funny."

By her sophomore year Christiane had not only met, through her clique of Persian friends, Brown's almost sore-thumb-obvious celebrity student, John Kennedy Jr., but had become one of his very best friends. Christiane—the serious and opinionated foreigner, her refugee status making her seem appealingly life-worn—was impressed that John had organized an anti-Apartheid rally on campus, and her approval mattered to him. After the rally, Christiane and John went with a group of friends to a campus burger joint. He took to calling her Kissy—so, soon, did all her close Brown friends—as did his mother. "She obviously got to know Jackie quite well," and spent weekends at Mrs. Onassis's Martha's Vineyard estate, Leila says. Christiane may have been too discreet to gush about becoming a houseguest of America's most iconic woman, a childhood idol of hers—"She was very natural; she never thought it was particularly amazing," Diana Bellew says—but when she went home to her family in London she opened up and "talked about John a lot," says Leila Amanpour.

"I have no brilliant explanation why [John and I] became close friends other than there was a 'simpatico' between us—his word," Christiane has said. She described some of the friendship's virtues: "There was never this conscious or unconscious one-upmanship between us. There was never a romantic twist, nor ever the hint of one. I think he saw me as solid, English, sensible, and reliable. I always gave him the truth and the most honest appraisal I could muster."

John does seem to have respected her toughness, dignity, and bravery. Christiane "wasn't hard. She was just sort of British and determined," he said, three years before his death. Regarding her family's displacement, "there was not one iota of self-pity" about Christiane. "She was very matter-of-fact, very stiff upper lip. You wouldn't have known what she'd gone through."

At the beginning of the 1981–'82 school year, John and Christiane were chosen to become housemates of a friend of John's from high school, Christina Haag, who was already living in a charming Victorian house at 155 Benefit Street, a lane of gas lamps and cobblestones in the historic neighborhood outside Brown's campus. Christina's other housemates had graduated; her friend Lynne Weinstein was moving in, as was a fraternity brother of John's named Chris Oberbeck. Chris was the instigator in inviting John and his friend Christiane to come in as the final roommates. It turned out to be a diverse group. Chris Oberbeck was a preppy and a bedrock political conservative, and both Christina and Lynne were arty, well-heeled young women, soon to become, respectively, an actress and a photographer. (Christina would in a few years' time become John's most significant girlfriend until Carolyn Bessette, whom he married.) In this already eclectic group, Christiane was especially distinctive: She was several years older than the others, the only foreigner, the only exile, the most politically aware as well as politically fervent—an unapologetically strong personality. She was also the only housemate not attending Brown, an inconvenience, especially since, not having a car or a U.S. driver's license, she had to intrepidly wrangle rides to campus.

Christiane was awarded the largest bedroom in the house (John got the smallest), and although at least one housemate "didn't perceive it this way," she "was sort of the mother of the house," as John once said. "She divided us all up into cooking and cleaning crews. She put a mop in my hand and sent me to clean the toilets." During her trips home to England, she would regale her family with how "she was the sort of organized one—we would laugh at how she said she made races for everyone to clean the house," Leila says, adding that the time at Benefit Street was "the *one* cooking phase in her life." All the housemates took turns cooking, with Lynne the most accomplished cook and John the most inexperienced, proudly mastering hamburgers. Christiane often cooked them Persian food, introducing her American friends to the glories of crispy rice with dill and yogurt, "and everyone loved it," says Leila. As a break from domesticity, the roommates frequented Mutt 'n' Jeff's down the block, which served all-the-rage sandwiches named for rock stars and politicians.

In the house, Christiane has said, "We had the most intense dinner table conversations. Reagan was president, and we endlessly debated his policies, from Star Wars to nuclear war. Chris Oberbeck was very Republican, and I had just discovered the antinuke campaign and so I was full of earnestness and righteous indignation at the thought this man might blow up the world. It all got very boisterous, and John, whose politics were clear" was "also an effective devil's advocate." John was liberal, but his approach, his Republican friend Rob Littell would say, was "sometimes surprisingly conservative" and "practical." At the table were often assorted others, since all the housemates were in and out of relationships, including Christiane, according to Leila.

Christiane by now was fervent in her desire to be an on-camera TV news reporter, specializing in foreign assignments. She started slow, with radio, walking into Brown's own radio station, WBRU, and volunteering her services as an intern. She ripped copy out of the newspapers for the station's news department and read news bulletins in the slotted breaks between the playing of a very well-curated selection of records and brand-new CDs (the station was rather ahead of its times), and when the station moved from one location to another, she pitched in with the packing and unpacking.

When Christina, Chris, and Lynne graduated in the spring of 1982, John and Christiane, by prior agreement, switched bedrooms—now he had the biggest and she, the smallest—and he populated the house with near replicas of the previous occupants: Cordelia Richards, a budding actress, moved in, along with John Hare and Rob Littell, both preppy, Republican-leaning jocks. They all called Christiane Kissy, and she was still acknowledged as the boss. "Like a den mother, or maybe a general, she laid down the rules and we followed them. . . . The house ran like a Swiss watch," Littell marveled in his memoir *The Men We Became.* Littell also called her "the smartest" of the housemates. "I usually ended up as a knuckleheaded 'counter' to Kissy's fiercely informed 'point,'" admitted Littell, who has otherwise described himself to others as so commandingly self-confident he could match John in looks and status. "I required constant assistance from John, who, while firmly on Kissy's side in nine out of ten debates, acted as the de facto mediator between us."

Christiane's forte was her air of command—her tough, natural leadership. She was the exotic, passionately political boss girl whose whip cracking could snap the most cocksure, privileged young men into shape. Which didn't mean she was without her vulnerabilities. One night, for example, she borrowed John's car to drive to the market for lemons needed for the fish she was making for dinner. She accidentally whacked her mouth with his key chain, chipping a front tooth. John teased her that a broken front tooth meant that her dream of being an on-camera reporter was over. She burst out crying.

One day in her senior year, Christiane walked into WJAR, Providence's NBC affiliate and leading TV station, and asked for a job. Jim Taricani, then and now the head of WJAR's investigative team, was immediately impressed with her. "She said someday she wanted to be a foreign correspondent, which was unusual for a young woman," he says. "She told me she spoke three or four languages. She was eager to work." She herself felt "really lucky," she has said, to be hired at all. Her first job was doing graphics for WJAR's weather reports. She's laughed about how "I was always putting up 'cloudy' when it was sunny, and the weather anchor would call me out on the air. It was a little humiliating."

After Christiane graduated, summa cum laude, from the University of Rhode Island, Taricani put her on real stories: investigations of the rampant drug trade in Providence, a major Mafia city, and in nearby glamorous Newport. "They miked me up with all these wires and sent me out to get a confession from some mobster; I didn't get close," is how she's told it. Taricani somewhat begs to differ. "We took a look at the jet-setters' use of cocaine in popular clubs. We did a story about cocaine use in Newport, called 'City by the C'—C for cocaine. Christiane went into clubs with a hidden camera and a hidden microphone and got the cocaine dealer to talk. She had the savvy to pull that off at a young age. She was an amazing, amazing young woman with great journalistic instincts. She had a *great* head about her. And she was pleasant, with a good sense of humor."

But one exchange has stuck with Taricani for all these decades. "One day she walked in and said, 'Oh, by the way, I should tell you: I'm dating JFK Jr.'" Taricani was flabbergasted. It was a startling conversation stopper, and out of character for this tough young reporter. Was it a variant on her "princess" story—a proximate reality? Christiane wasn't shy about her connections—her housemates knew that her family was friends with the Pahlavis, that she knew the Shah's wife personally. But it certainly made an impression on her boss. "I went, *Yikes!*" Taricani recalls.

IT WAS AT WJAR, toward the end of summer 1983, that Christiane heard about a fledgling TV network in Atlanta. As she has described, "All of a sudden [someone in the newsroom] said, 'There's this new thing, CNN—and we've heard some English accents [on it]. . . . And they basically said, 'You know, this is a great opportunity for someone like yourself who's foreign, who has a foreign accent.'" She seems to be ironically embellishing here, putting into her Providence colleagues' mouths her own well-grounded sensitivities about her non-cookie-cutter looks and voice: "'Who knows, maybe they'll take you, because you certainly don't fit in in the American spectrum of news'"—meaning blond, big haired, and unaccented. A friend for life she would soon make at CNN, writer-turned-producer David Bernknopf, vociferously agrees: "Christiane would never in a hundred million parallel universes have worked her way up the success ladder of a local TV route" and might not even have "ended up as an international correspondent of such renown had it not been for the weird timing" of the founding, in the earliest 1980s, of "this crazy, ridiculous, unique place" that was hungry for any and all talent, unconventional or not.

That radical idea—a twenty-four-hour cable news station—had been launched by Atlanta Braves owner Ted Turner and TV news service executive Reese Schonfeld.

A few years earlier—in spring 1980, in the most seat-of-the-pants way imaginable—CNN had started filling its temporary quarters in sleepy Atlanta, Georgia. "The kids in the newsroom were so young, they looked like they didn't have driver's licenses," says Lynne Russell, one of the first anchors to sign on. There were no health benefits; they couldn't afford to unionize. But Russell sees in retrospect, "If it had been unionized, it wouldn't be uniquely CNN. Because you go in to Ted Turner off the street and say, 'I have an idea.' And the next thing you know, you're carrying cardboard boxes in and you've got an office."

The network hired a number of African American anchors—Renalda Mews, Roz Abrams, Bernard Shaw, later Leon Harris—at a time when national ABC, CBS, and NBC remained fairly snow white. And it hired lots of women. With twenty-four hours to fill, CNN "didn't have the luxury of being an old boys' club," says one of the early hires, anchor Marcia Ladendorff. "They needed young and hungry." Female news professionals *were* hungry.

It was an astonishingly unpropitious start-up, and hardy pioneers who were present at the creation often compete with each other to tell stories, one more zany and improbable than the next. When early-recruited weatherman Flip Spiceland's taxi arrived at "this old condemned white house on Peachtree Street, I argued with the driver—this *couldn't* be the right address!" Yet it was. He got out, disbelieving, and sat on the "old, dilapidated cracked concrete steps" of what had recently been a halfway house for drug addicts. The permanent building—a former Jewish country club—was being renovated, but so late off the mark that when "they moved us into its basement," early anchor Don Farmer says, "they forgot two things: a men's room and a ladies' room." Flip Spiceland: "You heard right: *No bathrooms.* And a mud floor." Turner made arrangements for the staff to use the bathrooms a block and a half away at a low-rent motel; some chose the closer but less sanitary gas station.

In addition to the initial lack of bathrooms—which prompted one female anchor to quit in disgust—the new studios were directly below a wrestling ring. Through the months of rehearsals there was constant booming and crashing, everyone recalls. Two weeks to launch, Turner lost a satellite in space—it just disappeared. Ten days to launch, there was a money crunch—the only bureau now was Atlanta, not the previously planned New York; Washington, D.C.; Dallas; LA; and Chicago. Ellen Spiceland (who met and married Flip there) remembers that, between the lack of bathrooms and the hours ("I'd work twenty hours a day, sleep four, and go back to work") and the sudden defunding, "it was horrible— *horrible.* We were putting our careers on the line for *this?*" Says Dave Walker, who anchored the first night—June 1—with his wife Lois Hart: "Everybody told Ted not to [attempt CNN]. But he was a riverboat gambler." "It deserved its nickname Chicken Noodle News," says Don Farmer. "It was slapdash. It was also exciting, fun, and groundbreaking."

"We made it up as we went along," says Marcia Ladendorff. The personalities were volatile. Ted Kavanau, the founding senior producer, was "a kind of wild man," Reese Schonfeld admits. "Ted was an incendiary device," amplifies Ladendorff. "You never knew what was going to happen. One day, all of a sudden we hear this crazy shouting. Kavanau was on one side of the room, and the person he was fighting with on the other.

They were screaming, and Kavanau reached over and grabbed the other guy, and there was a flurry of fists and hollering. That was the tension and energy at CNN. Oh, and the midnight show Kavanau produced! He would set little 'bombs' to create crises so he could run in and fix them—that was his adrenaline rush." Kavanau says: "A lot of guys who worked late watched that show—it got a following." Kavanau once cohosted his show with Frank Zappa. Yippie radical Abbie Hoffman called the show while in hiding from the feds to say he was a fan.

"I anchored Ted's show a couple of times and I thought I'd have a nervous breakdown," says Marcia Ladendorff. "He would put the show together and then disassemble it while it was on the air. It was like a suicide mission every night. People were popping Valiums right and left. There was a rumor that a tech guy was peddling coke. I'd walk into the makeup room and—those little hand mirrors? I'd have to wipe them off. In the bathroom stall, you'd see marijuana in the tile grout. People would go out and spin around the block and get stoned and come back and do their newscasts. There were no rules! All we were interested in was making this ship float!"

Televised screwups were par for the course, says writer Sparkle Hayter. "Klieg lights fell in the middle of broadcasts. Bad-tempered people were seen pitching fits in the blurry background. Another time, a big thunderstorm knocked out our signal—or so we *thought*. The producer of *Prime News* decided to take this time to tell a few raunchy stories to the anchors while they waited for the signal to return. The switchboard lit up with people wanting to know why the chubby man was telling dirty jokes." On a different day, a news executive didn't think he was on the air "and so he responded with a big, dramatic fake heart attack." *Again*, the switchboard lit up. "CNN was patched together with chewing gum," says producer Maria Fleet, who was a fresh-out-of-college newbie like most everyone else.

But the craziness bred a fierce kinship among the staff. "It was such a weird start-up, such a freak show" that staffers were like resolute outcasts bonded together against the sane world, says David Bernknopf. "We were a small group of people filling those twenty-four hours, but we had a sense of mission and we were together all the time," says Sparkle Hayter. "We worked together, lived together in sprawling antebellum houses, dated each other, partied together, and those of us on late shift would grocery shop together at Winn Dixie at three a.m. It was very incestuous." "People throw around the word 'family' about certain organizations," Lynne Russell says, "but we *really* were."

After hearing from her WJAR colleagues that CNN would be hospitable to someone who looked and sounded like her, Christiane picked up the phone and called CNN and got to someone willing to preinterview her in the most off-the-cuff way. "They asked me ten questions on the phone, and I answered them all, and then they asked me, 'What's the capital of Iran?' I said, 'It's Tehran,' so I passed that test with flying colors."

And so in September 1983, with what she's colorfully insisted was little more than a hundred dollars and her bicycle, Christiane Amanpour arrived in Atlanta, a city of Confederate flags and Baptist churches. She would join the CNN family—becoming close to Bernknopf, Hayter, Fleet, and others. It would be her family for twenty-seven years.

Another young woman had gotten there first: come, seen, not exactly conquered—and then resolutely pushed on. This young woman was every bit as aggressive and ambitious as Christiane—in ways, even more so— but she and Christiane were as different from each other as two aspiring TV newswomen could be.

Her name was Katie Couric.

CHAPTER THREE

Little Sister Cheerleader to Pentagon Correspondent

Katie: 1957 to 1989

KATHERINE ANNE COURIC was born on January 7, 1957, in Arlington, Virginia, the fourth child of Elinor Hene Couric and John Martin Couric. Emily, Clara (called Kiki), and John Jr. were the three siblings who preceded her, each separated by roughly two years. Years later, Katie's husband, Jay Monahan, would kid her that she must have been "born on a sunny day," because the circumstances of her childhood were so normal and easy.

Katie's parents had different religious and ethnic backgrounds. The Omaha-raised Elinor was Jewish; her father was a successful architect whose parents had emigrated from Germany, and the family had spanned out in the Midwest and South, with one wing of it, the Frohsins, proprietors of a couture women's clothing shop in Atlanta. Katie's father was the great-grandson of an émigré from France who had been a cotton broker. John Couric grew up in Georgia and, after service in the navy, worked as a newspaper reporter and editor before eventually entering public relations.

Katie and her family attended a Presbyterian church, her mother having converted to Christianity before marrying John. It is unclear whether Elinor's conversion arose from personal conviction or marital compromise, but Katie has said that she herself had a "tough time" with some of the tenets of Christianity: "When our minister showed me a diagram of Jesus on a throne, surrounded by my family, I had a tough time with the idea that Jesus was more important than them. I didn't become a [church] member." Perhaps in this way she was mirroring her mother: Family was more important than fierce religious identity. Though Katie would abidingly continue to relate as a Christian, she grew to become fascinated with Judaism, especially after she went out into the professional world.

Elinor was more temperamentally and politically liberal than John. Elinor volunteered for Planned Parenthood. In another era, Katie has said, her mother "would probably be an ad executive or a stockbroker," adding, of Elinor's zeitgeist savvy, "She bought many shares of Trojan condoms in the safe-sex early eighties." Katie has characterized her father as "cerebral, gentle . . . thoughtful and intelligent, hardworking, a voracious reader, and a bit of a taskmaster who expected excellence from his children." Even the musing deliberateness and specificity of Katie's description of him hints at a parent different from the out-there and hip-shooting person she would become. Katie seems to have shared the directness of her mother—"Let them know you're there!" was one of Elinor Couric's mottoes for her kids. John Couric, by contrast, was formal, in a Southern, somewhat military way. When Katie made goofy, sometimes precociously bawdy jokes at the dinner table, Elinor would laugh, but John would plead to his wife, "Please, Elinor, don't encourage her." And, Katie has said, if her father "called to us and we responded, 'Yes,' he would say, 'Yes, *what?*' We were required to say, 'Yes, *sir.*'" Katie grew up being accustomed to a man modeling tradition and propriety, reining things in, tamping things down. This would resonate later, in her relationship with Jay Monahan.

Indeed, Katie Couric was a normal girl in the most normal suburb at the tail end of the last normal moment in America. The Courics managed to do something fascinating: They raised four *un*rebellious teenagers during America's most rebellious span of years. Katie frequently says, and her friends agree, that hers was "a *Leave It to Beaver* childhood." As one of those friends, Janie McMullen Florea, recalls, "No parents on the street were divorced." The wives in the Jamestown Elementary School and Williamsburg Middle School district of Arlington, including Elinor Couric, were predominantly stay-at-home moms who had dinner on the table when their kids tumbled in from after-school sports—Katie ran track and did gymnastics—and their business-suited husbands came rustling through the front door.

How different this was from Diane's parents, who had vaulted from Appalachian poverty to respectability, her mother brandishing fierce, aggressive perfectionism to show for it—and certainly different from Christiane's poshly cosmopolitan Iranian-British heritage and her family's sudden exile. Katie's eventual conquest of Morning—the immediate *rightness* of her fit as the sister stand-in for middle-class middle American women getting in some TV time before car pool—had a lot to do with her casually bone-deep understanding of her audience.

Katie idolized her older sisters, Emily and Clara, and she happily played the little sister card, courting their friends. "I used to memorize photos in the yearbook," Katie has said, "and then approach various students at football games with salutations like, 'Hi! You're Barbara McLaughlin. I recognize you from the picture in my sister's yearbook.'" Kiki's friends nicknamed Katie "Smiley." Katie also adored her cool, closer-in-age brother, Johnny, who was her confidant and partner in hijinks. As a major ABC producer later observed, "Katie has a 'guy'-like sense of humor"—blunt, baiting. Perhaps it came from her closeness with her brother. Neither Diane nor Christiane had a male sibling.

However implicitly formal, even stern, John Couric was, it was Elinor who was the family enforcer. Katie recounts that her mother once drove "her station wagon over to [classmate] Steve Elliot's house [after school], knocking on the door, dragging me out and throwing my ten-speed in the trunk, when all we were doing was smooching in the basement." The anecdote, in both substance and delivery, is very Katie: the flip, ostentatious candor; the portrayal of herself as a flirt and a scamp.

But the innocence she describes was real. The girls in Katie's posse—Sara Crossman, Betsy Yowell (now Howell), and Janie McMullen (now Florea), and, later, Barbara Cherney (now Andrukonis)—listened to the Monkees and the Cyrkle's "Red Rubber Ball," which was Katie's favorite song. They had crushes on the cute boys in that crowd of—as one friend describes them—"good, clean, popular kids" who eschewed the psychedelic counterculture that was lurking on the fringes. By high school, some of their peers in other crowds smoked marijuana, but that was mainly considered the province of the misfits. The girls played flashlight tag during sleepovers. Katie, Sara, and Janie serenaded their parents "with our versions of 'Lemon Tree' and 'Let Me Entertain You,' and Katie kind of directed the whole thing," says Janie Florea. They shopped at the mall at Tysons Corner, ice-skated at the Falls Church rink, swam at the Washington Golf and Country Club pool, hiked at Turkey Run, and set their hair very carefully for the Friday night dances at school. "For Christmas, we'd all have our lists of what we wanted, and one Christmas the four of us got the same banana-seat bicycle," Florea adds. "We called ourselves the Mod Squad." Another time, "We had a 'carnival' where we raised money— twelve whole dollars—for the United Givers Fund. The *Northern Virginia Sun* came out and took a picture of us on the steps of Katie's house. There was always a game of softball or kickball going on in the street, and the doors were open and we'd go from one house to the other."

Katie seemed to know, from very early on, that she wanted to be a television reporter. In 1970, when she was thirteen years old, "at cheerleading practice and in the hallways, she would hold a fake microphone in front of her face, and she would say, 'This is Katie Couric, reporting from Cairo,'" her friend Barbara Cherney Andrukonis recalls. "Katie always had a vision of being 'somebody' when she grew up." Adds her friend Betsy Yowell Howell: "In college, when we'd come home summers" and everyone else was cheerfully clueless about their futures, "she knew what she wanted to do: 'I want to go to New York and be on TV.'" The on-camera part fit her natural zesty exhibitionism, her mischief, her flair for the wry bon mot. The newswoman part suited her serious self—a self she aspired to, knew she possessed if did not always manifest, and spent her early career uphill-battling to be acknowledged for.

At Yorktown High, Katie had grabbed one of the rare eighth-grade spots on the mostly ninth- and tenth-grade cheerleading squad. The cachet of being a cheerleader, with its visible bravura, presaged that other, further goal. She'd practiced her older sisters' cheers over and over; she memorized the cheerleaders' names, both for ingratiation and for inspiration—and finally her shrewd determination paid off. She made the team. But cheerleading was just the beginning.

"She was in the limelight from a very early time in our schooling," says Barbara Andrukonis, recalling her bubbly friend as a track and field whiz who sang Broadway show tunes while playing them by ear on the piano; who was a ham, cracking everyone up while lip-synching "My Boyfriend's Back"; who was a gifted mimic, hitting it out of the park, if she did say so herself, with her Karen Carpenter imitation. Katie's knack for performance was deep—and her talent was not insignificant. She played Debussy and Chopin—the only one of her four siblings to keep up piano lessons—and she pecked out the music by heart, "like Irving Berlin," she would later say, "play[ing] everything in the key of C."

Katie excelled at school. She was elected senior class homeroom president and she earned placement in the honors society. With Emily and Kiki both graduates of Smith College (Kiki was now studying architecture at Harvard), Katie applied there as well in her senior year, feeling optimistic that she would be accepted for fall 1974 entrance: She was a double legacy, and her grades were good.

It was not to be. Smith sent her a rejection letter.

This wouldn't normally seem like a grievous loss. She was accepted to the University of Virginia, where Johnny was a sophomore. With its stately, bucolic campus established by Thomas Jefferson and its high academic standards, UVA was one of the finest state universities in the country. But the arrival in the mailbox of the thin envelope from Smith, indicating that her application for admission had been declined, was devastating to Katie, perhaps revealing how much she secretly feared her boisterous peppiness was less than her sisters' gravitas, and how high a bar she had set for herself. (So stinging was the rejection that she still talked about it almost ten years later. "Katie told me she had always wanted to go to Smith, and when she didn't get in she was heartbroken," says her Atlanta boyfriend Lane Duncan, who met her in 1982. "I said, 'Come on, Katie! UVA—it's a wonderful school!'" But she wasn't having it. "Katie was envious of her older sisters—she wanted to measure up to them and she felt she didn't.")

Katie reacted to the Smith rejection, and the inferiority and imperfection she inferred from it, in an extreme way: She became bulimic. She began a secret daily habit of bingeing and purging—eating large quantities of food and then repairing to a bathroom to vomit it all up. "I wrestled with bulimia all through college and for two years after that," she admitted in 2012. "I was struggling with my body image and feeling like I wasn't good enough or attractive enough or thin enough." She was wholesomely pretty, chubby cheeked, and barely five foot three. She was certainly not fat, but she was "curvy," as she puts it, and, like many other *Vogue*-reading girls who looked enviously at the three lissome Charlie's Angels on TV, she was deeply aware that the cultural ideal seemed to be "five-foot-eight and 115 pounds. It can be so difficult to embrace the body that you have if it doesn't fit with the ideal," she has said. "Women get praised for being super thin, so you keep striving to be that way." She began to experience "this rigidity, this feeling that if you eat one thing that's wrong, you're full of self-loathing and then you punish yourself, whether it's one cookie or a stick of gum that isn't sugarless. I would sometimes beat myself up for that." In the midseventies, little was known of eating disorders to which young women were especially prone. It would take Karen Carpenter's death from anorexia nervosa in 1983 to shine a spotlight on what came to be known as the "good girls' illness." But eating disorders were far from rare at the time.

As Katie entered the UVA freshman class of three thousand—along with some forty others of Yorktown's 540 graduating seniors—she was not alone in her secret habit. "Lots of us girls were bulimic or anorexic," says a female classmate. "If everything else spirals out of control, you've got food whipped." And what heavy food that Southern school had! There was almost a secret contest among girls "for barfing up 'grillswiths'—two grilled donuts topped with vanilla ice cream—usually eaten after a one-eyed bacon cheeseburger—fried egg on top—and sometimes pipn' hots [fries with gravy] at the 'UD,' the University Diner, consumed at two a.m. after fraternity parties."

Popular culture at the time was rooted in disco. The swirly, strings-heavy music in seamless rotation introduced a new kind of joyous but disciplined dancing and made strange bedfellows of disparate elements of urban culture: preening outer borough New York tough boys like John Travolta's character, Tony Romero, in *Saturday Night Fever*; dandyish African Americans in John Shaft suits; and denizens of the openly gay bathhouse scene.

But the culture of UVA in fall 1974 was not only *not* in tune with the current disco era but "it was as if even the sixties had never happened," says a woman with a background similar to Katie's. "You didn't wear jeans on campus, really." Coming from a middle-class public high school, "I couldn't believe all the boys in Lacoste shirts and khakis and the girls in these awful wraparound quilted skirts and headbands, dancing to 'Build Me Up, Buttercup,'" by the Foundations—the song that was all the rage. "For those of us"—Katie included—"who did not come from the Virginia boarding school culture, with boys named Schuyler and Tripp with III after their names, those of us who wore halter dresses and platform shoes on our first day of class, UVA seemed like time-traveling to another era." As classmate Michael Vitez, who also grew up in a middle-class neighborhood near D.C., puts it, "The longest distance in America seemed to be the ninety minutes it took to get from Washington to Richmond—it was a different world."

UVA had only started admitting women in 1970—four and a half years before Katie's class entered. It was still catching up from its time warp, this school with its tradition of wealthy but provincial Southernness. Unmarked graves of Confederate soldiers peppered the fields adjoining the campus; the school was still majority male, and there were even a couple of professors who refused to teach women. One was the esteemed regional history professor Virginius Dabney, named for the state his ancestors helped found, a tall and courtly direct descendant of Thomas Jefferson and of sundry Stars and Bars eminences. Professor Dabney was an (initially reluctant) opponent of segregation, but he'd been ambivalent about the civil rights movement; he defended the South when it was criticized, and he wrote a book contesting the notion that Jefferson had had a love affair with his slave Sally Hemings. According to a student at UVA during Katie's early years there, Professor Dabney firmly believed that

Mr. Jefferson's university should have remained all male, and he intended it to stay precisely that way. Other professors would teach women only if they came to class in skirts.

Katie's immersion into a school culture that was so conservative may well have carried a lesson for her about maneuvering in the "real," post-college world she would soon enter: America will change, but not that much. Her future ability to fit so perfectly into the expectations and approval of middle America during the first half of her fourteen years as *Today*'s star anchor may well have come from this understanding about the limits of change—the obdurate nature of tradition. Later, she would be punished by her loyal viewers for deviating from the image of her they had embraced so energetically early on.

The college's president, Frank Loucks Hereford, was a staunch traditionalist, and, says one then-student, "You got the idea that anyone who wasn't Southern, male, and straight was there under sufferance." UVA's sororities were racially segregated and many did not accept Jewish girls, and competition for the top houses was intense. Katie pledged one of the two most exclusive sororities, Delta Delta Delta—Tri-Delt—in which, a Kappa Delta says, "the joke was that their version of diversity was letting in brunettes. Katie was probably about as far out on a limb as they went: brown hair *and* from a public school in Northern Virginia *and* she declared one of the new, nontraditional majors, American studies. Imagine!"

On weekends, UVA became majority female. The students from the nearby "suitcase schools"—the all-women's colleges Mary Baldwin, Mary Washington, Hollins, and Sweetbriar—thronged in for parties. These girls were considered prettier and both more mysterious *and* more accommodating by the UVA frat boys who now had a surfeit of women to choose from; they scorned their weekday female classmates as "U-bags" and bragged they'd never date them.

The sexual politics of the mid-1970s were perplexing. There was a heady scent of mainstream-ascendant feminism in the air—Title IX existed; women were enrolling in law and med school in newly record numbers; the culture was energized by activists, like Gloria Steinem, whom teenage girls actually wanted to emulate; movies like *The Stepford Wives* showed, by way of horror movie hyperbole, what everyone finally understood that gender relations *shouldn't* be.

At UVA, even girls outside of the "I'm-going-to-be-a-teacher-but-mainly-get-married" inner circle wanted to fit in. As one explains it: "Here you had this über-traditional place that was filled with very, very smart women who wanted change, but not wholesale change. We didn't want to be Michigan or Antioch. We wanted to keep the cool traditions. We wanted to drink with the boys at the frats but not worry about date rape. We wanted to get into a good sorority but not because the Richmond debutantes approved of us. We wanted intellectual respect and equality— we wanted to be smart and outspoken—but we still waited on pins and needles to be asked out for the weekend on Wednesday night. Needless to say, we didn't always succeed with this confused agenda."

Katie, this sorority friend says, was as afflicted with this "confused agenda" as any other UVA freshman girl. She certainly partook of fraternity parties, which were frequent and raucous. Easter weekend was the school's big blowout—one year Jackson Browne performed and *Life* magazine took pictures. "Katie may have wanted to get into Smith, but she wouldn't have wanted to *go* to Smith," the sorority friend opines. "The Seven Sisters' time had passed. They weren't fun." This friend adds, "In order to do well at UVA, you had to be able to work hard and play hard, twenty-four/seven. UVA was very good at rewarding people who could handle that. Contemplation was not encouraged. Katie's a high-energy person. That's why she thrived there. Lots of other people burned out."

Kathleen Lobb met Katie when they were resident advisers in the same dorm. Kathleen was a junior, Katie a sophomore. Their shared background departed from UVA's more elite norm—"I went to a Catholic high school in Northern Virginia, which was very near the public high school that Katie attended," Kathleen says, "and one of my closest friends had known Katie since we were all little kids." They would become friends for life, and at UVA they shared the sense that they were at a school that "still had very much the aura of a Southern conservative institution, and yet the women's movement was exploding all around us. I don't think we had that much of a sense of being part of feminism in terms of our day-to-day life at school," but they wanted some of what was out there: careers as well as boyfriends, independence as well as security. Adventure, even.

Resident advisers counseled younger girls in the dorms, and Katie was a natural for the job. "She would stay up all night talking to a freshman girl who was depressed over breaking up with her boyfriend," a friend recalled. "Being an RA was a challenging experience and we just bonded," says Kathleen, who is now the senior vice president of Katie's Stand Up to Cancer. "She's a lot funnier than I am, but our senses of humor were similar. We had the same value system; we were both very close to our families." Kathleen was struck by Katie's determination to become a TV reporter. "In my circle of friends, it was pretty rare to have such a definitive sense of what you wanted to do from the beginning of time, like Katie did."

The way Kathleen heard it, Katie had told her father she wanted to be a reporter and he'd replied, "Go into TV; you'll make more money." But Katie's oldest sister Emily's journalism career also inspired her. Katie's talent for writing impressed Kathleen. "Katie was taking a graduate-level cultural and intellectual history course as a sophomore, and we were sitting together while she was writing a paper on witchcraft on her typewriter, and it was riveting. She got an A-plus in that course, so her talent as a storyteller was very apparent to me from the beginning."

In her freshman year, Katie joined UVA's paper, the *Cavalier Daily*. "She started as a reporter, her second year became an associate editor, then the faculty was her beat for a year," during which she did a series of profiles of professors. "She was a rock-solid legitimate staff member," says Michael Vitez, who became the *Cav*'s editor in chief in his senior year and went on to win a Pulitzer Prize at the *Philadelphia Inquirer*. The paper took its mission very seriously—its staffers considered the campus's weekly paper, *The Declaration*, "to be more conservative, more party line."

"I want to say this carefully," Vitez says, "but if you lined up everyone in the newsroom at the time and asked, 'Who will be the most successful?' you wouldn't necessarily have picked Katie. Because you would have thought, 'Who's the smartest?' and there were a lot of intellectuals"—many went on to estimable, serious newspaper careers. But, in retrospect, Katie's eventual outsized success makes sense to Vitez because "she was not just very attractive and hardworking, but she had a fabulous personality and was very quick on her feet, and she was forward-thinking to go into TV—CNN!—right away." He pauses to make a point more important than it may initially sound: "And that classic suburban background and that solid, nurturing home she came from made her really in tune with America and gave her the confidence to deal with lots of people."

During Katie's senior year at UVA, she was on the senior resident staff and was awarded the most coveted housing on campus, a rare "lawn room," one of about a hundred small suites—cramped, but with a fireplace—in the most historic part of the university. "She was a mover and shaker on campus," says Barbara Andrukonis, who attended UVA as well but was returning home after graduation and was engaged to her boyfriend.

By now, the tenor of the campus had changed. No longer was UVA purely the anachronistic rich Southern preppie haven it had been in 1974. Katie related as a feminist now—"I was one of those young women right smack in the middle of the women's movement who thought, 'I don't ever need to get married. I don't need a man.'" And the gay rights movement had arrived on campus. On the other side of the country, Harvey Milk, California's first openly gay political official, had just been assassinated in San Francisco. UVA boys who had trembled in their closets during freshman year were coming out now, and gay bashing—once an unremarkable staple of fraternity life—was drawing outrage. Katie became close friends with a gay student who was an editor of *The Declaration*. Both papers—*The Dec* and the *Cav*—came out for gay rights. UVA's new Gay Student Union demanded a meeting with President Hereford to discuss protection for gays on campus. When Hereford declined, saying he had a prior commitment to go to the theater, students howled at his tone deafness: Going to the *theater* as a way of ducking gays? In defending his refusal of the meeting, Hereford explained that UVA was predominantly heterosexual.

Students then reworded the earnest school song from "We come from Old Virginia, where all is bright and gay" to "We come from Old Virginia, where all is bright and the majority are heterosexual."

EVEN BEFORE GRADUATION, Katie had begun sending her résumé, such as it was, to D.C. network news directors. The place she had the best chance, she figured, was at ABC, where she had connections. (It helped to be local.) The D.C.-based executive producer of *World News Tonight*, David Newman, had two younger brothers who had been in Katie's sister Kiki's high school class. When Kevin Delaney, the deputy chief of ABC's Washington, D.C., bureau, didn't respond to her query, she called his office several times; his "officious" secretary, as Katie later called the woman, refused to schedule an appointment.

So Katie planned a guerrilla strike. She put on "my best dress-for-success outfit—you know, the blue blazer, the blouse, the completely geeky little bow tied around my collar that was almost obligatory wardrobe for any young, aspiring career woman at the time," she has said. She asked her mother to drive her to ABC so she could tour the newsroom. "My mother looked at me as if I were on crack."

Nevertheless, Elinor Couric obliged, driving Katie to the bureau in her cream-colored Buick station wagon. As Katie has described it, she approached the security guard and asked to see Kevin Delaney. The guard "chuckled" at the chutzpah of this girl with no appointment and turned her down. But she spied a phone in the waiting area, politely asked to use it, walked over, picked it up, and asked the operator to be connected "to Davey Newman"—of course, she was not on such casual terms with him, but the ruse worked. Newman answered the phone himself. Katie's words spilled out: "Hi, Davey. You don't know me, but your twin brothers, Steve and Eddie, went to high school with my sister Kiki, and I live down the street from your cousin Julie." The guileless appeal to personal ties, the brazen charm, the young voice—it *worked*. She asked to "come up to the newsroom and poke my head into the deputy bureau chief's office," she has recalled. "I think he was completely flummoxed," enough to say, "'Sure, come up.'"

Katie has told various versions of that story, always with her plucky charm highlighted. Lane Duncan remembers her saying something along the lines of, "I went through the back door, and while someone was open- ing it, I walked in and said, 'I think you need me to carry your reels.'" In all accounts she uses the same topic sentence: "I just kind of wormed my way in."

Whatever the details, she got to Delaney's office and begged him for a job. "I told him I really wanted to work at ABC News. I told him I had a considerable amount of work experience compared with many of my peers and I would be a real asset to the organization." Within a few weeks, she was hired as an assistant.

It was a—male—star-studded newsroom. There was Sam Donaldson, then the ABC *Sunday Evening News* anchor, who serenaded her with a lusty chorus of "K-K-K-Katie, beautiful Katie . . ." There was the network's former evening news coanchor Frank Reynolds, whose lunch order— usually a ham sandwich—she had to deliver. There was Brit Hume, then ABC's congressional correspondent (much later Fox News anchor), and *Nightline*'s Ted Koppel. In contrast to CBS's Washington newsroom, home to Watergate warriors Connie Chung, Lesley Stahl, Susan Zirinsky, Marcy McGinnis—and now, in a move that sparked staff fury, so-called Nixon apologist Diane Sawyer—the ABC bureau that Katie Couric entered was a den of testosterone, where the suited stars, she's recalled, "sat around drinking Scotch after the newscast." But there was an exception: the smart, elegant Cassie Mackin, ABC's Capitol Hill correspondent, who was covering Senator Ted Kennedy's campaign to unseat President Jimmy Carter. After having earned distinction as a hard questioner of Nixon dur- ing his run against McGovern, Mackin had been hired away from NBC by ABC News president Roone Arledge, who was on his way to becoming known as a money-brandishing poacher of female TV news stars, for the then unprecedented salary of $100,000 a year.

By now forty-one and still single, and a local girl like Katie (she'd grown up in Baltimore), Cassie Mackin defied every patronizing image of the never-married career woman the culture had presented. Katie seized upon Cassie as a role model. "I used to see her floating around the office—and she did float because she was this willowy blond. I used to think, 'Gosh, she's so neat! She's so smart!' As a young woman, I was proud of her, proud of her role."

"Cassie was enormously self-possessed and charismatic," recalls Richard Wald, who knew Mackin from her NBC years. "She was blond, striking looking, with great self-assurance. Whenever she'd interview a politician, she'd ask tough questions. She knew, and you knew that she knew, and she wasn't going to take any crap from you. But she wasn't overly aggressive," Wald says, puzzling out the subtle mix that, in 1980, kept appealing femininity importantly in the picture. "It was that self-possession" that most stood out, Wald emphasizes. Katie could tell, from Cassie's late hours and her long time on the Kennedy campaign trail, that she "sacrificed a lot" of personal life for her work. Katie admired that. As Lane Duncan, her Atlanta boyfriend, notes, even slightly later, "You could tell that her career was more important than any entanglement. It was clear that her career was first. She wasn't in the market for a husband."

Other ambitious young single female D.C.-based TV news reporters also looked at Mackin and saw that same complex combination—mostly awe-inspiring, but with a hint of warning poignance—that Katie saw. "You'd look at her and think, 'How can you be *that* beautiful and *that* smart, in one package?" recalls Susan Zirinsky. "But there was a little bit of the lonely-girl aspect to her, too. There was the beauty, and I had so much respect for her, but you didn't know what else was in her life."

The bureau's other Capitol Hill correspondent was a veteran on-air reporter named Don Farmer, whose wife, Chris Curle, was a TV newscaster in Tampa. As with many married couples in the news business, their careers kept them geographically separated. It was considered a conflict of interest for married news anchors to work the same market; most had commuter marriages.

Katie didn't let her junior position keep her from pitching story ideas—and she did so, again and again, to Farmer. "She was barely out of college—a desk assistant—and she was hanging out in the same area where I had my cubbyhole of an office, along with Ted Koppel and some other correspondents," says Farmer. "She would come in there and pitch stories to me that related to Congress. She would say, 'This would be a good story for you to do,' and more often than not they were good ideas. I don't remember any bad ones. She was young and smart and really eager. That bubbly personality: I got to thinking really highly of her." So did a higher-placed man Katie pitched stories to: ABC's Washington bureau chief George Watson, a Harvard alum and close friend of David Halberstam.

In June 1980, when Katie had been pitching ideas at ABC for less than a year, CNN had just opened its doors in Atlanta. Ted Turner's non-unionized, rules-breaking, initially bathroomless twenty-four-hour cable network—which Christiane would later come to—was on the radar for ambitious young people like Katie. It just so happened that—aside from looking for young people (requiring little salary), and aside from accepting staffers the networks wouldn't so easily accept, such as women, African Americans, and old-timers aging out in other markets—Ted and partner Reese Schonfeld had another hiring trick up their sleeves: They got expensive veterans cheaply by approaching married-couple TV pros—anchors, weather people—stressed out from constantly weekend-commuting between his city and hers. Lois Hart and Dave Walker were the first married couple who gratefully jumped to the Atlanta unknown in order to work together and quit their commuting lifestyle. Next, Schonfeld recruited Don Farmer, the ABC Capitol Hill correspondent who was so impressed with Katie, and his Tampa-based wife, Chris Curle. They would anchor CNN's two-hour crown-jewel afternoon *Today*-style show, *Take Two*.

As soon as Reese and Ted secured a line of credit and they re-upped the affiliate bureaus they had lost during their temporary money crunch, Reese asked Don Farmer and George Watson (by now also recruited to CNN) to recommend hires for CNN's D.C. bureau. "George and I suggested Katie," Don says. "She became part of our staff, an associate producer."

Katie has remembered this period as being overwhelming. It was,

"'We're gonna give you a break, kid.'" They told her to "go to the White House and talk about what the president was doing. It was like saying to me, 'Why don't you go play Lady Macbeth?' I was sooo bad! I had this sing-songy voice and I looked like I was in high school."

One morning the D.C. anchor failed to show up for the new seven a.m. spot, and unbeknownst to Atlanta, Katie was rushed in as a replacement. "Ted Kavanau—who hated Washington and was always fighting with George Watson about who had more time on the air—called me and said, *Look who's on the air!*'" Reese Schonfeld recalls, mimicking Kavanau's outrage at seeing an unprofessional novice. The story—which has been repeated many times—goes that Schonfeld then screamed, referring to Katie, "*I never want to see that girl on the air again!*" "It was a real confidence builder," Katie has said, with grim sarcasm. Schonfeld admits: "She looked eighteen. Her voice was quavering. I did call the producer and ask, 'Who put *her* on the air?' But I didn't say, 'Never put her on the air again.'" Reese says his actual words were "Never put *anyone* on the air again without calling me first," and he claims that, in the retellings of the story amid Katie's fame, his actual, more politic words morphed into the harsher ones.

As hurtful as Schonfeld's outburst may have been, Katie steeled herself against it. She wanted to leave D.C. for the network's wild and crazy action central. She also was having a flirtation with Guy Pepper, a good-looking young CNN producer engaged to a beautiful blond CNN anchor named Denise LeClair.

Looking at it from the perspective of 1980 *and* today, CNN producer Marcia Ladendorff says: "Katie flirted up a storm with Guy Pepper"—the two would indeed become involved—and once she got to Atlanta, she would also, more innocently, "flirt up a storm with Ted Kavanau." (Kavanau says, with some pride, that when he put Katie on the air—he takes credit for being the first to do so, in a series of spots in which she sparred with him in "cutting, sarcastic repartee"—she "told me that her parents thought she should marry me.")

Ladendorff continues: "Katie was pixielike. And she was very, very clever about who to get near and who to get to know. You can be the smartest person on the earth, you can be drop-dead gorgeous, but if you can't do the people-politicking, you're not going anywhere. This is not to put Katie down, but there are plenty of women out there who are probably smarter than she is and certainly more beautiful than she is, but when it comes to working the crowd," Katie beats them. "This is the age of shameless self-promotion. I do believe she does have substance. But all the substance in the world is not going to trump someone who is smart and savvy."

And Katie was savvy—and nervy. One day toward the end of 1980 Reese Schonfeld got a call from a D.C.-based CNN reporter named Jean Carper. "So Carper calls me and says, 'Katie's in my office in tears. [Producer] Stuart Loory just fired her. Can you get her a job?'" Reese respected Jean Carper—"She was one of the best reporters we had. I get Katie on the phone and she's crying and I say, 'I'm not going to override Loory, but I'll see if I can find you something here on *Take Two*." It turned out Farmer and Curle were thrilled to have Katie as a production assistant.

Only, Katie *hadn't* been fired by Loory. Katie had made up the story and faked the tears to get Schonfeld to offer her a spot on *Take Two*, which would get her to Atlanta, a better launching pad (and where Guy Pepper also happened to be located). "The whole thing was a setup! Katie played me!" Reese Schonfeld says today. "She *played* me!" Apparently she'd also played Jean Carper. Schonfeld learned the truth much later: "I called Carper and said, 'Did you get the story from Loory?' And she said, 'No! Katie just came in—her eyes were red and she was crying.'" Schonfeld pauses. He calls what Katie did "nefarious," and adds, "No one likes to be played for a sucker." Still, despite his words of anger and judgment, he involuntarily breaks into a small, admiring smile at Katie's chutzpah.

THE WAY KATIE operated wasn't the way women in TV news—especially "soft," featurey TV news—had ever acted before. Looking back, from the perspective of knowing that Katie would, starting in 1991, enjoy the longest and most successful run of any female *Today* host, it's as if she represents a 3.0 attitude: bald aggressiveness and caginess, as seen in the defiant refusal, even as a young, inexperienced rookie, to be cowed or thwarted by a dismissive D.C. bureau chief or his "officious" secretary, by a condescending security guard, or by a network head who'd just screamed that her career dreams were futile.

Katie's two predecessors as the female *Today* anchor had advanced their careers by very different means. Barbara Walters was beleaguered, battle-tested, battle-weary: the pioneer who cleared the path for others, but at personal emotional cost. Jane Pauley was, as she puts it, "reality-based," sensible, so inherently deferential that she lost a promotion she'd clearly earned.

Barbara Walters emerged from her *Today* show struggle with Frank McGee only to become embattled with Harry Reasoner, an even worse television partner. From 1976 to 1978, as famously the most expensive Roone Arledge hire, Walters became the first woman to coanchor an evening news show. Her cohost Reasoner *hated* this.

"Harry Reasoner was a male chauvinist. He once said to me, 'You're a great executive producer, but you have one failing: You hire too many women,'" says Av Westin, who was SOS'd to the show in 1978 to first defuse and then phase out the toxic pairing. At the time, Reasoner may not have been the only man affronted when Walters got the anchor job. Walter Cronkite, upon hearing about Walters's ascent, had the "sickening sensation that we were all going under, that all of our efforts to hold network television news aloof from show business had failed." David Brinkley harrumphed that "being an anchor is not just a matter of sitting in front of a camera, looking pretty," while Brinkley's NBC partner John Chancellor said he was glad Walters wasn't partnering with *him*. Yes, Walters was coming from the entertainment rather than the news division, but *Today* was a hybrid, focused on news as much as features, and TV news had been so inhospitable to experienced women that there wasn't much of a pool of candidates with durable credentials. That Barbara Walters would be the first female coanchor made sense.

By the time Av Westin entered the fray, Walters had been cohosting with Reasoner for about a year and a half, but the coanchors weren't talking to each other. "You're coming into a room where a bickering couple has just had a hell of a fight and the walls are still reverberating," was how Roone Arledge described the situation to Westin. Reasoner had been angry that Arledge had not only paired him with a woman, but, Westin says, "with Barbara, the *quintessential* woman who had made it, with extraordinary difficulty." As if to underscore the gender war, Walters had turned her office into an all-pink lair; even her typewriter was pink. "It was very feminine—strange in an old boys' newsroom," says Westin. And during one of their first newscasts, not only did Barbara—not Harry—interview Anwar Sadat, but Sadat (whose salary as Egypt's prime minister was about $12,000 a year) absolutely marveled on air—at peculiar, improvised length—at the million dollars that ABC was paying her.

When Av Westin arrived, Reasoner and Walters "had their own little coteries" that buffered them, to keep the broadcast from descending into "internecine warfare." The first words Westin heard, from one of Reasoner's allies, was, "'She owes him five minutes and twenty-five seconds!'" Reasoner had been keeping "a running clock of the amount of time each of them had on the air, and if Barbara had more airtime he wanted it back. That's how ludicrous it was." Barbara was soon "pleading, though not in words, '*Get me out of here!*'" She left the show "gun-shy," for *20/20*.

For all her battles, Walters, at that time and place, had little appetite for warfare. Says one who knew her well then, "She was the *most* insecure person! I was once at a dinner party to which she came, and she stood in the corner with her hands against the wall, touching the wall."

Jane Pauley, who took over Barbara Walters's job on *Today* in 1976, says that she coined the phrase to describe her female cohort, "The Class of '72" (as well as the term for her own too-long-for-TV tresses: "Bad Hair Day"). She is the first to say she benefited from Barbara Walters's struggles, and from Title IX, which sprang a door open exactly as she was walking toward it.

"Lucky" is a word Jane Pauley often uses. She was lucky to go to a top public high school in Indiana, to be a speech and debate champion and a political science major working for a political candidate, George McGovern, in a battleground state, at the very time, "the spring of '72, that the FCC added two words to the affirmative action clause to the qualifications

for hiring: '*and women*.'" One day a TV recruiter saw her addressing envelopes for McGovern and said, "'There's an opening for a reporter, and
they're looking for'—and I quote—'*a female-type person*.'"

Pauley was hired as an evening anchor on the local Indianapolis station, which provided another stroke of luck: On Memorial Day weekend,
the Indianapolis 500 draws a half million extra people to the city—
including many media types—and she was noticed by channel-flipping
media execs in their hotel rooms. Result? An invitation to join CBS's Chicago affiliate. A year later, in 1976, at twenty-five, she beat out two very
different opponents—sixty-year-old Betty Furness and thirty-year-old
Candice Bergen—to take over Barbara Walters's coanchorship of *Today*.

Jane joined Tom Brokaw on the show and was immediately popular.
Pretty, young, blond, and personable, she had what TV critic Tom Shales
called "red light reflex": The instant the cameras were on, she was, too.
She tightened her Midwestern drawl into a formal, crisp voice with concertedly authoritative cadence and timbre, which seemed to say, "I am a
professional," and which became the template for young female anchors.

Viewers may have assumed she was coequal to Brokaw, but, contractually, he was the host. "It was extremely obvious to me, and my employers,
that Tom was number one among equals. He is such a big personality! He
had gravitas when he was fourteen. He had just come off the White
House. He'd covered Watergate. With my sense of proportion, it would
have been absurd to try to persuade anyone that my four years in local
television was comparable to his work. I knew where I stood." Jane Pauley's acceptance of "where she stood" would be the biggest difference between her and Katie—that and the change in gender politics from 1976 to
1991. When in January 1982 the by then popular, experienced Jane Pauley
inherited a new partner, Bryant Gumbel, it was Gumbel who was anointed
sole anchor; Jane, again, was his "cohost."

By today's media-star measures, this would seem odd. Jane Pauley was
a staple in *People* magazine by then; she was respected and adored. Her
"bad hair" had settled into a thick and well-groomed blond pageboy, she
was dignified but charming, she was married to the actor-handsome
Doonesbury cartoonist Garry Trudeau, who manifested preppy whole-

someness as well as witty social criticism. She'd had a miscarriage (actually two; one was kept quiet) that had garnered public sympathy. Hadn't she earned the starring role? In 1980, when sports anchor Gumbel was appearing on *Today* in a secondary capacity, "I felt it was incumbent on me as a woman *not* to accept second-class citizenship. I made this rather impassioned argument to the president of NBC News, Reuven Frank and [four other] guys, that to *not* elevate me to full anchor role—for them to pass over a woman—would not look good. A confab was convened in Reuven Frank's office. They had to hear me out. My agent was not there. I was on my own.

"They took me seriously. These were thoughtful men." But: "I lost. I lost the fight." Even though most viewers did not know it, "Bryant, by contract, was the sole anchor. I could only be called 'cohost.'" Did he make more money than she did? Pauley laughs, ruefully. "I assume he got a *lot* more." She adds, "I'm not shufflingly grateful, but I know how lucky I was."

When her time came—and it would come in less than ten years from the day she moved to Atlanta—Katie Couric would not make Jane Pauley's mistake. As she has said, "I'm pretty convinced that the meek will *not* inherit the earth." And as a UVA friend of Katie's who went on to work in the thick of one of the most rarefied, most cutthroat hotbeds of media ambition told a friend, "Katie Couric is the most ambitious person, by far, that I have ever encountered."

WHEN KATIE GOT to Atlanta in early 1981, she worked prodigiously, moving in the short span of two years to assistant producer and then to daily talk show producer.

Take Two, the show she worked on—with her former ABC colleague Don Farmer and his wife, Chris Curle—mixed celebrity interviews with hard and soft news. Katie was twenty-four, but, as one of the network's evening anchors, Lois Hart, recalled thinking, "'Oh, my God, that girl looks like a teenager!' She looked so young compared to everyone else—even to me, and I was only thirty." Hart's husband, Dave Walker, remembers that, from virtually the moment she got to CNN, "Katie was *pleading* with people to get a shot on the air."

Katie met architect Lane Duncan because they both had apartments in a cozy building in Ansley Park, a neighborhood that attracted youthful careerists during those years that the city was just beginning to gentrify. She dated Duncan—a native Atlantan over a decade older than she— when her more regular boyfriend, a CNN cameraman, was out of town on assignment. "Lane was her secret lover," says a mutual friend from those days. "You know news business people; they had a lot of lovers, and so did Katie—well, she was a player."

Another Atlanta friend and young CNN colleague of Katie's, Diana Greene—at the time a serious Vermont girl who "didn't shave under my arms" and was culture-shocked by Atlanta—viewed Northern Virginia– bred Katie as, by contrast, having "the Southern girl's early attachment to makeup." Diana was also a bit taken aback that someone who wanted to be a serious journalist (and had "a more cush job"—daytime show producer—at CNN than did the more ostensibly serious Diana) would have *Vogue* magazines lying around her apartment living room. There was always that whipsaw in Katie: the contradiction between the slightly trivial or jivey or snarky—the makeup, the *Vogue*s, the wisecracks, the "player" dating habits—and her sincerely hurt feelings at not being taken seriously. There was always the friction between that *Leave It to Beaver*–referencing, enthusiastically cheerleading, undisguised sorority girlishness—a part of herself she brandished half with *I-gotta-be-me* pride and half with cheeky self-deprecation—and her ferocious ambition and abiding feminism.

"Katie was always ambitious," Diana Greene recalls. "Every day she arrived at work one hundred percent ready to go on camera—hair perfect, clothes, makeup—even though the impression at CNN was that they would *never* put her in front of a camera." It was "endearing" to Diana, the dissonance between what Katie wanted and how people thought of her, and that while Katie *looked* so organized and camera-ready, "she was chaotic. If you looked in her purse, she had a lipstick with no top. She wanted to be taken seriously, but she was *so* funny. She was the funniest person I knew."

"When people didn't think she belonged in front of a camera, it *energized* her," her childhood friend Betsy Howell believes. Lane Duncan saw this, too. "Katie was aware that people perceived her as not serious. She was hell-bent on proving something. She was constantly on. Her ON switch was turned there and there was no alternative." Lane would wonder, "Where's the REST button, Katie?" He also saw her teasing wit turn occasionally discomfiting. She could "tweak anybody about any subject and that caught us older people off-guard. Sometimes the thing that makes us most aggressive is that we're scared."

One evening Katie brought Lane to her CNN cubby and played for him a piece on the Amish, which she'd "finagled a chance to do, and went out and did," he says—producing, reporting, narrating, and filming it, although it never aired. He was stunned by the "thoughtful, solid journalism." He'd pegged her as a funny, sarcastic, bubbly girl; he hadn't taken her seriously. Now, here was "this paradox—she wasn't play-acting. I thought, 'This girl's *good!*' My perception of her really deepened."

Duncan also noticed that Katie, unusual for a newbie, kept track of the competing networks in town. "We'd drive past a station, and she'd say, 'Oh, they're on top of that specialty.' It was clear she knew who the good ones were and why."

Katie's reputation at CNN Atlanta was mixed. Everyone saw her energy and determination. Some saw her star power in its bud; others, her unquenchable faith in herself. "Katie *always* knew she was going to be big," says Gail Evans, who was vice president of talent at CNN during Katie's (and Christiane's) tenure and who was then the highest-ranking woman at CNN. But others weren't convinced. One of CNN's three news vice presidents was Sam Zelman, a *60 Minutes* producer hired by Ted Turner to give the network credibility. Zelman could hardly be called a sexist; in fact, "he insisted there be a woman on every show," says Reese Schonfeld. Which may be why it hurt Katie all the more that Zelman dismissed her. "Katie didn't impress me as a journalist at all," Zelman flatly says. "She was a television personality and that was her ambition. She was very personable and she talked quickly with a sharp mind, but she didn't have enough journalism background and moxie." Being written off like this hurt Katie, Diana Greene says. Despite "that unflappable quality" of hers, "she wasn't steely at all. She was very human. She was very vulnerable." Still, Katie at least gave the appearance of rising above the disdain. "She was always high energy, she did her own thing, and she tuned out the haters," is how Sparkle Hayter recalls it.

Even Katie's mentor at CNN, Don Farmer, referred to her to others there as "terminally cute." Some thought that Farmer and his wife, Chris—the mentors she trusted—were hard on Katie. "They were really tough on her, always promising something would happen which never happened; she may have remembered things charitably later," says one staffer.

If Christiane, who briefly overlapped with Katie's time at CNN, starting in 1983, was kept off the air because she was too foreign, too serious looking, too assertively knowledgeable—in other words, too big and strange for the niche—then Katie had the opposite problem. She seemed too eager, too cute, too funny—too small and ordinary for it.

Still, as different as they ostensibly were, the two had much in common. "Katie and Christiane were both comfortable in their own skin," Gail Evans says. "'I know who I am and I know where I'm going': You saw this in both of them. Everybody wants authenticity—that's what Cronkite had. They both had it." Also, "Katie and Christiane both know how to get inside a story and tell it properly. And they share irreverence. Christiane talks back to authority figures like no one else. Katie's irreverence is humor, her willingness to say anything despite the consequences."

"Katie was the best bump-line writer we had," says one of the senior producers, Judy Milestone, referring to the teasers used to promote a show's coming segments. As an assistant producer, Katie "really worked it, morning, noon, and night." She flew to Texas and did a piece on Gilley's, the bar with the wooden bronco that John Travolta had made famous in *Urban Cowboy.* She produced the piece and narrated it. "The piece was good but she wasn't. Her delivery wasn't good," Reese Schonfeld says.

Ted Turner had connections with Fidel Castro, and one of CNN's early "gets" was an invitation to film life in Cuba, essentially for the first time since 1959. This was Katie's first big production. She and Guy Pepper flew down and produced the series together, through which their secret romance, which eventually fizzled out, was first revealed to the others. Cuba in the early 1980s was in many ways jelled in aspic from the end of the Batista regime. Don Farmer and Chris Curle remember that, by a fluke, Katie and Guy got one of the only rooms in the Hotel Nacional that had a toilet seat lid. Don: "*That's* why she got so perky." Chris: "We knew then that she was going to be a star." (They tried to trade rooms with her, to no avail; Katie wouldn't budge.) Katie produced a piece on the town Hemingway had stayed in while starting *The Old Man and the Sea.* And when Reese pronounced it "'Brilliant! Wonderful!'" Curle recalls, "she couldn't believe it. She was excited." She also did a touching piece about *quinceañeras*, the coming-of-age festivities for fifteen-year-old Cuban girls, which showcased her ability to relate well to young women. After it aired, Gail Evans remembers "Katie running down the long hall of the hotel, shouting, 'I just got a call from WJLA in Miami! They saw it and they want me to come for an interview!'"

Reese continually rejected Katie as an on-air presence. "She was not a good performer, but she had great news intelligence. She was so quick and fast. When the freed hostages were coming back from Iran, she got film of them coming in and going out" of the White House but missed the crucial meeting of them with President Reagan. "So I say to her, 'Katie! You got foreplay! You got postcoitus! But you missed the climax!' And Katie immediately says, 'All I got was a quick feel, a cup of coffee, and wet sheets.'" Lois Hart: "Katie was serious about her work but she wasn't serious about herself." Reese: "She was so *likable.*"

That she was. Back in 1981—as opposed to the more macho-woman present—raw ambition in a young woman was most effective when softened by some typically female quality. For Diane Sawyer, it was that half-tongue-in-cheek blushing-maiden, poetry-quoting seductive charm. With Katie, it was what Michael Vitez was getting at when he mused about the benefits of her secure upbringing—she had a freewheeling everyday humanity that enhanced her little world. It was only a few years past the end of the seven-year stretch of the immensely popular *Mary Tyler Moore Show*, and while Katie was younger, feistier, and far less self-effacingly perplexed than the hugely likable fictional newsroom pivot Mary Richards, she filled a similar workaday and after-work peppy-good-neighbor role.

"Katie taught my daughters to speak Valley Girl," recalls Gail Evans. Of her six-year-old, whom she brought to work on days when school was out, producer Judy Milestone says, "Katie turned my son into a 'runner' and she taught him to Xerox and file. He adored her because she treated him as someone who had value while everyone else thought he was disruptive. She had a human touch." One neighbor of Katie's in her small and highly collegial Ansley Park apartment building was an elderly woman; Flip Spiceland noticed that "Katie would make it a point to take her out to dinner once a week and introduce her to us. She was always doing that kind of thing." Soon after encountering CNN colleague Diana Greene at the local laundromat, Katie, playing Cupid, arranged for Diana to meet an attorney friend of Lane Duncan's at Lane's gallery show. The man bought a painting, Diana was impressed, they dated—and they married. "Katie was good to everybody at CNN," Diana says. "She really was. She would know people's names. She would know the name of the person who fixed the vending machine."

That plucky generosity, that wholesomeness: There was a character-is-destiny side to Katie's nascent rise, Don Farmer began to see. Don evaluated her in the light of NBC's star anchor in Houston, Jessica Savitch. Though the two women—Jessica and Katie—never worked together or met, Don couldn't help contrasting them with each other. "I knew Jessica very well," he says. "She wanted to be *the* woman anchor." Ten years older than Katie, Jessica, a Philadelphia-raised blond as close to smolderingly attractive as a serious news anchor could be, was called the Golden Girl. She was undeniably talented, hardworking, and appealing. She rose swiftly in the ranks. She used the same tight, all-business anchor voice as Jane Pauley did to detract attention from her looks. (In fact, Pauley thinks that had Savitch not been under contract in Philadelphia in the midseventies, she would have been one of the strongest contenders as Barbara Walters's *Today* replacement.)

Jessica ultimately became a Washington correspondent for NBC. But she was a troubled woman, addicted to mood-stabilizing drugs (which once made her slur unintelligibly on the air), and her life took a number of very sad turns at the very time Katie's career was taking off. She endured a turbulent marriage, then, right on its heels, a second marriage that ended in five months when her new husband hanged himself, with their dog's leash, in the basement of their town house. Working daily with Katie while getting alarming bulletins about Jessica, whom he liked, Don Farmer found himself thinking about how the two women differed. Yes, Katie was fiercely ambitious, just as Jessica was. But, Don realized, "Jessica's was a hollow ambition," fed by a crippling lack of self-esteem. By contrast, Katie was emotionally healthy. "She took all the steps."

Savitch's story ended tragically. One early evening in the fall of 1983, Savitch, then thirty-six, was in a car driven by a news director with whom she was having yet another stormy romance. They'd just dined at a popular restaurant in New Hope, Pennsylvania, when they accidentally drove off a pier jutting into a canal that abutted the parking lot. Stuck in their car, they drowned in the shallow canal.

OF COURSE, Katie had demons of her own—bulimia, for one. As 1981 turned to 1982, Katie was combating—and eventually conquering—that condition with the help of a therapist. She was also seeing a voice coach to neutralize her "git"-for-"get" accent. She may have been frustrated that neither Reese nor his deputy Ed Turner ("a bad hire, a drunk," Schonfeld admits) would put her on the air and that Sam Zelman, the network's champion of women, appeared to disdain her. But, at twenty-five, she was pushing forward.

Then she received dismaying news. Her role model—the woman she'd been fascinated by at ABC in D.C., Cassie Mackin—had terminal cancer. She had left the network and was living with her sister in Baltimore. This woman, who had been so "enormously self-possessed, became

tentative as she became ill," Richard Wald recalls. "She stayed at home
for a long time, and she wasn't that forceful person [she had been]. It was
a very sad time."

Cassie Mackin died in November 1982 at age forty-three. "It happened
so fast—it was like a Shakespearean tragedy. This wasn't the way things
were supposed to be!" says Susan Zirinsky. The death rocked Katie—and
challenged her career-first priority. "I remember being so saddened by the
fact that she wasn't married and had no children," Katie said years later.
"While her pallbearers were famous people like Teddy Kennedy, I just
wondered how truly happy she was and if she died basically a lonely person. I hope not, but I remember thinking: Ten years from now, people are
going to say, 'Cassie who?' She sacrificed an awful lot, and for what? If you
ask people today, they wouldn't know who Cassie Mackin was. The idea of
chasing after this sort of illusionary fame made me realize that it was not
the most important thing in life." Katie was a traditionally raised girl and
a fantastically ambitious young woman. Cassie Mackin's sudden, sad, distinguished but lonely death made her feel that there were no clear answers, old or new. She would have to cobble together a life plan for herself.

Katie was promoted from *Take Two*'s assistant producer to full producer, replacing Louise Nobis, who many thought had been excellent. It
was surprising to some at the network that Katie got the job, and it was a
tribute to her political skills—being an operator counted as much as talent, and sometimes the two were too jumbled to separate. "I came to work
one day," says Nancy Battaglia, a senior staffer and Nobis's good friend,
"and suddenly Louise was gone—she didn't have a job! I was shocked.
Louise was in a *real* state of shock. But it wasn't my fight. The show did
very well under Katie."

Despite the promotion, or perhaps emboldened by it, Katie vented frustration to Don and Chris. Don says, "She got ticked off and said, 'What
should I do? I'm told I don't have a future on air and *that's* what I want.'
And we said, 'It's amazing and stupid [you were told that] but if it's true,
you should get the best job you can find in the best market and get on the
air.'" While some CNNers say the pair supported Katie and that she benefited from their support, others say they led her on. One major interna-

tional producer's take on it was: "They saw a threat in her, somebody coming up behind them, because Katie's personality was so perfect for Morning. They were autocratic and unfriendly." After Curle and Farmer left CNN, says a CNN writer, some of the staff threw a party to celebrate their departure.

Ted Kavanau—CNN's famous wild man, who got into fistfights just before airtime and who turned his late-night show into heart-attack central for the staff who had to abide by his adrenaline-rush-fomented need to simulate danger on air—put Katie on the air with him. The two did brief lead-ins to features. In the spots, Katie made snarky small talk (her idea); Kavanau responded in kind. "What I learned about Katie is, she's very charming, but she's tough," Kavanau says. "She's *tough*. She's *not* some innocent person."

During the run-up to the 1984 elections, Katie got a brief on-air moment, and it so happened that Al Buch, the new news director at Miami's WTVJ, was watching. This was not the same Miami station that had called her after the piece she had done in Havana, though perhaps that piece had lodged her in the consciousness of various nearby Miami news professionals. "She seemed like the quintessential *hostess*," Buch says, using an odd word for a stand-up reporter on a political piece, but a word that would certainly predict the most successful part of her future. "I decided she'd make a pretty good reporter for the Miami market"—a sexy market at the time, home to the hit TV drama *Miami Vice*.

"We were looking for a few reporters, and Al Buch came in with a tape Katie made," says WTVJ's president and general manager Alan Perris. Perris flew her to Miami and hired her. "I can't use the *p*-word"—perky—"because she goes nuts, but she absolutely was—delightful, smart, funny." Brian Gadinsky produced a WTVJ magazine show called *Montage*. He was twenty-seven, two years older than Katie, and while Buch was giving Katie a tour of the station that would be her new home, Gadinsky was struck "that an outsider was coming here, to this insular newsroom. It was very unusual for someone to come from the outside, and there was this thing of, 'Who is this girl and who does she think she is?'" Katie had lost weight by now and cut her hair and changed her on-air name to *Katherine*

Couric. "You could tell she wanted to get down to business. She was laser-focused, she wanted to get her chops here, she was here on a mission—she never saw Miami as where she was going to make her home," Gadinsky intuited. "Some people have found that off-putting, but to me it was attractive." In no time, she developed "charisma. It was palpable. You walked in, your eyes went over to her—her spark, her mojo."

At WTVJ Katie became an on-air beat reporter, eventually sometimes given early access to breaking stories by her new boyfriend, Bill Johnson, a director of public affairs for the Miami Police Department. (It was a mutually convenient relationship, in the same way her romance with Guy Pepper had helped her at CNN.) At work "she was serious, she didn't gossip, she was nice to everybody but she wasn't there to fool around," Gadinsky says. But after hours, Katie "was the life of the party" when she, Gadinsky, and other young staffers gathered at the hip bars and restaurants like Taurus and Monty Trainor's in Coconut Grove and the retro Biscayne Bay dance club in South Beach. A lot of her colleagues were, like Gadinsky, Jewish. She explained to Gadinsky that she was half Jewish but that her mother had converted to Presbyterianism when she'd married. Gadinsky teased her, "'Are you having half-seder on Passover?'"

To Alan Perris, Katie seemed irrepressible. She became (and remains) close friends with Lisa Gregorisch, who was in charge of the station's Fort Lauderdale bureau, "and when Katie and Lisa would come falling into my office once or twice a week, the Keystone Cops had arrived." In interviews she gave during her *Today* years, Katie has said she was frustrated at WTVJ. Perris acknowledges, a bit defensively: "I do remember Katie wanted to anchor the morning cut-ins and I didn't want her to. I thought she was more valuable as a reporter than in the studio." But Al Buch saw her frustration. "She was driven. She knew where she wanted to go, and some people she worked with—mainly one photographer—gave her a hard time about her aspirations. There were nights when I'd walk her from the newsroom to her car and she was almost in tears—in fact, she *was* in tears—that people couldn't see what she could do. I'd put my arm around her and say, 'Look, consider the source. You have a good sense of yourself. You're going to be just fine.'"

Katie may have put on a damsel-in-distress routine to Buch, but she was blunt to her peers. When her UVA friend Kathleen Lobb and two other girls visited her little Miami apartment, one of the girls asked, "So what do you want to do next?" The girl meant the question in an airy, open-ended way, not expecting a surge of entitled ambition. But "without missing a beat, Katie said, 'I want Jane Pauley's job,'" Kathleen recalls.

At WTVJ, the assignment she wanted the most, lobbied for, and finally landed was spending a night as a homeless woman on a street in Overtown, one of the worst neighborhoods in Miami. "She went in prosthetic makeup," Gadinsky recalls. "She became a bag lady. Just her and a shopping cart and her cameraman, Kevin Raphael." Granted, the move might be considered a stunt by an ambitious young woman. But "she was in danger," sleeping on that street, Gadinsky makes clear. "It was very ballsy of her, and she came back with a great story." She pushed for more. When on her day off two FBI agents were killed during a big shoot-out, she called the station and said, "Listen, I'm really close by. Can I go cover this? Please?" The station hewed to protocol: The story was given to a reporter who was on duty that day.

KATIE SOON TIRED of the limited markets of the South—even jazzy Miami—and wanted to go back to her home environs, in D.C. She heard about an opening for late-news general assignment reporter at WRC, the NBC local affiliate, which she applied for and got. WRC was more than a local station; it was deeply linked to the NBC Washington bureau. Her idol, Cassie Mackin, had been launched at WRC. (So too would be other, later female stars: Suzanne Malveaux, Campbell Brown, and most recently Savannah Guthrie.) When Katie arrived in early 1987, at age thirty, at her fourth TV station in seven years, she had her game down enough to not need a champion—a good thing, because, as Arch Campbell, then a producer at the station, recalls, "The news director who hired her, Jim Van Messel, and the general manager, Dave Newell, both left just as she came on board." Van Messel had been particularly enthusiastic about her, calling her "one of the most natural and spontaneous people on television," on the basis of clips of her work in Miami. "We were looking for somebody who could do live shots at eleven p.m. She exuded the personality we were looking for." Campbell continues: "She came to work totally unknown, with no one to protect her, yet she managed to thrive." She made the staff laugh by gossiping about her date with Larry King, "and how he'd tried to 'Roto-Root' her"—stick his tongue way down her throat, Campbell says. (Katie has told that story widely in the media.) She got an apartment in D.C. with young producer Wendy Walker, who in fact soon went on to produce Larry King, for years. Wendy remains one of her closest friends.

Katie seems to have felt this was an assignment she had to hit out of the park. "She was down and dirty about her job," Dana Rudman, a colleague of hers at WRC, told reporter Jennet Conant. "She looked young, but she could be very aggressive. When she wanted an interview, she pushed and pushed and pushed." Her energy and determination could apparently reach near manic proportions—Wendy Walker has recalled that sometimes Katie would close the door of her own hopelessly messy bedroom and Walker would "come home from work to find [Katie] sitting on my bed among papers and plates and cups. She'd have tried on all my clothes, and they'd be lying on the floor."

Bret Marcus was the news director of WRC, and he was a good friend of Don Browne, NBC's Miami bureau chief. Browne had noticed Katie's talent in Miami, knew of her tremendous tenacity, and wasn't surprised that she'd pushed Marcus for an anchor job at WRC. Browne had heard that, "wherever she was" (Atlanta, Miami), Katie had pushed for an anchor slot, and Browne heard "story after story that management at stations in those other cities didn't see it." Now, when she lobbied Marcus, he suggested she try her wings in a smaller market—say, Ohio. This suggestion—smug and tin-eared in retrospect—would become a famous piece of Katie lore when she popped up in the "small market" of New York.

Hearing of his friend Marcus's unintentional insult, Don Browne offered himself as a kind of counselor to Katie. He'd gotten a glimmer of

Katie's talent. "Katie had an edge," he says. "Katie had this inner self-confidence, this tenacity—people would knock her down but she never gave up. That smile, that determined set in her jaw—she *never* gave up. 'By God, I'm gonna wear those guys down and one day they're gonna *see* it.'" One of Browne's friends, Fred Francis, NBC's Pentagon correspondent, was impressed with Katie's work on WRC. Francis brought her to the attention of Tim Russert, the chief of NBC's national bureau.

Russert was looking for a second Pentagon correspondent and had interviewed a great many candidates. Russert was impressed with Katie, too—and offered her the job. Having had her high hopes dashed for so long, it wasn't instantly clear to Katie that, nine years after leaving UVA, *this* was the opening she needed. "So I'm driving down in Miami one day," Don Browne recalls, "and I get a call from Katie and she says, 'I need some advice. I have a job offer from NBC to be the number two at the Pentagon. It doesn't pay that much—what do you think?' And I said, 'Do it! Do it!' I said it twice, because she'd be working with Fred Francis—I loved Fred. I said, 'This is a great entry point to the network. *Do it now.*'" Influenced by Browne's advice, she accepted.

"When Katie became a Pentagon correspondent for NBC, all the CNN people rolled their eyes—'*Yeah, right,*'" recalls David Bernknopf, who was Christiane's close friend. "That whole 'perky' thing." Still, Bernknopf had run into Katie when she was in Miami, and he "realized, for the first time, that I might have underestimated her."

ONE WEEKEND IN 1988, when she was still at WRC, Katie was in New York visiting Kathleen Lobb. Kathleen heard that a UVA friend was having a party in D.C.—did Katie want to hurry back home for it? Yes, she did. She wanted to meet people. She was thirty-one. When she'd recently run into her Tri-Delt sister Beth Kseniak at the Democratic National Convention in Atlanta, she'd yelled out not "Hello!" but "Hey, Beth, you married yet?" When Beth responded with a surprised no, Katie yelled back, "Oh, good! Neither am I."

The party was full of lawyers. David Kiernan, a lawyer at the prestigious firm Williams and Connolly, came with his best friend, Jay Monahan. Neither one was a typical corporate attorney. David, who was as interested in medicine as law, would go on to medical school. Jay—handsome and dark haired with a slender face—was a romantic, an original. Though he grew up in the town of Manhasset on Long Island, New York, in an Irish Catholic family (his given name was John Paul Monahan III), he had early on become fascinated by the South. He attended the College of William and Mary in Virginia and became a lay historian of the Civil War, collecting antiques and memorabilia—including an assemblage of brass bugles—and he participated in reenactments. "Jay was the smartest guy I ever met," says Mandy Locke, the woman who later married his best friend, Kiernan. "He knew so much about the Civil War, about history." He was also an accomplished equestrian, an avid dancer at everything from swing to ballroom, and so accomplished a pianist, especially on classical compositions, that he'd been nicknamed "Liberace" by his bunk mates in the navy. There was a Renaissance man quality about him, Kathleen Lobb thought when she eventually met him through Katie.

At the party, David and Jay were both quite taken by Katie Couric, who was wearing a tight black dress. "But she gave her card to Jay, not me," David would later say. The oft-repeated story goes that when Katie found out that almost the whole group of men were lawyers, she mimicked gagging. Shrewdly, Jay said that he was a painter, not a lawyer. Katie "was taken with him right away," says Lobb. In fact, she described him to Kathleen in one telling adjective: "Heathcliffian."

Jay Monahan was disciplined and orderly—a "neat freak." Katie was disorganized. (So messy was she that when her mother walked into her apartment bedroom one day, she burst into tears.) Jay was the oldest of seven siblings; Katie was the youngest of four. Lane Duncan, her boyfriend in Atlanta, had keenly felt that "Katie was always *on*." This new man, Jay Monahan, perhaps provided, in his very character, a reality check—a brake—for Katie's freneticism. And he was family-minded, so close to his father he would ask him to be best man at his wedding. The first time Kathleen Lobb met Jay, at Katie's parents' house, "I remember watching him playing catch with Katie's brother John's son, and I had such a vibe of, 'This man is going to be a fantastic father.' I said that to Katie."

Jay asked for Katie's hand in marriage formally, by visiting John Couric, alone, man to man, while Katie and her childhood friends "gathered at our friend Tracy's house, waiting. 'It took so long!'" recalls Barbara Andrukonis. "We thought it was going to just take fifteen minutes, but it took two and a half hours. At some point Katie started to get nervous." It turned out that "Katie's dad took it very seriously. 'How are you going to make my daughter happy?' 'How are you going to provide?'" Here was an older, naturally traditional Virginia gentleman assessing a young, more consciously traditional, adopted-Virginia gentleman: a navy man to a navy man. "I've always had a weakness for Southern men," Katie recently said.

Katie Couric and Jay Monahan were married on June 10, 1989, at the Navy Chapel in Washington, D.C. After the ceremony, the newlyweds rode to their reception standing up and waving through the sunroof of a car. "There was a big UVA contingent," Kathleen says. "It was joyous and fun."

WHAT MIGHT IN RETROSPECT be considered Katie's biggest wedding gift was provided, accidentally, by Jane Pauley.

In September 1988, not long after Katie's engagement, Pauley went to the Seoul Olympics for *Today.* She was assisted by a recent Harvard graduate who was a temporary intern at NBC. "He was just awesome. He was simply amazing," Jane recalls of the young helper. "When the Olympics were over, his assignment was off." But after she returned to New York in early October, "I went to NBC and said, 'It's funny, this guy—*I can't let him go.*'" NBC kept him on at *Today* because of their star anchor's insistence. The deliberate, modest, moderate Jane Pauley is not one to take credit unduly. So when she says, as she does of this intern, "He owes his career to me," you know she is not throwing those words around lightly.

The young man's name was Jeff Zucker. He had grown up in Miami and had been the president of the *Harvard Crimson*. And when, three years later, he would almost literally bump into Katie even before she was hired at *Today*, some potential professional electricity would crackle between them. From then on, as Pauley says, "Katie and Jeff Zucker [would be] a partnership that cannot be underestimated."

PART THREE

PRIME TIME

CHAPTER FOUR

Brainy, Blond, Glamorous

Diane: 1978 to 1998

DIANE REMAINED at San Clemente helping Nixon with his memoirs for three and a half years, from August 1974 to mid-1978. (Her official ABC biography has been revised to show 1975 as the cutoff date for her time there, but earlier, real-time-reported accounts indicate that she was really there three years longer.) In fact, she and her beau Frank Gannon were the last staffers to leave. They had stayed there all the way through the revisions of Nixon's memoirs. The night Diane departed—it was July; she was thirty-two and a half years old—Nixon took out a special bottle of brandy and toasted her efforts on the book, and spoke emotionally and gratefully of all she, and Gannon, had done for him.

All that time that she was at San Clemente, CBS News vice president Bill Small had kept tabs on her. "Bill had already created the best Washington bureau ever," says Connie Chung. His on-air reporters included Dan Rather, Roger Mudd, Daniel Schorr, Marvin Kalb, and Bob Schieffer, as well as the worthy fruits of his and Dick Salant's crash-feminism: Lesley Stahl, Rita Braver, Susan Zirinsky, Marcy McGinnis, and Chung herself, who would imminently depart for NBC in LA. "Bill made us so aggressive, we were ready to kill each other," Connie says. "We were all competing with each other because we were the only people we wanted to compete with."

Small could not have expected that a Nixon loyalist like Diane would fit well into his elite crew of hubristic, triumphant Watergate sleuths—

who'd proudly called themselves "the Enemy of the President," and who were suffering what Connie Chung calls "post-Watergate letdown," because no story would ever be as important—but he didn't care. He went after Sawyer anyway, for all those four years. "I had a correspondent, Bob Pierpoint, who lived near San Clemente, and when Nixon abdicated," Small says, he put Pierpoint on the case. Periodically "Pierpoint would contact Diane, and she would say, 'We've got to finish the book.'" Small waited. And waited. "And finally Bob said, 'If you call her now, her part of the book is done.' I called her, and she agreed to come in to audition."

En route to the audition, Diane stopped in Louisville to see her mother and looked in on her ex-colleagues from WLKY. Bob Taylor, who'd supervised her as a weather girl, was now the manager at a stronger local station, WHAS. "Diane and I had a wonderful visit, and I said to her, 'We're ready for you in any capacity you want to be in.' And she said, 'You know, after having gone to D.C. and San Clemente, I would love to be home, and I would love to consider an offer. But I have one commitment to make. I have to visit Bill Small. I promised Bill when I left Washington that when I returned from San Clemente I would come back for one final visit.'" Taylor, sitting in his minor-market station, was nevertheless left gratifyingly "convinced, when she walked out the door, that she was coming back to Louisville." Such was Diane's ego-stroking charm.

Hearing of Diane Sawyer's pending audition at CBS, Bill Small's team was horrified. Dan Rather told Small, "Don't hire her!" So did Eric Sevareid—and Sevareid, one of Murrow's Boys and a regular commentator on Cronkite's nightly broadcast, "had a lot of clout." But that was just the beginning. Small and Don Richardson, his trusted assistant news director, had thought that the flak about hiring "a Nixon person" would come from *outside* CBS. Surprisingly, Small says, "that almost never happened. Most of the criticism came from our own people."

It was fierce. "Diane Sawyer was back from San Clemente, and all of a sudden CBS News is hiring her?—I remember the uproar," says producer Jennifer Siebens, who held many positions in CBS News over the ensuing decades. "CBS was right behind the *Washington Post* with the most in-your-face anti-Watergate attitude." "There was almost a revolt in the ranks at CBS News! Lesley Stahl was gonna quit!" recalls Sandy Socolow, Cronkite's producer, who reported to Small and who in fact signed Diane's hiring papers. "Diane came with this baggage. She was close to Nixon. And she wasn't a journalist. Here you had an organization"—CBS News— "that demanded five years of experience and all this journalism. And suddenly Small is picking a political person who had no experience. The Junior Miss of the United States, or whatever she was," is how Socolow and the CBS people derisively viewed this politically encumbered beauty queen and so-called reporter.

"It was that she worked for Nixon even *after* his resignation that caused the animosity," says Roger Mudd. "It's one thing to work in a political operation in the White House. But to continue with him even afterward meant she had some loyalty to this blemished, crooked president." So contagious was the protest that even Bob Pierpoint, who'd been essentially operating as Small's recruitment emissary all four preceding years, joined in.

"There was enmity. I caught a lot of flak," Small admits. "But I hired her." To those who raised questions, "My answer always was, 'She's intelligent, a good journalist, and a good addition to the staff,'" adding now that "it had nothing to do with her being a woman." (Av Westin, who'd defused the toxic pairing of Barbara Walters and Harry Reasoner, begs to differ on the latter: "I happen to be a cynic about a lot of this stuff. I believe that management was going to make it work for Diane because they needed a woman at CBS.")

And so, in mid-1978, Diane Sawyer flew back to D.C. and into the lion's den. This happened to be just when women her age were identifying with well-bred, smart, idiosyncratic, vulnerable, WASP urbanites—Diane Keaton in *Annie Hall*, Jill Clayburgh in *An Unmarried Woman*. The era of the sarcastic if polished feminist rebel, often with long, straight, center-parted hair and long legs in bell-bottoms (Gloria Steinem, Jane Fonda, Ali MacGraw in *Love Story*) was giving way to an updated version of discerning, distracted ladylikeness: a girl in a skirt. This shift of zeitgeist did not hurt Diane.

Arriving at CBS, Diane launched a preemptive three-pronged strike on her critics. She was an egoless team player, she worked immensely hard—tirelessly—and she purveyed her copious charm.

Some people say that she was made to do penance—even that she was hazed, as if she were a hapless fraternity pledge. "I know they humiliated her. They made her do all the crap duties they could think of. They really slapped her around," recalls a CBS veteran. "They made her do stakeouts, stand in front of Supreme Court justices' houses in the rain. But the buzz was, she was taking it and taking it and taking it." In other words, she knew she had to pay—and she did. (Bill Small denies that Diane was hazed. "Anyone who came in at the bottom was given the worst assignments, like sitting with a crew outside a house all day," he explains.)

She was not only uncomplaining but humble, the faceless leg-woman for colleagues. "She was selfless," says Roger Mudd, "and that quality in her, more than anything else, eradicated this feeling that this Nixon sympathizer was coming to work for us. I remember she was backing up at the State Department, and Marvin Kalb was the main diplomatic correspondent, and day after day she'd come in at four or four fifteen, and her notebook was filled with stuff she'd gather during the day, and she dumps it on the producer and says, 'This is what I've got'"—that is, giving it to the reporter with no strings attached—"never saying, 'I've got a story. This is my exclusive.'"

Her tireless work ethic kicked into high gear when two huge, dramatic, and confounding news stories broke just months after she joined the bureau. She threw herself into both.

The first, emerging on November 18, 1978, was so startling and tragic and out of the blue that the public had, literally, no template for it. A wild-eyed, dark-haired white "preacher," Jim Jones, had assembled a cultlike community called the Peoples Temple, largely populated by black Americans desperately loyal to him, on the island of Guyana. When a U.S. representative flew there with an investigative team to examine conditions, gunfire from Jones's henchmen greeted the delegation, killing five, before the inconceivable transpired: 914 members of the temple stood calmly in line to commit suicide, along with Jones, at Jones's orders, by way of cyanide dissolved in Kool-Aid. Many were adults who first subjected their children and babies to the potion (more than two hundred children were murdered) and then drank it themselves. The tragedy—which led to the now common expression "drink the Kool-Aid," to indicate blind obedience—ranks among the largest mass suicides in history, and was then the greatest loss of American civilian life in a nonnatural catastrophe, and would remain thus until September 11, 2001.

"When the story happened in Guyana, with Jim Jones, it was Thanksgiving weekend," Susan Zirinsky remembers. "Diane and I were at Dover Air Force Base, where all the caskets and the bodies were coming home. She was amazing. We were up for seventy-two hours. Nobody slept. It was, 'What *is* this?'" During the hectic production of the Peoples Temple suicide broadcasts, Zirinsky and Sawyer worked together intensely. "She was simply the hardest-working woman I had ever met."

Then, four months later, on March 28, 1979, alarms blared throughout the U.S. energy community: A partial meltdown had taken place at the Three Mile Island nuclear power plant in Pennsylvania. It was a fast-moving crisis—the most severe accident in American nuclear power history—confusing to the plant technicians and operators, the U.S. Nuclear Regulatory Commission, and the press alike. Diane—who had by then matriculated from leg-woman to on-air correspondent for *CBS Evening News*—threw herself into the complex story, punctiliously and determinedly reporting. Even the skeptical Sandy Socolow, who'd dismissed her as a beauty queen, was amazed. "She was great at ferreting out information. Everything about her was very professional. She worked night and day, and she was ready to go on the air morning, noon, and night. Everybody was just knocked out," he says. *The Encyclopedia of Television* would later report that Diane's "coverage of the Three Mile Island crisis assisted her in garnering heavy journalistic assignments which at the time were considered a challenge to male colleagues."

Diane further burnished her workhorse reputation at the outset of the Iranian hostage crisis in November 1979. She camped out for an entire week at the State Department. "I would sleep all night on two secretarial chairs, so I could get up at four a.m., stalk the halls, and see what I could get," she has recalled. This was actually reporter fanaticism doubling as a very smart move: Charles Kuralt, the deep-voiced, avuncular anchor of *CBS This Morning*, would cut to her live reports. And there was something about this elegant young female correspondent, in the State Department so early in the morning, that caused the executives in New York to sit up straight.

She was also assigned to the Republican presidential primaries, covering George H. W. Bush in his campaign against the ultimately successful Ronald Reagan. She was paired with correspondent Richard Roth, with Jennifer Siebens as their producer. Siebens, who'd been stunned when Sawyer was hired at CBS, was by now impressed. "She was very smart and unbelievably well-read," Siebens says. "She and Roth tag-teamed: One day one would do TV and the other radio. She did not pull attitude. She would carry the tripod, and they had a collegial relationship. After every campaign stop we'd get back on the bus or plane and they'd sit together and share notes. I remember being surprised she was such a good team player, because if you're assigned to the Washington bureau you can become a prima donna."

Within two-thirds of a year "everyone forgot the Nixon connection—she'd endeared herself" to the bureau, Bill Small says, with the satisfaction of one who'd made an unpopular bet that turned out to be a winner. "In fact there were several people who denied that they had ever objected to her. She won them over." Bob Pierpoint had not only stopped protesting Diane's hiring but was starting to claim that he'd "discovered" her. But, Small adds, "Dan Rather was the only one who came to me and said, 'Remember what I said to you before, Don't hire her? I was wrong.'" No one else said that.

The third prong of Diane's campaign—unleashing her charisma—helped silence naysayers. "She was a marvelous people person," Small says. "Well, let me put it another way: She had more charm than most men. A lot of male beginning reporters could find it difficult to become a member of the team quickly, but she did not. Part of it may have been her charm, part of it may have been beauty. She worked the 1980 conventions and was very good at getting people. I can't remember a time when we said 'Diane, get Senator Russell' or 'Get Senator Humphrey' and she failed."

Small was, in an innocent way, quite smitten by her. He frequently took her out to lunch—and when, on the one-year anniversary of his hiring her, she insisted that *she* treat him, she employed all her Southern charm. "You said your father always told you, 'Never let a woman pick up the check'"—Small denies his father ever said this but was tickled nonetheless—"but today I want to pick up the check." Small replied, "Only if *I* can pick the restaurant." She agreed. He promptly led her to Hot Diggity Dog, where, perched on stools, they elegantly dined on the best one-dollar frankfurters in the nation's capital.

Bill Small knew what he had. Diane was exceptionally attractive for a news reporter—and exceptionally smart. Told that so many people have called Diane "the smartest person I have ever met," a high-ranking female news producer frowns a bit at what she views as hyperbole and says, "People in television are not necessarily brilliant—we're not talking about people who went to Harvard Law or anything like that. There are some very, very smart people in television, but, in serious news, there are not very many beautiful blonds, and that is why Diane is talked about like that." But another television professional has a different take: "I'm not sure I've ever worked with a smarter person in my entire life. And not just intellectually smart. But smart about how to do a better job, or what questions to ask, or . . . how to *maneuver.*"

In 1981 Diane got an offer. Her early-morning State Department dispatches with Charles Kuralt had dovetailed with the network's reevaluation of its morning news program. The executives decided to restructure Kuralt's *CBS This Morning* as *CBS Morning News.* While NBC had *Today* and ABC had *Good Morning America*, the Tiffany Network had eschewed the morning news-and-features format in favor of a straight-news morning broadcast. Now they wanted to compete with the others, but with a still slightly more serious focus. They asked Diane to be the female coanchor, which would involve a move to New York.

Roger Mudd—originally skeptical about Diane—had become one of her big brothers at the D.C. bureau. By now he had left CBS, but while Diane was considering the offer, the two ran into each other at a Washington dinner party. "She said, 'They want me to come to New York, to do the morning news,'" Mudd recalls. "And I said, 'Don't go,' and she said, 'Why?' I said, 'Diane you haven't lived enough. You don't have enough experience. You haven't been through enough. If you're on the air and it's live and you've got to fill airtime, you need stuff that you've experienced to draw on. You should stay in the field another year.'" Spoken like a true old-timer, slowly and earnestly building a career.

But this was the beginning of a new age of TV reporters—younger, glossier, more oriented toward human interest stories—and while Roger Mudd may not have sensed this, Diane did. "She said, 'Interesting, interesting . . .'"—respectfully mulling the advice. "But she went to New York anyway. So the hell with Father Mudd."

NEW YORK LOVED DIANE. During her early years there, CBS chairman William Paley, a widower since 1978, showered attention on her—romantic attention, some believed. She befriended Henry Kissinger. At one point, she briefly dated Warren Beatty, the premier pursuer of any Girl of the Hour. ("If you win an Academy Award, he's right behind you," notes Arlyne Rothberg, manager of two of Beatty's most famous short- and long-term girlfriends: Carly Simon and Diane Keaton, respectively.) She settled into an apartment, but barely furnished it.

Even before she officially began at *CBS Morning News*, Diane used the imminent tenth anniversary of the 1972 Watergate break-in to score the interview she was destined to be granted—the interview she had earned: a face-to-face with her former boss Richard Nixon. Now she was the journalist—not the defender, not the employee. Perhaps Nixon hadn't fully grasped the difference when he agreed to the sit-down, and his oddly cheery prattling on about how "I want women to be like women," rather than like "witch"-like reporters, gave her a fitting, ironic opening. "She really pressed him about Watergate; she asked him about it in great detail. It was a very tough interview, and he was really pissed, but the interview certainly helped her with CBS," says someone who covered the event. She and Nixon had made advance plans to go out to dinner afterward; Nixon abruptly, angrily canceled.

It is fascinating that she—whose usual means were subtle and indirect—risked so explicitly signaling to her former boss that she was no longer an ally. Was she killing the past, cutting herself off from her loyal-employee and good-Southern-girl self? Or had she simply been as pragmatically opportunistic as any journalist with extraordinary access to a public figure would be?

Diane began dating Richard Holbrooke, who was just completing a term as assistant secretary of state for Asia and was now an investment banker with Lehman Brothers. Brilliant, handsome, self-assured—in fact, widely disliked for his arrogance—Holbrooke, two years older than Diane, had had a very impressive Foreign Service career, starting with his six years as a civilian attaché in Vietnam immediately after he graduated from Brown in 1962. By the time Diane met him, he was a superbly connected high achiever. He also had a somewhat unusual personal background: He had grown up in Scarsdale, the son of parents who avidly took him to Quaker meetings on Sundays, but both of them were Jews who had fled the Nazis, his mother from Germany, his father from Poland.

By several accounts, Holbrooke fell deeply in love with Diane. "He was head over heels about her," says a normally cynical journalist, adding that, as for her feelings for him, "it was hard to read Diane emotionally." (Even after they broke up, their closeness endured, according to one former network executive.) She kept her own apartment, but spent much of her time in his, an elegantly furnished suite of rooms in the Beresford on Central Park West. They also had a historic country house in the little-known town of Sandisfield, in Berkshire County, Massachusetts. Far worldlier than Diane when she arrived in New York, Holbrooke became "a pivotal part of her growth and her formation," says a woman who worked with her. "He wasn't just her boyfriend. He was for years her primary guidance counselor."

In October 1982 Diane began cohosting *CBS Morning News*, first, briefly, alongside Kuralt, then, and enduringly, partnering with Bill Kurtis, who had been a Chicago anchorman for sixteen years. Diane proved an arresting alternative to her competition, the two very popular female morning anchors—both, like Diane, blonds—*Good Morning America*'s

Joan Lunden and *Today*'s Jane Pauley. Lunden, an approachable young married woman with a two-year-old daughter, somewhat suburban in style, with fluffy short hair, was a native of Sacramento. Jane Pauley was the cheerleader-pretty debate team whiz with the girlish long tresses, the aura of Midwestern decency, and the earnest, crisp voice that directed viewers to take her seriously. She was married now to Garry Trudeau, and viewers had empathized with her about her miscarriage; soon they would watch her growing daily more pregnant with her twins—a girl and a boy. Lunden would bear two more daughters during her time on *GMA*; Pauley would bear a third child, a son. Over the whole second half of the 1980s, Pauley and Lunden were unintentionally embroiled in, as Pauley puts it, a game of "dueling pregnancies," their swelling bellies and their unavoidable forthrightness about their conditions finally erasing the last vestiges of puritanical TV. Pauley and Lunden would turn Morning into a format virtually synonymous with moms of young children—a template very welcoming to Katie Couric, who would ascend to the *Today* chair when she was five months' pregnant. Diane Sawyer was not only unmarried and not a mother but was also slightly more remote than the other two when she took her seat at *CBS Morning News*.

The difference was newsworthy. What *Time* magazine would later call Diane's "rich, honeyed voice" was "free of the severe tone affected by" Pauley. And in contrast to Lunden's and Pauley's "red light reflex"— eyes aimed straight at the lens—Diane's confrontation with the camera was beguilingly indirect. She was starting to "master"—and fine-tune as her own—what camerawoman Ginny Vicario describes as the "chin-down, eyes-up look of Lauren Bacall." She was also learning to "know how to control an audience and make you think you're her best friend," says former CBS executive Joe Peyronnin. In addition, there was the blond pageboy so reminiscent of the Breck Girls advertisements from viewers' awed childhood perusals of *Life* and *Look* magazines; the thick, sensual lips; the slightly Southern decorum; the lightly flirtatious laughter. Diane's persona had an alluring gentility and mystery—the counterpoint to Pauley's and Lunden's genial transparency.

And she appealed to men as much as to moms. As one man, considerably younger than she, who would later work with her at ABC, says, "There is something about Diane that is *romantic*." And a now veteran male CBS correspondent, then just starting out, says, "I used to wake up early in the morning just to watch her. She's the only person I would do that for. She was breathtakingly beautiful and incredibly smart, and the combination was really sexy." Media guys enjoyed the fact that powerful men she interviewed seemed disarmed, stripped of the shrewdness that governed other parts of their lives. "I remember her interviewing [Vegas casino powerhouse] Steve Wynn, and he was flirting with her, and you could tell he had *no* idea that someone like Diane would see him as a joke," says a male author.

Diane wisely sought to maximize both her exposure and her on-air responsibility. Just three years earlier, Roger Mudd had called her "self-less," a stance that had helped defuse the Washington bureau's initial tremendous animus toward her. Now she was self-*interested*. According to someone who witnessed the goings-on at the show, she wanted a presence equal to her cohost, the far more experienced Bill Kurtis (not for her, Jane Pauley's deference to Tom Brokaw), and she had in her corner a powerful proxy. "Richard Holbrooke did her dirty work for her," this staffer says, "and he drove everybody crazy. He was an obnoxious guy, but he could be charming too. He would call the executive producer *every* day to say, 'Why doesn't Diane have more to do? Why does Bill Kurtis get to do that?'" Kurtis had two producers; Holbrooke pressed for Diane to have two producers as well. Once, when Diane was returning from an interview in South America, Holbrooke called the show's female production assistant, yelling so much about her "letting" Diane ask certain questions (which had not shown her favorably) that the young woman was driven to tears, leading her friend, another news professional, to feel "shocked that the Diane I knew could have a control freak boyfriend like that."

But having a person to explicitly advocate for her while she retained a more modest demeanor was beginning to reflect a part of Diane's M.O. A dazzling indirectness—soon manifest as the most canny sense of strategy of anyone in the industry—would become, in terms of business politics, the quality that Diane is today most known for. She seems to have begun polishing that adaptation during this interval. "Seductive" is a word frequently used—often admiringly, sometimes not—to describe Diane. "Manipulative" is another. ("You could never pinpoint" that particular part of her emotional intelligence; "you just knew it existed," says a colleague.) But the chief term applied to her, which comes from her own playbook, is "leaves no fingerprints"—something that Diane's having Richard Holbrooke be her "bad cop," for example, might well have been meant to effect. "She *thinks* she doesn't leave fingerprints," says a person who was closely involved in the advancement of her career. "But she leaves *cat paw* prints on people's foreheads."

People in the news industry—including female executives—are fond of saying that Diane plays "three-dimensional chess." One takes the image further: "She's playing three-dimensional chess while you're *sleeping*. She's way ahead of you, by leaps and bounds. She has moves that [others in the business] could never rival." Such may have always been a talent of hers, though it seems to have taken off at this juncture, only to escalate. Diane's self-regard has never translated into that of a diva. Her disarmingly self-deprecating personality may be part of what people mean when they call her "manipulative." Diane's frequent mentions of her flaws, and her negative self-comparisons with her sister, Linda, became shrewdly endearing tropes. One example: "My sister is elegant," she said in a 1984 interview. "I was a kind of parody of elegance, always the one to fall down the stairs." (Linda Sawyer got married, had two children to whom Diane became and remains a devoted aunt, divorced, and remarried, and became a highly successful Manhattan Realtor. With her second husband, David Frankel, she recently bought Rosie O'Donnell's multimillion-dollar Connecticut estate.) Though her awe of Linda is no doubt genuine—she "idolizes, *absolutely* idolizes" her sister, says a former colleague—her highlighting that awe kept people from resenting Diane: her beauty, her success, her poise, her *luck*. And, colleagues believe, she couldn't have been unaware that such disarmament was the effect of her leitmotif-like paeans to her sister.

Keeping conversation away from herself was another way to deflect resentment. "In the South, your mother teaches you that when you're with a group of people, it's not about you. Your job is to make other people feel comfortable," says a former colleague. "Diane would *never* talk about herself. She would tell many stories and say funny things"—her Lily Tomlin imitation was a killer—"but she was never narcissistic in that 'Look at me! Look at me!' way. That's not who she is at all." And then there was her tone. "You never raise your voice. You always say it with a smile."

Finally, there was outright courtship. "If Diane thought you didn't like her, she went above and beyond" in trying to please. "Diane wants everyone to love her," says this colleague. "She's 'I'm going to make you all love me, and I'm going to make you all love each other. And it will be *great!*'"

At the same time, her enormous and sincere work ethic made it impossible for people to get the impression that, despite her silky charms, she was *ever* coasting. The compulsive perfectionism—or indecisiveness, or both—that would be Diane's forte was also coming into view. At *CBS Morning News*, a writer or producer would write a script for her, and then "she would rewrite it and record it," someone who worked with her there says. The piece would then be edited, and once she saw it "she'd want to change it, and change it again." People at the show knew that "she'd call you, *honestly*, at three in the morning, and she'd want to change it. *Five times*"—even for just "a three-minute piece." Often, all that work would be for naught: The piece would be put on the air in its original form. "She drove us crazy, but not in a bad way," the staffer says, adding, "Diane was very competitive and she knew exactly how to use her beauty and her smarts. While she and Kurtis were doing it, the show actually got to be number two in the ratings."

Diane's detailed thoroughness startled coworkers. "The phone rings early one Saturday morning," recalls another colleague from the show. "It's Diane. She says, 'Have you seen this fascinating profile in the Style section?' Now, this is the Style section of the *Washington Post*. She lives in Manhattan. There's no Internet yet. How the hell did she get her hands on the Style section of the *Washington Post* so early? But she did, and read it, and expected that I would have too. That's the kind of round-the-clock obsessiveness she had." She was also utilitarian. "Diane will only spend time with people who will be of service to her," this person adds. A former executive agrees: "Diane uses people. Every relationship has a purpose."

Diane was thirty-six years old—living with Holbrooke but with no apparent interest in marrying him (much less in having babies)—when, as one of her *CBS Morning News* features, she interviewed Candice Bergen. To at least one person who viewed the uncut interview, Diane seemed to use her conversation with this strikingly similar woman—they were the same age, they'd both attended top colleges (Bergen had gone to Penn); they were intelligent, discerning, beautiful blonds—to indirectly ratify an ambivalence she had. Bergen had been married to filmmaker Louis Malle for two years, and at that point had not yet had a child. "Diane spent half the interview asking her if she was going to have children. It seemed to me that she was looking for—that she really *wanted*—another well-known woman who was willing to say, 'I don't want kids.'" A male producer who knows Diane's round-the-clock work habits says, "She likes taking care of other people's kids. I feel a little sad when I see that because I think she could have been a really cool mom. But maybe she knows enough about herself to know it would be impossible for a child to get enough love from her, because she had too much to do."

In 1984 Don Hewitt, the creator of *60 Minutes*, the jewel in CBS News's crown, asked Diane to join the show as its first ever full-time female correspondent. Then, as now, *60 Minutes* was revered, the most esteemed newsmagazine show—or news broadcast—on the air.* In 1984, there was only one other newsmagazine, ABC's *20/20*, and it was considered to be more a "variety" show, as one producer called it—not at all in *60*'s journalistic league. Stunningly, for all its seriousness, credibility, and prestige, *60 Minutes* was also a moneymaker.

It was no small honor to be asked onto the show, which at the time was a latter-day Murrow's Boys enclave—"the quintessential boys' club," as

---

*In November 2013, *60 Minutes*'s reputation took an unexpected hit when a report that correspondent Lara Logan and producer Max McClellan did on the terrorist attack in Benghazi in September 2012 turned out to be based on the false claims of its featured interview subject and source.

many put it. When producer Ellen Rossen interviewed for a position there, one of the first things she was asked was, "Do you play poker?" Much worse, when film editor Patricia O'Gorman worked there, she explains, Mike Wallace "grabbed me from behind. I turned around and hauled off and *hit* him. He looked shocked, like, 'What did I do?'" (O'Gorman goes on to say, without specifically indicting that particular show, "I knew women who'd been pinned to the wall" by other bosses at CBS "and were afraid to lose their jobs.") CBS veteran Jennifer Siebens recalls that one day in the 1970s, as a young hire on the show, she "was walking down the hall to Cronkite's studio, and I suddenly heard somebody call out, 'Siebens! Did anybody ever tell you you have ugly legs?' It was this giant of the industry, a legendary producer whose work was amazing—a man of such seeming class, I was stunned. I was burning with humiliation and anger. I said nothing, but I wanted to say, 'Did anyone ever tell *you* you have a small dick?'"

Those sexist tales aside, "Diane charmed Don," a top CBS female producer surmises. But how? A male CBS producer who was powerful in the sixties through the eighties gives this blunt reason, under the cover of anonymity: "I had a discussion with a fellow—one in my peer group, an important guy at *60 Minutes*. And I said, 'What the hell is Diane's secret? She's always hired, for a lot of money, but she has no impact on the ratings.' And he laughed like hell, and he said, 'You gotta understand—the guys who own and run the networks all have the shiksa disease.'"

The fascinating paradox—the irony—about Diane is that, despite her lack of impact on the ratings, she was considered cost-effective because of her sheer labor, her workaholism. In 2008, twenty-four years after Hewitt pursued her, Disney president and chief executive Bob Iger, who is Diane's current boss, reportedly told someone that people put up with her difficult qualities "because she's an earner." In other words: "She will always work hard enough to be worth her pay." That same person vouches for her: "She gives her all, twenty-four/seven. In fact, she works too much. Especially on the road. She will work until three or four in the morning and sleep twenty minutes, and then go back out in the field."

Diane left the CBS morning show (Maria Shriver, Meredith Vieira, and Jane Wallace alternated in her spot alongside Kurtis) and accepted Don Hewitt's offer, joining Mike Wallace, Morley Safer, and Ed Bradley— and the media discovered her. In a *People* magazine profile, illustrated with a photo of Diane seated on her bed jubilantly throwing papers in the air, writer Margo Howard described her as "a thinking man's Angie Dickinson" who "got to the top with a formidable blend of smarts, drive, and earnestness" and "is extremely desirable for television because her manner is both authoritative and appealing." Howard made a zeitgeist point: "There is another component to Sawyer's rise, and that has to do with her aura of refinement. She is one of those highly visible women who communicate the old-fashioned ladylike values from which we have 'progressed.' Along with Meryl Streep, Glenn Close, and Shelley Long, Diane Sawyer is one of the Ladies of the '80s. They have all gained star status with a cultivated style that offers a connection to a gentler time."

AT *60 MINUTES* Diane continued to produce and report the kind of serious news that had, thus far, built her reputation. She did feature reporting on the AIDS epidemic in Uganda, where the air was buzzing with malaria mosquitoes; when not on camera, and with little else in the way of clean paper goods, she resorted to protecting her eyes from dangerous bites by covering them with sanitary napkins. She interviewed elderly legendary author James Michener and Corazon Aquino, the reformist female president of the Philippines.

She brandished her evolving interviewing skills—the gentility masking the toughness, armed by massive preparation—in grilling Vice President George H. W. Bush on Iran-Contra just as he was launching his presidential bid against Michael Dukakis. In fact, it was at *60 Minutes* that Diane began to think about the art of interviewing in all its amplitude, says Ira Rosen, who worked with her there, and later at *Primetime*. But she also learned the double standard by which women adept at hard news were somehow lessened by their foray into celebrity interviews in a way that their male peers were not. "Diane looked at Mike [Wallace], and he could go from interviewing a president to Barbra Streisand; he could do a comedian or Khomeini. She looked at that and said, 'Why the hell can't I be that way?'" In a few years she would spread her wings with Wallace-like breadth. But she didn't realize, Rosen continues, "that it was always different when Mike did it. He could be confrontational with Streisand. He did a piece on Tina Turner without people thinking it was softball." Doing a celebrity interview as a newsperson was "much harder for women," Rosen believes. "You're trying to avoid two traps—appearing soft and appearing unlikable, and the more you tried not to fall into one, the more you risked falling into the other."

Diane was now developing her unique way of putting a piece together, which she would elaborate upon for the next decades: amassing the transcripts, cutting them up into small passages, taping or stapling the strips into one long document to produce the narrative she envisioned, ordering the segments by marking them A and B and C and D, circling passages, and then having the whole piece reformatted, taping key words to her wall or, later, to her computer screen—a process that was "like an art form; *nobody* does that anymore," says her eventual protégée Anna Robertson.

Still, at *60 Minutes*, "I think it was a difficult time for her—with so many men. She had a hard time, to prove that, as the first woman, she could do the work," Anna Robertson says. But Jeff Fager, the current first chairman of *CBS Evening News* and a longtime former producer and still executive producer of *60 Minutes*, strongly disputes this. "Everybody respected Diane. They valued her on *60 Minutes*," he insists. "It's easy to fall back on the 'old boys' club,' and *60 was* an old boys' club—I don't think there's any doubt about it. But I don't think [sexism] is what happened to her," he says, citing as evidence the fact that Lesley Stahl, who arrived at *60 Minutes* in 1991, "loved it from the get-go."

So why wasn't Diane destined to stay? Fager explains, "I think she might have been too big for it. We"—*60 Minutes*—"are an ensemble. Every correspondent has to accept that there are moments they don't get their way. Whether you fit in at *60 Minutes* or not [hinges on] whether you can tolerate an ensemble rather than a star system. It's a zero-sum game. If one is happy, two or three are going to be unhappy. I think Diane bristled at that a little bit. I don't think it was the right fit for her. Some people work well in an ensemble and some people need their own show."

Whatever the reason, Diane was responsive when in 1986, two years into her *60 Minutes* tenure, NBC made a lunge for her. Someone close to the situation puts it this way: "Her contract was up and CBS had promised to get her things that didn't happen. NBC and ABC chased her at the end of her deal." In order to keep her, CBS raised her salary to $1.2 million and also arranged for her to substitute-anchor the *CBS Evening News* for Dan Rather. The plan greatly threatened Rather. An executive who worked closely with him asserts that Rather was so fearful that Diane could permanently replace him, he dismantled long-planned family vacations at zero hour just to keep her from going on air in his stead. "I saw Dan do that a lot, because Diane could anchor better than he did," the executive says.

In 1987 Diane traveled to the Soviet Union to participate in a CBS documentary, *Seven Days in May*, about the advent of glasnost. She was working again with Susan Zirinsky, with whom she'd energetically partnered on stories during her post–San Clemente days at the D.C. bureau. "We weren't going to get Gorbachev, but the centerpiece was a [hoped-for] interview with Boris Yeltsin, who had not yet been elected president but was really powerful," Zirinsky says. "So I'm sitting in this gorgeous office with two translators, trying to talk Yeltsin into doing the first Western television interview, where you're talking about breaking up the Soviet Union. I'm getting nowhere. Finally, I walk across the room and get to my backpack and pull out an eight-by-ten glossy of Diane Sawyer. I walk back across the room, I put it on the desk, and I tell Yeltsin, '*This* is who will be doing your interview!' He's a lush. He's lazy. But his face flushes, his ears flush. He goes, '*Da!*' and then the Russian word for 'certainly.' Diane flew in and we did an amazing interview." Zirinsky pauses. "But I must have rewritten that Yeltsin piece with Diane *fifty* times! She is a taskmaster!" (A few years later, when Diane had gone over to ABC, she called Zirinsky, who was, and is, still at CBS. "I had Yeltsin's home phone number," Susan says, and Diane knew this. So now "Diane said, 'Okay, I'm gonna ask you a question. Would you give me Yeltsin's number?' And I said, '*Fuck, no!*'" The women were now competitors.)

Yeltsin might have been surprised had he spotted his alluring inter-viewer at the Moscow airport, on her way home. As a witness tells it, Diane showed up "with her Coke-bottle glasses and her hair is not done and she's not dressed up." The airport officials "look at her passport, which has a glamour shot, and they don't believe that it's her."

Diane herself would make sly jokes about her charm offensives, giv-ing tips to the younger women with whom she worked. Like a parody of Helen Gurley Brown, she once said, "Always wear clothes in fabrics that men like to touch." She also cheekily admitted that she liked to wear high heels when interviewing shorter men because "men love it when you tower over them."

LOVE CAME TO DIANE IN 1986, when she was just turning forty-one.

Diane had taken her mother and her stepfather, Ray Hayes, on a trip to France, where her mother's doctor called her to warn her that the heart monitor Mrs. Hayes wore had transmitted an alarmingly high reading. So they planned to fly right back to New York; the night before the hastily planned return trip, Diane sat outside her "mother's door all night, listen-ing to her breathe, in a blind panic." The next morning, at the airport, Diane was in the Concorde lounge, "wearing a juice-stained turtleneck and ratty jeans," she has said, when Mike Nichols, the esteemed director, "walked up behind a potted palm and said, 'You're my hero.' 'And you're mine,' I answered, in a dazzling riposte."

Diane was still living with Holbrooke, and Mike—one year divorced from novelist Annabel Davis-Goff—was in a serious romance with a woman who is described by a friend of hers as a "diligent, hardworking" media professional. Though this woman was in a committed relationship with another man, she was seeing Mike on the side and it was the rela-tionship with Mike that mattered to her. "I think she thought she could become the next Mrs. Mike Nichols," says her friend, who knew the situ-ation well, adding, "I think she was really blindsided by the Diane thing."

At the time he met Diane, "I think Mike was very interested in chang-ing his life—and I mean consciously," says a friend of Nichols's. His career was in flux. Seven years earlier, his movie adaptation of *Catch-22* had been "his first failure. He had been the golden boy—he was untouchable" before that: Oscars, Emmys, Tonys. "Because he'd been such an early success, he wasn't used to failing." After that comeuppance, his track record had been uneven: some wins, some losses. "It wasn't that people weren't returning his phone calls," the friend stresses, "but still, he said, 'When you're a failure, you begin to understand what people are there for'"—that is, how readily you could be abandoned by fair-weather friends.

As for Diane, she was instantly taken with him. "In the first ninety seconds I knew. It's like the tonic chord: When you get there, you know you're there; there's no explaining it. . . . I knew before he spoke. I knew before he was walking across the room. I knew something was happening." She laughed at the ridiculous Hallmark card aspect of this, but reaffirmed: "I knew life was changing. . . . Not that anyone thought [a relationship] was going anywhere," because of their significant others, her relationship with Holbrooke and his with the media woman. "But I knew he was at the center of the dance."

That man, age fifty-five, who suddenly became the center of Diane's dance was enormously sophisticated. He had been married three times and had had a legendary, decades-long career in avant-garde comedy, theater, and film. He occupies an elite position at the intersection of quality popular culture, high culture, and high society. "When you speak to him, he says, 'Oh, Noël Coward said thus and such to me,' and 'George Abbott said this,' and 'Samuel Beckett . . . ,'" says a relatively new addition to the inner circle of the man who was first blessed with fame in the 1950s. "And the stars who've been in love with Mike! Meryl, Emma Thompson, Julia Roberts—there's an endless list. And Jackie [Kennedy Onassis]! She loved Mike—no question. She loved Mike. . . ." The sentence trails off knowingly.

Nichols was born Mikhail Igor Peschkowsky, of wealthy Jewish parents in Berlin. In 1938, at age eight, along with his brother, he was hustled off to safety in America, reuniting with his parents after they, too, fled the Nazis, just as Richard Holbrooke's parents had done before his birth. The Peschkowskys, who changed their name to Nichols, resumed a prosperous life in Manhattan, Mike's father becoming a successful doctor. Unlike the Holbrookes, the Nicholses owned their Jewishness. Even today, Mike Nichols will ask an opinion of a Christian friend by prefacing it with "What would a goy do?"

A childhood disease left Nichols's whole body permanently hairless; he has always worn a wig. His friend believes that "in some way he's still suffering from that disease." It's made him "not afraid of luxury. He's very funny about it. He appreciates every minute of the wildly luxurious life he's always lived," with his collection of horses and art and houses. "He doesn't take any of it for granted. It's fun for him—it's almost like he knows he doesn't belong in it." He's still in some way the boy "who deserved nothing—he had no hair, so how could he deserve anything?"

With his comedy partner, Elaine May, Nichols helped to pioneer the intellectual "neurotic" sketch comedy of the late 1950s. The long span of films he subsequently directed include *Who's Afraid of Virginia Woolf?*, *Carnal Knowledge*, *Silkwood*, and *Heartburn*, and the stage plays include *Barefoot in the Park* and *The Odd Couple*.

He is sophisticated personally as well as artistically. In the midsixties he was such a fixture at elite New York nightspots that morning planning meetings for *The Graduate*, his eventual directorial debut, often started at his apartment *before* he got home from his evening gallivanting. Yet people talk of his relationship to the very differently backgrounded Diane rapturously, none more so than the principals themselves. Nichols described an epiphany to Joan Juliet Buck: "I thought [at first that Diane and I] were brilliant but totally full of shit, so modest, so wise. It took me a long time to realize that, in the first place, [Diane] wasn't bullshitting, she was real. And then—to my astonishment—that I was real, too. And it was because of her. The way she saw me let me finally see that I was real, too."

As for Diane, according to her friend Mark Robertson, "I heard her say this: 'Everyone I've ever dated in my life, there was a piece of them that was right for me, that was intriguing and wonderful. But Mike was *all* the pieces of *all* of them.' And she felt it immediately." Diane has amplified this statement: When she met Mike, "I thought he was the most heart-stoppingly funny and limitless person I'd ever met. To be so funny and generous, it's a rare combination. And the connections he makes to the world—it really is like flying with the Blue Angels. I love it so much when we get into a cab in New York and within two blocks he'll have the cab driver, even if he only speaks Pashto, in stitches. You know what Napoleon said: 'A woman laughing is a woman conquered.' It's just some gift that comes from a very original view of the universe. And he's not judgmental about anybody."

After that first meeting of theirs in the airport, back in the city "we had lunch," Diane has said, "at which point I sort of did my performing seal number: 'You just have to let me interview you!' And he postponed seeing me again, and then it just sort of trailed off."

There was a good reason for the trailing off. Nichols, like his friends Philip Roth and William Styron, had become addicted to the sleeping pill Halcion, a sedative hypnotic that would later be linked to a mesh of side effects, from amnesia to suicidal thoughts, termed "Halcion madness." He'd gotten on the drug when he was in the hospital for a minor heart procedure, and had soon become dependent on it. "He had a nervous breakdown—he thought he was going to die," says a longtime friend from the theater world. "I went totally crazy" as a result of the drug, Nichols said. He thought he was losing all his money. He began to sell his prize collection of horses. He didn't call Diane right away after that first lunch because "I didn't want her to see me as I was. And as soon as I was okay again, I called her up. She had wondered what had happened to me and was sort of hurt. And then it went very, very fast."

Quickly, Diane broke up with Richard Holbrooke. "She just came home one day and told him. He was crushed; he was devastated," says a friend of Holbrooke's. She moved out of his apartment—and into her own makeshift one. Mike was shocked that, at the height of her glamour, Diane had no furniture. For such a successful woman, she had the most bare-bones life he'd ever seen. Diane admitted, "I have no taste. When I've had the option of going to a movie or looking at swatches, it wasn't even close. I'd rather send out for pizza and sit on my floor pillows." Mike broke up with the woman he was seeing as well, and Mike and Diane took a penthouse apartment in a Park Avenue hotel. Diane set to work to woo Mike's children, Max and Jenny. Over a nervous lunch, Diane asked Jenny, "What do you think of my marrying your father?" When Jenny, after a stage pause, answered, "Have you seen his feet?" Diane understood, with relief, that Jenny thought *Diane* was the catch.

Diane also wooed their mother, Annabel Davis-Goff, whom a friend describes as a "very charming, very cunning, extraordinarily quick Anglo-Irish woman—and a true intellectual—who does not suffer fools at all." When Diane—"with knocking knees," as she's recalled—arrived for a meal at Annabel's house, Annabel accidentally served her coffee with sour milk and then "began to recite all the people Mike could have married who were far worse than me." This "dance of wives," as Diane calls it, was a love match: Annabel took to "stocking Mike's country house with food," a friend says, "because otherwise Mike and Diane would starve over the weekend—they were both helpless." Diane does not disagree; in fact she's said that her relationship with Annabel was forged because "I'm so undomestic [and] there is no doubt in anybody's mind how little I know about the things she knows about." Diane stayed proudly undomestic for years into their marriage, leaving such niceties to Mike. "*He*," Diane's good friend Joan Ganz Cooney has said, "is the decorator—likes the paintings, the furniture." Diane did, after a fashion, eventually learn how to cook. ("She cuts out thirty-five different versions of the recipe," Mike has said, and then they cook together, the process being "very detailed and sometimes complex.") Today, Annabel, Mike, Diane, and the adult children have Thanksgivings together.

Holbrooke eventually married Kati Marton, an ex-wife of Peter Jennings and a stunning, self-possessed author and woman about Manhattan with a complicated background (parents who'd had to deny their Jewishness) that uncannily matched Holbrooke's parents' own. Marton and Holbrooke were a dashing, even intimidating, A-list couple, perfectly suited to each other. But on some level, for a man as used to winning as Holbrooke was, the early abrupt loss of Diane seems to have stuck in his craw. For example, years later, when Holbrooke was U.S. ambassador to the United Nations, he and Kati hosted a dinner for a Kentucky official. Diane was present. "He began his remarks by saying, 'Diane'—not 'Kati' but 'Diane'—"'and I welcome you,'" a guest recalls. "Everyone gasped. Then he couldn't stop doing it." Obviously, it wasn't as if Holbrooke went around actively pining for a long-dissolved romance (especially with a woman he remained friends with), but the sight of Diane that evening seems to have triggered one of those innocent yet revealing past-to-present time displacements. "He said 'Diane' instead of 'Kati' two more times," the guest recalls. "The room was full of very well-known people who were looking over at Diane. When he finished, nobody knew what to say. Diane went into the other room," defusing the awkwardness by "playing 'My Old Kentucky Home' on the piano."

Diane's ingratiation of Mike's friends seems to have been earnest and thorough. A celebrity friend of Mike's at the time says that when Diane and Mike became a couple Diane "did everything she could, in a political way, to win me over," including giving this person "lavish presents." The hardest people to charm were Mike's long-standing theater friends. "The arts circle thought that Diane was not up to Mike, and they *still* feel that way," says the friend, who has known Mike for fifty years, adding Jackie Onassis to the list of disapproving intimates. "Jackie was very covetous of Mike. She didn't like him dating Diane, just as [many years earlier] she hadn't liked him dating Gloria Steinem." Another Nichols friend agrees that, however long past their actual romance was, "Jackie didn't like" Mike being in love with Diane. "She was possessive. Mike was a love of her life."

DIANE SAWYER AND MIKE NICHOLS were married on April 29, 1988, in a private ceremony at a church on Martha's Vineyard, near the estate there, at Stevens Landing, that would become their primary retreat. The reception was held at the home of Carly Simon and her then new husband, the poet Jim Hart. "Mike," someone asked, after the ceremony, "is this your third marriage?" "My fourth," he corrected. "And is this your first, Diane?" the person inquired.

"This," Diane firmly declared, "is my *only* marriage."

Nichols's friend says, "Mike always says the same thing about Diane:

'She is the perfect wife.'" The friend enunciates that sentence, per Nichols, with each syllable given equal weight, as if to suggest intentional self-satisfaction—ironic because he is *not* being ironic. Mike himself has spoken movingly about his sincerity in almost a pious way. "My happiness in life really started with seeing my children become astonishing people," he has said. "But my *ultimate* happiness began in 1988 when I married Diane." Six years after that marriage, he was still analyzing its thrall: "Falling in love really does have a sort of going-over-to-the-other-side feeling to it. Giving something up. Dying. Giving up balance, equilibrium, some kind of safety, and just sliding through this unknown and slightly terrifying country, where you become unnervingly like the enemy." That latter touch is pure Nichols in its dark originality and come-to-think-of-it sense making. "The other side. Just belonging to somebody: the end of all games," he has said.

"I'm trying to think if I've ever seen them fight," says Nichols's friend, squinting, and coming up empty. The friend mulls it over. "If I did, it would be about such a minor thing, like, 'Why didn't you make those reservations?' They just don't. When they're irritable, they each accept blame for what's gone wrong. And I suspect it has more to do with Diane than Mike, because Diane isn't like *us*"—grandstanding males from hyperverbal cultures. "Her ego is not involved. She doesn't need to take attention away from him." Nichols told Mark Robertson: "Diane is the only person I've ever known in my very broad life who is without vanity." (Diane has said they so rarely fight that "once when we were arguing, he stopped in the middle of it and said, 'Well, this is sort of fun, *too*.' And it was!")

Yet colleagues have noted how similar their styles can be. Someone who worked with Diane recalls, "Harrison Ford was on *Inside the Actors Studio*, and he said he loved Mike Nichols because Nichols had the uncanny ability to point you in the direction where you need to go and get out of you what he needs to get out of you, and that you never feel his hand on your back the whole time he's doing it—the whole time he's pushing you in that direction. And that's Diane." Again: "No fingerprints." A writer who knows them: "Mike pushes actors as perfectionistically as Diane does producers."

Interviewers sometimes ask Diane why she never had children and if she regretted that she hadn't. Her friend Mark Robertson once overheard her say, "I would have had children earlier," under other circumstances, "but I chose Mike, and Mike already had three children with two other women, and he was fifty-eight when we married. And"—she stressed—"I chose him."

DURING THE YEARS that Diane Sawyer was rising at CBS, women at another network were organizing. In late 1984, when Diane was making her mark at *60 Minutes,* a group of women at ABC's Washington bureau— led by Carole Simpson, an African American correspondent who would break numerous barriers—was getting together for what Simpson called "bitch sessions." Fortune, and Don Hewitt, may have smiled on the de- serving Diane, but for other women in the field—many, far more experi- enced than she—it felt like Groundhog Day: Twelve years after Title IX and the effective early CBS protests (and hires), what progress had been made had hit snags or had been dialed back.

Over a dinner that stretched to seven hours, Simpson and eleven fe- male colleagues pooled their war stories and realized that, at ABC, "there were no women correspondents, no women in top management, no women vice presidents, no women bureau chiefs, no women senior producers on any of our broadcasts," Simpson said, describing the session to communi- cations professor Judith Marlane. "And this was 1984!"

ABC News president Roone Arledge had indeed spent lavishly on cer- tain female stars, including the by then deceased Cassie Mackin and, of course, Barbara Walters. Still, the across-the-board representation was paltry. Marlene Sanders recalls sharing her frustration with Simpson. "I said to Carole, 'You had to do the same damn thing all over again as we did!' We're reinventing the wheel and fighting the same fight!" Except this time it was different. "Carole's group had an advantage," Sanders says. "They had more women, they had more information. And they had numbers."

Numbers, meaning: *statistics.* Carole Simpson's husband was a vice president of a computer company, and he helped the women conduct a content analysis of every news broadcast on ABC. A graph was constructed, documenting the lack of women on the broadcasts. On May 9, 1985, Simpson and the others appeared at a banquet that Arledge was throwing, at New York's Westbury Hotel, to honor Barbara Walters. Their plan? To spring the graph on Arledge and the other self-satisfied executives during the festivities.

After Barbara Walters accepted her award and left the dais, Simpson stood up and said, "We think we have a problem here. We have a problem of institutional sex discrimination. We don't think it's any conspiracy to keep us off the air. You're not bad people. . . . It just probably hasn't crossed your mind." The graph was then displayed. Arledge and the other executives gave over the floor to the women, who spoke for three hours. The executives' "mouths fell open," Simpson recalled. "We really blew them away. Roone Arledge—I have to give him credit. He listened. He said, 'You know, I just really never had thought about it before. You're absolutely right.'"

Sanders, too, gives Arledge credit for accepting the evidence of Simpson's group. But she does not let the late, widely adored TV legend off the hook. Before he became president of ABC News, Arledge had been the head of ABC Sports (functionally from 1964; officially from 1968), and during that time, Sanders says, "The women [in Sports] came over to tell him that [that department] was sexual harassment headquarters. He knew, but he never did anything."

Simpson's group demanded a talent scout to find female correspondents and managers. Amy Entelis, a producer for Peter Jennings at *World News Tonight*, approached Richard Wald, who by then was a senior vice president at ABC. Wald challenged Entelis, "What makes you think you can do this well?" Entelis replied, "I don't think you guys have done such a great job so far. I think I could do better." With Entelis hired, ABC branded itself as a network that welcomed women. And more women *were* hired.

"Roone *had* listened," Richard Wald says, agreeing with Simpson and Sanders. And the fact that he listened seemed to ratify the sense he already had and had already seen pay off at the topmost levels—certainly with his hiring of Barbara Walters, who was now riding high at *20/20*: that women as on-screen presences were television news's future. Perhaps his listening also signaled recognition of a shift in what "news" actually meant. The now mature women's movement, the gay rights movement, the continuing search for equality for African Americans, the acceptance of psychology (serious, pop, or in between) as a lens, the acknowledgment of social-roles revolutions and human behavior trends as legitimate news, the upgrading of human interest and celebrity stories to newsworthiness (gone were the days when, six years earlier, Walter Cronkite had refused to make Elvis Presley's sudden death the lead story on his broadcast)—all these phenomena were in bloom. Stories that were "featurey," sociological, empathy-requiring were stories that female reporters had more experience with, and perhaps more of a natural touch with.

The ABC women, and Marlene Sanders, may have felt their complaints were twelve years unaddressed, but this year—1984—was a pivotal year. The previously unknown Oprah Winfrey beat Phil Donahue in the ratings and was galloping forth to a startling stardom, making women's personal issues a news category in itself. Donahue himself—who had primed the pump *for* Winfrey, turning emotional issues into non-sneer-worthy news (as perhaps only a beefy, heterosexual, heartland Irish Catholic man could most effectively do)—moved his show from Chicago to the bigger stage of New York. And Time Inc.'s *People* magazine celebrated its prosperous ten-year anniversary. The "numbers"—of viewers, of readers—associated with this blooming of human interest news must have been as striking to an astute executive as the damning stats on the ABC women's graph. The tantalizing numbers pointed to the same solution: more women's faces. Roone was "celebrity mad," scoffs Marlene Sanders. He wanted a female *star.* He knew who he wanted.

IN 1988 ROONE ARLEDGE decided that he *had* to have Diane Sawyer at ABC. Her contract was up for renewal at *60 Minutes*—again. He had pursued her before, and she had listened to his offer, but the right terms had never been met. "She was generating star power, and he was very attuned to that," says Av Westin, who was now producing Barbara Walters, with Hugh Downs, at *20/20*. "Roone had an expression" about the rarest TV talent: "The person 'comes through the screen.'" Diane Sawyer came through the screen, but, even more than that, "Roone was *besotted* with Diane," says a confidant of Arledge's. "One of his great regrets is that she never fell for him." Yes, he knew she was with Mike Nichols, but it didn't stem his crush on her. "He was a shy egomaniac."

"Roone went through hoops to hire Diane; it was a long courtship," the Arledge confidant continues. During that courtship's course, one day while Diane and Roone were exiting a limousine, Diane briefly took Roone's hand to steady herself. "'I thought I might have a shot at her,' he told me."

By now, this kind of fruitless crush on Diane was pretty generally shared by a lot of men in media—editors, writers, producers, network executives. What Gloria Steinem had been a dozen years before—the impossibly smart, classy woman in their elite milieu who they respected the hell out of but who was nevertheless undeniably a babe—Diane had now become. The essence of the term used four years earlier in *People*—that Diane was the "thinking man's Angie Dickinson"—was what we'd now call her personal "brand." Novelist Frederick Exley—one of those colorful alcoholics still being glorified as Macho Writer in the late waning season of same—made that point clearly in a cover-lined story he would do in *Esquire* a year after Roone started his pitch. The article was billed "The Decade's Last Piece About Diane Sawyer" (that blurb alone, in a December 1989 issue, said something about the buzz she'd been generating for years), and his interview with Diane was given a mock-pining headline: "If Nixon Could Possess the Soul of This Woman, Why the Hell Can't I?" (Diane played along. A pull quote from the piece trumpeted: "'You know, Diane, you have a flat ass,' I said. 'How can you say that?' she said. 'I've got a great ass.'")

Roone Arledge wanted to create something new: a live newsmagazine show—"telling news stories like movies, with swooping cranes and high production values, and a fabulous look created by [Arledge's star director]

Roger Goodman," a producer says—and he had the swagger and experience to do it. Says one who was close to this ABC action: "Roone was an impresario. He'd invented instant replay and *Monday Night Football* and *Wide World of Sports*"—*live* broadcasts were what he'd done best. "And he'd been the first person willing to pay an evening news anchor a million dollars: Barbara." He'd also nurtured Peter Jennings and Ted Koppel, *Nightline* and *20/20*.

"Roone *stole* Diane—and it was a gigantic coup," the insider makes clear. "It was practically 'I can make you a star': an old-fashioned spiel. Roone was a seducer. It was the ultimate charm meets charm. In fact, two people with the charm of Roone and Diane probably haven't been together in a long time."

To "steal" Diane, Roone enlisted the help of Phyllis McGrady, who'd been *Good Morning America*'s executive producer and was now running Barbara Walters's Barwall Productions. "When he first said to me, 'My wish list is Diane Sawyer,' I said, 'Are you serious? Why would she leave *60 Minutes* to start a show that might not work?'" Phyllis says. But by February 1989, Diane had essentially said yes to a reported $1.6 million yearly contract—an increase of almost half a million dollars a year over what *60 Minutes* had reportedly been paying her. (According to *Time*, in a cover story on Diane six months later, "The prospect of losing Sawyer so rattled CBS's bigwigs that they virtually handed her a blank check in an effort to keep her." For his part, Don Hewitt retorted that while Sawyer was "a monumental talent," he claimed that "her coming to the broadcast didn't do that much for us. And her leaving has not even remotely crippled *60 Minutes*.") An insider on the other side of ABC's wooing and negotiating table puts it this way: CBS's promises to Diane had not come to fruition and "she knew it was time to leave. One way or another she found a way to leave."

The new show would be called *Primetime Live*, and would pair Diane with Sam Donaldson. The peaked-eyebrowed newsman known for his audacious questioning at White House press conferences was the overcaffeinated yang to Diane's wry, ladylike, mellifluous yin. "A sonata for harp and jackhammer," Diane aptly called their pairing.

Phyllis McGrady had a series of lunches with Diane between February and April. The two women found that they had much in common: their Southernness (McGrady hailing from southwest Virginia), their dutiful daughterliness, and their insomnia, which paved the way for years of three and four a.m. work phone conversations. Diane had felt "confined" at *60 Minutes*, Phyllis learned. This new show would be a risk, but "Diane's not afraid of taking gambles. She said to me, 'The thing that's scarier than change is standing still.'" That seemingly Catherine Marshall–inspired sentiment impressed Phyllis. "When I've worked on a show and it's bombed, I sometimes have a tendency to hide under the table. But Diane, immediately, is: 'Okay, what are we going to learn from this? How are we gonna take what *did* work and put that into the mix?'"

Betsy West, who'd been one of *Nightline*'s several female junior producers, was hired as number two. The young *Nightline* women had called themselves the News Nuns because "we would come in at ten thirty in the morning for a conference call at eleven, and very often be there till twelve thirty a.m., doing an update for the show, and then turn around and go home and come back again. There wasn't much time in our lives for anything else but *Nightline*." Betsy thought "Diane felt liberated to break out of the formula. She'd come in my office in the morning with an article ripped out of a magazine with her inimitable scrawl: 'Can we advance this story?' 'What's behind this?' 'Can we do this?' She was always driving the story."

Roone brought his new star anchor to his star director's next-door office almost immediately—and Diane's glamour wasn't lost on Roger Goodman, who, in general, has the kind of effusively romantic way of talking more associated with Hollywood or the arts than the news business. "I'll never forget the day as long as I live," Goodman swoons. "Oh, my God! I've always been just in awe of her!" Days later, Goodman's four-year-old son broke his arm and Diane had a dozen balloons delivered to the boy's hospital room before Roger even got there. This would seal the ardor of the soothing, talented director who made anchors feel safe during live segments whenever they could say, "Roger's in my ear." Goodman worked mostly with Peter Jennings, who gave him secret on-air finger signs—Jennings straightening his tie meant "cut to tape"; Jennings scratching his nose with his *middle* finger meant he was really damn annoyed at something.

"I wanted to make sure that everything was perfect for Diane," Goodman says, and his own, charmingly over-the-top appreciation for her was rewarded by her diligence on the job. At the end of a trip to Russia soon after *Primetime Live* launched—during which Diane called Betsy West at four a.m., prodding her for research for her interview with a KGB chief—"Diane collapsed, in the most *beautiful* way, on a luggage cart, and I pushed her, sound asleep, through the airport."

Some at ABC found Diane's overtures off-putting. One major producer was surprised when, at their first lunch, she brought a gift "for my wife." Among the skeptics was Mimi Gurbst, the head of news coverage and a powerful figure but so controversial that when she left ABC in May 2010 to become a high school guidance counselor, the comments section of the *New York Observer*'s Web site, which reported her retirement, literally erupted with staffers' complaints about how she'd played favorites at the network and had cultivated a clique. "If Mimi liked you, you were golden," a colleague says. "I think Mimi was never a big fan of Diane's. Mimi was very up front, and she was smart enough to see Diane's manipulation (though she was also fascinated by it). I think Diane knew that, and she really went into overdrive to woo Mimi. 'Let's go to lunch!' 'I want to hear your thoughts!' 'I want to know what you're thinking!' *Desperate!* Sometimes that pays off—Diane has found out that it worked. But with other people it doesn't."

The most powerful person who remained impervious to Diane's charm was another woman at the network—the most powerful woman at the network: Anne Sweeney, who became president of ABC in 1996 and then went on to become cochair of Disney Media Networks and president of the Disney–ABC Television Group. News is a small part of Sweeney's domain. "I've heard her refer to her high-priced anchors as 'whiney anchors,'" says someone who worked there. "I don't think Anne *ever* felt she had to kiss Diane's ring in order to keep her own job and in order to succeed."

There was a familiar face among Diane's new colleagues at ABC. During part of her time at CBS, she had as an intern a former *Harvard Crimson* editor named Ben Sherwood. Very tall, handsome, palpably ambitious, from a wealthy Beverly Hills family, Sherwood was fascinated by his boss. When, soon after his internship with Diane at CBS, he left for Oxford as a Rhodes scholar, he kept a photograph of Diane on his desk. When Diane landed at *Primetime*, Ben arrived as a producer there—serendipity!—and his fascination escalated. Sherwood saw his boss—now Diane the Star—strolling around the offices, slurping Diet Coke "in her sweatpants and her thick glasses, amazingly normal," remembers another colleague. Sherwood and that colleague would wonder together, "Was this an affect, a pretense? Or just her being relaxed? She was *so* charming. Is she playing the role of 'charming Diane'? 'Diane-of-the-people'? You didn't know if she was self-absorbed—or totally the opposite. She was a very interesting psychological character. Ben asked me about it. He asked me, in general, 'What *is* she?'"

The fascinating truth is, people weren't sure. At this point, Diane's serene mysteriousness had become a thing of wonder. "You feel like there's not a sincere bone in her body," one colleague says. A colleague who worked with her at this time says: "People who've known Diane for twenty years don't know who she is; her core is impossible to touch. But it doesn't take away from her talent—in a way, it *helps* it." At a memorial service for a colleague who'd passed away, this person adds, industry insiders were "rolling their eyes" because Diane's eulogy was "insincere *but beautiful*." Another colleague agrees: "I can't say that I really know who 'Diane Sawyer' is. I don't think *she* remembers. But the real Diane—*Lila*—comes out when she has a few drinks and sings."

Ben Sherwood was fascinated. He was fascinated by power well wielded, anyway. He would soon be termed "aggressively aspirational" by the *New York Observer.* He is called "very cunning and manipulative" by a friend. Was he struck by his affinity to Diane, or was he learning from her charm and skills? Were both things happening? The two would have many do-si-dos in their future.

. . .

EARLY ON, Phyllis McGrady left *Primetime*—because of a family emergency, she said—and was replaced by Rick Kaplan for the show's August 1989 launch. Toweringly tall, known as an incredible producer with a huge ego, Kaplan stayed at the helm for years, steering the show from its wobbly beginnings to its galloping success, which Diane doggedly drove. (The "live" aspect, proving unworkable, was ditched and the name shortened to *Primetime*; *L.A. Law* was its formidable contender.) As for Donaldson, "Diane got along well with Sam and she thought he was amusing, but she was competitive with him, too," says a staffer. "Sam had an evening news mentality—if you gave him ten minutes for a story, he'd fight you for an extra thirty seconds." Still, "it wasn't a fair fight; the balance of power was in Diane's favor."

Phyllis McGrady had brought in Ira Rosen from *60 Minutes*. Diane wanted to do big investigative stories, and Ira encouraged—and helped shape—her desire. (Many of the pieces were also produced by Robby Gordon.) Picking up on the issues he knew she cared about, "I simply said to her, 'Why don't you focus on investigatives meaningful to women: day care, mammograms, pap smears, deadbeat dads,'" Rosen says. "'You can be the Nellie Bly of our time.' She said, 'I get it!'" She'd likely had a version of that same idea on her own. "A couple of days after this talk with Rosen, Diane came in with her hair chopped off. The managing editor said, 'Oh, my God! What did Diane do?'" But by hacking off the Breck Girl pageboy to the no-nonsense chin-length bob, "she consciously decided, 'If I'm gonna go down this road, I don't want people to focus on my beauty or my glamour.'" That wasn't her only savvy image-conscious move. She also had her set's look toned down. A staffer: "She said, 'It's got to be a raw set, because if it's polished, I'm too slick.'" She instinctively knew how to maximize her desired self-presentation.

Diane juggled her two worlds seamlessly—the sweatpants and Nellie Bly stories in the office, the sophisticated evenings with Mike and his friends, sometimes with campy repartee. One friend recalls a dinner party "with Mike and Slim Keith and John Guare—and the very *raffi-*

née, high-gay repartee. Diane was in her element. 'Oh, John!'" she crooned, in parody, to playwright Guare. "'Come and lick the whiskey off my lips.'" On the night of Mike Nichols's sixtieth birthday, "I said, 'Wait a second, Diane, it's eleven thirty and you're throwing him a party and you're here with *me* in the editing room?'" Ira Rosen recalls— during which, as ever, she was nibbling plastic-bagged okra, collard greens, and salty potato chips: Southern snacks as comfort food. "And she looked at her watch and said, 'Oh, my God—I gotta go!' And she runs to the bathroom and comes back looking drop-dead gorgeous in makeup and heels and is out the door."

Even more than she had at *60 Minutes*, Diane intensely microman-aged stories, honing them to their essentials. Being questioned by Diane about a piece was like "going through a PhD review," says Rosen, noting that the need to rigorously justify minute aspects of a piece improved its quality. Gratuitous lines, filler, sloppy inferences—these were cut. How-ever, the last-minute aspect of some of Diane's revisions could yield mis-takes. As she reworked a story dangerously right up to airtime, her attitude would be "naughty, devilish—but *I* would be a nervous wreck," a co-worker recalls. "She's, 'I *wonder* if this could move . . .' And she'd walk back to the edit room. And somebody was hovering around, saying"— desperate voiced—' "*Why* move that? It reads *great*, and we're on the air in *five* minutes!' She'd say"—airy voice—"'Oh, no, I think we can make *one* change. . . .'" Inevitably, sometimes passages would be in the wrong order. "She'd say, at zero hour, "'We haven't been introduced to this char-acter, have we?'" The change would be hectically made, "and then, after the show aired, we were, 'Did you notice we introduced a character *twice?*' Or somebody's talking and you have no idea who because the introduction was afterward."

She did this "with *every* story," the person says, beleaguered even in remembering it. "The show would be over and she'd say, 'Well, I guess we cut it pretty close.'" Did anyone stand up to her? "No. David Westin was notorious for not doing so. Westin accommodated her."

Diane's relationship to David Westin, who came in as president of ABC News in March 1997 after Arledge retired, is much remarked upon. Westin was a lawyer by training, not a talent person—"Diane showed him the ropes," a producer says. Notably, Westin, like Diane, came from a religious Protestant family in a noncoastal city—in his case, Ann Arbor, Michigan. But Westin's upbringing was more devoutly Christian than Diane's was; as a boy, he went to church three times a week (she went on Sunday and sometimes to one midweek meeting) and his denomination forbade card playing, drinking, smoking—even watching movies.

Diane championed David Westin at the very awkward beginning of his tenure. He was having an extramarital affair with Sherrie Rollins, the wife of Republican political consultant Ed Rollins. Diane smoothed the way for Westin, talking him up when his personal scandal made many at the top tiers of ABC angry. "You would see the two of them whispering in the halls," a producer says. Some believe she was essentially responsible for getting him the job. More, she personally supported him and Sherrie when they shed their respective spouses and decided to marry, and she initiated him into the social sphere he coveted. "David Westin was a climber," says one producer. Says another staffer: "Their social circle widened through Diane. David and Sherrie were really beholden to Diane," because of Diane's and Mike's top-drawer-elite milieu and connections.

David and Sherrie decided to get married on the Vineyard, and Diane and Mike flew them there, to their wedding, in a private plane. Diane made many of the arrangements for the Rollins-Westin nuptials, and, according to one former anchor, "Diane personally took care of Lily, the Chinese daughter that Sherrie and Ed Rollins had adopted. Diane gave them her and Mike's house for their honeymoon, and she took Lily somewhere else" so the newlyweds could have some privacy. Some people at ABC were surprised by these expansive gestures. A female eminence says, "He's your boss! You don't do that! It made me want to throw up, Diane being so unctuous." As for Westin's being charmed by the largesse and glamour, "Well, shame on him," this person continues. "You're president of News!" When Sherrie Westin became pregnant, Diane reportedly accompanied Sherrie for her ultrasound. Says a former staffer, "Everything about David and Sherrie was tied to Diane—tied to making Diane happy."

Still, the work was always paramount for Diane. Investigatives, interviews, human interest pieces: Diane brought "an intensity to every story," recalls Betsy West. "She never phones it in. She doesn't pick and choose. She always goes where she needs to go to crack the nut of the heart of the story. She's a complex thinker, and that's part of what made it challenging to work with her. She will push and pull to make sure a story has the nuance she thinks it deserves."

Somehow it all paid off. Ira Rosen: "She won a Peabody for her story on pap smears, and we won an award on the day care centers story and the deadbeat dads story, and the story about Russian orphanages won a DuPont Award." Diane also spent two days and nights in a women's maximum-security prison for a major special—one particularly strong story—and she investigated the mistreatment of mentally handicapped patients at a state-run home, along with an influential feature on the high incidence of pharmacy prescription mistakes. The era's Nellie Bly she was, indeed, becoming.

Ironically, one of Diane's most powerful investigations—of grossly unsanitary conditions at Food Lion markets—proved that sometimes her attempts at charm could backfire. The show, which aired in November 1992 and won a journalism award, showed numerous *Primetime* reporters who, armed with tiny hidden cameras, acquired jobs in the meat and deli departments of various branches of the rising supermarket chain. Working undercover, they documented stunningly unethical and unhealthful practices: redating old meat on its plastic wrappers, washing meat in dirty water, and so forth. The sensational broadcast, vivid because of the surreptitious photography, caused Food Lion's stock to plunge; the formerly fast-growing chain made plans to close more than eighty stores.

Food Lion sued ABC—not for libel, but for unfair methods of reporting—and in 1997 the case went to trial. Diane was flown down to Greensboro, North Carolina, to testify before a jury of exactly the kind of regular Southern folks she had grown up among. She was utterly charming and, of course, she seemed to be highly impressive on the stand. But the jury found ABC guilty on two counts: fraud and breach of duty of loyalty, manifested by the use of the hidden cameras and the ABC reporters' misrepresentation of their identities. After the verdict was announced, the jury was interviewed on television. One of the jurors, a grandmotherly woman, smiled as she said that a key mistake for the defense was having "the great Diane Sawyer" take the witness stand. *We're not a bunch of starstruck simpletons*, the juror seemed to be saying.

Diane finally won her first Emmy at *Primetime*—at *60 Minutes*, "she'd been the Susan Lucci of Emmys," always nominated, never winning, says a colleague—for her piece on the Menendez brothers. The shocking saga of the siblings—two privileged, handsome young men who murdered their mother and father in cold blood in their Beverly Hills home in August 1989—was a kind of shot across the bow, signaling a phenomenon that no one explanation could account for: the emergence of sensational, media-begging crime stories, which would transform the decade's television. The trend's apotheosis was the O. J. Simpson story, which NBC "owned," covering the story to the saturation point in 1994 and 1995.

In June Diane embraced the "magazine"—as opposed to the "news"—aspect of the show with celebrity interviews that sparked criticism. The first was a heavily advance-promoted interview with Michael Jackson—who had just privately settled his notorious child molestation civil lawsuit, brought by a thirteen-year-old boy—and Jackson's wife, Lisa Marie Presley. The interview was denounced by *Vanity Fair* writer Maureen Orth, who accused Sawyer, and ABC, of bending journalistic standards. Jackson, Orth argued, was given free rein to proffer a one-sided version of events, without challenge, and ABC allowed Jackson to dictate many of the broadcast's conditions, right down to the lighting. It was an undeniably gimmicky segment—the credibility of already-far-gone, whisper-voiced Michael Jackson, married to Elvis's daughter in what none could imagine was a genuine marriage, was implicitly shaky—but Diane firmly insisted that she had done her journalistic due diligence.

Fans of the "classy" Diane took this interview—and, earlier, her interview with Donald Trump and his bride Marla Maples, in which Diane prodded Maples to answer a question about their sex life—as warning that the elegant highbrow interviewer was not above going pop. Sensational celebrity interviews could actually be a smart career move, in fact.

They're "what make people talk about you," says a CBS correspondent. "And then, in this perverse reversal, *you* start to become more a celebrity, and then the power allows you to get to *other* people," many of whom are *not* pop figures. But such interviews could also exemplify what Ira Rosen meant by the no-win situation of female newsmagazine stars. From then on, Rosen says, "sometimes Diane was trapped between, 'Am I more Peter Jennings, or am I more Barbara Walters?' Sometimes she ended up splitting the difference." Eventually, as the years of her nonstop multigenre career ensued, and as she could be more selective about the celebrities she chose, she could do *both* well.

Diane was now doing double, even triple, duty at ABC. She appeared on *Turning Point*, a show launched by McGrady that gave over a whole hour to one strong narrative. She did special investigations. She substitute-anchored for Peter Jennings on *World News Tonight* and for Ted Koppel on *Nightline*. Her dedication was rewarded in early 1994, when her compensation rose to $4 million a year. Even at that price, Arledge considered himself lucky to have retained her—there was heavy competition from CBS, NBC, and Fox, with Rupert Murdoch reportedly offering her $10 million a year.

By now, over at CBS, Connie Chung had broken the unofficial dictum against women anchoring the six-thirty news, which had been first poorly tested by Barbara Walters's humiliating experience with Harry Reasoner. Connie had star power, and NBC had been ashamed to have recently lost her to her original network, CBS. CBS had her coanchoring the *CBS Evening News* with Dan Rather. But Connie's triumph didn't exactly count as besting Diane, since Rather made no secret of his dislike for sharing the spotlight. He undermined Chung, openly complaining, for example, that *she* got to cover the Oklahoma City bombing. "People have told me that it would not have mattered if I were a man," Connie says. "He would not have wanted to share that chair because he had owned it before. He wasn't about to give half of it up voluntarily. I can understand that." But Rather wasn't the one—or the only one—who judged Chung as undeserving of coanchorship. Jeff Fager, the current head of CBS News, says, "Connie is one of the best people I've ever known. But she was junior to Dan in journalism. It should not have been perceived as a man-woman thing. I don't think they were equals, journalistically."

Eventually, Fager says, "it blew up—and blew up badly," when Connie made an embarrassing faux pas interviewing Newt Gingrich's mother. Chung had asked Kathleen Gingrich how her Speaker of the House son perceived First Lady Hillary Clinton. Kathleen Gingrich declined to answer the question until Chung encouraged her to "whisper" her reply, "just between you and me." Then Mrs. Gingrich said, "She's a bitch." Though Chung never promised confidentiality—and the cameras were rolling—Mrs. Gingrich insisted she thought she was speaking off the record. During the ensuing outcry, a CBS reporter says, "Dan knifed Connie." So, by the middle to late 1990s, the only two women (Walters and Chung) who'd ever anchored the vaunted six-thirty news had been cochairs to men, to whom both were considered journalistically inferior. And both women had, essentially, been run off the newscasts.

Diane's *Primetime* was not immune from political infighting, and Diane could act as a healer. Ira Rosen says, "When our show was floundering around, she, through her force of will, would get everybody in the same room until we solved the problem." Still, there was also the opposite of healing—the fate of Sam Donaldson, for example. Sam was very popular with the producers—"Everybody loved Sam," one says. Affection for him increased when, shortly after he had cancer surgery, he did a particularly grueling story on a survivalist living in the wilderness. Yet as soon as it aired, a staffer recalls, "Diane called everybody and said, 'That was a really terrible piece—let's make sure it doesn't happen again.'" Then "Diane started saying"—this staffer affects a concerned whisper of a voice—"'Sam *really* should be in Washington. . . .' So Sam was moved to Washington—in Diane's mind, he was *exiled* there. She always has a three-dimensional chess game going on, and that chess piece went to Washington." As for Sam himself, the crisply gruff newsman who was born in 1934 has admitted that he ate his humble pie—but that maybe it was good for him. "When I got into the business there weren't any women at all," he marveled, at some point after the incident. "And [though] I've never thought of myself as being sexist-in-the-extreme," still, "being sixty-two," some attitudes inevitably developed and remained. Being "teamed up with Diane" meant he was "competing with a woman who can and does beat me. I've had to read [in the media] for years how Diane is the main anchor and I'm the minor anchor." He's "had to accept that," he said, adding that his being in D.C. while she was in New York made that acceptance—that bit of ego deflation—easier to bear.

Finally, there was the matter of executive producer Rick Kaplan. "'Rick is so mean to me!'" Diane moaned to a colleague. "But Rick wasn't mean to her!" says the colleague. "'Mean' was Rick's sending the editors home at four a.m." (The video editors eventually staged an "intervention" with Diane, not because of their late hours but because of her seconds-before-airtime changes of the pieces.) Kaplan was dismissed ("Diane left no fingerprints," an insider says, but she was behind the dismissal) and Phyllis McGrady, with whom Diane by now had a long relationship, returned as executive producer. (Some believe that Phyllis's earlier leave-taking from the show had not been entirely voluntary.) "Diane just gets tired of people," shrugs a producer whom she wanted as her own. Says another, "Here's the key: Diane is always looking for the magic bullet, where somebody will push her creativity and she will be the most famous broadcaster in history. Once she works closely with you and she sees your strengths and weaknesses, she's like a vulture on the weaknesses. So suddenly Rick Kaplan wasn't good enough." A writer who's worked for her agrees: "She's a roving searchlight always looking for the next brilliant person, and TV is littered with her rejects. And she has the unbelievable gift of killing you with silence," in terms of getting people who work for her to work harder. "Diane uses silence better than anyone I know."

But the biggest clash at ABC during the *Primetime* years was the abiding competition—some would call it warfare—between Diane and Barbara Walters. In her memoir, Walters writes:

Diane and I struggled to figure out what to do, especially when we were competing for the same newsmaker or celebrity for our respective news-magazines. We each had a booker to help pave the way with a potential guest's lawyers, press agents and other handlers. Then we would come in for the last round of phone calls or meetings. Our bookers were notoriously competitive. Diane and I were more polite.

Walters may have been exaggerating the politesse—at least in terms of how the women expressed things in private.

Their rivalry had begun as soon as it was announced that Diane was coming to ABC with her own newsmagazine, *Primetime*, which competed with Barbara's *20/20*. "Barbara felt betrayed by Roone—*betrayed*," says one who was close to Walters during those years. "Barbara was the queen of ABC News. Roone Arledge was her mentor—well, not exactly her mentor, but the big chief and very dominant. Barbara always assumed she had worked so hard for this position—and now she was usurped by Diane."

Indeed, part of it was a sheer—and understandable—generational clash. Barbara had been the pathbreaker, and she had fought for everything she had attained. Richard Wald remembers, of her leap from tea pourer to anchor at *Today*, "She figured out ways to get things on the air. She figured out how to get high-profile show business people on. She *produced herself*. She built the show." The women who came after her, in Morning and in celebrity interview prime-time newsmagazines, "didn't have to create it. Barbara had done that hard work. Barbara *invented* the formula." So of course this charming, beautiful new star—Diane—might seem, to super-competitive Barbara, like someone who'd glided through a door that *she'd* knocked herself out pushing open at an earlier time when women in TV news weren't getting any breaks.

Then there was what colleagues could see as Barbara's "wounded" quality; her surprising personal shyness, so intriguingly the opposite of the "old-time Hollywood type, Louis B. Mayer" élan she appeared to project. In her day-to-day work years earlier, she had been "very shy, terribly shy—*head-down* shy!" says a woman who worked closely with her during her battlefield years against Harry Reasoner. "Very insecure, very driven, very loyal—and she worked harder than anyone else."

Now Barbara was facing *another* unbelievably hardworking female, and one who seemed—to this older woman with the outsider's complex—

intimidatingly blessed. "Barbara referred to Diane as 'That Girl,'" says someone who worked closely with Barbara when Diane came on board. "She would become very agitated" during booking wars, "and there would be terrible conflicts. President Clinton or whoever the person was, Diane had already put in a request and Barbara would be livid.

"Roone would not resolve it. His number two would pull her hair out and roll her eyes. And we'd all have to sit in a room. We'd have to negotiate. It would never be 'fair.' And Barbara would talk about Mike Nichols. And it was so interesting, because Barbara would say, '*I* don't have a husband who's a Hollywood director!' And I'd say, 'But you're Barbara Walters!' And she would say, 'But I don't have what she has! That Girl can book everybody! I don't have these dinner parties. I don't go to Martha's Vineyard. I don't even have a house. I rent Felix Rohatyn's in Southampton.'" And yet by Barbara's own standards, this wasn't quite true. Walters had her own axis of connections. For much of this time, and certainly when Diane arrived at ABC, she was married to Merv Adelson, owner and CEO of Lorimar Productions. Adelson was one of Hollywood's most successful producers of network television series—*The Waltons, Dallas, Knots Landing, Eight Is Enough*—and an emerging billionaire. Theirs was a commuter marriage, which lasted from 1986 to 1992.

Still, the colleague felt Walters had a point about the subtle status differential. "There *was* a New York media elite, and Barbara always felt like an outsider, and that feeling is what drove her. Barbara felt Diane had tools she didn't have."

The women's styles were radically different. Diane could "go down to the edit room and chat with the producer and work on a script—she loved that people saw her as part of the team," the colleague says. "Barbara would never, ever do that. Barbara saw herself as a Gloria Swanson in *Sunset Boulevard* character. People would come to her office—the editor, the writer. She'd say, 'I don't know how to do this.' One of them would push the button for the tape for her, and she would be more regal. She considered this her position, which she'd worked so hard to get. She didn't see herself going to the cafeteria."

Yet for all that "regal" attitude, Barbara would turn into a pious, intimidated hopeful in the presence of Peter Jennings. Barbara would sit in Jennings's office "with her hands folded on her lap, like a schoolgirl," this colleague continues. Jennings had an "imperial" attitude. During the production of a piece on the Olympics diver Greg Louganis, who'd just come out as gay, Jennings dispensed his advice, "and I think Barbara even had a notepad in her lap." After the Louganis piece aired, Jennings told Walters, "'I'm glad you followed my directions, but there are certain things you *still* need to know about editing.' He was very officious and arrogant. It deflated her—*deflated* her. I felt very bad for her."

Walters's reaction to Jennings points to a bigger problem, one that women in the industry say hardly gets discussed: For all the competition between women doing similar work on the same or rival shows, the biggest competition—and the worst treatment and strongest barriers—came from their male colleagues. Peter Jennings is singled out for his arrogance and condescension. He was "the most rude, officious, thought-he-was-God's-gift-to-women man, *but* also the smartest, most experienced international reporter," says a female former news star. Cowed as Barbara might have been by Jennings in 1995, two years later, at Princess Diana's funeral, "Peter and Barbara were at the desk together and he kept talking over her," says an ABC witness. "And Barbara would say, *'Let me talk!'*" Down the line, in 2001 and 2003, Diane would also have issues with Peter's imperiousness. Thus, whatever combat Diane and Barbara had with each other, "the men were worse," says an ABC woman. "Ted Koppel, too. His attitude with women was, 'I'm sorry, did you say something? Do you have a brain in your head?' Peter and Ted were cold and condescending to women," including their top peers.

Diane and Barbara expressed aggression differently. "Diane was very evasive, elusive, demure," says the ABC newsmagazine insider. "Barbara was the opposite." An on-air personality puts it this way: "Diane was a stealth bomber. You never knew what was going on. Barbara was a tough cookie—beyond-the-pale tough! The toughest! The *queen*! She was straightforward. She'd say it to your face, not to management. I like straight shooters, even if they're going to kill me. They'll stab you in the front, not the back." This person adds, "And Barbara and Diane *were* de-

termined to kill each other—to wipe each other off the face of the earth."
(A junior producer demurs, saying, "It was in ways a healthy rivalry.")
They fought over Robin Williams, Al Gore, Henry Kissinger—so many
"gets" in the hectic circus of time-sensitive weekly TV. When there was
tension over who would interview Mary Kay Letourneau—the Washington State teacher and married mother of four imprisoned for having sex
with the twelve-year-old student with whom she eventually had two
babies—David Westin threw up his hands and said words to the effect of,
"We are *not* doing it. *We don't want it.* Everybody, *stand down*," says someone involved in the fracas. So legendary was their competition that in
2002, at Roone Arledge's funeral, when it came to the ordering of eulogies,
an insider recalls Frank Gifford whispering, "Is Barbara speaking first, or
is Diane speaking first? And are they *fighting* over it?"

Yet for all the rabid competition and inner-office-whispered angry
words, the two women respected each other's work, and they showed a
graciousness on camera. When Barbara did an enormously moving special
on transgender children—several years before the issue became well
known—Diane said of her, on air, with a musing smile, "Any time there's
a beating heart, there's Barbara. . . ." It was an unmistakably admiring
remark and it came from Diane's own beating heart.

Also, the competition between these two women was no sharper than
that of competing newsmen. ABC people recall Koppel and Jennings—
however close friends they may have been—nevertheless being "nasty
and competitive with each other. Koppel would be wailing on Peter, putting him down," says a female producer who witnessed those incidents,
"but you just didn't hear about *that*." An even more closely held secret was
the back-biting between the top male anchors at CBS: The likable, folksy
Bob Schieffer was vocally "resentful of Dan [Rather], just as Dan had disliked Cronkite," says a CBS star correspondent. Over the months of Rather's travails during "Memogate," when his report on George W. Bush's
time in the Texas Air National Guard was being unmasked as deeply
compromised and he was losing his anchorship, "Bob took opportunities
on his own to trash Dan," despite his reputation for great loyalty to him.
But the male versus male competition—even the back-biting—was not as

seized upon or gossiped about—everyone prefers a good catfight. As for Rather himself, he was "so competitive," says a producer who worked with him, "he would kill Tom Brokaw and Peter Jennings, and vice versa." Adds a CBS News reporter, "Dan would kill *anybody* who looked like he wanted his job. Dan felt threatened by people"—as he had, earlier, by Diane—"and if he did, he'd cut you off at the knees."

AT SOME POINT in the middle of the 1990s, Richard Wald was installed as the official Barbara-Diane mediator; he would enforce the "head of state rule," deciding which interviews went to Barbara and which to Diane. "Diane was always trying to get something Barbara didn't have," says a colleague, adding that when Wald ruled against Barbara, sometimes "a black cloud would come out of Barbara's office."

But Diane emitted a black cloud, too. She once referred to Barbara as "that terrible person." Another time she phoned an on-air personality at home and said, "Barbara is saying nasty things about you"—which took the person, a friend of Walters's, aback. When Walters nabbed the Monica Lewinsky interview—one of her biggest gets (she scored it by being "very maternal," says an insider—"'Oh, you're so young to go through this. . . .'")—Diane snapped at an aide who was working with Walters: "What are you doing with *that woman*?" "Diane always insinuated that Barbara was like a street fighter, going after things in an inappropriate way," says one who witnessed this behavior.

Still, Diane herself was fragile and could sound as hurt and wounded as Barbara did. A musical performer once heard her complain to a *Primetime* producer, "You know, if I got Al Gore for *60 Minutes*, Mike Wallace and Don Hewitt would hug me, but I didn't get anything from you. What do I have to do—beg?" The plaintive, seemingly out-of-character remark was not an isolated instance. Might these producers, whom Diane had asked for reassurance, have been proxies, of a sort, for her harshest critics? Mike Nichols was one of them. "She wants desperately to please him and for him to be proud of the work she's doing," says one who has worked with her. But there was no sterner or more abiding critic who could get to Diane than her mother. Diane's mother criticized her for being too hard on Whitewater prosecutor Kenneth Starr—Jean Sawyer Hayes respected the evangelical conservative. Her mother's criticism had seemed to startle and deflate her, since her interview was a hard-won scoop. Even more to the point, when Diane covered the Kentucky Derby and stayed at her mother's house, another staffer met Diane there in the morning and saw Diane— as a close adviser heard the story—walking down Mrs. Hayes's stairs looking almost despondent. "What happened?" the staffer wanted to know.

Diane revealed the answer: Her mother hadn't liked the way she'd made her bed that morning.

DIANE DROVE HERSELF HARD—unsparingly hard. And she pushed her staff to the limit. As the four, five, seven, finally nine years of *Primetime*—which in its last years merged with *20/20*, making the competition between the women all the keener—wore on, "you'd hear these stories" from Diane's loyal staff, said one in a position to hear them. "They'd say they were working too hard, they were burned out. And once in a while they'd say, 'I'd like to be reassigned.'"

Unbeknownst to Diane, her own reassignment was being plotted. In December 1998, a secret meeting was convened at ABC to stanch the "hemorrhaging" of ratings of *Good Morning America* and to consider firing its lackluster hosts Lisa McRee and Kevin Newman. By now Diane's brief stint at *CBS This Morning* was beyond the viewing public's memory; she was associated not with Morning but with Evening, as representing sophisticated, sometimes pop-laced, seriousness. "But the whole point of the meeting was to challenge our assumptions and not do the same old, same old," says one attending executive. At the meeting, David Westin was adamant about Diane: "You don't play your queen!"

Westin had taken that position in a separate conversation with Shelley Ross, who had just signed on as *GMA*'s new executive producer, tasked with wooing a highly resistant Charlie Gibson back to the show after a half year's absence. Ross, a former *National Enquirer* writer and a hard-charging producer—fairly young, petite, highly voluble, very story smart and creative, always fashionably dressed—had grown close to Diane while working on the Menendez story. It was Ross who had hatched the startling idea that Diane could come over and revitalize *GMA*.

Ross wasn't present at the secret meeting when Westin made that proclamation. But someone else who was present said, "Okay, let's dissect that." Diane's considerable negatives for the job were detailed, says an executive who was present: "She's not a morning person. She doesn't do 'live' well." Rather, "she was a scripted performer"—all wrong for Morning. "Think about it: *60 Minutes*, not live. *Primetime Live*—live for little bits. . . ."

And then there was Diane's persona. She wasn't a Joan Lunden or a Katie. "She's not perky. And she's not a mother—being a mother is important for Morning. Once a woman goes through a pregnancy and has a baby in full view of the public"—as Lunden and Pauley had—"everybody feels she's her best friend. Diane seemed unattainable. Was she too glamorous? Too sophisticated? Too 'aspirational'? Viewers could be turned off by that."

But once the small claque in the meeting laid out every single downside—every last negative—a funny thing happened. "We went from, 'Holy shit, no way! There's *no* way you risk Diane Sawyer!' to realizing that she fit most of the criteria better than anyone else." After all, "Diane had unimpeachable journalist credentials. She had deep curiosity, experience, name recognition. She had interviewed the most important people in the world. And we had just come off of two people"—Newman and McRee—"where we couldn't really brag about anything they'd covered."

By meeting's end, Diane had emerged as the surprising choice—the risk-all-to-gain-all choice.

Why? Because there was a war going on and ABC was the clear underdog. That war was Morning, and ABC was desperate to topple the undisputed Empress of Morning.

And that was Katie Couric.

CHAPTER FIVE

America's Sweetheart to Premature Widow

Katie: 1989 to 1998

THE YEARS 1989 TO 1991 were very busy and very lucky for Katie Couric—though luck, in her case, was often the meeting of serendipity (and others' bad fortune) with an ingrained-but-struggled-with cluster of personal qualities that she managed to turn to her advantage.

Katie's marriage to Jay Monahan was fresh. The couple had bought a historic house in McLean, Virginia, where she was getting used to his neat freak ways, and he to her messiness. (Katie initially resisted her ex-roommate Wendy Walker's advice and didn't hire a maid. Husband and wife had a big blowout one night when Jay found one of Katie's cereal bowls—full of hairs from their Persian cat, Frank—under his pillow.) And she was adjusting to Jay's participation in Civil War battle reenactments, which had initially sounded "really weird" to her, she admitted to journalist Lisa DePaulo. "I used to tease him about it," she said. "'If you think I'm gonna be following you around in a hoop skirt and snood, you've got another think coming.'" Reassured that Jay wasn't one of those fanatics who thought the war was still going on and who "urinate on their uniform buttons to make them look old," Katie settled on thinking of him as a "Civil War scholar."

Jay was a rising criminal defense lawyer for Williams and Connolly. Katie was still covering the Pentagon, and in December 1989 she flew to

Panama to report on the American invasion to depose dictator Manuel Noriega.

The following summer and fall, her beat got even hotter: Saddam Hussein had invaded and annexed Kuwait on August 2, 1990. Five days later, Operation Desert Shield commenced, with American forces, heading a UN-authorized coalition of thirty-three other countries (many only symbolic participants), landing in Saudi Arabia to prepare to defend Kuwait. Operation Desert Shield turned into Operation Desert Storm in January 1991; in less than two months of aerial bombardments and ground attacks, the mostly U.S. forces beat back Iraq's incursion. The United States was supported by Saudi Arabia and Egypt. Notwithstanding that the presence of U.S. troops in the country that housed the sacred shrines at Mecca and Medina became a purported final instigation for Osama bin Laden, never since has a war on Arab soil been so casualty- and hate-free for America.

When Katie arrived in Saudi Arabia during Desert Shield, it was shockingly novel to be a female American reporter in the world's most sternly fundamentalist Muslim country. CNN had sent an all-female team, with whom Katie and her NBC crew shared quarters and swapped tales. The three-woman CNN posse included a young reporter with whom Katie had briefly overlapped in Atlanta—Christiane Amanpour—as well as Maria Fleet, a sound editor who had personally liked Katie at CNN, had found her eminently talented, and had been "irked that they called her a lightweight and not a serious journalist" there. Katie was wittily "self-deprecating" during her time in Saudi Arabia, Fleet recalls, quipping that merely enduring the assignment raised a female reporter's status. "As a woman, you come here as a six and you leave as a ten," Katie said. Katie was actually in the early stages of pregnancy, but she hadn't revealed it to anyone—she hadn't wanted this assignment scotched.

The Gulf War was an unexpected star-making occasion: CNN went from ridiculed Atlanta second-rater to the leader of international television news broadcasting. It would also catapult the career of Katie's one-time CNN-mate, Christiane Amanpour. As for Katie, coming back to D.C.

for Christmas as a "ten" instead of a "six" advanced her lifelong effort to be taken seriously. The generosity of her senior NBC reporting partner at the Pentagon, Fred Francis, helped as well. "Fred didn't look at her as competition," Katie's career mentor Don Browne says. "He looked at her as, 'This is great.' He was very supportive. We were in the middle of attacking Iraq. She was really coming on strong. The Pentagon was a hot story." Accident though it was, "Katie's timing was spectacular, and *she* was spectacular."

By now, Katie actually had a dual role—Pentagon correspondent and *Today*'s national correspondent. Her duties expanded when Don Browne, who had a particular interest in diversity, became executive news director at NBC in New York. Among his hires were soon-to-be-stars Deborah Roberts, Elizabeth Vargas, and Ann Curry. He'd kept an eye on Katie, remaining a sounding board as Katie took over the Pentagon position. "Katie and I were now in regular touch—we were like old home week," he says.

Tim Russert believed in Katie's potential, too. "She was articulate, direct, and there was a real wholesome appeal," Russert said. But Browne was especially sensitive to the way Katie, like many outside-the-box strivers, tended to imitate some imagined mainstream newscaster "ideal." At the Pentagon, and before that, "Katie was trying to replicate the traditional white male journalist role, and for her to be credible at it, she had to shut down the very thing that eventually made her great," he says. "The on-camera part of Katie was *not* Katie. Katie as a *person* was incredibly infectious, funny, charismatic. But it all shut down" when the microphone was in hand and the network camera was running. The striking difference between the real Katie and the performing Katie made Browne believe that her long ordeal of being rejected could potentially work to her benefit—she still had that off-duty raggedy realness; it hadn't been ironed out. "The fact that she *didn't* anchor is the greatest blessing!" he stresses, looking back now. "When you anchor, you become manufactured—you're told how to dress, how to turn, how to speak." Anchors from midsized markets looking for better jobs often didn't get them, Browne says (he'd nixed more than a few himself) because they were too smooth, too undistinctive. "Katie never got manufactured. She had a nat-uralness, a rough-around-the-edges charm that was authentic and not polished."

If only he could find someone who could bring out her true self *on* the air.

A SHIFTING TIDE at NBC News would help. In midsummer 1989, the division was in woeful shape. *Nightly News* seemed permanently stuck in third place, with Tom Brokaw limping behind Peter Jennings at ABC and Dan Rather at CBS. The network hadn't managed to launch a truly suc-cessful newsmagazine, despite many efforts. And perhaps most direly, in terms of advertising dollars, the *Today* show had fallen to number three in the ratings. "It's a little counterintuitive, but we had weak ratings in a key demographic: young women," admits Jane Pauley, who'd epitomized that very cohort throughout her long tenure. "I'd been on the show twelve years." It was logical that they'd want someone new.

There was a rising-star contender: Deborah Norville, a Georgia native who had made a mark for herself on TV news in Chicago. Jack Welch, the bombastic chairman of General Electric, which now owned NBC, "was a huge fan of Debbie Norville's when she did her early news," NBC's *News at Sunrise,* Pauley says. At twenty-eight (Pauley, by contrast, was thirty-nine), Norville had a cool, blond, pageant-level beauty that was a slightly more upscale version of the local-anchor paradigm. She was also a solid journalist. Jane Pauley graciously (at least from this distance of years) concedes that "Debbie was fabulous. She was gorgeous, smart, ambitious—and a very good reporter."

So Norville was tapped to replace Pauley. But *how* she was worked into the *Today* show mix was unnerving at best. She was "pushed in," Pauley says. "Debbie did *not* push herself in—it was not her doing. But it was done"—by the network producers and executives—"in *such* a ham-handed, ham-*fisted,* awful way." One day, September 5, 1989, Norville, hired as *Today*'s newsreader, suddenly appeared on the couch next to Pauley and Gumbel, as if she were a third anchor.

"I felt blindsided," Jane says. "Nobody had warned me, and it struck many viewers as, 'Oh, my God, does that look awkward or *what?*'" Worse, it seemed like a slow-motion dismissal notice. Jane says, "I recognized what was happening: My role was being diminished significantly, in a way that would absolve NBC from having to" be explicit about it. "I would just be allowed to sit further and further in the background—and then I'd be gone."

Every Tuesday, from early September through mid-October, Jane Pauley fought with her bosses to let them "settle" her contract. She wanted to have an on-air celebration of Deborah's new role as her replacement, and then she would leave the show while collecting the salary that NBC was contractually obligated to pay her. Pauley couldn't stand the humiliation—or that the tabloids were turning the episode into a catfight. But NBC, she says, thought that paying her to leave would set a bad precedent, even though it had been done when Stone Phillips left *Dateline*. Then Pauley got an idea: She would host an evening newsmagazine, justifying her payment while being able to exit *Today*. NBC went for the plan. (The show would be called *Real Life with Jane Pauley*, and it would end up being short-lived.) So on October 27, 1989, the baton was passed: An emotional Jane Pauley handed Deborah Norville the alarm clock that Barbara Walters had given her fourteen years earlier.

On January 1990 Norville officially became Bryant Gumbel's coanchor.

NBC tried to muster optimism about Norville. Dick Ebersol, the senior VP in charge of *Today*, called Norville's arrival an "appeal to women" (he regretted that word choice after she was wrongly smeared in the media as being the young encroacher on a much-loved female veteran) and touted her "unique talents in being able to think on her feet and project cohesiveness"—vague and less than rousing praise. But network spin didn't matter. What mattered was how Norville would be welcomed by the viewers—and by the notoriously challenging Bryant Gumbel.

Gumbel was a tough partner for a rookie female. "Bryant was the only person in television who said, 'I don't care if you like me; I care if you respect me,'" says someone who's worked closely with him. "He didn't pander to the audience. He would never have a Sally Field moment—'You like me! You like me!' He was a different type of guy." Indeed, months earlier, a memo written by Gumbel in which he'd spoken ill of weatherman Willard Scott had been leaked to the press. Gumbel didn't apologize for it.

As the winter of 1990 turned to spring, it was clear that the viewers weren't warming to Norville—and neither was Gumbel. Panicked producers rushed in likable former baseball star Joe Garagiola as a third on the couch to try to build camaraderie. It didn't work. "Implosion" was a word staffers now whispered in the 30 Rock halls.[*]

Meanwhile, Browne, with Dick Ebersol and recently hired NBC News president Michael Gartner (who had had a background in serious newspaper editing), had been considering Katie for Norville's old job as *Today* show newsreader. During one of Katie's visits to New York to meet with the executives about the newsreader job, she stopped in first to see Kathleen Lobb, who was working in an office in Rockefeller Plaza, right near NBC. The two women were practically jumping up and down. "For both of us, it was, 'Is this *really* happening?'" Kathleen says. They remembered Katie's hubristic words in Miami: *I want Jane Pauley's job*. Then, after meeting with the executives, Katie ran into Jane herself. "Katie stopped me in the hall and asked some advice. I don't know what I said, and I doubt she remembers it, either," Pauley says. "But there was a certain *inevitability*; I just *felt* it. She was a go-getter, and she had all the ingredients."

It was decided that, instead of becoming newsreader (Faith Daniels got that job), Katie would become *Today*'s national correspondent— "which meant they wanted to get her on the air a lot, and have her travel

---

*Morning show audiences become so loyally attached to their hosts that even the most popular shows are punished for what seems like a cruel expulsion. In 2012, when Ann Curry left the *Today* show—with a teary good-bye—to be replaced by Savannah Guthrie, fans took out their anger on Matt Lauer, who had always enjoyed huge popularity on the show that Katie's fourteen-year tenure made unbeatable. As a result, *Today*'s ratings plummeted and *GMA* grabbed the number one Morning spot. In April 2013, *Today*'s public relations train crashed when it was revealed that *Today* had essentially removed Curry. The term that was used on NBC in 1991 resurfaced in 2013: implosion.

and do stories," says the then young man who also bumped into her during one of her earliest NBC interviews. It's hard to overestimate how important not merely the hallway meeting but everything after it would be. That young man was Jeff Zucker.

Jeff Zucker had been Pauley's intern—the one intern she'd insisted *Today* hold on to. Then, at twenty-four, he was a *Today* junior producer. He was nicknamed "Doogie Howser" because he resembled the sitcom character. People thought him talented, bold, and brash—"hyperkinetic" is a word some used. He still vividly recalls that chance meeting in the hall with Katie. "I was wearing white Keds sneakers," Zucker says, and she—this young stranger, striding along with her out-of-towner hair and in her corny dress-for-success suit—"completely made fun of me for wearing them! She *totally* teased me." He was struck, as if by lightning, with her brazenness, her brio. If she had so much sassy, ad-libby confidence in an office hallway, imagine how that would translate on air.

"So what happened was, I raised my hand to be her producer," Jeff continues. "I wanted to do something new. And she seemed like the fresh new thing."

When Zucker raised his hand, Don Browne called on him at once. From the day Katie became NBC national correspondent, on June 11, 1990, in spot after spot—reports, promos, live tags—Jeff Zucker guided her from the control booth. "We began seeing a transformation taking place in Katie," Browne says. "She was growing before our eyes." Katie Couric and Jeff Zucker would, simply, be one of the most formidable news star/ producer combinations of the last twenty-five years of television.

Zucker explains their magic synergy in an understated way: "We were both young and eager and ambitious—and we were in the right place at the right time. I had a sense of what she was really good at: being herself, being natural without trying to play the role of 'anchorperson.' She was the girl next door who wasn't afraid to ask the questions that everybody wanted to ask. So I told her to do that. I saw she could be great. I think she saw in me someone who gave her confidence. She sensed I was there to help her look great, that I was completely looking out for her. She knew I had her back."

In just weeks, Browne got a sense that "Katie and Jeff were the perfect complement to each other, the perfect couple. Jeff had great instincts. He recognized the hidden talent in Katie. Katie gave him what he didn't have": a chance to pull an underutilized personality out of a pat mold, to bring out the essence of "the *off*-camera Katie we all loved." And "Jeff gave her what she didn't have": a total advocate—the energy and loyalty of a gifted, hungry, very young producer. "He saw the bigger picture of what she could be. He fought for great stories for her," Browne says.

The synergy between the two was even greater—and, in a sense, perhaps less innocent—than people thought. Jeff was Katie's producer when she went to Saudi Arabia during Desert Shield. Someone who worked closely with the two of them daily reported to a colleague that when Katie and Jeff were together, "it was like no one else was in the room—I was invisible. Katie and Jeff spent every minute—their entire stay in the Gulf War—planning to take over the *Today* show. It was a very clear plan between Jeff and Katie."

Not surprisingly, between her Pentagon stand-ups, her reports from exotic countries, and her increasing national correspondent spots, Katie was now getting such visibility that Jay's best friend and Williams and Connolly colleague David Kiernan kiddingly suggested that he change his phone listing from Jay Monahan to Jay Couric. "My husband is traditional, but he's proud of me, so he was amused by that," Katie said. "Traditional," "proud," "amused": Was there a hint of possible crisis looming in the marriage? Kiernan's joke may not have been that funny to Jay or Katie.

In January, Katie was asked to sit in for Norville during Norville's maternity leave. "It was exciting, but it was obviously complicated because Katie was pregnant herself"—at the end of her first trimester, Katie's friend Kathleen Lobb recalls. "She was living in a rental apartment on Third Avenue in the Sixties. I remember going there and hanging out and reading baby books with her. It was definitely a lot to contend with. But she and Jay both were, 'Let's just *do* it!' They were *determined*." Katie accepted the offer to substitute. It was like a dress rehearsal.

Deborah Norville's two-month maternity leave started in February

1991; Katie was in the "And sitting in for" slot. Weekday mornings she had to meet the NBC car downstairs at five a.m. Just as it had been for Pauley and Lunden and Norville, morning sickness was *not* an option. Being completely alert despite the expectant mother's prohibition of coffee was a necessity. Her hair was the same short mop-top that had been practical for spur-of-the-moment trips to Panama and Saudi Arabia—she had no time to cultivate the more "feminine," beauty queen mane of Pauley and Norville. Her pregnancy-pudgy face beneath the bob gave her the look of a jaunty tomboy. (One TV critic would speak of her "sandlot grit.") Her clothes were not chic, and her awkward, end-of-first-trimester body lines—when you don't "show"; you just look fat—made them less so. *"Be yourself,"* Jeff Zucker exhorted. "Ask the questions everybody wants to ask."

Each weekend either Jay commuted to New York or Katie went back to Virginia. On top of everything else, they had just bought an eighteenth-century farmhouse in the Shenandoah Valley, as a country home, in addition to their McLean house. There Katie and Jay managed to entertain friends on weekends. While Katie pored over research for the upcoming week's interviews and Jay practiced for his trials, they attempted to relax. He indulged his love of riding horses and playing the piano. Everyone played board games and the word-association game "salad bowl," a kind of variation on charades (still a Katie favorite); they watched fireworks and went apple or strawberry picking, depending on the season. "Katie was more the cutup and Jay was more the straight guy, completely, but they had a lot of fun together," says Mandy Locke, who had just begun dating David Kiernan.

Deborah Norville gave birth to a son on February 27. A month later she was photographed in *People* magazine, breast-feeding the infant. Breast-feeding was certainly respectable; still, one network executive huffed to *People* that Deborah's breast-feeding photos were "self-serving and embarrassing" to NBC, driving home the priggishness of the brass— or else exaggerating what they might have thought would be acceptable-sounding outrage as a pretext to get rid of her. Soon after, Norville announced that she would be spending a year at home with her baby.

Katie had bested her.

"Katie was *so* good," it was decided that "Deborah just wouldn't come back," Don Browne says. "When we saw Katie with Bryant, and Jeff in the control room, we *knew* we'd found the answer." The realization came in rapid-fire stages. "First it was disbelief. Then it was excitement. And then it was, '*Holy crap!*'"

AT EXACTLY SEVEN A.M. on Friday, April 5, 1991, *Today*'s rainbow/sun logo and familiar staccato theme music backdropped a new intro, one devoid of Norville's name: "This is *Today*, with Bryant Gumbel, Katherine Couric, and Joe Garagiola." (During her substituting for Norville, Katie had been announced as "Katherine" but called "Katie." Soon it would be only "Katie.")

When the music stopped, Gumbel was blunt: "In case you haven't gotten the message, Katie is now a permanent fixture up here, a member of our family, an especially welcome one. Deborah Norville is not." (The unfortunate ordering of some of the phrases may or may not have been a Freudian slip.) "We had some good times here, and we wish all the best to Deborah and Karl and their new baby. Katie, welcome aboard."

"Thanks. I'm thrilled to be here," Katie responded. "And I guess that means you're stuck with me." Pause. "Or maybe I'm stuck with *you*."

Neither Deborah nor Jane would have sassed Gumbel in her second sentence as coanchor, but Katie was clearly able to handle him, right from the start. In fact, Katie delivered a lot of impact with that rejoinder: She proved she could handle Gumbel. She slyly indicated that Gumbel's remark about Norville may *not* have been unintentional. And she showcased her improvisational skills.

But that was just her opening salvo in her fight against Morning's sexism—more was to come. "Katie was the first woman to demand equal treatment in terms of what story she could do," says TV news content critic Andrew Tyndall, whose *Tyndall Report* is considered essential reading within the industry. "She would still do the soft stories, but she demanded Gumbel do an equal number of the soft stories and that she would get an equal number of hard stories." As Katie has explained: "Not to sound too Helen Reddy–ish, but I felt I had an obligation . . . for the women who were watching, to have an equal role on the show." Tyndall continues: "This was a breakthrough—the first time on a morning program that there were no sex-role stereotypes in the assignments between a man and a woman." The condition "was understood when she took the job."

Indeed, one of Katie's most pugnacious interviews—and the one that she still calls her most unpleasant—was among her first: David Duke, the Ku Klux Klan leader who was trying to tone down his image and run for public office in Louisiana. "It was very contentious," she'd later say. "I read his quotes back and he denied them." Still, Katie pushed back at the prevaricating racist: "You said, 'I think the Jewish people have been a "blight" and they deserve to go into the "ash bin of history." '" When Duke tried to dissemble, Katie leaned in and firmly said: "Well, that was only six years ago." She took Duke on, quote by quote, pressing him as he grew angry. Some media critics actually thought she came down too hard on him.

Katie's refusal to be ghettoized in fluff threw Gumbel just slightly off his game. He was "fascinated" with Katie, Tom Brokaw surmised. An un-named "industry source" expounded to the *American Journalism Review*: "[Katie] comes in a package that's a little deceiving at first. I think Bryant [now] understands that he is going to have a female there who is competition for him. Jane had to sit there and take a lot of grief, take a back seat and not do a lot of solid interviews. This isn't the case with Katie." "Zucker helped, too," Don Browne says. "Jeff could manage Bryant. Bryant is very strong, but he needed a strong hand, and Jeff and Bryant got along well." Zucker was made executive producer of *Today* at age twenty-five. Thus, the show now had a perky woman (and virtually every article written about Katie in those first few years included the *p*-word, often using the protestation "Don't call her perky!"),* who, from the start, held her own

---

* "It's not the word itself so much as the way it sounds that's so ridiculous," Katie ultimately said. "I looked it up in the dictionary recently, and the definition I can live with: 'briskly self-confident, jaunty.' That's not so bad."

with a partner known to seize impatiently, even contemptuously, on any perceived weakness in a woman. That strikingly *"tough"* quality that CNN's tough guy Ted Kavanau had found in Katie was now serving her with another tough man.

KATIE'S RELATIONSHIP with Bryant would grow thornier as the years wore on. But at the very beginning of their time together, "Katie did a lot for Bryant—softening him up, making fun of him," says one who worked closely with them at a high level. "He became a lot better hosting with Katie." Did Bryant acknowledge her positive effect on his screen persona? "No," the colleague says, but then adds, on the basis of long experience in the format, "When you have two people on a show, you have an actor and you have a reactor. Bryant was the actor—he drove the show. Katie was the reactor." That's how they started out. As the show's reactor, "you wait your turn," this television veteran says, emphatically.

As her methodological talks with Zucker in Saudi Arabia indicated, Katie Couric was not one to wait her "turn." She hadn't waited when she was an inexperienced beginner pushing hard against closed doors, so she certainly wouldn't wait now, with a prestigious perch and with the wind at her back.

And what wind it was! It is hard to overtout the splash that Katie made—how naturally she took to the role of *Today* female anchor, how well she updated it, how quickly the public seized on her as an intimate. Fans sent her christening gowns for her baby, fretted over her hair ("You have it puffed up on the left side, then combed at a straight forty-five-degree angle," one fan wrote) and her clothes ("That multicolored outfit you wore on March 12—it was gawd-awful," another complained) like busybody aunts who only want the best. Media critics gushed ("She hit *Today* like a meteor; suddenly she's the savior, just by punching Bryant Gumbel's arm": the *Washington Post*) and gushed ("a Cinderella ascent!": *American Journalism Review*) and gushed some more ("She skyrocketed right to the top": *Redbook*). And *really* gushed: "The hard part is finding a flaw. She's the everything gal. She's an apple a day. She's real, she's natural, she's totally at home on the air. She's a godsend, that's what she is. Thank you, God": the *Washington Post*'s Tom Shales again. More soberly, astutely—and archly—Bruce Weber limned her in the *New York Times* as:

> petite and tomboyish, pretty but not glamorous, cheerfully collegiate . . . conversationally deft, ever vigilant for the opportunity to quip and gibe. On the air this translates into a precocious competence, a crossbreed of authority and chatty hip: the video offspring of, say, Walter Cronkite and Martha Quinn on MTV. She carries on impressively in the important world of adults, somehow without appearing to be important, or, for that matter, adult.

IN THE NOW TIME-HONORED tradition of Pauley, Lunden, and Norville, Katie lumbered to the end of her pregnancy on the air. "It was slightly bizarre gaining thirty pounds in front of millions of people, but I guess it's fine as long as you don't pose on the cover of *Vanity Fair*," she remarked, referring to Demi Moore's notorious nude shot (and demonstrating, as she would in every introductory interview, a skill with one-liners that could match a late-night TV host). She gave birth to a daughter, Elinor Tully Monahan (Tully was a name on her mother's side), on July 23, 1991. She and Jay were elated. After a two-month maternity leave, Tom Shales hosanna'd her September 9 return to the show as "brighten[ing] the program by several thousand watts," going on to say that "Couric puts [*Today*] blissfully over the top," and adding that "perhaps no one is quite so deliriously ecstatic about Couric's return as NBC News, which is otherwise in terrible shape and which hopes the wildly likable co-anchor will help restore *Today* to its long-lost first place among morning programs." Shales noted that, on Katie's first day back, she interviewed Defense Secretary Dick Cheney and "cranky legend Katharine Hepburn," the latter one of Katie's favorite interviews of all time.

A month after she returned from maternity leave, Anita Hill's testimony at Clarence Thomas's Supreme Court confirmation hearings thrust the coanchors onto opposite sides of that bruising national debate, which was blaring from TV sets in public places, stunning the country with surreally vulgar talk (pubic hairs on Coke bottles?) that was delivered with prissy matter-of-factness by staid business-suited witnesses, starchy congresspeople, and straight-faced anchors: a crazy eye-rubber of a televised circus.

Bryant Gumbel was not merely a golf-playing man's man who scoffed at "women's lib"; he was also (though this was rarely remarked upon) a highly accomplished black man who, as such, had reason to be angered on behalf of another highly accomplished black man who was calling the testimony mounted against him a "high-tech lynching" of an "uppity Negro" who dared speak his mind. Almost any other brand-new white female coanchor might have paused at the edge of such sensitive territory and been reticent to support the feminists' freshly minted heroine Anita Hill. But Katie pushed right in, and she and Bryant had on-air exchanges that provocatively strained the niceness quotient of Morning.

During her first year, Katie rigorously interviewed conservative columnist turned token presidential candidate Pat Buchanan (accusing him of being on an "ego trip") and serious third-party candidate Ross Perot (he bristled at her relentless questions). She had the first interview after the Gulf War with General Norman Schwarzkopf—conducting it in Saudi Arabia. It helped that she was perceived as cute and harmless by older gentlemen who wandered into her web with their expectations low. She even crowed about this convenient fact during one of her earliest, and boldest, triumphs: a *gotcha* interview with President George H. W. Bush. In a very real sense, this interview was the equivalent of Diane's interview with her former boss Richard Nixon, and one that Christiane would soon conduct with Bill Clinton. In each case, the young newswoman came into a conversation with a president and was either underestimated (Katie with Bush), or unknown (Christiane with Clinton), or asked hard questions of a man who had expected, instead, loyalty and deference (Diane with Nixon). In each case, the great man was caught unawares and the reporter got the goods.

The triumph unfolded this way: Katie was at the White House to be taken on a tour by First Lady Barbara Bush—a tiresome "women anchor's" chestnut of an assignment. *Today*'s cameras captured a peppy Katie in red, a dowagerlike Mrs. Bush in deep blue—and, midtalk, the casually attired president, stopping by merely "to congratulate Barbara" on her fine disquisition about the antiques. Seeing an opening, Katie pounced on a surprised George Bush with substantive questions—which he answered—about the Iran-Contra scandal, about his Democratic opponent, Governor Bill Clinton of Arkansas, and about much more. Katie was so unrelenting that Mrs. Bush resorted to pulling her husband away. "Aren't I great?" Katie couldn't resist zinging the president. "I'm one of these less contentious reporters who can convince you to stick around and talk with me because I'm so easy." The joke was on him—and everyone who'd ever underestimated her. Katie later said of this interview, "I was trying to prove my manhood."

Receiving Katie's transmission in real time, Zucker made a brazen decision: He withheld commercials to run her grilling of the cornered chief executive, uninterrupted, for a stunning nineteen minutes. At the end of the segment, "it was eight forty-five in the morning, so we weren't going out for drinks" to celebrate, Zucker says, "but there was a sense in the White House driveway, where we met up afterward, that that had been an incredible moment. It was a very significant event in Katie's career—it made people see that she was able to react to any situation on her feet. And it helped cement our relationship." That interview "made" Katie, says an NBC colleague. "No question that she saw the opportunity and just went off script. That's perfectly in character with her being curious, inquisitive, loud, and boisterous."

Morning is the hardest of all the TV formats because it necessitates dozens of polar swings, from silliness to seriousness, all crisply sequenced and authoritatively delivered within right-down-to-the-second-tight time spurts. It involves interviewing minimally prepped guests—most of them, TV naifs—economically, and live. Being a Morning anchor is like being an actor playing a half dozen different characters in a two-hour-long one-man stage show. Katie just had a knack for it, and its built-in ironies matched her wit. Of sharp-right-turning from saxophonist Branford Marsalis to a report on domestic violence, she alliterated: "From Branford to battered women, this is the life I have chosen. Or maybe it's the life that's chosen me." In the rush of magazine interviews that the NBC publicist booked for her, America's new darling, she played along, polishing her girl-next-door brand, with remarks that some regarded as contrived and calculated and others deemed authentic: "My friends call me the Energizer bunny—I keep going and going and going." "I guess I'm wholesome." "I think I'm attractive, but not *too* attractive." She *liked* the attention. She *liked* being famous.

But there was a price. Katie was a traditionally raised woman with a traditional husband, and as Ellie began crawling and walking, something felt not right about having a long-distance marriage—her nights in New York with baby and nanny, her piles of research for the next morning, her Lean Cuisine, and her eight-thirty bedtime. And the separation was rough on Jay. "It's really hard," she'd muse. "I miss him terribly during the week. And he misses me, too. It's harder for him, because I have Ellie with me. He really misses her." Guilt and unease bobbed beneath the surface of these peppy interviews.

Mandy Locke and David Kiernan spent time with Jay during the week in D.C. "Fortunately for Katie, Jay had a very demanding job," Mandy says. "He was very busy during the week, which helps when you're missing someone. But on the weekend, when I'd see them together, it was mostly regroup time—let's hang out in our sweatpants all weekend, we'll go to the farmers' market, get together as a family, 'cause it's hard." As Katie herself told an interviewer, "It was hard enough [managing the two careers] when we were together. But, now, being separated, and dealing with the whole head trip of this job, it's *really* hard." "Hard" became a theme. Their commuter marriage *was* "hard," Katie's childhood friend Betsy Howell says. "But Katie respected the fact that Jay had his job down here and needed to stay. She made sure she respected his choices and life."

"Sometimes Jay and I will sit back and kind of evaluate what's been going on," Katie said during this time, "and if it feels like my life is starting to lose its balance, he'll call my attention to it." *He'll* call *my* attention:

It was *he* who noticed the preoccupying whirlwind that Katie's new role had become. It was *he* who had brought it to *her* attention.

Katie, too, would fret over her "instant fame thing." She was careful to say, in 1992, "My husband is terrifically supportive and very secure in himself," but then she added, with a candor rare for women in the public eye, "But sometimes he'd like to get more attention. I wish he *could*." She and Jay would be walking down the street, or they'd enter a restaurant for a quiet meal, and people would look at her in that new, excited way, and "he'll say, 'Your RF'—recognition factor—'is very high today.'" She summed it up: "We are dealing with a lot."

Part of "a lot" might have been the disorientation of a woman in a situation for which her *Leave It to Beaver* childhood, to use her expression, left her unprepared. Elinor Couric had been a stay-at-home mom in a community of stay-at-home moms. All the cheerleader exhortations of these now entrenched new times—the "You've come a long way, baby!" of the sixties, the "I am woman, hear me roar" of the early seventies, and those that followed—could not make up for the fact that she had never, in her childhood, seen this brave new way of being a wife and mother modeled. "It's a constant struggle," she said, "to make sure I'm not becoming too immersed in this show to spend enough time with my family."

The early nineties was a beat before the two-career "commuter marriage" was widespread enough, and sufficiently lauded as a "trend," for its inconvenienced practitioners to feel at least a safety-in-numbers consolation. It was a decade before the phenomenon of upper-middle-class women outearning their husbands was too common to make men feel ashamed.[*] And it was two decades before *many* women did outearn their husbands and before graduate school enrollments by gender suggested that this might be a persistent fact of American life. Katie was a hugely ambitious,

---

[*]Katie, who had started at *Today* with a salary of about $500,000, used every opportunity to procure raises commensurate with her contribution to the network. When in 1994 a threatened Roone Arledge boosted Diane Sawyer's compensation to $4 million, Katie pushed for, and got, a healthy though undisclosed raise. By the end of her tenure at *Today* Katie had a four-year contract worth $60 million to $65 million.

aggressive young woman in terms of her work, but in terms of her personal life she was poised on the front line of a vanguard she hadn't sought or wanted. When she'd looked at Cassie Mackin ten years earlier, she had always seen a split, a quid pro quo, a warning: Ambition and success could stanch or jeopardize a woman's personal life. Not every ambitious young newswoman would have been so alert to that, but Katie was.

At some point in 1993, Jay, almost inevitably, gave up his position with Williams and Connolly and moved to New York so the family could be together. This was not a small sacrifice. But in New York, in the Central Park West apartment he and Katie and Ellie now shared, he kept his life stubbornly Virginian: He started with a new law firm, Hunton and Williams, that was based in Richmond; he began writing a history of a place—the Shenandoah Valley—that he adored; and he kept up his love of horseback riding by going to the Claremont Stables, just off Central Park, early every morning. Clearly, he was almost touchingly holding fast to the distinctive identity he had crafted for himself, as if to proclaim that he would *not* be subsumed in his wife's persona.

Magazine articles appeared mentioning that "Katie was the main breadwinner." None of this could have been easy. Still, Jay continued to play the role of the somewhat courtly man of taste. "He was great; he would teach me about antiques," says Lori Beecher, who had just started as Katie's associate producer and would become one of her confidantes. "I was interested in learning about antiques, and Jay would help me. And if I was moving, I would show him an apartment" under consideration. Lori relied on Jay's educated opinion and advice. "He was very supportive and kind and easy to get along with."

But toward Katie, not so much. As Katie whirled into greater and greater celebrity, Jay was judgmental—sternly vigilant about her character and providing, as ever, an important corrective to her disorganization, says a man connected to her work at NBC. "Jay was in charge," this man says. "She respected him. He knew her before she was a star. And he ran it"—their life, her schedule—"with a hard fist. He didn't take any bullshit. Made sure she showed up. Made sure she was disciplined. Made sure she was honest." This man adds, bluntly, "Katie is not organized enough to do a show like the *Today* show. Professionally, Katie did a lot for Jay," imminently getting him into lucrative TV-commentating arrangements. "But he made it so she could function." Another man, a soon-to-be network head, muses, "It's always struck me: These women who are so strong, they still need a guy. They tend to have one guy who's key to anything they do." Clearly, some would dispute this statement, but for Katie, Jay Monahan clearly did fulfill real needs.

Katie consolidated her style and her power throughout the early nineties, partnering with Jeff and personally going after competitive stories. "There have always been bookers, so it's not like the 'get' thing was invented by us," Jeff says. "But Katie was incredibly willing to get on the phone, to get on a plane, to put herself out there—to convince these people to talk to her." (Later, when she went to *GMA*, Diane would be stunned that her famously unfailing charm was one-upped by Katie's and *Today*'s practiced ability to woo talent for Morning.) She also produced her own taped pieces—turning her interview with Woody Allen into a walk through Central Park and her inquisition of Paul Newman into a game of pool. These were a toe dip into the full-scale theatrical capers that would later seal her brand: flying across Rockefeller Center as Tinkerbell on Halloween, trading places with Jay Leno and hosting *The Tonight Show* for a week, arriving as Nurse Ratched at weatherman Al Roker's house as he was preparing for a medical test.

Toward the end of 1994, Bryant Gumbel renewed his contract for two more years, and when he did, Katie made a tactical error, according to the TV veteran who had dubbed Katie the "reactor" to Bryant's "actor." In this man's view, in a morning show pairing, you, as the reactor, "wait your turn" to try to turn the tables. But, he says, "after Bryant signed that deal, Katie was unable, or unwilling, to wait. So she began to push—for more stories, for bigger stories, more airtime." Broadly hinting at a conflict upon which he declines to elaborate, the man says, "It was *very* unwelcome. It was a very, very sad thing, that she couldn't wait—that she couldn't wait her turn."

But all this talk of "turn" taking sounds so retro and antifeminist. Besides, wasn't Bryant Gumbel the ultimate male chauvinist? This man instantly answers: "*She's* the one who put it [that image of Bryant as the male chauvinist] on the street," fixing his face in the kind of grave stare that wordlessly suggests what Ted Kavanau had said: *She is tough. Katie is not some innocent.* Other women, indeed, have termed Gumbel a male chauvinist. (One who temporarily worked on the show confided that Bryant was very hard for her, as a woman, to work with, and that friendly Willard Scott took the edge off Bryant's condescending coldness.) Katie might have been the one to secure the impression of Gumbel's being a chauvinist, because her spin machine with the press was so good.

Katie had a trusted and experienced live-in nanny named Nancy Poznek, a woman several years older than she, who had previously worked for Mick Jagger and Diana Ross. It is standard practice for members of the household staffs (and often the professional staffs) of celebrities to be required to sign confidentiality agreements, but apparently Katie did not ask Poznek to sign one. She was enormously dependent on the nanny, who did many tasks for Katie, aside from caring for Ellie; thus Poznek observed the Couric-Monahan household at close range, including Katie and Jay's fights, and the incredibly busy life Katie had, sometimes manifest in sloppiness at home. Poznek initially came to Katie's defense when a reader of *People* magazine wrote a letter criticizing Katie for being a partially absent parent—an accusation that is very painful to any working mother and that, of course, is never made about working fathers. Poznek's rebuttal ran in *People*'s October 4, 1993, issue. The letter briefly mentioned the "dilemma of all working mothers," which Katie shared, but declared that—"without hestitation"—Katie "is there for her daughter at the important and not-so-important times in her daily life," giving vivid examples.

But after Nancy did that good deed, the relationship soured. Apparently, Nancy told Katie the negative things Jay had said about her, including his mocking of her fame-inflated ego. For this or other reasons, Katie fired Nancy—"for cause." Nancy retaliated by selling a story about life with Katie to the supermarket tabloid *Star.* It included this unattractive, though hardly damning (in fact, oddly endearing), description of the exhausted morning star for whom neatness was never remotely a habit: "She drinks milk straight from the carton with the refrigerator door hanging open. She eats ice cream and has to be told to wipe the chocolate mustache off her face. She peels her clothes off in one motion and leaves them wherever they land. She's so tired on weekends that sometimes she doesn't bother to bathe."*

Whatever disputes Jay and Katie had—and no one, including Katie, denies that their marriage was fractious during these years—they were committed to each other and wanted one or two more children. In early summer 1995, they were thrilled to learn that Katie was pregnant again. By now Jay was segueing into a new field, and one that directly competed with Katie: He was becoming a legal commentator on television. Criminal defense lawyers were suddenly *celebrities*. The unprecedented phenomenon of the O. J. Simpson case had created a market for lawyer-pundits, who analyzed daily and opined nightly—their patter and makeup, exhortations and arguments as theatrical as those of any TV star. Jay Monahan, handsomer than most, became a commentator on NBC News, MSNBC, and CNBC; that all these networks were divisions of his wife's network must have led to complicated feelings on both of their parts. He became a guest on the show that was the prime minter of criminal-defense-lawyers-as-stars and was the evening watercooler for the O. J.–obsessed: *Geraldo*.

Caroline Couric Monahan, known as Carrie, was born on January 7, 1996. With the birth of her second child, Katie, who herself had two cherished sisters, saw her life move closer to an ideal sealed in childhood. More, everything Katie loved about her husband was thrust into emo-

---

*In 2005, Nancy Poznek was sued for aggravated harassment by her subsequent employer, Carol Feinberg, for writing letters to Feinberg's friends and family (including to Feinberg's young son), imparting negative impressions of Feinberg. The lawsuit claimed the nanny "embarked upon an intentional and malicious campaign to harm, harass, and disparage her." Noting that the plaintiff's free speech rights outweighed the "potential damage to the plaintiff," and that the lack of "face to face interaction between plaintiff and defendant" defrayed the threat of a breach of peace, the judge ruled in favor of Poznek and stanched the lawsuit. *New York Post* reporter Dan Mangan interviewed both Poznek and Feinberg; despite the lawsuit lodged against her by Poznek, Feinberg told Mangan that Poznek had been an excellent nanny.

tional high relief, with the marriage's gnawing complications relievedly and abruptly pushed aside. Katie has remembered the day she and Jay brought the baby home from the hospital, when New York was in the midst of a massive blizzard: "Settling into our warm apartment, [Carrie] was napping with me and Ellie, [who was] then four and a half, while Jay played a Brahms lullaby on the Steinway piano that we had bought each other for our birthdays, which were two days apart. This was deeper and more satisfying than any happiness I'd ever experienced. This was pure, soul-filling contentment."

Still, the marriage "had a lot of problems" at this point, says a then close NBC colleague. "She was becoming an international superstar. It was harder and harder for Jay to control her. All of a sudden everyone knows who you are. You're one of the biggest stars of television, generating five, six, seven hundred million dollars of revenue a year. It is difficult to stay as you were—the perky, wonderful, caring person. Everyone's telling you how great you are, how important you are. It turns your head. Jay tried to turn it back."

During the summer of 1996, not long after returning to the show from her two-month maternity leave, Katie conducted another substantive gotcha interview with a presidential contender. Senator Bob Dole was running against President Bill Clinton, and Dole and his wife, Elizabeth, had written a memoir about their marriage. At the time, their union involving two major careers and no children was unusual (and, in some eyes, laudable) for a late-middle-aged Republican politician. To promote the book, and to try to cut into Clinton's large lead among women voters, they were appearing on *Today.*

Katie's friend Mandy Locke, Elizabeth Dole's deputy press secretary, helped arrange the interview.

Just as she had with George H. W. Bush and Barbara Bush, Katie cut to the chase, going beyond the expected female interviewer niceties to the red meat. Dole had accepted considerable campaign donations from the tobacco industry, and now, in various campaign appearances, he was claiming (in 1996!) that tobacco was not addictive. "I guess what I'm trying to say, Senator, is that some people think, from your comments that you've made of late, that you're being an apologist for the tobacco industry," Katie said. "That somehow they have you in their pocket."

Katie's aggressiveness startled the couple. "Elizabeth Dole kept taking her microphone off and saying, 'I thought we were here to talk about the book,' but Katie kept her cool," Mandy recalls. It was Senator Dole who lost his cool. He angrily accused Katie of being part of the "liberal media," even suggesting that her questions were "violating FCC regulations."

The next day, when the piece aired, Mrs. Dole's main press secretary, Kate Bush, heatedly informed Mandy that the interview most certainly did '*not* [go] well' I was in an awkward position," says Mandy. Then Mandy got a call from one of Katie's assistants, who said, "Hi, I'm just calling because Katie wanted me to make sure you're still talking to her." Mandy laughed then—and she laughs now. "I said, 'Of course I'm still talking to her! She was just doing her job.' She's a serious interviewer. But her gift is, when she gets into these really stressful, high-stakes situations, she injects calm and humor." The next day, having gotten the preliminary "all clear" from Mandy's staffer, Katie called Mandy and, to be doubly sure, asked, "'Are you still talking to me?' She had to put her job first, but she was still concerned about our friendship."

ONE DAY IN OCTOBER, Jeff Zucker walked into Katie's office without the confident élan that he usually projected. His mood surprised Katie— what was this about? Barely three months earlier, Katie had been at Jeff's wedding to Caryn Nathanson, a *Saturday Night Live* executive. They were a happy couple. Jeff had a good life. But his face now projected something very dark. "I remember going to her office to tell her that I had colon cancer," Jeff says. "I was just diagnosed and [had to make plans for] my surgery." He was thirty-one years old.

When he told Katie his news, "she immediately sprang into action and wanted to find the best people to treat this." She made phone call after phone call, to every contact she had in the medical community. "I ended up finding the doctor who treated me on my own," Jeff says, "but she was very eager to help—she jumped in instantly."

Three months into Zucker's long medical ordeal, which included sur-gery and chemotherapy, a sea change came to *Today*: Bryant Gumbel decided to step down after fifteen years. That Katie hadn't "waited her turn" had something to do with his decision. She had become the star, she had Jeff Zucker on her side in many ways, and there was tension between her and Bryant. Although Bryant has claimed that he and Katie never exchanged an uncivil word, Katie is more forthright. "There was a lot of creative tension," she would later say, stagily amending, "Well, there was tension. I don't know how *creative* it was."

The show's newsreader, the smooth, urbane, good-looking yet un-threatening Matt Lauer, took Bryant's place. Lauer, then thirty-nine, the son of a New York businessman, had spent his postcollege years following the standard television career path: stints in a series of small and medium markets—Richmond, Providence, Boston, Philadelphia—then landing at NBC in New York, where he eagerly plugged holes by substituting and weekend-anchoring for Morning, newsmagazine, and news, as well as newsreading on *Today*. "Now *Katie* was the actor and Matt was the reactor," says the NBC veteran who'd first mentioned those terms of art. "Eventually, it would come full circle: Matt would not 'wait *his* turn.' What goes around comes around."

But at the outset, the big difference between Katie and Matt was in punctuality. Allison Gollust, then a *Today* publicist, says, "Matt left his house at the same exact time every day—four forty-five a.m. He got in the car. It took six minutes to drive to the studio. He'd be in the studio at three minutes to five. He liked having that time between five and seven to be in his dressing room and his office. Katie, on the other hand, liked to get there at the very last minute. She was more of a six-fifteen type of girl." Some say that Jay made certain that six fifteen was the absolute *latest* she left.

Shortly after Matt replaced Bryant, Katie scored another coup: an in-terview with Palestine Liberation Organization leader Yasir Arafat. She and her producers flew to D.C. for the scheduled meeting, but when Arafat didn't show, Katie rounded everyone up for a tension-relieving photo. Re-calls one of the people in attendance, "So we all got into the picture—the producers, the crew, the cameramen, and Katie—and it was Katie's idea to have us all pulling our hair out. It was very Katie: '*Aahhh!* What am I gonna do?' Making the best of the situation."

The interview finally took place a few days later, back in New York. "Katie asked a lot of tough questions, which made [Arafat and his minders] uncomfortable," says one witness, of the interview that was also being covered by Lisa DePaulo of *George* magazine. At one point Arafat screamed at Katie, "Lies! Big lies!" "Then tell us what the truth is, Chairman Arafat," Katie said sweetly. "Ask your government to tell you the truth!" he retorted. Even the State Department observer could tell the chairman did not like, or expect, the question. When it was all over, Katie said, "Thank you, Chairman. I enjoyed talking to you. Now get some rest."

Arafat said, "Katie, I am sorry I got angry."

"Hey, that's okay," she informed the head of the PLO. "I can take it."

Katie and Jay had traded their Shenandoah Valley country house for a beautiful spread in the horse country of Millbrook, New York, a two-hour drive from Manhattan. They loved the house and were able to grab some peace there, away from the attention of the city. Mandy Locke, who would soon be engaged to David Kiernan, thought the weekends in Millbrook were magical, more relaxing than those at the Shenandoah Valley house. Everyone would sing show tunes—"*any* show tunes; Katie loved them all," Mandy says. (A number of years later, when asked what she would be if not a newscaster, Katie unhesitatingly answered, "lounge singer," and during a "dream jobs" segment on *Today*, she sang with Tony Bennett.) One time, "we became the Trapp Family and we were singing from *The Sound of Music* all night." During another weekend, Jay described every movement of the 1812 Overture, then played the piece—gloriously—on the piano. Mandy saw what so many did: Katie was fun and pop; Jay had a certain romantic majesty about him.

But Kathleen Lobb has a less idyllic memory. Her first time in Millbrook, she recalls, "Katie and Jay were telling me about this completely bizarre, terrible thing that had happened to Jeff. 'Can you believe it? Thirty-one-year-old Jeff Zucker has colon cancer?'"

. . .

EARLY 1997 STARTED WITH no alarm bells. Sure, Jay "had lost a lot of weight," Katie said in a conversation with Larry King in 2000. "But, you know, in this weight-obsessed culture, we didn't really think that much about that"—losing weight was *good*. "He was working nonstop, and he was very fatigued. He was traveling back and forth from Los Angeles"; jet lag seemed the obvious culprit. "We had two young children, a two-career family. We just thought we were both exhausted [and that] Jay was particularly exhausted." It made perfect sense.

One morning Katie was on the *Today* set when an urgent call came in from the babysitter: "Jay was doubled over in pain. I said, 'Let's get him to a doctor right away.'" Katie rushed to meet Jay at the office of her internist, since Jay didn't have a regular New York doctor. ("He was, you know, a healthy, athletic, forty-one-year-old guy," she has said, "so he didn't really even have regular checkups.") A diagnostic test was scheduled. Still, the two felt reassured; the doctor said the magic words, and Katie and Jay took them in with great relief: "Don't worry. *It's not cancer.*"

Some days later, Kathleen Lobb was traveling through New York with an old mutual UVA friend named Julie—Kathleen, Julie, and Katie had been resident advisers together—who was briefly in town from Alaska. Kathleen and Julie called Katie's apartment from a phone booth to suggest getting together. "We thought, 'We'll just catch her at home,'" Kathleen says. "When no one answered the phone, I thought, *This is weird*. It was a time of day when she would have been back from the studio, and Jay had something of a work-at-home schedule, and they had the babysitter for their young daughters." Kathleen pauses. "I had a little sense of foreboding."

The next day Kathleen tried to reach Katie at work. "I couldn't get her, so I called Lori Beecher, because they were very close friends. I said, 'What's wrong?' Lori was being cryptic, because Katie had asked her not to speak about it. But she said that Katie and Jay were *both* off the air"— Katie had someone substituting for her at *Today*; Jay wasn't on *Geraldo*. Not good.

"I called their apartment, and Katie's dad answered the phone. He said, 'Jay has colon cancer.'" Just like Jeff Zucker. Kathleen's heart sank.

Then came worse news: Jay's cancer was advanced. Katie has said she can't even remember how she learned the prognosis—through a phone call? In the doctor's office? "It's a blur. It's a blur because it was a nightmare."

Katie shared her news with Jeff, and, Jeff says, both of them felt "it was unbelievably coincidental that Jay and I both suffered from the same cancer. She immediately swung into action, as I had seen her do with me, to try to do everything she could." Katie herself said her attitude was, "You know, we're going to fight this thing! We're going to do everything we can! I sort of took the role of cheerleader, and the person providing all the hope and the positivity."

Mandy Locke and David Kiernan came up from D.C. for Jay's surgery. The visit was painfully ironic: They had recently become engaged, and David had just asked Jay to be in their wedding. From then on, "because Jay and David were so close, we would all spend a lot of time at the hospital."

Katie continued doing her show. Her viewers had no idea that Jay was sick and "only her closest friends knew what she was going through. She did not wear her heart on her sleeve," says Lori Beecher, who worked with her daily. "She was always professional." The man who saw the tough and disorganized Katie—who says she'd needed Jay's "hard fist" and had not waited her turn to go from "reactor" to "actor" on *Today*—says that Katie was emotionally girded at work during this time, and that this was her way. "Katie will never let you see her cry," he stresses. Jeff Zucker emphatically disagrees: "I've seen Katie cry *a lot*. On screen and off screen."

The minute she left the set at nine a.m., Katie would switch into research mode. "She would spend *hours* calling experts, doctors—figuring out what drug was being tested where, what experimental treatment was happening where," Lori Beecher explains. "She was doing research constantly. She so very desperately wanted to find something that would help him—*anything!*" Mandy Locke adds: "She kind of had a team of friends, mostly people who she worked with, who helped her get in touch with every doctor, every clinical trial. Every waking moment that she could be spending on it, she was." David Kiernan was by now a doctor as well as a lawyer, "and he said that, after a month, 'Katie's knowledge of colon cancer has already surpassed mine,'" Mandy recalls.

For Katie, life was now divided between the normal world and her own world—a realm of unique and unbidden pain and a medical language she had never expected to be speaking. As she put it: "It's these parallel universes when someone you love is sick." Your world becomes "this completely foreign place involving radiation and tumor markers. Outside, people are buying sweaters." The irony was painful—and angering. She would watch "people walking down the street and talking and pushing baby carriages and having lunch with friends, and you would think, How can their worlds go on? Mine has been completely turned upside down. Don't they know what you're going through?"

Then came the ultimate heartbreak: Jay's illness was terminal.

The reaction, Mandy says grimly, "was *wordless*."

Jeff Zucker: "There were a lot of tears."

Still, Katie would not give up. Having taken the role of the "cheerleader," it was so "hard," she has said, "because I don't think I was ever able to express how devastated and concerned and upset I really was in this very dire situation. I wanted to take the role of, 'We can beat this thing!'" When she talked to old friends, she let her guard down. "She was just very somber, in an almost preoccupied way," says Betsy Howell.

As for Jay, "he never wanted to admit" things were as bad as they were, says Mandy. "Jay wanted to keep trying. He wanted to keep fighting." Kathleen Lobb: "It was just terrible. But he was the type of person who needed to continue to live his life and be hopeful about his prognosis, even though it was very dire. I think it was important to Jay and to Katie to maintain a semblance of the normality of their lives."

To maintain that "semblance of normality"—to resist surrendering to hopelessness—Katie kept working. "I think, in a way, it was a refuge for me, to come to work every day, to keep kind of a normal schedule," she said later. "I thought that was so important for Jay and for Ellie and Carrie." But it was challenging. "I would be reading copy off the teleprompter and thinking about Jay, or somebody would be answering a question and [I would] think about Jay." "I think without that job, she would have gone crazy," says a person at the show who was close to her at the time. "That job was her salvation."

Mandy and David frequently traveled to New York to spot Katie at Jay's bedside. "We were able to say, 'Katie, go home and take a nap! You've been here for twenty-four hours!'" Mandy says. "Especially when I was with David, she'd say, 'Okay, I'll go home.' She had this huge job and had two kids"—Carrie was not yet two—"and she was caring for a terminally ill person." As the weeks wore on, David would often go up to New York to spend a day or a weekend with Jay "so Katie could sleep."

Then "Jay's cancer spread to his brain," Kathleen Lobb says, "and it was creating problems with his vision." Katie was impelled into a mindset of "Get all the records! Go see this person!"—this specialist, that specialist. Having to find myriad specialists on her own as her husband's cancer was spreading rapidly was, she felt, "insult added to injury when you've already had your world turned on its head." Katie concluded that "there *has* to be a better way to deliver patient care," Kathleen says. Later, when she became as much a cancer patient advocate as a news star, Katie helped devise a solution to the maze of specialist research she'd been through: an integrated approach by which all the specialists a colon cancer patient may eventually need are worked seamlessly into a program and brought to the family by a "patient navigator." Katie devised this approach, along with Jay's gastroenterologist Mark Pochapin, when she founded the Jay Monahan Center for Gastrointestinal Health at New York Presbyterian Hospital.

At some point Katie was talking to Jay about how meaningful the Millbrook house was to her. He said that he hoped she would hold on to "happy memories" of their time there. That was a way of telling her he knew that he was dying.

"He suffered *so*," says Kathleen Lobb.

"He did not go gently into the good night," Katie herself said. "He fought until the bitter end."

Jay entered Lenox Hill Hospital in early January 1998 and held on for weeks. He died there on January 24, 1998.

"When Jay died," Janie Florea says, "Katie was so stricken by grief, she was numb." One of the last things he said was, "Nothing really matters but your family and friends." Katie never forgot that.

Jay's funeral was held at St. Ignatius Loyola Catholic Church in Manhattan. Judy Collins sang "Amazing Grace" and "Battle Hymn of the Republic." Katie was too emotional to deliver the eulogy she had somehow managed to write. Her oldest sister, Emily, stood up at his funeral service and read it on Katie's behalf to the packed pews of mourners, in a clear, feeling-full voice. After the funeral, Emily didn't want to leave Katie and Ellie and Carrie all alone, so she had her teenage son Jeff move in with them for a while, to help with errands and housekeeping and babysitting—and to provide family connection and warmth.

Katie took a monthlong break to be with her daughters—Ellie was six and Carrie had just turned two. When she returned to *Today* in late February, she was wearing Jay's wedding ring on a chain around her neck. She thanked the viewers for their thousands of cards and letters—they had heard about his death, and about the cancer that had preceded it, in the media. She spoke briefly and touchingly about Jay. "He was everything I ever wanted," she said. Then she got back to work. It was a powerful, understated, and dignified reentry. Television critics and viewers were moved and admiring. Katie Couric was now viewed as heroic.

KATIE HAD ALSO now entered a new phase in her life. Jeff Zucker explains, "How can you not change? She became a widow and a single mother to two young girls at a very young age. I think it made her life more difficult, more complicated. She had the means to deal with all that, so that was very fortunate, but it certainly affected her. It made her more of an advocate, more of a philanthropist, a fighter for those causes. Which was great." Zucker pauses, then adds, "Jay and her father were the two most important men in her life, no question."

"When Jay died, that left a tremendous void in her life," agrees the

NBC man who spoke of Katie's reliance on Jay's judgment and discipline, but he adds a darker emphasis: Jay's death "changed Katie. Katie was no longer the person she had been. And look—I don't know a lot of people who could function [as she did] when the husband gets sick and dies and leaves two children. But Katie has not recovered from that. She is nowhere near the person she was. I'm not saying that maybe Jay could have lost control, or that they didn't have a lot of problems. But there are two lives of Katie Couric—with Jay, and without Jay. And all the bad stuff was without Jay, *after* Jay. Katie right now is a person who only cares about Katie Couric. She doesn't care about anything else." It is hard to reliably analyze this, but suffice it to say that, both in her and in those close to her, Jay's death left a hole far deeper than can be readily seen in Katie's public persona.

Certainly, now, Katie's own visceral understanding of tragedy allowed her a deeper grasp on sensitive stories. In early October 1998, Matthew Shepard, a twenty-two-year-old gay student at the University of Wyoming, was brutally attacked in a rural area outside Laramie, tortured, pistol-whipped, and left hanging on a fence. Soon thereafter "all the networks were pursuing an interview—everyone had heard the story," remembers a *GMA* producer. "It was a very competitive situation." Matthew's parents, Dennis and Judy Shepard, chose Katie, and Katie flew to Laramie and sat with them at the hospital, questioning them sensitively while Matthew fought, in vain, for his life. Katie's recent time in critical care units and her loss of Jay gave her a natural understanding of what the Shepards were going through.

A few months after Jay's death, Katie had lunch with Lilly Tartikoff. An elegant former ballerina, Lilly was the widow of NBC Entertainment wunderkind Brandon Tartikoff, who had overseen or reordered the development of the shows that made NBC: *Hill Street Blues*, *L.A. Law*, *Law & Order*, *Cheers*, *Miami Vice*, and *Seinfeld*. Brandon had died of Hodgkin's lymphoma in August 1997. Several years earlier, Lilly's young daughter Calla had been seriously brain-injured in a freak car accident in Lake Tahoe when Brandon was at the wheel. Calla had required intensive therapy to regain her speech and movement, and the young girl was still in rehabilitation when Lilly and Katie sat down to dine.

Lilly Tartikoff was now an activist and philanthropist for cancer and other health issues, and this inspired Katie. Katie said to Lilly, in effect: "I want to use my bully pulpit—my platform on the *Today* show—to help demystify all the treatments for colon cancer: colonoscopy, sigmoidoscopy, *all* of it." Colorectal diagnostic tests were considered too embarrassing, and colonoscopy was wrongly presumed to be too painful, to consider or even discuss. Those tests might have saved Jay. Colon cancer, if caught early, is very often curable. Katie wanted *some* silver lining, for others, from Jay's tragedy.

The need for action was especially acute now. Jeff Zucker's colon cancer had returned. Still, Jeff was Jeff—positive and aggressive. He was *not* letting cancer get in the way of his life—he and Caryn were creating a family; they would ultimately have four children. He would triumph over the illness, in his professional and personal life.

During their lunch, Lilly told Katie that, before Brandon's death, the two of them had begun working with the venerable Entertainment Industry Foundation (EIF)—a charity founded in 1942 by Cecil B. DeMille, Samuel Goldwyn, and Humphrey Bogart—on a promising cancer research project that had just started bearing fruit. With a lead grant from Aetna, they were funding the work of Dr. Dennis Slaman, the chief of hematology and oncology at UCLA, who had developed a drug, called Hercepten, that was found to effectively treat 30 percent of women with the most aggressive form of breast cancer. Under the direction of the EIF's president and CEO Lisa Paulsen, and with the energy of the Tartikoffs and others, the organization had moved beyond medical philanthropy to sponsoring scientific research. "You should meet Lisa," Lilly told Katie.

"And so," Lisa Paulsen recounts, "Lilly called me and said, 'Will you meet with Katie Couric? And let's see if we can help her develop an initiative that will fund a colon cancer campaign around awareness and bring together some of the best and brightest scientists in the country to fast-track great colon cancer research.'"

When Paulsen met Katie, she says, "We just immediately fell in love with each other. She is absolutely hysterical. We knew we could do something really extraordinary to make colon cancer a first-tier issue for this country." During their second or third lunch date, "Katie said, 'I think I'm going to have a colonoscopy on the *Today* show.' I said, 'Yeah, right.' Katie said, 'No, *really*!'" After taking in Katie's wild idea, "I said, 'That is *genius*!'"

Then Katie and Lisa began mapping out their path. They would be joined by others—Katie would bring a great many of them in—but it would start at this lunch, with the belief that a very high-profile woman in television and an experienced female fund-raiser in Hollywood could change the way money for cancer was raised. Over the next fourteen years, Katie's intense efforts with the EIF, including Lisa and eight other women with whom she founded Stand Up to Cancer, and through partnerships with universities and hospitals—would raise $320 million to date for cancer research and services. That figure breaks down as follows: the National Colorectal Cancer Research Alliance, which Katie established with EIF, has raised $36 million, with part of the funds used as seed money to open the Jay Monahan Center at New York Presbyterian/ Weill Cornell Medical Center; more than $261 million has been pledged to EIF's Stand Up to Cancer initiative since it was cofounded in 2008; Katie personally donated $565,000 to the University of Virginia Cancer Center; and, later, in her role as honorary chair of the campaign to fund the Emily Couric Clinical Cancer Center there she helped raise $25 million in private donations. Katie Couric and Lisa Paulsen would be a formidable combination, with Paulsen herself having overseen the increase of EIF's charitable giving from $1.8 million to over $100 million.

DESCRIPTIONS OF KATIE would change, and the disparaging adjectives would change—from "perky" to "lazy" and "overpaid" and "unserious." And, eventually, worse. She was thin-skinned, to be sure. But she could take it. Her eventual singular effect on Americans' awareness of colon cancer would be a priceless public service. She knew what she had done, and what mattered, and who the best part of her was, criticism be damned.

CHAPTER SIX

From Atlanta to Bosnia:
A Crusader Is Born

Christiane: 1983 to 1999

CHRISTIANE'S TIME AT CNN in Atlanta started inauspiciously. She was passed over for the first job at the network that she applied for—in the electronic graphics department, run by Nancy Diamond. Diamond, today a Fulton County councilwoman, laughs at the fact that, yes, back in September 1983, she rejected Christiane Amanpour. ("It's a running joke every time she wins some international award.") At the time, Diamond explains, "we had a nice conversation, and I think she was older than I was and I felt uncomfortable grilling her, and all the languages on her résumé jumped out at me, but I ended up telling my supervisor, 'I'm not going to take the time to train somebody who's not going to be here for long.'"

Nixed for electronic graphics, Christiane started in a lowly position "on the foreign desk because—I kid you not—I had a foreign accent." (Her friend and CNN-mate David Bernknopf says, however, that she "wanted to be" on that desk.) Like so many others, she found the network lovable not despite but because of its difficulties—she would later cite its "barely meeting payroll" with affection.

Christiane made friends with Maria Fleet, Sparkle Hayter, and Amy Walter, as well as Bernknopf, all of them sharing what Bernknopf describes as an "almost communal life. You could call it a fraternity-sorority. There was dating, there was hanging out, there was going to movies."

Still, the very confident, forthright, ambitious new addition to that "communal life" was slightly mysterious. "I always had the sense that Christiane wanted people to think she'd gone to Brown," Bernknopf says of those early months. "It was kind of like pulling teeth to get her to say it was really the University of Rhode Island. Not that she ever lied—she said, 'Oh, yeah, I lived with a bunch of people from Brown.'" Her conflicting status markers made her hard to place. It seemed "that Christiane was having money troubles—which was funny, given her family upbringing—but she used to ride her bike to work," and was known to ask to borrow a car more than once. Maria Fleet says Christiane was "*always* borrowing cars." One of their crew finally asked, "Christiane, do you even have a driver's license?" When Christiane said no, Bernknopf said, "'Much as I love you, Christiane, I'm thinking it's not a good idea to let someone who doesn't have a driver's license borrow my car, especially when you can barely ride your own bicycle.' It took a lot of guts to ask to borrow a car, not really knowing how to drive!" Despite her seeming money problems and her scrounging about for wheels, "Christiane once bought a Picasso, at an auction or a gallery," recalls Fleet, whose small apartment in the Midtown neighborhood was near Christiane's equally compact flat. "She was very proud and pleased. I distinctly remember her saying, 'You've got to see this *Picasso!*'" Still, she didn't *dress* like a Picasso owner. "Her clothing was very workmanlike, simple, cheap," says David. "She wore jeans. Clothes just weren't very important to her."

Of the many new friends she made among the other CNN staffers, none would eventually be more significant than young producer Liza McGuirk, who remembers first coming upon "this young woman with the bottle of Fantastik and paper towels, polishing the foreign desk, *literally*. She was willing to do whatever she had to do. Early on, one of the foreign editors wasn't particularly fond of her." Christiane herself has spoken of this obstructionist editor, without using her name. "I am sorry to say my first boss was a woman," she has said. "You'd think that would have helped me, but it didn't. If I had thought I would get a sympathetic hearing from her—some female solidarity—I was sorely mistaken. She hated me and my ambition. *She made fun of me.* She said, 'You'll never make it at CNN. You've got to go somewhere else and start.'" A half dozen current and ex-CNNers unqualifiedly identify this foreign editor as Jeanee (pronounced Jen-Ay) von Essen, and four of them say she had a negative opinion of Christiane. Von Essen was Christiane's bête noire all the way through, and battling the roadblocks "was character-building stuff," Christiane has said. To be sure, Christiane had an even higher-placed nemesis at CNN: executive Ed Turner. Sparkle Hayter says he "was just dead set against her becoming a reporter. 'Not as long as I'm here,' he famously said." Liza McGuirk says, "Ed Turner was incredibly uncomfortable around Christiane."

But the immediate obstacle was von Essen. David Bernknopf says: "Christiane was given just the worst kind of grunt work by Jeanee"—to wit, the desk polishing—"and I think Jeanee had no interest in Christiane ever getting ahead or being anything more than a secretary." Amy Walter perceived that von Essen's and Ed Turner's attitude was, "'Forget it! You will never get on the air!'" and that, in response, "Christiane basically said, '*Fuck* this! I want to do what *I* want to *do*!'"

Bernknopf parses the office politics: "A lot of these folks who came in had their little groups of people that they brought in. Jeanee was not really a superstar of international coverage. At CNN, jobs were given out—including to me—[on the basis of] 'Can you breathe? Can you be here at really bad hours? Want to work for very low money?' So Jeanee brought in her little group—people who would kiss up to her, defer to her. And one thing about Christiane: Even as a secretary, she was never gonna kiss up to anybody, and she won't defer to anybody." In fact, Bernknopf was taken by his new female friend's brazenness. "She's gonna tell you exactly what she thinks. She will just get right up in somebody's face if she thinks they're not being honest. I'm trying to think if I ever worked with anybody else who used their physicality that way. Not that she would ever strike someone, but squaring her shoulders and leaning in and maybe even using her finger once or twice. Letting people know very quickly, 'Maybe you can bullshit *other* people, but you are *not* going to bullshit me.'"

Christiane was impatient. She knew she understood more about Iranian and Middle Eastern affairs than many of her superiors in that shallow-benched department. "We had a guy named Mark Leff, who had been a foreign editor at CBS," Bernknopf continues. "Every time there was an international story it was, 'Let Mark do it. He knows what he's doing.' Christiane saw that, and she knew she could do better. She knew where she was going and she intended to do it, and she wanted to be on the air right away. And that might have caused some friction."

Von Essen resented Christiane's forthrightness, and she was threatened by it, several people say. "Jeanee really held her back," says another coworker. "Christiane was a hard worker, always coming up with ideas— obviously she had ambition. She started writing on the side, and she spoke all these languages and had this personal history—her family being run out of Iran—but Jeanee was very picky about who did what. She would not give Christiane the opportunity to try reporting. She would not let Christiane go anywhere."

As von Essen blocked her advance, Christiane tried to go around her. "She knew exactly what she wanted to do, to the point of making a nuisance of herself," Eason Jordan, who later became CNN's senior vice president for international news, recalled. "She badgered people." She even tugged the sleeve of Flip Spiceland—"and there I was, a weatherman!" Spiceland says. "She picked everybody's brain all the time—*all the time*. She would go into the break room, into the lunch room, and go from table to table and talk to every single person she could. She just wanted it *bad*, as if she knew: This was where she belonged in life."

Gail Evans, the highest-ranking woman at the network at the time, who had seen the star potential in Katie, was greatly impressed by Christiane. "There was something a little bit breathtaking about her. She had an aura of authority, of determination, of intellectual competence." Two senior members—anchor Marcia Ladendorff and senior producer Sam Zelman—who had dismissed Katie—were struck by Christiane as well. "Christiane took a totally different approach than Katie. She was very much interested in establishing credibility and was very professional, and she was not much running around trying to find the spotlight, which is how I would characterize Katie," Ladendorff says. (Katie and Christiane overlapped at CNN for less than a year, and the two striving young women were not friends there.) Another anchor, Bob Cain, became friends with Christiane because they had "our alma mater, WJAR, in common." He recalls that "she stood out for her somewhat British accent and Iranian Farsi heritage—that and her obvious intelligence. She was neither self-effacing nor arrogant—she was a straight shooter." But Diana Greene—who was Katie's friend, and who had seen both Katie's ambition and her social generosity—believed that Christiane had keen power sensitivity. "I was the same level as Christiane, so I wasn't important to her," Greene says. "Christiane knew where the power base was. She was interested in the people who could bring her to the next level."

For her part, Christiane has downplayed her ambition in favor of a narrative that has her combating prejudicial obstacles. "I had to lose the ability to hear the word 'no,'" she has said. "*No*, as in, 'Your name is too unpronounceable to be on television.' '*No*, you've got a foreign accent.' '*No*, your hair is black, for heaven's sake, and very unruly. Don't you know you have to be a blond to be on television here?'"

According to Bernknopf, Christiane stuck it to von Essen. "Oh, *yeah*, especially at the end" of Christiane's time as von Essen's employee, "it was open warfare. She would have a fight with Jeanee or a producer, and she'd be very up in their faces and 'I *know* what I want to do here!' And as soon as that producer was out of sight, she would turn to us [as if to say], 'Well, *that* really worked well!' She knew she'd gone over the line. She would laugh—and she does have a great laugh, full, deep, and mischievous—about how crazy it was that she'd been so aggressive."

Christiane "finally got away from Jeanee and became a writer, like I was," says Bernknopf. At last some movement was possible. "We could do voice-overs on weekend stories. They would look around the room and say, 'Who can voice this story about the Middle East today? Christiane, you busy? Can you write this up and go track it?' So you wouldn't get on camera, but it was close." One time "she managed to convince whoever she had to convince to be allowed to do a backgrounder on Iran," recalls Maria Fleet. She was so excited. "'Marie! Marie!'—she called me Marie— 'would you shoot a stand-up for me?' So we went out into the CNN parking lot" and filmed Christiane's CNN on-air debut against that "generic background of vague trees." A few years later, when the two women and camerawoman Jane Evans—the three female musketeers—were in Kuwait and Saudi Arabia together, at the start of Christiane's brilliant career, they laughed about the parking lot stand-up.

DURING ONE BRIEF PERIOD of weeks in 1984, a trio of almost operatic tragedies rocked Christiane's life. First came the deaths of two female gay friends of Christiane's, a CNN tape deck editor named Wendy, whom a mutual friend recalls as "brilliant, indefatigable, very funny," and Wendy's quiet, retiring girlfriend. Wendy had been telling Christiane and others that she was going to break up with her girlfriend but kept putting it off because her girlfriend was "fragile." Wendy was killed in a traffic accident. Shortly afterward the girlfriend, feeling she couldn't face life without her beloved (and having no idea that Wendy had been planning to break up with her), killed herself. It was shocking for everyone in their circle, not least for Christiane.

These shocks had barely dissipated when, one night, a houseguest of Christiane's showed up at Sparkle Hayter's apartment door "distraught," Sparkle recalls, to report that she had been alone in Christiane's apartment when a phone call came in relating that Christiane's adored uncle had been executed. "The friend wanted to give me a heads-up because Christiane was coming over to my place that day before work," Sparkle recalls. "We were both on late shifts then. I went out and bought vodka and mix so we could have cocktails before work, which we never did any other time—in fact, that's the only time I remember Christiane having a drink. She had one only. It was also the only time I saw her cry." Many of Christiane's relatives (and her beloved childhood nanny, to whom she remained close for decades) had been able to get out of Iran, a number of them painstakingly extricated through international rescue services. But this uncle hadn't been so lucky, and now, a full five years after the revolution, he was murdered. "She was in a very grim mood, as you can imagine, but at work that night she just buckled down, did her job, wrote her stories, and said nothing about [the execution] to anyone at work, as far as

I know. But she and I talked about it—and about Wendy, and about life—a *lot* that year. People who don't know Christiane's private side think she's tough, even hard, but she's not. She feels everything deeply. She's not tough, she's not hard, but she is very strong." To Sparkle, Christiane personified the art of "keeping an open heart without having your heart broken fatally."

However, all was hardly somber during Christiane's last two years in Atlanta, 1984 and early 1985. Diana Bellew, who had been at Cambridge while her best boarding school friend was in Rhode Island, moved to Atlanta to work in a Chinese porcelains gallery. She moved into Christiane's tiny apartment. The girls were always broke—so much so they not only didn't have an air conditioner, but, for a while, "we didn't even have any *fans*—it felt like 150 degrees." Of course, Christiane was carless "but, luckily, she had these nice friends at CNN who had cars. And she used to get our landlord to drive her to the farmers' market to buy food." Diana, meanwhile, "was the only white person on the MARTA," the bus, "to my gallery job in Buckhead—white people didn't go on buses in Atlanta in those days." Diana recalls, "I used to cook every night—chicken and potatoes, because I'm Irish, or veal marsala, or pasta—because Christiane got home at eleven p.m. Then we would eat. But it wasn't so bad because, after that, Christiane's friends would take me dancing in Midtown." Usually Christiane abstained—"she'd be at her desk working"—except for weekends, when they'd all go to the club where there was a Prince impersonator singing "Purple Rain" and then to "another where RuPaul was discovered." CNN colleague Amy Walter would hang out with them. "We made no money, so we would hit the bars at happy hour and have the hors d'oeuvres as dinner," Amy recalls. "Diana and I would go up to any guy and dance. Christiane was always much more reserved. Diana was the wacky, goofy one. I was in the middle, and Christiane was very solid, but when she did cut loose, she had a great, delightful sense of humor."

The dynamic between the two onetime New Hall roommates had shifted radically in eight years. Diana now seemed frivolous next to the internationally concerned, hugely ambitious, and now notably un-looks-conscious Christiane. Christiane would lecture her old roommate, "You should put as much time into thinking about your career as you do about your hair!" Amy Walter says, "Christiane got more and more serious as time went on. She had found her calling. Diana and I were more social."

Diana and Christiane did have fun hanging out with their buddy Ray Nunn, the ABC local bureau chief. Ray was black, and he drove an expensive car—and their presence all together served to remind them that they were in the South. "We'd arrive at restaurants," Diana says, "the black guy in the white Porsche getting out of the car with the very white Irish girl and the Middle Eastern—or maybe she was Hispanic?—girl." People in that still provincial city did a double take at this "mixed" group. "Christiane did *not* like Atlanta," Leila Amanpour says. "She would rather be in New York."

In July 1984, Christiane got a break—she was sent to the Democratic National Convention in San Francisco. Diana remembers that her friend was thrilled not just by the opportunity, and the excitement, but perhaps also by the fact that, for the first time ever, a woman—Geraldine Ferraro—was being nominated for vice president, sharing the ticket with Walter Mondale.* Christiane had always lobbied to get on the air, but now she really pushed hard against what she would call "Fortress No." Her fellow countrywoman Parisa Khosravi, who was higher up and would eventually become a major CNN executive, knew "she wanted to go up to New York. She was writing down here [in Atlanta]; she kept on wanting to get on air and not all the bosses were supporting her, because of her funky name and accent—the whole bit. She was not your typical on-air person; she was told that. She was going to quit and go to New York anyway." Parisa, both of whose parents were Iranian, and who grew up there (she would gently make fun of half-Iranian Christiane's "adorable," imprecise Farsi), immediately bonded with Christiane. Aside from their ethnicity and their status as exiles from the Revolution, they would have in common both ambition and an instinctual international perspective that

---

*In another first, the convention was chaired by a woman, Kentucky governor Martha Layne Collins, who happened to have been the home economics teacher at Seneca High when Diane Sawyer was a freshman there.

others could attain but not quite so effortlessly feel. They would produce many stories together, they would marry at approximately the same time, and they would have their babies at close to the same time. Christiane would have closer CNN women friends—Liza McGuirk, for one—but Parisa was as close to a CNN *sister* as she would ever have.

Liza McGuirk got herself in a position to break the stranglehold. In 1985—after much "angling, angling" on her own behalf—Liza was made the head of CNN's small New York bureau's assignment desk. Her friend Christiane immediately saw an opening, and she started "begging me to bring her up—to give her a shot—because I was assigning reporters," McGuirk says. "I talked to Burt"—then vice president of CNN Burt Rheinhardt. For the plan to work out, someone had to overrule Ed Turner, who oversaw the day-to-day operations of the newsroom, and who "had said he didn't want her on the air—Ed said the same thing about Katie Couric at the time." David Bernknopf adds, "If you looked at the list of people who Ed Turner thought would be great stars and the people who he pushed aside . . . the people pushed aside were generally much better."

But both women, McGuirk and Amanpour, kept pressing. "Christiane was pleading her case to Burt and I pled her case to Burt—just for her to be on air, just for her to learn on the air. Obviously, an Iranian young woman with an English accent is not the first person you cast as a reporter, but somehow we talked him into it. I was pretty close to Burt—he loved both of us. I think he just did it because he loved us." (At the memorial service for Rheinhardt, who died in May 2011, Christiane expressed her gratitude to him.)

CHRISTIANE MOVED TO NEW YORK in 1985 and roomed with McGuirk in Liza's cousin's "fabulous" three-bedroom apartment in a doorman building on Tenth Street and University Place in Greenwich Village. Liza gave Christiane weekend assignments—cleverly, Bernknopf notes, "on the theory that the executives were probably not watching much on the weekends and they might not even see who was on the air. And even if they did, they wouldn't care because it was only the weekend: 'Okay, who else are you gonna get to work for free on a weekend?'"

Christiane went out on corny, local-newsy stories, Liza says—"stuff like Coney Island hot dog–eating contests." Christiane sometimes did her stand-ups, as one who saw the clips recalls, "wearing a crazy flowered jacket with big, huge shoulder pads." Liza definitely had her friend's back while Christiane was working out the considerable kinks in her on-air persona. "Ed Turner was incredibly uncomfortable with Christiane, and with another guy I was using, a neophyte, too—he didn't like either of them. I would say, 'Ed, just *who* do you want me to send out?'" She was challenging her boss while buying time. "Anyway, Christiane got better." She mastered the storytelling part of her new job "pretty quickly [but] it takes a couple of years to get any kind of comfort level on air. She started developing her comfort on camera, and with the voice and the edit processes—slowly. Gradually, the protests [from Ed Turner] died down."

Meanwhile, Christiane never stopped pushing for better assignments. Finally "somebody said, 'Okay, Christiane, let's talk about making you a full-time reporter,'" Bernknopf recalls. "Now she was not just covering stupid features but *real* news." "A huge door had opened for her," says Parisa Khosravi. "General reporting or fill-in reporting, just to kind of break through—that was sort of the start of her reporting career. And when we used to chat, she always said, 'Send me out there! I want to do some international reporting.'"

Christiane, meanwhile, remained close to her family members, who were all still living in London. One day her mother, who was in constant touch, had to deliver heartbreaking news. Her youngest sister, Leila, then eighteen, had been riding her bike down a country road in East Anglia when a car slammed into her. In a lifesaving measure, her right leg had just been amputated above the knee.

Christiane quickly went into a mode that few had seen her in before. Obtaining an extended "compassionate leave" from CNN as soon as she could, Christiane flew over "to be by my side for quite a long time—a couple of months," recalls Leila. "She was a massive help—a great source of strength." Before leaving New York, Christiane had rounded up encouraging letters to Leila from other young amputees, explaining how they had overcome their disabilities. "She brought over great letters that people had written," including one from Teddy Kennedy Jr., who'd lost his leg as a boy to bone cancer, as well as a "great" one from then Paralympics track-and-field star Dennis Oehler, who had become an amputee at twenty-four following an automobile accident, just as he was about to start playing professional soccer. "I still have those letters," Leila says.

Christiane's decision to take such a break from work seemed touchingly out of character to her family members. Lizzy Amanpour says, "It surprised me—and I'm her sister—that Christiane took all that time off to be with our younger sister after that accident. People's impression of her is as very ambitious and driven and nothing would stand in her way. So it was really a shock that she would take that much time off."

Christiane's nurturance of Leila was not gushy. "Christiane did not break down into tears," Leila says. "She was very strong and really encouraging" as Leila moved from hospital to home and made the challenging transition from treatment to rehabilitation. "She said, 'You're going to walk. There's amazing new technology. You're going to be fine.' I especially remember her saying, 'You can either look at this as an obstacle or as a challenge.' It was brilliant—it was just what I needed to hear—and I obviously went for the latter."

When she got back to New York, "Christiane was *so* determined to get out of America and go international," says Liza. "She was an operator and an excellent spokeswoman on her behalf. She was constantly, *constantly* lobbying to go overseas." Even her staunchest champion, Liza, thought that goal was wildly out of reach. So she was blindsided when, in 1989, Christiane's dream came true: "She was assigned to our Frankfurt bureau as a producer, and soon after that as producer-reporter," says Parisa Khosravi. Liza says, "I don't remember who made that decision to send her to Frankfurt, but I remember I was, 'Whoa, how'd she pull *that* off?'" Lizzy Amanpour believes, "I think it was a question of timing. She was the only person at CNN who said yes to Frankfurt. It was for her an opportunity to go abroad but it was not considered a particularly great posting."

Yet from the distance of decades, Bernknopf believes Frankfurt meant, "'You're qualified—go out in the world and do stuff.' But even then nobody expected that they were going to get this brave, bold, dogged reporter who seemed to be fearless, not afraid of power."

Except maybe Christiane herself. "I don't think she predicted she was going to become the most famous correspondent in the world," says an executive who met her then. "But I also don't think she was surprised."

Of course no one could foresee the events that would thrust Christiane onto the world stage. Within a half year of her Frankfurt posting, Saddam Hussein, the ruler of Iraq, long the archenemy of her native Iran, would invade Kuwait, instigating what would ultimately escalate into the Gulf War. Along with two female colleagues, Maria Fleet and Jane Evans, Christiane would head off into that war zone—the first of many. "And the rest," Parisa Khosravi says, "is history."

Two dinners seem to bracket that posting to Frankfurt, that moment when Christiane's life changed, placing her on the threshold of renown. The first took place in New York, Diana Bellew recalls. Christa D'Souza, Christiane's friend from London and Brown, by now a correspondent for *Tatler*, was in town, and the three young women went to the opening of Lucky Strike, the new venture of a hot restaurateur of the era, Keith Mc- Nally. Madonna sat a few tables away. Losing her cool, Diana "let my mouth hang open" at being so close to the Material Girl. "Christiane and Christa both said, 'Stop doing that—you're so embarrassing!' But then Christa looked over at me and said, 'What kind of dressing is she putting on her salad?' And I said, 'You just told me I'm not allowed to look! And now you want information?'" Christiane—the former starstruck teenager, her celebrity scrapbooks long gone—stayed unimpressed and above it all.

At the second dinner, in London, Diana joined Patricia Amanpour and Christiane, visiting from Frankfurt, at a Covent Garden restaurant. "And this time it was Christiane, not me, who was sitting with her mouth open," Diana says. "She was gawking. She didn't say anything—she just stared." The object of her awe was a woman seated nearby whose rapid ascent in TV news she may have longed to emulate. The woman seemed golden, having just been "stolen" away from one major network to be a star at another.

The woman in Christiane's gaze was Diane Sawyer. And Christiane was, fittingly, fastening on her just as her own star was beginning to glimmer.

KATIE COURIC CALLED the Gulf War a proving ground that made a female journalist a "ten," giving her the credibility to open better doors. But for Christiane, it was a novitiate, an induction into her true vocation as an international correspondent. In a double Cinderella moment, the war would thrust CNN, once called the Chicken Noodle News, and Christiane herself, the network's in-the-right-place-at-the-right-time reporter, into the public eye.

Christiane's sense of vocation would soon be truly tested in a far more thankless conflict in Bosnia. "Nobody else wanted to go to Bosnia, so we ended up going there," CNN cameraman David Rust recounts—the "we" being he, Christiane, and several close colleagues. Rust would become a stalwart in Bosnia and one of Christiane's closest teammates there, documenting the dangerous, frenetic conflict at close range. Rust and Christiane would survive many near misses together.

The two of them and the CNN team—as well as a coterie of committed others from different networks, photo agencies, and newspapers—covered the conflict so intensely, starting in early 1992, that, Rust says, "I spent more time with Christiane in Bosnia for two and a half years than I did with my wife and kids."

It was in Bosnia—in reporting on the explicit targeting of the Bosniak Muslims by the Serbs (and, at some points, to a lesser extent, by the Croats), and in revealing the atrocities committed upon civilians, including the raping of women—that Christiane was affirmed in her mission. She has flatly said: "I consider Bosnia the most important thing I've ever done."

First, though, Saudi Arabia.

In August 1990, three CNN women met up in Egypt to form a team.

Maria Fleet would be the sound woman and editor. Jane Evans would be the camerawoman. They'd both flown in from Rome and were in Egypt to film the Arab League's meeting there. Christiane Amanpour winged in from Frankfurt. She would be the reporter.

They'd all been told that Saudi Arabia was "unrepresentative of the Middle East—it's more conservative than any other country," says Maria Fleet. "So, in preparation, we bought all these big, long swatches of fabric, so we could wrap our head and cover our hair." It turned out the women only needed to be seriously covered up when they wandered into "the most conservative areas or when we went into a mosque. Mostly, we wore Western clothes. Because Saudi Arabia was asking for the U.S.'s help, and we were doing them a huge favor by giving it to them, they relaxed some of the rules—we did not have to wear *abaya*," the head-to-toe black garb with eyeholes. "We wore pants and loose blouses—not jeans and tight T-shirts," but it was close enough to what they'd be wearing at home.

The team had a male producer, Jim Miller, whom they adored and who was especially useful since women in Saudi Arabia weren't allowed to drive. As it was, "the Saudis were taken aback by the fact that CNN would send a team of women here." Still, in worldly places like downtown Dhahran—the point from which the U.S. troops deployed to the desert bordering Kuwait—"the Saudis kind of loved us." The three women befriended Prince Adel al-Jubeir, the soon-to-be-ubiquitous representative of the kingdom on American TV, whose vulnerable, beady-eyed face was often capped by an official royal headdress and who later became Saudi Arabia's ambassador to the United States. Adel wore jeans when he hung out with Christiane, Jane, Maria, and Jim. And in a play on the kingdom's role as "Keeper of the Three Holy Mosques," he anointed Jim "Keeper of the Three Holy News Babes." So felicitous was this time that Christiane discovered, as she put it years later, "I have found it has been a great advantage [to be a woman reporter] in . . . Saudi Arabia. . . . Being a female correspondent, having a female crew with me, has been an amazing door opener."

Christiane appears to have been a bit of a femme fatale during this time, romantically vied for by *New York Times* reporter Neil MacFarquhar and CBS correspondent Bob Simon, who was married. In the 2006 novel of former *New York Times* Cairo bureau chief MacFarquhar, *The Sand Café*, recounting this time in Saudi Arabia, the character, Angus Dalziel, who seems to be MacFarquhar, becomes besotted by Thea Makdisi, a witty, provocative TV journalist for a cable network. Thea Makdisi is equally flirtatious and one-of-the-guys-like and is given to flashes of righteous disgust at the Saudi oppression of women. Thea is of Lebanese-Swedish heritage and she grew up in Beirut, and her subtle looks grew on men. "At first glance she did not strike Angus as beautiful. Her complexion was olive . . . but not distinctly exotic . . . and her nose, bending slightly over a little bump, was one that a less confident woman might have had reshaped. She was about five-foot-nine with unruly, light brown hair cropped off at the neck." Other than the "light" brown hair, the description fits Christiane. But even closer than the physical description and the proximate stand-ins for Christiane's Iranian-British heritage and her childhood in Tehran is the dead-giveaway fact that Thea works with two other women—Christiane, Maria, and Jane were the only all-female crew during Desert Shield—and that she tells Angus that she was told, at her network, "'You're foreign, you should go work for the Foreign Desk'" and that "some senior producers doubt I will ever overcome my slightly foreign looks and accent, but I am determined to prove them wrong": almost literal real-life quotes of Christiane's.

Angus's rival for Thea is an older network producer named Aaron Black—charming, experienced, and ultimately captured by Saddam Hussein's troops after the start of the war. Aaron Black seems a clear stand-in for CBS's veteran war reporter Bob Simon—even before *The Sand Café* was published, rumors had swirled that he and Christiane had had something of a romance. In the novel, Thea is charismatic and confident—she "arouses attention wherever she goes," the jacket copy raves.

Operation Desert Shield was all about waiting—the U.S. and coalition soldiers were getting ready to repel Saddam Hussein's aggression. And although "there was worry that Saddam would invade" at any time, Maria says, a lot of it was fairly unanxious waiting. Romances notwithstanding, Christiane, Maria, and Jane did many nearly identical nonstories about live-fire exercises, with Christiane intoning, as Maria recalls it, "'These are the men of the First Cavalry Division . . . ,' and they were always men. The U.S. military did not deploy women." (Women were, however, used in close-range support capacities in the Gulf for the first time in any U.S. war.) "One time when we stayed overnight in the desert, we might have been the only women in the contingent. We had to take showers in little makeshift wooden booths." On the air, "we could never say where we were"—location was a military secret—"which was about a mile from the Kuwait border. It was all so controlled—kind of a dog and pony show." The government wanted the media to do a *"rah rah* cataloging of military might—there was not a lot of journalism involved, unless there was a visit from Norman Schwarzkopf.

"But at a certain point, one of the soldiers we were interviewing made an aside about a [weaponry] supply side problem they were having, so Christiane's ears perked up and she made a story out of it," Maria continues. "A photographer from *Time* magazine—this older, seasoned guy— got very angry at her and tried to get her not to report it because she was reporting against the military. Of course she didn't get intimidated by him. She did the story."

Along with the military cheerleading, Christiane, Maria, and Jane produced human interest stories. "Because we were women, people let their guard down—they think you're less threatening, so you can get more information and more access," says Maria. They reported on Saudi women who organized protests to be able to drive. (That effort, which has been ongoing ever since the war, is periodically refueled, with brave Saudi women circulating clandestine petitions and flyers in beauty parlors, and is just as regularly rebuffed by the Wahhabi-beholden government.) They reported on women who owned businesses. They shopped for gold jewelry in Bedouin bazaars, and they socialized with the Westerners who worked for the oil conglomerate Saudi Aramco and lived in the large, gated compounds where women could not only drive but could wear bathing suits in mixed company—"and where all the houses had the exact same floor plan, with a room in the back where everyone made alcoholic drinks," forbidden in the kingdom, Maria explains.

"But mostly we spent time in the desert. We always wore those sleeveless vests with all the pockets"—a look Christiane would trademark in her broadcasts. "For some reason," Maria says, "she had very limited clothes: three shirts, which she kept rotating and laundering and rotating. She was developing her style" based on an eschewal of style. "From the beginning, she was self-assured. She was a *force.*"

CNN itself became a force the night—January 17, 1991—that the coalition bombs started falling in Baghdad. "Everybody took our signal to get the coverage," Fleet says gleefully. "It was golden for CNN! The people who had called us Chicken Noodle News for years were now begging to use our signal!" Iraq launched Scud missiles—initially feared to have chemical warheads—into Israel and Kuwait. Now that the war had started in earnest, Christiane did live stand-ups for the suddenly not only respectable but also on-the-money CNN, just as the missiles flashed in the sky. "She showed her stuff," says Parisa Khosravi. "Her reporting was outstanding and memorable. She had nerves of steel."

Soon Christiane left Saudi Arabia for Baghdad. She was ready for a real challenge.

David Rust had been part of the CNN team in Baghdad around the time the air war started. Much of the team, including Rust, returned to Amman, Jordan, the next day, leaving correspondent Peter Arnett and a small crew. When Rust and the others returned to "the embattled city," as Rust recalls, all hands were needed for intense, round-the-clock reporting. But two members of the team had gone briefly on holiday. One was Nic Robertson, a British satellite engineer who'd joined CNN in 1989, and the other was his fiancée.

Robertson would quickly return, soon to become Christiane's Bosnia producer (and eventually an iconic and prolific conflict broadcaster). Their abrupt departure left the team "with only one photographer and one reporter, and we were unable to do all the work that needed to be done," Rust says. "CNN decided to ask Christiane if she was willing to risk travel to Iraq to help with the coverage.

"She *jumped* on it," Rust says. Rust had seen Christiane in a CNN "gag reel" shot in New York. The more she had tried to be mock-serious in the film, the more she'd cracked up. He'd been fascinated by this posh-British-accented woman, "endearing" in her inability to keep a straight face. But the Christiane who flew to Baghdad was different: all business. "She wanted to be there. She came in to help Peter out and did whatever was asked of her. My sense is she liked to be in the center of stories—and this *was* the center. She was amazed when the bombs burst," but not in a bad way. "To Christiane, danger was just an obstacle that had to be overcome to provide a top-notch story." He adds, "She worked extremely long hours, under very difficult circumstances, and she never complained."

The Iran-Iraq crisis was close to her heart; her family's exile to England had been due not merely to the Revolution but also to the breakout of that war. While in Iraq, she covered the dilemma of the Kurdish refugees on the border of the two countries, left over after the end of that long and still resonating conflict.

By now, "things in the Balkans were heating up," Rust says. "Yugoslavia had begun to break apart when Slovenia and Croatia declared independence. There was a ten-day war in Slovenia, but the war in Croatia was more prolonged and severe." Christiane went to Croatia and "was totally immersed in the story by the time I got there," he says. "The famous pictures of the prisoners of war? Guys at the camp, all skin and bones? She was right on top of that"—she'd already gotten into Bosnia briefly—"when I went in to join her. It proved to be a particularly brutal war for journalists. Between Croatia and the beginning of the Bosnian War, we lost so many—a *ton* of people were killed." There were more journalists killed during the Vietnam War but over a much longer period of time. In 1991 alone, twenty-three journalists were killed in Croatia (thirty in a five-year period). By contrast, in Vietnam, sixty-three journalists lost their lives over a twenty-year period.

CHRISTIANE AND DAVID RUST were both in Croatia intermittently during its ten-month fight for independence, from early March 1991 to early January 1992. A male reporter with whom David was working had begged off. "He promised his wife he wouldn't go to the hot spots." So that reporter left, but Christiane—a single female and neophyte hungrily acquiring experience (she had also, briefly, flown to Russia to cover the breakup of the Soviet Union and the war in Tbilisi)—did not demur.

"As tensions spread, it was obvious that Bosnia would be the next area of conflict," David says. "The Croatian war was a sort of warm-up. Everybody knew that something *big* was breaking out in Bosnia."

Bosnia declared its independence from Yugoslavia in late February 1992. In the new multiethnic state, officially called the Republic of Bosnia and Herzegovina, a slender plurality—44 percent of the population—were Muslims (called Bosniaks), one-third were Orthodox Serbs, and 17 percent were Catholic Croats, who had essentially already declared their independence. The idea of this unified new nation was violently rejected by the Orthodox Serbs, under the leadership of Slobodan Milosevic. War broke out, with Milosevic's forces—the Army of Republika Srpska—pitted against the Bosniaks' Army of the Republic of Bosnia and Herzegovina.

A month after rejecting a brokered peace, in early April, thirteen thousand Srpska soldiers, armed with every kind of weapon—from sniper rifles to rocket-launched bombs—laid siege to the capital city of Sarajevo. In early May, the Serbs went further, blockading the city, and the Croats launched their own attacks against the Bosniaks. The Bosniaks were outmanned and overwhelmed.

The Siege of Sarajevo, as it would come to be known, lasting nearly four years, would be considered the longest assaultive military blockade of a capital city in the history of modern warfare. Eleven thousand civilians were killed and fifty-six thousand were injured, 10 percent of both figures being children.

This is the conflict that Christiane—by now a rising star—threw herself into.

A community of reporters, photo agency still photographers, cinematographers, and producers assembled, starting in the late spring of 1992, at the Sarajevo Holiday Inn. It was located on what was immediately nicknamed "Sniper Alley" because of the proliferation of Serbian marksmen along the route to the center of town, where the one television station was located. Nic Robertson was there. David Rust was there. So was Ron Haviv, a twenty-seven-year-old NYU graduate who, despite his low-key, unswaggering demeanor, had already been captured and beaten and almost killed in two other conflicts where he'd bravely aimed his camera. Among the photographers in this core group were Gilles Perez, Chris Morris, and Haviv's close associate Luc Delahaye—actor-handsome, French, especially gifted with color image. Joining them later was chic, witty Emma Daly, reporting for the *Independent*. She and Christiane—both British, female, single—would meet up at the reporter-filled bar on the ground floor of the building housing the Associated Press office (nicknamed "Love Hotel" because it was a former brothel), bonding over the special challenges of women covering war.

The group was soon joined by Mark Phillips, a cameraman from CNN Australia who would begin to work closely with Christiane (eventually being captured with her by the Taliban in her 1997 ordeal). Like the other cameramen who'd weathered Bosnia and other hard-core conflicts, Mark would soon be called a "shithole specialist"—a "term of endearment," he stresses, which masked the considerably less sentimental calculation, made by the Atlanta bosses, that only such seasoned war dogs were fit for dangerous assignments "because it cost CNN $30,000 to $100,000 to get us *into* these places and CNN didn't want to invest money in people" who would be unnerved by whizzing bullets.

But they were all unnerved. Pierre Bairin—the soft-spoken, gay Belgian videotape editor who had known Christiane in Zagreb and was drafted to join her in Bosnia, eventually becoming her producer and confidant—says that he resisted fear during his time traveling Sarajevo's Sniper Alley, but then, "when, after a month there, I got back to my hotel room in Croatia, and it was so peaceful in comparison, I started to *cry*."

The oldest war dog there, at forty-five, was the charismatic Reuters contract photojournalist Kurt Schork. War reporter was a fourth career incarnation for Schork, a onetime Rhodes scholar who'd previously been an executive with the New York Metropolitan Transit Authority, an aide to presidential candidate Michael Dukakis, and a successful real estate developer. Impatient with the constraints of actually reporting for a news bureau, "at some point he'd decided to send *himself* to Sarajevo," working for Reuters on his own terms, says Emma Daly. Kurt grew very close to Christiane, and all the others, who learned from him and loved hanging out with him at the Love Hotel bar. "Kurt was amazing," says Ron Haviv. "He would show up somewhere and after a couple of days everybody else was showing up because of the respect he had from his peers and his ability to find stories that needed to be documented." "Kurt was very smart, very dry, with a very dark sense of humor," adds Emma Daly. He would blast Dire Straits' "Brothers in Arms" on his portable CD player in honor of the solidarity they all felt—and *had* to feel.

Schork was slyly competitive. "He would write his stories even before the UN briefing"—the source for others' stories—"and he would kick the AP reporters' asses," says Emma. But he was also a profoundly romantic character. "He was a natural ascetic who adored women and usually rose before dawn to read literary novels—he was a great fan of Michael Ondaatje." The story he reported of a Bosnian Romeo and Juliet—a Serb man and a Muslim woman, both twenty-five, gunned down for their love—was among the most moving narratives to come out of the anguish of that conflict. It began:

> Two lovers lie dead on the banks of Sarajevo's Miljacka River, locked in a final embrace. For four days they have sprawled near Vrbanja bridge in a wasteland of shell-blasted rubble, downed tree branches and dangling power lines. Bosko is face-down on the pavement, right arm bent awkwardly behind him. Admira lies next to her lover, left arm across his back.

The crew became inextricably close. Pierre would soon introduce Mark Phillips to the woman Mark would marry, and Pierre would become the godfather of their child. Ron Haviv and Christiane would each briefly leave Sarajevo, in December, for Mogadishu, Somalia. "We ended up covering three genocides together: Somalia, Bosnia, Darfur," Ron says. "It would become, when we'd run into each other, 'Of course *you're* here, too.'"

Still, no one in this grab bag of likely and unlikely war dogs possessed the idiosyncrasy, glamour, and chutzpah of camera operator Margaret

Moth, who was a senior member of the CNN team. The previous half century of wars yielded a dazzling dozen or so female journalist legends— camera operators, still photographers, and reporters—among whose ranks Moth incontestably belonged. There was Margaret Bourke-White; there was Lee Miller, the Poughkeepsie-raised *British Vogue* model and Man Ray paramour turned World War II photojournalist who'd snapped a photo of herself in Hitler's bathtub. Add them to Martha Gellhorn, Oriana Fallaci, and Gloria Emerson: in aggregate, a jewel-boxful of women of war whose quality of work and personal panache made up for their small number by a quantum of a thousand. At the end of the twentieth century, there would be two other excellent candidates for this elite sorority. One was the *London Sunday Times*'s Marie Colvin. Half blinded in the line of duty, the hard-drinking, aggressive, and exquisitely vain Colvin wore an eye patch—along with designer lingerie under her flak jacket. She would eventually be killed in February 2012 after smuggling herself into Syria to do dangerous reporting on Bashar al-Assad's crackdown on the rebels. The other draft pick for this dazzling group? Hands down: the Sarajevo gang's Margaret Moth.

One of New Zealand's first professional female camera operators, she was born Margaret Wilson but changed her name to Margaret Gipsy Moth. By the time Moth got to Sarajevo she was already a legend: After seven years as the aggressive, exotic bird at a Houston, Texas, TV station, she had gone on to cover news for CNN—in the Middle East, in India, in the crumbling Soviet Union. She'd jumped out of planes barefoot; she'd shot footage of rebel warriors while they were aiming guns at her head. She was a striking beauty, with fine features within a long, heart-shaped face, framed by tousled, curly black hair that tumbled well past her shoulders. She possessed a fashion model's figure—and vanity, often virtually starving herself for her looks. She rimmed her eyes with quarter-inch-thick black eyeliner, producing the effect, against her milk white face, of a Goth-tinged Elizabeth Taylor in her prime—or Grace Slick in Jefferson Airplane's 1967 posters.

Moth was forty-two when she joined the Sarajevo group. She chomped cigars, drank everyone under the table, played a game called "Who Would

You Rather Sleep With?," proffering amusingly ridiculous choices for colleagues she queried. She was a role model to and supporter of women, especially Christiane—the *one* female colleague who, like she, had been an
aggressive, black-haired, English-accented, "foreign" duck out of water at
a TV station in the American South.

In those early days of the Siege of Sarajevo, the team did not have armored cars.

CNN dealt with the potential danger to its staffers the cheap way: by
dividing the risk among the reporters, placing teams of journalists on
three-week rotations.

Christiane was on rotation in the United States when, one day in July,
Margaret Moth went out for a routine drive down Sniper Alley, with her
head and lens stuck out the window of the car, taping the scene. As she
was taping, a bullet whizzed at her—*right* at her. It shot through her
cheekbone and exited the other side of her jaw. The bottom of her face was
partially blown off.

The press crew was shocked—even panicked. Moth was immediately
medevaced out of Bosnia and flown to the Mayo Clinic in Minnesota. According to David Rust, who was on vacation at the time, "They decided to
evacuate the whole Sarajevo team out when Margaret was hit—they
wanted a new team, because the trauma" resonated so intensely with all
the other crew members. Moth's grievous, maiming injury shook the team
members to their core. Parisa Khosravi recalls that, along with deep worry
for Margaret, there was the strong, silent—shared—feeling: "'Oh, my
God, if this could happen to *her*, then it could happen to any of us.'"

Parisa rushed to the Mayo Clinic to see Margaret, "who was very conscious. Her head was the size of two basketballs. I gave her a pen and
paper, and the first thing she wrote was, 'I want to go back to Sarajevo and
look for my teeth.'" Moth later told Emma Daly—when she eventually
returned to Sarajevo*—that she'd put her finger to her lower face right
after the blast "and all I could feel was my tongue." No skin or lips or bone.

---

*Margaret Moth continued working, despite her injury and its complications, until and
after she was diagnosed with colon cancer in 2007. She died in 2010, at age fifty-nine.

Christiane, about to go off on a scheduled vacation to a Spanish island, also immediately flew to the Mayo Clinic to see her wounded mentor.

After considering suspending its Bosnia coverage, CNN decided to stay the course. An international desk assignment editor phoned Christiane and asked: Would she fly back and rejoin the team there? People were "surprised," David Rust says, when Christiane said yes. Parisa Khosravi probed her friend about the choice, for her own safety. "Are you *sure?*" she asked Christiane. "Are you *sure* you don't want to take a break and rethink?" After all, CNN—however dependent on her it may have been—didn't *order* reporters to war zones; reporters had to volunteer for the postings. "And here was a story where they were outright targeting journalists— that realization is what changed it for all of us," Parisa says.

"It was very dramatic; it was a decisive moment. Christiane gritted her teeth, and then she said, 'I'm going back.' Seeing Margaret with her jaw shot out steeled her to go back to Bosnia."

Here's how Christiane has explained her decision, fighting back tears: "I said yes because I couldn't say no. I said I'd go back" to Sarajevo because "we did the work for her. We did it because [Margaret] was our champion, and we wanted to be *her* champion." But she also said this: "I know to this day that if I hadn't said yes, then I probably never would have gone back, and I never would have done this career."

THOUGH THE WHOLE CREW covered the war together, Christiane's passion and pushiness, and her emerging prominence with CNN, kept the coverage going and made the Bosnian atrocity known to America. "She reported the hell out of that war," says Emma Daly. And Bob Simon says, "Christiane was probably the best correspondent covering Bosnia, and she was certainly more dedicated than anyone else. She became completely devoted and committed to that story."

But the depth and breadth of all of that would come later. For now, in July 1992, with Margaret Moth in the hospital, David Rust says he "called the CNN international desk to get details, and then I volunteered to join Christiane" and return to Sarajevo. A week after Margaret's shooting, he met Christiane in Zagreb, where she "was already following a breaking story involving detention camps, or what the Serbs euphemistically called 'transit' camps." What was to become known as the "ethnic cleansing" of Bosniaks by the Serbs had begun. In one camp, "a British television crew got images of prisoners that looked a lot like photos taken in Nazi concentration camps toward the end of World War II."

On August 14, Christiane and David flew from Zagreb to Sarajevo. At the airport they ran into two fresh arrivals in Bosnia, both from ABC: Diane Sawyer's *Primetime* partner Sam Donaldson and producer Dave Kaplan. Christiane greeted Sam and Dave collegially, and the four of them planned to meet up at the Holiday Inn. The ABC folks were accompanying then Yugoslavian prime minister Milan Panic into town. Donaldson entered Panic's armored UN vehicle, while Kaplan hitched a ride with another TV crew. That car was unarmored.

Minutes after the car in which Kaplan was riding turned onto the highway, out of the airport, a sniper bullet pierced the car. The bullet penetrated Kaplan's back and exited through his chest. He died almost instantly.

At the Holiday Inn, and at the bar at the Love Hotel, this news of a fresh sniper assassination of a journalist (on top of the recent injuries of fourteen other newspeople) was received with ashen faces, fists clutched around shot glasses, steely resolve, submerged fear, and sorrow. Christiane had rescheduled her missed vacation for three weeks hence. But after Kaplan's killing, redoubling her conviction, she canceled it for good. She was in for the long haul. She must have anticipated then—in her bones, in her heart—what she would later put in words: that Bosnia was "where I became myself as a reporter, where I learned how to use my voice, where I learned what it means to have someone's back and for them to have yours; where we risked our lives and sometimes our sanity . . . [and] forged the closest of bonds."

Because of the sniper killings, CNN instituted a new policy: Reporters and crew would travel only in armored vehicles. In most cases they wore bullet-resistant vests and helmets. As an additional safety measure—and an act of community—the media outlets organized the Sarajevo Agency

Pool, whereby the news bureaus rotated being on duty and shared the fruits of their news gathering with the others, thus mitigating the risk. "So many lives were saved through this," Emma Daly says.

The danger was escalating. As David Rust recalls,[*] "Although there was activity every night in the Bosnian capital, this night"—August 24, ten days after Kaplan's death—"was different. The intensity of the shelling and small arms fire was far greater than any previous night. Explosions were constant. Because it was too dangerous to go outside the hotel at night, we were forced to cover the battle from inside the hotel. While Christiane and Nic [Robertson] gathered facts and tried to file reports over satellite phone, I went to the upper floors and tried to use nightscope to get pictures of the firefight.

"Mortar shells exploded close enough to the hotel to spray shrapnel into the windows. Through the broken windows in many of our rooms you could hear rounds from AK-47's whiz by, some lodging in the metal frames of the windowsills. The battle lasted throughout the night and into the early morning hours. It got so intense at one point that we decided to protectively load up our armored car with supplies and equipment that we"—Christiane, David, and Nic—"felt were essential in case we needed to abandon the hotel and seek shelter somewhere else."

Nevertheless, by day's end, they filed their story—Christiane filing audio reports over the phone until the early hours of the morning. Sleep was impossible; their rooms were on a low floor, where the tank rounds could easily pierce the windows and walls. So, sitting in the hall outside Nic's room, the three talked all night as the sounds of warfare pounded all around them. When the sun came up, the sleepless trio, fueled on bad coffee and much adrenaline, left the hotel. The national library was ablaze. In the previous twenty-four hours, twenty people had been killed and over a hundred wounded on the Bosniak side alone.

David and Christiane drove off to do a story at a playground about the

---

[*]Much of this account has been taken from the diary David Rust wrote nightly in Sarajevo—encrypted, in case he was captured or a checkpoint guard asked to examine his belongings—portions of which he generously volunteered to share for this book.

children of the war. This was a heart-stopper. Some of the children's little friends had already been killed. As Christiane gently probed the children, David filmed, noting in his diary that "they had very nice faces, including one that was disfigured by a mortar blast—she still smiled a lot. I also got pictures of two little boys with plastic rifles that featured homemade sniper scopes." The plight of the children was one of the reasons Christiane felt—as she'd say much later, even after she'd seen so much crisis—that "Bosnia [remained] the most emotionally wrenching and physically arduous story I've ever covered or been through in my life. You just see terrible stuff all the time. If it's not bodies, it's children bloodied and battered, old men and women injured. . . . [W]e saw houses burned and people inside, charred like barbecue, and mosques and churches dynamited."

Just as Christiane was wrapping up her piece, "War Through the Eyes of Children," she and David got news that a colleague, BBC's Martin Bell, had been hit by shrapnel. She and David drove—past a stretch of highway the British were now calling "Murder Mile"—to the BBC studio's "feed point," where Christiane filed the story in time to make the morning newscasts—getting *this* story out to an America that had barely heard of Slobodan Milosevic or even Bosnia now seemed urgent. Then they rushed to the hospital to see Martin Bell and to wish him well (he eventually fully recovered) before he was medevaced to England. Returning to the hotel, Christiane, David, and Nic had to drive on back roads to avoid heavy shelling. "We did see a fire burning about a half mile behind the hotel but felt it wasn't worth chasing," David wrote.

The three of them later met in the lobby for dinner. No sooner had they begun to eat than a bomb was detonated, very close by. "Soon, there was increased fighting all over the city. It was dark outside except for flashes from explosions, tracer rounds, and fires." Christiane wrote the copy while Rust and BBC cameraman Rory Peck taped the fighting through the upper-floor windows. (Less than a year later, Peck would be killed while on assignment.) For three hours "artillery shells, mortars, and machine-gun fire lit up the darkened neighborhood," David recalls. "There were tracers and loud bangs with echoes almost continuously. It reminded me of a scene out of *Apocalypse Now*. Those glass windows in the room that were still there would shake after each explosion. You could often hear the individual rounds whiz by when they were close enough."

Christiane took the tape and went live with it on CNN International. "Despite the fact that the [Atlanta-based] anchor could *hear* loud explosions in the background, he asked Christiane, 'Are you in any personal danger?'" In an impatient, emotional voice, Christiane retorted: "*Everyone* in Sarajevo is in personal danger!"

The risks continued, unabated. "Our armored car was hit by small arms fire over nine times," says David. "Once it was taken out of commission by a fifty-caliber machine gun that tore up the engine compartment. We also encountered snipers a number of times while on foot. Once, we were doing an interview with a French officer in charge of airport detail, and a sniper shot hit, right off the wall, about four feet above our heads. Cement flew! So we moved to another location." Christiane kept interviewing and David kept taping. "That was pretty typical," he says.

Another time, Christiane has recalled, when Serb "gunners on the hills figured out" she and her team were reporting on, of all things, the starving animals in a zoo (they'd been abandoned when the zookeepers ran for their lives), she kicked in a building and took refuge in a doorway, and as they too ran for cover, "all I could keep saying to [them] was, 'If you die, I'm so sorry, I'm so sorry, I'm so sorry.'" She later realized that, by being "too busy apologizing," she had cleverly tricked herself from fearing her own possible death. "The minute the shooting stopped, we ran out of there." Yet another time, CNN producer Judy Milestone conducted an Atlanta-to-Sarajevo phone interview with her. "I could hear gunshots," Judy says. "I asked Christiane, 'Are you okay?' Christiane said, 'I just ducked behind a door.'" What Ron Haviv and the other photographers and videographers appreciated was that "she wasn't just doing stand-ups from hotels; she was in the front lines with the rest of us. There were not a lot of TV people who would do that."

Then there was Mostar, where for nine months Bosnian Croats had been shooting, shelling, and hemming in the Muslims "under extraordinarily bad conditions," says David Rust. "Christiane wanted to see for herself what was going on in Mostar, and she decided we should follow a UN food convoy"—these were allowed in only at the pleasure of the Croats—"into the city. The convoy entered, and workers started to unload flour and cooking oil. Before they could start to distribute supplies, the trucks were surrounded by townspeople. They came out of buildings heavily damaged by war. We found many residents living in basements of buildings that were without running water, heat, or electricity"—this was in the middle of winter. Then Christiane wanted to see and report on old Mostar, "a no-man's-land and the scene of the most extensive destruction in the city. We were told it was dangerous to go there." They went, cautiously, anyway.

They had a Muslim guide—their lifeline in hostile territory—and he was skittish. The only way to get to the no-man's-land was over a questionably viable bridge. "We worked our way through the town, past shell-damaged buildings and somewhat close to the entrance to the bridge. As soon as we got there, our guide ran from the cover of the buildings and crossed the bridge. Unfortunately for us, we had to follow him. He had guided us to the bridge and we needed him to get us back to the food convoy. Our only choice was to follow him across"—amid gunfire.

"Christiane made the first dash for the other side. I stayed back to videotape the crossing. It took nearly forty seconds for her to run from the safety of the last building, across the bridge, and finally to a building on the other side. Normally, that's not a long time, but when you're being shot at, it's an eternity."

Rust could see that the bridge was a wreck. "It had been shelled often and many parts were missing"—yet those gaps were hard to see because the planks were snow covered. You had to just "forget about the snipers" because "one false step and [you'd] be making a seventy-foot plunge into a deep, ice-cold river with swift-flowing water."

But he and Nic made it safely across, after Christiane had. On the other side, the Muslim and Croat armies were virtually on top of each other. "As we ran through the trenches, several shots and a couple of rockets were fired, and inside one of the buildings I heard soldiers on both sides shouting at each other. I couldn't believe the opposing sides were that close."

After taping and reporting, they gingerly picked their way back over the rickety bridge, "one at a time, and then we raced back to the convoy." After that, Sniper Alley and the Holiday Inn felt like relatively safe havens.

"It's shocking how normal things become," says Emma Daly. She and Christiane—who both wore jeans and parkas and bare faces while the Bosnian women around them (many of them fixers and translators) were slathered in makeup and tottered around in high heels—talked about how this war disabused them of dependence on what now seemed like trivial luxuries. "It became normal to walk into a room at night and *not* reach for the light switch, because there was no electricity. It became normal to live without bathing for several days. Our great friend and colleague Allan Little of the BBC said to me one winter, 'We've all heard of dying from hypothermia, but nobody ever died of smelling bad—so, no, I am *not* taking my clothes off to wash in my windowpane-less hotel room [in twenty-degree weather].' It became normal to drive on the sidewalk because there were no traffic lights, traffic rules, or"—during heavy shelling—"traffic."

Harder was getting used to friends' near misses. A sister newswoman, Elizabeth Neuffer of the *Boston Globe*, was attacked by the Bosnian army but, fortunately, was rescued at zero hour by a UN crew. (Neuffer was killed in a car crash in Iraq in 2003.) Harder yet was seeing the raped women and the constant civilian casualties. "People would be killed running out to try to get food or standing in line for water," Emma recalls. And the children had gotten so used to war, "they would play games based on the real circumstances of their life, like, 'I'm the sniper, you're the victim, and that's the ambulance.' Or, later, they'd play the humanitarian aide worker game: 'Here, pretend this rock is your bowl of rice.'" Emma and Christiane had a hard time shaking off the images of the children in hospitals, like the blind little girl "with both hands cut off." Christiane has said, "Seeing children victims of the genocide was more than I could tolerate. Children who'd deliberately been scoped through a sniper's sights and killed: It's a kind of horror that you don't believe is possible." Amid the horror, they felt so helpless, so frustrated by the paltriness of their own contribution as journalists, a disappointment that the people they were covering vociferously and contemptuously seconded. "After someone was shot and one of us would show up," Ron Haviv says, "people would spit on us and say, 'Leave! You're not doing anything to help us. We don't want you here!'"

The crew sought relief in abandon. "I remember Christiane dancing on the table, to funky music, at an AP party," says Emma. The Love Hotel had a great party space downstairs, and since the UN would always refer to the "warring parties" of Bosnia, any reporters' bash held there was inevitably called the "Warring Party." After one wild evening, a noted correspondent drank so much that he passed out in the street—"in the middle of the gutter. We actually put a pillow under his head," Emma says.

They imposed after-hours *omertà* on war talk. "At one point when we were sitting around drinking and chatting I said, 'Can we institute a ban on Bosnia Bore at dinner? Can we please just talk about really random things that have nothing to do with this war?'" Christiane escaped into corny romance novels. "Christiane said, 'You *have* to read this *really* good book!'" She thrust it at Emma—*The Bridges of Madison County.* "I came back and I was outraged. 'I can't believe you made me read this book—it's horrible!' And she was, 'No, no! It's good! You have to keep reading!' She really does have this sappy, romantic side." Perhaps, Emma thinks, Christiane liked the book so much because the photographer protagonist was said to have been inspired by Jim Nachtwey, one of the most distinguished war photographers of his generation. "Jim was very tall and handsome and very, very nice," Emma says. "We all had crushes on him."

A better escape was real-life romance. Christiane became seriously involved with the dashing Frenchman Luc Delahaye, the two repairing, during their off rotations, to an apartment in Paris. Romances among war zone reporters are their own kind of treachery. Vulnerability, attachment, and preoccupation—the staples of love—only leave the combat reporter disadvantaged in the quest for the focus so necessary to live another reporting day.

"Christiane had a lot of boyfriends on the road, and she wasn't thinking about getting married," her sister Lizzy says. "I don't think she was particularly discreet about her romances," shrugs Pierre Bairin.

.   .   .

CHRISTIANE AMANPOUR. CHRISTIANE AMANPOUR.
American viewers—and international viewers, the vast majority of CNN's
audience—got used to the battlefield-type credit line under the nightly
reports, got used to the sight of the woman with the messy dark hair in
the flak jacket or parka, standing against the darkened sky, holding the
microphone and giving passionate nightly reports in a loud, crisp, plummy
English accent, with the sound of distant bullets sometimes popping in
the background. How different this all was—where *was* Bosnia? who *were*
the Serbs? who *were* these besieged people, their victims? (*Muslims*
in Eastern Europe?)—from the other news that Americans were really
paying attention to in 1992 and 1993: the transfer of the presidency from
a terse-talking aristocratic establishment Republican to the first baby
boomer chief executive, a voluble hail-fellow Arkansas New Democrat
with a blond named Gennifer in his not-so-distant past. The historic
handshake on a podium in front of the White House between lifelong
enemies Yitzhak Rabin and Yasir Arafat. And the tabloid grabbers: Amy
Fisher shooting Mary Jo Buttafuoco!

"Now to Christiane Amanpour, in Sarajevo": The Atlanta anchor's
handoff was both anticlimactic, amid this gaudily competitive parade,
and beseeching.

"Christiane tried to pound it home to CNN that we had to stay
there and cover this story," says David Rust. "It wasn't a popular war in
America—we didn't have a dog in the fight, it wasn't a place we got our
oil from—but she knew it was important for historic reasons. She was
very, very persistent." She relentlessly worked on Steve Cassidy, who
was in charge of CNN's international desk, and Eason Jordan, who oversaw all the network's international operations. "I think her push and her
drive made them keep agreeing with her that it was important."

Ron Haviv was Christiane's partner in pushing the story, refusing to
let it die, refusing to leave Sarajevo. As a conflict zone reporter, "you'd
either just say, 'I can't handle this anymore—I'm just a voyeur and there's

244 THE NEWS SORORITY

no point,'" he says. "Or people like Christiane and myself and others
would get so angry. Anger was the motivating factor to keep going, basically throwing these images in front of the Americans, in front of the
politicians, and saying, 'You can't say you don't know what's happening—
we're showing it to you!' She was going live, every night, from Sarajevo.
Day one, day five. 'This is what's happening.' Day thirty, day fifty. Day *one
hundred*." Christiane kept at it because she says she felt, "I cannot believe
this is being allowed to happen." The war was "being fought against civilians, in the cities, people's homes, not on the battlefield. The United
Nations [eventually] said that there has never been a war in modern times
that has affected so many children. It is horrifying, and savage."

After a while Christiane was so upset and frustrated that other
media—newspapers, networks—were not paying more attention to Bosnia that, after a particularly brutal day in Sarajevo, she did a piece entitled
"Just Another Day." She and David Rust massed together highly graphic
video of carnage in the city, and between snippets she would look at the
camera and say, "It was just another day in Sarajevo." More shelling, more
sniping. "It was just another day in Sarajevo." She said it again and again.
"The package was so effective," David recalls, "that the day after it aired,
an aircraft full of journalists arrived at the Sarajevo airport, and several
mentioned that they had seen her report and felt compelled to cover the
conflict."

As the siege wore on, and the "medieval conditions" the Serbs forced
the Bosniaks to live under (as the war tribunal prosecutor would later
describe them) intensified, "some of the most compelling stories occurred
in the [Muslims'] so-called 'safe havens' established by the UN," Rust
says. One such "safe" town was Gorazde, where the Muslims, "surrounded
by hostile troops"—the Serbs and the Croats—struggled to survive for
months with little contact from the outside world. (The Croats had been
initially aligned with the Bozniaks but that relationship had now fallen
apart.) "Even the UN convoys could barely get in."

It was Christiane's decision to try to get into Gorazde. As she, Nic, and
David approached the city, they confronted the Bosnian Serb troops, who
were stunned to see them. The Serbs were "very unhappy" with Chris-

tiane's anti-Serb slant. A Serbian official had "a look of amazement" that she'd dared enter Gorazde. "We quickly proceeded down the road," David says. "Our excitement turned to disappointment"—not fear, but disappointment that they might not get the story—when it was "explained that both the Croats and Muslims had extensively mined the area. They said the Muslims would meet us on the other side of no-man's-land but that the Croats didn't know where the land mines had been placed. We decided that walking across an unmarked minefield was too great a risk." Ultimately, "we contacted a nearby UN facility and were told we were very lucky to be out."

In May 1994, via satellite from Sarajevo to the televised CNN Global Summit, Christiane asked President Bill Clinton—live, for the world to see—"Mr. President, my question is: As leader of the free world, as leader of the only superpower, why has it taken you . . . so long to articulate a policy on Bosnia? Why, in the absence of a policy, have you allowed the U.S. and the West to be held hostage to those who do have a policy—the Bosnian Serbs—and do you not think that the constant flip-flops of your administration . . . set a very dangerous precedent and would lead people such as [North Korea's] Kim Il-sung . . . to take you less seriously than you would like to be taken?" Here was Christiane, giving what David Bernknopf calls her familiar "withering, unpleasant, nothing-held-back" response—scolding the president of the United States. More important, this was Christiane establishing her moral authority and insisting the leader of the free world do the same. Here was a war being waged on civilians, grave harm and injustice being done—why was the president dithering?

Clinton at first seemed stunned by the steely criticism from a not very well-known female reporter. He came right back at her, using his first defense: his trademark, mildly threatening finger wag. "No, but speeches like *that*"—Christiane's nervy tirade—"may make them take me less seriously than I'd like to be taken," he said, eyes narrowed. "There have been *no* constant flip-flops, *madam.*"

Parisa Khosravi was sitting with Christiane while she was arguing with Clinton, via remote, and she recalls that, when Clinton seethingly called her "madam," "Christiane had to *hold* her face to keep her composure" and keep from breaking up into the "nervous chuckles" the two women collapsed into later.

Right after his sarcastic fillip, Clinton shifted into his default mode: empathetic, co-opting charm, with bitten-lip apology. "That poor woman has seen the horrors of this war, and . . . she's been fabulous," he said. "She's done a great service to the whole world [and] I do not blame her for being mad at me." As characteristically endearing as Clinton's contrition may have been, he wasn't just doing it for effect. He was correct in praising Christiane for doing "a great service to the whole world," and his endorsement of her in that significant manner caused others—in the media, in diplomacy, in public service—to also look at her as a force for morality in public policy. Ron Haviv believes that U.S. and British intervention in the Kosovo War, which started in February 1998 and lasted a year and a half, "started much faster because Clinton and Tony Blair were like, 'We can't keep seeing these images again. We can't keep seeing Christiane—Here's Christiane Amanpour, again, on television, doing the same thing she did in Bosnia three years ago.' So they were embarrassed into reacting much, much faster."

In addition to putting the government on notice, the exchange with Clinton "raised Christiane's profile dramatically," says David Rust. And it came at an accidentally propitious time. Less than one month later, on June 12, Nicole Brown Simpson and Ronald Goldman would be found stabbed to death in a Brentwood courtyard. O. J. Simpson would be arrested and arraigned. He would attempt to flee in a white Bronco, and he would be jailed. Suddenly every other story that Americans had been following, and to which networks were channeling resources, was shoved aside for this one. Christiane Amanpour—freshly anointed as a tough talker to the president—would be a voice crying in the wilderness, protesting that, along with the ethnic cleansing of the Bosniaks and the Siege of Sarajevo, there was also a horrific genocide under way in the African

country of Rwanda. How could the media focus so single-mindedly on the
O.J. case while these global humanitarian catastrophes were occurring?

Later Christiane would say she was "ashamed" by the ineffectuality of
her effort to promote coverage of these horrors. "It drives her crazy to see
the kind of superficial stuff that passes for news," says David Bernknopf.

After all, journalists were putting their lives on the line for these
important international stories. Five months after the start of the O.J.
saga hijacked media attention, in November 1994, Ron Haviv and Christiane's boyfriend Luc Delahaye were driving around, taking pictures, in
Krajina, which was controlled by Serbian rebels. They drove past "some
secret missile silo," Ron recalls, where they were stopped, aggressively, by
Serb militiamen and arrested.

"We were handcuffed together and driven off and interrogated and
beaten up," Ron says. The captors performed "mock executions on them."
Then Ron and Luc were separated by their captors. "I don't know what
happened to Luc, but I was punched in the face, batted over the head, told
I would be killed and that they would kill Luc, too. It was pretty scary."
At the time, Ron was on the Serbs' "death list," and Christiane—also considered their enemy—"was very worried that I would get her boyfriend
killed." For twenty-four, then forty-eight hours and counting, Delahaye's
and Haviv's whereabouts were unknown to their colleagues (and to the
U.S. State Department). Ron: "We just disappeared. We were just *gone*."
Fevered, behind-the-scenes negotiations began by "the French government, the U.S. government—I'm sure Christiane had a lot to do with
them. Even the Russians got involved." After three days, Ron and Luc
were separately driven to a bridge on a densely foggy night. Each was
pushed out of his respective captors' vehicle and "we were just left there,"
groping for the low, slim railings over a raging river. The French came
and rescued Luc; the Americans came and rescued Ron.

Christiane's reunion with Luc was almost certainly emotional and
passionate, but "Christiane and Luc broke up at some point quite soon
after that," Emma recalls, explaining that "having a successful or long-
standing relationship in those conditions is extraordinarily difficult. The

story is so consuming, it really sucks up every part of you. You don't really have much left for anybody else." Christiane subsequently had a Sarajevo-based love affair with French journalist Paul Marchand. (Marchand would dramatically evade abduction while on assignment in Algeria in 1997; years later he would commit suicide.) Little about war reporters' circumstances—and, sometimes, their temperaments—was undramatic; tragedy dogged so many. A recent academic study has shown that the rate of post-traumatic stress disorder for ex–war reporters is almost as high as that of military veterans.

"For Christiane," having a relationship with a fellow correspondent "was now even more complicated because she was so visible," Emma continues. "On the one hand, that new visibility made her powerful and gave her leverage with the State Department"—she *had* helped Haviv and Delahaye be freed. On the other hand, her increasingly intense and increasingly televised public invective against the Serbs made them hate her on the level that diplomacy doesn't have time to reach: the hair-trigger, spontaneous, someone-could-kill-her-at-any-moment level.

The capstone atrocity of the Bosnian conflict was the July 1995 targeted killing, by the Serbs, of eight thousand Bosniak men and boys. This attack, the Srebrenica Massacre, would later be officially cited as genocide. (The conflict would end with a negotiated peace four months later, in November 1995.) Having covered it and the events leading up to it, in the winter of 1994–1995, with Christiane, Pierre Bairin says it was hard for them to process "people transported in buses, separated in the middle of winter, with very little clothing. Ethnic cleansing—it was horrendous." Outraged, Christiane pushed the story onto a public that was being stuffed, morning, noon, and night, with the O.J. Simpson trial. Now she was starting to be called—even in some quarters of the State Department—strident and nonobjective.

Christiane didn't give a damn. "Once Srebrenica happened, it was a massacre too far, and our Western governments, after showing a deplorable failure of collective will, finally got their acts together and did something about it. But they might not have done it if we were not reporting it," she said. A year later she would shoot down the "nonobjective" charge, saying: "Objectivity means giving all sides a hearing. It doesn't mean treating all sides equally. The overwhelming number of atrocities were committed by the Bosnian Serbs. The Serbs shelled civilians, sniped small children, and committed torture, rape, and murder against civilians. That's not war; that's war crime." David Bernknopf says: The "this side says" and "the other side says" approach to stories like Bosnia "almost physically made her have a conniption fit. 'Would you cover the *Nazis* that way?' she would say."

ESPECIALLY TOWARD THE end of her time in Bosnia, Christiane confronted resistance from another quarter—which wasn't unexpected, but was now very strong: envy and resentment from male war reporters, both the seasoned ones *and* the young ones. "Men were jealous because she was a woman with bravado, doing things that these big macho guys wouldn't exactly do," explains Pierre Bairin.

Someone else who observed the situation close at hand goes further. "Nobody had wanted to go into Bosnia; they thought it was a dangerous place. The London bureau of CNN had totally refused to go." Then, as Christiane and her team began getting this story, "a lot of the guys" who hadn't gone "criticized her a lot—they wouldn't admit she was very good. They said nasty stuff. They made stuff up."

Over drinks at pubs, the men who'd begged off war coverage would say, to one particular man who was joining her team, "'Why are you doing this? You'll get killed.' It was kind of like, 'Play on *my* team, not hers. There's more weight behind one side if we all get together. Then none of us will go in [to Bosnia] and she can't do it anymore.'" Essentially, they were trying to sabotage her work. The older guys could hide behind the boast, "'I've *done* my war.' One guy in his late forties even said, 'I told my mother I'd never go anywhere dangerous.'" The man who heard this says, "I kind of had to look at the ground and chuckle. The younger jealous guys were particularly bitchy and bastardy. They would say, 'Oh, she's seeing this guy; try to spread a rumor.'"

Female correspondents were sometimes derided by their male counterparts for using charm for access, Emma says. The unstated retort to the "please?" and the smile to the driver, the fixer, the guard at the checkpoint, was "Guys wouldn't do that." But Mark Phillips says, "Christiane would probably kill me if she knew that I said this, but she never flirted with anybody. That was never her thing, and some other correspondents did that."

As her prominence grew, *60 Minutes* did a feature on Christiane—and this really set off some of the grumbling men. CNN wasn't supposed to have stars—"The *news* is our 'star,'" Ted Turner famously decreed—but here Christiane was: famous. What's more, she was *enjoying* it. "She was excited when Mike Wallace came" to do the story on her, a CNN team member says. "She walked around with this Cheshire cat grin." The other reporters also felt—and she seemed to realize—that the *60 Minutes* segment on her "was a *60 Minutes* job interview as well.

"She was becoming a star, she was pulling in the numbers—and management didn't know how to handle it," the team member says. "You've got to remember: The people who came to CNN were old network guys who'd done their time at the networks and who couldn't make it at the networks. We used to go to the Emmys and joke, 'You never win anything.' And all of a sudden *she's* competing with these guys—and *winning*."

WOULD SHE LEAVE CNN for one of the big networks?

The answer came in June 1996. Christiane renewed her CNN contract, turning down offers from the major networks. "Roone wanted to have Christiane very badly. Several times in the midnineties, he went after her, but we never got her here [at the time]," says an ABC executive. But she also cut a fairly unique deal to do four or five big foreign investigatives a year for *60 Minutes*, for a million dollars. When Leslie Bennetts of *Vanity Fair* asked Don Hewitt about the unusual "half a loaf" deal—why didn't they court Christiane more heavily and put her on as the needed younger female?—Hewitt, who had waxed defensive when Arledge stole Diane Sawyer away from him nine years earlier, barked ferociously: "I don't give a fuck what the perception is! I don't play the younger bullshit game! You're telling me what the people in the industry say? Most of them couldn't find their asses with both their hands! I don't play the gender game! I play the reporter game!"

Whether Hewitt was protesting too much or hoisting the battered Murrow/Cronkite banner, Christiane began, in 1996, a course of nonstop two-network globe-hopping. She based herself in London, "which always felt like home to her," says Bella Pollen, the novelist who would become her close friend there in subsequent years. From 1996 through 1998, she did stories in, among other places, Israel, Cairo (where at the Pan-Arab Summit she interviewed Jordan's King Hussein, Libya's Muammar Gaddhafi, and Egypt's Hosni Mubarak), Africa, Eastern Europe, Afghanistan, Iran, and Cuba.

In Cuba she worked with her friend David Bernknopf. "She started asking people—and they recognized her—about the reality versus what the government was telling them, and some people started yelling at her and it got quite heated: 'We don't want to be portrayed this way! It's your fault, you Americans!' But she kept asking them," says Bernknopf. She even took the long drive to the home of a Cuban citizen who, "probably at some risk to himself, gave a shockingly honest interview" about how "'the government promises us things but we have nothing.'"

With Parisa Khosravi, she worked doggedly for weeks to get the first interview with Iran's brand-new president, Seyyed Mohammad Khatami. As Christiane conducted the interview—both women using their respectively excellent (Parisa) and good enough (Christiane) Farsi to make out the words of the man now called the Smiling Mullah—"we were looking at each other," dumbstruck, Parisa says. "'Did he really say what it sounds like he just said? *That he apologized to America for the hostage taking!*' In the car we listened to the tape and said, 'Boy! Big news here!' We went back to the hotel and listened to it again, and the translators were poring over it and—Yes! That *is* what he said! We called Atlanta and told our bosses. '*He apologized!*'" The new political leader of Iran had just expressed regret to the Great Satan for the most aggressive, sustained, and humiliating recent event in American foreign relations.

Christiane and Parisa couldn't wait to see their major scoop—which

252 THE NEWS SORORITY

was so personally meaningful to them as Iranians—go top of the news. And it should have. Except that day—January 17, 1998—filling American TV screens instead was the image of a hitherto unheard-of, broadly smiling, wide-faced, pleasant-looking, thick-dark-haired young Los Angeles woman: Monica Lewinsky.

In Ghana, Christiane and the young American producer Andrew Tkach—with whom she would spend a decade developing many gut-wrenching *60 Minutes* pieces all over the world—made their way, in part by dugout canoes through a river full of crocodiles, to the remote villages of the Upper Volta River where a traditional form of slavery called Trokosi was still practiced. They were on the track of an important exposé: a "spirit," a traditional priest and very powerful personage in the community, was said to be enslaving, sexually and otherwise, a seven-year-old girl who had been indentured to him by her grandfather. This was an illegal but widespread custom in this region. "We saw this little girl," clearly overburdened, "carrying large objects. Christiane looks at the priest and, rather than making social peace to get the story, she just points right to the girl and demands to know, '*Is this one of your slaves?*' And the priest said yes, and she just let him *have* it." Not every reporter would berate a powerful priest in a far-off country where the reporter was a barely—and warily—permitted intruder. But Christiane did just that. "She was able to express her outrage so clearly." (The abuse was reported to a human rights agency.)

"In stories like these, when you interview people whose lips were chopped off so they couldn't tell secrets, whose limbs were cut off so they wouldn't inform on the rebels"—as he and Christiane did in a piece on child soldiers in Uganda—"the emotions are overpowering," Tkach says. "You definitely get sucked into their world." The child soldiers story was particularly painful, showing, as it did, not just cruelty but a moral dilemma. The youthful Ugandan strongmen "would empty whole schools, kidnap the children, and take them into northern Uganda or southern Sudan and use them as slaves or cannon fodder. Christiane and I went to one school," headmistressed by a brave nun named Sister Rachele, "which had been emptied. One hundred and thirty-nine girls had been taken.

Sister Rachele followed the trail left by candy wrappers, because the kidnapping soldiers *themselves* were children. She followed the candy wrappers for an hour or two into the jungle and fearlessly confronted the commander. He forced Sister Rachele to make a deal with the devil—he said, 'You pick the [finite number of] girls you want to take back.' How do you interview somebody forced to make a moral choice she finds abhorrent but which means saving lives? Christiane did [the interview] with great sensitivity. One of the girls escaped. We talked to her [too]. You put it into a compartment: 'This is really important. This is something the world should know. We are privileged to witness this; it is our duty to tell it well.'" That self-reminder is just as important as the team bonding— "the cameramen, the soundman, the producer, the correspondent Christiane, the translator, maybe an assistant producer: You become a family and you share things. That's how you deal with those searing emotions. Because sometimes you want to cry."

In Rwanda, she and Tkach entered a surreal purgatory: a mammoth, airport-hangar-like detention center stuffed, from ground to ceiling, with men incarcerated for crimes they had committed during the recent genocide. It was so crowded and oppressive that even the guards wouldn't enter—they merely opened the door for Christiane, Tkach, and the cameraman, and then they vanished. The arena "was stacked—five decks of people, all men," Andrew says. "In each of those decks," hundreds of "faces peered out at us. It was so tense with humanity, and with such an overpowering stench. But there was Christiane, asking these men accused of the most horrible crimes what they had to say about the atrocity. Without coddling them. Without *needing* to be coddled."

Whatever their assignment, "Christiane was able to do all the heavy lifting," Tkach says, thanks to her discipline and stoicism. "She wasn't complaining about being covered in flies. She was only thinking, 'Are we getting the story? Is this working?'" In the years he worked with her, "the only time I saw Christiane flinch wasn't when we were in any kind of danger or warfare." Rather, it was "when we did a nonpolitical piece, in Gabon, on gorillas being repatriated into the wild. A dominant male adolescent gorilla—they're powerful!—jumped on Christiane's back and started pulling her hair and nipping at her clothes. Her face was, 'I'm *really* scared, but I don't want to blow it. So I won't do anything. I'll keep my fear in.'"

But Christiane was hardly battle-scarred into stoicism about all that she had witnessed. While in Africa, she met Paul Rusesabagina, the manager of the Mille Collines Hotel in Kigali, Rwanda, and one of the heroes during the genocide. A few years later, when she and her friend Bella Pollen were in London, watching the movie detailing his heroics, *Hotel Rwanda*, on TV, "we sat slightly awkwardly side by side on the couch and I had to try terribly hard not to cry," Bella says. Christiane blurted out, "'I knew that man!' Afterward we had a cup of tea and she said, 'I was struggling so hard not to cry in front of you because I would be embarrassed.'"

Christiane's emotions *would* eventually come out, and in a fairly quick, three-year succession. As her friend Bella Pollen explains the change: From late 1997 to 2000 Christiane "fell in love, got married, had a child, and fell in love with being a mother." She had been prepared for war and human tragedy. *This* transformation came as much more of a surprise to her.

PART FOUR

SWEEPS

CHAPTER SEVEN

The Cool Drink of Water Versus the Girl Next Door

Diane and Katie: 1999 to 2005

DIANE SAWYER—the queen—was in play. In December 1998, *Good Morning America* was in free fall. Three years earlier, *Today* had broken *GMA*'s eight-year winning streak to seize the number one Morning slot, thanks to the addition of Katie. She and Matt were a perfect nineties morning mix—suave and bouncy, neighborly and urbane, in seemingly effortless sync with each other. And with Jay's death in January 1998 and Katie's poignant return from bereavement leave in March, her popularity was exponentially magnified.

That same month, March, David Westin had replaced Charlie Gibson at *GMA* with young Kevin Newman. Charlie had anchored Morning at ABC since 1987 with Joan Lunden and had now been cohosting with Lisa McRee for a year. He was a serious reporter, providing weight and a certain avuncularity as counterpoint to the women with whom he was paired: Both Lunden and McRee were blonds who had started out as local anchors. As such, he was a bit above it all; he didn't procure the "gets." He let the producers get their hands dirty with that.

Charlie's departure at age fifty-five was not meant to look negative. The show threw him a big on-air going-away party. But, says a then senior producer at ABC, "Charlie had been very convinced" that the network felt "his time had come and gone and it was time for someone new." He himself later tartly admitted, "My sell-by date had arrived."

The new team—McRee and Newman—were poised to ascend. The trouble is: They didn't. By late October, that was clear. "They felt junior, they felt small," says someone who was an ABC executive at the time about how they resonated. McRee hadn't been ABC's initial choice to replace Lunden. The network had performed "a low-level steal," according to the ex-executive, taking Elizabeth Vargas from NBC to give her Lunden's job. (Vargas and Katie hadn't gotten along—"Elizabeth was never going to inherit over there.") But instead Vargas became the newsreader, and the anchor job went to Lisa McRee, a Texas-raised news anchor who'd worked the Dallas and Los Angeles markets. "Lisa was very good live—she was brilliant in terms of ad-libbing and thinking on her feet. But she fell short on real depth and gravitas," says the executive. "It's not that you have to have gravitas, but you have to be able to interview the president *and* put on a Halloween costume, and do everything in between. She wasn't big enough to fill the job."

As for Kevin, "he was a very good broadcaster, very smart," the ex-executive says. "And very good looking." But "he was Canadian—that's a little more reserved. When the World Series happened, he didn't know how to get excited because he wasn't American. That certainly wasn't the only reason" ABC wanted to replace him, "but it was just emblematic."

In early November 1998, the ABC brass turned to Phyllis McGrady, who had long worked with Diane. "They said, 'What can you do to the show?'" Phyllis recalls. "I said, 'It's hemorrhaging. Why put a Band-Aid on the show; it's hemorrhaging pretty critically.'" Big changes—at least one if not two new anchors and a new producer—were needed, Phyllis felt.

Shelley Ross from *Primetime*, who was brought in as executive producer, flew from LA to New York to win back Charlie Gibson, whom she would be meeting for the first time. As soon as she landed, she learned that Charlie wouldn't meet with her. A former ABC executive explains: "Charlie can be impenetrable. He's crusty and tough, and I think he brought a lot of feelings to the table" during this rewooing, including old ones of "not having been well thought of by Roone." "He had a chip on his shoulder," someone who worked with him adds. "For eleven years, he was a rock-solid anchor and he got the big interviews, but the show was always about Joan Lunden. She was the blond and the star." Then, to add insult to injury, McRee, the *newbie* blond, remained while he was let go.

On the flight home, analyzing Charlie's rebuff, Ross got clear signals that he probably "didn't think he could turn *GMA* around with Lisa McRee—the show was *so* damaged," she says. Then it struck her: "Having the best prom date would get him back. Having *Diane Sawyer* as cohost—he wouldn't say no to that!"

Shelley picked up the Airfone and called Diane to explore the prospect. "Diane's first reaction was, 'I think my time to do the morning show has come and gone'—she'd already done CBS Morning—'and I think you'll find there's somebody else out there who's better suited,'" Shelley recounts. Diane had just turned fifty-three. "I knew she was saying she thought she had aged out of a morning show. There were all these young perky anchors; they had never hired somebody at Diane's age. I said, 'Diane, I don't agree.' I gave her part of my spiel"—about how ageless she was and what her star power could give to the show—"when she said, 'But I would do anything to help the news division.'" To Shelley, that felt like a yes. "She really wanted to do it—to redefine a morning show."

Shelley had already had a prior conversation with Diane, when Shelley had left *Primetime* for *GMA*. She had told Diane she wanted to change the news cycle, establish *GMA* as a new flagship. "There was nothing to damage one's news credentials," in Shelley's formulation. There was also this: Airtime is oxygen to highly successful TV news stars. The prospect of two hours of almost unrelieved airtime a day—ten hours of it a week—may well have had an irresistible pull on Diane even beyond the pull of duty to the news division. Yet, according to Shelley, Diane's interest was more in dropping the invisible wall between an anchor and her audience; she wanted to be less formal with viewers, who saw her as somewhat uptight on *Primetime*. Still, helping the news division was no small consideration. Because *GMA*'s ratings had dropped with Newman and McRee, the local affiliates were threatening to take back the seven to nine a.m. time slot. The revenue at stake was hundreds of millions of dollars. And Diane would not have to leave *Primetime*—she could continue to contribute as much as she wanted—in order to take *GMA*. "In a nutshell," Shelley says, "Diane's yes wasn't about the *GMA* anyone knew. She was committed to the *GMA* that we were going to *build*."

Shelley, still in flight, then called Phyllis and said, "Phyllis, I've got the answer." That answer was the *GMA* Dream Team. Phyllis said she would talk to David Westin. When Phyllis didn't call back, Shelley called her again—and Phyllis said that Westin had responded, "In the game of chess, you never expose your queen."

After Shelley landed in LA, Diane called her and said, "I haven't heard from anyone yet." Shelley assured Diane: "You will." Shelley then called Phyllis *again* and said, "Diane *really* wants to do this!" That led to the hastily scheduled secret meeting when the ABC executives, overriding David Westin's original objection—or bringing him around to their thinking—decided that, yes, they *must* play their queen after all.

It was two days before Christmas. They now had to make an official offer to Diane—urgently. Westin and McGrady went to Diane's Fifth Avenue apartment. "But I can tell you," says an executive who had been in on the secret meeting, "there was always an escape hatch for Diane." The offer was structured so that "Diane could always say, 'I'm out of here' if the ratings were looking" bad. The offer "allowed her to always say, 'I never said I was going to stay. I only said I was coming for three months.' Diane's very much like that," says a strategist. In seriously considering saying yes to *GMA*, "she was taking a flyer—she was jumping off a cliff to do this."

Phyllis and David launched into their pitch. As Phyllis recalls it: "We said a Diane Sawyer and Charlie Gibson pairing is a major statement that immediately sends the message: 'We're serious. These are two of our top people who are now going to be anchoring this morning program. *Good Morning America* is a show that's been on ABC for a lot of years. It's been number one, it has a lot of tradition, and it's sort of lost its way.' And this is signal to say: 'We are back. And we're back in a big, big way.'"

One stumbling block was that Diane "didn't really know Charlie," Phyllis explains. "They knew each other to say hello, but they'd never worked together. So it was kind of like, 'Do you really think so? I'm not so sure.'"

Even though Shelley had gotten the strong sense that Diane wanted it, Westin and McGrady felt they had to keep pressing their case—and they did so. "The viewer doesn't know what *we* know—that you're *funny*, that you have a great sense of humor, that you are so curious about everything. A two-hour program every day allows you a huge, huge canvas," Phyllis reminded her friend. Did that appeal to Diane? "Of course!" Phyllis says. "We kind of knew it would appeal to her. And yet it's live. It's a lot of show—two hours a day." Diane was intrigued, but "she still wasn't sure"—not atypical musing and equivocation for Diane.

A day later, on Christmas Eve, while everyone else at ABC was dashing out for holiday festivities, Charlie walked into Diane's office and they puzzled out a plan, like two kids making a double dare. "I said to Charlie, 'I'll do it if you'll do it,'" Diane's recalled. "And he said, 'I'll do it if you do it.'" They each took up the other on the dare.

And that was that.

Their agreement was kept strictly confidential over the two-week holiday period. Then, on January 4, 1999, the media got the announcement via a conference call. Phyllis, who was on the call, remembers, "You could actually hear reporters *gasp*. It's the only time in the years that I've been involved in television where something *really* stayed a secret."

THE NEW TAGLINE of the show was "Start Smarter," making a virtue of the cohosts' maturity and reporting heft. But what ABC viewers saw at seven a.m. on January 18 was warmer and folksier than "smart." Charlie, a known quantity on the show for a decade, nevertheless reintroduced himself, essentially to set up Diane's reintroduction to an audience that had never seen her as a morning coffee cup holder, doing light fare while viewers were packing lunches and helping their children dress for school. "I'm Charlie Gibson, from Evanston, Illinois," he said. Whereupon the glamorous, classy blond at his side said, smiling, "And I'm Diane Sawyer, from Louisville, Kentucky." Everyone who knew Diane—Diane of the sweatpants and Coke-bottle glasses, the okra and salty potato chips, the Norman Vincent Peale and Catherine Marshall mottoes, the Methodist hymns and the obeisance to her indomitable mother—knew how central that identification actually was. Now perhaps America would get a glimpse of *this* Diane, too.

KATIE AND DIANE would now be locked into one of the more fascinating rivalries in morning TV, imbued with two very different kinds of star power: "Diane was the glamour girl—the tall, cool drink of water—and Katie was the girl next door," says a staffer. Both were almost killingly competitive. In fact, when Roone Arledge learned that Diane had accepted *GMA*, the retired ABC News chief, who still carried a torch for her, called Diane to tell her *not* to take the offer, which was announced as open-ended and temporary, because, as a confidant of Roone's relates his words, "You're *so* competitive, you won't leave until you beat *Today*." He was 90 percent correct in his prediction: Diane would stay for ten whole years, including a window of time, in 2004 and early 2005, when she was a hairsbreadth away from trumping Katie.

Though she virtually glided with great success (aided by her massive work ethic) into supposedly harder forms of broadcast journalism, Diane had to push and pull to get Morning right. An immediate challenge was that morale at *GMA*, which had three million fewer viewers than *Today*, was at a nadir. McGrady says, "Basically, you go into battle every single day—and they [*Today*] are a worthy, worthy, *worthy* opponent! Shelley was the right person to go into battle on a show that was defeated because she is a warrior—'Hel-*lo*, we are *going* to *get* on the phone! We are going to *get* that booking!' She brought the staff back to feeling: We can win! And Diane was the right person, because she is very competitive." Says the senior staffer, reflecting the starting-on-a-dime angst they all faced: "Diane and Charlie were up against Katie and Matt, America's Sweethearts! Who'd been doing it so successfully for five years! And we were up against Jeff Zucker! Jeff Zucker, who's *so* smart!"

But recharging the staff was just a start. Diane had a "big learning curve" in front of her, three separate people—including Phyllis McGrady and Shelley Ross—say, all of them using that phrase. The learning curve roughly broke down into four components: tone and image, technical performing skills, accelerated "get" bookings—and a way to manage the competition with Katie.

First, the tone and image: Says the ABC person who attended the secret meeting, "The warmth that you've seen recently in Diane's specials with Rihanna and Jaycee Dugard—when she started at *GMA*, she didn't have that." (The speaker is referring to the very concerned-toned and insightful November 2009 exclusive interview Diane did with Rihanna, the first one the Barbadian pop star gave after her near strangulation, nine months earlier, by her then boyfriend Chris Brown; and the highly sensitive July 2011 interview Diane did with the Northern Californian young woman who was kidnapped, at eleven years old, in 1991 and held captive for eighteen years before returning home, with her two daughters, to her family in August 2009.) The senior staffer agrees: "At first Diane had trouble with that Morning emotional connection. It really took her time. It was a slow, gradual process. She didn't want to do the girl stuff, the fashion and makeup. She's a serious journalist." It took a while "for the Ice Princess to melt." Wardrobe changes helped her image: She took off her *Primetime* blazers and started wearing sweaters to appear softer and more accessible.

A bigger challenge was learning Morning stagecraft, the executive says. "Diane also didn't have the performing skills to do a two-hour, live, moving-parts program. She had to find the technical skill to do a job that, despite looking easy, is extremely, *extremely* difficult." The senior staffer says: "Morning shows just have a different cadence." One of those cadence-related technical skills was the mastering of the cut-to-the-chase live interview. In live Morning, you don't have time for warm-up questions, there are no do-overs, and you have to cram a lot into a short interview while giving it a polished thoroughness. "You don't start with question number one," says Shelley Ross. "You start with question *three*." In mid-March, two months after Diane started, boxing promoter Don King was on the show with fighters Evander Holyfield and Lennox Lewis, right after their Madison Square Garden bout that was, controversially, declared a draw; many believed that Lewis had really won. While Charlie interviewed Holyfield and Lewis, Diane delivered King a knockout punch by asking, "'So, did you fix the fight?' I almost fell out of my chair! And I know it blew Charlie away," says Shelley Ross. "She started with question *six*! That was the moment I knew Diane's learning curve was over."

Wrangling "gets" was more of a street fight in Morning. Someone associated with the show recalls, "Diane was used to very little competition, other than Barbara. If she wanted a guest, she got it. Also, with *Primetime* and *60*, she could work for weeks and weeks on things; Morning was immediate. And Katie and Matt and Jeff were so entrenched." Diane learned the "muffin basket lesson" early on, says the senior staffer. Up at four a.m. browsing the *Wall Street Journal* for stories, Diane came upon the tiny mention of a little boy who had accidentally stabbed himself in the heart with a pencil and whose mother had miraculously saved him. Diane "snapped her fingers" for the story. Though *GMA* instantly hustled a crew out to the remote Midwestern location, mere hours later the TV monitors in the Fishbowl (the broadcast's den of activity) displayed . . . mother and son on *Today*! "We're, 'How is it possible they're on the *Today* show? And—I'm not kidding—it was reported to us later that they'd said, 'Well, the *Today* show sent us a muffin basket.'" A muffin basket then became de rigueur. Still, "every single one of those little stories was incredibly difficult" to steal from *Today*.

In keeping with Diane's dignity, her booking team was decorous. As a close observer says, "She never wanted to—and we never put her in the position—of" starting a woo with, "'Oh, you don't want to talk to Katie or Barbara; you want to talk to *me*.' It was never, 'Oh, *they're not* the right person to talk to.' She was always, 'Let me tell you how I'm the best person to tell your story.' We never sent flowers to anybody and signed her name if we didn't first ask her or tell her, 'Here's how we need to do this.' We didn't put her on the phone without a plan or a strategy: 'Here's what this person needs from you.' We didn't ask her to write a note that was anything other than, 'You're in my thoughts.' It was very clear to us, although maybe not blatantly expressed, that we really never did anything to dishonor her name." Shelley Ross adds, "She never put herself in a position where she was directly competing with Katie. Charlie took *those* stories. We never let it be an 'Okay, guys, compare and contrast Katie and Diane.'"

A prime example of this strategy was the show's Columbine coverage. There had been two multiple-fatality school shootings before the one at Columbine High School in Littleton, Colorado. One had taken place in West Paducah, Kentucky, and the other in Jonesboro, Arkansas, so a terrible "trend" was in the offing. But somehow this incomprehensive tragedy—in which twelve middle- to upper-middle-class students, in a non-Southern state, were killed and twenty-one were injured by two of their peers, Dylan Klebold and Eric Harris, who then killed themselves—felt especially devastating, especially relatably suburban. It also seems, in retrospect, as if it were the ominous a starting bell for events that followed: at Virginia Tech and, later, in Aurora, Colorado, and Newtown, Connecticut—just as the Menendez brothers had been for O. J., and as Clarence Thomas/Anita Hill had been for Bill Clinton/Monica Lewinsky.

GMA had sent Charlie and a team to Columbine, but they had reported back: "None of the families are talking." Yet two families did talk to Katie—in an extraordinarily moving interview, which was followed up by an interview about the catastrophe, for *Today*, with President Clinton. So Shelley flew to Washington and, insisting to President Clinton's spokesman Joe Lockhart that "the White House can't have a favorite network," Shelley pushed for—and got—"*GMA* Live from the White House," a two-hour town hall meeting on the subject of school violence, with the president and first lady and survivors of school shootings across the country. Diane and Charlie co-moderated that, but first there was a one on one with the president, and it was a shrewd accommodation to hand Charlie a plum assignment—one that would wind up on the front page of the *New York Times*. Diane, with her wise strategizing (actually, she and the producers less elegantly called it her "law of the jungle" reasoning), thus acknowledged that the audience identified *GMA* as Charlie's show—one that he had cohosted for a decade, and one on which she didn't want to appear to be encroaching. It was never clear whether "crusty" Charlie appreciated Diane's deference; he would soon, according to the ABC executive, have tensions with Diane about her taking the show "down-market" and would feel that "here was *another* blond" overshadowing him after Joan Lunden had done so. For her part, Diane reacted to the White House town hall's success with typical rumination, brooding over glitches, real or imagined. "The bigger the success, the more tortured she becomes that we won't maintain the momentum," Shelley Ross says. "The morning our *GMA* reporting got on the front page of the *Times*, Diane called and said, 'Why did we pass on the Donny Osmond autobiography?'"

But it was Katie's *Today* piece in Columbine that stands out as one of the most affecting stories ever to run on morning TV. Just as he had done with Katie's impromptu interview with George H. W. Bush, Jeff Zucker canceled the commercial breaks and let Katie's conversation run overtime. Michael Shoels, the African American father of one shooting victim, Isaiah Shoels, and Craig Scott, the white brother of another, Rachel Scott, had never met. At first that worried Katie: "I just didn't feel" the surprise value for each of them "was appropriate under the circumstances," she said. But she would later describe the interview as "just bearing witness to something: these two people talking about what happened and holding hands and comforting one another." She told producer Yael Federbush that the Columbine interview was "one of the most profound and spiritual moments she'd ever had."

Watching the poignant fifteen minutes unfold on the studio monitors, with the snowy Colorado background, Federbush recalls, "Matt said that everybody on the set had to remember the last time they swallowed—you just stopped breathing." At *GMA*, a staffer remembers watching Katie pull it off, "and what she was able to get wasn't just a great story but *all* the human emotion that she was so good at and Diane didn't have yet."

In the new Diane versus Katie war: point, Katie.

MANY HAVE NOTED how the two women's styles crisscrossed over the ensuing years: When they would later resume their rivalry in 2009, this time as evening news coanchors, "Katie was more all-business and Diane was the more emotive," a former *GMA*-er notes. Meanwhile, Diane's ef-

fect on Katie started subtly in the crushingly competitive forum of Morning. "I think when you're number one you're just there to be knocked off,"
says Shelley Ross, whose helming of *GMA* eventually made that a near
reality. Soon Katie started dressing more like Diane. "The sweaters . . . ,"
Shelley says. "One day, after Diane started wearing pencil skirts and
twinsets, Katie came out wearing the same outfit—we all noticed." Over
the next few years of their intensifying competition, many people would
credit the change in Katie's style—from reassuringly, mildly dowdy
young suburban mom to cosmopolite in leather jackets and short skirts—
to the presence of silky Diane a dial switch away. But that "cool drink of
water"—that woman of the soigné evenings amid playwrights and literary eminences with her icon husband—was learning from Katie, too:
how to be cheerfully facile with kitchen segments, how to smile broadly
when a chimp climbed on her back (that segment provided inspiration
for a scene in the movie *Morning Glory*, with Diane Keaton playing the
Sawyer-like role), and how to gasp in incredulity that the average wedding now cost a whole gosh-darn $15,000. ("I thought, 'Oh, yuck,'" at the
insincerity, recalls one major CBS reporter who saw the segment while he
was Exercycling at his gym.)

Within a year, Diane *got* it. "She would always be saying to me,
'Where's the heart? Where's the heart?'" says her protégée, junior producer Anna Robertson. Actually, Diane was not only attracted to stories
with heart, but she made deep and meaningful friendships having nothing to do with their television utility. For example, Diane met teenage
cystic fibrosis patient and poet Laura Rothenberg "one day when she was
visiting someone in a hospital" and Laura was in an adjoining ward, Anna
recalls. "Laura was very ill; she needed a lung transplant. Diane became
friends with her *off* the air—it had nothing to do with on-camera. They
kept this friendship going for years," right up until Laura's tragically un-
timely death, at twenty-two, in 2003. Diane's viewers didn't know about
her mentorlike friendship with Laura, which perhaps was Diane's way of
giving to a poetry-minded young girl the affirmation that she, at that age,
had received from her Seneca English teacher Alice Chumbley. The viewers didn't know the many acts of philanthropy Diane performed—the

hospitalizations she paid for, the flowers and food she sent to producers' mothers who were having operations in far-off states. Or that she tutored a high school girl several mornings a week.

Similarly, Katie's viewers didn't know that she mentored Harlem girls by way of the Big Sisters program for years, and that, as Katie's daughters Ellie and Carrie got older, they did as well. Or that she was godmother to the severely autistic son of a junior colleague, once spending a weekend with him when he was in crisis, another time dashing from the studio to his eighth-grade graduation ceremony. They *did* know that she'd flown her girlhood posse—Betsy, Sara, Janie, Barbara—to New York to be on *Today*, get makeovers, and attend a Broadway play. But they didn't know that when they were all relaxing at Katie's Park Avenue apartment, a knock came at the door, in accordance with a special treat she'd cooked up: There, to borrow a cup of sugar, stood the generation-earlier football hero star alumnus of their rival Arlington, Virginia, high school: Warren Beatty.

Diane and Katie may have sharply competed for gets and may have eagle-eyed the tiniest fluctuations of the overnights in the horse race for viewers for their rival shows—which provided the lion's share of advertising dollars to their respective networks—but they also had private lives that cut against both the triviality and the avarice that their work could all too easily, and inaccurately, be reduced to.

In terms of content differences, there was a counterintuitive switch between the shows during this period. Says TV analyst Andrew Tyndall: "There came to be a huge difference in the first half hours. On *Today*'s, there would always be a longer, harder, more political news bloc than on *GMA*. *Today* would use Tim Russert much more than *GMA* used George Stephanopoulos. The type of news *GMA* would put in their first half hour was much more tabloid—true crime or celebrity trials or human interest, rather than politics or foreign policy."

The senior staffer at *GMA* says that Charlie Gibson found certain stories that the others wanted to do "tabloidy" and he disapproved of them. But "Diane was incredibly smart, and she was a very keen observer of popular culture, and she knew that she was willing to get her hands dirty with us versus his 'I don't want to touch this with a ten foot pole' attitude.

She knew that 'tabloid' stories were changing the direction of our country. She wasn't the first to raise her hand to do them, but she *was* quick to say, 'We *have* to do this.'"

Still, there was one "asset" (though painfully unwanted) that Katie had in 1999 and 2000 and Diane lacked, and that was her fresh young widowhood. It had helped to get her Matthew Shepard's parents and it had helped her get the Columbine story. Whether intentionally or not, Katie's career benefited from the narrative of her widowhood, some people in the industry noted. Yet a widow's grief is real, as is all that comes with it. "Shortly after Jay died, Katie said, 'We should all just love each other more and better—life is short and uncertain. We should just spend more time loving each other,'" says her friend Barbara Andrukonis. The repetitive and pious nature of those remarks are not typical of pithy, snarky Katie. Perhaps the sentiment felt too real—and fatigued, and tinged with remorse for the fights they'd had before he received his diagnosis—to be wished away with wit. But Katie brought that life-worn solemnity to whatever interviews her personal circumstances had earned her.

IN MID-1999, while Diane was getting her Morning sea legs, Katie moved herself and her girls from the apartment she had rented with Jay to a twelve-room Park Avenue co-op. For a year and a half after Jay's death, Katie didn't want to uproot Carrie and Ellie from the home they'd shared with their father. But now, she had "lost the lease" on the Central Park place, as Katie told *Good Housekeeping*. She *had* to move.

"It was time to buy an apartment," she said at the time. "But it was a very scary thing for me to do all by myself, without Jay." Bringing Jay's essence into the new apartment and somehow keeping him in their lives was a big part of the move, just as it was a big part of Katie's wider life. She became godmother to the son that her good friend and producer Lori Beecher had given birth to—whom Lori and her husband had named Jay. With her new friend Lisa Paulsen and her longtime friend Kathleen Lobb, she was beginning work on a memorial to her husband, the Jay Monahan Center for Gastrointestinal Health.

Describing the new apartment to *Good Housekeeping*, Katie said that she made the girls' rooms especially "sweet" and cheerful. Like a typical seven-year-old, Ellie had been uncomfortable at camp the summer after her father died; that desire not to be "different" had masked her grief. But when Ellie took a framed photo of her father—looking particularly handsome, Katie noted—in his navy uniform into her new bedroom, "after a while she came into the kitchen and she had been crying." With her girls, Katie noted, the emotion "just crops up at unexpected times. There are days when [Ellie] can talk about Jay and be upbeat and fine about it, and other times I think she's really, really missing him so much." Given all this fresh experience, Katie helped developed a curriculum, for her daughters' school, for children who lost their parents.

Katie dotted the apartment with Jay's military memorabilia. The brass bugles and military helmets lined the shelves. A life-size mannequin of a Napoleonic-era soldier that Jay had bought just weeks before his death was given pride of place in the dining room. Carrie, who was now three, took one look at the dummy and said, "Jay!" Katie, who had found the mannequin "creepy" when Jay had purchased it, now saw it as a symbol that her late husband was "watching over us and protecting us."

In talking so openly about her widowhood and her children, Katie was viewed as being admirably honest and providing a service to other young widows. Alternately, to cynics in her cutthroat business, she was strongly thought to be exploiting her personal tragedy to reinforce her likability in the face of fresh competition from the glamorous, childless Diane. Although Katie has frequently mused that she always thought she would end up "like Florence Henderson on *The Brady Bunch*," with a second husband and a blended family, and though she went on to have other boyfriends—some more serious, others called "boy toys" by the tabloids—she remained single for fifteen years.

Soon, Diane took over her own booking. "She would be on the phone—with lawyers, with everyone for hours," Phyllis McGrady says. Shelley Ross: "Booking, booking, strategizing, looking ahead." Charlie continued to have Shelley and the staff do his booking, but Diane was hands-on and a perfectionist.

At the dawn of the new millennium—the first anniversary of Diane's arrival at *GMA* and, for Katie, the culmination of their first year of rivalry—the contrast in the two anchor teams' images was clear: Diane and Charlie were the mature wise couple, Diane speaking slowly and earnestly and, while enjoying herself, emanating a comforting warmth. By contrast, Katie and Matt were the younger couple, people viewers with school-aged kids might want to take a vacation with, and maybe blow off steam with at a blackjack table while a babysitter watched the kids: he affable and not quite slick, she everybody's sassy best girlfriend.

The different images and delivery of the two women were important. Morning gets a heavily female audience, and it did matter which woman the viewers *liked* better—it made a significant ratings difference. Also, women are more variable when it comes to their style—clothes, hair, and so forth. How they look matters on Morning TV—a lot. The Morning men, on the other hand—always in a suit and generally with short hair—pass more or less unnoticed on this score. Competition between the female hosts existed in guest wrangling, too. Sometimes a guest chose between Katie or Diane because she or he *liked* one or the other so much. Such was the case with Darva Conger, who chose Diane over Katie because, according to a *GMA* senior staffer, "Darva just *loved* Diane!" Darva, a pretty blond nurse, had won *Who Wants to Marry a Multi-Millionaire?*—one of the first of the reality shows—and had soon found out that her insta-husband was not only *not* a millionaire but had a shady past, having once had a restraining order filed against him by a former fiancée.

At around the same time that Diane and her staff were high-fiving over countless small but important triumphs in Morning-world, Katie had bigger internal worries. In the terminology of the man who believed that morning shows have an "actor" and a "reactor" and who felt that Katie changed for the worse after Jay died, Matt Lauer had "paid Katie back" for not having "waited her turn" with Bryant. Matt wasn't waiting *"his* turn" anymore, either. "The worm turned," this person says. Matt's attitude was, "'Hey, she's gonna be gone, *I'm* the future'—and he demanded more and more." This might have felt especially more justified to Matt now that Katie was becoming so late for work that her driver often had to call her from the car in front of her apartment, at six fifteen, to get her going, while Matt had been in the studio for a full forty-five minutes. Did his superior punctuality—his professionalism—not justify more aggressive anchor prominence on his part?

Katie's life now was a tight jigsaw puzzle of demands. The good thing about a morning show was that her hours coordinated with her daughters'—she went to bed as early as they did. And she made time for their activities, even if it meant dashing back and forth from studio to school to studio. Her friend and Park Avenue neighbor-mom Pat Shifke says that Carrie and Ellie "would do their dance recitals in the morning assembly. Katie would go to *Today*; she'd find out the timing, she'd leave the show, rush in, and get to the assemblies—she made it there for *all* of them. You'd see her on the show in the morning when everyone else was taking their time to get to the assembly." And then, once she was seated with the other mothers, heads would turn in surprise and "people would say, 'I *just saw* you on TV.'"

THE MATT-OVER-KATIE momentum had actually started two years earlier, just after Jay died. On January 27, 1998, Matt had scored one of the most-watched *Today* interviews in years: his sit-down with First Lady Hillary Clinton in the midst of the Monica Lewinsky scandal. It was there, seated across from Lauer, who handled the interview with just the right combination of solicitousness and authority, that Hillary had used the initially startling but eventually meaningful term "vast right-wing conspiracy." Around that same time, Matt had lobbied for and landed a very expensive yearly weeklong feature, "Where in the World Is Matt Lauer?" In it, Matt popped up—amid lots of aggressively advertised hints and fevered guessing—in exotic places all over the globe: Egypt, Greece, and Australia the first year; Mt. Everest in Nepal, Italy, and China the next. Now he was moving into year three of the star-making franchise, with trips planned to Hawaii, Spain, and Zimbabwe.

That same year, Matt, who'd been divorced ten years earlier from a TV producer, married beautiful Dutch model Annette Roque in 1998; the pair were often mentioned in the New York social columns. Matt and the man he'd replaced, Bryant Gumbel, were golfing buddies, and over time they became best friends. Matt and Annette would have three children. In 2006 Annette Roque Lauer filed for divorce from Matt, then withdrew her petition, and the supermarket tabloids would periodically blare rumors of his infidelity and their marital woes on their front pages. (Matt and Annette denied the rumors of infidelity.) As for Bryant, he would weather a very acrimonious divorce from his wife, June Gumbel, in 2001 and marry his longtime girlfriend Hilary Quinlan a year later. But somehow the considerably more turbulent personal lives of Katie's male coanchors didn't hurt their careers in quite the same way that Katie's normal, postwidowhood dating would turn her, over the years, in the Morning public's judgmental eye, from All-American Mom to an edgy, vaguely unsympathetic, somewhat older single woman.

Matt and Katie's relationship was complicated. It's not exactly that they were openly competitive, or even *only* competitive. One who worked very closely with them saw something more utilitarian and more subtle: "It was mutual respect/dependence. It was oddly codependent, because they needed each other, to protect each other from executives, from events, from schedules. They were two people in this bottle together, and they needed a certain relationship. But at the same time they could be at odds on who would get a certain interview, who was getting more time." Furthermore, in a morning show ensemble, this insider continues, "everybody has a role. It takes on the feel of a family. So Katie happily played the role of the demanding female star. Matt was the steadying hand—the brother. Al [Roker] was sort of the clown figure, and Ann"—Ann Curry, the newsreader on the show from 1997—"was the studious cousin. Ann was a very nice person. She and Katie got along well," this person, who witnessed them daily, says.

Others, however, have contested the view that Katie and Ann got along well. As a person at ABC always heard it from friends at NBC, "Katie was a bully and Ann was the victim." Katie often threw Ann off balance by criticizing Ann's clothing choices just before they went on air. According to several people at NBC, Katie was changing—she was now developing a reputation for twisting her snarkiness into meanness. Later, when Katie went to CBS, staffers coined a term for a tactic that, one says, "was Katie's forte. We called it the '*compli-insult*.' She would look at someone and say, 'I really think you're clever, but why is your script so horrible?' She was *mean*. And nobody was safe from her zinging."

IT WAS WHEN MATT was planning his third "Where in the World Is Matt Lauer?" segment that Katie determined to make the "crazy" idea she had shared with Lisa Paulsen come true: She would have a colonoscopy on live TV.

The idea of foisting the viewing of a rectum-penetrating exam on viewers while they were eating breakfast (not to mention risking America's Sweetheart's image by having the procedure performed on *her*) would have been beyond unthinkable had it not been for Katie's personal ownership of the colon cancer issue—and her sheer insistence and force of will. "Katie's the type of person who, when she's very passionate about something, doesn't rest until it's done," says Allison Gollust, the *Today* publicist on the project. "She decides she wants to make a difference in something and she relentlessly pursues. Jeff was on board from the start. I'm sure he would have been supportive of it even if he hadn't been through colon cancer himself, but the fact that he had been made it particularly significant."

First, with the help of Jay's physicians and the gathering team working on the Jay Monahan Center, Katie convinced the U.S. Senate to make March 2000 the first annual National Colorectal Cancer Awareness Month. In concert with that, she and Jeff designed two weeks of coverage about colorectal health—a completely new term for the viewers. This, Katie made clear, was the second leading cause of cancer death in the country and would lead to over fifty-seven thousand deaths the coming year. But those deaths were *preventable*, she stressed. When found in its early stages, colorectal cancer was 90 percent curable, yet almost half of those Americans who should be screened for it (those over age fifty) were not.

To show how easy and painless that screening was, Katie—though under the recommended age for screening (she was forty-three, and Jay had been forty-two when he died)—underwent the entire process live for the audience, step-by-step: the preparation the night before, arriving at the doctor's office, getting anesthesia, and then the procedure itself. Lying on her side on the gurney, with her still pixie-short hair grazing the top of her open-backed gown, Katie lapsed into mild unconsciousness and the inside of her rectum became the star of her show to nine million morning viewers.

The segment had a huge impact. A team of researchers at the University of Michigan and the University of Iowa compared the number of colonoscopies performed by four hundred gastroenterologists in twenty-two states during twenty months before Katie's colonoscopy with those performed in the nine months after she had the procedure. The number of colonoscopies, they found, had increased by 20 percent—and more women and more younger adults were having the procedure than in prior years. In their article in a July 2003 issue of *Archives of Internal Medicine*, the researchers called these salutary changes "The Katie Couric Effect."

Just after Katie's on-air colonoscopy segment, Jeff Zucker was promoted from *Today*'s executive producer to president of NBC Entertainment. In May 2000 Jonathan Wald (who is the son of Richard Wald, the veteran producer at NBC and ABC who had dealt with the change in attitudes toward women in the business from the fifties through the seventies) came over from *NBC Nightly News* to produce *Today*. Wald saw that Katie was actively searching for substance now. "She wanted to be taken more seriously. She would often say, 'I feel that the show has gotten too frivolous.' There was a frustration, a chafing" against the mold she'd been set in for so long. "She's the prototypical kid sister who always has something smart to say, speaks her mind—and wants attention. But you can't be the kid sister for that long—at some point, you grow up."

And at this very point, a painful impetus to grow up arrived: her sister Emily's pancreatic cancer diagnosis. This was quietly shattering to Katie. A second possible imminent loss of a loved one to cancer? How could it be? It was. By now Katie had somehow come to terms with what sometimes felt like a bargain fate had dealt her: uncanny success in her professional life; horribly unfair loss in her personal life. Emily was bravely dogged in fighting her disease. Katie prayed that her sister's determination would be enough. At the same time, the anguish made her years-long repetitive work on *Today* seem trivial. Her real life was too big for her television life. She was open to anything that would put the two in alignment.

It was also at this time—perhaps not coincidentally—that she started her first serious post-Jay relationship, with a man many thought she should have married and with whom she should have established that "Florence Henderson" life. He was Tom Werner, a Harvard graduate, an enormously successful television producer, and the co-owner of the Boston Red Sox. Seven years older than Katie, Werner, reared in a prosperous New York family, had been a programming executive at ABC in New York in the seventies. But his success—and his influence on the culture—came in the eighties, when he and his producing partner Marcy Carsey opened Carsey-Werner Productions and created the era-defining and stereotype-shattering sitcom *The Cosby Show* and later the equally high-quality *Roseanne*, which humanized blue-collar life. Through other shows, Werner and Carsey also helped launch the careers of Robin Williams, Tom Hanks, and Billy Crystal. The year before he met Katie (on a blind date arranged by her agent, Alan Berger), Werner had been honored by the Museum of Television and Radio.

Tom was perfect for Katie in many ways—a "catch," as it were—and she could be considered his mediagenic and accomplishment equal. Unfortunately, however, though Werner was separated from his longtime wife, he didn't file for divorce until shortly after he met Katie, and with this relationship, and that particular gossip-vulnerable aspect of it, the *National Enquirer* entered Katie's life, plastering her on its cover in a *gotcha!* way. The earlier *Star* story depicting her as a fatigued working mother, drinking milk from the carton with the refrigerator door left open, may not have been flattering, but it was certainly identifiable to exhausted women. This, now, was a different kind of tabloid glare. It would be the first step in turning Katie's image away from her ossified Girl Next Door and Plucky Widow roles. Now she was a complex woman who was living an altogether appropriate life, but who, in the mind of a public who could

LEFT: Even before she started elementary school, Lila Diane Sawyer was enrolled, by her mother, Jean, in a series of talent classes. Here, the little Louisville girl is artfully doing a Flamenco-style dance.

RIGHT: Diane's crowning as America's Junior Miss in 1963 looks like a lovely, jelled-in-aspic peak moment of a vanishing time. It was—and it was complex. Not long after winning the crown, she saw it as a liability in a changing culture—and at a northern Seven Sisters college. But the inspiration she received from the pagaent's den mother, Catherine Marshall, would inspire her throughout her career.

Diane's employment with Richard Nixon, through most of the 1970s, during his presidency (here) and at San Clemente after his resignation, remains a part of her résumé that has long puzzled many. She admired him during his tenure ("What a considerable presidency it would have been without Watergate," she later mused). After his disgrace, she stayed with him because, she said, "If I didn't come through for him at a time when he needed me, I couldn't live with myself."

In 1981, Diane moved from D.C. to New York to cohost CBS's morning show, first with Charles Kuralt, here, and eventually with Bill Kurtis. Thus began her glamorous years, when powerful men had unabashed crushes on her and she was called "the thinking man's Angie Dickinson." Yet her extraordinary drive and work ethic were the opposite of what one would expect from an anointed golden girl.

On the surface, the 1990s-long co-reign of Diane Sawyer and Barbara Walters as the twin queens of the ABC newsmagazine world was, as this early photo suggests, equitable and sisterly. But behind the scenes there was such heated competition over high-profile "gets," a veteran producer had to be called in to referee. Barbara called Diane "That Girl" behind her back and bemoaned her connections. Diane disparaged Barbara's street-fighter tactics.

When Diane married Mike Nichols (here they are in 2005) in 1988, he corrected someone who asked him if this was his third marriage. "This is my *fourth* marriage," he made clear. Diane, then forty-two, corrected the same interlocutor by saying, firmly, that this wasn't her first marriage, "this is my *only* marriage." Even people whose usual mode is cynicism and who find Diane challenging professionally are reduced to rapture when they talk about the love that the iconic director and Diane evidence for each other. She's said she knew, "in the first ninety seconds" of meeting him—in the Concorde lounge—"that my life was changing," that "he was the center of the dance."

When it was announced, in January 1999, that Diane was to become cohost of *Good Morning America* (with Charlie Gibson, here beside Diane in 2002), TV industry watchers—and viewers—were shocked. This elegant, "aspirational" woman who wasn't a mom and seemed more elite than approachable was an odd fit for morning TV. But she took to it magnificently, and her short-term appointment lasted a highly successful decade, during which she expanded her skill set and allowed Methodist Diane of Kentucky to emerge from beneath the urbane, sophisticated overlay.

Diane's December 2002 interview with Whitney Houston was one of several that she conducted with celebrities dogged by controversy, including Mel Gibson and Rihanna, during which her mature skill as an interviewer and her downplaying of her own once-distracting glamour allowed the subject to reveal striking vulnerability. During this conversation, the troubled singer—once America's music-video sweetheart—used bravado and arrogance to dispel rumors that she had had a drug problem. But Diane bore down, shrewdly declining to play the Polite Blond Lady (a tactic that had worked in smoking out Gibson's bellicose bigotry). Her combination of concern and toughness led Houston to an epiphany she painfully shared with America. When Sawyer asked her who the devil was, the singer, in a near whisper, admitted, "The devil is me."

Diane, the committed world-circling journalist and fevered perfectionist, would not miss a chance to fly to a far-away crisis—in this case, the East Indian tsunami that struck in late December 2004—even if it meant trading off something crucial: desk time on *Good Morning America* during a crunch moment in the show's long-fought-for ratings race against *Today*. Here, Diane watches purified water being loaded onto the USS *Abraham Lincoln* off the coast of Sumatra, Indonesia.

When Diane ascended to *World News* anchor over the 2009–10 holiday season, it was as if every accomplishment in her thirty-year-long TV news career had led seamlessly to this capstone moment. She spent her first month on the move: grilling Iranian president Ahmadinejad in Copenhagen, helicoptering around Afghanistan with General Stanley McChrystal, and commandeering a series of aircraft to get to the Haiti earthquake.

LEFT: "Senior Katie Couric gives the stands her fantastic smile," announces the caption of the 1974 Yorktown High yearbook. Katie was a cheerleader for most of her high school years in Alexandria, Virginia, as well as senior class president. The *Leave It to Beaver*–like childhood she lived as the wisecracking kid sister of three siblings with a working dad and stay-at-home mom would later serve her well in personifying a Middle American everywoman with a wry edge.

RIGHT: When Katie (here, in demure dress and pearls) joined the team at brand-new CNN Atlanta in the early 1980s, she was thought to be stunningly young-looking even by fellow junior colleagues. Some dismissed her as peppy and lightweight; others saw the powerful ambition that lay beneath that convenient veneer. In 1982 she surprised senior colleagues by being promoted to producer of CNN's *Today*-style show *Take Two*, anchored by Chris Curle (the platinum blonde at far right) and her husband, Don Farmer (back to camera).

When Barbara Walters was the first female star of the *Today* show, despite the fact that she created the entire template, she was barred by her cohost, Frank McGee, from asking the first, second, third, and fourth questions (he got those) of any guest they jointly interviewed. When Katie became the show's new female face in 1991, it was instantly clear that she had authority—and suffer-no-fools repartee—on a par with the male cohost, the famously arrogant Bryant Gumbel. Here, in 1994, the woman who broke down the door and the woman who came in with not a shred of timidity—and made herself arguably the most successful anchor in the genre's history—have a tête-à-tête in Rockefeller Plaza.

After Katie met lawyer Jay Monahan at a Washington party in the late 1980s, she described him to a friend as "Heathcliffian." The ambitious, peppy, messy on-the-rise TV star married the neat-freak man of accomplishment, gravity, and originality in June 1989. Two years later, Katie's rocketing to stardom, amid their starting a family, raised inevitable challenges to their marriage. Here they are in early 1997, right before a shocking diagnosis of advanced colon cancer changed everything. Jay died in January 1998.

Being a mother meant a lot to Katie. Unlike the way Diane or Christiane felt about it as their careers progressed, motherhood was something that she was never going to do without. Here, in March 1996, Katie—who two months earlier had given birth to her and Jay's second daughter, Carrie—poses with their four-and-a-half-year-old, Ellie (center), and Ellie's friend.

From the beginning of her tenure as *Today* cohost, Katie had had it stipulated in her contract that she share equally the substantive interviews with her male cohost. Early in her career she had scored a strikingly successful interview with President George H. W. Bush, virtually ambushing him with questions he wasn't expecting. Here, in April 1999, she takes on President Clinton.

In the history of TV news stars and producers, few pairings had been as instantly inspired and relentlessly successful as that of Katie Couric and Jeff Zucker. They met when she, a novice at NBC New York, ran into the junior producer in the network hallway and cheekily insulted his shoes. Over the ensuing decade and a half, Jeff was one of the few people who would tell the truth to the strong-willed and increasingly powerful Katie, even though "she's not gonna admit that I'm right," he says. And "even if she doesn't like" what he might have to say. Such an occasion was the one punctuated by this farewell-to-NBC kiss in 2006.

Katie's last day at *Today*—Wednesday, May 31, 2006—was, as Matt Lauer promised, "like an episode of *This Is Your Life*." There were snippets of her at all the stations she'd worked at throughout her career; a witty video clip pointing out her infamous lateness; a highlights reel of her most memorable moments—from inciting Yasser Arafat's wrath to flying as Tinkerbell through the Plaza—to this bouquet of flowers from a young fan. Now she would go on to her summer listening tour and in the fall, at forty-nine, she'd become, via *CBS Evening News*, the first woman to solo-anchor any network evening news show.

Katie's early autumn 2008 three-part interview with vice-presidential candidate Sarah Palin changed her luck at the *CBS Evening News*, where she had very briefly soared, then hit a she-can-do-no-right patch, and now was struggling with lackluster ratings, resentment from her far-less-compensated CBS News colleagues, and lack of challenge. Katie's knowledgeable, insistent probing of the Alaska governor yielded some cringe-inducing answers (Palin could not name a single newspaper that she read or a Supreme Court opinion she disagreed with) and also showed Palin to be more hard- than middle-right on some important social issues. The interview series affected the outcome of the presidential election and won Katie the Walter Cronkite Award for Excellence in Television Political Journalism from USC's Annenberg School.

By April 2010, when this photo was taken, Katie had been anchoring the *CBS Evening News* for three and a half years. She had recovered from a bad low, had gained stature with her Palin interviews, had deftly provoked Mahmoud Ahmadinejad into going out of his way to decry special status, among war crimes, for the Holocaust, and had been the first anchor on the ground during the catastrophic January Haiti earthquake. But her show's low ratings—which had existed even before she was expensively drafted to save the day—augured ill.

Christiane Amanpour was nineteen and living in London in 1977 when this photograph was taken at her close friend Diana Bellew's house in Hampshire, England. The two girls, who had "met cute" (they originally couldn't stand each other) at convent boarding school three years earlier, were now best friends. With her long, Farrah Fawcett–styled hair, her post-high-school job at a London department store, and her fascination with the Swedish pop group ABBA, "Kissy," as Diana and her family called her, was not someone one might expect to become the world's most passionate conflict zone journalist.

Christiane's years driving home to CNN viewers the atrocities against the civilian population in Bosnia, in the early to mid-1990s, were fundamental to her development as a fearless reporter and advocate for international justice. She has said, "I consider Bosnia the most important thing I've ever done." Her relentless stand-ups—such as this early one in front of a cemetery in 1992—forced Americans to know about the targeted deaths of children and the rapes of women in the country they'd barely heard of. As her equally dedicated colleague, war photographer Ron Haviv, says, "Anger was [our] motivating factor. She was going live, every night, from Sarajevo. Day one, day five....*Day one hundred*."

Christiane—the daughter of recent Iranian exiles who'd left all their worldly goods in their villa when the Revolution came—had become close friends with John Kennedy Jr. when he was at Brown and she was at the University of Rhode Island. They were housemates and confidants, and she frequently joined him and other friends at his mother's elegant home on Martha's Vineyard. Their post-college friendship—exemplified by this undated photograph—and mutual admiration deepened. When she was newly pregnant in the summer of 1999, she and her husband, Jamie, spent what she's called "a very happy, lovely, normal, friendly couples weekend" with him and Carolyn on Martha's Vineyard. Days later, when his small, self-piloted plane got lost over—and ultimately plunged into—that same island's waters, John and his wife were dead.

After a rather whirlwind courtship and a January 1998 engagement (Christiane's flouting of her diamond ring on the airstrip almost cost her, at zero hour, a long-planned assignment in Iran), Christiane married Jamie Rubin, Secretary of State Madeline Albright's spokesman, in August 1998. Their dual-religion wedding was held in the Italian lakeside town Bracciano. The Catholic ceremony was performed at the Church of Santo Stefano; the Jewish one at a castle, Castello Orsini-Odescalchi. The public wasn't (and isn't) used to this Christiane—the veiled bride.

Christiane's breaking-news cut-ins were a familiar sight to viewers of CNN shows such as *Wolf Blitzer Reports* during her long tenure as the network's chief international correspondent, between the end of her Bosnia coverage in the late 1990s and her departure for America in 2007. She reported from a dizzying array of countries in Europe, the Middle East, and Africa— sometimes taking a quick flight from one country, where she was reporting for *60 Minutes* on CBS, to a different country to cover a major crisis for CNN. In March 2004, she rushed to Madrid to report on the backpack bombing that killed 191 train passengers, igniting Europe's sense of vulnerability to terrorism.

Here, Christiane is in Tehran, properly head-scarved, as any Western newswoman must be, reporting on the Ashura holiday season, when, according to Shi'a Muslim tradition, people walk through the street and whip themselves with chains to reenact the suffering of the martyr Hussein. During one of the observances being filmed for CNN's documentary *God's Muslim Warriors*, Christiane "was sitting next to a woman who was hugging her emotionally," her friend and producer Andrew Tkach recalls. The Iranian-raised daughter of a Muslim father, "Christiane played right along," understanding the woman's fervor as only a person who intimately knew that culture could.

Christiane had not necessarily thought of getting married, or having a child, during her independent years reporting in war zones. Her two younger sisters knew that their onetime virtual "second mother" wasn't a gusher over babies. When she was pregnant, Christiane was even honest about the certainly welcome but still mysterious feelings of maternal love. She even macho-kidded (with one eye trained on men who'd have loved to take her place in war zones) that nothing would change; her baby would simply wear "bullet-proof diapers." But once she had her son, Darius John—here, at age eight, with his parents in New York in 2008—everything changed. Her love for her child was as surprising and all-encompassing as her decade in dangerous war zones had become routine. She became the ultimate conflicted modern mother: juggling serious, travel-dependent work she was passionate about with possessive, hands-on care of a child who meant the world to her.

If Christiane played the native daughter in Tehran, in another Muslim country she reported from on numerous occasions—Afghanistan—she was all-Western. Here, she is talking to enrollees at a U.S.-government-built school for girls in the Jalalabad Province during the filming of CNN's *Generation Islam*, which was produced and aired in 2009 after Christiane had made her—rocky—return to state-side CNN.

When the Arab Spring broke out in all its early euphoria in January 2011, stealing headlines and airtime from every other event, Christiane, by now host of ABC's *This Week*, did what everyone expected she'd do: She became the only reporter to interview the intensely beleaguered and soon-to-be deposed Egyptian president Hosni Mubarek, a scoop that engendered jealousy throughout her industry.

If Christiane had been passionate about pushing Americans to care about Bosnia, she was just as passionate about getting them to care about the unending humanitarian crises in Africa. "There is a big prejudice" in American news "about telling news from Africa," she said; it was one of her prime missions to bust through that aversion. From the late nineties to the present day, she has repeatedly shone the spotlight on heartrending tragedies—most of them with children as victims—on the continent. But she felt guiltiest about the U.S.-media-ignored genocide in Rwanda, which took place mostly while she was busy in Bosnia. In 2008, she returned to Rwanda to film the special *Scream Bloody Murder: Rwanda* about the genocide. The jubilation she felt in experiencing the native kids' resilience resonates in this picture.

turn from magnanimous to judgmental quickly, was romancing a still technically married man. In this regard she was crossing a bright red line.

THE STORY THAT MORNING would claim as its historical epitome of peerless reporting of history in real time—and the story that everyone on Morning would dearly wish *wasn't* there for them to claim—would come on a beautiful late-summer day.

It was the second Tuesday after Labor Day. Katie emerged from her car at 30 Rock at 6:45 a.m.; Diane had been working at the ABC office since before dawn. By 8:00 a.m. it was looking to be that rare meteorological meeting of cloudless sky, crystalline visibility, and no humidity. "Katie had even remarked on what an impossibly beautiful day it was—I think her expression was 'heartbreakingly beautiful' day, without any knowledge of what was to come," says Jonathan Wald.

Good Morning America had cold-opened its broadcast with Charlie trumpeting the fact that jury selection was starting in the murder trial of Andrea Yates, the Houston mother who'd drowned her five children in a bathtub. Next to him on the couch in a bright red dress, Diane mused in awe about Michael Jordan's fresh declaration that he was, once again, returning to basketball. Over at *Today*, Matt cold-opened with the Jordan news, and Katie—next to him in a chic black dress, the bangs of her newly blond-highlighted hair flipped over her forehead—cracked wise about it: "What's that Dolly Parton song? '[she paraphrases]—Here You Go Again.'"

Both sets of anchors were just wrapping up their two-hour shows when urgent, surreal images appeared on the monitors. Matt was chatting with an author about a book on Howard Hughes when Jonathan Wald said into his earpiece, "A plane's hit the World Trade Center—we need to get out of this interview." Over at ABC, just after 8:48 a.m., Diane announced, in a slow, assiduously calm-keeping voice, "We want to tell you: We just got a report that there's been some kind of explosion at the World Trade Center. We can't confirm any of this. But you're seeing the live footage. We just got a report that a plane may have hit." This was the North Tower. They relayed a phone call from a person who had escaped one of the buildings.

Meanwhile, back at NBC, *Today* did an extensive interview with an eyewitness, Jennifer Oberstein, who had just emerged from the subway at the nearby Bowling Green station when the mysterious explosion occurred. A field producer got her on the phone with Katie and Matt at 8:54. Oberstein's persistently emotional words—contrasted with Katie's and Matt's controlled, precise queries—gave the first hint that what had happened was catastrophic.

"We have a breaking story to tell you about. Apparently a plane has just crashed into the World Trade Center," Katie announced. "Jennifer, can you tell us what you saw?"

"It's quite terrifying!" Oberstein said. "It's unbelievable! It's mind-boggling! . . . I've never seen any fire like this in the air! It's like the top twenty floors! It's horrible! I can't describe it!"

"Do you have any idea what kind of plane it was?" Katie pressed. "We're getting reports that an airplane hit the buildings."

Jennifer: "We were all saying around here that it's so strange that it was a bomb and so high up!"

"Jennifer," Katie continued calmly, "can you describe it for us?"

Matt now entered the conversation: "Jennifer, it's Matt Lauer. Have you seen anybody taken out of the building? Have you seen any ambulances?"

"The smoke is incredible!" Jennifer continued.

"Jennifer," Katie pressed, "do you have any idea what *kind* of plane it was?"* Before she could answer, Katie was fed the latest—erroneous—information in her earpiece, which she duly reported: "Right now we're getting information that it was a small commuter plane."

Now Matt started analyzing for viewers—as they simultaneously viewed the footage—the angle of entry and the fact that both sides of the building showed damage. He astutely noted that it must have been a larger plane to make that impact. Jennifer kept obsessing: It was "a big ball of fire!" Katie filled time by saying that onlookers were "obviously

---

*Oberstein's continued mention of an explosion while not mentioning having seen a plane eventually made this snippet of a videotape a favorite among 9/11 Truthers, who insist that the September 11 attacks were an inside job.

horrified. Commuters were obviously devastated. And we have to surmise because of the time that there were people in the buildings."

At 9:00 a.m. Matt speculated that this could be an "intentional act."

Of course, the plane that hit the tower was American Flight 11 from Boston, hijacked by al-Qaeda terrorists—the first of four planes to be overtaken. Over at ABC, at 9:03, the monitors showed the second plane, later identified as United Flight 175, heading into the South Tower. At 9:04, Diane solemnly said, "We had seen the plane circling in from another direction. Charlie, I don't know if it was the same plane, but Charlie, did you—?" And then she clarified it as "a *second* plane coming around the other side." In a YouTube clip containing unaired audio material from the broadcast, people can be heard screaming, "A *different* plane! Oh, shit! *Another* plane! Oh, shit! *Oh, shit! Oh, shit!*"

Charlie echoed, "That looks like a second plane."

"*Oh, my God*," Diane said softly.

"So it looks like some kind of concerted effort to attack the World Trade Center," Charlie concluded, just as Matt had done over at *Today*.

Unlike Pearl Harbor, unlike John F. Kennedy's assassination, the terrorist attacks of September 11, 2001, marked the first time that world-stopping events occurred in real time during morning television. "Morning *owned* that story," says a producer at *Today*. That day, and as the next days marched on in a shell-shocked city, "the morning shows did a much better job than the evening news." And what events that first half day brought! They were confusing, conflicting, surreal, and frightening—not merely these two attacks, but the third plane, American Flight 77, hitting the Pentagon at 9:37; the collapse of the South Tower of the World Trade Center at 9:59; the collapse of the North Tower at 10:28; the fourth plane, United Flight 93, headed for the Capitol, crashing to the ground in a field in Pennsylvania at 10:07 (after televised reports that it had been *shot* down by government-ordered U.S. aircraft); and the forced grounding of every single commercial plane from U.S. skies.

Amid the horror of the day and the days that followed, there was the strong relief at ABC that Diane was in that chair beside Charlie. Says the senior staffer: "Once they knew it was a terrorist attack, you really saw their humanity—the water in the eyes." Says the executive who was in on the December 1998 vetting meeting, "When 9/11 happened, we were like, 'This was *so* the right decision,'" hiring Diane for *GMA*. "That was the turning point in a lot of people's minds. The notion of having Kevin and Lisa take the country through 9/11 . . ." The thought trails off. The tragedy tested Diane because "she had to be live. This was a moment of: Throw it all out there! Bring *everything* you've ever covered—and all your knowledge and all your sensitivities. With people not knowing where their relatives were, people being fearful," the public needed gentle, authoritative gravitas. "Diane pulled it off. She found her tone, she found her sea legs. She was *brilliant*."

The sheer war zone emergency of it all brought out the gonzo reporting chops Diane had nurtured at CBS in Washington, D.C. As soon as she was off the air, she grabbed Anna Robertson and said, "'We've got to get down there immediately!'" Anna recalls. "By the time we got down there everything was blocked off. We had to wiggle our way down there and get as close as possible. We took off our shoes and *ran*. We just reported there *all night*." Diane saw a fellow with a video camera and drafted him on the spot. The man, one Bucky Turco, was standing with what he called "my shitty camcorder" and recalled that "Diane asks me to join her film crew; there's evidently a 'media blackout' around Ground Zero and they need some guerrilla camera work. They give me a paper towel roll to conceal the camera." Diane told Turco: "Do your best. I'm walking away to distract attention from you. Just keep shooting *everything* you can shoot." As for the other ABC staffers: Charlie tried to get to the site by ferry in the Hudson River, but was not able to; George Stephanopoulos and his producer rushed downtown, and the two men "returned to the control room," Shelley Ross recalls, "covered, head to toe, in white residue from the building collapse, as if they'd been rolled in flour. They would have been killed had they not been pulled into a store in time."

Continues Anna Robertson: "Diane and one of the producers, Dennis O'Brien, ran into the rubble, and she pulled out a bunch of documents—financial records, people's items. We went live on the air with that. We just covered *everything*. Peter Jennings and Diane did the show live from the site that night." Phyllis McGrady: "Diane stayed up all night" and did the show the next morning on no sleep.

Katie was down at Ground Zero, too, surveying the apocalypse in a hard hat. Yael Federbush says, "Everyone just had to kick into gear. It was all hands on deck—we all came to the studio, we worked around the clock. I remember calling hospitals and trying to find out how many injured there were and there were no numbers" because there were virtually *no* "injured." Among the most poignant images of the story were the lines of empty ambulances outside the class-A trauma center hospitals; the queues of citizens standing for hours to give blood when none was needed because almost everyone in those buildings, and everyone on those planes, had perished; and the desperate "MISSING!" posters of fresh-scrubbed good-looking young faces plastered on building walls all over the city. Shelley Ross says that, during these early days, "around the office you'd see someone on the phone suddenly keel over sobbing." It was a common occurrence at *Today* as well.

The morning staffs and producers on both shows worked unceasingly; the coverage was wall to wall. Yet despite the sense of profound emergency and need for team spirit, there was rank-pulling at ABC. According to one who worked closely with Peter Jennings, Jennings was as imperious now as he had been at Princess Diana's funeral, when he'd crowded out Diane and Barbara. After the first night, Jennings blocked Diane from the most in-the-trenches coverage, and, in a puzzling nitpick, he even strongly recommended that she take her customary vase of flowers off her desk because he thought such a touch was inappropriate under the circumstances. But Charlie Gibson was worse. About the fifth or sixth day after 9/11, Charlie complained that Diane had been reading more of the show's "cold opens" than he was. (The reading of the cold opens at *GMA* was generally randomly alternated, according to such minor factors as whether Charlie or Diane came out of makeup first.) To appease Charlie, Shelley Ross immediately told Gibson he could read all the cold opens from then on, and she instructed the writers to adjust future scripts. His behavior in the face of the tragedy was "so petty as to be pathological," an insider says, and it suggested the depth of his resentment of Diane. Explains another insider: "Charlie was a serious person and a war horse. He had been kicked off the show earlier and he got pulled back in, and he went back in, head down, good-soldiering on his way—and Diane got all the attention and she controlled it."

The rivalry between Diane and Charlie would erupt more significantly—and secretly—in 2005, and again in 2009.

SEPTEMBER 11 WAS FOLLOWED by the anthrax attacks of September 18—attacks leveled against the TV news media itself. Letters containing the lethal, highly air-transmittable bacteria arrived in the newsrooms at ABC News, NBC News, and CBS News, among other sites, and security was tightened and nerves were on edge while everyone, Diane and Katie included, went about their now twelve- to fourteen-hour days reporting on the still very pressing catastrophic attacks of the week before. Soon, a number of anthrax letters were mailed to Senators Tom Daschle, Patrick Leahy, and Russ Feingold and their staffs. Many people initially believed that these attacks were the second part of an al-Qaeda one-two punch. It was only later determined that the anthrax attacks, which killed five people, including some postal workers, had been the work of domestic actors.

On October 15 Katie took a leave from work and rushed to her sister Emily's bedside, where she and the rest of the Couric family remained during her painful last three days. Emily died on October 18, and at the funeral at St. Paul's Church on the UVA campus, Katie spoke movingly to the two thousand mourners of her sister. "She taught me not about dying but about living," Katie said, as bell-clear to this gathering as Emily herself had been less than three years earlier, reciting Katie's eulogy for Jay at his funeral. With true Katie bluntness, she didn't hedge from issues others might leave out, such as the irritating fame disparity between the revered and accomplished oldest and once scrappy younger sibling. "Emily found it mildly annoying when she was asked, 'Are you Katie Couric's sister?'" she told the mourners, a sentiment Katie later seconded, with rare anger in her voice, when talking to Larry King. "The truth is, I've always been and forever will be so proud to say I am Emily Couric's sister."

Betsy Howell remembers that Katie seemed to be feeling "disbelief that this had happened again," and she was especially concerned about how this would affect her parents—her mother now seventy-eight, her father eighty-one. Later Katie wrote her childhood friend Janie McMullen Florea a note, thanking Janie for coming. In the note, Katie let her hair down, as only one could to an intimate, by adding a remark in the high Katie vernacular: "What can I say other than this is a big suck sandwich?"

The terrorist attacks of September 11, the anthrax letters, Emily's death, Katie's impatience with her bedeviling curse of the perky persona: "Everything was pushing Katie to be more serious," a senior staffer for *Today* says. "This was a moment in Katie's mind that cemented how important she wanted her role to be." In her interviews, "she gravitated naturally to people like Ann Richards. I remember her coming back and telling me once, 'Ann Richards says the show isn't as good as it used to be.' She gravitated to Condoleezza Rice, she gravitated to Hillary Clinton. Before 9/11 she had been aware of the frivolous parts of the show being frivolous." After 9/11 that awareness of hers became exacerbated. "That was it—we increased the focus on hard news." Both of the morning shows did a sobering swivel from watercooler tabloid fare, forced to acknowledge that this was a different time.

This person sees this period as "the height of Katie's power zone, the top of her game at the *Today* show," when Katie achieved "the transformation from singular star of that morning genre to a powerful person seeking something more." Indeed, in mid-December 2001, Katie got a kind of Christmas present: She signed a contact "reaching beyond $60 million for the next four and a half years," wrote Bill Carter in the *New York Times*—the largest contract ever signed in TV news. Some estimates put the total at $65 million for the four years. Katie's agent Alan Berger had skillfully solicited outside offers to get the auction up that high. One came from Don Hewitt, bidding on behalf of *60 Minutes*. DreamWorks tendered an offer, as did AOL Time Warner. Katie's $15 million to $16 million a year remuneration would include both salary and stock in NBC's parent company, General Electric. For this record-breaking paycheck, she would also be expected to do occasional evening specials, matching Diane's continuing evening specials and interviews for ABC. (Ten years later, a reality check: Matt Lauer's 2013 salary was $25 million, roughly $9 million more per year than Katie's was then.)

Katie's staggering salary was made public—and she was proud of it. In retrospect, leaking the figure would prove to be a mistake. A male executive from a different network puts a very negative spin on the disclosure, reflecting the feelings of many at the time: "Katie was 'over' the day she signed her last contract with the *Today* show. When people knew that she was going to make as much as $65 million, she was no longer the girl next door but a rich, recently bereaved, skirt-up-to-her-crotch, hair-changing woman. It can offend you all you want for me to put it that way, but it is a *fact*."

Indeed, stoked by the news of her glamorous new salary and glamorous boyfriend, the media started sniping at Katie's hair and clothes, which enraged the women at *Today*. Says someone who worked with Katie, "Do they do that to *guys*? I haven't noticed them commenting on the ties, the slicked-back hair" of male anchors. "'He used to have a middle part, now he has a side part.'" Allison Gollust adds, "And they'd do it to Diane, too. 'Here's what Diane wore. Here's what Katie wore.' We'd think, 'They don't do it between Charlie Gibson and Tom Brokaw in the evening!' Katie had no problem with Diane. You'd see them at events together and they were perfectly cordial. Yes, their shows were rivals. There were hundreds of millions of dollars at stake—everyone wanted to be number one. But to turn it into a catfight—Katie always thought that was just a very sexist way of looking at it.

Despite the sniping, Gollust explains, Katie had in fact made an effort to dress modestly. "Katie was famously frugal. She was like Michelle Obama is now, with her J.Crew style of dress, although it was Banana Republic back then. She understood the importance of connecting with a regular audience. She wanted to look real—she wasn't shopping at Chanel."

Through 2002 and 2003 Diane and her team capitalized on Katie's fans' disapproval of how Katie had grown and changed, sleekened and prospered. A new "Beat Katie" ethos emerged at *GMA*, according to one observer—born of the feverish workaholic girl power of Diane, Shelley, and Phyllis. "They were the triumvirate," this person says. "That was real power, the three of them! McGrady, Ross, and Sawyer: These three women would sit at night and talk in circles about everything, *forever*—dissect a show again and again. They fed off each other in a brilliant and pathological way. I'd think, We're doing a morning TV show—we're not saving the world! Look at Matt Lauer—he does his job. You don't have to sit all day long and say, 'Oh, my God, that set that we did on the 7:40 segment didn't really make sense.'"

Diane's middle-of-the-night reach-outs to her writers grew more intense. "EEK!" "OMG!" "ARGH," her e-mails would girlishly begin. "This would go on forever," the staffer says. But don't many controlling, top-of-game media leaders behave this way? "It's not even close—not even close. It was *endless*," this person says. So, apparently, was Diane's holding of her highest-level staffers to supposedly impossible standards—like, some of them theorized, the standards her mother had held for *her.* "A title for Diane's own book should be *Less Than Perfect*," quips this person, whom Diane liked. (A producer who worked with Diane on her specials would see Mrs. Hayes drop by the studio every so often; Diane would instantly pull herself up to full height and attention. "Her mother was the boss!")

But the diligence paid off. That July, when first eighteen and then a remaining nine miners were trapped deep below the earth's surface in the flooded Quecreek Mine in Pennsylvania for three days—with a harrowing and uncertain rescue attempt in play—it was *GMA*, not *Today*, that got the hero miners smiling at the seven a.m. cold open. Diane's Kentucky roots and loyalty were her impetus to get this story, and it worked.

Most striking was her December 2002 *Primetime* interview with Whitney Houston, the pop music superstar now facing rumors about drug use and eating disorders. Even though she'd agreed to the interview, she was defensive and slightly combative. If Diane had attempted this sitdown seven years earlier, her more ingratiating style—the one she'd used with Michael Jackson and Lisa Marie Presley—would not have worked. She might have seemed cloying, even weak. But now, the relentless experience of her ten weekly hours of live Morning had taken Diane's skill and added to it a get-to-the-point quality she hadn't had—or needed—before.

This Diane was more formidable—sympathetic, but formidable. Pointed and concerned. Minimally made-up for this interview, Diane found the right way in. You could tell she felt for Whitney when she raised the rumors of the singer's drug use, but Diane was not cowed by Whitney's confrontational tone. Admitting to overusing drugs and alcohol, Whitney essentially bragged that she was too rich to use a drug as lowly as crack cocaine. Diane's sober face and pointed silence was just right for that stunning, sad remark. (The interview, disturbing when it aired, seemed tragically prescient when, ten years later, Houston died of an overdose in the bathtub of the Beverly Hilton hotel.)

Both Houston and Sawyer were dressed in white for the interview. Both women had sung in church choirs. When Diane asked what the biggest "devil" in Whitney's life was, the loaded noun seemed unforced—it seemed mutually understood. Houston's eyes misted. She dropped her bravado, more in relief than defeat. Her tone of voice suggested she'd been waiting for someone to ask her that question, but it had to be the right someone. In a powerful, poignant confession, Whitney Houston answered that the "biggest devil" in her life "is me."

Katie, meanwhile, was inciting animus within *Today*. She was arriving so late now that "it became a joke," says a senior staffer. "But she was so good that *that* was the problem. She was able to swing right in: Show up, be in the shot, do the tease, and then go into makeup during the news and get final touches on. But she was making everybody's life miserable." In November 2002 Jonathan Wald was fired—allegedly for making the show too serious and taking too long to get back to the cooking segments—and replaced by Tom Touchet, who had been an ABC documentary producer and a line producer for Shelley Ross at *GMA*.

Steadily, *GMA* was closing the ratings gap. From 1999, when Diane came on board, to the end of 2003, *Today* flattened or decreased in both main viewer categories (adults twenty-five to fifty-four, and households) while *GMA* soared. This was a significant threat to *Today*, which was the biggest money earner of any show on any network, its ad revenue holding at $250 million annually, three times more than *GMA*'s.

The competition between *GMA* and *Today* "was like a relay race, it was tremendous, it was moving like the wind," says an ABC staffer. "There was *definitely* a fight to overtake *Today*," Anna Robertson concurs. The executive who had attended the December 1998 play-our-queen meeting adds, "The challenge of that show is something that could have been a disaster. And the fact that Diane mastered it, that she figured out the skill set, the booking, the relationship to Charlie, which is very complicated," was a tribute to her doggedness. It was also a tribute to Shelley Ross's work as executive producer. And to the entire team.

Still, as close as she got, "I think Diane was completely baffled by the fact that she could never make it over Katie in the morning," says a senior staffer. "She knew deep down that there must be *somebody* out there who had all the answers, if we could *just* find them. She thought, 'Why can't we find our own Jeff Zucker? Who is the next Jeff Zucker?' There *was* no next Jeff Zucker. Jeff Zucker is Jeff Zucker." Allison Gollust thinks that "the times that *GMA* got closer to us was probably more a reflection of when the *Today* show got lazy than *GMA* doing better. Or it was a combination. Not to take anything away from *GMA*, but Katie and Matt, in those chairs, were just an unbeatable combination. I've studied them for fifteen years—they *know* what people want to see."

COMPLICATING THE MORNING war was the actual war that was starting now—Operation Iraqi Freedom. When, in March 2003, President Bush announced the decision to invade Iraq, Katie flew to Saudi Arabia and did *Today* from there, while Diane, in her fashion, took a more in-the-fray approach in *GMA*'s coverage. "Diane and I literally just went to the airport, sat in the Virgin lounge, and said, 'Okay, should we try to go to Jordan or should we try to go to Kuwait?'" says Anna Robertson. "'How do we best get into Iraq?' You didn't know if you *could* get in. So we just called people from the airport and said, 'We're going; this is the plan.' We ended up going to Kuwait." There, they hired a car and driver to get them into Iraq—"Diane is putting on her drugstore makeup in the back of the car with her little compact and we're driving into the desert. We really had *no idea* where we were going. We got to the American military base and all the sirens went off and everybody put on their masks and we interviewed soldiers. This was definitely dangerous—we didn't have the right equipment and at the time no one knew if Saddam had weapons of mass destruction. Diane was fine. She mostly worried about the crew. If she had been alone, she'd have done anything—she's fearless." Soon after, Diane and Anna returned to Iraq to interview the notorious female weapons scientist known as "Dr. Germ," a scoop produced by Shelley Ross. Anna: "It was a crazy adventure."

But during one of these trips to Iraq, Diane, again, confronted—and sidestepped—the hauteur trap of Peter Jennings. Peter suggested that he, as anchor, ask Diane an on-air question, but Diane had learned her lesson from his treatment of her during 9/11 and his abiding treatment of Barbara Walters. According to an observer, "Diane said something like, 'No! I'm not going to do that'"—converse with Jennings on air—"'because he will say, "No, you're wrong." He will intentionally make me look foolish.'" In less confidential settings, Diane had a deft and witty way to get back at Jennings. "To make fun of him at events, she would say, 'Oh, captain, my captain!' That was a dig to Peter. It said: One, you're not educated. And two, *I'm* the captain," says one who's worked with both of them.

Ben Sherwood, Diane's protégé at *Primetime*, had worked his way up the producer line to handle Tom Brokaw at *NBC Nightly News*. According to a *GMA* insider, he was up for executive producer of *Nightline*, and "when he didn't get it, he left," returning to LA to write a book, the bestselling novel *Death and Life of Charlie St. Cloud*, which became a movie. (It didn't hurt that Sherwood's wife, Karen Kehela, was an executive with the powerful production company Imagine Entertainment.) During this time—2003, early 2004—"Ben, who was as cunning and seductive as Diane, really wooed Diane. He sat at home, he finished writing his book, and he wrote her e-mails" as an unofficial adviser. "'Why did you do this?' 'Here is where I think you're going wrong.' *That's* how he wormed his way in" to her favor.

The beginning of the year 2004 was intense for Diane. On the heels of the release of Mel Gibson's controversial *The Passion of the Christ*, Diane taped her interview with Gibson, which aired on February 16. "It was very, very complicated," Anna Robertson says, editing "five hours of tape" of a "very intellectual" nature down to a piece that was fair. "Diane feels a great responsibility to people who entrust her with their stories." Gibson narrowly denied charges that he was anti-Semitic—he said that "to be anti-Semitic is a sin." But the fervor with which he threatened Diane when she asked him about his father Hutton Gibson, a proud Holocaust denier—"He's my father. Gotta leave it alone, Diane. Gotta leave it alone"—and the subtly fearful snap back of the head of this genteel WASP wife of a Holocaust escapee when Gibson leveled that threat, spoke volumes. Diane played Mel Gibson the opposite of the way she'd played Whitney Houston—she used her Decorous Lady card instead of her Serious Dame card—and her shrewd choice would grant her another, stronger crack at Gibson a couple of years later.

In February 2004, during *GMA*'s post–Academy Awards broadcast, Shelley Ross made a split-second decision to lead the coverage with Charlize Theron, who had won Best Actress for her depiction of a serial murderer, instead of Charlie Gibson's interview with Best Director winner Peter Jackson. Theron had a dramatic personal backstory: In their native South Africa, her own mother had shot her abusive husband, Charlize's father, dead. Charlize had been in the house at the time, protected by her mother's action. She was infinitely more photogenic than the messy-haired, then hefty *Lord of the Rings* director, and the interview Diane had done with Theron was a rare one in which the actress had discussed her mother's act of lethal self-defense. Still, Diane's interview with Theron was an earlier-taped interview while Charlie's with Jackson was Oscar-night current. Initially, Shelley relented and agreed that Charlie's piece could lead, but it wasn't yet sufficiently edited, so Shelley made the call to go with the Theron piece. Soon afterward, the *New York Post*'s Page Six planned to run an item stating that Charlie was angry at Shelley "for tricking him"; he did not believe his piece wasn't ready (though Ross says she never heard uncivil words from Gibson about her decision). Ross had the opportunity, during ABC's negotiation with Page Six, to "pre-trade" that upcoming negative item about herself for a negative item about movie reviewer Joel Siegel having a tantrum at an Oscars event. But, feeling that Siegel, a cancer patient, had enough problems without an embarrassing gossip item, Shelley declined to trade her own Page Six slam for Siegel's. Partially as a result of that Page Six slam against Shelley—and despite the fact that David Westin, over a recent lunch, had just signed Shelley to a hefty new $3 million *GMA* contract—Shelley was suddenly "reassigned" back to *Primetime*. For her part, Diane told Shelley that, for the sake of unity with Charlie, she regrettably couldn't step in.

Some at *GMA* thought Diane failed to protect her longtime producer by letting the bad press stand unchallenged and for not stopping the reassignment. (By contrast, "Diane's friend Oprah would have gone to bat for a loyal producer," one senior staffer says.) The sudden loss of the powerhouse producer came as a shock to Morning as a whole. But someone who later came to the show reasons, "The trouble was, Shelley and Diane were too much alike. When you have an executive producer and an anchor who are *both* very creative and who *both* want you twenty-four/seven, it's really like working eighty-eight/seven. Diane and Shelley together were too much pressure on the staff and the show. Only one of them at a time could be in a place like that or it was going to break. And Diane wasn't going to be the one to leave. So it had to be Shelley."

Now Ben Sherwood came in as *GMA*'s new executive producer. He was lucky. The momentum that Shelley Ross had built for the show got a boost through a stroke of ABC prime-time programming fortune: The debut of instantly popular *Desperate Housewives* in October made more evening viewers leave their dials on ABC when they went to bed. Now *Today* was in serious trouble—at one point the *GMA*-to-*Today* gap was closed down to forty-seven thousand households, a miracle from the standpoint of Diane's January 1999 initiation.

In a sense, *GMA*'s edge in the tightening horse race may have been compromised by Diane's own perfectionism—her insistence on being a journalist, covering far-flung international stories, while also being a morning anchor. The catastrophic Indian Ocean tsunami hit over the Christmas holidays. Diane made a trip to the devastated region, and, says Anna Robertson, who accompanied her, "she kept going and going and *going*. We would fly over decimated areas. We didn't sleep for *days*." And when she did catch shut-eye, "she was sleeping in the back of a Jeep. But that's just how Diane is." There was a problem with getting out of Malaysia and back to New York; Diane and Anna ended up hitching a ride on a seatless C-130 cargo plane. "This is a woman who really puts herself in the zone," says Phyllis McGrady. When she would go off on intense assignments to dangerous locations, "Mike gets extremely worried. His own work is very different and he's very protective of her—he *loves* her. He's called and said, 'I'm very worried. I haven't heard from her, Phyllis. Have *you?*'" Once, before a trip, he called David Westin and worriedly asked, "Is she really going to be safe? Is she *really* going to be safe?"

Perhaps in the wake of the exhausting tsunami coverage, "Diane got a little lax [on *GMA*] after Christmas," an insider recalls. "The show was doing really well for six or eight months," since Sherwood came on. "They were really firing on all cylinders. Diane, Charlie, and Robin [Roberts, the newsreader] were golden. *Desperate Housewives* was a huge hit and there was great cross-promotion on that." But "after Christmas we came back and we lost our momentum. We all talked about it. We couldn't quite figure out how to get back that fighting feeling."

Eventually—inevitably—"Diane started losing confidence in Ben. Then it got progressively worse. I don't know that there was a point where she didn't talk to him, but she had gone through that with other EPs," the insider says. Ironically, it was only after *GMA* mysteriously started—at least privately and internally—feeling the 2004–2005 postholiday morale slump that the New York media jumped on its rival's misfortune. The trigger point was *Today*'s firing of Tom Touchet and replacing him with sports producer Jim Bell, in April 2005.

On April 25, an Alessandra Stanley story ran in the *New York Times* under the headline "*Today* Seeks Yesterday's Glory." It was as coolly venomous a piece as the *Times* ever published, and in those largely pre–social media days, it went viral by word of mouth. Stanley spared Diane just marginally less scorn than she heaped on Katie with her catty opening line:

> Something has to be very wrong with NBC's *Today* if viewers are turning to ABC's Diane Sawyer as a refreshingly wholesome, down-to-earth alternative. . . .

Then she lit into Katie:

> [Katie's] on-air persona has changed, along with her appearance and pay
> scale. But lately her image has grown downright scary: America's girl
> next door has morphed into the mercurial diva down the hall. At the first
> sound of her peremptory voice and clickety stiletto heels, people dart
> behind doors and douse the lights.

Stanley reprised her swipes at Diane near the end ("Her golden good
looks never change" and her "poised, creamy insincerity . . . never varies
or falters"), but taking down Katie was the main point. This included
the crediting of a flamboyant fashion correspondent's rather histrionic
complaint that his recent firing from the show after a kidney transplant
had been like being "shot at the crack of dawn" and "left in a gutter to
bleed."

"It was all true!" says someone who was at *Today* shortly before this
epic takedown was printed. "And that is what made it so painful to Katie.
Had it been wrong, you would have laughed it off. 'Disgruntled ex-
employee?' Are there any *gruntled* ex-employees who *don't* have an ax to
grind? And is anyone ever grinding anything *other than* an ax? But it was
so close to home that I think it really hurt her. And you should have seen
the dragnet of '*Who* could have been the source? *How* did this happen?'"
that ensued, with Katie fruitlessly demanding to know who had spoken to
Stanley.

A female former CBS producer says, cynically, "We producers have a
term for something anchors get. We call it 'the disease that comes out of
the front of the lens'—and the longer the time you spend looking into the
lens," the more you are susceptible to that malady. It may best be described as a public-attention-stimulated exaggeration of one's personality
in the service of self-interest and as a result of the necessary rapacious
competition that comes with the territory.

People in the business note that the difference between Diane and
Katie is reflected in how they've fought over gets. When a friend of Diane's, a public figure, was being pursued by Katie's people, the wooed

eminence got a call from Mike Nichols, who said—in a very nice way, to be sure—that he and Diane would essentially cut off all social contact if their friend appeared on *Today*. That threat of permanent silence from Diane *"hurt,"* its famous recipient reports, adding, "Diane has hurt me *many* times" and "Diane's very sharp sword, which is hard to see because she's so lovely, can cut you to the quick." It was pure Diane—no finger-prints, yet *all* fingerprints—and it was stunningly effective: Diane's worried friend turned *Today* down cold.

Here, by contrast, is recklessly blunt, snarky Katie: When, in May 2005, a woman named Aleta St. James gave birth to twins at fifty-seven, a get war broke out between Katie and Diane for the mature new mother's exclusive. Diane won; St. James chose *GMA*. Soon after, Katie minced no words. Within earshot of people in the control booth, Katie loudly mused: "I wonder who she blew *this* time to get it." Converting Diane Sawyer's famous penchant for figurative seduction into such graphic and improba-ble sexual terms may be common office banter, but it was startling for someone of Katie's stature to be so unmindful of her image. Says one shocked witness: "You can *think* those things, but to *say* them? And where everyone can hear them?"

By now, Katie was being aggressively, secretly courted away from *Today*, to far more prestigious pastures than morning TV. Andrew Hey-ward was the president of CBS News in 2004 when he first approached Katie to discuss replacing Dan Rather—thus becoming the first ever fe-male solo anchor of a six-thirty news show. It was "probably Leslie's" idea, Heyward says gingerly—others make that statement more forcefully—referring to Leslie Moonves. Moonves was president of CBS and—as many people, especially those at CBS News, make a point to stress—a product of Hollywood, not of the news business. Says a longtime CBS News producer: "The Katie decision was taken *outside* of the news division. The news divi-sion had *no* voice in it—you really need to understand that."

Heyward: "Katie was one of the few superstars in the business, and it was known that at a certain point her *Today* show deal was going to be up. Leslie was very eager to reinvent the news." Heyward agreed, believing, as he puts it, that "this tradition of the evening news anchor who hands down wisdom like tablets from Sinai" needed to give way to "a relationship between a journalist and her viewers" that was "more peer-to-peer and more authentically based," less dependent on "the trappings of authority." One way to do so would be "to name somebody of her stature—and there was almost nobody else of her stature." To say you want "'somebody *like* Katie Couric,'" as Moonves seems to have said, "*means* Katie—there's nobody like Katie *but* Katie."

By some accounts, the first confidential overtures were made in early 2004. One of the "preliminary discussions" took place at Katie's apartment, as is customary in these cases since, as Heyward explains, "we were not allowed to negotiate with her—she was still under contract [to NBC]. But you're permitted to get acquainted, to have exploratory conversations about things that might be interesting in the future." At this meeting, which Heyward and Moonves attended, Katie's agent Alan Berger was also present. There was another meeting "at Leslie's apartment," Heyward says. "And I met once with Katie at her apartment. There might have been more [meetings] than that."

The meetings were kept secret even inside CBS. Although CBS famously never had an anchor succession plan—on principle, says a long-time CBS man ("We've never *tried* to 'make stars'; if you *became* a star, whether it was Dan or Ed Bradley or Mike Wallace, it was because of what you *did*")—it was thought, among the anchor-in-waiting senior correspondents, that "Scott Pelley and John Roberts desperately wanted it." (Pelley eventually succeeded Katie.) It was even widely thought that Heyward was actively championing John Roberts—at least until Moonves made his crush on Katie clear.

CBS News was known for being a proud, hard news, tight-budget, family-style network—a place that was difficult to get into but where, once you did, you spent your entire career; a news division that prided itself on using less money and fewer cameras than its rivals but always got a better story. It was housed in the least prepossessing, most unglamorous Manhattan physical studio and office space of the Big Three. (It's a "dumpy old building," says the CBS man—in the lonely, far west reaches of Midtown, hard by the car showrooms.) People spent their whole careers there and it had a very conservative turnover system. As of September 2004, CBS News had had only three six-thirty anchors in its entire history: Douglas Edwards from 1949 to 1962, Walter Cronkite from 1962 to 1981, and Dan Rather after that.

During her courtship by Moonves and Heyward, Katie had the upper hand. She "very understandably had a lot of options," Heyward says. He refers to the "tensions between opposing forces" involved in considering bringing her in as anchor. "On the one hand, you have a very noble tradition of the evening news. On the other, you have the need to continue evolving and innovating—and you have her unique skills." Katie was concerned she'd lose something in the bargain. "It would be less a showcase for her versatility, her ad-lib ability, her sense of humor, her effervescence. I think she wanted to make sure that she could play a role in influencing the future of the *Evening News*," to retain a little of her Katie essence. Yet the idea of becoming the first solo female six-thirty news anchor was overwhelmingly compelling. Not to mention the fact that, as a *Today* colleague says, "After fifteen years, maybe she thought, 'If I have to do *one* more story on hormone replacement therapy, I'll blow my brains out.'"

Then, in September 2004, the unthinkable occurred, for a newsman of Dan Rather's stature. On a midweek *60 Minutes* report, a scant two months before the presidential election between George W. Bush and John Kerry, Rather revealed scathing memos about President Bush, supposedly written during his service in the Texas Air National Guard. The memos' validity was suspect; upon rigorous technical analysis, they were determined to be counterfeit. CBS quickly offered a retraction. Rather hung on, defended the memos, and fought for the veracity of his story. "I like Dan, but he wouldn't let go of it," a female producer says of the effort to dislodge him from the chair. But as his error grew undeniable, Rather agreed to step down.

In March 2005, after twenty-four years as *CBS Evening News* anchor, Rather signed off the air. Rather's ouster was the capper to the "extremely traumatic" period of Memogate (as it came to be called), says a longtime CBS man, who adds, "They tried to historically *erase* Dan." Images came off walls. "If you walk through the halls of CBS today, you can't find a picture of Dan Rather. It's very strange when somebody who's been the heartbeat of the place for so long is shown the door, it's slammed behind him, and they try to pretend like he was never there."

Bob Schieffer became interim anchor as "a desperation thing," says the CBS man. The fellow late-middle-aged hard news Texan had been nicknamed "Deputy Dog" because he had for so long been second in command "and was shrewd enough not to get in Dan's way, because Dan would have *killed* him." Now Schieffer was thrilled to finally get his day in the sun. "He took everyone out to lunch and spent the whole time talking about himself. You'd walk down the street with him and people would walk up and shake his hand and he'd be beaming." On top of that, "after a rocky few months, Bob hit his stride. The numbers went up. The mood in the place brightened." Increasingly, people thought: Why don't we keep Schieffer on as anchor?

But Moonves and Heyward were strongly "in favor of the new." And so here was CBS News—regarded as the most boys' club–like of the three networks in terms of its internal behavior, and the one whose six-thirty newscast drew the oldest, most male, and most rural viewers—secretly planning to put Katie Couric in the anchor chair.

Katie had done her share of interviews with political news makers at *Today,** and had covered such major stories as the Rodney King riots, the Oklahoma City bombings, and the fiftieth anniversary of the Normandy invasion. But her Morning persona clung to her tightly.

---

*Among them: Shimon Peres, Benjamin Netanyahu, Yasir Arafat, Geraldine Ferraro, Jerry Falwell, Pat Buchanan, Madeleine Albright, George H. W. Bush, George W. Bush, Laura Bush, Jeb Bush, Janet Reno, Warren Christopher, Richard Holbrooke, Christine Todd Whitman, Newt Gingrich, Condoleezza Rice, King Abdullah of Jordan, Bob Dole, Leon Panetta, Dick Armey, Nelson Mandela, Colin Powell, Tony Blair, Tariq Aziz, Norman Schwarzkopf, Anita Hill, Dan Quayle, Ross Perot, Joe Biden, Mikhail Gorbachev, Ariel Sharon, Bill Clinton, Hillary Clinton, John McCain, Dick Cheney, Sandra Day O'Connor, Henry Kissinger, John Kerry, and John Edwards.

As a result of Rather's Memogate, Andrew Heyward left CBS News in November 2005. The incoming news president was Sean McManus, the chairman of CBS Sports, who would now be president of CBS Sports *and* president of CBS News. A by then twenty-five-year CBS news veteran says, "I think most people in the news division weren't familiar with who Sean McManus *was*."

Heyward says, "When I handed off to my successor, Sean McManus, in the fall of 2005 we actually went to Katie's apartment together." However that meeting at the apartment may have gone, senior CBS staffers think that, as one male correspondent puts it, "Sean was probably the worst possible executive" for Katie. "He's a very uptight guy, and I don't think he handles women well at all, and Katie's very in-your-face."

ON AUGUST 25, 2005, Hurricane Katrina struck. Katie flew to New Orleans and broadcast in the street, the floodwater up to her knees. Then she repaired to the Superdome, where, among the teeming dispossessed, was a man named Glen Henry, who couldn't find his family. He looked into the NBC camera and plaintively wailed, "Katie, help me!" She tracked down his family and reunited them.

Diane rushed to New Orleans, too. Outdoing Katie in the reporter true grit department, Diane—and Phyllis McGrady and Anna Robertson— "slept in a car," Phyllis says, "because there was *no* place to stay. We only slept for an hour or two" before heading to the worst-hit parts of the city and to the Superdome.

Meanwhile, back in New York, machinations continued that would roil all three networks—not just NBC, Katie's current berth, and CBS, her would-be home, but also Diane's more comfortable habitat, ABC. As for Christiane, she would embark on the most emotional experience of her life and the most intense schedule of travel in her career.

CHAPTER EIGHT

Home from War, Still in Battle

Christiane: 1997 to 2007

LIKE MANY WOMEN who had found their calling in a particularly all-consuming, aggressive, "nonfeminine" career after being raised in a traditional happy family setting, Christiane had consciously chosen work over serious love during the years in Bosnia and just afterward. It was a pragmatic, not a wounded, decision. "I couldn't have done my work if I'd been married or had a kid," she later said. "All my energy, my emotion, my intellect went into my work. During the nineties, people would ask me, 'When are you going to settle down?' and I'd say, 'I don't think I'll ever have a child.'" Those close to her knew this. Christiane "wasn't a gushy baby kisser and would have been all right if she never married and had children," says Lizzy Amanpour. "We thought we would never get married," says Diana Bellew. "I remember chats with her—a wistfulness, a sense that 'this'"—marriage—"'isn't going to be for us.' But we weren't crying over it. We weren't really sad." They were matter-of-fact. "I had made my life working and living in Rome, and Christiane had her big old career—and that was just how it was."

But then something changed. "I knew Christiane was looking for love at some point," says Emma Daly. Christiane has put it this way: "There came a moment where I flipped the switch and said, 'Okay, self. You can be proud of the work you've done. You wanted to be a foreign correspondent, you're a foreign correspondent. Maybe now it's time to look for some personal happiness and fulfillment. It took me a couple of years, but I consciously changed myself."

Christiane turned thirty-seven in January 1995, when Bosnia was still ablaze. There was a small window of time for childbearing, as Christiane, Emma, and all the other female war reporters well knew. If you worked these dangerous international assignments too long, you risked never having children—if, indeed, you wanted them. But if you did want kids and you did want to continue your career, as Christiane was now beginning to feel—well, there was no easy answer. One major consideration was how much risk you'd then be willing to take: "There's a lot more eyebrow raising if you're a mother" covering wars, says Emma, who now, as a parent, has a desk job. "Whereas if you're a father, everyone assumes you'll carry on. Why would you stop just because you have a family?"

Another risk was the culture itself, in which men had infinitely more time to be attractive as potential mates than women. On January 12, 1997, when Christiane turned thirty-nine, she called her old friend Liza McGuirk from her hotel room in Bulgaria, as Liza, who now had a husband and child, remembers it. "She was talking about how the power had been turned off in the entire city and it was freezing cold. I remember saying, 'Boy, that really sucks. It's your birthday and you have no power.'

"And I thought to myself, 'Has she made too many sacrifices?' It was the first time I ever thought: 'Sometimes you don't get it all—and she might not.' I hung up the phone feeling really sad. Feeling like: Had it been worth it for her? If you're [almost] forty in pitch-black, freezing cold Bulgaria—and *I* am the first call you make?" Liza remembered how, a dozen years earlier, the *Newsweek* cover headline warning that a single forty-year-old woman had a better chance of being killed by a terrorist than getting married had sent her and her friends "into a black depression."* She and Christiane had talked at the time about how the arti-

---

Newsweek apologized for the article twenty years later, in 2006. It turned out that the dire prediction in the 1985 Harvard/Yale marriage study that had been the basis for the sensational cover line was not borne out in the ensuing years. Women over forty were, indeed, getting married.

cle had been "a disservice to womankind." Now, on her friend's birthday, she wondered if their umbrage had been too idealistic.

That birthday and phone call provided a wake-up call to Christiane, too. She made the decision to start consciously looking for love. Then, about six months after what she has called "that turning point," she met Jamie Rubin. Jamie (James Philip) Rubin was the brother of Elizabeth Rubin, who was freelancing for *Harper's* magazine when Christiane met her in Sarajevo. The Rubin siblings had grown up in Larchmont, a comfortable town in Westchester County, their father the prosperous owner of a small publishing company, their mother a medical school instructor who helped students interview psychiatric patients. A graduate of Columbia, where he also earned a master's degree in international affairs, Jamie Rubin, at thirty-seven, was chief spokesman for Secretary of State Madeleine Albright.

Jamie had never been married—like Christiane, he had been so absorbed in his work that "he never had time to date," according to one friend, British writer Peter Pringle. At least not date *steadily*, by apparent choice. Jordan Tamagni, a college friend who became a speechwriter for Bill Clinton, remembered being struck by the sight of the "tall, handsome, brash" Columbia student driving around "in a beautiful green Mercedes convertible." Jamie seemed to have always been confident; he has said that he realized he could "talk to anyone about anything. I didn't hang out only with the nerdy, smart kids, but also with the sports jocks." He developed a passion for politics while at Columbia. Reagan had just been elected, and—mirroring Christiane's concerns about Reagan, voiced at the Benefit Street dinner table—Jamie became obsessed with nuclear weapons, which he thought would be recklessly used by the new president. His postcollege job was at an arms control think tank; by the end of the 1980s he was then senator Joe Biden's foreign policy adviser. Albright was quick to hire him when she was appointed secretary of state.

"Women in D.C. thought Jamie was hot—a very attractive guy who could have had a lot of beautiful women," says a female NPR producer, who adds that people were surprised by his romance with Christiane. In fact, when Christiane's family met Jamie, "my mom and sisters were shocked at how good looking he was—we were quite astounded," says Lizzy Amanpour.

Jamie had a forceful personality. "Jamie's highly intelligent, extraordinarily articulate, but he's a difficult character, like all interesting men are difficult," is how Christiane's new friend Bella Pollen would come to view him. Such men "have their fair share of neuroses and baggage; they have a lot of stuff going on in their heads; they're opinionated and contrary, fun to be with but not easy." The words "arrogant" and "ego" had been bandied about in descriptions of him in Washington, D.C.'s media and gossip circles. He liked to dress well. He was socially well connected. He was a highly effective spokesman for Albright, and he did his job with appropriate aggressiveness. He had an evident degree of self-importance: Years later, when he was hired for an executive position at Bloomberg, the media empire of New York mayor Michael Bloomberg, Rubin, unlike other equally credentialed executives there, couldn't abide the egalitarian open-space setting. "Jamie is *not* a cubicle guy," a friend of his says, citing this as a reason that he left.

Christiane and Jamie first briefly met through his sister, but it was four years later, in July 1997—six months after her concerted attempt to look for love—that they both found themselves on board a State Department plane bound for Bosnia. Jamie and his boss had been, as diplomats, as passionate about justice for Bosnia as Christiane was in her role as that embattled country's premier reporter. On the plane, Christiane was in the press section, and Jamie was sitting with Secretary Albright. Lizzy Amanpour says, "He passed a note down to her to say, 'Will you go out for a drink with me?'" Emma Daly recalls, "Christiane was a little freaked out about this. I remember her saying, 'What should I say? 'Cause he's the spokesman for Madeleine Albright.' I said, 'Go for it. See what it's like. See if you have a good time.'"

When they disembarked in Bosnia, Christiane and Jamie went to a bar and ordered margaritas. From there, says Emma Daly: "It all happened very quickly. They were pretty besotted and it took off like wildfire." Liza

McGuirk: "From the minute she met him it was very clear: This was very different. It wasn't as if Christiane didn't have her share of suitors, but Jamie was definitely right for her from the first second."

As for Jamie, when he got back to the United States, he told a friend, "I've never felt this way." He was smitten by a woman whom he didn't name but then said, "Turn on CNN now and have a look at her."

Christiane's family saw that "Jamie really made her laugh. And they were intellectually compatible," says her sister Lizzy. "They had passionate conversations about what was going on in the world." The Amanpours were "very, very happy" for Christiane.

Each was traveling on separate work schedules. "They spent as much time as they could meeting in places where they could be together," Lizzy says. One rendezvous was in Italy, where they attended Diana Bellew's fortieth birthday party, at a historic castle on a lake just outside of Rome. Another was in D.C., where they attended a book party for Sally Quinn, long the social doyenne of the nation's capital, who would soon become a close friend.

Less than three months after that party, in January 1998—four months after her harrowing encounter with the angry Afghan Arab in Kabul—Jamie and Christiane took a vacation to the island of Tobago. As they walked on the beach one night, he rustled in his pocket for the box that contained a gold-and-sapphire ring he'd recently bought in Paris. Then he dropped on one knee in the sand.

Days later, Christiane was in London, about to fly to Iran for the interview she and Parisa Khosravi had worked so hard to obtain with President Khatami. Mark Phillips would be her cameraman. "We'd heard a rumor that Christiane was getting engaged to James Rubin," Mark says. Since "Rubin was the spokesman for the secretary of state, the word was, 'Don't say anything to Iran because we don't want to blow that interview.'" The interviewer's intense relationship with a member of the secretary of state's team could look suspicious. "So at Heathrow we're loading all the stuff, and we could see Christiane coming across the tarmac—and she's holding her finger up in the air and pointing to her finger! And we're going, 'Shut up! Shut up! You're not supposed to tell anybody!'" For the tough, mature, worldly Christiane Amanpour, the image of her flaunting her engagement ring is incongruous, if endearing.

The wedding was scheduled for August. Lizzy says, "At that age you realize if you meet somebody you really love, you get married quickly." Christiane and Jamie considered marrying in London but decided Rome would be more central for their far-flung friends and family. They chose the lakeside town Bracciano, where Diana Bellew had had her birthday party. The castle, Castello Orsini-Odescalchi, was just right for the Jewish ceremony that would be held after the Catholic ceremony was held at the nearby Church of Santo Stefano.

Habitué that she may have been of shelled-out Sarajevo hotels and African flophouses, Christiane now paid fussy attention to detail. She spent so much time comparing tablecloths with the wedding planner that, Diana recalls, "Jamie got really bored and wandered off and came back a few minutes later and said, 'Is the great linen debate over yet?'"

The wedding was very nearly derailed at the last moment by world events, perhaps fitting for this particular power couple. On August 7, 1998, the day before the ceremony, al-Qaeda forces drove truck bombs through the gates of the U.S. embassies in two African capitals—Dar es Salaam, Tanzania, and Nairobi, Kenya—leading to 223 deaths and 4,000 people injured. But even in the face of this major terrorist attack, Christiane and Jamie decided not to call off the wedding. "We were truly distraught," Christiane has said. "We thought we had to do something, but you only get to get married once. It was almost inevitable that such a thing happened at our wedding. When people like us take vacation, our worst nightmare is that something should happen," she said. "It was a credit to them to go on with it," says Parisa, who attended. "Christiane and Jamie knew that the world could go on without them."

The wedding was "an incredible cross-cultural thing," Diana says. "Christiane's dad and some cousins from Iran were the Muslim contingent. There was the Catholic ceremony, and then the Jewish one, with Jamie's friends holding the poles of the chuppah." Christiane wore a round-necked white sleeveless silk dress with a short, tiered veil, her hair pulled back to show dangly earrings. Among the guests were John Kennedy Jr. and his wife, Carolyn, present just as Christiane had been at their small wedding two years before in a tiny church on Cumberland Island, off the coast of Georgia.

MARRIAGE WAS STRANGE new terrain for an international correspondent. "Christiane was not used to being in a committed relationship," says Lizzy Amanpour. "She'd had lots of relationships on the road." But marriage to Jamie *"changed* her. It made her more patient."

Just after their wedding at the end of 1998, Christiane was scheduled to go to Iran with Liza McGuirk and Pierre Bairin to begin reporting an intensely personal documentary called *Revolutionary Journey.* Liza was particularly excited to go. She had taken time off from work during this period and Christiane had talked her into getting back into action. "Only a friendship with Christiane would allow one to go from a PTA meeting to hopping a plane to Tehran," Liza says. "Pierre and I got there first. We checked into the Homa Hotel and that day's headline in the *Tehran Times* was 'Zionist Rubin Condemns Iran.' And I remember Pierre and I looking at each other: Is she gonna be able to come into the country now that she's married to Jamie?"

Not only did the trip work out, but it was the first of several such trips, some filmed during her ensuing pregnancy, in which Christiane showed her native country most hopefully—marveling at the plethora of newspapers of many political persuasions on the street—and most personally, proudly showing off an Internet café owned by her cousin, where young Iranians were not opposed to America but, rather, *hungry* for news about it. The head-scarved Iranian girls smiled at the American cameras, and Christiane, herself in a green head scarf, looked straight at the lens and said, "I was *their* age when the Revolution began." In the most heart-stopping portion of the three-part special, she returned to what was left of her childhood home and greeted her father, embracing him, and a cousin. The once lovely house was "a ruin," as Christiane's father aptly put it—"a shell" of its former self, she said. She walked from wrecked room to wrecked room. Only now, twenty years after the Revolution, had her family been able to reclaim it. It was a poignant stocktaking by an exile whose family had lost so much yet had survived intact, and whose expulsion had impacted Christiane's ambition in ways that benefited the world.

CHRISTIANE AND JAMIE wanted a baby, and, considering her age, there was no time to wait. She determined that pregnancy would not slow her down. At just about the time she became pregnant, in June 1999, Christiane traveled to Bangladesh with Andrew Tkach to investigate how UNICEF had made a colossally fatal mistake. "They'd put in," explains Andrew, "a million hand-pump wells so the people would *not* get waterborne diseases. But nobody had tested the water and there was arsenic in it," resulting in "the largest mass poisoning in history." Standing on the banks of a river, with footage of women and children near a well, Christiane reported that "the road to hell is paved with good intentions. . . . When UNICEF first started its safe water program twenty-five years ago, it helped to nearly halve the number of child deaths in Bangladesh. Before that, hundreds of thousands of children like these were dying every year from diseases like cholera and diarrhea, found in the dirty surface water. But no one suspected that the clear water in the new wells would simply replace one poison with another. . . . The poison was arsenic."

Christiane then turned her microphone over to University of California researcher Allan Smith, who said, "This is the highest risk of cancer that we know of from environmental exposures. . . . [O]ne in ten may eventually die of cancer." Christiane's transition from a reporter in literal war zones, those of bombs and grenades and intentional genocide, to a reporter in humanitarian war zones—those of tragedy, oppression, cruelty, and hideously *accidental* killing—had begun.

Getting to the crisis site in Bangladesh was sluggish and challenging—"twenty trucks trying to get over one huge river, currents, huge traffic jams!" Andrew recalls. Finally, impatient Christiane took control. She leapt out of her and Andrew's stalled vehicle, stormed to the front of the crush of inert convoys, and took over directing the flow of vehicles—imperious attitude, hand signals, and all. "She jumped up and literally became the cop. 'You go first! You go second!'" She ordered them and they obeyed. "It was just natural to her. And it was funny!" Andrew laughs, in memory. Later, the crew gave her a present: a Bangladesh traffic policeman's baton.

Almost right after finishing that story in Bangladesh, Christiane and Jamie flew to Martha's Vineyard to spend a weekend in early July with her close friend John Kennedy Jr., his wife, Carolyn, John's cousin and best friend Anthony Radziwill, and Anthony's wife, Carole. Anthony was severely beset by cancer, and the celebration was thus bittersweet, but they all managed to have a good time—"It was a very happy, lovely, normal, friendly couples weekend," as Christiane would recall it. They all went back to Manhattan, and Christiane hugged John good-bye as he and Carolyn boarded his small plane to fly to Toronto (with his flying coach on board) on a quick business trip—a "mission," as Christiane called it, for *George*, the magazine he'd founded and was editing.

Days later Christiane would pick up her phone and hear the ominous news: John, Carolyn, and Carolyn's sister Lauren Bessette had taken off on a subsequent trip in John's plane—this time, without his flying teacher on board. They were headed for the Hyannis Port wedding of John's cousin Rory Kennedy to Mark Bailey. While in flight they disappeared over the water; their plane could not be located. Christiane stifled her dread in order to go on Larry King's broadcast to talk about her dear friend—trained in war zones, she said she was *still* holding out hope that the three would be safely found. Never before had she violated the privacy of their friendship to talk about John, she made clear. She described him as a "loyal and generous and faithful guy, and if you look at his friends, they are all the people who have been with him for the last nearly forty years of his life." She spoke admiringly of his "big risk" in launching, and succeeding at, a magazine where "many people [would be] just delighted to see somebody like John fail."

Her optimism was not justified, of course. The plane had crashed and no one had survived. Days later, she attended John's funeral mass at Manhattan's St. Thomas More Catholic Church, after the private burial at sea that the three received off the coast of Martha's Vineyard. She was now two months' pregnant. If her baby was a boy, John would be his middle name.

Still, as with many accomplished working women who did pregnancy later and were seriously enmeshed in their work, she knew enough to let incipient motherhood sneak up on her in its own time. It wasn't real until it was real—that's what many modern working women feel. And she was one of them—maybe, given the machismo pervading her field and the cynicism of the men in it who were waiting for her to falter, she took that attitude to unrealistic extremes. "I was very cavalier when I was pregnant," Christiane has admitted. "I was a little over-the-top. I was, 'Nothing will change. I'll take my child with me. All I need is some bulletproof diapers.'" She felt the way many professional women who are pregnant feel but do not always admit: the surprise of it all, the foreignness, the trust that some feeling will come over you that you don't yet understand but you will welcome when it does. "Motherhood is a very strange concept," she admitted. "It'll take time to figure it out because I never intended to have children—that wasn't one of my goals. Everybody is saying it changes you radically, so I'll wait and see." A strikingly honest statement.

When Christiane was five months' pregnant, she traveled to Russia to exclusively interview Mikhail Gorbachev on the occasion of the tenth anniversary of the fall of the Soviet Union. When she was more than eight months' pregnant, she traveled to Iran with Parisa Khosravi to do a story about the elections there. She was now CNN's chief international correspondent, and that meant ceaseless travel. "It was hot," even in February, "and there's always an extra layer of hijab to wear, and that *does* help disguise a pregnancy," Parisa says. "But Christiane was running around in Iran, covering the election, eight months' pregnant!"

Christiane and Jamie's son was born on March 24, 2000. They named him Darius John: Darius for the great Persian warrior who fought the Greeks in 490 BC; John, of course, for John Kennedy. Christiane wanted Darius christened a Catholic. Jamie did not object.

. . .

NOTHING TOOK Christiane Amanpour more by surprise than how she would feel once she had a baby. She hadn't quite expected to fall in love with being a mother. She didn't fully anticipate the wave of emotion.

At first she tried to deny it in mixed company. David Bernknopf recalls: "Right after Darius was born, I talked to Christiane about whether she wanted to go back out into the field and do the kinds of dangerous stories that she was doing," he says. "Initially she downplayed the danger completely. 'No, no, it's important! I want to go back out.'" Christiane, as a female journalist who'd witnessed sabotage attempts by jealous male counterparts, needed to be on her guard. "I think she denied it to me and I think she denied it to *herself* at first, because she wanted so much to *not* have that vulnerability. Christiane did not want people to say, 'Oh, now she's had a baby, now she's a mommy—now she's weaker.'" Bernknopf's assessment of his friend matched what Christiane herself has said: "I was conscious of being a woman and not letting them say, 'Now you're a mother and you can't do this anymore. Let the guys do it.'"

Still, however she talked to others, something *was* different. "The minute my child was born, everything changed," she later admitted. "There's a love inside you that you never knew existed. There's a protectiveness that you never knew you were capable of." Christiane made these uncharacteristically sentimental and personal remarks to Oprah Winfrey, who, of course, has been known to coax emotion from anyone. But then Christiane continued, more defiantly: "And there's no way in hell I would take my child to the places I go! That would be completely irresponsible. I'm also much more concerned about my [own] safety, and surviving."

The risks of her field were underscored for her two months after Darius was born, on May 24, 2000, when Emma Daly called Christiane with the terrible news that Kurt Schork, their adored Bosnia buddy, and Miguel Gil Moreno de Mora—a gangly, charming, devoutly Catholic Spanish lawyer turned cameraman they were so fond of—had been killed on assignment in Sierra Leone. Christiane's affection for Kurt is strikingly evident in a photo of the two of them that appears on his memorial page—she's smiling in a giddy, hammy high-school-best-friends-in-a-yearbook way. "We were all sort of in collective shock," Emma says. Christiane felt "devastated—I was really angry, she said. "They were killed telling a very important story, but does anyone know where Sierra Leone is? How many stations—how many networks—aired their footage?"

Christiane sent her condolences to Miguel's family in Spain and journeyed to D.C. for Kurt's ceremony, which took place after his cremation. Half of Kurt's ashes were buried at the Sarajevo grave of the Romeo and Juliet lovers whose moving story he had shared with the world.

Losing these two colleagues together fortified Christiane's motherhood-borne incentive to somehow stay safe while still doing powerful stories. And there would be more to come, less than a year later. "In 2001 another very close friend of ours was killed, along with two Reuters people and an Italian journalist, driving from Jalalabad to Kabul," Emma says. The three "were pulled out of the car and shot and tortured." On top of this tragedy was the indignity of some people's judgments. "People said, 'What were they thinking, driving down that road without an escort? Why didn't they have soldiers with them?'" To have friends risk their lives for stories, get killed—and then get blamed for "irresponsibility": This was a cruel irony.

CHRISTIANE AND JAMIE had had a commuter marriage the first fourteen months—she based in London, he in D.C. But when George W. Bush became president in January 2001 and Jamie was thus freed of his job, Jamie moved to join Christiane in London. "London was Christiane's spiritual home," says Bella Pollen, who would become her best friend there. Now Jamie entered that spiritual home.

Christiane and Jamie became part of a social circle of accomplished young Londoners of aristocratic heritage—Bella and her husband prime among them. Though she continued to travel to dangerous places, intent on her journalistic mission, Christiane's life was now fuller, more bifurcated—and also, perhaps, more conflicted. In London, the grungy war dog receded (only to be trotted back out when on assignment) and an adult version of the elite boarding school girl reemerged. As with her time in Providence—among friends who were nobility, real or metaphorical—this was a kind of homecoming.

Arabella "Bella" Pollen was an attractive new friend to Christiane. The daughter of British aristocrats, Bella had spent her childhood shuttling between a family estate in Scotland and a town house in Manhattan. She was an accomplished fashion designer—she'd had her own line (Princess Diana was a client)—who then turned to writing novels, including two, *Hunting Unicorns* and *The Summer of the Bear,* that were greeted with critical praise. With her second husband, the publisher David Macmillan, a grandson of Prime Minister Harold Macmillan, Bella presided over a lively blended family in several homes, including an English country mansion that was featured in *Vogue.* This was the world that Christiane and Jamie slipped into, with their move to London.

Before she met Christiane, Bella had researched her, as preparation for writing her protagonist—a tough-minded female war correspondent—in *Hunting Unicorns.* "I came across an interview Christiane had given on the death of the news—how entertainment was taking over real news. I was struck by how passionately she felt. Then, quite by chance, she was friends with friends of mine in London, and I met her at a small dinner. She read my book and loved it and gave me a quote. Then we started to bump into each other at our local farmers' market and began chatting over vegetables," and "because she was close friends with people who were also *my* close friends, we became a gang for five or six years. We'd meet a couple of times a week for movies and family Sunday lunches, and slowly we made the jump to close friends."

Bella and the other Londoners were taken by how down to earth Christiane was. In a crowd of Brits of casual privilege, Bella saw that "Christiane's not remotely rarefied. She's the furthest thing I know from being a snob. She has no time for kiss-ass or fakery." She was earnest and happy in her new London life. Christiane, says Bella, fell in love not only with her baby but also "with being a member of the community": the young-prime-aged English gentry. And this life was "pretty much the polar opposite of what she'd been doing most of her adult life—being a passionately independent roving reporter."

Christiane tried to puzzle out the dual—the dichotomous—nature of her life with Bella. "We talked fairly extensively about" the change in her circumstances from single reporter to social wife and mother. "She was passionate about her work in the field, but it brought loneliness at times—and worry about Darius." Christiane displayed her feminine side with Bella. She was "incredibly giggly—game for anything. In Colorado," where Pollen and Macmillan have a house, "we're cooking up a storm," and even though Christiane "can't boil an egg, she's in the kitchen wearing a funky vintage apron and a pair of weird Walmart slippers we've given her for Christmas, with her hands stuck up the back a raw turkey, trying to stuff the damn thing—laughing her head off. She has a deeply silly sense of humor. She is *much* the opposite of Jamie, who has a much more cynical, less hopeful take on the world than she does. In fact, of *all* the people I know, especially in London, Christiane is the *least* cynical by a very long way."

Was it motherhood, and a new relish of stylish domesticity, that softened this once impatient and confrontational warrior? Did flattery at being included in a tony circle make her more ingratiating? Or was the fact that she *really had* effected change for desperate people as few other journalists had what made for the optimism that Bella found in Christiane? Whatever the reason, over the ensuing years Christiane seemed to want—to *need*—the contrast of genteel hospitality she shared with Bella to soften—or to glamorize, or to reward—her breakneck investigative work. Bella says: "One minute we're at the local Chinese mani and pedi; the next minute she's in camouflage and embedded with soldiers in Afghanistan. *My* toenails are still looking pink and neat while hers are encased in hobnailed boots in a war-torn country."

For the first six years of her son's life, Christiane—simultaneously doing work for *60 Minutes* and as CNN's chief international correspondent—traveled to more international trouble sites than ever before in her career. Never had she worked so hard. She flew off from London to do stories in Sudan, Chad, Sierra Leone, Ethiopia, Kenya, Darfur, Israel, Palestine, Jordan, Iran, India, Afghanistan, Pakistan, Iraq, Kazakhstan, Moldova, Kosovo, Italy, France, Spain, Russia, Ukraine—and Washington,

312 THE NEWS SORORITY

D.C., and New York—rushing back to London between each crisis report in each hot spot and each hard-fought-for interview with a controversial leader in a private room. Her sister Lizzy says, "I've noticed this with people: If your personality is driven with work, it's *also* driven with being a mom. That's just your personality—you are a driven person. She is like that with Darius. Her responsibility to Darius is the *number one* thing in her life. You can tell he means everything to her. She doesn't like going away; it worries her. But at the same time, it fires her up. She feels incredibly passionate about doing a mission," an investigative justice story. "When she's engaged on that level, she just *goes* for it."

During a portion of their time in London, Jamie took a position as television host on a British show. According to an American network executive, it wasn't a good fit. Still, says Bella, "I never got the feeling that their agreement was that Jamie was a househusband. There is absolutely a sense that they have equally important careers—Jamie is passionate about politics, passionate about his time in office—but because of the vagaries of his job, because the Republicans came to office, it was the right time for her to return to England [in 2000]. If you're a politician at the top of your game as Jamie was, then being out of office—during the Bush years, eight years of having to sit and twiddle your thumbs during the best years of your life—is really tough." Christiane has been somewhat defensive about Jamie's time in London while she had such an intense work schedule. When Oprah provocatively quipped, "I read he just gave up everything for you and put on an apron," Christiane retorted, "He's not a househusband—that's a myth. He worked for a private company and wrote speeches. Post 9/11, he became Jamie Rubin, the voice of Americans overseas." Whether or not that last remark of Christiane's may be slightly hyperbolic, Bella says: "London was very receptive to Jamie. We Brits can be very snotty about the U.S.A. and its foreign policy or sometimes lack of it, but here was Jamie—*brilliant* on foreign policy."

When Darius was around six months old, Christiane traveled to a desolate part of southern Sudan with Andrew Tkach to do a *60 Minutes* report on the fact that there existed a safe, effective medication to cure the area's great child killer, sleeping sickness, but commercial forces were keeping it unavailable. It was like being in Bosnia again—Christiane risked her life to take the trip. "We were flying into a war zone in a charter plane," says Andrew. "There were men with machine guns on trucks. The rebels were not going to shoot us, because they'd invited us, but there was no communication in advance. They had all their weaponry on the grass strip"—hence a misidentification of the plane could have been deadly. Once they safely landed, deplaned, and picked up their gear, "the African pilot, who was like a cowboy, took off again and 'buzzed' us—he flew *just* over our heads. He thought it would be fun to give us a haircut."

They were now in "the most remote part of Africa"—a shell of a city, Yambio, where "there was not a single moving vehicle, just bombed-out trucks that children used as playgrounds." From there, they hopped into the Land Rover of a female Colorado doctor, Mickey Richer, the hero of the piece. "We had to go still deeper into the bush," to a burned-out old clinic where Richer was doing her best to care for the victims of an outbreak of fatal sleeping sickness—with the only drug available, a horribly corrosive one. Christiane and Andrew witnessed children wailing in pain while being injected with malarsoprol, which had been developed forty years earlier. "It was like shooting antifreeze into the children's veins," Andrew says. "It was very painful for us to watch. We were viewing extreme human suffering. There was another medicine, DFMO, that was a hundred percent safe and effective." But, as Christiane herself later said, one of the big companies producing the drug, Aventis, "was stopping making it because it simply wasn't cost-effective to make it—for poor Africans." Christiane, Andrew, and Dr. Richer felt sheer outrage, and their goal was to use the *60 Minutes* piece to shame the drug company into donating a supply of the drug to the suffering children. And that's what happened after the story aired, on February 11, 2001: Aventis (soon to be renamed Sanofi-Aventis) donated a five-year supply of DFMO and made a $25 million donation to the World Health Organization. (Eventually the Bill and Melinda Gates Foundation took over the funding.)

Christiane flew back to London in a safer plane than the one she had arrived in. This story out had been worth the risk.

Working outside the network system as she did, both by virtue of her

314 THE NEWS SORORITY

international location and her personality, Christiane was always a strong advocate for the stories she wanted covered. She was now considered the best-known foreign correspondent on TV, so the uphill fight she'd had with getting Bosnia covered was over. She had a unique relationship with *60 Minutes*: She was the first two-network correspondent they'd ever hired, and she could call Don Hewitt any time she wanted—he deeply respected her editorial advocacy. She pushed for stories about crimes against humanity, about the oppression of women and children in developing countries, about unjust and unjustified wars, and about her native Iran.

In September 2001, Christiane returned to Africa—to Sierra Leone—to shoot a *60 Minutes* story. She and Andrew were doing their second story on child soldiers, this time on children who were tattooed by the rebel army, in big block letters on their foreheads and chests, to keep them from running away. Christiane had already interviewed the doctor who was in the process of removing the tattoos, and now, late on a Tuesday afternoon, she was just sitting down with the scarred children themselves—a very delicate task, and a wrenching one.

The cameras were rolling on Christiane, gently talking to a child, trying to get him to open up about the painful physical disfigurement he'd endured, when an urgent call came in on Christiane's dedicated CNN satellite phone: "There's been a plane crash in New York. Please call." Andrew's thought was: "What does that have to do with us? There must be CNN crews that can handle a breaking news story in New York." He called them back and politely but firmly said, "Thank you, but we will continue our work." Minutes later came a second, more urgent message: "Need Christiane back. May be a major terrorist attack."

This, of course, was September 11. CNN chartered a helicopter out of the capital of Sierra Leone, picked her up, and got her to the airport to fly to London, where she reported live—first there, and then in Afghanistan—for her primary network. In Afghanistan for many months after 9/11, camplike conditions prevailed for the reporters. There were no hotels. The crews lived in the security compounds, and all cooked and ate communally. It was a little like Bosnia all over again.

Soon afterward, Christiane covered Pakistan—Pervez Musharraf's Pakistan, our freshly bribed ally in our brand-new "War on Terror." In that hotbed of pro-al-Qaeda sympathy, where many of bin Laden's lieutenants were hiding or in the American line of fire, any reporter could have met the awful fate of Daniel Pearl, especially a "trophy" reporter. "But she went in there," Parisa Khosravi says. "She went in there with a very tight schedule—a *very* tight schedule." Christiane was then in the habit of wrapping up assignments quickly, in order to get home to be with her child. Parisa could empathize, as she, too, would soon have a baby, and their conflicting loyalties were as twinned as their backgrounds. "Regardless of the story, she did *not* change her absolute commitment and rules about how she raised Darius," Parisa emphasizes.

On the heels of her Pakistan coverage, Christiane flew back to Afghanistan, to do two *60 Minutes* reports with feminist themes. Terrible conditions still existed for women there, even after the overthrow of the world's most brutal antiwoman regime. Returning to the country that had been shorn of the Taliban in name only took guts for Christiane, considering that, on her last trip, a Taliban soldier had, for nearly three hours, circled her and repeatedly promised to kill her for being an Iranian and a Western woman. Christiane and a cameraman entered a special wing of the medieval-looking prison that was reserved for women escaping honor killings by their families for such "crimes" as resisting arranged marriages or being seen holding hands with a beau. The women were held there, for indeterminate periods of time, for their own good: to protect them from families culture-bound to kill them. Christiane conducted interviews with women, some of whose faces were protectively obscured. Then she traveled to a home where a twelve-year-old girl answered— "more with her eyes than with words," Andrew recalls—the sensitive questions Christiane asked about her sexual abuse by the much older man to whom her family had married her off in order to pay off a debt.

Christiane confronted the new chief justice of a high tribal court about these cases. Forced marriage was now technically illegal in the post-Taliban Afghanistan, but Sharia was still the law. Right behind the chief justice—as he spoke vaguely of a "new" Afghanistan—was something disconcerting hanging on his office wall: "a whip, for the people publicly whipped for adultery," Andrew recalls. "He wasn't ashamed of it."

In a final piece in Afghanistan, Christiane interviewed a Tajik family returning from exile to their newly liberated village. The Tajiks were the main ethnic group within the Northern Alliance, loathed by their foes, the Taliban. "We rode on their truck with them"—those memorably televised dilapidated vehicles brimming with fifty feet of roped-together clots of a family's total belongings. "The towns they were returning to looked like Berlin after the war—not a wall standing, just rubble," Andrew says. But the ex-exiles were jubilant. One beaming returning resident was thrilled to find his "house"—even though now it was merely a roofless hole. He creakily pulleyed up an inaugural cup of water from a hundred-foot-deep well that was part of a two-thousand-year-old irrigation system on his reclaimed land. How clean could this water be? Nevertheless, the happy returnee "passed the metal cup to Christiane" for her to take a ceremonial sip for the camera, Andrew recalls. "She looks at me for a second: *Should I do this?* There were obvious sanitary questions—animal waste, for one. And some of those wells had been poisoned" by the departing Taliban. But the Tajik man had "smiled so broadly, Christiane knew if she made a face like, 'I don't think so,' it would have destroyed the relationship and also destroyed the moment on film."

So she took the risk. "She drank it. She was a trouper."

Still, Christiane was also becoming more demanding—with her CNN stories, anyway, if not necessarily with her *60 Minutes* ones produced with Tkach. "She got a reputation as time went on as being somewhat difficult to work with," David Bernknopf says. "As she got more known and more experienced, she had power—and she insisted that everybody work to her standards. She would not take any crap from anybody back in Atlanta about the direction of a story." This would prove a double-edged sword, but for now Christiane's powerful reputation intimidated people. Kathy O'Hearn was now producing CNN's brand-new *American Morning*. This tall, commanding woman learned to hold her own with the toughest of male colleagues when, years earlier, she was the second female camera operator ever hired by a network. Now she found Christiane "tough as nails" in dictating what time slot she wanted to be in. "She was not gonna buy anybody else's characterization of where she should be," says Kathy, "and if I whispered in her ear, 'I only have two minutes for you, okay?,' she'd ignore me and go on for four minutes if that's what she needed. She cut a daunting figure." She was tough, cocky, life-risking, in-the-field *famous* Christiane—and she was being indulged by daily-grind studio-centered Atlanta.

But the balance of power wouldn't always stay this way. Coming home to the States would mean playing her game differently. Did Christiane know that?

One CNN writer at the time notes that "after September 11, Walter Isaacson, [then] president of CNN, was trying to get all the reporters in the Middle East to skew their stories more favorably to Israel. The reporters were complaining, and I remember Christiane just going to the producer— she is pretty fearless; some of the news brass were afraid of her—with a story about a village where the Israelis came in and decimated it. She did one giant story about how bad Israel was, and I think she put a call in to [the Israeli] side but she didn't include their quote. And there was all this flak" before the story aired. "'Where was the other side? Why didn't she have an Israeli point of view?'" The writer laughs, and explains, "The producers just *aired* it!" Christiane had the power to push a piece through.

Yet the hubris that Christiane was used to wielding, allowing her to get away with such behavior, would come back to bite her a few years later. "She rarely criticized herself," says someone who was high up at CNN. "She'll rarely take the blame. Nothing's ever her fault."

CNN DISPATCHED CHRISTIANE to Iraq when Operation Iraqi Freedom began in March 2003. "Of course you're here. Of course I'm here. How could we *not* be here?" she and Ron Haviv said when they bumped into each other in Baghdad. The minute the statue of Saddam came down, they and all their colleagues "knew immediately that things were going downhill," Ron says. "I remember Christiane saying: 'No intervention on the looting. No martial law . . .'" She and Ron agreed that the U.S military's failure to implement these measures was a mistake "They won the war easily, but they immediately screwed up the rest of it."

Christiane was utterly unafraid of tendering criticism of the Iraq War, even in venerable company. At some point after it became clear that there had been no weapons of mass destruction in Iraq—those weapons being, of course, the very pretext for our invasion—and that Judith Miller's prewar reporting about the weapons for the *New York Times* had been off the mark, Christiane and Jamie spent a few weeks in the Hamptons. Darius attended a day camp there, as did a child of Emma and Bill Keller, who was then the editor of the *Times*. While sitting around watching their children play, Emma Keller mentioned complications at the paper that had arisen from the reporting of Judith Miller and others.

Christiane shot back, "Well, they [those *Times* reporters] got us *into* this war, *didn't* they?"

Roughly around this time, Christiane, Andrew, and their *60 Minutes* crew journeyed to places that *did* possess weapons of mass destruction: Russia and Kazakhstan. "The Soviet Union had the biggest biological weapons program, which they continued all the way into the Gorbachev era," Andrew explains, on the basis of Christiane's and his investigative work. "The U.S. had a program as well, but we dismantled ours, but the Soviet Union did not. We had access to these Soviet bioweapons, because Americans were paying for their cleanup, and the main testing and production site was in Kazakhstan.

"We ended up in this room—'the most dangerous room in Kazakhstan,' our guide told us—where the biological remnants of altered smallpox pathogens were stored." Protection against harm or accident was shockingly primitive and minimal. "They'd built a wall around the building, but that was it. The only security was the old Russian system where they melt a candle over a door sealed by two strings to prove that nobody's opened it." The twenty-first-century world's bioweapons were protected by nineteenth-century folk safety.

Dressed in extremely inadequate protective wear provided by their

Kazakh hosts—little more than hospital surgical greens—Christiane, Andrew, and their camera operator entered the chamber. The guide "brought out test tubes with pieces of cotton inside them," each marked according to the lethal pathogen the tube contained. "He was arguing that, basically, they needed help to secure them." But while the guide was thundering around making his case, "any of those vials could have been dropped and broken. We looked at each other: *What are we doing here?*"

But they knew just what they were doing: "Telling a story."

AFTER THAT QUIETLY harrowing brush with toxic substances, Christiane embarked, again with Andrew, on a deeply feminist double-subject investigative report in India about the country's "missing girls"—India's dearth of female babies—and one bold young woman's solo fight against the illegal exploitive dowry system, which drives all money from women's to men's families' pockets.

In their reporting, Christiane and Andrew found a link between two alarming practices. One was the practice of "silent abortions": the destruction of female fetuses—a custom that, although illegal, was so strong one village in Punjab had virtually "no girls" and had to bring them in from Nepal. Related to this, they found, was the culturally resilient practice—again, against the law, since 1961—of a family's having to spend its entire life savings to marry off a daughter. With such a dilemma—losing all their money to marry off a daughter—why wouldn't desperate families choose to have only boy babies? Together the stubborn customs helped to create a virtual holocaust of female infants. Christiane stood outside a penitentiary housing convicted mothers-in-law telling *60 Minutes* viewers, in her uncompromising voice, that seven thousand to twenty-five thousand young women were murdered every year by "greedy husbands" trying to extort more dowry money. "To avoid crushing debts that go with marriage, many Indian families are now aborting all their girl babies," she bluntly said.

The capstone of the piece was footage of a family brawl at the nuptials of a brave young woman named Nisha Sharma, who called off her wedding at the last minute because her groom-to-be's family was trying to extort more dowry. The powerful piece, "For the Love of Money," won an Emmy.

The trafficking of young women from money-starved ex-Soviet states was another under-the-radar crisis that Christiane brought attention to. Moldova had the highest incidence of girls being lured to Mediterranean countries with promises of glamorous jobs, only to be enslaved. Christiane and Andrew found a Moldovan girl who'd been absconded to Italy, where she'd escaped her pimp. "We interviewed her in a shelter, her face hidden," Andrew says. "Then we went to Moldova and found her family on a farm within a town of wooden houses and horse-drawn carriages. Christiane made an easy rapport with the parents." When she put them on the phone with their daughter—who could not yet leave her safe house in Italy—"the outpouring of emotions was *so raw.*"

Another feminist feature Christiane and Andrew produced was a profile of Iranian human rights and women's rights lawyer Shirin Ebadi, just before she won her 2003 Nobel Peace Prize. Taking advantage of the brief thaw in Iranian-U.S. rancor during Khatami's presidency (which would end in August 2005), Christiane and Andrew were able to shoot footage in a courtroom where Ebadi was representing a divorced woman who had lost custody to her husband, per the Islamic law. Ebadi's client's child had been tortured and killed by a stepbrother and stepmother. Revealing the Islamic Republic's laws was risky for Christiane, who already had a complicated relationship with her country of origin, but she *had* to take that risk.

Andrew always saw a bit of charming proprietariness, and vulnerability, in Christiane whenever they reported in her native country. She instinctively knew how to react during Muslim religious ceremonies, such as the passion plays held during Ashura, the celebration of Shiite martyrs. On one such occasion, "we went to a big barn far in the country—we had to drive a whole day to get there—and Christiane, all covered up, was sitting next to a woman who was hugging her emotionally. Christiane played right along." And "she was proud of the cuisine. We would go to restaurants and she would order for everybody. She would ask me, 'What do you think of this place?'" Andrew felt "she was asking: 'Is my enthusiasm for Iran objective? Is there enough appetite for foreign news here that *isn't* just about headlines but is also about the humanity?'" She loved her native country. She was *of* it.

Pierre Bairin, who produced her CNN stories there, perceived that the "Iranian government had a love-hate relationship with Christiane. She's a famous Iranian abroad, so they like that. But they know she's going to ask the tough questions. They're kind of proud of her, but at the same time they don't like her because she's not saying the party line."

ON MARCH 11, 2004, Christiane rushed to Madrid, where 191 people had been killed in a terrorist attack on a train by way of backpack bombs. Whether or not the culprits were radical Basque separatists or members of al-Qaeda was long investigated and tormented over—and never definitively established. The attack made Europe unsettlingly mindful of its even greater vulnerability to terrorist attacks than America was because of its proximity to the seats of Islamic terrorism and its countries' multicultural makeup.

Two months later, in May 2004, Christiane flew to Africa again for one of her most touching, powerful investigatives. Just as the UN was deeming the conflict in Darfur, in western Sudan, a genocide, she pushed her way into an extremely closed-off region to report on what was transpiring there. Ron Haviv, himself an expert at sneaking into hot spots, marvels: "Just getting *into* Darfur is not easy! The logistics of working in a place as remote as Darfur were daunting." Christiane herself said: "Darfur is barely accessible to outsiders. With great effort, the UN and Human Rights Watch [had] gained access." Ron continues: "It takes a long time to get visas—stacks of paperwork" are involved. "I'm sure she had to charm lots of government officials to get in. And then to broadcast her report *live*—there's a whole bunch of technical stuff that had to happen. And it's expensive. The fact that she could convince CNN to spend the money on a story that obviously very few people cared about, even though it's kind of become a cause célèbre to some degree—that was pretty impressive. It was an indication of her reputation, to be able to say: 'I care about this story, and this is worth people covering, and worth making sure that people understand.'"

On May 12, 2004, Christiane stood outside the Farchana refugee camp in Chad—already crowded with seven thousand refugees, while more were flooding in—and brought this catastrophe to the world in her familiar impassioned tones: "The hellish scene in northern Chad where people are fleeing the vicious but little-publicized war in western Sudan's Darfur region has been called the worst humanitarian crisis in the world today. . . . Children are dying of preventable causes, like diarrhea or lack of water and health care." She spoke of the systematic rapes of women and girls, the burned-down villages, "the ethnic cleansing conducted by the Sudanese army." Ethnic cleansing: She would *always* report on an atrocity that included that ultimate heinousness.

This was Christiane at her best—and her most effective. "I'm sure people donated after that report," says Ron Haviv. Parisa Khosravi says that the fact that "people *do* respond to these stories, on so many different levels"—the United States, the EU, the UN, NGOs, grassroots organizations—is what kept Christiane flying off from London to do them. "She really takes exception to people saying, 'Americans don't care about international news,'" Parisa says. "She is all about fighting that perception," which can lead to American networks saying, "'Okay, then we *won't* cover international news.'" She refused to let that perception become a self-fulfilling prophecy—and that's largely what the immensely challenging first five years of her working motherhood were all about.

Toward the end of 2004, Christiane and Andrew journeyed to Fallujah, a city in Iraq that had become, in Andrew's words, "a hotbed of radicalism," therefore leading to a number of casualties perpetrated, often unintentionally, on Iraqi civilians by the U.S. military. "What the army would call 'collateral damage,'" says Andrew. The U.S. military occupied Fallujah a month after the March 2003 invasion; bloodshed ensued; a year later Iraqi forces reseized it, leading to two reinvasions by U.S. forces. It was not an easy place for a member of the U.S. military to be safe—or to *not* veer into hair-trigger reactions or the temptation to go rogue.

Digging out a story in which the U.S. military was, accidentally, to blame for the deaths of children might have been emotionally awkward for Christiane, given that "she had almost a fan club in the American military" by now, says Andrew. Servicemen and -women "were constantly stopping her to take pictures with her, to get her autograph. She was a star to them, and I think it's because she empathizes with the grunts. She knows what war is like. She knows it's not what any soldier finds pleasure in but, rather, is forced to do. But even in the situation where there is a natural empathy between Christiane and soldiers, it wouldn't stop her" from being objective and aggressive to find the truth, however badly it reflected on U.S. soldiers.

Christiane and Andrew had heard a rumor: A family of Iraqi chicken wholesalers who supplied food to U.S. soldiers had been driving to market, had been mistaken by U.S. soldiers for insurgents, and had been fired upon by the soldiers. The U.S. military spokesman denied the rumor. "We decided to investigate," Andrew says. He and Christiane were driven around the armed-to-the-teeth town by a soldier with an AK-47. Once Christiane and Andrew got confirmation of the incident from a pro-U.S. Iraqi police chief, the U.S. military spokesman conceded that the chicken truck siege might have happened, but that it was an accident. This did nothing to lessen the fact that Fallujah *was* dangerous to U.S. soldiers and contractors. Andrew: "This was the same place where, a couple of weeks later, Iraqis strung up four U.S. contractors on the bridge and burned them."

Aside from those found dead in the impetuous gunfire the Americans had rained upon the chicken truck, two boys—one, the chicken purveyor's son—were missing. Christiane and Andrew visited the family of one of the missing boys and filmed the conversation. "They were extremely gracious," Andrew says. After further prevaricating, the U.S. military spokesman admitted that children might have been killed in the assault on the truck. Christiane eventually found the military hospital where one of the family's two missing boys—listed as an "enemy combatant"—was lying in a bed, his legs shattered. The boy was compassionately interviewed.

Between the family, the badly injured boy, the equivocating U.S. military spokesman, the local Iraqi chief of police, the streets full of tense armed soldiers, both Iraqi and American—between all these diverse players in the web of conflict—"our report showed how war touches *all sides*."

Tragedy would eventually touch the cameraman—Paul Douglas—who filmed that scene as well. A year and a half later, he and four others would be killed by an IED in the Sunni Triangle. Douglas would be the first black journalist to be killed covering the war in Iraq; his colleague, CBS reporter Kimberly Dozier—seriously injured in that same attack—was one of a number of female journalists to be badly wounded in the same conflict in which Christiane risked but escaped that same fate.

A NEWS FLASH erupted on July 7, 2005, that was jarringly close to home for Christiane. During Monday's morning rush hour, the London subway was attacked by four bombs—ignited, in quick succession, by members of a local al-Qaeda cell. Right after that, a London bus was blown up by a fifth bomb. Fifty-two people, and four of the bombers, were killed, and seven hundred were injured. Christiane did stand-up and reporting on this terrorist attack for CNN, and the cross fire of anger that pulsed within her and her family's home city—both the radical Islamic cells and mosques operating openly there *and* the outright discrimination against foreign-born Muslims by many native Britons—moved her, so much so that this woman born to a British mother and a Muslim father decided to produce a documentary on the phenomenon. She began work with CNN producers on the film, which would be titled *The War Within*. As Andrew Tkach, who had now moved over to CNN and produced the project with her, describes it, it was about "the war within the Islamic community in the UK—the fight between forces of moderation and extremism, and the Islamophobia that was becoming a force. We followed a former radical who was now working to bring people to their senses. Christiane feels strongly that those are the forces that need to be supported." While working on this project, she began talks with CNN to produce yet another series of documentaries exploring the bellicose absolutism in each of the major religions: how what salves and redeems—religious faith—is also a creator of divisiveness, hate, and warfare.

While she was working on the first documentary and conceiving the second, she flew to Kenya to undertake, for CNN, another of her powerful advocatory investigatives, "Where Did All the Parents Go?," about the devastating orphaning of young African children due to the continent's AIDS epidemic. "There is a big prejudice" in American news "about Africa and about telling news from Africa," Christiane has said. It was one of her prime missions to bust through that prejudice, that aversion to news about the continent's desperate need and pathos.

"According to the United Nations, there are 12 million AIDS orphans in sub-Saharan Africa alone, and in four short years that number will skyrocket to 18.4 million," she now announced, looking somberly into the camera. She continued, explaining that, whereas pregnant American and European women have medication that can prevent the passage of the AIDS virus to their babies, only 10 percent of pregnant women in Africa had access to such treatment. This, a doctor she interviewed rightly said, was simply "unacceptable death."

The stories she was trotting the globe to report had a clear theme. Consider: The twelve million and counting AIDS orphans in sub-Saharan Africa, themselves at risk of infection and death. The frightened boy with the shattered legs and the dead brother in the Fallujah hospital. The child soldiers in Sierra Leone with tattoos on their foreheads. The children wailing from excruciating treatment for sleeping sickness in Sudan. The trafficked Moldovan girl telling her story in her Italian safe house. The Iranian divorcee whose child had been tortured to death in her ex-husband's mandated custody. The raped twelve-year-old Afghani child bride hiding from almost assured honor murder. The massive number of female fetuses aborted, and the dowry-blackmailed women and their families, in India. The hundreds of thousands of Bangladeshi children made ill and killed by arsenic in their water. It was no coincidence that Christiane became a champion of children and women after she became a mother, Parisa Khosravi believes. "You can't help it," Parisa says. "*I'm* a mother. I certainly saw stories differently after I became a mother, because you can 'put' your own child there. Christiane has always been committed to stories about women and children, but having Darius probably reinforced her even more."

Parisa saw Christiane juggle the stories and mothering during these years, with increasing intensity and stress. "She is an incredibly hands-on mother," Parisa says. "She knows every hour where Darius is and what he is doing and his programs. She's talking to every caregiver and the teacher—and the fact that she's managed to have this kind of international field career, with its demands, and get a good few years of it with a child—she has talked about it to me. And I *saw* the change. She would not take every assignment." For those she took, "she would go and stay at the length" it required to fastidiously complete the reporting, but "it was not endless, and she and Jamie coordinated it so one of them was always there with Darius." Parisa is adamant: "Regardless of the story, Christiane did *not* change her absolute commitment to and rules about how she raised Darius."

Christiane herself has described the abiding push-pull during dangerous assignments this way: "I've said, 'Please, God, let me get through this and I'll never do this again.' And then I do it again."

IN JANUARY 2005, two months from Darius's fifth birthday, Christiane had a chance to do an exclusive interview for *60 Minutes* that would bring her closer to what was beginning to feel like a necessary goal: an easier working life, without the need for such regular bargainings with God. Viktor Yushchenko, a handsome reformist, had run for president of Ukraine. His wife, Katherine, was a reverse immigrant, an American who had moved back to that once proud country whose capital was Kiev: Her parents had been USSR-era Ukrainian immigrants who had fled to Chicago, where Katherine grew up. Months before the election, in early September, Yushchenko fell mysteriously and critically ill. He recovered enough of his health to continue the campaign, but one symptom was durable: His smooth facial skin was horribly pocked and disfigured; it was as if he'd instantly become another man, thirty years older.

Then came the December election. Yushchenko's rival, the government-favored Viktor Yanukovych, "won," but there was widespread belief that the election had been rigged, and it was proved that Yushchenko's near death and disfigurement had been the result of dioxin poisoning. An idealistic Orange Revolution—strikes, protests, civil disobedience—sprang up to support reform, honesty, and the defaced Yushchenko. In a second runoff election in January, Yushchenko was deemed the winner by a healthy margin.

Christiane's exclusive with Viktor and Katherine—set in a historic Kiev cathedral that had been destroyed by Stalin but had been rebuilt as a symbol of the new, free Ukraine—was a kind of chance to audition to become a Barbara, a Diane, a Katie: the handsomely paid, serious but accessible, heartstring-tugging star female interviewer gently probing a simultaneously specifically personal *and* also resonantly inspiring story out of the political hero of the hour and his wife. It was an audition for a next step she wanted—one without the nonstop travel, the constant separation from Darius, the *danger.* How would she do on it?

She put her characteristically slightly confrontational touch on the questions. "You challenged people about your face," she said. "You said that your face is everything that is wrong with Ukraine. What did you mean by that?" He answered, "People cry when they see my face, but my country has also been disfigured. Now we'll bring both back to health." Then he said, of the face in the mirror, with a wistfulness evident even in the sentence structure, "*This* Yushchenko I'm still not used to." The interview was strong. Yushchenko's last line—"To die is not very original, but to live and carry on, that's special"—was proof of greater Russia's stubborn genius for literary expression. But in it Christiane revealed what would prove to be a limitation to her advancement from field correspondent to anchor/analyst: her lack of warmth, when it was needed, with government leaders. She was deeply sympathetic with suffering children; her clipped mien instantly evaporated in their presence. But with powerful officials she was crisp—and crispness was not always the optimal mode with interviewees, even with heads of state. Barbara, Diane, and Katie knew this in their slightly more emotive, domestic-broadcast-seasoned bones; they could match their interviewees' level of sentiment expertly. The annoying double standard—that women doing hard and soft interviews had to tread water in that delicate netherworld of the interrogative-but-*also*-sympathetic: Barbara, Diane, and Katie knew it; they had lived it. Diane had threaded the needle with Whitney Houston, Barbara with Monica Lewinsky, Katie with the Columbine families. Christiane—who'd been an outsider—didn't get it quite as instinctively. Yushchenko's responses were more reflective and musing than was Christiane's tone of questioning. For an interviewer of an injured political hero, this is not a good thing.

Christiane's AIDS orphans piece aired in July 2006. Around this time, she and Parisa began having deeper talks than they'd had before. "I don't want to say 'philosophical,' but 'What does it all *mean*?'" was a question they mulled. For one thing, leaving Darius behind was so very hard, but the need to tell the stories was also deeply compelling, on a public service level. For another, there was the clash of realities. Christiane and Parisa talked about how "shocking to the system" it was to be "in one part of the world that is incredibly devastated and then catch a flight—and five hours later be in London at a café. You think: 'Look what I just left! Why do I have this opportunity and those people don't?' And you look at the conditions in the third world countries. And you stop yourself if you're ungrateful or angry, next to what these people are going through. And that is a lot where" their conversations started to go: "*What is that bigger purpose?* And, with that perspective, how do we do things differently? It's doing a gut check on yourself continually: 'Yes, we've given voice to the voiceless in so many places around the world, and that's wonderful, but: *Am I doing what I'm meant to be doing?*'"

It had been, after all, during the filming of the piece on the AIDS orphans that Christiane had most acutely confronted the conflict of work versus mothering. Darius was taking piano lessons, something that delighted her and made her proud, and he was preparing for a children's recital back home in London at the very time that she and Pierre Bairin had secured unprecedented CNN access to a charity hospice in Addis Ababa, Ethiopia, that had been founded by Mother Teresa's religious order. The nuns took in eight hundred people who were dying in the gutters from AIDS and tuberculosis, and they housed, fed, and cared for them. "It was a big coup for us," Pierre says. "They had never allowed a camera inside," not even when Bono and Angelina Jolie had visited. When Pierre returned from his "recking"—reconnaissance—trip and showed Christiane the footage of the life-giving services in the home, "she cried, it was so dramatic."

But there was a problem: They could only shoot on one day—a Sunday. The very next day was Darius's piano recital. "It was a big dilemma for her, but she solved it," Pierre says. "She paid for a chartered plane to take her from Addis Ababa to Nairobi so she could make the British Airways flight from Nairobi back to London that same night. It cost her a lot of money, but she refused to compromise on either the story or her motherhood."

Christiane's change came in careful measures, though. "There are situations now where I've heard her say, 'No! I'm *not* gonna go there! I'm going to stay with Darius and watch his school play!'" says Bella Pollen. "But at the same time, she has to square that with her desire to be in the thick of the action."

Saddam Hussein's first court appearance—in Baghdad, in October 2005, on charges of killing and torturing 140 of his own people in 1982—was one such irresistible occasion. "It was a huge story," says Tony Maddox, CNN's chief of international reporting. "All the media outlets in the world were clamoring" for the sight of the arrested dictator brought in in chains and prison jumpsuit. "Almost no reporters got in. But Christiane showed up that day, and I *knew* it would be *her*" who was allowed inside to see Saddam screaming in rage at his accusers. "All the other news organizations were furious. She was thrilled! She was filing every few minutes. She was so pumped up. It was like someone just out of college, that kind of excitement."

IN LATE 2007, Christiane and Jamie arranged to move back to New York, with the general expectation that an anchoring job awaited. Darius was now seven, and in those seven years of her motherhood alone, she had—aside from her justice and crisis stories—conducted interviews, many of them exclusive, with figures such as Tony Blair, Jacques Chirac, Pervez Musharraf, Jordan's King Abdullah, Mahmoud Abbas, Syria's president Bashar al-Assad, and Yasir Arafat. Her documentary about Islam in the UK, *The War Within*, had been aired to praise.

She had also reported *God's Warriors*, her other documentary, an ambitious six-hour series about how "the three monotheistic religions—Judaism, Christianity, and Islam—were related, but also how the forces within those traditions were using religion as a political weapon," Andrew Tkach explains. Christiane had traveled to six countries to film the three separate installments of the series, which aired one after another in late August 2007. While some appreciated how uniquely suited she was to the project—"Nobody could have done that multipart documentary better than her: her father is Muslim, her mother is Christian, her husband is Jewish. How many people have that kind of perspective?" says Parisa—others would not feel that way. She would attract criticism for the series, and it would dog her.

"God's Jewish Warriors" aired first. In it Christiane covered the radical Jewish group that intended to blow up Islam's sacred Dome of the Rock in Jerusalem in order to derail the peace talks between Israel and Egypt; she looked at evangelical Christian supporters of Israel; and, most controversially, she conducted interviews with people who believed that America's Israel lobby was supportive of Jewish settlements on the West Bank. In "God's Muslim Warriors," which aired the following night, she profiled the late Sayyid Qutb, the self-martyred Egyptian "father" of today's Islamic fundamentalism; she delved into the Iranian Revolution; and she discussed women's rights, and the lack thereof, in Islamic societies. "God's Christian Warriors" was the concluding segment. She interviewed American conservative evangelicals and conducted the last interview with Jerry Falwell shortly before his death.

The series rated tremendously high for CNN, attracting more than six million viewers over the three nights. But that fact—on the face of it a great boon to Christiane—was undermined by one particular problem that would linger: Christiane was criticized by Fox News and some pro-

Israel groups for, as the Committee for Accuracy in Middle East Reporting in America put it, "equating the extremely rare cases of religiously inspired violence on the part of Christians and Jews with radical Islam's global, often state-supported, campaigns of mass killing" and for "presenting highly controversial critics of Israel and the so-called Israel lobby and doing so without challenge." Even MSNBC's Dan Abrams, that network's general manager, felt enough entitled umbrage to call the series "the worst kind of moral relativism" and "shameful advocacy." Abrams publicly carried on at length about Christiane's report, saying, "I felt the journalism behind it was shoddy" and "I felt very strongly that in its totality it was unfair." He did, however, he concede that "it was a very successful, well-rated documentary for CNN," which of course was Abrams's network's competitor.

Christiane had been confrontational with Walter Isaacson about day-to-day Mideast coverage, but that had been an internal CNN matter. These specials, timed as they were as a kind of calling card for Christiane's return to New York—where CNN was now headquartered, in a gleaming new building in Columbus Circle, a clear power statement—had the potential to make her seem too left wing and too insensitive to American political and religious sympathies. There are few more abiding taints for an American journalist or public servant to bear than that of having a bias against Israel, yet, after all the fine and arduous work that Christiane had done for a decade and a half, this charge was now the chief one surrounding her. With *God's Warriors*, she had taken an impolitic risk—but then, taking impolitic risks was what Christiane often did.

She had won numerous awards.* Queen Elizabeth named her a Com-

---

*To date, Amanpour has won eleven Emmys, two George Foster Peabody Awards, two George Polk Awards, the Edward R. Murrow Award, the Walter Cronkite Award, the Courage in Journalism Award, the Goldsmith Award, the Fourth Estate Award, and she played a major role in two DuPont Awards given to CNN. She has been the recipient of honorary doctorates at the University of Michigan, Northwestern University, Amherst College, University of Southern California, Emory University, and Georgia State University, and an honorary graduation class membership at Harvard. She has received honorary citizenship from the city of Sarajevo and has been named the Persian Woman of the Year, among numerous other awards and fellowships,

mander of the Most Excellent Order of the British Empire. *Time* maga-zine named her the most influential foreign correspondent since Murrow himself.

That Christiane Amanpour should be able to trade constant war zone hopping for a high-status anchor/analyst chair seemed self-evident to many. Others had done it before—Murrow, Cronkite, Peter Jennings—following years of war zone reporting on a par with hers. If ever a reporter had earned her right to a post at an anchor/analyst desk, it was Christiane Amanpour, many thought. Such advantage was *rightly* hers. No other in-ternational correspondent of her generation had done this as long and as well and as passionately as she had.

She arrived in New York with an appropriately entitled feeling.

---

including one named for fellow journalist Daniel Pearl, murdered by terrorists in Pakistan, and another named for fellow journalist Anthony Shadid, who died in the course of duty under hardship in Syria.

CHAPTER NINE

First Female Anchor

Katie and Diane: 2006 to 2009

IT WAS DIANE, not Katie, who was supposed to have been the first solo female six-thirty anchor. And she almost was.

In the earliest days of February 2006—while Les Moonves was tendering his secret preemptive CBS offer to Katie—Diane made a secret move of her own.

The *World News Tonight* anchorship had been in play, amid tragedy, for ten months, ever since April 2005, when Peter Jennings announced he would resign to undergo aggressive chemotherapy for lung cancer. Charlie Gibson had pitched in as interim anchor, as had Elizabeth Vargas. After Peter's death on August 7, Elizabeth Vargas and Bob Woodruff had rotated duties, and in December Woodruff was named Jennings's replacement. But a month later, on January 29, 2006, Woodruff was seriously injured by an IED in Iraq.

Says someone who knows: "Diane went to Westin as soon as Bob Woodruff was injured and said, 'It has to be me.'" But the airtight secrecy of Diane's request for the job was compromised by a leak to a minor trade bulletin, "and so Diane said, 'It can't be me. It's ruined. It has to be Charlie.' She didn't want it to look like she was big-footing Charlie. She didn't want to look like she'd killed Charlie's dream." This would seem to be classic Diane: the chess game *and* the decorum. The "no fingerprints" code had been violated. Someone else—a person less concerned with image than Diane, someone who wouldn't care about a possible media storm of "She pushed for the job and then got it" stories—would not have pulled back from so delicious and well earned a possibility as the anchorship. But Diane wasn't like that; *how* a thing was done was just as important as *that* it was done. The Southern woman in her would not abide looking as if she had elbowed Charlie out, and the chess player in her would not abide so clumsy and risky a move. So she undid the move. (Remarkably, the small, off-line trade bulletin leak got no attention. Such accidental secrecy "never would have happened today," says the source, when media industry gossip runs in a twenty-four-hour-a-day Twitterverse.)

Besides, "Diane *liked* Charlie. She's not a bad person—she's just incredibly ambitious," this witness continues. Still, despite her own hand in the goings-on, "she was very angry" that it hadn't worked out. Furthermore, "she was completely bat-shit that Katie was the first female anchor. It will *always* eat away at Diane that Katie was the first."

Apparently not knowing the details of Diane's approach and retreat, the media was puzzled by the situation. In his *New York* magazine article, "Charlie the Conqueror," Joe Hagan wrote: "When Diane Sawyer did not get tapped to anchor ABC's *World News Tonight*, it could have been reasonably assumed that she must not have wanted the job. Otherwise, what could explain the decision? She's the network's most bankable news star, and she has made no secret of her desire to handle weightier fare than what she can get away with on *Good Morning America*." When Hagan asked Diane herself if she'd wanted the anchor job, for which he felt she'd earned "first dibs," she waxed elusive. "'Yes and no,' she told me, as we sat in her office. 'No and yes.' . . . Faced with [the] choice . . . she slipped into Hamlet mode, unsure of how to balance her loyalties and self-interest. Which . . . is what gave her *GMA* co-host Charlie Gibson the chance to land the job himself. . . . Gibson had none of Sawyer's ambivalence." Hagan went on to say he'd probed Westin and Sawyer "over many conversations," and in these talks, "Westin says that he gave Sawyer the chance to take the job, but she wouldn't. This is his official position and it squares with Sawyer's official position . . . [e]xcept of course that she did want it." Hagan provocatively observed that, when he interviewed her, "instead of being content with this state of affairs, Sawyer seemed very much at loose ends."

Three and a half years later, Diane would get her due. Diane was ever strategic, waiting for the right time to strike—the opposite of Katie, who dove into, or pushed herself into, opportunities. Diane revealed too little, and indirectly; Katie revealed too much.

Thus, for now, Charlie assumed the anchorship. (The show's name was changed to *ABC World News*, the "Tonight" shorn.) Diane was mysterious about her feelings and her strategy. "The Golden Sphinx . . . has been more inscrutable than ever," reported Rebecca Dana in the *New York Observer*, adding that a source told her, "Diane is keeping her cards extremely close to her chest" and "None of us has any idea what she plans to do." That was certainly the view at the time. But a staffer who has spoken to Charlie Gibson over the years describes the 2006 to 2009 events more dramatically—and unflatteringly to Diane: "In *Gladiator*, one of the senators advising the mad emperor says that certain sea snakes lie very still at the bottom of the water. They let their predators get very close—and *then* they strike. When Charlie got the anchor job, Diane went quiet like a sea snake."

When Charlie ascended to *World News* anchor, Robin Roberts became Diane's *GMA* coanchor, an appointment that would not have been possible without Diane's approval. "What other woman would have invited another woman to that desk? I can't think of another. That's pretty generous, in that world," says her friend, producer Mark Robertson. The pairing was immediately successful. The two tack-sharp, elegant Southern women—both raised by powerful, proper, controlling mothers to whom they were complexly obeisant (Lucimarian Roberts criticized Robin's shade of lipstick just as Jean Sawyer criticized Diane's hair)—had a rapport that was genuine, and dated back several years: When Robin's father, a former Tuskegee Airman, died in October 2004, Diane took a day off *GMA* to arrive at Robin's mother's Biloxi, Mississippi, doorstep at nine a.m. on the day before the funeral, "in big sunglasses, hair pulled back," so no one would notice her, Robin has recalled, bearing pots of gumbo from the Robertses' favorite restaurant "so when we came back from making arrangements we'd have food at home."

The white woman/black woman symmetry had a comfortable genius to it—for Diane, it might have even been a forty-five-years-later Seneca High come full circle. During a joint interview with *Ladies' Home Journal* editor Diane Salvatore, when asked if they talk about how race affected their friendship, Diane instantly straight-manned: "You mean . . . I'm *white?*" Then, through Robin's and Salvatore's uproarious laughter, she protested: "But . . . did you see me dance?" Diane and Robin's friendship would deepen over the years. When Robin stayed up all night after the shock of her breast cancer diagnosis in 2007, "Diane called and said, 'Go to bed—*I'm* on watch now,'" Roberts says. "She was relentless in finding me medical information."

In fact, Diane's generosity has been quietly known within her circle of colleagues for years. She is such a good friend that "if you get sick, *forget* about it—she's calling a van to the rescue," says someone who is otherwise critical. Ira Rosen concurs: "She is simply the best foul-weather friend in the business. If, God forbid, something bad is happening in your life, she will go through every doctor she knows. When Anthony Radziwill was dying of cancer, she spent days on the phone [calling doctors and] trying to save his life." She did the same for a colleague who had pancreatic cancer. Private school tuitions for kids of single moms she barely knows, beach camps for children who never saw an ocean, surgeries for family members of a studio tech and an elevator operator, all done anonymously, with the recipients not knowing the source: "You could fill a stadium with the people she's helped," says Mark Robertson. On long international flights, she'd often force her first-class seats on her young producers while taking their coach seats. Eventually, when she took over the anchorship of *ABC World News*, she bought the whole staff gym memberships, each one including a trainer.

Still, "the problem with Diane," says a person who worked with her around this time, "is she causes so much pain" through her relentless pushing of senior staffers. "There are people at work who believe the people who got sick got sick because of her. Whatever it is that drives her breaks as many people as it helps." "She gets every executive producer she's worked with fired when she gets tired of them, and she never wants it known she's had anything to do with it," claims a man who suffered this fate, probably exaggerating for effect or from wounded feelings. "Diane presides over a kind of imperial court like in *I, Claudius*," contends one particularly arch ex-staffer, adding that Charlie Gibson cautioned this person, in 2003, about the flip side of her seductive charm: "When the mighty light of Diane shines on you—so brightly, so briefly—I am giving you the strongest possible warning: *Don't fall for it.*"

IN FEBRUARY 2006, while Diane was making her secret and then self-withdrawn bid to be anchor at ABC, Les Moonves was making Katie a secret preemptive offer of about $15 million a year to be anchor at CBS. This was twice the salary that Dan Rather had made—and, says a foreign bureau worker, Rather's salary had itself just recently, before Memogate, "been doubled—and at a time when the TV news business model had already been incredibly stressed, not to mention with the recession coming." Fifteen million dollars a year for an anchor—and an anchor who was considered more a "celebrity," not a longtime hard news dues payer? And coming from outside to a network that, as Marcy McGinnis puts it, was so familylike, "people at other companies marvel to me in conversation that people stayed at our news division for so long." All this would be a lot for the CBS News staff to stomach. Besides, "some *Evening News* staffers were making ten dollars an hour and working sixteen-hour days, doing major research," says one who was there at the time. Moonves apparently didn't think of the staff morale, not that it might have mattered to him.

As the offer from Les to Katie was going forward, Jeff Zucker, who was now president of NBC's entertainment, news, and cable group and was thus back in control over the news division that subsumed *Today*, tried to hold on to his friend. "Obviously, I was leading those conversations to try to get Katie to stay. I offered her a lot of money and a lot of opportunity for her to stay at NBC," Jeff says, declining to explain "opportunity." *Newsweek* reported that he offered her $20 million and Fridays and summers off. "Well, that didn't happen," he rebuts, then seems to take it back: "But yeah, I think that's a pretty accurate reflection of what we had on the table for her—and there was other stuff. I was sad for NBC. And I had to protect NBC."

But others in the know have a different recollection of how badly NBC wanted to keep—or reclaim—her. The man who said Katie had not "waited her turn" and that Jay had kept her in line says, "At no time did NBC come in to try to top Moonves's offer. Once she got that offer, NBC made no attempt." And a confidant of Katie's and veteran producer puts it another way, saying, in 2009, when rumors started to swirl that Katie might leave CBS to return to NBC, "*No one* at NBC wants Katie to come back." Whatever the case, Meredith Vieira was quickly tapped. "We didn't go down a lot of roads," says an NBC insider. "It would be Meredith or Ann [Curry]."

Whether or not NBC animus existed against Katie at the time or later, Jeff, who knew Katie's talents better than anyone, argued with her—benignly, he says ("There was never a contentious conversation")—about whether or not her move would be successful. "She went in" to the CBS anchoring "with a lot of hope. She wanted to fit the evening newscast more to her personality, which was my point all along—*I didn't think it fit her personality*," Jeff says. "You can't fundamentally reshape the programs. I thought it wasn't the best fit for her talent. I told her that. Katie trusts me because I tell her the truth," even though "she's not gonna admit that I'm right. Even if she doesn't like it, Katie knows I'm telling her the truth for her own good." Katie herself characterized Jeff's advice, and her response, this way: He "told me it was the worst idea he'd ever heard—he thought it was the wrong format, that I should have my own show, that it didn't use my quote-unquote talents. I listened—and I had my doubts—but I've always trusted my own gut, and ultimately I did what was right for me. That's the way I've lived my whole life."

All of these conversations were taking place while Jeff and Katie and Lisa Paulsen put together their plan for their first Stand Up to Cancer multichannel telethon, which turned out to be tremendously successful and would be repeated year after year. NBC, CBS, ABC, and CNN observed the "blockade"—the first proactive rather than reactive (the latter meaning a response to a crisis such as 9/11 or Hurricane Katrina) one in television—whereby these networks turned over all their prime-time programming for one night to star-studded fund-raising. Only Fox refused. (But Fox participated in Stand Up to Cancer's 2010 and 2012 blockade telethons, along with, respectively, eighteen and twenty-two cable stations.) "Let's raise money for The Colons!" was Katie, Lisa, and Jeff's battle cry, explains Lisa, "The Colons," irreverent shorthand for colon cancer patients. "Let's raise money for *all* the body parts!"

On April 6, during the last minutes of *Today*, Katie announced that, in what would turn out to be less than two months, she'd be leaving the show. Matt then poked through her script and stage-asked, "Did it say anywhere [in the script] *where* you're going? If you were a guest on the show, I wouldn't let you get away with that." Katie smilingly rejoined: "I know— it's the worst-kept secret in America." And it was: The business press had been dropping hints. "I'm going to be working on the *CBS Evening News* and *60 Minutes*," she replied to Matt. As coyly as she may have put it, the news broke *huge*, eclipsing even the day's political stories. *Newsweek* both limned the reason and unintentionally personified the dated absurdity of the newsiness with its question, "Will viewers accept their evening news from someone wearing mascara?" However, they importantly qualified that "Couric is cut from entirely different cloth than any of her predecessors, including the handful of women co-anchors. She's the most up close and personal news broadcaster ever on television." The article continued, "We've seen her inside and out—literally," referring to her colonoscopy. "We know her kids and her deceased husband. When she's dating a new man, she makes the gossip magazines."

Regarding the latter, Katie and Tom Werner had broken up. In a few months, just as she was starting as CBS anchor, Katie would begin a years-long, eventually live-in romance with entrepreneur Brooks Perlin, a Connecticut-raised Williams College graduate sixteen years younger than she. The good-looking, athletic Perlin, not infrequently photographed in sports attire, could fairly be called a "hunk." As worthy as his trendy endeavors were—marketing "green" construction materials was one—he did not emanate either the dignified panache of amateur historian and classical pianist Jay Monahan or the estimable success and power of Tom

Werner. Many accomplished women choose younger men, but sixteen years qualifies as *much* younger, and some of the pair's vacations—for example, staying at the Sun Valley home of Las Vegas casino emperor Steve Wynn—fed into a meme that was not synonymous with Katie the Serious Newswoman. To her credit and her detriment, she did not seem to care. In fact, when, two and a half years later, she gave the commencement address at Princeton (whose sports teams were the Tigers), she opened with: "I've been called a cougar a lot lately, but now I'm proud to be a tiger." Being in-your-face in owning the tackiest personal aspersions lobbed against her by the lowest tabloids in the first sentence of her address to the graduates and faculty of a premier Ivy League university: This was Katie, and you kind of had to love her for it. But you also had to *fear* for her, for that kind of wholesale thumbing of proper image could work for men, but a woman who rocked the "appropriateness" boat was leaving herself wide open.

The *Newsweek* piece, which was written by two men, Marc Peyser and Johnnie L. Roberts, trotted out sexist clichés—"Couric cries regularly" (which contradicted what the *Today* man has said of her off-air toughness)—and asked if "the girl next door," which Katie had stopped pretending to be for the last half of her *Today* tenure, to the partial disapproval of the public, could "succeed as a network news anchor."

"Welcome to a very special edition of *Today*," Matt intoned, at seven a.m. one brink-of-summer morning. "Now, after more than fifteen thousand interviews, millions of laughs, and countless cups of coffee, Katie is saying good-bye to us on Wednesday, May 31, 2006." The theme music boomed. Katie—in a low-V-necked white jacket, her voice hoarse—kidded Matt about how controlling she was. "*You? Controlling?*": He was mock-aghast. Both the affection and the edginess in their long TV marriage resonated. The show would be, Matt promised, "like an episode of *This Is Your Life*."

And in terms of her professional life, it was. A reel was unspooled of snippets of Katie's early intros from her positions at CNN D.C., CNN Atlanta, WTVJ Miami, and NBC D.C. and pre-*Today* New York. Her generic concerned-and-serious enunciation, expression, and cock of head in every one of those intros was stunning for what was lacking: the completely original woman America had come to know over fifteen years. Don Browne had been right: The brevity of her tenures in front of each of those other cameras—her "failure" in each of those markets—had kept that standard-issue anchor persona from taking root. She was able to come to *Today* as a total original.

After a video clip of her driver calling from the NBC car at her apartment house curb, pleading with the half-asleep Katie to get her out of bed, Matt and Al joked about how late she arrived every morning, always inconceivably ready to go at five of seven. A very effective reel of sharply edited takes of her tough journalistic combat—*punch! punch! punch!*—as she pinned to the wall Yasir Arafat, Kofi Annan, Bob Dole, David Duke, George H. W. Bush, H. Ross Perot, Pat Buchanan, and Laura Bush pulled viewers up to their full height about who she really was as a power interviewer. Next came those moments—Katie as Tinkerbell, flying through Rockefeller Plaza on Halloween; Katie dancing with Al Gore, with Patrick Swayze, with John Travolta; Katie singing with Tony Bennett, with queen of the backup singers Darlene Love, and (along with Matt and Al) with Stevie Wonder—that had already risen like cream to the top of viewers' memories.

Barbara Walters watched the May 31 show—and the preceding shows, from April 6 on—with the rue of a pathbreaker who would never, understandably, quite stop licking her wounds. She mused in her 2008 memoir:

I can't help but contrast my experience with what happened to Katie Couric when she left NBC. There was little uproar over the salary CBS was giving her, a reported $15 million a year. NBC gave her the most glorious send-off—a three-hour retrospective preceded by two weeks of tributes, messages from celebrities and high-profile politicians, special music written for her, and past clips of her work from her years on *Today.* There was a gala going-away party and an equally warm welcome awaiting her at CBS. . . .

Perhaps my experience was the price of being first, and in a very different time. Back in 1976 you could freely attack a woman for wanting to do a so-called man's job, especially in the holier-than-thou men-only news departments. Many people still believed that women were supposed to know their place—and stay in it. There were few women in front of the camera and fewer still in any kind of executive position. Today . . . that same attitude would not only be politically incorrect, but the backlash would be enormous.

Walters's misty-eyed hurt failed to take into account that many at NBC were thrilled and relieved to see Katie go, and that her "welcome" at CBS would turn out to be more complicated than "warm."

ONE PERSON WHOSE BLESSING KATIE definitely wanted was Walter Cronkite. "Katie wooed and won Walter," says his forever producer, Sandy Socolow. "He was a big fan from afar, and when it was announced she was becoming *CBS Evening News* anchor, she took him out for dinner a couple of times." Cronkite, in his dotage, was highly susceptible to charm. "He fell in love with Katie," Socolow says. He'd been impressed that "she covered the Pentagon and other hard news." Now, during the dinners, "he fell in love with her even more than before. She paid attention to him. And he's an egomaniac."

Katie embarked on a summer "listening tour" across America. Patterned after Hillary Clinton's listening tour when she decided to run for the Senate from New York, the series involved Katie flying to a variety of cities and taking questions, in auditoriums, from a diverse pool of citizens (selected, by CBS affiliate staffers, from people who'd filled out applications) about what issues mattered to them. Several insiders believe that that pretentious gimmick of a "rollout," which was the brainstorm of Moonves and CBS spokesman Gil Schwartz, was a mistake. One industry authority believes Katie would have been better served spending the summer honing her broadcasting skills. Bob Schieffer was an expertly conversational broadcaster, able to pack nuance into a folksy but serious sentence, while Katie read what her writers wrote for her. "Katie liked puns, and real people don't talk in puns—it [ended up being] cutesy writing," another CBS producer says. At the very least, as Andrew Tyndall puts it, Katie's listening tour and CBS's massive fanfare created inflated expectations.

It also let Katie, prone to be stoked by attention, increase her brio about, and up the ante on, the Moonves-blessed incipient change of format. "This is not your grandfather's newscast," she told *Good Housekeeping* as she began to prepare for the show, for which she would also serve as managing editor. "I think people are ready for an anchor who's multidimensional, who's not so detached. I hope I do this job with humanity and heart. And intelligence." By the time Kurt Andersen interviewed her, in a welcoming *New York* magazine piece—"Humor Is the New Gravitas"—just before her *Evening News*'s first broadcast, she was saying things that, while certainly A-for-effort in terms of thinking outside the box, were, in hindsight, flashing danger signs of what six-thirty news viewers *didn't* want to watch. One key innovation in the broadcast was to be a ninety-second commentary by both ordinary citizens and well-known opinion purveyors, called "Free Speech." Aside from the difficulty of reining in a verbal essay (especially by a non-media-trained speaker) to the tight time limit within the twenty-two-minute-long broadcast, there was Katie's trendy wish list for guest speakers: director Nora Ephron, popular novelist Carl Hiaasen, and urban liberals' favorite TV pundit-host, Jon Stewart. "I love Jon," Katie said. "He and I have talked about" his appearing on her broadcast "down the line."

Says a woman who'd worked with Dan Rather, "Moonves misjudged the market. He thought if he brought the *Today* show to nighttime, they'd increase the audience." Says a CBS News producer: "They wanted to *reinvent* the evening news." "They" were Les Moonves, Sean McManus, Couric, and the producers. The venerable six-thirty news broadcast had been a classy fixture of the American conversation almost since the beginning of television, but it was also a relic of another era: before twenty-four-hour cable and the Internet, which gave the news in real time; before the complicated, constantly in-flux schedules of modern life. Especially at CBS, the audience for the six-thirty news was old and aging; Moonves's and Couric's planned "reinvention"—whether a creative move or a desperate one, whether admirably conceived or ill conceived—was a bold risk, a shoving of all poker chips to the middle of the table.

Whatever would happen—and a lot *would*—one had to admire Katie's insistence on retaining her own personality and her defiant eschewal of affectation of any kind. Just as she was taking the reins, she told *Glamour*, "I think most people equate humor with intelligence and comfort in one's own skin. I'm proud I have these qualities. It's funny, through all this discussion of gravitas, I realized I don't really *want* to have gravitas. I want authenticity. I want good journalism—but gravitas is sort of a pretentious word." Her goal, she went on to say, was "to make news compelling. So much of it feels like *newzak*, news that's just there but doesn't sink in or register." That latter point was dangerous. It was one thing to stick to her guns as an authentic, pomposity-loathing broadcaster—that was her persona; that was Katie. It was another to think that the essential aspects of the packaging and broadcasting of the six-thirty news had to be changed—that was the content and form of the show, and it involved the expectations of viewers who had been watching the show for a long time.

Katie's executive producer, hired by McManus, was Rome Hartman; Hartman's second in command was Paul Friedman, brought over from ABC, where he had worked with Diane and, most significantly, with Peter Jennings, next to whom Friedman seemed to believe all other anchors, especially female ones, failed. The highly experienced Friedman was key—and temperamentally stronger than Hartman. "Sean hired him over because Sean didn't know what he was doing; he only knew sports," says one CBS senior staffer, a woman. That staffer and the Rather aide—both women—and a longtime CBS man outline how unfortunate the choice of Hartman and Friedman ultimately was in the show's launch, which was rockier than it seemed to the outside world.

Hartman, who had been at the network for years, came in from *60 Minutes*. "Rome is about as straight-arrow as you get," says the CBS man. "Traditional news guy, no nonsense. Not a good sense of humor. Not mean or anything, but kind of a military-like presence." Yet there was some-thing about Rome that Katie may have sensed she could control, believes the female Rather aide, who also, provocatively, says, from observation, "I don't think Katie liked men. She surrounded herself with weak men." Hartman "was weak," declares veteran Richard Wald, who, like so many, watched with interest. Says an NBC producer, "Rome was a hand-holder. He had no power." The CBS senior staffer: "Rome couldn't control Katie, and [the innovations] were her ideas. Except 'Free Speech,' which was a horrible, ill-conceived idea, a Journalism 101 exercise. Paul Friedman was behind 'Free Speech,' and while he was very smart and very persuasive and could be charming, he was an angry man."

The CBS man remembers the Katie-and-Rome process: "The show would be structured one way at nine a.m., before Katie arrived. At one, when she arrived, the whole show would change. She'd say, 'Oh, no, we're not doing that. We're doing *this*.' Rome didn't think the way she did. So he would then spin it back the other way. You'd end up with some kind of in-between, neither fish nor fowl. That's why the show was a mess. Most of us were going, 'What *is* it? What do you really want?' I can't tell you how hard the executive producers tried to figure out how to make this work around her. They all tried to figure out, 'What is Katie's greatest strength? How can we highlight that, and still make it a hard news broadcast?' Which is what our audience wanted. They tried in many different ways." In the end, it was thought that Rome couldn't contain Katie.

If there was confusion with the Katie-Hartman relationship, there was outright conflict in the Katie-Friedman relationship, and it augured minor disaster. The senior staffer is blunt: "Paul hated Katie, and she hated him. She *hated* him. She told me that, and she let Sean know." In the end, because of Hartman's weak helming and Katie's and Friedman's strong negative feelings for each other, "nobody ended up respecting Sean. He came across as very weak."

But far beyond hurting McManus, the retooled show would be *Katie's* Waterloo. Animus she had skirted for decades at NBC would now be pel-leted at her at CBS.

.   .   .

YET AT THE very beginning, all seemed shiny. On Tuesday, September 5, 2006—when, at six thirty p.m., none other than Walter Cronkite's* stentorian voice announced "the *CBS Evening News*, with Katie Couric," and the first female solo anchor, in white jacket over dark shell, said, "Hi, everyone," in front of a sleek new set—there was a sense of utter jubilation from the CBS News brass. "A high-ranking executive was standing right next to me and he was, '*This is it!*'" says the CBS man. "The management completely drank the Kool-Aid. They were all *convinced*."

In that first broadcast, between delivering the news, Katie interviewed *New York Times* columnist Thomas Friedman about the war on terror, and she showed photographs of Tom Cruise and Katie Holmes's four-and-a-half-month-old daughter, Suri, a day in advance of their exclusive cover story in *Vanity Fair.* Says the senior staffer: "The tone was set that first day, with the Suri baby pictures. Too fluffy. Too *Today* show." As she signed off, a long shot showed her standing, leaning casually against her desk. You could see her fashionably fairly short (but not very short) skirt and her appropriately high (but not too high) heels.

The CBS executives' elation continued that week, "because they saw the numbers," says the CBS man. "They had promoted the hell out of it. They had spent a fortune advertising it. Her numbers the first week were *unbelievably huge*." Thirteen and a half million viewers (which was more than half of the then twenty-five million six-thirty network news viewers) watched that first show, and the numbers pretty much held for the week.

Katie's retooling, as Joe Hagan would later describe it in *New York* magazine, gave the news "a chatty, friendly vibe and a bright casual at-

---

*Katie personally asked Cronkite "to do the opening 'announce' on the broadcast, which he did for no money," says Sandy Socolow. "About six months after Cronkite died, they took Walter's voice off and they had Morgan Freeman doing it. I realized: They must [have been] paying Morgan Freeman—he's not doing it for free." The difference between the iconic news anchor's volunteered work and the actor's presumedly paid work was quietly revelatory to Socolow, indicating how the TV news business had changed from public service to commercial enterprise.

mosphere never seen before at 6:30 p.m. There were fewer headlines, more news features and off-the-cuff reactions from Katie." The CBS man: "Katie thought if you brought in a show that was more human or friendly, people would relate. Deep down, she's not a hard newsperson. *She's not.* That was reflected in the broadcast she went on to do." (This is an assessment three female CBS News producers independently affirm. She could do hard news—announce it, report it, conduct hard news interviews—but hard news was not her passion; it was not, at base, who she was.)*

Jeff Fager, current first chairman of CBS News, perhaps puts it best: "Newspeople become celebrities, but celebrities don't become newspeople. It's an important distinction. Someone who's a celebrity shouldn't be brought in to anchor a newscast." He was speaking in the hypothetical, but his meaning, especially considering its timing (Fager made this comment, in an interview for this book, shortly after he assumed his current position and mere days before it was announced that Katie was leaving as anchor), seemed clear: Despite her previous experience with hard news, Katie had a personal celebrity quotient that was unusually high, according to the old template for a traditional news anchor, and this was distracting.

Things changed quickly. Over weeks, and then months, "the executives watched the air come out of the tire and a lot of the press turned and Katie was just getting hammered and couldn't buy a break—it was pretty brutal," says the CBS man.

As the ratings sank and the grumbles—from traditional serious-news professionals, affiliates, and critics—increased, quick, urgent, nervous repairs were made. The friendly "Hi, everyone" was replaced by a dignified "Hello, everyone." The closing shot that showed Katie's legs was scrapped in favor of a seated shot. "Free Speech" clearly didn't work—Socolow and Cronkite had watched the segments and thought, says Socolow, "'Holy

---

*As *CBS Evening News*'s managing editor as well as anchor, Katie was entitled to tell the bureau chiefs, via a representative in a daily conference call, what news stories she wanted covered on any given night. But one of the participants on those calls, a woman, says that, conveyed in the daily calls from the New York producers, there had always been "lots of 'Walter wants'"—a special news story Cronkite wanted covered—as well as "'Dan wants.' But there were very few 'Katie wants.'"

cow! A guy in Colorado saying the Columbine massacre was the result of godlessness . . . ?' 'Free Speech' made no sense at all." It was dropped with a thud. Katie's voice was called "grating." The celebrity gets went unappreciated: Two and a half weeks in, Michael J. Fox came on, right after Rush Limbaugh had mocked his Parkinson's symptoms and accused him of being a "faker" in a public service commercial. "Fox was a big name and Katie got him because of who she was," says the senior staffer. "Yes, it was a news story," because of the Limbaugh attacks. "But I'm not sure our news audience cared about Michael J. Fox."

Cronkite was upset at Katie's version of the broadcast for abandoning its audience—and its principles. "It was a disaster," Socolow bluntly says, sharing Cronkite's opinion. But, in hindsight, Socolow is somewhat sympathetic. "Katie went through a rough debut. They had a lot of false starts." They tried to make the *Evening News* "like the local news"—a stinging put-down. "The 'wisdom' was to make it viewer-friendly, to go for younger viewers," which made no sense to Socolow and Cronkite. The average age of *CBS Evening News* viewers "is sixty-one or sixty-two. Yet they're always trying to 'youthify.' But look at the ads—they're all for medicines, like Viagra, for older guys who can't get it up! It's stunning. The advertisers have a better view of the audience than the people putting on the show." (Socolow gives this personal aside to illustrate what Katie was up against: "I have three children, in their forties"—the demographic Katie and her producers sought. "They have not read a newspaper in who knows how many years. They do not watch the evening news. They get all their news off the Internet.")

Seven months in, in April 2007, the failure of the experiment was pretty clear: The numbers had plummeted by almost two-thirds from the first week's figures, to 5.5 million viewers, the lowest for the program in twenty years. (Though that low viewer figure would be reprised in early September, the number would soon slightly improve, to six million to seven million viewers a night.) "It was unfair" that Katie was publicly blamed, says the CBS man. "But I gotta say: When you fashion yourself as a celebrity—which she does; she *lives* by that—then you are completely at the mercy of a celebrity beating. I don't think" her new colleagues at CBS News "were particularly sympathetic to her when" it fell apart. "It was, 'This is *your* game. You brought your game to our place. So don't look at *us* to save your butt.'"

Bob Schieffer makes a bit of the same point, indirectly but leadingly. "The whole thing with Katie is so delicate, and so anything I would say would be misconstrued," he says, possibly referring to the fact that he had been named in an article as a possible leaker of anti-Katie information. Still, he continues: "I was really part of the Welcome Wagon for her. And because, after me, the ratings went into the toilet, this would be misunderstood." Couching his words in seeming diplomacy, Schieffer appears to be saying: I, longtime CBS News man, brought the numbers *up* in my year and a half as interim anchor. I was gracious when Katie replaced me— *and then she failed.*

Others in the news department shared the sentiment. "The resentment was virtually immediate," recalls the CBS man. "The burden was on her. People were waiting to see her disprove the reputation she arrived with. You've gotta be conscious of the fact that you're making at least ten or fifteen or twenty times more than anybody else on the show."

As well, CBS spent other money on her. "*All* the money went to her—it wasn't just the salary," says the senior staffer. "They hired all these people to come with her—producers, a creative director," and others, including a makeup artist. This is not an unusual situation in, say, a high-stakes, game-changing entertainment division show. But for old-school, frugal, earn-your-way-up CBS News, it was new. "CBS putting a lot of money into her meant they didn't put it into the physical plant, they didn't put it into the story gathering. It was hard for other people to get raises." Even more: Some eminent correspondent stars at *60 Minutes*, where Katie also was doing stories, were asked to take salary cuts. Ed Bradley was asked to take a decrease before his death, two months after Katie started. Morley Safer took 30 percent less salary (for fewer working hours), and Lesley Stahl was asked to take a half million dollars less in salary.

The CBS man: "You know the saying, 'Of those to whom much is given much is expected'? I don't think she understood that part. To be sure, she tried in a couple of ways. Katie can put on a charm offensive if she wants to. It was like: After there's a divorce in the family and your father gets remarried, in comes the stepmother . . . and she's smiling at you the whole time. But really, she doesn't give a *shit* about you. She cared about you only as much as it affected her.

"She expected that everyone was working for her and was extending her brand," he continues. "She started a blog, Couric & Co. And [people at CBS] said, 'Do you want to blog on it?'" But this man's attitude, and that of others, was: "'I'm not contributing to her blog! If I want to blog, I'll create *my own* blog. I'm already giving enough to Katie's show!'" Having once been asked to yield his producer to her when he was in the midst of a big story, he refused, saying, "'She *cannot* have my producer! She's taken everything else in this building!' She'd have three-camera shoots, which were just *unheard of*" at the proudly nuts-and-bolts CBS News. "Some of us would have trouble getting a camera because they were all with Katie."

Others complained that, as the senior staffer puts it, "If you worked really hard for her, she might not even recognize it, or she might end up criticizing you." The Rather aide, who said she spent "a lot of time chasing Katie to do her homework," says, "You'd write all this stuff for her and then she would read it and say it wasn't what she wanted, and you'd say, 'Katie, I have it in my notes that this is *exactly* what you asked for,' and she'd be angry."

The CBS man: "So it was her world versus everybody else's."

Katie and the team she brought over from NBC felt the animus—they felt ganged up on—and their reaction, says one team member, was this: "CBS was not supportive. There is a mentality there that your success is somebody else's failure. At NBC, your success was everybody's. It was a different culture."

As justified as much of the staff's reaction to Katie seems, was any of it tinged with sexism? Would a very highly paid male morning person have been greeted in such a dukes-up way? Would he have been compared with a devious stepparent? Would "the burden," as the CBS man put it, have been on him, from the start? Would the transfer of resources to the star—as excessive as they may have been in this case—have been quite as acutely noticed and resented?

It's hard to entirely disentangle the button-pushing uniqueness of Katie—and her behavior, and the money involved in her arrival—from a possible deep-seated double standard. Even women who were critical of Katie say that, as one female producer puts it, when Katie entered, "it was an *incredibly* sexist time at CBS News. We had *no* women correspondents. They had fired so many of them. In our LA bureau they fired five women and kept all the men. And Sean McManus was impossible. He was *such* a guy's guy, he could not even talk to a woman. He could not look a woman in the eye. He was uncomfortable around women, except for" one female executive brought in from another network who "acted like a little kitten" in his presence, this female staffer asserts. "It was a very macho atmosphere. You'd go to those meetings and they would talk about golf. The national editor once said, 'You women should play golf more.'" A woman responded: "'You know, you work five days a week; the other two you want to spend with your kids.'" This female producer continues: "And Paul Friedman was the *most* misogynistic. At one meeting someone said something like, 'Well, we could have a woman do it.' And Paul said, 'Ah, women—the *other* race.'" Perhaps he meant this facetiously, but it was not perceived that way.

Indeed, a remark that Friedman made one day, early in Katie's tenure, drove this home, quite astonishingly. CBS News has an internal audio line called the McCurdy; everyone in the New York offices can hear over it. One day, during the beginning of Katie's tenure as anchor, Friedman made a comment over the McCurdy during rehearsals. Friedman had, of course, been at ABC and had worked with Diane at *Primetime*. With the whole staff listening, he said, over the open McCurdy, about Katie: "The only person I've seen who looks worse without her makeup on is Diane Sawyer."

"I was blown back in my chair," says a female producer. "What did it say about a man in senior management that he didn't know he shouldn't say that, of his boss, out loud?"

. . .

ULTIMATELY, THOUGH, in terms of her relations with her new colleagues, it was Katie's seemingly flaunted unfriendliness to them that most of them deeply resented and felt hurt by. During the holiday season, "Katie held a huge Christmas party for her entourage only, which anybody on the second floor," where many of the producers were, "could see. When Dan was there, every single person on the second floor got a Christmas present, which Dan paid for with his own money." By contrast, Katie and her private guests "were singing and exchanging gifts, but we old guard got nothing. We would walk by and think: 'What are we, chopped liver?' She drew a very, very clear line in the sand."

It's important to pause here and do yet another sexism reality check about the behavior of the anchor of CBS in relation to his or her staff. Yes, Dan Rather, a lifetime CBS man, may have given everyone holiday presents, but, says an executive who worked with him, he also "expected the waters to part for him" and he sometimes enlisted a CBS News producer to walk him across the street to ward off fans. And he was thin-skinned and temperamental: "I've seen Dan scream into a telephone at Leslie Moonves because he was angry at perceived slights," this producer adds.

Katie's show was a risky, ambitious, and expensive experiment: to reinvigorate—to *change*—the news, to pull in a younger audience. That experiment didn't work. And she—the highly paid star in a budget-strained TV news era—met with a relentlessly conservative national CBS audience and a stubborn difficulty in shedding her female morning star image, a stumbling block that male stars like Charlie Gibson and Tom Brokaw had not encountered when they moved from Morning to Evening. She also demonstrated a tin-eared approach to her new colleagues at the proud and family-like organization, and she demonstrated a lack of initiative in taking her role as managing editor of the *CBS Evening News* seriously. ("Traditionally, the anchors of the evening newscast not only had the title of managing editor, but they *are* managing editor," says one who worked at CBS News. "They show up early during the day, have a hand in which stories are being covered. They read the script, talk to the correspondent about the script. They have *enormous* impact—some would say too much." By contrast, "Katie was out doing other things. She was being a star.") She was easy to blame, and she wasn't un-blame-worthy. And her salary made her particularly easy to resent.

There was also the damned-if-you-do, damned-if-you-don't factor, which tends to afflict risk-taking people in power who are experiencing suddenly downward trajectories. In March, with Katie's numbers sinking, public and media criticism of her zigzagged from the charge that she was too soft . . . to the charge that she was too hard. Interviewing John and Elizabeth Edwards together for *60 Minutes*, in their first joint interview since their decision for John to remain in the presidential race despite Elizabeth's incurable cancer, Katie asked tough questions about how responsible to the electorate the decision to continue to run really was. Some thought Katie's attitude was "callous," "hostile," and "cold."

But a year later—for what it was worth—Katie was vindicated: It was revealed that Edwards had had *at least* a fleeting affair with his campaign videographer Rielle Hunter (and, of course, it was later revealed that it was more than fleeting and that Hunter had had his baby) and that Elizabeth—at the time of Katie's interview with them—*had* known about the indiscretion, any ultimate revelation of which could have sunk the Democrats had Edwards become the Democratic nominee for president. Given this new information, Katie's toughness on them in March now seemed retroactively justified. Katie, with her strong interviewer's instincts, had sensed that the Edwardses had been disingenuous about *something* during that conversation; she just didn't know what it was—and her toughness on them was a bit of a smoke-out, a probe.

Katie's toughness was displayed to the public, too. The Katie-who-never-lets-you-see-her-cry—the wry counter of slights, always invigorated when underestimated or dismissed—came through in Joe Hagan's *New York* cover story. "I think [it] bugs people even more that I'm not a woman on the verge of a nervous breakdown" over the bad press and ratings, she said, with startlingly frank bitterness. "It's probably disappointing to some people."

In private, Katie—who had recently turned fifty—was now begin-

ning to actively and repeatedly compare herself to the embattled but energized Hillary Clinton. Katie deeply related to Hillary; she felt she was
being pummeled as first female anchor just like Clinton was being pummeled as first major female presidential primary candidate. Moreover,
she saw, through her own experience and sensitivities, what even many
women didn't see until after the 2008 election: how many casual remarks
about Hillary Clinton were sexist. A female producer says, "We would be
at meetings, Katie and I, and she would say to me afterward, 'I know that
you feel the same way that I do'" about tossed-off remarks by the men in
the room about Hillary's appearance. "It was a little bond" they had,
this female producer and Katie seeing what others did not see. Katie's
feminism—wryly expressed—came out during these difficult months at
CBS News, in remarks such as, "I've . . . decided [that] 'gravitas' . . . is Latin
for 'testicles,'" and "What is the word for a male diva? A *divo*?" The complicated fact is that even those women at CBS who saw Katie as deficient
in certain things—solidarity with her colleagues, full-bore seriousness
about hard news—appreciated her serious feminism.

Katie protested the bullying of girls at her daughters' Manhattan private school several years before teen bullying became a high-profile issue.
And at work, "Katie would correct me when I would say things that were
not gender-friendly," says a female producer who didn't otherwise find
working with her fulfilling. This producer adds, "She's very aware of
these issues. She's very pro-woman. It's her and her girls—her daughters,
Ellie and Carrie. She wanted to be the first woman in that anchor chair to
empower other women—that was real."

IN MARCH 2007, Rome Hartman was fired, and Rick Kaplan was hired
to straighten out the show. This was the same Rick Kaplan whom Diane
had had dismissed from *Primetime*. Rick came in as the tough, forceful
savior. "When Rick came, things calmed down, without a doubt," says the
CBS man. "Things had been coming off the rails for Katie—she was
flailing, she was getting hammered in the press—and I think she kind of
looked at him and said, '*You* do it.' He held her in check. He's big and

loud—those are his weapons—but he's really a pussycat. He's like a big little boy. And when she'd push the line he'd look at her and say, 'No! We're doing it *this* way!' He protected her and solidified things and the criticism stopped." Rick himself puts it this way: "I went back to some basic journalistic principles. Katie and I just decided we were going to raise the bar big-time. We were going to show off her interviewing skills and her journalistic skills. We were going to make the evening news all it could be."

The senior staffer: "I like Rick, but people lived in fear of him. He would blame people for things. He would start screaming for no reason." Still, for all his commanding machismo, Katie could—and did—overmatch him. Once, in a moment of exhausted candor, Kaplan confessed to a colleague, "'You *can't* tell Katie what to do.'"

Now, with Rick at the helm, gone were the failed innovations. Back the show went to being a straight, conventional six-thirty news show with Katie reading the news. She was being an appropriate good soldier, but it was a waste of her personality, and she more than anyone knew it. She turned her social media into virtually a stand-alone entity. She started a monthly column, interviewing notable women, for *Glamour* magazine, and the editor who worked with her on it found her and her designated staff helper as cooperative as many of those CBS colleagues found them both uncollegial.

She traveled more—the aim was to get dramatic international stories for hard news credibility and buzz. She flew to Baghdad and Damascus, "and worked very hard there," says a foreign staffer, "and interviewed General Petraeus and the other [top brass], who fell all over themselves for her." During her time in Afghanistan, Katie spent her off time fretting over getting just the perfect food for her father's upcoming ninetieth birthday, for which relatives were assembling from far and wide. "Where can I get the best Southern biscuits?" she wrote her friend Pat Shifke. Pat wrote back: "I cannot believe you're in Afghanistan—Kabul Katie— e-mailing me about the biscuits!"

Meanwhile, Rick Kaplan had noticed something about Katie's inter- view skills: "Katie is a master of follow-up questions," he realized. "She listens really hard. If you leave her an opening, she will follow up brilliantly." If he was to resurrect her, they'd have to find an interview subject where her perennially unexpected skill would have spectacular effect.

WHILE KATIE WAS going through this year-and-a-half-long roller coaster, over at ABC Diane was doing some of her strongest work—and taking the strongest control of her content. The loss of the anchor position to Charlie, the great disappointment aides say she felt when Katie, not she, became the first female solo anchor—whether or not these losses impelled her to redouble her competitiveness, those months of late 2006 through mid-2007 were *hers*. As Rebecca Dana put it in the *New York Observer* at the beginning of this period: "The big jobs—the Diane Sawyer–sized jobs—have passed by," going, of course, to Charlie and Katie. "[B]ut the big stories are there. And Ms. Sawyer has been getting them."

The first change was a change in producers, which had occurred in June 2006. Ben Sherwood, with whom Diane had been dissatisfied during *GMA*'s previous year's close but ultimately fruitless race with *Today*, left and was replaced by Jim Murphy, who had worked for Dan Rather for five years and then had created Bob Schieffer's broadcast at Katie's new home, CBS. Given his years with Rather, coming in to rescue a morning show may have felt like small potatoes to Murphy. "Jim didn't care if Diane liked him or not," says the female *GMA* insider who knew how upset Diane was that Katie had become the first solo anchor. "Jim told people, publicly, that he didn't care. And I'm going to bet that's probably true: that he really didn't care. And *that* made her crazy. She goes *bananas* if she can't woo you." An associate says Diane once barked at Jim, in a wounded, angry voice: "'You were married to Bob. You were *so* married to Dan! *Why won't you marry me?*'"

But it was Ben Sherwood's leaving that would be, in the long run, more consequential than Jim Murphy's entering. "Ben resigned suddenly when it was clear his head was on the block," says someone who knows him well. "He is personally wealthy," so holding on to the job wasn't something he needed desperately to do. "He told some story about 'important family reasons' for returning to LA. But, really, he had to go crawling back to LA with his tail between his legs." Meanwhile, Diane told at least one person afterward, "Ben is just *so weak*," indicating that the choice to "resign" had not really been Ben's.

But others whom Sherwood talked to heard a different story—one that gives Sherwood more agency in the decision. "Ben told me he gave up working with Diane six months after he got [to *GMA*], because it was just too hard," says one in the know. "He just wanted to get away from her. But then," this person adds—fast-forwarding, "he spent the next five years figuring out how to get back in her good graces."

With her new producer, Jim Murphy, Diane racked up a series of important stories. First was her second Mel Gibson interview, in mid-October.

Three months earlier, Gibson had been arrested while drunk driving well over the speed limit on the Pacific Coast Highway. The arrest itself was less inflammatory than Gibson's words to the arresting officer: "Are you a Jew? The Jews are responsible for all the wars in the world."

Diane was her charming but tough self with Mel Gibson—and he walked into her traps. A "Gibson insider" had told Nikki Finke, herself Hollywood's most insider journalist, that Gibson had "needed someone who'd hit him hard," given the events of the summer. "But she was f——harder on him than I could imagine. I was cringing. No other TV journalist would have been that hard on him." (This was an odd comment, possibly meant for spin, because Diane's earlier interview with Mel had had a gentility to it. He had warned her to stay away from criticizing his father, and she had acted startled. It is probable that Gibson's people thought Diane would be *easy* the second time, not tough, and when their prediction backfired, they spun it thusly to Finke.)

This was the first interview in which Gibson confessed his alcoholism, but that admission—that he had fallen off the wagon over the summer— was the easy part. He dismissed his anti-Semitic raving at the officer as the "stupid rambling of a drunkard"—the last time, he'd weakly said that anti-Semitism was a "sin." But, importantly, he partly justified his rant as having come from the fact that the Israel-Lebanon conflict was going on;

he also said that he was hurt and mad that Jewish leaders who had thought his *Passion of the Christ* would stir anti-Semitism had never apologized *to him* after the film's release.

Gibson said people had a "choice" whether or not to forgive him and that he felt "powerless" if they didn't. As for his most controversial assertion made to the officer, Gibson did not take it back. Diane pushed him by saying that there was a difference between asserting, as he had to her, that the Middle East was a "tinderbox" and saying, "The Jews are responsible for all the wars in the world." Gibson gave no ground: "I think that they're not blameless in the conflict," he said, and a sentence or two later he *repeated* that statement. Gibson talked about his stunned realization that American Jews might be afraid he'd "go goose-stepping" toward them and physically attack them. Aside from subscribing to the old canard that Jews are fearful and timid, he didn't seem to understand that fear of Hitler-like annihilation was not, in 2007 America, the fear or the issue. The fear was that such casual anti-Semitism would go unpunished. The point was that he should have apologized and he didn't.

Diane's interview, which aired in *GMA* and nighttime portions, showed a nervous, perspiring Mel Gibson in all his grand contradictoriness: woebegone, hotheaded, defensive, startlingly clueless for a man who'd been perched for a long time at the highest levels of PR-engined Hollywood, and bizarrely selectively repentant. Few interviews with *any* celebrity revealed so much.

Then Diane went to North Korea for a week. She filed reports for *Good Morning America* and for *World News* on everything from nuclear weapons to women's sports. In that most closed of countries, she pushed past the government minders. "She kept saying, as we were driving along, 'Can we stop, can we stop? Can we talk to that rice farmer, just for five more minutes?'" producer Margaret Aro, who accompanied her, recalls. "She was very pushy about it," because if she'd waited for the interviewees the minders had chosen, she would have had only pat, approved answers. "She was practically hurtling" with her translator, Margaret says, "running into a rice paddy to ask what the people thought of the U.S."

More foreign travel ensued: to Syria and to Iran, in the latter to conduct—in proper head scarf—her first interview with Mahmoud Ahmadinejad. When the excessive cost of all this foreign travel on the *GMA* coffers was raised, Diane was tough. "Man, we're gonna really blow the budget," a functionary worried. According to someone who was within earshot in the studio, she shot back: "Don't you ever talk to me about money in a company that paid a hundred and ninety million dollars to an *idiot* to make him go away!" She was referring to Walt Disney CEO Michael Eisner's departure payoff to Creative Artists Agency cofounder Michael Ovitz, whom they'd briefly hired. Someone in the room laughed at this remark, agreeing that she had a point.

Then, and on other occasions, Diane's anger took listeners aback. One time, when a staffer opined that Diane seemed unhappy, she seethed, unconvincingly, "I am the *happiest* person I know!" She appeared to be in overdrive—work and more work, perfectionism and more perfectionism had always been her response, and now that she was in her early sixties, with forty full-time years in the workplace, that mode seemed to intensify, not to lessen. When someone noted that she worked too hard, she snapped that the person didn't appreciate "my Calvinist work ethic!" It was not like her—the utterly charming and deftly self-deprecating Diane—to be snappish; perhaps she'd been criticized for this penchant of hers one too many times over one too many years for her not to be sensitive about something she now must have known that others not only marveled at but also made wisecracks about.

The overnight workers in the newsroom were powerless when Diane would call at one a.m. with a story she'd just seen on the *Drudge Report* or the BBC. "Is anyone working on it?" she'd demand. When the answer was no, she'd say, "Well, send somebody out to work on it." And, says one who knew of these events, the overnight person would "immediately start hiring freelance producers all around the world. There are some restrictions on what you can do, but she never listened to them." And having "answered the phone at one a.m. long enough, you'd realize ABC would now have to be wasting ten thousand dollars for something that was not going to go on the air. But if you didn't do it, and if she found out you didn't do it, she would triple your agony for the next few weeks by calling in at one a.m. more often, wanting more stories, checking back to make sure you were working on them."

Word leaked out of the studio that a few staffers who were, as one of them said in earshot of a third person, "so stressed out and burned out by what she put them through" expressed their feelings to her. "Diane listened—"she teared up, she got upset." But the complaint remained. As one put it, "That's what it's like working for Diane. All the time, you feel that you can't do enough. You'll never give enough. And you'll just do this until you break."

Few on the outside knew this. What *was* visible, from 2006 to 2009, was a morning and newsmagazine star in her practiced prime. What had once been called her "rich, honeyed voice" had, with age, taken on an automatically emotional tear-in-the-throat quality. Her Lauren Bacall approach to the camera was now more eyes-straight-ahead, more welcomingly forthright. She expanded her franchise of social issues investigatives, which she had minted with her "modern-day Nellie Bly" pieces, as Ira Rosen had called them, at *Primetime*, and which she had refined on *GMA*. And she turned that initially feared liability for Morning—her childlessness—into a virtue: If Walter Cronkite had been America's Uncle, Diane Sawyer was becoming America's Aunt. Right after September 11, she had poignantly interviewed the full complement of pregnant widows from those terror attacks, and at the one-year and the five-year (and eventually the nine-year and the ten-year) anniversaries she had the widows and their growing children back on *GMA*, her gushing (especially at how much the children resembled their late fathers), and their bonding with her, as feel-good as it was sincere.

Now she focused on impoverished children. She traveled home to Louisville to do a special, "Calling All Angels," on Maryhurst, a shelter for the state's most abused and neglected girls. Louisville was always—ever—home for her: Her mother still lived there. A local park, Tom Sawyer Park, was named after her father. She traveled to her Seneca High reunions. She received kudos and awards from her fellow Seneca alum, Louisville's mayor (and eventually Kentucky lieutenant governor) Jerry Abramson. And she had never forgotten the lessons she and her classmates had faced during their young, improvised stumbling from segregation to integration. That even now, in the mid-aughts, such cruelty, by way of poverty, remained in Louisville was painful to Diane, and she was determined to expose it. Says Anna Robertson, who worked on the special with her: "It was heartbreaking, what these kids had to go through, getting circulated through foster care home after foster care home. Their resilience was amazing." Diane won the Robert F. Kennedy Journalism Award for that investigation.

Next she went to Jamaica. She interviewed an HIV-positive young woman living in poverty; when her reluctant driver hesitated to enter the most gang-ridden area of Kingston, Diane virtually threatened him: If he wouldn't drive there, he could move over and *she* would take the wheel of the car.

After that, with producer Claire Weinraub, she profiled children in destitute families in Camden, New Jersey, for a *20/20* special, "Waiting on the World to Change," which aired in January 2007. Twice Camden had been rated America's most dangerous city. Thirty drug arrests could take place inside Camden's municipal borders within three hours. The city had record-high homicides and a plethora of random gunfire, burned-out lots, and abandoned buildings. It was Diane's idea to spend the night with one of the profiled families, on a hand-me-down couch in their living room. "Diane fell asleep right away; *I* didn't," says Claire, remembering how nervous she was while Diane was relaxed. "She got up in the morning and right away started doing interviews. No makeup. It was very low-key. We shot most of it ourselves."

On the heels of the Camden piece, Diane pushed to do a similar special on the impoverished children of Appalachia. If Maryhurst had felt personal, this was even more so. "It was something she had wanted to do for a long, long time," says Anna Roberston. Her parents' stories of their own hardscrabble childhoods had made her sensitive to the pain of the region, whose problems had only deepened over the decades; central Appalachia now had three times the poverty rate of the rest of the country, the shortest life span in the nation, plus epidemic drug abuse, epic rates of cancer and depression—and record toothlessness.

Diane and Claire followed four children and their families over the course of two years. "She was pretty indomitable about shooting from five in the morning until eleven at night," says Claire. "At the end of one very long day she wanted to drive an hour away, way up in these winding hills in Inez, Kentucky, to visit this woman, Dinah, who we were profiling." Dinah, an impoverished woman raising her four grandchildren, "was in choir practice at this little ramshackle church. It was called 'the Homecoming Church.' It was where President Johnson had declared the War on Poverty." Once inside the church, Diane took a seat in the pew "and listened to the sermon and sang along to the hymns." The cameraman hadn't arrived, which didn't seem to matter to Diane. Perhaps the Homecoming Church represented a kind of homecoming for Diane herself.

The *20/20* special—"A Hidden America: Children of the Mountains," which Jon Banner, who would become Diane's *World News* executive producer, calls "one of the most disturbing hours in television I have ever seen; *nobody* had seen [the dire poverty it revealed] before"—generated action: editorials as well as corporate donations of medical aid. It won a Peabody Award and a Robert F. Kennedy Journalism Award.* After it was completed, Diane planned, with Claire, her next in the series—"A Hidden America: Children of the Plains"—about the grinding poverty of Lakota Indian children in South Dakota. She kept going on this theme, next throwing herself into a special about children growing up in gang-ridden Chicago. "Children of the Plains" aired in October 2011, and the Chicago piece—"Don't Shoot, I Want to Grow Up"—aired in October 2012 and included a discussion, with members of gangs, about solutions to urban violence.

The "cool drink of water" was now a newscaster known for her empa-

*In addition to winning a string of DuPont, Peabody, Emmy, and Robert F. Kennedy Journalism awards for her long body of work, Diane received the USC Distinguished Achievement in Journalism Award, was inducted into the Broadcast Magazine Hall of Fame and the Television Academy Hall of Fame, and received the IRTS Lifetime Achievement Award, which is considered the grand prize of the Investigative Reporters and Editors Association.

thy. She was producing, with these specials, the same passionate, accessible sharing of stories of hardship and grit that Catherine Marshall, her America's Junior Miss mentor, had shared by way of her 1950s bestsellers. The tagline Diane came up with for "Children of the Mountains"—"In the dark of Appalachia, sometimes the measure of strength is how much you can hold on to hope"—might have been a line from a Catherine Marshall book.

MEANWHILE, OVER AT CBS in the summer of 2008, Katie was enduring her workmanlike middle passage—the innovations and criticism had been stanched, but her broadcasts were undistinguished, and CBS, number three when she'd taken over, was *still* number three, behind Brian Williams's number one NBC broadcast and Charlie Gibson's ABC second place. Then some startling political news transpired. As the *New York Times* put it on August 29, "Senator John McCain astonished the political world on Friday by naming Sarah Palin, a little-known governor of Alaska and self-described 'hockey mom' with almost no foreign policy experience, as his running mate on the Republican presidential ticket."

Nicolle Wallace, the McCain team's designated Palin handler, set up major network interviews for Palin. Charlie Gibson went first, in early September. Palin came off poorly prepared, her geniality only accentuating her ignorance. (When Charlie asked her what she thought of the Bush Doctrine, she asked, "In what respect, Charlie?") But Gibson's stern impatience and condescension was so off-putting, the Republican vice presidential nominee seemed sympathetic by comparison. McCain senior strategist Steve Schmidt felt Palin had survived the interview—it was "not an A," he said, but neither had it inflicted "significant damage." (That interview had, however, included Palin's instantly infamous quote, "You can actually see Russia from land here in Alaska.")

When Katie got her shot at Palin two weeks later, the chemistry was different. In gender, age, and—handy, shopworn—image, the two seemed more evenly matched. In fact, Palin later claimed, on *Oprah*, that she'd understood that the interview "was supposed to be kind of lighthearted, fun, working mom speaking with working mom and the challenges that we have with teenage daughters." Well, Palin was wrong. First, Katie, and Rick Kaplan, saw this as a potential game-changer for the show, a chance to remind everyone of Katie's interviewing acuity and persistence. Second, "Katie thought Palin was *such* a fake," says a CBS producer who talked with her about the experience afterward. "Katie thought she had really seen through her" during the interviews, which began as a walk-and-talk near the UN and then continued in a studio sit-down. Mainly, Katie was palpably knowledgeable, and never had her talent for unexpected fastballs been so effectively parlayed.

The interview was broadcast in three parts over three nights: first on the economic crisis (Lehman Brothers had just declared bankruptcy), on international affairs the next night, and finally on domestic and social issues. In the first portion, Palin struggled to hold her own against Katie's calm, relentless challenges. Despite what Palin said, polls showed that most Americans were looking to Obama, not McCain, to solve the economic crisis; would Palin support a moratorium on foreclosures? Couric asked. When faced with a question about the proposed $700 billion stimulus plan, Palin's answer was so incoherent, a *Newsweek* columnist described it as "a vapid emptying out of every catchphrase about economics that came into her head." And when Katie asked Palin when, in McCain's twenty-six years in Congress, he had ever been in favor of government regulation, the stumped Alaska governor sarcastically offered to find some examples *later*, "and get them to ya."

The foreign policy segment was worse. Palin muddled her generalized and uninformed responses, lost her composure (she would later say she just wanted Couric to "go away"), and, most memorably, when Katie asked her, and re-asked her, and *re*-re-asked her, what newspapers she read, Palin could not name a single periodical. One writer put it this way: "Katie peeled Sarah Palin like a raw carrot." It was on the basis of this interview that the Obama campaign began, as campaign manager David Plouffe put it, "to see in our research not merely a cooling off in terms of people's views of Palin but downright concern about her qualification."

It was in the third segment, on domestic issues, that Couric showed her feminism straight up. But she also showed partisanship. It could be argued that she pushed Palin past Palin's own avowed generalized feminism— "I'm a feminist who believes in equal rights . . . I'm absolutely for equal pay for equal work. . . . It's obvious there are some double standards here," Palin said—into a place where there was little room for Palin's points of view. For example, Katie prodded Palin on the Lilly Ledbetter Act, which indeed dealt directly with fair pay for women, although Palin, like almost all conservatives, opposed it strongly. Then Katie questioned Palin on abortion and contraception. Palin said she was not opposed to contraception, and that she would never punish a woman for having an abortion. But when Couric pushed her to take a stand on whether a fifteen-year-old who had been raped by her own father would be entitled to an abortion, Palin responded that she would always counsel to "choose life." (Hardright abortion opponents oppose incest exceptions, and Palin's use of the word "choose" was tellingly moderate.) Katie pressed Palin on homosexuality, and Palin went out of her way to say, "One of my absolute best friends for the last thirty years, and I love her dearly, happens to be gay," pointedly sneering at tokenism by adding, with likable emphasis, "And she is *not* my 'gay friend.'" Yet she termed homosexuality a "choice" rather than an orientation. Katie pushed Palin to explain her Wasilla church's harsh view on gays, and Palin distanced herself from an egregious antigay event at the church. But, troublingly, Palin, while declaring respect for science, said evolution should be a subject for "debating" in schools. She also couldn't identify a single Supreme Court decision with which she disagreed.

Was Katie using Democratic criteria to question—even vet—Palin? It could be argued that she was. Was there a "gotcha" element to this portion of the interview? For conservatives: almost certainly. Did she nevertheless help to pinpoint those beliefs of Palin's—on homosexuality and creationism, and possibly, though less clearly, on abortion in cases of rape and incest—that were beyond the pale of even center-right *Republicans?* Also: yes.

Katie's interviews with Palin were considered highly revelatory, and they proved to be a sharp—negative—turning point for voters' perceptions of Palin's qualifications. For the interviews, Katie was awarded, in March 2009, the Walter Cronkite Award for Excellence in Television Political Journalism from USC's Annenberg School. The judges termed Katie's Sarah Palin interviews "a defining moment in the 2008 presidential campaign." Given all the pearl clutching that had taken place in high-toned journalistic circles over Miss Morning's ascent to the Great Man's chair, what better *literal* validation was there than the Cronkite Award? A friend of Katie's from NBC says: "Sarah Palin vindicated Katie. So many times" in the previous two years "people had said, 'Oh, Katie's *out.*'" Now, she finally wasn't. As well, Sean McManus's much-whispered-about failure during those first seven months of Katie's tenure evaporated as he proudly, if opportunistically, announced, "We congratulate Katie.... [Her] journalistic achievements are unique, unmistakably her own, and in keeping with the highest tradition of Walter Cronkite and CBS News excellence."

A month before the award ceremony, Katie had gotten her game back in a different way, in an exclusive interview with America's hero of the moment, US Airways pilot Chesley Burnett Sullenberger III—known to the world as just "Sully." On January 15, Sully had safely, brilliantly landed a commercial plane on the Hudson River right off Manhattan after a flock of geese had jammed the plane's engines following takeoff. The media became consumed by Sully rapture, and the Sully mania—making a hero of a gracious, older white male saving a plane full of travelers—was even, in its way, a peace flag to a badly divided country. Katie returned to her early *Today* show self to engage with the pilot warmly but not gushily.

Yet despite the validation from her journalistic peers and the display of her unique skills, some noticed an apparent melancholy in Katie. One female staffer noticed that "it seemed important to her that she had a boyfriend"—the handsome Perlin. "We were walking down to the sports control room" one day and she blurted out, in a complete non sequitur, "'I have a *boyfriend*, you know!'" The staffer thought Katie said that to signal her own invulnerability, but of course it only had the opposite effect. Her older daughter, Ellie, was away in college now; Carrie was a high school girl, separating from her mother as all girls do. The tight bond they'd had since Jay's death—it had always been "me and my girls"—was now loosening. "It can be lonely," she admitted to a magazine.

At the end of May, Katie gave the commencement address at Princeton, and it was delightfully Katie in her truest, smart-feminist form. It turns out she was the first woman to ever give the address, a fact she nudged the school about: "All these years, and only one woman?" she asked the fellow cap-and-gowned assembly. And "you actually asked [actor] Bradley Whitford of *The West Wing* before you had a woman? I understand the concept of casting a wide net, but great women like Madeleine Albright, Sally Ride, Mother Teresa, Ellen DeGeneres—all bested by a fake political adviser to a fake president? And then you had Stephen Colbert, a fake TV anchor? Actually, Stephen could be a *real* anchor . . . with just a little more product in his hair."

In September, Katie obtained an interview with Mahmoud Ahmadinejad just before he addressed the UN, in which she used an ambush style she'd honed early in her career. Of the Holocaust, "you have called it a lie," Katie said to the pock-faced leader. "And I'm just curious"—the sarcasm was pure Katie—"I have some photos, dead bodies from a German concentration camp taken by the Associated Press, Mr. President." She brandished the image, caught by the cameras. "Is this photo a lie?" The Iranian president then asked her why this "particular" historical event among many was "so important to you." She said, "Because you're denying it happened." Instead of simply dodging her questions, he foolishly let himself be piqued by Katie's aggressiveness in brandishing the photos. "In World War II, sixty million people were killed," Ahmadinejad retorted. "Why are we just focusing on this special group alone?" He had fallen into her trap. With that provocative, extraneous comment, he was *highlighting* his anti-Jewish feelings and his suspicion that any U.S. reporter was promoting Israel's cause. Katie had used what was by now an old trick of hers on a new target: She had pulled a striking new confirmation of unsurprising sentiments out of a major troublesome world leader, yielding a newsworthy sound bite.

Her talent was beginning to show in her new anchor post. Too bad plans were now being secretly made to scuttle her.

CHAPTER TEN

Two Out of Three and
Then Three Out of Six

Diane, Katie, and Christiane: 2008 to 2011

ON SEPTEMBER 2, 2009, the TV industry and the world of media women were jostled with another bit of momentous news: Charlie Gibson announced that he would retire, in three and a half months, from his anchor duties at *ABC World News*. It was finally time for Diane to take over as anchor. Two women anchors, where just three years earlier there had never even been one! The *New York Times* aptly headlined its story "At ABC, an Anchor Shift; for TV, an Image Shift," with TV reporters Bill Carter and Brian Stelter cautioning that the somewhat revolutionary news that "two of the three main network anchors will be female" was qualified by the fact that being a woman anchor "in the past has punished others, like Barbara Walters and Connie Chung."

In a sly aside, Carter and Stelter called Diane "the longtime—some would say long-suffering" host of *GMA*. Over at the *Washington Post*, Howard Kurtz wrote a story with a lead (almost undoubtedly given to him by Diane's camp) that made Diane sound like she was looking out for her colleague's interests. "When Diane Sawyer was approached last Thursday about taking over for Charlie Gibson as ABC's evening news anchor," Kurtz authoritatively wrote, "her first words were about her friend and former broadcast partner: 'Can't we talk Charlie into staying?' Sawyer asked ABC News President David Westin." Kurtz reported that it was "only after Westin assured her that he had tried and failed to persuade . . . Gibson not to retire" that Diane agreed to take the anchor post.

Behind the momentous news was a bit more drama than was evident—and behind the media-fed story of Diane's concern and generosity things had gone rather differently.

Charlie Gibson's resignation e-mail to his *World News* colleagues and staff was strikingly emotional, even pained. He wrote: "It has not been an easy decision to make. This has been my professional home for thirty-five years and I love this news department, to the depths of my soul." David Westin then sent his own e-mail, crisply saying what hardly needed to be said: "Diane Sawyer is the right person to succeed Charlie and build on what he has accomplished. She has an outstanding and varied career in television journalism, beginning with her role as a State Department correspondent and continuing at *60 Minutes, Primetime Live,* and *Good Morning America.*" Jon Banner, who would become her executive producer, puts it this way: "When Charlie retired, it was sort of a natural for Diane to come over. There was nobody who was more qualified to step into that chair, and in some cases she was probably more qualified years beforehand."

Exactly. She had been qualified "years beforehand," and Charlie's e-mail's high emotion might have betrayed something: an involuntary aspect of his resignation. As for Westin, as one insider says (as others also have), "Diane controlled Westin. She had a grasp over him. A lot of people felt that, in the final years" of his news division presidency, their relationship had been strained after she did "*not* get the job after Peter left." He had been indebted to her—she had championed him for president during the rocky patch that had included his extramarital affair. Some presumed he now felt bad that the effort to hand the anchor reins to her had been botched and that Charlie had gotten the anchorship instead.

Here is what the ABC insider says really happened, rather than Charlie resigning: "In the summer of 2009 Charlie had lost his momentum and Diane moved in for the kill." The person says this account came from Charlie himself. "Charlie told people that he was called into David's office and told, 'You're out.' I don't know what language Diane used to pull that off."

. . .

DIANE AND KATIE were different enough, temperamentally and in work ethic and reputation, that caution did not have to be taken by Diane for her to not repeat the errors of the Katie rollout—an excessive good-bye week at the morning show, too much advance promotion of the new anchorship, touting of her salary, a radically experimental and personality-tailored news broadcast. Still, the lessons of Katie's disastrous first six months at least served as a consolation prize for the fact that Diane was the second, not the first, female anchor. And, yes, the gender issue was unavoidably there in the minds of the press and the network publicists—and the public. If a man succeeded Charlie, there wouldn't have been such acute comparison; when there are so few women at the top, the distinctions become more powerful.

Diane's transition from Morning to six thirty would be concertedly business as usual, a reflection not only of her caution and fine-tuned sense of strategy but also of what ABC had learned from Katie's overhyped transition. "Besides," as an NBC producer who watched both launches closely says, "Diane is older and more respectful—and from the South. She knows how to ease her way into your living room. Katie has a more feisty, sly, jokey, winking-at-you persona. Katie's *not* soft. And Diane's salary"—about $14 million when she started (estimated at $17 million by 2012)—"was never talked about, if you noticed. She wanted it that way."

Still, personality cues were sprinkled about, like tasteful favors at a low-key party. Diane's farewell show on *Good Morning America*, in mid-December 2009, featured Robin Roberts almost tearfully saying, "I'll miss my Louise," referencing her and Diane as the do-or-die gal twosome in *Thelma & Louise*; some golden oldie moments of Diane tumbling into full-bore Morning (the chimp on her back, for example); and a multi-hanky surprise appearance by the 9/11 widows and their children. Thus Diane left *Good Morning America* as the person she had become *on* that show: the encouraging female relative, the "aspirational" lady who—surprise!—really *did* let her hair down. (The private send-off party was more sophisticated: In the gag reel, ABC's investigative reporter Brian Ross was made up to portray Mike Nichols, and he was locked in a furtive embrace with Katie. Says an ABC staffer: In the original gag reel "we [filmed] Mike [himself] kissing Katie. Mike agreed to do it as a joke. But that version got nixed," and the Brian Ross–as–Mike-with-Katie scene was substituted. It isn't clear on whose say-so the scene was nixed. However, the staffer adds, suggesting that it might have been Diane who demurred, "Katie takes risks and Diane doesn't.")

DIANE ENTERED *ABC World News* as the serious, hard news workaholic *and* as the earnest Methodist who'd transformed into a social issues reporter.

The tough reporter part of her was reflected in her second interview with President Ahmadinejad, conducted in Copenhagen in December 2009, three months after Katie had done her own interview with him. Diane sped to the Denmark-bound plane right after she hugged the last *GMA* staffer good-bye; she was *not* messing around, not putting any daylight between her departure from one gig and ascent to another. She was to grill the Iranian leader on his nuclear program, and there was showcase-potential competition among female interviewers with Ahmadinejad, whose imperviousness to the conventions of Western-media politesse had made as his statements as easy to mock his button-shouldered, short-sleeved khaki shirts. Christiane had had the first, and most penetrating, interviews with him, and Katie's baiting of him over the Holocaust pictures had been effective theater. Diane made "precision" of preparation the name of her game with him, says Margaret Aro: Just before sitting down for the interview, to clear up a tiny research inconsistency that no one else on her staff had noticed, Diane insisted on getting on the phone with Mohammed El-Baradei, then the head of the International Atomic Energy Agency.

Diane confronted Ahmadinejad with the United States's recently obtained documents about Iran's nuclear plans—she waved them at him, just as Katie had waved the Holocaust photos. He angrily dismissed them as having been "fabricated" by America. She also took him firmly to task for detaining three young American hikers—two young men and one young woman—who had gotten lost and accidentally ended up inside the Iranian border. Diane's tone made it clear that she felt it was preposterous that the hikers could be spies. Ahmadinejad's calm assertion that they *could* be spies drove home to viewers the intransigence that the American public had come to identify with him. (The female hiker was released after over four hundred days; the men would end up spending almost eight hundred days behind bars.) It was a take-no-prisoners interview, and Diane premiered it during her first week as *World News* anchor, laying down the gauntlet: She would be a strong, world-traveling reporter-anchor.

But her opening evening broadcast also featured a different facet of Diane—her *other* side, as it were. She did an inspiring story—an appropriate pre-Christmas piece—about the Brattleboro, Vermont, First Baptist Church and its pastor, Suzanne Andrews, who, along with her congregation, had decided to sell the church's prized Tiffany windows in order to be able to accommodate more homeless people in its shelter. The museum-quality windows were less important than helping the destitute—*this* was the Diane Sawyer of St. Mark's Methodist Church and St. David's Methodist Church in Louisville, choosing to tell *this* story.

The next evening she told viewers that her report had caused many of them to call the church and donate money, thus at least temporarily saving the windows.

Diane called this a "miracle," which irked media critic Andrew Tyndall, who says, "Calling something a 'miracle' with not a single word about how much money was raised, or how firm the promises were, and saying, as she did, that 'when we showed you this last night, somehow we just *knew* this could happen': That isn't journalism, it's inspirational propaganda."

Throughout her months and then years at *World News*, Diane would combine the hardest-won hard news and international exclusives with service-to-the-populace features on health and living. "She's an advocate for the audience," Jon Banner says, adding a point similar to the one Andrew Heyward made about Katie: "The idea that we are a bunch of people sitting behind a desk telling you"—stentorian voice—"'Good *ev-en-*ing' is not who we are as a country and not who the audience wants us to *be* anymore."

Sometimes Diane's approach bordered on feel-good inspirational. Spirituality was something she was not afraid to occasionally inject into news, Tyndall says. This was heartland Diane, Methodist Diane, and over the years of her anchoring, that tinge of spirituality would become "the ABC News 'house style,'" and not exclusively a female province: Diane's star correspondent and "heir presumptive," David Muir, would report on the occasional "miracle" right along with her. (For example, in August 2013, Muir reported that multiple witnesses in rural Missouri saw a priestlike man come to the aid of a young girl trapped in a car after a crash. Photographs did not reveal any such man, making his "miracle" status all the stronger, Muir implied. The mystery man was credited by the girl's parents and others with helping to calm and save her.)

When Diane came on board during the holiday season of 2009–2010, she had her hands full—and then she made them fuller. Barely back from Copenhagen after her Ahmadinejad interview, she went off to Afghanistan in early January. As Jon Banner, who accompanied her, recalls, "We were there for four days" at the start of the "surge." "She got amazing access to General [Stanley] McChrystal—did some off-camera intelligence briefings with him, flew around on battlefield circulation," talked to people on the Kabul streets *sans* bulletproof vest.

"And we were sitting in the newsroom," on January 10, "and we found out about the Haiti earthquake"—7.0 on the Richter scale, devastating on the impoverished country. The original death toll figures fluctuated wildly (eventually, it would be reliably estimated that between 100,000 and 150,000 people were killed, with many more injured). "It was pitch black outside, there were no private planes in Kabul, but Diane would not take no for an answer," Banner says. She finally found a plane from Kabul to Frankfurt, and another from Frankfurt to New York. She and Banner and a few others then got a JetBlue flight from New York to Santo Domingo, Dominican Republic, and there boarded a small prop jet. "There were six of us and we got all the way to the Haitian runway but were turned back"—the airport was closed. Back in Santo Domingo Diane be-seechingly convinced the pilot of a small helicopter—"the tiniest little chopper I have *ever* seen," Banner says—to crunch her and the medical editor, Richard Besser, "who's about six foot six," into its miniscule hold and fly them to Haiti.

Diane's zeal had a competitive aspect: Katie, with the advantage of having flown directly from New York, had beaten her to it, becoming the first major network anchor on the ground in Port-au-Prince. Katie gar-nered powerful interviews, stirring with initial-report immediacy. As Katie would later recall, "When we landed on the tarmac, the first person I saw was a woman in a wheelchair whose head was completely bandaged in bloody rags. She was one of the lucky ones. . . . I asked her compan-ion where she had been when the earthquake struck. 'She worked at the Citibank building,' he told me," referring to one of the more well-built structures in the country. "'It's been flattened.' . . . Haiti's President René Préval was also on the tarmac. He wasn't wounded, but he seemed lost and wondered aloud when help would arrive." Katie was driven through the streets of Port-au-Prince. "It's so hackneyed to say it looked like a disaster film, but when that's your only frame of reference, it's difficult to come up with adjectives other than 'surreal.' A building completely intact stood next to one that had pancaked. People were working with tiny pickaxes in a slow, painstaking way to dig through the rubble. Some walked through the streets on a kind of mass exodus to nowhere. It was strangely silent. No ambulances, fire trucks, or rescue workers. As I quickly learned, these services don't exist in Haiti." Notably, Katie—effectively—employs the opposite perspective from authoritative, crisis-zone-saturated Christiane: Katie exaggerates her American Mom naivete ("when that's your only frame of reference," "as I quickly learned"), her abashed provincialism, and her eagerness to learn, coming eye level with her armchair viewer.

The race between Katie and Diane in Haiti was on.

Diane and Richard Besser were eventually joined by the others, in-cluding Jon Banner and Robin Roberts. The hotels were destroyed. They set up camp at the airport. "We slept on baggage carts out in the open the first night and in a building that could have been toppled by aftershocks, sitting upright in chairs," Banner continues. "It was as unglamorous as it could be." If Katie had the advantage of seeing the destruction first, Diane had the advantage of immediately experiencing conditions as close to those matching the residents' as any major anchor could be forced into. Diane interviewed with no place to change or shower. She didn't worry about herself, Banner says, but she was "very concerned" for the Haitians. "'Where was the aid? Where were the ready-to-eat meals? The tents? The water purifiers and water supplies?' We did a *Primetime* special that night and she took the lead in anchoring."

All this—Copenhagen, Afghanistan, Haiti—within her first three weeks as *World News* anchor.

BUT IF THE FIRST MONTH OF 2010 felt like a triumph for women in TV news—two out of three anchors, female—there was a hidden down-side. The rising tide did *not* lift all boats. The TV news economy, interna-tionally, was in trouble. On February 1, 2010, CBS News instituted "massive layoffs, worldwide," says a then foreign bureau principal. One New York staffer estimates the number as "about a hundred" employees in a wide variety of capacities, including technical. Of this number, eight female producers were let go, and "four of the women, all over the age of fifty, worked directly for Katie's broadcast," whether out of London, New York, or Los Angeles. One was fired and the other three dismissals were termed "voluntary retirement" and came with monetary compensation, but one of those three women insists "it was *not* 'voluntary'—we wanted to keep working. And not one of us got a note or a phone call from Katie. Great big feminist—she lets them fire eight women while she compares her-self to Hillary Clinton," this woman says, bitterly. "That's 'convenient' feminism."

As it happened, the March issue of *Harper's Bazaar* hit the news-stands the very next day after the eight female producers were dismissed, and in it was a breezy interview with Katie, illustrated by a movie-star-glamorous photo of her in a chic, one-shoulder-strapped beige sheath. Now, fashion magazines do that sort of thing all the time, and network publicity departments *like* them to do it, and anyway, the photo completely failed to capture Katie's essence. But to the CBS News staff reeling from the layoffs, the accident of timing was bad, as was the magazine's Web-embedded promotional video of, as one high-level female staffer recalls it, "Katie dancing around like she was twenty and saying she has 'the best legs.'" It is hard to overestimate the pain that many CBS senior staffers—including women—felt at the cuts in the reporting budget while the elephant in the room—Katie's phenomenal salary—remained. Irrational though it might have been, it felt like Katie was rubbing in her privilege while so many women saw themselves, or their friends, clearing their desks and saying good-bye.

By the same token, and the same accident of timing, the movie *Up in the Air*—about an executive, played by George Clooney, who flies around the country firing people—had just been released. Says the laid-off staffer, "Katie thought it would be 'fun' if the *Evening News* did a piece about it. None of the senior producers had the balls to explain to her why that was inappropriate, but they did call the assigned correspondent to tell him he had to include the premise of the film in the first graph of his piece because they did not want Katie to have to say the words 'fired' or 'laid-off.' The piece ended up not airing—but because news got in the way, *not* because Katie realized how insensitive it would be." A female senior staffer says the widespread feeling was: "Les has to have his head examined!" Even when CBS had known bad fiscal days were coming, "they hired *her* for fifteen million!"

WHILE DIANE WAS fine-tuning her show during its first year, she explained the stories in practical terms, and her injection of a citizen-eye-level service component came to be its leitmotif. Executive producer Jon Banner would call her practice of having correspondents sit at her desk and converse with her "experiential broadcasting; she was an advocate for the viewer." When the BP oil spill happened in April 2010, "she was really driving our coverage and was reminding our audience—on a daily basis, with *passion*—how much oil was spilled" and how that spillage was affecting the fishermen and the community. Once, while home visiting her mother in Louisville, she encountered a neighbor who stepped off a curb and broke her femur; she came back and talked to the medical editor— and ended up doing an investigative segment on a drug that was supposed to increase bone strength but, under certain circumstances, when taken by older women, actually made bones more brittle.

TV cognoscenti would marvel that, by 2010, onetime Morning Katie had become all business while formerly restrained Diane was now acting like your neighbor and leading with her heart. As Andrew Heyward says, "If you'd arrived here from Mars and were told, 'Here's a quiz: One is a regal news superstar and the other is the girl next door. Here are the evening news scripts. Match them,' you would fail."

In mid-October, when thirty-three Chilean miners were rescued alive after sixty-nine days trapped underground—the longest successful rescue operation ever—Diane devoted exceptional airtime and passion to the story of the valor of the miners and the rescue team. As the daughter of a historic mining community, she felt an emotional tug. Still, even beyond that, a lesson—that people's character *matters*—seemed to inspire her to dwell on the story, according to Andrew Tyndall, who drew a far-reaching conclusion about her worldview, even her politics. "No evening newscast dedicated more time and resources to the event than ABC's *World News with Diane Sawyer*," Tyndall wrote in his newsletter, and the "human nature" rather than "public policy" angle was behind the appeal of the story for her.

Tyndall continued:

Her enthusiasm for the Chilean story—and the lessons she learned from it—vindicates this analysis. It is a commonplace . . . to refer to Fox News as the conservative network. Yet Fox is as committed as any liberal to the concept that . . . governments and institutions are both the causes and the potential solutions of society's problems [while a] conservative is skeptical that the human condition is susceptible to social engineering. Sawyer is the true conservative. For her the world is personal, not programmatic, inspirational, not partisan.

Diane was not politically conservative—her politics were intriguingly vague ("My husband has said he doesn't know my politics," Diane recently said)—but Tyndall had caught something in her character that went all the way back to childhood and that validated her mother's values.

Meanwhile, over this whole second six months of Diane's anchorship, and unbeknownst to her, a potentially power-upending development was in the works behind the scenes. In Los Angeles, "Ben Sherwood quietly approached" Anne Sweeney, the president of ABC, says a friend of Sherwood's, and suggested himself as someone who could help Sweeney find a replacement for David Westin. Westin was being eased out of his news division presidency, people in the know believe, even though this wasn't officially acknowledged. ("His relationship with Diane had cooled dramatically," says a senior staffer, positing this as one possible reason for the easing out.) "Ben's a very good student; he learned from the best—Diane," this friend says. Another insider describes what happened: Brian Grazer, the producer with whom Ben's wife, Karen Kehela, worked, called top Disney ABC boss Bob Iger "and got Ben into the process as a consultant" to Sweeney for the purpose of discreetly finding a new president. Producer David Doss's name had been bandied about. But Doss was known to have an explosive temper. "And then Ben did a Dick Cheney," the insider says, referring to how George W. Bush's vice president self-chose himself when he'd first been tasked with heading up the search team. The Sherwood friend uses the identical coinage: "He Dick Cheney'd himself in"—he suggested *himself* for the job. "And I would imagine that one of the selling points with Anne was that Ben had a long history with Diane but now wasn't beholden to Diane." Things had changed since his involuntary leaving of *GMA* years earlier. The friend puts it bluntly: "With Ben, I don't think he gives a rat's ass" about what Diane wanted or wants. "I don't think he cares."

Ben Sherwood had been Diane's intern, then her staffer, then her executive producer. She had been responsible for his dismissal. Now he was her boss.

In December 2010, exactly a year after she came on as anchor of *ABC World News*, Ben Sherwood replaced David Westin as president of ABC

News. The insider felt then and feels now, "Ben's gonna stick it to her. She will pay dearly. She might have met her match in Ben."

One week after this revelation, Diane received equally startling news but of a far more personal and tragic nature: Richard Holbrooke suddenly died. Holbrooke—by now the Obama administration's special representative for Afghanistan and Pakistan—had taken ill at a meeting with Secretary of State Hillary Clinton and had been rushed to the hospital with a tear in his aorta. Twenty-four hours of surgery could not heal the wound. "He was such a pivotal part of her growth and formation," says one who worked with her. "He wasn't just a boyfriend" before Mike. "He was for years her primary counsel. She'd relied on him.

"David Westin had a series of [farewell] dinners with the anchors and Diane didn't go. I'm told she was completely devastated" by Holbrooke's death. In her subsequent memoir *Paris: A Love Story*, Holbrooke's widow, Kati Marton, wrote of how, at Holbrooke's memorial service at the Kennedy Center, "I noticed a tall, blond woman, alone and hunched inside her black coat—Diane Sawyer, Richard's partner for many years before I came into his life. She had written me the briefest and most generous note. 'At the core of Richard Holbrooke,' Diane wrote, 'was his deep love for you.' I walked over to say thank you. Tears were streaming down her face and we exchanged a wordless embrace." Diane had been charming and tactful with that note, some people thought—for, they believed, *she* had been the great love of his life.

CHRISTIANE MADE A major move—to New York City—in 2008. Sure, she had lived there back in the late eighties when she was doing weekend reporting on the Coney Island hot dog–eating contests and rooming with Liza McGuirk, but now she was coming back as probably the most well-known and well-regarded foreign correspondent in the world.

Her tenure started out auspiciously. She and Jamie were swept into an influential social circle—she was a hero; powerful people wanted to be her friend. The pair became close friends with D.C. social maven Sally Quinn and her husband, legendary *Washington Post* eminence Ben Bradlee, and with ABC president Robert Iger and his wife, newscaster Willow Bay. While a producer with whom Christiane would soon work believes she continued to want to go out into the field as a reporter—"I think she missed the traveling but was excited about trying something new"— another whose path she would cross believes, "She wanted the anchor's life now. She didn't want to spend her entire adult life in shit holes. She wanted to be home with her family and go to parties at Bob Iger's house."

Indeed, a CNN person who was in on discussions between Christiane and the top executives at the network, and in discussions among the executives themselves, characterized her and their goals this way: "Christiane had put in her time as a frontline correspondent. She had been extremely courageous—physically courageous. And now, having done that for twenty years, she deservedly felt it was time to morph into the next phase of her career. To [us at CNN] that meant doing documentaries, which we had had her start to do." This person is referring, of course, to the *God's Warriors* series, as well as the important documentary she was determinedly preparing for the network on a subject deeply important to her reporter's heart: genocide. (The documentary aired in December 2008, timed to coincide with the sixtieth anniversary of the United Nations convention to prevent genocide and punish its perpetrators.) "She's primarily a reporter in the field," this person continues. "But in *her* mind that meant sort of retiring into a position as a grand dame interviewer." *Grand dame* interviewer? It is a bit startling that Christiane's desire to be an interviewer was described, by people within her home network, with such aspersion. Sure, she had a certain hauteur. But her abidingly serious work would seem to render even low-key snark unfair.

Being an interviewer was "her dream job," this person continues, and she was "driven by [the fact that] she's got a child now; she doesn't want to risk her life. That's certainly justifiable. It makes perfect sense. But the thing is that being a great interviewer is an entirely different skill from being a field correspondent." Murrow and Cronkite and Jennings, of course, had made the leap. But the times were different, not to mention the fact that network dynamics were different for men in that male-dominated world. Christiane had spent her best—her strongest—years outside the system. She had defied Walter Isaacson (who was no longer the president of CNN; now Jonathan Klein was); she had let her stories run overlength. In malarial dens and overcrowded HIV wards and Taliban football fields and mass murderers' putrid prisons, she'd done her thing—boldly, bravely, with little interference. She had done all this from thousands of miles away from cubicled offices. Coming into the world of suits and office politics—a world she'd last encountered years before by way of fights with Jeanee von Essen, the world that Diane and Katie had *always* navigated, in their very different and differently canny ways—put Christiane at a disadvantage she may have forgotten about, or perhaps she even may have felt above.

The thinking at CNN was that being a "great interviewer" meant being an "analyst, someone who helps us understand *why* things happen. That's different from being a person who stands at the front line and tells us what *is* happening," the CNN representative continues. "Christiane was great at the latter. No one was better. She was great at getting there, and chasing the rabbit—riding along the way" of a galloping international news story. "What was required now, if you're going to shift into a different specialty, you have to *learn* the specialty. It's a different set of skills." In other words, the CNN executives were deliberating about her desire for her "dream job" and privately concluding that Christiane would have to, figuratively speaking, "go back to school."

Meanwhile, for the final installment in the *God's Warriors* series—"Buddha's Warriors"—Christiane interviewed the Dalai Lama, flying to India, where he has lived openly since he fled Tibet in the 1950s. Just as the interview was beginning, all the power went out in a thunderstorm. As they all sat in darkness, "the Dalai Lama lets out the biggest laugh," says Andrew Tkach, who produced the segment. The CNN team interpreted the laugh as: *"This is God's will!"* Christiane was taken by how the Dalai Lama "mesmerized" his followers. But the message of the impeccably timed thunderstorm, the power outage, the total darkness, and the fecklessness of destiny might have augured her own fate: Once she returned to New York, she would not get the CNN "dream job" she wanted.

While Christiane was doing "Buddha's Warriors," CNN hired Fareed

Zakaria, the young Mumbai-born Harvard PhD who had been the managing editor of *Foreign Affairs* and the editor of *Newsweek International*, to be its one p.m. Sunday news analyst. One o'clock Sunday was the perfect hour for a CNN news analysis show—you'd get the news-interested viewers coming off the morning major network news roundups (*Meet the Press*, *This Week*, and *Face the Nation*) and the noon replay of *State of the Nation*. The executives were very impressed with Zakaria's ability to, as one puts it, "listen to disparate strands and then come up with his own insight."

Management broke down the differences between the two this way: "Christiane's famous for going out, being *on* the story, while Fareed is parallel in his ability to sit in his office and pull together—synthesize—the underlying meaning of those events. She knows her subject very well, but she doesn't approach these stories in an intellectual way. Like [that of] many foreign correspondents, her knowledge is experiential but it's not analytical. Great foreign correspondents love to be the witness—they have to have the front-row seats at these events—but they don't want to spend a hell of a lot of time chewing them over; they want to go on to the next one."

Christiane was angered by their reasoning. "She didn't buy this explanation that he was great at what he does and that she does something entirely different," continues the person who heard the management conversations. She was very offended that we had hired him to do what she saw as her dream job." Her attitude was: "'Why did they hire him and not me?'"

Further, she didn't buy management's patronizing view that "none of us ever doubted that she would be able to master" the kind of news analysis that Zakaria was doing, "but it was going to take work." To someone who had risked her life all over the world—as Zakaria had *not* done—the idea of this vague additional "work" in the total safety of a studio must have seemed absurd, if not insulting. At least some in management viewed her attitude as arrogant and entitled, an appraisal that would likely not have been the case with a man. "It was difficult for her to imagine" that this one p.m. news analysis spot "wasn't just going to be handed to her. She would say things like, 'Do you know that I'm the world's best-known foreign correspondent?' And, 'I'm extremely well known all around the world.'" The response from management: "'Yes, we know. You're Christiane Amanpour—we all get that.'" Management's sense remained that "in order to maintain that thing that stands for excellence and reliability and accuracy, you've got to work it."

Clearly, this infuriated Christiane. "She wanted her prime-time, agenda-setting show on CNN in the U.S.—where all America would watch her." The executives had "no doubt she would get there." But, continues the insider, they "wanted first to see her learn, to make her mistakes in a low-wattage environment—*in the back*."

As part of that "in the back," Christiane was offered a daily half-hour show on CNN International, which would be broadcast only overseas, and she was also offered a "compilation" show on American CNN, on Sunday afternoon at two, right after Zakaria. Both shows would be called *Amanpour*. The U.S. show would weave together the best of her daily international shows. Both shows would debut in 2009.

It took a long time for Christiane to find the right executive producer. She and CNN talked to what someone in the process recalls as "a long line of people—a *lot* of different people—for months," starting in November 2008. Finally, in late March 2009, she chose the highly experienced Kathy O'Hearn, who had gone from CNN to ABC and had recently left executive producing George Stephanopoulos's *This Week* to work on ABC's 2008 election team. Kathy was a friend of Christiane's new friend Willow Bay, and Kathy and Christiane had worked together, via international phone line, when Christiane was in Afghanistan and Kathy was producing *American Morning*. (Christiane had authoritatively told Kathy what time slot her piece would run in, brooking no disagreement.)

Kathy immediately sensed the challenging newness—everyone did. "Christiane had done just about everything under the sun, but she had not anchored a show. She had anchored from war zones, she had done specials, but she had not anchored a regular daily talk show." Another producer puts it more negatively: "She's remarkable at what she *used* to do. Everybody gets her doing *that*." Would they get her doing *this*? This producer privately thought, and says some others shared the thought: "She's not really an American anchor."

384 THE NEWS SORORITY

Many things about the pending new CNN *Amanpour* shows were not ideal. "Two o'clock was a horrible time" for Sunday, Kathy O'Hearn says. By that time, after all the morning politics and policy shows, people were already off doing Sunday errands; they'd had enough TV. But she and Christiane didn't fight the unfortunate time slot—"we knew we weren't in a position to get one p.m. But we *did* fight to do it live. CNN wanted us to prerecord the shows because it would save money. But Christiane was very fierce about making sure we got to do it live, which is what gave it such a powerful vitality."

So already, in mid-2009, Christiane was not getting what she felt she deserved from the network for which she had done so much: She was being told she had to "work" to learn to be an analyst. She lost the prized one p.m. slot to Zakaria, whose live round-table-style show—touted by CNN as a "weekly global get-together," with Fareed "boiling down, without dumbing down, complex issues"—was similar enough to hers that it was reasonable to worry that she'd feel redundant to viewers. And she had to fight to get her daily and weekly shows live. Management felt enthusiastic about her Sunday time slot: She would inherit "the perfect audience," the insider recalls their thinking. "Anybody who's watching Fareed and liking Fareed would stick around for Christiane's show." But Christiane felt that *she*, not Zakaria, was the main draw.

Still, despite these setbacks, Kathy says she found Christiane's attitude to be very positive. Having encountered the my-way-or-the-highway Christiane several years earlier, "I was surprised at how warm and welcoming she was," Kathy says. "And how it was very much 'just between us girls.' And she wanted to include everyone on the staff at editorial meetings. If it was an intern who said, 'Shouldn't we be doing this story?,' she wanted to hear it."

And Jamie, too, was involved in the show's preparation. "He was almost a member of the staff," O'Hearn says. "The week before the launch, we were over at her house, the whole team brainstorming over bagels. Jamie would float in and say, 'No, that doesn't make any sense,' and then he'd float out for an hour, and then he'd come back in, sit down, and listen." (He continued to be hands-on after the show started broadcasting.

"He'd call the control room and say, 'Hey, Christiane just mistakenly called the foreign minister the finance minister.'")

Bringing international news to Americans—news that educated State-siders felt they needed to know but couldn't curate and assess on their own—was the point of *Amanpour*. "She was excited about changing the concept of a Sunday show to be a bigger embrace of international news," says O'Hearn. "She wanted to analyze the way power was perceived and wielded, and to be a passionate voice for women across the globe. And children—she was always touched by the children. She wanted to give a voice to the disenfranchised. She's *fierce* about exposing injustices. It's not a false posturing. It's real."

BOTH SHOWS LAUNCHED IN SEPTEMBER, and in advance of them Christiane appeared in TV promotions that simultaneously promoted the network itself. Over dramatic music there was a shot of a distressed baby. Then came her half-screen-wide face—the hair styling and makeup that hadn't been part of her previous image made her freshly glamorous at fifty-one—staring into the viewers' eyes. In her passionate, authoritative voice, she intoned: "You have seen the destruction caused by natural disasters. Witnessed the atrocities of war. You have listened to world leaders and leaders who want to rule the world. You have heard from men of God and men who kill in God's name. Gazed into eyes filled with hope and seen hearts consumed with hopelessness. With CNN, you have followed the facts from around the world. Come with me and see where the story takes us next."

On September 15, the day before the show aired, Christiane appeared on Stephen Colbert, in what would become her post-down-parka uniform: smart dark blazer over crisp white shirt. Colbert raved about her exotic last name. She demurred that "it was a name that I was once told would never make it to television." No! he countered. Her name was like "cozying up with a snifter of brandy in a Swiss chalet!" She said, of her new venture, "This is dangerous. This is scary." She wasn't kidding. *War zones* were her territory.

Though O'Hearn felt she had "Scotch-taped" together the best of the daily international shows to make the weekend U.S. show, it did not feel like a compendium. With Christiane live at her sleek new desk emblazoned with "AMANPOUR," the viewers received a digest of what and who was important in the world that week. In a sense, Sunday *Amanpour* was like *Omnibus*, the Ford Foundation–sponsored Sunday TV show hosted by Alistair Cooke between 1952 and 1961, or, more recently, the *MacNeil/Lehrer News Hour*, which turned into the *PBS News Hour*: a program meant to educate Americans about serious issues. In *Amanpour*'s case, she also introduced them to opinion-givers they might not know. Aside from foreign policy experts and world leaders, Christiane liked to interview little-known female heroes of the developing world, such as Liberian peace activist and Nobel Peace Prize winner Leymah Gbowee, as well as activist American women journalists on international issues, such as Amy Wilentz on Haiti. She also featured and conversed with underexposed young Iranian American women, like Farnaz Fassihi, the award-winning journalist for the *Wall Street Journal*; Shirin Neshat, the filmmaker and activist who had recently gone on a three-day hunger strike at the UN to protest the Iranian elections; Azadeh Moaveni, the author of *Lipstick Jihad* and *Honeymoon in Tehran*; as well as *très* hip, gay Muslim reform advocate Irshad Manji, a kind of Rachel Maddow for Islam, with whom Christiane engaged in a standing-room-only conversation at Manhattan's temple of talk, the 92nd Street Y. In fact, for younger Iranian Americans in the media—both women and men—who had repatriated to the United States as children with their parents after the Revolution, "Christiane was a role model for us," says Karim Sadjadpour, a young man who is an analyst at the Carnegie Endowment. "Most Iranians we saw were doctors, engineers, pharmacists. But Christiane was on television! So it was, 'Yeah!' You would call your cousins: 'Turn on CNN!' She was like Madonna!"

During the Sunday show's first week on the air, "when there was still an air of mild chaos," Kathy recalls, Christiane nevertheless came out swinging. The show scored a major, volatile get: an interview with Robert Mugabe, the prime minister of Zimbabwe, who was responsible for the killings of ten thousand to twenty thousand people. "Mugabe hadn't done an interview in about twenty-five years. Why on earth he agreed to an interview with Christiane, of all people, I'll never know!" Kathy says. "He came in with a really scary contingent of men in uniforms, and they stood around the studio in a way that was meant to be intimidating." But Christiane "pinned him to the wall," repeatedly questioning him about the political foe who'd been jailed without cause. Mugabe was "angry and uncomfortable and flummoxed and dumbstruck. *He could not answer.* Sitting in the control room, I almost started to feel bad for him. It was an incredibly dramatic moment."

Others followed, the tough alternating with the inspiring. Elias Khoury, a Palestinian whose son, a Hebrew University student, had been killed by a Palestinian terrorist while jogging, was honoring his son by funding an Arabic translation of Israeli author Amos Oz's novel *A Tale of Love and Darkness.* Christiane had Khoury and Oz on the show together, but her blunt questioning made the meeting far more than a mere feel-good hour.

In other shows she grilled Ehud Barak, Hamid Karzai, Tony Blair, Tzipi Livni, and representatives of countries from the Caribbean to Eastern Europe to Africa. "We did topics that nobody else was covering," says Kathy. "The secession of South Sudan from Sudan. The looming global water crisis. Sexual slavery in India. The selling of wives in India." Christiane had brought her decade and a half of fieldwork into the studio.

Was the show a little too worthy, a bit too wholesome for Americans to flip on after brunch? Christiane's voice was unalloyed, erudite English—was there an intimidation factor there? "It was very successful in a quiet way in the States," O'Hearn says, pointing to an industry index—the C3—that tabulates how long people stay with a program through commercials, and how much it's DVR'd. "It had incredible numbers that way, and it was a blow-away hit overseas."

But "overseas" didn't count so much, and management saw things differently. "Her show, creatively, was not that strong in the beginning. She wasn't that comfortable as an interviewer," says one who listened to the executive conversations. "The ratings were pretty weak. She was not growing her audience off of her lead-in. And her show was either losing viewers from Fareed's show or she was holding flat and Fareed's audience was slightly growing. So it wasn't impressive ratings-wise, but that was okay." Management "never, ever gave her a hard time." They did things "to tweak the show." They were confident it would improve.

But Christiane, says this source, blamed her placement after Zakaria's show for the problems. "She began insisting that it was because of the lead-in—it was wrong to put these two shows back-to-back; people were tired of foreign news by the time her show came on."

While these conversations were going on, the *Amanpour* staff threw a surprise fifty-second birthday party for their boss. They made a secret gag reel. "We took the Beatles tape, 'You say it's your birthday,' and we wore ridiculous hats and danced around, mouthing the words. We found footage of her from when she first started at CNN, with those huge-shoulder-padded jackets. We put those in. We had her son, Darius, in there playing air guitar. Then we surprised her. We brought her into the morning meeting and said, 'Christiane, you have to look at this tape first, it's a big problem—Atlanta is saying we can't use it.' She said, 'I don't have time.' But we insisted. Then the crazy birthday tape played. It was hilarious. She laughed out loud. She was really touched. It was a perfect birthday." And fitting for a pioneer at the network for over a quarter of a century.

But that affection didn't translate into any moves by management to elevate her exposure. Zakaria was promoted from his one p.m. slot to ten a.m.: the star spot, right there with the major Sunday shows. Why? "Fareed had been on the air about a year and a half before Christiane came. The thinking was, 'Okay, Fareed has worked out his kinks—he's gaining momentum. It was the most DVR'd show on our schedule, and that was a sign that the audience really didn't want to miss it. So let's create more opportunities for the thing to be seen.

"Christiane was *flabbergasted*." The CNN insider says that her attitude was: "'Why aren't I getting that time? Here's this man—he's an interloper—and I've been at the network so long!'" They tried to soothe her by saying her show would improve as Zakaria's had improved; "it was only a matter of time." But there were other considerations, too. While she'd been doing her specials and documentaries, others had become stars.

Again, the CNN source says the sense was: "She's an iconic figure, but, at the same time, the biggest international stories of late, where we had really distinguished ourselves—the Haiti earthquake, the first tsunami, the famine in Niger—she was at the periphery. It was Anderson Cooper. It was Sanjay Gupta. Soledad O'Brien—those were the people who were getting on the planes there. And they were doing a phenomenal job."

Something had gone wrong. To an idealistic outsider, Christiane seemed to have a stellar career trajectory—combining network loyalty and years of unparalleled international reporting—that would have resulted in a just reward: a favored-time anchorship. By contrast, Peter Jennings's career was an example of what could go *right*. He'd been an international reporter who made it into the most prestigious anchorship, at six thirty p.m., way back in 1983, a post he'd kept until slightly before his death twenty-two years later. The two were similar in many ways: Christiane instinctively preferred war reporting to desk work; so did Jennings, says one who knew him well. Christiane was thought by some at New York's CNN to be "imperious," and that rubbed them the wrong way. Peter Jennings was undisguisedly imperious, but that had done him no harm; in fact, his hauteur awed normally cynical male producers and intimidated seasoned female news stars. Christiane was criticized for being insufficiently sympathetic to Israel—a long-standing beef against Jennings, but one that never hurt him. Jennings's former producer Paul Friedman says that Jennings was "a perfect mixture of all the things you need to be a successful anchor. He was knowledgeable, authoritative, credible, handsome, spoke beautifully, maintained his calm under pressure, was able to orchestrate coverage of live events unscripted. And he knew so much. He read voraciously, he took notes voraciously." And he was invaluably connected to international leaders, especially in the Middle East. Most of those qualities could be ascribed to Christiane, who, after all, merely had her eye on a far more modest goal: the one p.m. Sunday slot on CNN.

Especially given her moderate goal, Christiane felt "dismissed"—and this, people at CNN saw, "really rankled her." But CNN management's tin ear toward their longtime prestige reporter left an opening for other suitors. What CNN's executives may have been too cavalier or literal-minded about, Christiane's friends Willow Bay and Bob Iger were reverential toward. CNN's insults to Christiane became a great opportunity for ABC to make a bold hire.

In March came a blast of media-world news: Christiane was hired away from CNN to host ABC's *This Week*, taking over from Stephanopoulos. Her choice as the host of a show that was overwhelmingly national rather than international was widely termed "surprising." She would be the first woman ever to solo anchor any of the major network Sunday morning talk shows, with the fascinating exception of the person who invented the genre, little-known broadcast pioneer Martha Rountree, who turned radio's *The American Mercury*, which she had created, into TV's *Meet the Press* in the medium's infancy: 1947.

Christiane would be the first female solo of a Sunday morning news roundup show in sixty-three years.

When CNN staffers heard that Christiane would be leaving, they were, one says, bereft. As for the sense among the executives, the management insider says: "ABC really wanted her. It was a big risk, but she believes in herself in a big way. And to her credit, she said, 'You know, I'm gonna take a chance.'" Management "totally understood [and] didn't want to get into a pitched battle over salaries." It wasn't quite "Don't let the door hit you on the way out," but it certainly sounded as if they weren't willing to fight for her.

In contrast to CNN's permissive if blasé attitude, Christiane herself was very emotional about leaving CNN. A beat after the news went public, Christiane wrote this poignant private e-mail to her colleagues:

> To My Family at CNN,
> I am stunned and humbled by all your words and thoughts and good wishes. I have been bobbing on a tide of poignancy, enveloped in the amazing outpouring of love and affection from my friends and family at the place I call home.
> For nearly 27 years it has not just been a privilege but an unparalleled pleasure . . . a great, rollicking, earth-shaking,

world-shaping adventure . . . to be part of CNN, which is not just a company but an institution that has changed the very way we live. From the beginning the excitement was overwhelming as Ted Turner strode around declaring, "I WAS CABLE BEFORE CABLE WAS COOL."

And then boldly exhorted the establishment arrayed against him to "Lead, follow or get out of the way." He led, we followed and the rest had to get out of the way!

From being shut out of the first White House stake-outs 30 years ago to the barely met payrolls, CNN and all of us, the army of true believers, did what no one ever imagined one organization could do, pioneering, transformative, indispensable to this day.

From the very first day I walked into the newsroom at Techwood, September 1983, I have been proud to climb the ladder CNN put in front of me, every hard-won step of the way. Not just proud, but thrilled to bits. I feel truly fortunate to belong to the most supportive, amazing, dedicated and inspiring people from the leadership to my colleagues in every corner of the company.

I never get tired of recalling the heart-stopping events we have all covered and brought to the world, from the Wall coming down, to the first Gulf War.

She wrote movingly of how she'd found her calling—and the depths of colleagueship in Bosnia, where she'd learned to

never never wav[er] from the mission: to report the truth, no matter how difficult and dangerous; to be the eyes and ears of our viewers in the United States and around the world, to tell people's stories and be a constructive and positive force in society, a force that tries to make a difference.

That's what CNN is, that is what I am so proud to have been part of, proud to have helped shape. And happy to have had so much fun all along the way.

That's the mission I have been trying to continue with my phenomenal team at our eponymously named program here. So why am I leaving? In my heart I am not. This has been the most difficult of decisions. I am simply taking the next challenging and difficult but exciting step. I believe more than anything that knowledge and familiarity with important international news and events abroad are fundamental to Americans today. This rare chance to take international news to a broader base here in the United States is one that I felt I could not turn down. I will take everything I have learned, and loved, here at CNN and put it into action!

And the network I love will have you, your hard work, your heart, your vision and your faith. Keep doing CNN's important work, without which the world would most definitely be a poorer place. Never forget who you are. Never forget what CNN is. Never forget how we all together changed the world.

From the bottom of my heart I thank you all, and I say only "au revoir," not goodbye,

Christiane

And so by the beginning of autumn 2010, two of the three solo evening anchors were women, and one of the three Sunday morning solo hosts was a woman. That was three out of six when, five years earlier, there had been none.

Richard Wald, who'd watched all the changes over the decades, thought Brian Williams—the now minority male at six thirty—"had a great line" he used when he talked about his profession to credulous young students and cheerlead them past ambition-stanching stereotypes in the process. Patronizingly exaggerated though it may have been, Williams had said "I want to tell schoolchildren, 'You *don't* have to be a girl to be an anchor.'"

CHRISTIANE'S DEBUT ON *THIS WEEK*—now renamed *This Week with Christiane Amanpour*—on August 1, 2010, was met with a complicated and hard-to-parse early reaction. She placed a decent if not stirring second of three major Sunday morning network shows among the highly valued twenty-five to fifty-four demographic. Yet, factoring in other viewer age groups, her show was in *last* place.

The early reviews were polarized. Alessandra Stanley, who had earlier evinced almost gleeful ridicule for Katie and mild contempt for Diane, approved of Christiane's "panache and a no-nonsense briskness," and termed it refreshingly welcome in this more genial, schmoozy context. In her *New York Times* review titled "A TV Host Challenges a Guest. That's News," Stanley applauded Christiane for holding up the discomfiting *Time* magazine cover of Bibi Aisha, the young Afghan woman whose nose and ears had been cut off by her husband, while sharply demanding of guest Leader of the House Nancy Pelosi, "Is America going to abandon the women of Afghanistan?" This was Christiane throwing out her global feminist red meat. This was also Christiane treating Pelosi with the same scolding bravado she'd so effectively (and name-makingly) visited on Bill Clinton over Bosnia. Stanley noted Pelosi's being "startled" and giving "fractured, politic answers" to the new host's defiant challenge. And, citing the conventional wisdom purveyors' "surprise" and "negative" reactions to internationalist Christiane's selection for *This Week*, Stanley saluted her freshness and intelligence. "Ms. Amanpour is not an election expert and hasn't spent her life covering Washington politics, but she is smarter than many of those who have," Stanley declared, with comradely defiance.

On the opposite end of the opinion spectrum, the *Washington Post*'s Tom Shales seized on Christiane's deficits with a sarcastic vengeance. Calling her "The Grand Duchess Amanpour from her Royal Barge Overseas" and describing aspects of her debut show as "ludicrous," he assayed: "With pomp and panoply befitting a visit from a foreign dignitary, ABC raised the curtain on its newly revamped *This Week* program and introduced in a big way the superstar . . . Christiane Amanpour, veteran CNN foreign correspondent now uneasily relocated to a desk job." He called her "miscast" for the role, her "highly touted global orientation coming across as inappropriate and contrived" on a longtime domestic-issues show.

The media gossips also took shots. Christiane, just yesterday an above-it-all global heroine, became fodder for the Beltway natterers. The *New York Post* wrote: "The knives are out for Christiane Amanpour at ABC News' D.C. bureau. Since the ex-CNN war correspondent began anchoring *This Week* in August, she's upset some co-workers by being a 'distant outsider,'" sources said. Anonymous sources ripped into her for her aloofness: "It's not like other war zones that you can parachute into. She is very cold and distant with the other bureau staff." Others complained about her lack of experience covering U.S. politics.

Christiane's shows seemed to oscillate according to her strengths and weaknesses. The controversy surrounding the proposed construction of an Islamic community center very near the site of the destroyed World Trade Center—the Ground Zero Mosque, as the project was called—afforded her the chance to present, in early October, as close to a healthy fight as one ever sees on TV. With nine guests—from conservative Christians to a conservative imam, to an Iranian intellectual who fled the Ayatollah and a young Muslim-turned-Christian-turned-Muslim scholar, to an American anti-Islamist, to two parents of 9/11 victims with two different positions, to the liberal imam sponsoring the mosque and his wife, an American Muslim feminist—Christiane confidently rode herd over the frankest town hall imaginable, and one in which, even though things got emotional, every speaker had a valid argument. Right-wing Web sites, which had had it in for Christiane for years, called the program biased, but it was bracingly multisided, genuinely thought-provoking, and strikingly cosmopolitan. Only she could have curated such a palate of speakers and moderated it aggressively and deftly to its Emmy-nominated acuity.

On the other hand, Christiane's January 2011 show after Gabrielle Giffords was shot displayed her at a disadvantage. Though her interview with the eyewitness intern Daniel Hernandez was strong, gathering together and chatting with other, secondary witnesses showed that transplanted *Morning* was *not* her métier. She tried too hard. She wasn't natural. Without intending to, she sounded too high-toned to have what was essentially a space-filling, bread-and-butter human interest conversation with regular Joe and Jane residents of the mall-strewn American Southwest.

Eventually Rick Kaplan was called over from CBS to ABC to save *This*

Week with Christiane Amanpour. Kaplan, of course, had EP'd for Diane at *Primetime*, and then he'd been called in to save Katie's CBS broadcast. With Kaplan's rehiring at ABC, some women producers privately— angrily—marveled that hot-tempered executive producers like Kaplan and similarly ever employed David Doss (neither man was shy about screaming at staff) continued to get reemployed, whereas the talented Shelley Ross, who had boosted *GMA*'s numbers to near parity with *Today*, had been doggedly implied as "difficult" in Page Six items.

AS FOR THE GABRIELLE GIFFORDS STORY, it would be Diane who came to "own" it, interviewing the recovering hero congresswoman and her astronaut husband Mark Kelly with animated, empathetic ease. Later that year, *World News with Diane Sawyer* kicked off a series, "Made in America." Correspondents went out into the heartland, finding factories and companies that were creating jobs. For two holiday seasons in a row— 2011 and 2012—Diane and her correspondents launched a campaign: If every American spent just sixty-four dollars more on items with the "Made in America" label, Diane told her viewers, two hundred thousand new jobs could be created in the United States. Producers at other networks weren't sure if this was sweet-spot hitting for a financially depressed America—or if it was jingoistic. Viewers liked it, and they liked Diane, who gave up little of her glamour to be the purveyor of both hard news *and* empowering service. But still she lagged behind Brian Williams. And Katie lagged behind both of them.

It was hard not to think that Brian Williams's being a man—and the hand-picked Brokaw heir (both all-American, handsome, genial)—had something to do with his abiding fortune, ever since he assumed the NBC anchor chair in December 2004. Williams was a consummate pro, to be sure. And, yes, he was self-assured and very likable. And his coverage of Hurricane Katrina had won him and his team a Peabody Award. But his tone was slightly unctuous. Those who felt Diane was too creamy would— if they were being honest—have a hard time disputing that Williams was close to a male equivalent. Like Katie, Brian Williams was "real." He goofed around. With NBC's blessing, and help, he had cultivated an enter-tainment persona (Katie had cultivated hers on her own), by way of not only comic stints on Tina Fey's TV-news-spoofing sitcom *30 Rock* but also guestings on *Leno* and *Late Night with Jimmy Fallon.* Yet people didn't criticize him for that, as they had criticized Katie.

Furthermore, Williams's résumé was significantly lighter than Di-ane's years of serious social justice investigatives and her enormous bank of international leader interviews, and it was lighter than Katie's output as well. And, unlike Katie, with her overseas work as a Pentagon correspon-dent in Kuwait, Williams had not had international experience before he started to be groomed by NBC to become Brokaw's heir in the mid-1990s. In fact, both Katie and Diane had had longer runs on national TV than Williams had. He had spent midcareer time at local Fox, CBS, and NBC affiliates (in D.C., New Jersey, Philadelphia). Nothing wrong with that, of course. But in the high-barred world of highest-level network TV news, it's not a distinguished career arc. Nor had Brian Williams ever been in the thick of war, unlike Christiane, who chose to throw herself into the dan-gerous mix of many international conflicts.

Still, in 2010, Jon Friedman, the well-regarded media columnist for MarketWatch.com, called Brian Williams the new Walter Cronkite. Fried-man explains, "He has the appeal and gravitas in this century as Cronkite had in the last one," adding that "viewers trust Brian more than any other current anchor, just as people did with Cronkite. The viewers"—judging by the ratings—"clearly respect him. And they like his air of informal-ity," something, apparently, a handsome, confident, high-suburban white male can pull off in network news—even if Katie, with her nightly "Hi," couldn't.

AT THIS SAME TIME that Williams was consolidated well in front of Diane and Katie, Christiane made an effort to wade into the conversation about American politics, not always successfully. Her *This Week* lagged behind David Gregory's *Meet the Press* and Bob Schieffer's *Face the Nation* in the same way that an international show hosted by either of those seasoned, jousting national news relishers would have lagged behind the show Christiane had just left at CNN. *This Week with Christiane Amanpour* "just didn't fly—it was too big a political year," reasons Kathy O'Hearn. "An anchor is not Christiane's natural habitat," Bella Pollen adds. "She's a field reporter—and if they were smarter, they'd send her out more."

MEANWHILE, KATIE'S POOR viewership numbers weren't moving. By late fall 2010, CBS News was buzzing with gossip that Katie had finally pushed too hard against her prime champion, Moonves. Says the CBS man, "She was trying to pressure Les to put [a two-year extension of her contract] on the table." Katie was a great communicator. She lived out loud. Whether or not the two-year extension from CBS was real or mere media bait, the sense within CBS was that Moonves felt she had gone too far in putting that out to the media.

Still, as 2010 turned to 2011, intranetwork politics—as well as national news—was dwarfed by cataclysmic world events. The year 2011 started with massive anti–Hosni Mubarak protests in Cairo. All three women—Katie, Diane, and especially Christiane—were involved in the coverage. But another female journalist was to bear the horrific brunt of a terrible object lesson: what could happen to women reporting crises in anti-Western countries.

At the outset of February, Katie flew to Egypt to cover the momentous events in Tahrir Square during the heady and tumultuous days of the Arab Spring. It was dangerous for reporters. Pro-Mubarak mobs attacked Anderson Cooper—he could be heard saying he'd been "hit" through the crush of assailing bodies who were angry at American newspeople. Cooper reported: "My team were set upon by the crowd. There was no rhyme or reason to it—it was just people looking for a fight, looking to make a point, and punching us." Later that same day, Katie's friends watched, through the TV screen, a similar crowd engulfing Katie as she tried to report into her microphone. "We were nervous," says Katie's cancer charity partner Lisa Paulsen, as the hordes drowned out her words and her feed got cut off. The media site Gawker posted the video, with the caption:

"Here's 'America's Girl,' Katie Couric, narrowly escaping as the mob circles her. Don't threaten our national lady-mascot, Egypt. *Just don't.*"

Christiane was set upon, too—the crowds ran after her crew, shouting anti-American slogans and smashing the windshield of the car in which she was being driven. This was Christiane's meat—she'd been here before, in similarly fraught situations, in the Arab world, in a way that few of her competing colleagues had been. She would pull a scoop out of this, the most defining international story of the season.

When Ron Haviv saw Christiane in Cairo during what both battle-scarred journalists felt was a great moment of democratization, "I got that sense" that she was happy to be in the field again. "I definitely, definitely got that from her," he says. "It was such an uplifting and positive experience. Journalists were literally jumping up and down" at what seemed, at the time, a jubilant sprouting of democracy that had a chance of succeeding.

Mark Phillips knew that Christiane would be the *one* journalist to deliver an interview with the besieged longtime president who was now in the turbulent midst of being overthrown. "She had interviewed Mubarak years before," he recalls, "and she'd walked into the room, and Mubarak, who was a flirt, had said, 'I see you in Bosnia and I see you in Africa and Somalia and now I see you with me!' And she kind of smiled and said, 'Thank you,' which helped. Never in her interviewing did she go after people in a vicious, nasty way." So now, in frenetic Cairo, Mubarek granted her, and her alone, a sit-down. The cameras were not rolling (though still photos emerged of them talking), but the interview was exclusive nonetheless. "The reason he talked to her was because he knew, from all those years of engaging with her, that she never twisted the words," Mark Phillips says.

Emerging from the interview in the palace, Christiane spoke, live, on camera to Diane, who was sitting behind her anchor desk in New York—and America learned the words and sentiments of the suddenly most reviled leader in the region through the conversation between a female news anchor and a female star foreign correspondent. In a dramatic, empathetic voice, Diane announced that Christiane had gotten "into the palace encircled by chaos" and that, in order to get there, she'd had to "move through those rioting thugs in the street, threatening death to the journalists . . . an *incredible* journey on this breaking story."

"Well, it was an extraordinary experience," Christiane picked up, strong-voiced but far less emotional, on feed from Cairo. "Obviously, he is embattled and he hasn't been seen [by the public]. . . . He said, 'I feel strong . . . I will die on Egyptian soil.' He said, 'I'm not fed up and want to retire, but if I retire now there will be chaos, and I am afraid the Muslim Brotherhood will take over." Christiane continued: "When I asked him if he felt betrayed, he did the shrug. He didn't answer one way or another," but he eventually told Christiane that "President Obama didn't understand the culture here."

Diane asked, "What does he think about the violence?"

Christiane replied, "He blamed agitators. . . . He even suggested the Muslim Brotherhood was behind it." He said, "'I'm very unhappy with that violence. I don't like to see Egyptians fighting Egyptians.'"

Christiane's Mubarak scoop—eight days before he forcibly stepped down and the Brotherhood took over the country—incited jealousy within the industry. As her friend David Bernknopf said, "The work she did in Egypt just blew everybody away. There may not be another American reporter who is as well sourced internationally."

"I'm a reporter at heart . . . in the field, not an anchorperson," she admitted to Market Watch's Jon Friedman, explaining the triumph but also articulating her dilemma. She had landed the "dream job" she'd wanted, at a major network. But its primary subject, national news, was *not* her wheelhouse. *This*—international news—was her wheelhouse. But it involved dangerous travel, away from her son.

A week after Christiane's Mubarak interview, a most brutal attack upon another female journalist occurred. Lara Logan was sexually and physically assaulted by multiple men, right in the open, in Tahrir Square. It was a hideous attack. "Suddenly, before I even know what's happening, I feel hands grabbing my breasts, grabbing my crotch, grabbing me from behind," Lara told Scott Pelley on *60 Minutes*. "I think my shirt, my sweater was torn off completely. My shirt was around my neck. I felt the moment that my bra tore . . . and . . . they literally just tore my pants to shreds. I didn't even know that they were beating me with flagpoles and sticks and things, because I couldn't even feel that. . . . The sexual assault was all I could feel . . . their hands raping me over and over and over again. . . . They were tearing my body in every direction at this point, tearing my muscles. And they were trying to tear off chunks of my scalp—they had my head in different directions."

For nearly half an hour Logan put up what fight she could. "I [had] no doubt in my mind that I was in the process of dying," she said. But thinking about her two children at home in Washington helped her focus on staying alive.

That attack gave Christiane serious pause. "It's clearly an appalling thing to have happened. I think it's every woman's nightmare," she said several months later, adding, with a somewhat stiff upper lip: "I am grateful that nothing like that ever happened to me, and I spent my long career covering those kinds of events and much worse."

Logan's attack, as heinous as it was, did not inhibit other women journalists, who were taking the same kinds of risks reporting international stories. "I feel very badly for her, but I don't think she's a martyr because of it," says one female print journalist who has been embedded in Iraq several times. "These are the risks we take. Men in our field take different risks." To have a woman in a situation where she's helping to determine coverage, even at this risk, is an important thing—a leap from the old days when well-meaning Av Westin refused to let female reporters go to Vietnam.

SUFFICIENTLY UNINTIMIDATED by the message of intimidation sent by Lara Logan's vicious rape, Christiane stayed in the Middle East and schemed to get an interview with Libyan leader Muammar Gaddhafi. She wrangled both the Mubarak and Gaddhafi interviews in the middle of—of all things—planning a luncheon, at her Central Park West apartment, for her friend Bella Pollen.

The clash between what Bella has described as Christiane's "two diametrically opposed lifestyles" was rarely more evident. Christiane seemed as intent on hosting the ladies' party (in advance of the publication of Bella's *The Summer of the Bear*) as she was on getting the interviews with the two most despised dictators in the Arab world. It was a marker of her valuing of friendship. The planning had started while Christiane was in Cairo. "She was in a car, literally being shaken by rioters in Egypt," Bella says, "and I was shouting [through the phone], 'The luncheon doesn't matter! We ought to forget the whole thing!' And she said, 'No! I'm going to be there!'"

Then, several weeks after the Mubarak interview, Christiane was in Libya, making efforts to get to Gaddhafi, while insisting to Bella that the luncheon would go on. Bella: "I said, 'This is ridiculous! Stay safe! No one will mind if you cancel when you've got the scoop on Mubarak!'" But Christiane would not be daunted. She did her interview with Gaddhafi, starting her broadcast in a helicopter over Tripoli, then sitting with a virtually unbodyguarded Gaddhafi at a beachfront restaurant on Tripoli's Mediterranean coast. She was face-to-face with the dictator, who, in his trademark brown robe and headgear, was "looking every inch the larger-than-life character he had honed," Christiane said.

She dove right in, asking him about the nine protestors against him who had been shot to death. "They love me! My people love me!" He laughed and scoffed. "But if you say they love you, why are they capturing Benghazi?" she shot back. When she reminded Gaddhafi that the leaders of the United States and Great Britain were asking him to step down, he laughed. She gingerly accused him of using force against his own people. "Your own airline pilots—at least two—have defected," she pressed. He laughed again.

When Bella arrived in New York from London, while continuing to protest about the luncheon, Christiane sent her a message: "'I've found this flight that flies me to London and then Munich and then'"—Bella exaggerates—"'the moon!' Christiane arrived at JFK at three a.m." on the day of the luncheon, "and by seven a.m. she was up and moving tables to seat thirty probably very nice people she'd *never* met before," all the while "simultaneously talking to her network because she got this Gaddhafi exclusive."

.   .   .

RIGHT AFTER THE PRO-DEMOCRACY RIOTS in Egypt came the earthquake and tsunami in Japan, in March. Diane flew to Japan—she was the only evening anchor to report live from the dangerous locale—and she took an inspirational approach with the coverage. With no makeup on, but her face aglow with admiration, she visited a shelter, a maternity hospital, and other sites. The Japanese called this "the storm without pity," she said, on her March 14 broadcast. These resilient people provided a "master class in enduring crisis." She explained that both the Shinto and Confucian faiths placed a premium on the idea of community and that a key phrase in their spiritual teachings was "to come together in one body."

The poetry and philosophy that she had read at the little creek near Seneca High—that "*so* earnest" idealism she'd once mocked in herself—had become embedded in her broadcasts. The accretion of world catastrophes she'd witnessed and reported on had made her broadcasts more, not less, humane, even at the risk of seeming sentimental.

One of her later *GMA* producers thought that she'd been—and has been—hiding her true self on the air. "She fakes being less smart than she is," this person says. "She fakes being more 'feminine' than she is. She fakes being more 'Midwestern' than she is. That JCPenney-shopping white woman who just left the farm and, 'Oooh! Look! I'm telling you the news'? That's *not* Diane Sawyer. She's the most sophisticated, intelligent woman I know. She should be a tough broad on the air. She won't do it." Maybe. But she had found an alter ego or, more likely, pulled up a part of herself, that was equally genuine. She had, indeed, become America's Aunt—America's *glamorous* aunt—and she played that role in Japan when she spoke to a brand-new mother who had gone into labor just as the devastating tremors had hit, and when she marveled at the other young mothers who had patiently waited with their babies "*for three hours*"—her now familiar slow syllables, her admiring emphasis—without complaint. Earnestness and compassion amid tragedy: This was her theme. Many viewers loved Diane. Others thought, as a highly placed female producer at a rival network says, "She'd given up on men." They weren't watching her in great numbers, anyway—she had ceded that territory to Brian Williams and, later, to Scott Pelley as well. This rival female producer concludes, perhaps too sweepingly: "Diane is doing her whole news broadcast for women."

This view dovetailed with what Andrew Tyndall had called Diane's "inspirational" and "spiritual" focus, an assessment essentially seconded by Paul Friedman. Friedman wrote, in the *Columbia Journalism Review,* that "ABC emphasizes stories it considers most relevant to its viewers' lives, plus lighter news and features, in a program built around the dramatic (some say melodramatic) delivery of Diane Sawyer." That's one way to look at it. Another is that Diane, in this story and others, was using a crisis—here, the tsunami—to illustrate the civility that people can muster in the face of difficulty, and thus showcasing the message she had lived herself and that she had exhorted to her despondent friend after his relative's death in the car crash: *"Turn your pain into purpose."*

So Diane was integrating spirituality and service into her broadcast; Christiane had achieved the unsurprising coup of an exclusive interview with the besieged Mubarek; and Katie—fresh from Egypt and rescuscitated by way of the lingering effect of her Palin interviews—was trying to hold on to her anchorship against a steady drumbeat that it was imperiled. They were respectively innovating, successfully competing, and working hard treading water. And each of them was doing so without ratings on their side, and with significant criticism. Reaching the top may have been triumphant, but it was also perilous.

PART FIVE

CANCELLATION

CHAPTER ELEVEN

"Any White Male in the Chair . . ."

Katie, Christiane, and Diane: 2011 to 2014

BY EARLY 2011, Brian Williams at *NBC Nightly News* had eight million viewers, Diane Sawyer at *ABC World News* had seven million, and Katie at *CBS Evening News* had five million. From the beginning of Katie's and then Diane's tenure, Williams was always ahead, even though the focus and quality of the three broadcasts and the three news divisions were almost interchangeably similar.

Paul Friedman says the unrelenting gender and number order was not an accident. "We had research at CBS that made it very, very clear that Katie was suffering because she was a woman. Eighteen to twenty percent of the people, in one of the pieces of research I saw, said they'd never watch a woman anchor the news." "Never" is pretty extreme. Friedman reasons: "There's still a certain proportion of the population that finds that women don't have the credibility." Indeed, Cronkite's producer Sandy Socolow says, "You need some voice from Mount Olympus. That's what's missing now." Socolow doesn't put a gender on that Olympian voice, but many traditional viewers may fill it in as male.

By late 2010, the conventional wisdom around CBS News was that "we could put *any* white male in the chair and get better numbers" than Katie's. So says the CBS man who had had much to say about Katie's rocky entrance to the network. Even a female producer there offers this cynical truth, adding "white man *with white hair*" to the depiction of the ideal anchor. Paul Friedman, again: "[We] believe[d] Scott Pelley would get better ratings than Katie, only because he's a male. He's not necessarily better than she is.

He's not necessarily a better reader. He's not a better *anything*. But he *is* a male, and his ratings should go up." When he replaced Katie, in mid-2011, *CBS Evening News*'s ratings did go up: Within three-quarters of a year of Pelley's becoming anchor, the show gained almost a million viewers.

By mid-2010, much of CBS News management—even those who'd been on shaky ground during Katie's rough passage and had been vindicated by her Cronkite Award—were not averse to getting rid of her. The CBS man: "I had heard rumors that Sean and Paul had wanted her out before [the 2010 midterm] election but that Les had said no. Moonves did not want the controversy of her leaving. But everybody else in the news division was done—*finished*—with her, and her numbers were bad." People were asking, "'Why is she staying?' But Moonves was basically saying no because he was terrified that *he* would be tagged with this failure. It would always be blamed on him."

One person who would not countenance any media games with Katie was Jeff Fager, the highly respected executive producer of *60 Minutes* who had experienced Katie's work on his show and was more than unimpressed. Someone who's worked at *60 Minutes* explains: "He just doesn't like her. If you go to *60*, you can't take it as a sideshow. You can't walk in here like you own the place." Another who worked at the show says: "The rap on her there was: Katie is lazy. She doesn't put out the effort to make a piece better. She won't struggle with you in the edit room, like Diane or Lesley always did. But if something was wrong, Katie would be quick to blame the producer."

In December 2010 it was rumored that Moonves was talking Fager into replacing Sean McManus. Moonves would be giving Fager the job of CBS News first chairman, a position Fager didn't necessarily want, while allowing him to keep his role at his beloved *60 Minutes*. The CBS man: "Apparently what Moonves did was: He was tired of all the stuff with Katie. So he went to Jeff and he said, 'I want CBS run like *60 Minutes*.'" While the talks between Moonves and Fager were apparently taking place—and with *CBS Evening News*'s ratings down to 5.73 million viewers a night (down almost a full 25 percent from when she took over)—an article appeared in Bloomberg News asserting that Katie would be willing to take a pay cut from her $15 million to stay on. Though the unsourced article made it sound as if "both sides" agreed that her salary needed to be reduced, the item seemed to unmistakably come from the Couric camp. Only her spokesman, Matthew Hiltzik, was quoted, saying, "Katie is enjoying herself at CBS and is proud of her award-winning show"; CBS's spokesperson declined to comment. The piece sent the message to the public: It would now be churlish of CBS to not agree with Katie's generous willingness to take a pay cut for a quality show that she loved. It was—almost transparently—a way to pressure CBS into agreeing to renew her contract. Planted items like this were said to have annoyed Moonves, but, nevertheless, it was thought within CBS News, he did not want to appear the heavy or be tagged with her failure.

In February 2011, mere days after Katie returned from Egypt, Jeff Fager was officially named first chairman. The correspondent: "I think what Moonves got with the deal was, 'It's not *my* choice to fire Katie. It's Jeff's.'" In an interview with a trade magazine right after he took the job, Fager—diplomatically and with protective vagueness—said that he didn't know whether Katie wanted to stay on as anchor but that he intended to talk to her about what was "best for both parties." Then, immediately afterward, in his *Daily Beast* column, Howard Kurtz reported that "CBS has asked Katie Couric to stay on as anchor after her lucrative contract expires at the end of May, a source familiar with the situation [says]." Some suspected that the item was floated by Katie's camp. Floated or not, this item was said to really have annoyed Fager. If Katie was behind it, "She made a big mistake doing that to Jeff," says a senior producer. "You don't manipulate Jeff. He does not care"—meaning: He won't play defense against media-lobbed versions of events. "I know Katie wanted to stay—not forever, but through the 2012 election, this person continues." But Fager's ascent seemed to seal her fate. The CBS man says, "Everybody knew: Once Jeff was in, Katie was out. The minute Fager got the job, she was done." "But," says someone from NBC who had not always been her fan, "to defend Katie Couric—and I *will* defend her—*CBS Evening News* was in third place when she got there. And they're still in third place. If CBS News is so great, how come they're in third place? How come the boss of CBS thought they needed Katie Couric to get out of their doldrums? How come, if CBS News was so great, they didn't have anybody to replace Dan Rather? All good questions." Even better questions, perhaps: Since the *CBS Evening News* had won the Murrow Award for Best News Broadcast of 2008 and Best News Broadcast of 2009 (this in addition to Katie's Murrow Award for the Sarah Palin interviews), why were they so eager to dump her?

While plans to let her contract run out were being made, Katie and the media continued to play the it's-*her*-choice game. On March 23 she appeared on David Letterman and he teased her about the signs she was putting out about wanting to leave. The Cronkite-Rather chair was "not like a temp gig," he chided, and the *Los Angeles Times* entertainment blogger credulously assented enough to her scenario to write that "Moonves may not want to be publicly pursuing" Katie, since she "clearly has made [her] mind up" to leave. Meanwhile, the insiders at CBS News felt otherwise: The choice was not Katie's.

It's interesting. In order for Diane to attain the ABC anchor chair, Charlie Gibson had to be out of the way. The story went out that she'd reluctantly taken the job only after Charlie assured Westin he wanted to leave. In a kind of opposite scenario, Katie was, for all intents and purposes, booted by Fager and Moonves, yet the official story was that *she* had left *them*. Two different egos—one with no fingerprints, and the other one, filled with bravado. Two very different women.

In Katie's case, though, there was perhaps more reason than mere pride for her to will that the choice be hers. Her entire career had been based on her nerve and chutzpah. She had broken down doors, sometimes literally. She knew what she wanted—she had chosen for herself. As Rick Kaplan had said, "You can't tell Katie what to do." In this wider context of agency, Moonves's wooing of her for the anchor seat at CBS had been one of the first times she'd let someone *else* choose something for her and at least partly talk her into it. One could say that he'd used her to create an experiment based on three novelties: a solo female six-thirty anchor, a morning star in Cronkite's chair, and an attempt to draw in a more youthful audience. Now that the experiment had failed—and now that her return to her show's prior format had not brought about a sufficient course correction—she was collateral damage in his misbegotten experiment.

Who could blame her for *not* wanting to look passive and tossed aside? She wanted agency, and if she couldn't have it as literal truth, she would take it symbolically, for the sake of her self-esteem, her brand, and for the sake of other women who looked upon her as a pathbreaker.

On April 26, 2011, an exclusive and highly newsbreaking (even if not entirely surprising) piece ran in a publication that Katie had selected. It was bombshell titled: "Katie Couric: I Am Leaving *CBS Evening News.*" "I have decided to step down from the *CBS Evening News,*" Couric announced to the interviewer, with the change going into effect in a month and a half. "I'm really proud of the talented team on the *CBS Evening News* and the award-winning work we've been able to do in the past five years in addition to the reporting I've done for *60 Minutes* and *CBS Sunday Morning.* In making the decision to move on, I know the *Evening News* will be in great hands, but I am excited about the future."

That she made the decision seem as if it had been hers when in fact it had been Fager's and Moonves's is not what bothered the CBS News people; they understood the politics of face-saving and they knew that Katie had one of the best publicists in the business. They also knew she had one of the best instincts for publicity in the business, and that she had pre-rebranded herself for the return to human interest coverage by, just now, publishing a book, *The Best Advice I Ever Got*, a compilation of inspirational, feel-good essays from the people she spent years interviewing, with the proceeds going to charity.

No, what bothered the CBS News people is "that she announced it in *People!*" marvels the CBS man, with a tone of disgust bordering on admiration. Like it or not, Katie had had the nerve to break the stuffy rules of Hallowed News Anchor. She even went further: Perhaps thumbing her nose at "serious" critics whose disapproval had dogged her throughout her five years as *CBS Evening News*'s anchor, she celebrated her departure from the show by capping off her last night as anchor, in May, at a Manhattan karaoke bar. There, she did a rousing performance of "Build Me Up, Buttercup," the anthem of UVA's early preppy parties—"still dressed in a blue power suit," as the *New York Post* pointed out, and fresh from the broadcast, no less. An on-air CBS reporter, speaking for colleagues as well, privately noted, of her choice of song, "That's just about her speed." Katie's in-your-face "owning," as it were, of her sorority-sister past may have been a statement: I am immune to your shortsighted put-downs of me for being insubstantial and perky; in fact, I'll *load* you with evidence for your snobbism—I'll get there *first*.

But the karaoke night told only one side of the story. There was also a sad side to Katie's loss of the anchorship, shared by her and her female colleagues. Three days after the announcement that she would be leaving, Katie was in London, covering Kate Middleton's wedding to Prince William. The female CBS staffers and producers—even those who'd had trouble with her enormous salary and her complaints about the CBS ladies' room and her star-who-waltzed-in-from-another-network attitude—even these women found themselves emotional that the first solo female six-thirty news anchor had failed to gain traction, that this landmark move would go down as a failure. "We were incredibly sad," says one producer, a hardened pro. "A female correspondent and I were sitting in the hall, talking to Katie—and we both started to cry." Katie, unhappy herself, tried to console them. "She said, 'You're gonna be okay, you're gonna do fine. But still, I wish it had worked out.'" Katie paused and then said, wistfully: "'Think of how cool that would have been . . .'"

All three women agreed: "Yes, we overestimated America," one says, speaking for their shared sentiment.

"She did a great job anchoring the news," says Rick Kaplan, about the blow dealt both of them. "And it was heartbreaking—*heartbreaking*—that she didn't do better" in the ratings department. "She deserved better. She deserved *way* better. She should have been in first place."

Katie's last broadcast, on Thursday, May 19, featured a low-key farewell reel, all the more poignant for its brevity. Over the Beatles song "In My Life" was a montage of clips of Katie with Obama and McCain during the 2008 campaign; with Palin, of course; with the survivors of the Virginia Tech shooting; with Ahmadinejad; with Sully; in a helicopter over the California wildfires; in Egypt and Japan; getting George W. Bush to say he wished Abu Ghraib had never happened. It ended smartly with Clint Eastwood obliging Katie by saying, "Go ahead—make my day."

"And to all of you watching, thank you so much for coming along with me on this incredible journey. From *CBS Evening News*, for tonight, I'm Katie Couric. *Good night.*" And then the woman who had been America's first female solo six-thirty news anchor was off the air.

KATIE SET OUT to craft a syndicated afternoon show—the revenue available from this genre, Daytime, could be enormous. So was the risk. But Katie would imminently have the best partner for the venture: Jeff Zucker. After climbing the professional mountain at NBC to the topmost perch—president and CEO of NBC Universal—Jeff had met his stumbling block just as she was meeting hers: His disastrous decision, in 2010, to push Jay Leno down to ten p.m. and give Conan O'Brien Leno's eleven p.m. slot had cost him his job. When he was eased out (with a handsome payoff), he reunited with the now unemployed Katie.

Katie and Jeff—the dream team duo—took meetings with suitors, who eagerly courted them. The bosses at CNN were "blown away" by Katie, says a person who "took her to meet one of our executives" and "she just dazzled him. She had a good dozen strong story ideas—they ran the gamut from science to international to pop culture." Two executives were "so impressed."

In the spring of 2011 the media was buzzing about where she would land. Despite CNN's heart on its sleeve at the time, the NBC man who had been Katie's critic (saying she hadn't waited "her turn") would turn out to be somewhat prescient in describing the situation at the time: "Katie Couric can go to CNN and triple their ratings without doing anything. But basically how she feels is, 'I'm never going to go to another place to save it.' She was called in to save CBS and that didn't work. So she's labeled a 'failure' at CBS. The *Today* show has never done better than without her. They don't want her back." His assessment illustrates this fact: Highly paid news stars—and news-plus-entertainment stars—have as much to lose as to gain when they're called in to use their stellar brand to rescue a wobbly project or niche or network.

This man, like others, saw the risk Katie was looking at in mid-2011. "With a daytime syndicated show, she's now going to be compared to

Oprah Winfrey, and she cannot possibly reach those heights." (Even Oprah had stopped reaching her own heights. At her peak, in the 1990s, she could pull in thirteen million viewers a day; by the time she ended her show in May 2011, she had more than halved that number, down to an average of six million viewers.) "Either Katie rights this [failure] trajectory with her syndicated show or it's over for her." (His remarks would prove to be accurate.) Oprah had just left the air in a massive multiweek ceremonial send-off, and even her reduced-by-her-own-standards numbers had been an important impetus to shows that followed.

"One of the things holding Diane Sawyer up was the Oprah Winfrey number at four o'clock. With television, it's all about the flow"—the segue from one hit show to another show on the same network that profits from the dial setting. Among industry insiders, the smart money was on Katie going to ABC—joining Diane at the network where Diane had been a queen for twenty-two years. A female news star who'd long worked with Diane, and who had quickly failed in a format that Katie had better succeeded at, narrowed her eyes and said, of the prospect of Katie and Diane (seemingly power equals) being at the same network: "Katie will not know what hit her"—alluding to Diane's creamy politicking, her no-fingerprints perfection.

Indeed, ABC president Anne Sweeney made a big, expensive woo of Katie—and won her—for a reported whopping $40 million a year. It was soon announced that Katie would be bringing her syndicated show to ABC in September 2012. Excitement reigned. So did apprehension. In getting a three p.m. show with Katie, the ABC local affiliates were losing out on a competitive offering—a talk show hosted by Queen Latifah—and some feared that the charismatic actress-singer would do better with their viewers than the charismatic Morning queen and recently rebuffed news anchor.

THE SUMMER OF 2011 was hard for Diane. The loss of Oprah as a lead-in from four to five p.m. hurt her. Even more, so did Scott Pelley's replacement of Katie as *CBS Evening News* anchor. Earnest, chiseled-featured, with prematurely white hair at fifty-four (the same age as the departing Couric), Pelley was, like Rather and Schieffer, a Texan. He was almost militarily stiff; he projected decency and manliness. He'd been a CBS newsman for over twenty years—a correspondent on major stories, like the 1993 World Trade Center bombing and the Oklahoma City bombing two years later; a *60 Minutes* hand; and the network's chief White House correspondent. With the selection of Pelley, Fager seemed to be saying: We are going back to the old CBS ways. (Although some things had changed: In Pat Shevlin, Pelley acquired the first ever female executive producer of *CBS Evening News.*)

With Pelley at CBS, Diane's viewership fell. It wouldn't take long before gossip began to circulate around ABC that Diane was, as an insider phrased it, "putting out the story that she [was] dissatisfied with the editorial direction of the show." It was also known that Mike Nichols was having health problems and that Diane's mother—the indomitable Jean Sawyer Hayes—was not well. Further gossip inside ABC had it that, as the onetime friend of Ben Sherwood's says, "It's in the budget that she'll be let go" as anchor, probably to be replaced by one of her main correspondents (and anchoring substitute) David Muir.

Muir would be far less expensive. This person says, "I can't imagine she would willingly walk away—her entire history is the acquisition of power. There are three reasons she [will be involuntarily] going: One, she makes too much money"—an estimated $14 million to $17 million a year—"and no one should be making that much money at a show that's not making money. Second, evening news viewers are sexist. Scott Pelley is doing serious news that no one wants to hear yet his ratings are good because he's a man." Third, relating to Sherwood's and Sawyer's history, this person says, "What goes around comes around." Another person who knows Sherwood well and keeps up with ABC information says that when he became president of the ABC news division, in some subtle form or another, "Ben lorded it over Diane."

CHRISTIANE ON SUNDAY MORNING was suffering a fate similar to Diane's. Before Christiane took over, *This Week* had for years been number two, right behind the unbeatable *Meet the Press*. Now, by her anchorship's one-year anniversary—August 2011—it had slipped and *Face the Nation* became number two. Christiane was in last place. In the fall, rumors of her demise started to churn. As fall deepened into early winter, they got louder.

On December 13, it was announced in the *New York Times* that Christiane was leaving her anchor position at *This Week*, to be re-replaced by George Stephanopoulos, and that she would return to CNN, but to CNN International, a station somewhat hard to find on the U.S. television dial. The dismissal from *This Week* was face-saved for her by the announcement that, "in a unique arrangement with ABC News, Christiane will continue to report for [ABC's] news programs, as well" as "global affairs anchor." But this arrangement was announced by CNN, not ABC, and it was not "unique"—she had already divided her time between two networks, CBS and CNN, for years. Still, the CNN representative continued: "We could not be happier than to welcome back to the CNN organization the leading international journalist working in television news, who also happens to be our longtime colleague and friend."

This last sentiment was undoubtedly sincere, except its warmth disguised the fact that she would *not* be in the main CNN America lineup; she would *not* have her own easy-to-find-on-the-dial show, like Anderson Cooper, Sanjay Gupta, Fareed Zakaria, Piers Morgan, Wolf Blitzer. She would be "international." This was not without great reach—her new show would be broadcast in about two hundred countries, as well as being seen in America, on the CNN International station, for two half-hour segments, at two p.m. and five p.m. She had always been international when she was in the field, and she'd used it to her advantage, both in having the relative freedom to select atrocities and little-known stories of injustice to cover—and in some places, like Bosnia, becoming *famous* and crucially influential for it. Now, without having compromised a bit of her integrity or her credibility, she was nevertheless slipping further into the background. Her earned opportunity to be a widely watched anchoreditorialist had been unsuccessful.

What was perhaps most ironic, but yet unremarked upon, from a historical perspective, was this: Edward R. Murrow and Walter Cronkite—

major war reporters—had advanced from their field-reporter positions to permanent hallowed anchor (for Cronkite) and permanent hallowed commentator (for Murrow) desks, with respect and authority and *safety*, which they had rightly earned.

And yet, in our current age, when feminism has supposedly triumphed, a major war reporter returned to war zones—a mere two months after giving birth—and then spent seven subsequent years going back into high-risk zones again and again and again. Yet she—having been dismissed from her major network weekend news roundup show— faced a choice of lessers of evil: a daily TV posting where few in America would see her, or the default option that those men had not even needed to consider: a return to the active, dangerous "male" world of war. She took the former choice.

Christiane would be back working with her good friend Liza McGuirk, but she was essentially off the center of the U.S. television stage. This new international show, again named *Amanpour*, debuted in April 2012. "It is where she belongs," said Liza, in an interview for this book a month before the show's launch, admitting that "the fact is, it's getting harder and harder for journalists to find a place where they can do serious international news, but the responsibility [felt by] these people whose entire lives [have been spent on such news] is overwhelming. Christiane herself knows this." Ironically, despite the shortage of venues for serious international news, there was no shortage of young people inspired into that career—*by* Christiane, as Liza's in-box showed. "There's a Christiane *cult*. I get flooded with résumés from them: young women, and men, who grew up watching her on CNN and went into the news business because of her, the way people in my generation did because of Watergate."

MEANWHILE, KATIE'S SYNDICATED three p.m. show, *Katie*—with the tagline "Talk That Matters"—launched on ABC in September 2012, with Jeff Zucker working with her on it. The promotional photo of Katie for her new show was, appropriately, a 180-degree turn from short-simple-haired, unsmiling Katie the News Anchor. This Katie looked ten years younger—subtle, repeated plastic surgery and artful Botox are part of every TV personality's stock in trade, men included. She had her hair curled slightly under her chin. Her winsome smile was oddly non-Katie-like—too saccharine for any earlier iteration of her personality. After snarky, jokey Morning and all-business Evening, this picture obliterated both sides of her personality; in it, she seemed to be trying too hard to be Daytime. But then—like Christiane, who had faced a poor choice—Katie was stuck with a poor choice, too. The experiment she'd been wooed by Moonves into trying had failed, and she could not go back to Morning, which had been her most successful slot. Although she had recently done a week's worth of filling in for vacationing Robin Roberts at *GMA*—which had her vying for ratings with her longtime partner Matt Lauer—it was generally understood that the past was the past, and her guest-hosting was merely an homage, a wink—and a frank ratings-wars stunt.

You had to hand it to Katie, in a way—she followed the format she was in. The positive interpretation? She was a pro, a good soldier, free of pesty ego, shaping her visual image to audience expectation. The negative one? She was a chameleon: confusing, perhaps slightly untrustworthy. Also, Daytime was frankly lowbrow—certainly in comparison to Evening, but also more so than Morning. She was going from highest to lowest, and taking a bet: She would give up status in exchange for a lucrative syndica-tion, *if* her show was a success.

Daytime syndication involves complicated math. Affiliates pay mar-keting fees to carry the show, and *Katie*'s fees were high—thus the risk was elevated at the outset. The two markers of a new syndicated show's succeeding are: its ability to equal the viewership of the show it follows in the Daytime lineup (different shows, depending on the market), and how well it does next to the show that had formerly been in its time slot on the network (also often a different show for each market).

Katie had a great first week—huge promotion, high viewership. When she strode out onto her new *Katie* stage, in her chic blue sheath and sky-high heels, frankly expressing her nervousness, the small, close-in audi-ence of women applauded wildly. One could almost see her calibrating what her former colleague at NBC had said: This was her last shot; she could not fail here. One perhaps could also regret that she'd left evening news for Daytime, in which audiences of women (the word "housewives," while sexist, seems not only apt for Daytime, but desired) applauded wildly.

Maury Povich, Sally Jesse Raphael, Montel Williams, Tyra Banks: These were the second- and third-rate wannabe Oprahs, past and present, some laughing to the bank and enduring, others short-lived. Steve Harvey was successful. Ellen DeGeneres had proved you could be a fresh daytime interviewer with staying power and dignity, but she was an entertainer, not a newsperson. Katie had to wedge herself into a tight space: Be the best of her funny, personality-driven, great-interviewer self without letting her show descend to the sometimes ratings-driven, inescapable lower end of the genre's wobbly bar. Her immediate competitors on the other networks were Harvey, Jeff Probst, and Ricki Lake.

One of Katie's earliest shows was the essence of the best the show could be: an hour with Aimee Copeland, the lovely young University of West Georgia graduate student who, four months before, had fallen off a trip-line over a rural river and been ravaged by flesh-eating bacteria, losing parts of all four of her limbs. Katie's show—Aimee's first ever interview—was up there with the best of *Oprah*: from the footage of the accident and horrific aftermath; to the rousing, no-dry-eye welcome of Aimee appearing for the first time publicly, walking on her custom walker, across the stage; to the sit-down with Katie. Copeland's stunningly positive attitude was one of those rare times when the word "inspiring" is not an empty cliché. Finally, there was the ultimate *Oprah*-like touch—a surprise present: a customized van, as a gift from a munificent donor, for Aimee to drive.

About a week later, Katie did a show that was very personally important to her: on the underdiscussed epidemic of dating violence. Katie had been deeply shaken by the May 2010 murder of UVA star lacrosse player Yeardley Love following a rageful, drunken beating by her boyfriend, fellow student and athlete George Huguely, who had had a largely undisclosed history of violence. (Huguely was convicted of second-degree murder.) Yeardley Love had not only attended Katie's alma mater but she resembled Katie, physically and in her outgoing personality. On the September 20 show, Yeardley's mother and sister told Katie how they had expressed their concern about Huguely to Yeardley and urged her to get a restraining order against him. It was a powerful show—a high point for Daytime—blending a "get" (the family) with tragic human interest and a service takeaway about the prevalence, and need for prevention, of dating violence.

In another early show, Katie did a paired interview with Sheryl Crow and Jessica Simpson, minting an idea—offbeat pairings—that would be a viewer favorite. Bill Carter of the *New York Times* announced that, in her first week, she "scored the best initial rating number for a new talk entry since *Dr. Phil* in 2002." But Carter warned, "Ms. Couric has bolted out of the gate with great ratings before, however. For her first newscast as the anchor of *CBS Evening News* in 2006, she attracted an enormous audience" after a similarly "enormous promotion campaign," only, of course, to plummet. *Katie*'s high ratings would last for the show's first several months.

The show settled into a format with what seemed to be four quadrants. First, there were celebrity interviews a few days a month—the substantial (Barbra Streisand, Susan Sarandon, Alicia Keys, Olympic medalist Gabby Douglas, Jessica Chastain, Celine Dion) and the cheesy (Howard Stern, Judge Judy, Bill O'Reilly). Sometimes she put the celebrities in fun pairings (Billy Crystal and Bette Midler) or unexpected back-to-back twofers (Kerry Washington and Mike Tyson, Magic Johnson and Kathy Ireland) that brought in two different potential segments of her audience. Shows about serious social issues (autism, transgendered children, domestic violence, eating disorders, Facebook COO and *Lean In* author Sheryl Sandberg talking about women and ambition) and serious tragedies (Hurricane Sandy, the mass murder of children at Sandy Hook Elementary School in Newtown, Connecticut) constituted the second genre. The third category encompassed tabloid scandals and sensational theme shows: "Amanda Knox's Boyfriend Breaks His Silence"; "Shocking Medical Mistakes"; "Married to a Monster"; "Dying to Be Beautiful—Beauty Trends That Prove to Be Lethal." Lightweight service, feel-good features, and girl talk rounded things out ("The Hair Show"; "The Friendship Show"; "*Redbook*'s Hottest Husbands"; "Kate Middleton Look-alike and Ordinary People in the Spotlight").

In November 2012 Katie learned that her show was losing Zucker, who had been tapped to become the president of CNN in January 2013. It was an unfortunate loss: Over the next number of months, replacement EPs were signed and dismissed and replaced. But by now Katie had a happy romance going with a man who was closer in age to her (six rather than sixteen years younger): John Molner, a handsome banker and partner in Brown Brothers Harriman.

In late January, *Katie* scored its newsiest scoop: an appearance by Notre Dame football player Manti Te'O, who had garnered great sympathy months earlier by playing a game despite the fact that the love of his life, a pretty girl named Lennay Kekua, whom he had never met in person but had spent many hours with over the Internet and phone, had taken seriously ill and died, at around the same time that his grandfather had also passed away. When the Web site Deadspin revealed, in January 2013, that Kekua was a fictional character, the public turned on Te'O, believing he had staged the fake drama as a sympathy and publicity stunt. Then a close friend of Te'O's confessed to creating the hoax. Many people remained cynical . . . until the wholesome Samoan American athlete appeared with his parents on *Katie* and came off as an excessively naive, good-hearted young man who had probably been conned, triggering wider understanding that "catfishing," the creation of false Internet persona, was not an uncommon phenomenon. Katie's questioning was tough—or, rather, *seemed* tough—but the fact that she and Te'O shared Matthew Hiltzik (Katie's publicist and Te'O's crisis consultant) would have arguably constituted a conflict of interest if she had been interviewing him on her evening news, as opposed to her afternoon, show.

THE PERIOD DECEMBER 2012 to January 2013 brought much change, epiphany, and questioning for the three women. Katie was dealing with the shock of Jeff Zucker leaving her show and also with the triumph of the Te'O get. Diane was facing four things at once: Mike's temporary health challenges, her ninety-three-year-old mother's declining health, and the need for Diane to care for her in her off time, and Barbara Walters's announcement of her intended 2014 retirement. There were also nagging rumors that, in covering the 2012 presidential election night with her ABC teammates, she had been tipsy—footage that had gone viral indicated that she was not at her best. Ultimately, there was no way of knowing whether she had excessively celebrated earlier that evening (Election Day, November 6, was also Mike's eighty-first birthday) or whether she was just exhausted.

Christiane had just come off a meaningful, and personal, story. It had started the previous summer. Tasked with yet another special set in the Middle East—this one for ABC, on her new contract—Christiane did something new: She drafted her twelve-year-old son to be her companion, including on-screen. Darius Rubin himself wrote an endearing blog post, which pulled a curtain open on Christiane the correspondent *and* mother, that duality she'd struggled with so intensely for the first seven years of his life and which remained a mystery, if not wholly unknown, to most people. Katie, after all, had shared her motherhood, frequently, with her viewers; rarely did she not talk about her daughters when interviewed in magazines. Few of Christiane's viewers even knew she had a child—that's not what they tuned in to her for. So, whether or not many CNN.com viewers read it, Darius Rubin's words were a kind of offering: Here I am, and here's my mom. She's not just a serious, world-class international journalist sparring with dictators and tyrants; she's a woman cajoling a preteenage boy to give up his summer to hang out with *her*:

> This summer, my mom was planning a trip to Egypt to explore the history of the Bible. She wanted me to come with her, but I wasn't really excited at first. I wanted to spend the summer hanging out with my friends and didn't feel like taking a 30-hour trip to the middle of nowhere. But my spirits were raised when I realized I got to have my own Flip camera and to be one of the "assistant" film crew everywhere we went—that was pretty cool. And when we finally did get to Egypt, I knew going was definitely the right decision. It was an amazing trip.

Darius went on, in his blog, to say, "I even got in some target practice from the air when I tried to spit into a river from the balloon (Mom was not happy with my efforts)." A quite endearing touch.

Darius described his mother as being "pretty shocked" that the man (disguised as a Bedouin) who drove them through the Egyptian desert had a gun, in case any marauding thieves approached the car. "But I was never scared," Darius assured, charmingly macho and in control at twelve. "The driver seemed like a pretty capable guy, and I thought he could protect us. I didn't want to be kidnapped or anything, but the whole experience was kind of exciting because it felt like being in a movie."

Christiane's—and Darius's—special, *Back to the Beginning*, which vivified the Bible from Genesis to Jesus, aired right before and after Christmas 2012. As part of its narration, Christiane said that, although she had spent much of her career covering bloodshed and strife in the region, "the three Abrahamic faiths mean more to me than war and suffering. Judaism, Christianity, and Islam have come together during some of the happiest and most important moments of my life. In fact, my son Darius is the embodiment of these three faiths in one. You see, I grew up in Iran, the child of a Christian mother and a Shiite Muslim father. I attended Catholic church in Tehran right up until the Islamic Revolution. The man I married is Jewish American, and we were wed by a priest and then under a Jewish chuppah. And now, the blood of these three great peoples runs through the veins of my son." For those who wished to see it, this was a different—a wholer, more intimate—Christiane than anyone was used to.

In June 2013, Christiane took a further step in putting her family first while continuing to work: She and Darius and Jamie, who had recently quit his latest job as chairman of the Port Authority of New York and New Jersey, moved back to London. London: her "spiritual home," as Bella had called it. London—home to Patricia and Mohammed and Lizzy and Leila and Fiona.

ON JANUARY 29, 2013, several media outlets broke a story that Diane was, as the *New York Daily News* put it, "seriously considering retirement as early as this year." The online gossip wing of the newspaper reported that "'[s]he has discussed'" the option of retirement with "'a few close friends and some people at ABC,' said our insider. She said she'll be ready to hang it up not long down the road. She loves work and what she does and has endless energy, but she's overwhelmed with personal problems and she is thinking about leaving to take care of her family." (ABC immediately, reassuringly refuted that report.) From the tone of this and other parts of the statement, it seems to have come from a close colleague and champion of Diane's and may well have been a kind of preemptive, no-fingerprints-all-fingerprints strike in case Ben Sherwood *did* replace her with Muir. *I'm quitting, not being fired* was the message. As with Christiane's anger at CNN for subordinating her to Fareed Zakaria and her subsequent move to ABC's *This Week*—and, especially now, her moving "home" to her family's city, London; and like Katie's interpreting her dismissal from CBS as her own decision, here was a case of Diane attempting to control her career's own narrative. Predictably, a representative for ABC said, "That's a bunch of nonsense. As we made clear, Diane's plans for 2013 haven't changed in any way."

Three and a half months later, in mid-May, Barbara Walters announced on *The View* that she would be retiring in May 2014. Bill Carter wrote, "Like Johnny Carson, another television standout who took charge of his exit from the national stage, Ms. Walters is picking her television end date exactly one year in advance: over the next year she will participate in a series of retrospectives on ABC prime-time news programs and her home on *The View*, seeking, she said, 'to say goodbye in the best way.'"

Two and a half months after that announcement, triumphant news came out. As the *New York Times* put it in a headline, "ABC News Dethrones NBC in Crucial Ratings Race." Here came Brian Stelter's nut graph, a stunning, seeming victory for Diane, and all women anchors:

> ABC's 6:30 newscast, *World News with Diane Sawyer*, bested *NBC Nightly News with Brian Williams* among 25-to-54-year-old viewers last week, ending a winning streak of almost five years by NBC and rekindling interest in the once-predictable ratings competition.

But much farther down—in the second-to-last paragraph—came *this*:

> In a twist that television industry gawkers immediately homed in on, the victory was shared by Ms. Sawyer and one of her regular fill-ins, David

Muir. That was because Mr. Muir substituted for Ms. Sawyer three nights last week—the same three nights, it turned out, that ABC beat NBC in the all-important ratings demographic. Mr. Williams prevailed, barely, on the two nights that Ms. Sawyer was at work.

It was a stinging irony. After all these years of women's gains in the news business—*still*, the only way a woman could beat out a man on the six-thirty news was by way of another man sitting in for her. There was an even greater irony—or inconsistency, or even, one might say, a kind of lack of network's gratitude toward the anchor: In 2013, *ABC World News* won the Murrow Award for best news broadcast of the year. Yet this was the year that the possibly defensively self-generated rumors of Diane's retirement were most pointed. Similarly, *CBS Evening News* had won the Murrow in 2008 and in 2009, yet that hadn't helped Katie: a year and a half later, she was out the door.

Stelter ended the article with the suggestion that Muir (or George Stephanopoulos) was "widely seen" to take over for Diane. "For now," he hastened to say, "that is purely theoretical; Ms. Sawyer . . . has given no signal that she plans to step down soon."

Few would say that Diane's floating of the rumor of her retirement thoughts was not a good move under these circumstances. And as Barbara's May 2014 retirement date neared, she could easily leave the anchor chair—to Muir, or someone else—and waltz into Barbara's position.

WHILE DIANE WAS absorbing this humiliation, Katie was enmeshed in drama. The high viewership of *Katie* had fallen off. The show was renewed for a second season, which would start in September 2013, but it was the third season that was in question. The *New York Post* picked up industry gossip. "The show was oversold at syndication and hasn't lived up to expectations," said one source. In other words, of the two key things that had to happen—that it would hold or improve on the show it followed in most of its markets and that it would do better than the previous show that was in its time slot in the market—neither had happened in enough of the markets. "Oversold" meant that its licensing fees had been too high to make it worthwhile.

Several speakers said that Jeff Zucker's departure had left an understandable gap, with staff confusion and staff cuts. It was widely—and credibly—rumored that Katie was very unhappy with the lower-end stories. The woman who had spent her life triumphing over those who'd underestimated her intelligence and her seriousness could not have been happy with the silly shows, which undercut, within months, a hard-earned reputation she had taken years constructing.

Perhaps most damningly, another site, that of Perez Hilton—a kind of Elton John of Hollywood gossips—quoted an ABC source as saying that the show was "an unmitigated disaster" and that Katie was "dreadfully boring." She'd been the opposite of boring—she'd been a rocket that lit up morning TV—during the first half of her tenure at *Today*. But that had been nearly two decades ago. It takes effort to figure out what's wrong with a show that hits the doldrums, and it takes commitment to fix it. According to someone in the know, it seemed that Katie didn't want to put in that effort. Meanwhile, ABC president Anne Sweeney was said to be unhappy and disappointed over the failure of Katie's show, because she was the one who'd wooed her. Furthermore, the affiliates were "furious," the insider says, "because they could have had Queen Latifah or someone else instead of Katie."

Rumors circulated that Katie would join Jeff at CNN—she denied them—and that she would take Barbara Walters's place on *The View*— she denied those, too. An unusual (and unfair) splash of subsequent dissing came her way by people in a less, and then *far* less, exalted perch from which to criticize her than, say, Sam Zelman at CNN had been. "Is she a legitimate journalist? She used to be on the *Today* show," said Jennifer Aniston—ironically, an actress with the same career longevity as Katie, the same durable, sometimes frustrating (but very well-utilized) girl-next-door image, and the same undersung versatility, the ability to rotate between popular and serious roles. But perhaps the lowest blow came in August when Kim Kardashian, at one of the rare points in her dubious but enormous notoriety when she was actually sympathetic: when she'd just had her baby, North West—blasted Katie for hypocrisy. Katie had sent Kim a baby gift, a not unwise gesture for any afternoon talk show host. But shortly thereafter, in an uncharacteristic lapse, she'd apparently told a reporter for the supermarket magazine *In Touch Weekly*, "I don't understand—why are [the Kardashians] so famous?" This was clearly a question that much of America had asked, but Kim seized on it. She tweeted: #HateFakeMediaFriends and #MayIHumblySuggestYouNot SendGiftsThenTalkShit.

Katie Couric apologized to Kim Kardashian. In fairness, any interviewer in popular media would be well served to not make an enemy of this woman who, like it or loathe it, guaranteed crowds, press, and ratings. Still, the apology seemed a humiliating fillip at a humiliating moment for the woman who had been the first solo anchor. It was easy to fall far fast.

A week after the scold from Kim Kardashian, Katie did what turned out to be the smartest thing she could do, days away from the debut of her second season of *Katie*: She got engaged. Not that it was insincere—she and John Molner were in love, her friends were delighted for her, she had been a widow and single mother for over fifteen years. Not that it wasn't perfectly and responsibly timed for the whole mom-and-daughters family: Ellie had graduated from college, Carrie was about to leave home to start college, they would be happy to know that old mom would be taken care of. The first day of her second season, Molner appeared onstage with a bouquet of flowers for Katie. The women in the audience were appropriately thrilled. Two days later, Katie did a split-the-difference show—dethroned reality mom Kate Gosselin in the first half as low-bar bait; then Julianne Moore as a snarer of the secret-daytime-TV-watching elites.

As for Christiane, she remained in fighting, idealistic character, instinctively repeating the personal memes that had pushed her to prominence and admiration as a conscience among journalists. During September 2013's heated debate over Syria, when much of the country, and President Obama's own party, was at the least leery of intervention, Christiane's passion about the simple moral need to intervene in a case when a dictator was using chemical weapons against his own people was singular. She was as dramatic as anyone had seen her in many years—since Bosnia, since Rwanda, since Darfur.

On a televised panel with liberal *New York Times* columnist Charles Blow, strident blogger Andrew Sullivan, and *Newsweek*'s Paris chief and Middle East regional editor Christopher Dickey, Christiane said: "I can barely contain myself at this point. How many more times do we have to say: Weapons of mass destruction *cannot* be used. And as bad as it is to decapitate somebody, it is by no means equal. We can't use this false moral equivalence about what's going on right now. They tried to do it in the Second World War. They tried to do it in Bosnia. They tried to do it in Rwanda and they're trying to do it now. There is *no* moral equivalence."

When Blow and Sullivan tried to cut her off, she angrily insisted that she be heard out. "*Wait just a second!*" she thundered. "The president of the United States and the most moral country in the world based on the most moral principles in the world—at least that's the fundamental principle that the United States rests on—cannot allow this to go unchecked, cannot allow this to go unchecked!"

It was as if all her years covering atrocities—atrocities tucked away behind the American political news and the tabloid news, atrocities Americans didn't know about in places that didn't "matter," atrocities her friends had died reporting and photographing—it was as if all those sights and sounds, injustices and life lessons came flooding back to her now, filling her with an urgent desire to scream out to America, once again, how important it was not to ignore them. Then she added, "Fifteen, sixteen years later, President Clinton is *still* apologizing for Rwanda."

Something was jarring—even offensive—about this televised exchange, and that was Andrew Sullivan's attitude. When Christiane heatedly spoke of what she perceived as America's obligation to the people of Syria, Sullivan—a blogger who probably had never dodged sniper fire— patronizingly soothed and chastised her. "Stop being emotional!" he ordered. "It's not emotion," she responded. "It's not emotion! *We have turned our eyes away from the most terrible crimes!* It's not emotion!" The exchange was a reminder that women who report serious news still face double-standard knee-jerk complaints about maintaining "manly" calm and objectivity in the newsroom.

Later, Christiane tweeted an explanation for her outburst: "My passion based on justice and the moral imperative & indeed America's proud history of now-forgotten humanitarian intervention." The phrase "now-forgotten" leaps out. It is wistful. Wistful about the era she pioneered; wistful, perhaps, about her own stellar accomplishments.

One particularly important accomplishment occurred five days after that heated conversation about Syria. On September 7, Christiane scored an interview with the new Iranian president, Hassan Rouhani, who'd been sworn in in June. After she, Katie, and Diane had all had at the punching bag that was Ahmadinejad, each skillfully and differently revealing his anti-Westernness, pie-eyed zealotry, and woeful anti-Semitism, there was a new leader, and Christiane, fittingly, got him first.

In the interview, Rouhani's first English-language televised message to the United States, the Iranian president offered not only "peace and friendship from Iranians to Americans," he also made clear that he wanted to negotiate with the West (with the approval of the country's supreme leader, Ayatollah Ali Khamenei). Most significantly, at the end of the interview—in polar opposition to the years of his predecessor's Holocaust denial—the new president said: "I have said before that I am not an historian, and that when it comes to speaking of the dimension of the Holocaust, it is historians that should reflect on it. But in general I can tell you that any crime that happens in history against humanity, including the crime the Nazis committed towards the Jews, as well as non-Jewish people, was reprehensible and condemnable as far as we are concerned."

Christiane proudly touted the scoop on Twitter and Facebook. At last, here was sweet exoneration for her beloved native country.

Just before Christmas 2013, Katie received an unattractive holiday present: Her show was being canceled (effective after the June 2014 conclusion of its current season). She subsequently announced that news and said she would be leaving the network. Disney/ABC and Katie both declared it a mutual decision, which most people read as a tactful way of saying that ABC had dumped Katie after difficulties with the show that, indeed, she herself had been unhappy with. The joint statement read: "We're very proud of everyone's contributions to making *Katie* the number one new syndicated talk show of 2012–2013, and we look forward to the rest of the season." Katie *did* have someplace to go: She would become the chief global news correspondent for Yahoo News—albeit at a considerable decrease in salary. But it was hard to miss the fact that Katie was leaving her third major network in seven years. Still, there was another way of looking at it: She had tried every format—Morning, Evening anchor, Daytime. She'd done the grand rounds of national TV—of Old Media—briskly and thoroughly (if not always successfully), as few other broadcast stars ever had. Was it not time for her to finally move to New Media, which she'd been toying with for longer than her peers had?

Yahoo CEO Marissa Mayer announced: "Katie's depth of experience, her intellectual curiosity and her charisma made her the perfect choice to anchor Yahoo News and the whole Yahoo Network." Which brought up something else: the uncanny match between fifty-six-year-old Couric and thirty-eight-year-old Mayer. Couric was a relatable *and* controversial woman who had gleefully pushed the envelope in a way that had provoked needed conversation about why powerful women in serious business were so criticized for their personal lives, their clothes, their incomes, their beaux, their karaoke singing, their six-thirty on-air "Hi," their choice in magazines.

In taking over that conversation, Mayer was advancing the provocation in a manner commensurate with the times. Every bit as much a boat rocker as Katie, Mayer had thrown herself and her bridegroom, venture capitalist Zachary Bogue, an unusually ostentatious two-day wedding. She customarily dressed in foxier designer clothes than those worn by most businesswomen. Tapped to lead Yahoo when she was newly pregnant, Mayer had immediately announced she would be taking a very short maternity leave and would be working all the way through it. Then, once she returned to the Yahoo campus with her newborn and baby nurse installed in a suite she paid for herself, she demanded that those Yahoo employees who were specifically innovation tasked *not* telecommute but, rather, had to be on campus daily. (The mommy blogs and opinion Web sites exploded:

Was this CEO tough-mindedness, or elitist hypocrisy? Was the criticism of her for this edict sexist? Or was it appropriate anger that regular working moms were being thrown under the bus?) But, beyond the mere provocative, Mayer (formerly a senior executive at Google), like Couric, had been brought in to rescue a failing once stellar brand (Yahoo had stumbled badly, just as CBS News had); Mayer, like Couric, had represented a feminist triumph in that ascent of hers; and, just like Katie, Mayer—with all eyes on her—had initially fumbled the task before getting her sea legs.

Maybe Yahoo would be Katie's last hurrah. Or: Maybe these two similar women would be a dynamic inventive combination.

FOR DIANE, THE NEW YEAR—2014—started out with a fair amount of attention. In a published conversation with her friend Lee Woodruff (Bob Woodruff's wife), she confronted the rumors that had been brewing about her retirement. "I'm still here and I'm loving it," she said. "I would be delusional not to think that at some point I will want to step down. And I'm sure there will come a time when people will say"—unconsciously, she mimics Meryl Streep accepting her last Oscar—"'Her? Again? Still?' But right now my job is giving me the opportunity to wake up in the morning and say, 'What if we . . . ?' 'Why don't we . . . ?' 'Look at this!' or 'Somebody's got to do something!'" These exclamations, these proddings, that curiosity, that intense team leading: These had been, for decades now, pure Diane.

But at the same time, in January 2014, Andrew Tyndall, who had never been a fan of Diane's broadcasts, released a scathing content analysis report that was seized upon by the media. Headlined *"ABC World News* Is Certifiably Disneyfied," Tyndall's invective started off by saying that "2013 mark[ed] the year when *ABC World News* rejected the mission of presenting a serious newscast. ABC covered all four of the major domestic policy stories least heavily [of the three major networks]: the Budget debate, the Healthcare rollout, Gun control, and National Security Agency surveillance. Same with foreign policy: ABC spent the least time on the civil war in Syria and its chemical weapons disarmament, the military coup in Egypt, and on Afghanistan." He added that Diane's broadcast had bumped up its coverage of sports, entertainment, and true crime, especially the George Zimmerman case and madman Ariel Castro's "hell house" in Cleveland, Ohio, where three young women had been held captive for years.

Clearly, this was not all about Diane—in media coverage of Tyndall's blistering report, Ben Sherwood was called out for "fluffing up" *GMA* in order to successfully overtake *Today*, and as news division president, Sherwood had the ultimate responsibility. And some media people (who relentlessly gossiped about Tyndall's report) went further, speculating, as one put it, that the news softening had all come "from Burbank" and that ABC president Anne Sweeney had "a grand plan to homogenize all aspects of Disney's TV empire, not only within ABC News (making *GMA* and *World News* and *Nightline* similar) but also across ESPN and A&E, making journalism more like SportsCenter and reality TV."

But Diane was the implicit primary target of the criticism. ABC News's spokesperson retorted to the *Tyndall Report*: "Our mission is to give our viewers information that is relevant to their everyday lives. Winning the Murrow for Best Newscast in 2013 and enjoying our best season in five years"—Diane's show placed second in viewership, between front-runner Williams and Scott Pelley—"is far more meaningful than Tyndall's method that confuses quantity with quality." In his rebuttal to ABC, Tyndall seized on the network's own phrase "relevant to their everyday lives" as proof of his characterization. Indeed, Diane's early executive producer Jon Banner had said that Diane was an "advocate" for the viewer and that the era of the news anchor speaking stentorially from great Olympian heights was over while the era of anchor-as-peer, interacting with experts and correspondents to help real Americans, was now appropriate.

It was hard not to get the feeling that "relevance to everyday lives" was code for soft and female—a lesser frame for the presentation of news—whereas any suave, reasonably experienced, likable man in a suit could much more easily slide into the characterization of being an Olympian Cronkite. Meanwhile, Diane—completely unconcerned with Tyndall's put-down—continued on with her social issues specials, having honed her specialty of focusing on America's endangered children. For example, her January 31 *20/20* special "Young Guns"—deftly coreported and hosted by her potentially imminent heir, David Muir—showed the shocking danger of leaving guns where children can find them, and the idiocy of "teaching" toddlers how to use firearms. Tyndall and other critics be damned; Diane, with her lifelong goal to "be of purpose," was *all in*.

Validation came for Diane in early spring 2014. During the week of April 7, her *World News* narrowly beat Brian Williams's *Nightly News* by twelve thousand viewers—in the prized twenty-five-to-fifty-four demographic, ending, at least for that one week, Williams's unbroken five-year-long winning streak.

But that triumph proved insufficient. On June 25, 2014, in an announcement that rose to the top of the news and went viral, ABC reported that Diane would be leaving her *World News* anchorship in August, to be replaced by David Muir, with George Stephanopoulos lead-anchoring during elections. She would still do her special interviews, such as the one she conducted two weeks earlier with Hillary Clinton. The announcement was strictly ABC's; Diane offered no comment.

Less than a week before that, on Saturday, June 21, Katie married John Molner in the backyard of her East Hampton home. Her daughters, Carrie and Ellie, and John's two children spoke at the small ceremony. The *New York Post*'s Page Six pointedly noted that neither Matt Lauer nor Jeff Zucker was among the fifty guests. Katie's syndicated afternoon show had signed off mere weeks before; she was—for now, at least—entirely off television.

BUT WHAT DOES it all mean? It could simply be true that, for the ever dwindling viewers of network six-thirty news—and the even more dwindling numbers of those who feel they really *get* their news that way rather than use those shows for an authoritative summation of the spots and blips of news they've been receiving in real time all day long on their mobile devices—a man in a suit is *always* going to be the preferred news giver. That America could keep on changing—Hillary Clinton can be the most viable candidate for president; Janet Yellin can head up the Federal Reserve—and, indeed, a woman can finally become president of a major network's news division, as Deborah Turness did at NBC in May 2013. Yet one oddly particular niche would somehow, irrationally, always be reserved for a rearguard opinion: Only a *man* can be a "real" TV news anchor.

Female media critics, in particular, have noted how distinctively hard the climb has been for women, and how attenuated or ironic have been the victories. On the occasion of Barbara Walters's retirement announcement, Alessandra Stanley wrote in the *New York Times*: "In the era of Diane Sawyer, Katie Couric, and Christiane Amanpour, it's hard to believe that there was a time when the networks considered the evening news too important to entrust to a woman." And, four years earlier, when Diane became the second solo female anchor just as the network six-thirty news was becoming outdated by cable and the Internet, Stanley wryly opined: "As in other fields, women seem to break through the glass ceiling just as the air conditioning is being turned off in the penthouse office suites."

But there's another way to look at the seemingly anticlimactic nature of these women's triumphs—and their long reigns: The punctiliousness, focused ambition, and high quality of work these women had to master and refine in order to earn places that were long more easily, and with lower bar, given to men made them superior strategists and more dogged professionals. They've prevailed for so long because they *had* to be better.

As reporters and communciators of that which was beyond their control—the news of the world—and as women in a tremendously competitive professional arena in which their gender was an impediment, their ability to strongly control what they *could* control has been central to their success. Each has been self-aware and self-powering in a different way, and their careers offer lessons in female survival. We have seen how Diane used her intense work ethic, her charm and mystery, her witty self-deprecation, and her staged humility to win over workplace skeptics, to neutralize colleagues' resentment, and to endear herself to viewers. Whether she followed her fiercely sensible mother's post-widowhood advice or found the way herself, she married late for her generation, regional background, and copious opportunities—but it has been a nurturing and career-enhancing marriage, and she used the fact that she did not have children to her benefit, both by way of the additional time and undivided focus it afforded her and in enabling her to craft a persona as America's Aunt: deeply admiring of the quotidian pains of family life amid crisis, concerned about young celebrities' destructive behavior.

Katie was more straight-on, more aggressive. She used her innate toughness and the relatability born of her embrace of her American Girl identity to crash through impediments and to wedge herself into opportunities. She was easily mistaken as unexceptional, and, while such appraisal hurt her, she turned the chip on her shoulder into a self-motivational tool and used her penchant for being underestimated to sneak up on—and trump—the patronizing eminences she interviewed. Once she had power, she cemented a brand—based on her unique combination of normalcy and edginess—that gained her an enormous fan base. But though she could have coasted, she went for more; and when the risk she took did not pay off, she continued to mine her options, pragmatically ignoring the status order of industry elitism.

As for Christiane, her resilience and savvy were honed by being an exile—an emissary from a rich, complicated, international culture, improbably imported to the most provincial Southern city that could still host a major media upstart. She relished defying the rules—she was foreign, seemingly uncaring about her looks, confrontational—which only kept her down until she could find the loophole in the system that let her claim the niche for which she seems to have been destined. Her bravery and idealistic fervor were shrewdly counterpointed by a cool temperament. She relied on the autonomy afforded her by foreign postings, amassing an unassailable reputation and charisma that enabled her to make story choices independent of network interference. It was when she had to play by the inside rules that her toughness met its match, and it was when she was given the chance to be vaunted American Host that she fell prey to U.S. audiences' wariness toward women with accents and attitude. Still, true to character, she refused what for others might be a route and a trap—that of "selling out." Instead, she retained her integrity even while lowering her wattage.

There's a flip side of resilience—and that is vulnerability. Jeff Zucker says, "All three of these women are strong, but they're still very vulnerable. It's a very hard business, to put yourself out there" where millions see you daily, "every day, on the line. And be graded every day by people who have never had the courage to do this. Having the courage to put yourself out there every day: it says something about all three of these women."

Ginny Vicario, the first female camera operator ever hired by a network, who has collaborated with them all, takes it further. She says: "Diane, Katie, and Christiane have worked their asses off. But with that hard work has come compassion, in the stories they've told, in the stories they've chosen to tell, and in their lives. Power has not taken that away. If anything, it has increased it."

All three of these women modeled a reality of success that was different from past models. The more powerful they became, the more interested in people they became. They remained profoundly committed to telling the stories of ordinary Americans, unfairly beseiged victims, people in cataclysms and crises, fascinating celebrities both worthy and spoiled, world leaders both benign and heinous. They passionately kept up their commitments to their families, friends, and needy strangers through both improvised and formal philanthropies. They remembered what they had pushed past—grief, danger, tragedy—and the more they saw and reported, the more they folded the new experiences into those primary lessons. As intensely competitive as they have been, each of them had a moral brake on runaway power. They asked, "Where's the heart?" (Diane) or they considered their network colleagues their cherished "family" (Christiane) or they knew that that "other side"—the "payback" side—of their luck and bounty existed (Katie). Whatever their idiosyncrasies, whatever their egos, whatever their aggressiveness and ambition, they retained an experienced kernel of humbling reality, and it controlled their choices and their consciences.

From Three Mile Island to the Arab Spring, from the Gulf War to Bosnia to Iraq to Syria, from Columbine to 9/11 to the Haiti and Japanese earthquakes, from Matthew Shepard to Whitney Houston to Hosni Mubarek, from cancer awareness to corruption to genocide to childhood poverty, we got the news from them.

And we also got from them what is underneath the news, what is underneath *all* news: We got humanity.

ACKNOWLEDGMENTS

THE BOOKS I WRITE are journalistic rather than narrative nonfiction. For the most part, I let my sources tell much of the story, as they knew and lived and appraised it; so I am first of all dependent on them—and, secondly, I am grateful to them. First the "dependent" part, as relates to this book: Most of my sources have spent years—in many cases, decades—employed in television news. I've observed this world avidly through the TV screen and through the lenses of women's issues and a changing American culture: the latter, subjects I have written about for many years. But the *professional* world of television news is one I have only just entered. I mapped the territory—I learned its cadences, rituals, values, and jargon, its earnestness and cynicism—through interviewing these people, who gave me their insights and memories. Then there's the "grateful" part: I am grateful to them because every professional milieu is its own ecosystem, with powerful people to be feared and protected and secrets not often shared with outsiders. My sources took risks in telling me tales out of school, without which my book would have been incomplete—and boring.

Many of my sources spoke for attribution; some requested anonymity; some toggled between a desire to be quoted in one or many instances and a wish to remain a blind source in other cases.

Needless to say, there were many people who turned down interviews or sent word that they would not be interviewed or did not respond to my interview requests. No hard feelings—we who do this work are plenty used to this.

As for why I did not interview Diane, Katie, and Christiane: Basically, I was not able to. I was told at the outset that Katie would not give an interview, and my request to view Diane in the run-up hours to *World News*, which might have included or have been followed by an interview, was turned down. By the time I secured Christiane's interest in this project, for the sake of balance and uniformity, I decided not to request an interview with her. Also, there is this: Negotiating for prized interviews sometimes involves ceding a certain amount of control, or feeling in some way influenced by a bond established with the subject about whom one is objectively writing. I was not willing to do the former, and I felt concerned that I would be too easily susceptible to the latter.

Here, in alphabetical order, are my sources. I thank you all.

JERRY ABRAMSON, Leila Amanpour and Lizzy Amanpour (great thanks to the Amanpour sisters, for opening a window upon a unique family, and with such elegance and courtesy), Barbara Andrukonis, Magaret Aro, Pierre Bairin, Dr. Shaul Bakhash (I am honored to have the benefit of your authoritative command of recent Iranian history), Jon Banner, Nancy Battaglia, David Bauder, Lori Beecher, Diana Bellew (thank you for the New Hall yearbook, the wonderful photograph, and your witty candor), David Bernknopf, Aviva Bobb, Don Browne, the late Frances Buss Buch, Bob Cain, Arch Campbell, Leesa Campbell, Connie Chung, David Cosby (very grateful for your and the late George Unseld's memories of the painful segregation of old Louisville), Christine Craft, Jim Crunkelton, and Chris Curle.

Bruce Dalrymple, Emma Daly, Christine Davidson, John Dean (I feel I *lived* the Nixon White House's view of Watergate through you and Gerry Warren), Nancy Diamond, Lane Duncan, Haleh Esfandiari (it was an honor to interview you), Gail Evans, Jeff Fager, Don Farmer, Yael Federbush, Patricia Fieldsteel, Maria Fleet, Jon Fleischaker, Marc Fleischaker, Janie McMullen Florea, Marie Fox, Jon Friedman, Paul Friedman, Brian Gadinsky, Lee Goldstein, Allison Gollust, Roger Goodman, Tom Goodman, Judi Lempert Green, Diana Greene, and Tom Hampton.

Lois Hart, Ron Haviv, Greg Haynes, Sallie Schulten Haynes, Sparkle Hayter, Andrew Heyward, Melanie Howard, Harry Jacobson-Bayer (thank you for the wonderful Seneca High photographs), Sherry Jacobson-Bayer, Beth Johnson, Rick Kaplan, Ted Kavanau, Parisa Khosravi, Marcia Ladendorff, Susan Lasalla, Chet LeSourd, Kathleen Lobb, Mandy Locke, Alice Chumbley Lora (special thanks—and admiration), Tony Maddox, Bob McDonald, Celia McDonald, Marcy McGinness, Phyllis McGrady, Liza McGuirk, Milton Metz, Judy Milestone (thank you for the great photo), Milt Miller, Gig Moses, and Roger Mudd.

Pat O'Gorman, Kathy O'Hearn, Jane Pauley, Lisa Paulsen, Alan Perris, Joe Peyronnin, Beryl Pfizer, Mark Phillips, Cammie Plummer, Bella Pollen, Tom Porter, Stewart Robensen, Anna Robertsen, Mark Robertson, Ira Rosen, Shelley Ross, Ellen Rossen, Ken Rowland, Lynne Russell, and David Rust (thank you for your real-time, encrypted diaries of those hazardous years in Bosnia and your fact-checking assistance), Karim Sadjadpour, Marlene Sanders, Bob Schieffer, Reese Schonfeld, Ed Shadburne, Pat Shifke, Jennifer Siebens, Bill Small, Martin Snapp, Sandy Socolow, Jim Smith, Ingrid Soudek, Ellen Spiceland, Flip Spiceland, Jim Taricani, Bob Taylor, Andrew Tkach (thank you for the CDs of Christiane's perilous African and Asian investigative journeys and your fact-checking assistance), Andrew Tyndall, the late George Unseld, Ginny Vicario, Michael Vitez, Jonathan Wald, Richard Wald, Dave Walker, Amy Walter, Gerry Warren, Claire Weinraub, Betsy West, Av Westin, Bruce Whelihan, Sam Zelman, Susan Zirinsky, and Jeff Zucker.

THANK YOU to my thirty-five unattributed sources. You know who you are. Your insights were invaluable and I deeply appreciate your trust in me.

THANK YOU to the Gatekeepers: those who were crucial to my gaining access to approved sources. For Katie, that means the estimable (and very nice) Matthew Hiltzik—and his team, including Rachel Adler, Rachel Reichblum, and Jillian Taratunio. Matthew, I know you started warily, and with unpleasant memories of another author's book. I sincerely hope this book has justified the faith extended to me. For opening the door to many people who worked with Diane, I have two ABC women, past and present, to thank. Cathie Levine, I so appreciated your coming *to me* when you heard I was doing this book (that's the dream of respectful unauthorized biographers), and Julie Townsend, I greatly enjoyed working with you as well. Thank you, too, most recently, Van Scott. For Christiane: At ABC, Emily Lenzner and Natalia Labenskyj empathetically heard my plans for this project—and Heather Riley ultimately opened the door. Maggie Thomas at CNN was an abiding helper/conduit for many matters Amanpour, as was Neel Khairzada. Appreciation to you.

Thank you so much, Haleh Bakhash, for introducing me to your remarkable parents, whose historical perspectives on Iran from the 1950s through the Revolution were invaluable. Thank you, the always generous Shirley Velasquez—my valued compadre in much of my work over the years, for assembling a tremendously useful scrapbook of clips on all three women, and thank you to the cheerful and very sharp Megan Pedersen for putting my Bibliography in better order than I could. Rebecca Webber, also a longtime colleague—an outstanding, and gentle-mannered, researcher: Thank you for the astute fact-checking on the Watergate section—and more. Megan, Rebecca, and Shirley: Thank you for the yeoman's work on that bane of authors everywhere, the Source Notes. Elisa Petrini—dear friend and editorial brilliance: Gratitude for helping me come up with this formulation—and for reading and advising on my drafts, for noticing things I failed to notice, and for keeping my spirits up during some difficult patches. Bettina Stammen, photo researcher par excellence: gratitude for skillfully finding and acquiring the rights to images. Thanks, too, to Shana Darnell, photo editor at Turner Image. And thank you, Karen Mayer. Oliver LeSeur—thank you for being always available, in the middle of the night, on weekends, whenever computer emergencies and glitches occurred (and, of course, they always occurred at the most fraught junctures). Props, too, to Regina Alexander of Village Digital, for always being there—again, sometimes in the middle of the night—to aid this digital Luddite.

Leaving the best—and most important—for last. I deeply thank my agent, Suzanne Gluck: Your power and respect within the industry and your advocacy for your writers is matched by your down-to-earth menschiness. I am so glad I am your client and that we are friends—you are a caring, empathic wise-woman *and* a blunt straight shooter, and I always know you have my back: a dynamite triple combination. Suzanne's terrific assistants at William Morris Endeavor, Eve Atterman and Samantha Franks, were always so helpful—and delightful.

Ann Godoff was a dream editor. I mean that literally: For many years I had dreamed of doing a book for Ann, widely known as one of the most astute and prestigious editors in the business—and how lucky I was to get this opportunity, and for just the right book. Ann's peerless insight, her perfectionistic attention—and her kindness (toward me and toward the people I am writing about)—made this challenging process go down easier than it might have, and she taught me a lot in the bargain. I had written the entire book, but something about its launching chapters wasn't quite right, and a conversation you and I had—a profound but simple point you passionately offered as we spoke in your office one October day—not only made me see how to adjust the frame but emotionally validated my entire thesis, enabling me to elevate the book's very meaning. Thank you.

Benjamin Platt made everything that goes along with the production of the book pleasant; I felt in such good—and reassuring—hands with you. Sarah Hutson and Yamil Anglada, thanks you for the expert publicity.

My sister Liz Weller, vice president of legal at a major cable network, has been my sage cheerleader for all the years of effort on this book. She is my best friend in the universe and I don't know what I would do without her. My lifelong friends, writers Carol Ardman and Eileen Stukane: ditto. Writing an unauthorized triple biography of highly respected people exacts wear and tear on the sometimes-faint-of-ego, and all of you were there for me. And a pinot grigio toast (deviled eggs on a platter) to my fellow Good Witches: Lisa DePaulo, Judith Newman, and Aimee Lee Ball—who make doing this work, day in and day out, at our high-pitched level, feel invaluably supported—as well as delightfully snark- and gossip-filled. In addition, I, like many another hunched-over wordsmith, have discovered the unique life-perk that is Facebook, which, for me, is a little like getting to host a salon with a *This Is Your Life* cast of characters. (If Facebook had existed decades ago, I could have skipped psychoanalysis.) So a big HEART emoticon to all my buddies in my customized virtual universe of Likes and links and Comments.

My husband, John Kelly—author of beautiful, powerful, lauded books on the Black Death, the Irish Famine, and, out very soon, Churchill in 1940—was the one who, as I was conceiving this trio and racking my brain for the exactly right third, suggested Christiane: a brilliant—the hiding in plain sight! the *but-of-course!*—round-out for this triad. It pays to be married to a man who follows international news, present and historical, more than his provincial wife does. When you are two long-married writers, your relationship is one part putting up with each other's outsized idiosyncrasies; one part telling the other (*sometimes* politely) to be quiet when they're procrastatingly riffing while you're in the middle of composing a sentence . . . and a third part: a lifesaving, unequaled feeling that *No other human on earth knows what I have gone through!* Right after you finish a book, you forget all the other crap and behold in your mate only that majestic last thing, in rather the same way that, after hours of labor in a hospital maternity ward, you forget everything else and behold *just* the baby.

And, speaking of babies, my book-finishing "bonus," so to speak—the best in the world!—was provided by my wonderful, beautiful daughter-in-law and my terrific, handsome son—respectively, Rebecca Sinn and Jonathan Kelly (these two young magazine powerhouses are possessed of far more maturity, stability, and common sense than John and I ever had at their age): Jack Dawson Kelly. Jack's arrival on the night of November 9, 2013, was a major-network-regularly-scheduled-program-interrupting event rivaling anything Diane or Katie could lead a broadcast with or any white-peace-flag-flying burst of great news that Christiane could report from a war front. Darling Jack: ShaSha loves you so much! And you have the *most wonderful* parents.

And, finally, Diane, Katie, and Christiane: For four and a half years, your lives and your work have inspired this humble biographer. As a fellow story-chasing news grunt, workaholic, worrier, perfectionist, pushy dame (and, Katie, as a fellow former high school cheerleader), I have had the unique experience of writing about massively—deservedly—successful women in a field close enough to my own for me to understand it on an involuntary, granular level, but also different enough and on such an (envy-tempting) exalted plane that I had to do a couple of tonic, instructive head pivots to get just the right perspective. I hope you ladies like this book. Even if you don't like every single bit of it—it would be *bad* if you liked every single bit of it—I hope you secretly admire my reporting and wonder how the hell I got some of the stories. But, mainly, I thank you for what studying your lives and careers has taught me about craft, resilience, character, the ethical and effective way of using ambition—and the moral value of remaining a real-deal female human being despite constant, ungodly pressure.

—SHEILA WELLER
April 2014

SOURCE NOTES

As much as I could, without impeding the narrative, I have quoted my named sources, and indicated where statements and ideas came from the blind sources, within the pages of the book itself. The use of the present verb form—"he says," "she says"—indicates that I interviewed the speaker. The present perfect tense form—"he/she has said"—indicates that the quote came from another media source.

Because I did not interview Diane, Katie, or Christiane, I am listing, and giving the references for, the quotes I used of these women that came from their interviews to members of the media or in speeches or books. These are listed under the heading "Quotes from the Principal Subject [or Subjects] Obtained from Media Sources." (The slightly shorthandeded sourcing here—writer, magazine, Web site, or book—will point the reader to the more extensively identified source that is listed in the Bibliography.)

I am also listing and indicating the media source of quoted remarks in the text made by *others* (colleagues of the women, friends of the women, TV critics, writers, and so forth) that came from other media as opposed to secondhand references in my interviews with attributed or anonymous sources. They are listed under "Quotes from Other Speakers Obtained from Media Sources." Here, I indicate the speaker's name in front of the quote.

Where used in the text, Diane's, Katie's, and Christiane's words in their many major televised interviews with public figures, political figures, celebrities, victims of crimes and natural disasters, and so forth (garnered from transcripts and/or YouTube) are generally indicated in the Source Notes, but, in many cases where their actual words are not quoted and the mention of the interview in the text is minor, I am sparing the reader endless citations of these women's incredibly substantial body of work. A more comprehensive account is in the Bibliography. (And, truth be told, the most comprehensive bibliography in this regard is Google.)

Similarly, in a book about reporters who are engaged with the news of the world—and who have been on television for hours a day for decades—a

multitude of (largely Web-searchable) sources were consulted for the factual details of the minor and major news events and the biographies (and, in some cases,
obituaries) of the people they reported on and interviewed and the colleagues
they interacted with professionally. This pro forma research and fact-checking,
usually conducted through Web searches, is not included in the Source Notes and
is shorthandedly referred to in the Bibliography. In most cases, this research
filled in accounts I obtained from interviews I conducted with the people (producers, bureau chiefs, directors, news camera operators, assistants, colleagues,
friends, bystanders) who were party to Diane's, Katie's, or Christiane's reporting
of, or connection with, these news stories.

I owe a debt to a number of journalists who have long specialized in the
media and especially television. Their work, much of it cited in the Bibliography
and sometimes called out in the Source Notes, greatly informed my understanding of TV news as an art, craft, public service, business—and horse race. Thank
you: Ken Auletta, Alessandra Stanley, Bill Carter, Joe Hagan, Meryl Gordon,
Brian Stelter, Jon Friedman, Kurt Andersen, David Carr, David Bauder, Mary
McNamara, Tom Shales, Jack Shafer, Howard Kurtz, and Rebecca Dana.

TWENTY-SECOND TEASERS: AN ARC OF A STORY IN EIGHT SOUND BITES
Author Interviews:
Sandy Socolow, Av Westin, Connie Chung, Don Browne, Susan Zirinsky, and an anonymous
    source.
Quotes from the Principal Subject (and Other Speakers) Obtained from Media Sources:
"Audiences are less . . . woman's voice": Reuven Frank, speaking in 1970. Quoted in
    David H. Hosley and Gayle K. Yamada. *Hard News: Women in Broadcast Journalism.*
"Martha Gelhorn . . . 'was the effort.'": Christiane Amanpour, "2000 Murrow Awards
    Ceremony Acceptance Speech."

INTRODUCTION: **The News You Give Begins with the News You've Lived**
I. Pushing Past Grief
Among the People the Author Interviewed Are:
Greg Haynes, David Cosby, Alice Chumbley Lora, Bob McDonald, Celia McDonald, Ken
    Rowland, Ed Shadburne, Jim Smith, the late George Unseld, Mark Robertson, Anna
    Robertson, Phyllis McGrady, Jon Banner, and various anonymous sources.
Quotes from the Principal Subject Obtained from Media Sources:
"There were sometimes only pennies . . . *real* bruises in that life": Judith Newman, "Diane
    Sawyer," *Ladies' Home Journal.*
"Growing up, I didn't . . . I had *proximate* ones.": Ibid.

II. Pushing Past Danger
Among the People the Author Interviewed Are:
Mark Phillips (profound thanks for describing the siege in detail), Emma Daly, Sparkle

Hayter, Pierre Bairin, Liza McGuirk, Lizzy Amanpour, Bella Pollen, and various anonymous sources.

Quotes from the Principal Subject Obtained from Media Sources:

"I have spent . . . most military units": Christiane Amanpour, "2000 Murrow Awards Ceremony Acceptance Speech."

"Never be afraid. . . . *Use* it": "Christiane Amanpour's Address to University of Michigan Commencement," University of Michigan News Service.

Quotes from Other Speakers Obtained from Media Sources:

Emma Bonino: "*No one* was in charge. . . . situation of random terror": "Taliban Briefly Detains EU Commissioner," CNN Interactive World News.

Richard Cohen: "If you walk . . . zoning violation": Macon Morehouse, "Foreign Affair," *People.*

III. Pushing Past Tragedy

Among the People the Author Interviewed Are:

Lisa Paulsen, Kathleen Lobb, Lane Duncan, Diana Greene, Gail Evans, Pat Shifke, and various anonymous sources.

Quotes from the Principal Subjects Obtained from Media Sources:

"my first four decades . . . psychic payback": Katie Couric, *The Best Advice I Ever Got.*

"I feel like a human piñata . . . successful and female": George Rush and Joanna Molloy, "Profile in Couric: Bashed but Unbowed," *New York Daily News.*

"Before you gag . . . other side": Katie Couric, *The Best Advice.*

Quotes from Other Speakers Obtained from Media Sources:

Katie's NBC colleague, Barbara Harrison: "smiles on their faces . . . each other": Jill Smolowe, "Gone Too Soon," *People.*

CHAPTER ONE: **Louisville Idealist Becomes Nixon Loyalist**

Among the People the Author Interviewed Are:

Stewart Robensen, Marc Fleischaker, Jon Fleischaker, Tom Hampton, Bruce Dalrymple, Mark Robertson, Harry Jacobson-Breyer, Sherry Jacobson-Breyer, David Cosby, the late George Unseld, Lee Goldstein, Alice Chumbley Lora, Sallie Schulten Haynes, Greg Haynes, Jerry Abramson, Chet LeSourd, Aviva Bobb, Judi Lempert Green, Beth Johnson, Leesa Campbell, Marie Fox, Sandy Socolow, Joe Peyronnin, Martin Snapp, Ed Shadburne, Ken Rowland, Bob Taylor, Milton Metz, the late Frances Buss Buch, Marlene Sanders, Beryl Pfizer, Richard Wald, John Dean, Gerry Warren, Bruce Whelihan, and various anonymous sources.

Quotes from the Principal Subject Obtained from Media Sources:

"Every place you would look there would be . . . not for a minute thinking there was anything they couldn't do": Judith Newman, "Diane Sawyer," *Ladies' Home Journal.*

"Linda [was] a saint . . . time I was tiny": Ibid. "We had this little group . . . so, so earnest": Ibid.

"seismic wake-up call . . . her faith like that": "Still Dreaming Big," Guideposts.com.

"When the other girls were getting . . .": Margo Howard, "*60 Minutes*' Newest Correspondent," *People.*

"I went to my first . . . or five times in college": "Diane Sawyer: Beauty in Coke-Bottle," ABCNews.com.

"I felt that the journalist's . . . about taking responsibility": Robert Sam Anson, *Exile: The Unquiet Oblivion of Richard M. Nixon.*

"I was able to listen . . . was such an education": Kevin Sessums, "Diane Sawyer on President Nixon," Parade.com.

"get up in the morning when . . . cataclysm": Ibid.

"Bruising, nerve-deadening torment . . . because I seemed to have everything on file": Ibid.

"What a considerable presidency . . . without Watergate": Howard, "*60 Minutes*' Newest Correspondent."

"thought it was so strange . . . It was about pain" And "He also had a courtly feeling. . . . of a certain kind": Ibid.

"I went away by myself . . . I didn't know what was next": Lee Woodruff, "The Latest News on Diane Sawyer," LHJ.com.

"His world had collapsed . . . couldn't live with myself": Newman, "Diane Sawyer."

"I had a sense of duty . . . and then get to walk away when someone is living in defeat": Sessums, "Diane Sawyer on President Nixon."

"No matter how they got [to that defeat] . . . I just don't think that's the person I can be: Newman, "Diane Sawyer."

"Everybody talks about his awkwardness with social talk . . . And it happened over and over again": Frederick Exley, "If Nixon Could Possess . . ." *Esquire.*

Quotes from Other Speakers Obtained from Media Sources:

Nora Ephron: "was a dress rehearsal . . .": Nora Ephron, "Nora Ephron's Commencement Address," Wellesley University, 1996.

Nancy Hanschman Dickerson: "because it seemed . . . shopping and food columns": Anthony Fellow, *American Media History.* Cengage Learning, 2009.

Marya McLaughlin: "Oh, *now* I understand. If a 707 crashed this afternoon, you want me to take my camera crew to the pilot's house and . . . ask [his widow] what she would have cooked for dinner": Judith Marlane, *Women in Television News Revisited.*

Richard Nixon: "Those chambers are small . . . a space capsule with men": John Dean, *Blind Ambition.*

Barbara Walters: "The fact that I was there . . . experienced superstars . . . a lot of feathers": Barbara Walters, *Audition.*

"in the president's entourage . . . a nodding acquaintance but no real contact": Ibid.

Sources Particularly Helpful to the Author:

On the history of women in TV news:

Judith Marlane, *Women in Television News Revisited.*

On the Nixon White House during Watergate and Nixon at San Clemente:

Robert Sam Anson, *Exile.* John Dean, *Blind Ambition.*

CHAPTER TWO : **The Secret Princess Becomes the Exile in Atlanta**

Among the People the Author Interviewed Are:

Lizzy Amanpour, Leila Amanpour, Diana Bellew, Gig Moses, Shaul Bakhash, Haleh Esfandiari, Jim Taricani, David Bernknopf, Lynne Russell, Marcia Ladendorff, Flip

Spiceland, Don Farmer, Reese Schonfeld, Dave Walker, Ted Kavanau, Sparkle Hayter, Maria Fleet, and various anonymous sources.

Quotes from the Principal Subject Obtained from Media Sources:

"very shy . . . what they were saying": Oprah Winfrey, "Oprah Talks to Christiane Amanpour," *O, The Oprah Magazine.*

"falling off . . . gave me no choice": Ibid.

"My father was standing . . . consciousness began": Christian Amanpour, "Revolutionary Journey," Amanpour.Blogs.CNN.com.

"My first 'big break' . . . upside down": Christiane Amanpour, "My First Big Break," Mediabistro.

"We lost home . . . *everything*": Ibid.

"I quickly decided . . . my driving force": Ibid.

"I loved every . . . values and culture": "Christiane Amanpour's Address to University of Michigan Commencement," University of Michigan News Service.

"all the things . . . philosophy, political science": Ibid.

"slightly miffed . . . '*bomb* Iran'": Ibid.

"I have no brilliant . . . I could muster": Laurence Leamer, *Sons of Camelot.*

"We had the most intense dinner table . . . also an effective devil's advocate": Laurence Leamer, *Sons of Camelot.*

"I was always . . . little humiliating": Christiane Amanpour, "My First Big Break."

"They miked me . . . didn't get close": Ibid.

"All of a sudden . . . 'spectrum of news'": Christiane Amanpour, "2000 Murrow Awards Ceremony Acceptance Speech."

"They asked me ten questions . . . flying colors": Ibid.

Quotes from Other Speakers Obtained from Media Sources:

John Kennedy Jr.: "wasn't hard. She was just sort of British and determined . . ." and "there was not one iota . . . what she'd gone through": Leslie Bennetts, "Woman o' War."

John Kennedy Jr.: "was sort of the mother of the house . . . to clean the toilets": Leslie Bennetts, "Woman o' War," *Vanity Fair.*

Robert Littell: "sometimes surprisingly conservative . . . practical": Laurence Leamer, *Sons of Camelot.* Robert T. Littell, *The Men We Became: My Friendship with John F. Kennedy, Jr.*

Robert Littell: "Like a den mother . . . the de facto mediator between us": Robert T. Littell, *The Men We Became.*

Sources Particularly Helpful to the Author:

On Iran before and after the Revolution, my interviews with:

Shaul Bakhash, Clarence Robinson Professor of History at George Mason University, author of *The Politics of Oil and Revolution in Iran* and *Reign of the Ayatollahs: Iran and the Islamic Revolution.*

Haleh Esfandiari, director of the Middle East program at the Woodrow Wilson International Center for Scholars and author of *Reconstructed Lives: Women and Iran's Islamic Revolution.* (In May 2007, the Iranian-born and -raised Esfandiari, then sixty-seven and by then an American, was detained and interrogated in the country while visiting her ailing mother, was falsely declared a U.S. spy by the government of President Mahmoud Ahmadinejad, was threatened with death, and was imprisoned in solitary confinement for three and a half months. She was released after intense American and international diplomatic pressure.)

On Christiane's life in the Benefit Street house:

Christina Haag, *Come to the Edge*. Laurence Leamer, *Sons of Camelot*. Robert T. Littell, *The Men We Became*.

CHAPTER THREE: **Little Sister Cheerleader to Pentagon Correspondent**

Among the People the Author Interviewed Are:

Janie McMullen Florea, Barbara Cherney Andrukonis, Betsy Yowell Howell, Lane Duncan, Michael Vitez, Kathleen Lobb, Richard Wald, Susan Zirinsky, Don Farmer, Reese Schonfeld, Marcia Ladendorff, Ted Kavanau, Av Westin, Jane Pauley, Lois Hart, Dave Walker, Diana Greene, Gail Evans, Sam Zelman, Chris Curle, Judy Milestone, Nancy Battaglia, Al Buch, Brian Gadinsky, Alan Perris, Arch Campbell, Don Browne, David Bernknopf, Mandy Locke, and various anonymous sources.

Quotes from the Principal Subject Obtained from Media Sources:

"When our minister . . . member": Tom Junod, "Katie Couric: What I've Learned," *Esquire*.

"would probably . . . safe-sex early eighties": Katie Couric, quoted in *Life with Mother*.

"cerebral, gentle . . . excellence from his children": Ibid.

"Let them know you're there": Katie Couric, *The Best Advice*.

"Please, Elinor, don't encourage her . . . "Yes, *sir*"": Ibid.

"I used to memorize . . . 'my sister's yearbook'": Ibid.

"her station wagon over to . . . smooching in the basement": Katie Couric, *Life with Mother*.

"I wrestled with bulimia all through college . . . this rigidity . . . I would sometimes beat myself up for that": Luchina Fisher, "Katie Couric: 'I Wrestled with Bulimia.'" ABCnews. com., and Lesley Kennedy, "Katie Couric Admits to Bulimia Struggles," More.com.

"I was one of those . . . 'I don't need a man'": Judith Marlane, *Women in Television News*.

"best dress-for-success outfit . . . 'Sure, come up'" and "I told him . . . asset to the organization": Katie Couric, *The Best Advice*.

"sat around drinking Scotch after the newscast": Lisa DePaulo, "Killer Katie," *George*.

"I used to see her . . . proud of her role": Judith Marlane, *Women in Television News*.

"'We're gonna give you a break, kid' . . . real confidence builder": Lisa DePaulo, "Killer Katie," *George*.

"I'm pretty convinced . . . inherit the earth": Katie Couric, *The Best Advice*.

"I remember being so saddened . . . the most important thing in life": Judith Marlane, *Women in Television News*.

Quotes from Other Speakers Obtained from Media Sources:

Sam Donaldson: "K-K-K-Katie, beautiful Katie . . .": Lisa DePaulo, "Killer Katie," *George*.

Walter Cronkite: "sickening sensation that . . . show business had failed": Nichola D. Gutgold, *Seen and Heard*.

Dana Rudman: "She was down and dirty . . .": Jennet Conant, "Don't Call Me Perky," *Redbook*.

Dana Rudman: "She looked young . . . pushed": Ibid.

Wendy Walker: "come home from work . . . lying on the floor": Ibid.

CHAPTER FOUR: **Brainy, Blond, Glamorous**

Among the People the Author Interviewed Are:

Connie Chung, Bill Small, Bob Taylor, Jennifer Siebens, Sandy Socolow, Roger Mudd, Av
  Westin, Ginny Vicario, Joe Peyronnin, Patricia O'Gorman, Ellen Rossen, Ira Rosen,
  Anna Robertson, Jeff Fager, Susan Zirinsky, Mark Robertson, Marlene Sanders, Richard
  Wald, Phyllis McGrady, Betsy West, Roger Goodman, and various anonymous sources.

Quotes from the Principal Subject Obtained from Media Sources:

"I would sleep . . . what I could get": Margo Howard, "*60 Minutes*' Newest Correspondent,"
  People.

"My sister is elegant . . . to fall down the stairs": Ibid.

"mother's door . . . a blind panic" and "wearing a juice-stained . . . dazzling riposte": Joan
  Juliet Buck, "Live Mike," *Vanity Fair.*

"In the first ninety seconds . . . center of the dance": Ibid.

"I thought he was . . . not judgmental about anybody": Judith Newman, "Diane Sawyer,"
  Ladies' Home Journal.

"we had lunch . . . sort of trailed off": Ibid.

"I have no taste . . . floor pillows": Ibid.

"with knocking knees. . . . far worse than me": Rita Wilson, "Diane Sawyer: Truth &
  Beauty." *Harper's Bazaar*

"I'm so undomestic. . . . about the things she knows about": Newman, *Ladies' Home Journal.*

'Well, this is sort of fun, *too*': Lee Woodruff, "The Latest News on Diane Sawyer," *Ladies'
  Home Journal.*

'I've got a great ass': Frederick Exley, "If Nixon Could Possess," *Esquire.*

"A sonata for harp and jackhammer": Richard Zoglin, "Star Power," *Time.*

Quotes from Other Speakers Obtained from Media Sources:

Richard Zoglin: "rich, honeyed voice. . . . affected by" [Pauley]: Richard Zoglin, "Star
  Power," *Time.*

Margo Howard: "a thinking man's Angie Dickinson . . . connection to a gentler time":
  "*60 Minutes*' Newest Correspondent."

Mike Nichols: "I thought . . . I was real, too": Joan Juliet Buck, "Live Mike," *Vanity Fair.*

Mike Nichols: "I went totally crazy": Joan Juliet Buck, "Live Mike," *Vanity Fair.*

Mike Nichols: "I didn't want her . . . went very, very fast": Ibid.

Joan Ganz Cooney: "*He* . . . is the decorator. . . . the furniture": Joan Juliet Buck, "Live
  Mike," *Vanity Fair.*

Mike Nichols: "She cuts out thirty-five . . . sometimes complex": Jesse Green, "When in
  Doubt, Seduce," *New York.*

Mike Nichols: "My happiness . . . married Diane": Jesse Green, "When in Doubt, Seduce,"
  New York.

Mike Nichols: "Falling in love . . . the end of all games": Joan Juliet Buck, "Live Mike,"
  Vanity Fair.

Carole Simpson: "We think we have a problem. . . . hasn't crossed your mind." Judith
  Marlane, *Women in Television News.*

Carole Simpson: "mouths fell open. . . . 'You're absolutely right'": Ibid.

Richard Zoglin: "The prospect of losing Sawyer . . . an effort to keep her": Zoglin, "Star
  Power."

Don Hewitt: "a monumental talent . . . remotely crippled *60 Minutes*": Ibid.

Sam Donaldson: "When I got into the business . . . accept that": Judith Marlane, *Women in Television News.*

Barbara Walters: Diane and I struggled . . . Diane and I were more polite: Barbara Walters, *Audition.*

Sources Particularly Helpful to the Author on Specific or Provocative Details:

On Diane and Nixon after she went to CBS:

Robert Sam Anson, *Exile.*

On Barbara Walters's ex-husband Adelson's Mafia ties:

Bryan Burrough, "Remembrance of Wings Past," *Vanity Fair.*

On Carole Simpson and the ABC women's confrontation with Roone Arledge:

Judith Marlane, *Women in Television News Revisited.*

On Diane's romance with Mike Nichols:

Joan Juliet Buck, "Live Mike," *Vanity Fair.*

On the subject of Mike Nichols's and others' problems with the drug Halcion:

Gina Kolata, "Finding a Bad Night's Sleep with Halcion," *New York Times.* Joseph O'Neill, "Roth v. Roth v. Roth," *Atlantic.*

On criticism arising from Diane's interview with Michael Jackson:

Maureen Orth, "The Jackson Jive," *Vanity Fair.*

On the subject of Diane's career trajectory over these years:

Ken Auletta, "Promise Her the Moon," *New Yorker.*

CHAPTER FIVE: **America's Sweetheart to Premature Widow**

Among the People the Author Interviewed Are:

Maria Fleet, Don Browne, Jane Pauley, Kathleen Lobb, Jeff Zucker, Andrew Tyndall, Mandy Locke, Betsy Yowell Howell, Lori Beecher, author's off-the-record conversation with a Jane Pauley maternity-leave substitute during an interview with her for *McCall's* magazine, Allison Gollust, Yael Federbush, Janie McMullen Florea, and various anonymous sources.

Quotes from the Principal Subject Obtained from Media Sources:

"used to tease him . . . make them look old": Lisa DePaulo, "Killer Katie," *George.*

"My husband is traditional . . . amused by that": Katie Couric, *The Best Advice.*

"This is *Today* . . . stuck with *you*": *Today,* April 5, 1991, YouTube. "Katie Couric Talks," *Larry King Live.*

"Not to sound too . . . role on the show": Nichola D. Gutgold, *Seen and Heard.*

"It was very contentious . . . six years ago": Peter Johnson, "Couric's Good Mornings," *USA Today.*

"It was slightly bizarre . . . *Vanity Fair*": Jennet Conant, "Don't Call Me Perky," *Redbook.*

"I'm one of these less contentious . . . easy": Lisa DePaulo, "Killer Katie," *George.* For the Katie-Bush interview: Bill Carter, "The 1992 Campaign," *New York Times.*

"I was trying to prove my manhood": Ibid.

"From Branford . . . that's chosen me" and "I think I'm . . . but not *too* attractive": Elisabeth Bumiller, "What You Don't Know About Katie Couric," *Good Housekeeping.*

"My friends call me . . . going and going": Judy Flander, "The Two Faces of Katie Couric": *American Journalism Review.*

"It's really hard . . . really misses her" and "It was hard . . . *really* hard" and "Sometimes
  Jay and I will . . . attention to it" and "My husband . . . dealing with a lot" and "It's a
  constant . . . my family": Jennet Conant, "Don't Call Me Perky," *Redbook.*

"Settling into our . . . soul-filling contentment": Katie Couric, *The Best Advice.*

"I guess . . . tobacco industry": Adam Nagourney, "Dole Criticizes Role of Press," *New York
  Times.*

"There was a lot . . . *creative* it was": "Katie Couric Talks," *Larry King Live.*

"Then tell us what the truth . . . I can take it": Lisa DePaulo, "Killer Katie," *George.*

 "Jay had lost a lot of weight . . . Don't worry. *It's not cancer*": "Couric Talks," *Larry King
  Live.*

"It's a blur . . . hope and the positivity": Ibid.

"It's these parallel universes . . . buying sweaters.": Ibid.

"people walking down the . . . you're going through": Katie Couric, *The Best Advice.*

"cheerleader . . . 'We can beat this thing'": Couric Talks," *Larry King Live.*

"semblance of the normality . . . a question and [I would] think about Jay": Ibid.

"He did not . . . until the bitter end": "Colleagues Turn Out to Mourn with Couric,"
  Associated Press.

Quotes from Other Speakers Obtained from Media Sources:

Tim Russert: "She was articulate . . . wholesome appeal": Roxanne Roberts, "Yipes! It's
  Katie Couric!," *Washington Post.*

Dick Ebersol: "appeal to women" and "unique talents . . . cohesiveness": Edward Klein,
  "NBC's Great Blond Hope," *Vanity Fair.*

Tom Brokaw: "fascinated" and "This isn't the case with Katie": Judy Flander, "The Two
  Faces of Katie Couric," *American Journalism Review.*

Letter from a fan to Katie: "You have it puffed up . . . it was gawd-awful": Roxanne Roberts,
  "Yipes! It's Katie Couric!," *Washington Post.*

Tom Shales: "She hit *Today* . . . Bryant Gumbel's arm": Tom Shales, "Top of the Morning,
  Katie!," *Washington Post.*

Judy Flander: "a Cinderella . . .": Judy Flander, "The Two Faces of Katie Couric," *American
  Journalism Review.*

Jennet Conant: "She skyrocketed . . .": Jennet Conant, "Don't Call Me Perky," *Redbook.*

Tom Shales: "The hard part is finding a flaw . . . Thank you, God": Tom Shales, "Top of the
  Morning, Katie!," *Washington Post.*

Bruce Weber: petite and tomboyish . . . for that matter, adult: Bruce Weber, "Home with
  Katie," *New York Times.*

Tom Shales: "brighten[ing] the program . . . place among morning programs": Tom Shales,
  "Top of the Morning, Katie!," *Washington Post.*

Poznek letter and lawsuit: "Feinberg v. Poznek," Justia U.S. Supreme Court Center. Dan
  Mangan and Dareh Gregorian, "Hasty Nanny's Mud Blitz," *New York Post.* "Letters,"
  People, October 4, 1993.

CHAPTER SIX : **From Atlanta to Bosnia: A Crusader Is Born**

Among the People the Author Interviewed Are:

Nancy Diamond, David Bernknopf, Maria Fleet, Sparkle Hayter, Amy Walter, Liza
  McGuirk, Flip Spiceland, Gail Evans, Marcia Ladendorff, Bob Cain, Diana Greene,

Diana Bellew, Parisa Khosravi, Leila Amanpour, Lizzy Amanpour, David Rust (including—received with appreciation—passages from Rust's Bosnia diaries), Ron Haviv, Pierre Bairin, Mark Phillips, Emma Daly, Judy Milestone, Bella Pollen, Andrew Tkach, and various anonymous sources.

Quotes from the Principal Subject Obtained from Media Sources:

"on the foreign desk . . . a foreign accent": Christiane Amanpour, "2000 Murrow Awards Ceremony Acceptance Speech."

"barely meeting payroll": Christiane Amanpour, "To My Family at CNN," private e-mail.

"I am sorry . . . 'somewhere else and start'": Christiane Amanpour, "2000 Murrow Awards Ceremony Acceptance Speech."

"was character-building stuff": Ibid.

"I had to lose . . . 'to be on television here'": "Christiane Amanpour's Address to University of Michigan Commencent," University of Michigan News Service.

"I consider Bosnia . . . ever done": Ibid.

"I have found . . . an amazing door opener": *Piers Morgan Tonight*: "Interview with Christiane Amanpour," June 22, 2011, transcript.

"I said yes . . . done this career": Jessica Ravitz, "Fearless to the End," CNN.com.

"where I became . . . closest of bonds": Christiane Amanpour, "To My Family at CNN," private e-mail.

"Bosnia . . . and churches dynamited": Jane Hall, "Q&A with Christiane Amanpour: On Life Near Death: In Bosnia for CNN," *Los Angeles Times*, July 14, 1993.

"all I could keep saying . . . ran out of there": Oprah Winfrey, "Oprah Talks to Christiane Amanpour," *O, The Oprah Magazine.*

"Seeing children . . . don't believe is possible": Jane Hall, "Q&A with Christiane Amanpour," *Los Angeles Times*, July 14, 1993.

"I cannot believe this . . . horrifying, and savage": Ibid.

"Mr. President . . . like to be taken" and "No, but speeches . . . *madam*" and "That poor woman . . . do not blame her" and "great service to the whole world": "Christiane Amanpour Questions Bill Clinton," YouTube.

"Once Srebrenica . . . not reporting it": Suzanne Goldenberg, "Somehow I Don't Feel It in My Gut," *Guardian.*

"Objectivity means . . . war crime?": Oprah Winfrey, "Oprah Talks to Christiane Amanpour," *O, The Oprah Magazine.* Christiane Amanpour, "2000 Murrow Awards Ceremony Acceptance Speech."

Quotes from Other Speakers Obtained from Media Sources:

Eason Jordan: "She knew exactly . . . nuisance of herself": Leslie Bennetts, "Woman o' War," *Vanity Fair.*

Fictional male character through narrator's voice: "At first glance . . . at the neck": Neil MacFarquhar, *The Sand Café.*

Fictional male character through narrator's voice: "arouses attention wherever she goes": Ibid. (Also, on the subject of this roman à clef: Christopher Dickey, "Love and Rockets," *New York Times Book Review.*)

Don Hewitt: "I don't give a fuck . . . reporter game": Leslie Bennetts, "Woman o' War," *Vanity Fair.*

Additional Sources Helpful to the Author:

Marie Brenner, "Marie Colvin's Private War," *Vanity Fair.*

"Margaret Moth: Obituary," *Wichita Eagle.*

Jessica Ravitz, "Fearless to the End," CNN.com.

CHAPTER SEVEN: **The Cool Drink of Water Versus the Girl Next Door**

Among the People the Author Interviewed Are:

Phyllis McGrady, Shelley Ross, Yael Federbush, Anna Robertson, Lori Beecher, Betsy Yowell Howell, Lisa Paulsen, Kathleen Lobb, Pat Shifke, Allison Gollust, Jonathan Wald, Janie McMullen Florea, Andrew Heyward, and various anonymous sources.

Quotes from the Principal Subjects Obtained from Media Sources:

"I said to Charlie" and "'I'll do it if you do it'": Ken Auletta, "The Dawn Patrol," *New Yorker.*

"I just didn't feel . . . and comforting one another": "Katie Couric Talks," *Larry King Live.*

"It was time . . . without Jay": Joanna Powell, "Katie's Haven," *Good Housekeeping.*

"came into the kitchen and she had been crying" and "just crops up . . . missing him so much": Ibid.

"watching over us and protecting us": Ibid.

"like Florence Henderson on *The Brady Bunch*": Ibid.

"She taught me . . . living" and "Emily found it . . . sister" and "The truth is . . . Emily Couric's sister": "Katie Couric Talks," *Larry King Live.*

Quotes from Other Speakers Obtained from Media Sources:

Charlie Gibson: "my sell-by date had arrived": Meryl Gordon, "Duel at Sunrise," *New York.*

Bill Carter: "Reaching beyond $60 million . . . and a half years": Bill Carter, "Katie Couric Signs NBC Contract Said to Be Largest in TV News," *New York Times.*

Alessandra Stanley: "Something has to be . . . douse the lights": Alessandra Stanley, "*Today* Seeks Yesterday's Glory," *New York Times.*

Among the YouTubes and Transcripts of Interviews Conducted by Diane and Katie:

Katie Couric Columbine Interview: "Columbine Interview: NBC_630," KatieCouric.com. "Katie Couric Talks," *Larry King Live.*

"Whitney Houston and Diane Sawyer," *Primetime,* YouTube.

Sources Particularly Helpful to the Author on Specific Subjects:

On Katie Couric's colonoscopy:

"The Katie Couric Effect": "UM Study: Katie Couric's Colonoscopy Caused Cross-country Climb in Colon Cancer Checks," University of Michigan. Amber J. Tresca, "Colorectal Screening Gets 'The Katie Couric Effect,'" About.com.

Katie's cancer charity work: Jay Monahan Center for Gastrointestinal Health, MonahanCenter.org. EIF: National Colorectal Cancer Research Alliance, EIFoundation.org.

On the competition between the two shows and anchors:

Ken Auletta, "The Dawn Patrol," *New Yorker.* Bill Carter, "Katie Couric Signs NBC Contract," *New York Times.*

Meryl Gordon, "Duel at Sunrise," *New York.* Alessandra Stanley, "*Today* Seeks Yesterday's Glory," *New York Times.*

On September 11, 2001, and aftermath:

YouTube clips of *Good Morning America* and *Today* openings plus first twenty minutes of
coverage on September 11, 2001. Michael D. Lemonick, "Bioterrorism: The Next
Threat?," *Time.*

CHAPTER EIGHT: **Home from War, Still in Battle**

Among the People the Author Interviewed Are:

Diana Bellew, Lizzy Amanpour, Emma Daly, Liza McGuirk, Bella Pollen, Parisa Khosravi,
Mark Phillips, Andrew Tkach, Kathy O'Hearn, David Bernknopf, Pierre Bairin, Ron
Haviv, Tony Maddox, and various anonymous sources.

Quotes from the Principal Subject Obtained from Media Sources:

"I couldn't have . . . had a kid" and "All my energy . . . 'ever have a child'": Oprah Winfrey,
"Oprah Talks to Christiane Amanpour," *O, The Oprah Magazine.*

"There came a moment . . . consciously changed myself": Ibid.

"We were truly distraught" and "We thought . . . should happen": Nicholas Kralev, "You
Can't Hurry Love," *Financial Times.*

"I was *their* age when the Revolution began": Christiane Amanpour, "Revolutionary
Journey," Amanpour.Blogs.CNN.com.

"the road to hell . . . arsenic" and "highest risk . . . die of cancer": Christiane Amanpour and
Ed Bradley, "The Best of Intentions: UNICEF," *60 Minutes.*

"a very happy . . . weekend": "A Tribute to JFK Jr.," *Larry King Weekend,* CNN.com
(including transcript from July 15, 1999, interview with Christiane Amanpour).

"loyal and generous and faithful . . . forty years of his life" and "many people . . . John fail":
Ibid.

"I was very cavalier . . . 'bulletproof diapers'": Oprah Winfrey, "Oprah Talks to Christiane
Amanpour," *O, The Oprah Magazine.*

"Motherhood is . . . wait and see": Nicholas Kralev, "You Can't Hurry Love," *Financial
Times.*

"I was conscious . . . 'Let the guys do it'": Christian Amanpour, "Find the Thing,"
California Women's Conference.

"The minute . . . everything changed" and "There's a love inside . . . capable of" and "And
there's no way in hell . . . surviving": Oprah Winfrey, "Oprah Talks to Christiane
Amanpour," *O, The Oprah Magazine.*

"devastated . . . aired their footage": Christiane Amanpour, "2000 Murrow Awards
Ceremony Acceptance Speech."

"He's not a househusband . . . voice of Americans overseas": Ibid.

"To avoid crushing debts . . . all their girl babies": Christiane Amanpour and Mike Wallace,
"For Love and Money," *60 Minutes.*

"The hellish scene . . . health care" and "ethnic cleansing . . . Sudanese army": Christiane
Amanpour, "Sudan's Hellish Humanitarian Crisis," CNN.com.

"There is a big prejudice" and "about Africa and about telling news": Hanna Ingber Win,
"Christiane Amanpour on Her Genocide Documentary," *Huffington Post.*

"According to the United Nations . . . 18.4 million": Christiane Amanpour, "World Fails to
Save Africa's AIDS Orphans," CNN transcript.

"'Please, God' . . . I do it again": Suzanne Goldenberg, "'Somehow I Don't Feel It in My
Gut,'" *Guardian.*

"You challenged people" and "You said that your face . . . mean by that" and "People cry
    when . . . back to health" and "*This* Yushchenko I'm still not used to" and "To die is not
    very original . . . that's special": "Yushchenko: Live and Carry On," CBS.com.

Quotes from Other Speakers Obtained from Media Sources:

Peter Pringle: "he never had time to date": Malcolm Morehouse, "Foreign Affair:
    Christiane Amanpour and James Rubin Find Love on the Run," *People*.

Jordan Tamagni: "tall, handsome . . . Mercedes convertible": Ibid.

Jamie Rubin: "talk to anyone . . . the sports jocks": Mark Francis Cohen: "Flack Like Me:
    Jamie Rubin's Ego-System," *Capital Style*.

"equating the extremely . . . so without challenge": Felix Gillette, "MSBC's Dan Abrams'
    War of Faith Against CNN," *New York Observer*.

Dan Abrams: "worst kind of moral relativism" and "shameful advocacy" and "I felt the
    journalism . . . shoddy" and "I felt very strongly . . . unfair" and "it was a very
    successful . . . documentary for CNN": Brad Wilmouth, "MSNBC's Abrams Hits CNN's
    Amanpour for Defending Islamic Fundamentalism," NewsBusters.com.

*Among the Many Transcripts and Videos (Some Provided—with Gratitude—by Andrew
Tkach, Others Web-Accessed) of Christiane's International Stories Described and Quoted from
in This Chapter:*

"Billion-Dollar Business," *60 Minutes*.

Christiane Amanpour: "From CNN's Chief International Correspondent Christiane
    Amanpour: Sudan's Hellish Humanitarian Crisis," CNN.com.

Christiane Amanpour and Ed Bradley, "The Best of Intentions: UNICEF," *60 Minutes*.

Christiane Amanpour and Mike Wallace, "A Million Men, Women and Children," *60
    Minutes*.

Christiane Amanpour and Mike Wallace, "For Love and Money," *60 Minutes*.

Christiane Amanpour and Mike Wallace, "The Women of Afghanistan," *60 Minutes*.

Christiane Amanpour and Mike Wallace, "Weapons of Mass Destruction," *60 Minutes*.

Christiane Amanpour and Morley Safer, "Scars of War," 60 Minutes.

Christiane Amanpour and Morley Safer, "Thou Shalt Not Kill," *60 Minutes*.

Christiane Amanpour and Steve Kroft, "Sleeping Sickness," *60 Minutes*.

Christiane Amanpour and Steve Kroft, "Sunni Triangle," *60 Minutes*.

Christiane Amanpour and Steve Kroft, "Trokosi: Young Girls Sent into Slavery," *60
    Minutes*.

CHAPTER NINE: **First Female Anchor**

Among the People the Author Interviewed Are:

Mark Robertson, Ira Rosen, Marcy McGinniss, Jeff Zucker, Lisa Paulsen, Sandy Socolow,
    Andrew Tyndall, Richard Wald, Jeff Fager, Bob Schieffer, Pat Shifke, Rick Kaplan,
    Margaret Aro, and various anonymous sources.

Quotes from the Principal Subjects Obtained from Media Sources:

"You mean . . . I'm *white*" and "But . . . see me dance": Diane Salvatore, "Robin Roberts and
    Diane Sawyer: Soul Sisters," *Ladies' Home Journal*

"told me it was the worst idea . . . my whole life": Susan Dominus, "Hey, Katie—How's
    That New Job?," *Glamour*.

"it's the worst-kept secret": *Today*, Wednesday, May 31, 2006, YouTube.

"I'm going to be working on the *CBS Evening News* and *60 Minutes*": Ibid.

"I've been called a cougar . . . proud to be a tiger": Katie Couric, "My Speech to Princeton."

"This is not your grandfather's newscast" and "I think people . . . And intelligence": Jenny Allen, "Taking a Chance on Herself," *Good Housekeeping*.

"I love Jon . . . down the line": Kurt Andersen, "Humor Is the New Gravitas," *New York*.

"I think most people . . . pretentious word" and "to make news . . . sink in or register": Susan Dominus, "Hey, Katie—How's That New Job?," *Glamour*.

"bugs people . . . disappointing to some people": Joe Hagan, "Alas, Poor Couric," *New York*.

"I've . . . decided [that] 'gravitas' . . . 'testicles'": Alex Weprin, "Katie Couric," TVNewser.

"What is the word . . . *divo*?": Susan Dominus, "Hey, Katie—How's That New Job?," *Glamour*.

"It can be lonely": Jenny Allen, "Taking a Chance on Herself," *Good Housekeeping*.

"All these years, and only one woman" and "actually asked . . . in his hair": Katie Couric, "My Speech to Princeton."

Quotes from Other Speakers Obtained from Media Sources:

Joe Hagan: "When Diane Sawyer . . . *Good Morning America*" and "'Yes and no' . . . Sawyer's ambivalence" and "over many conversations" and "Westin says that he gave Sawyer . . . she did want it" and "instead of being content . . . loose ends": Joe Hagan, "Charlie the Conqueror," *New York*.

Rebecca Dana: "Golden Sphinx . . . ever" and "Diane is keeping her cards . . . chest" and "None of us . . . plans to do": Rebecca Dana, "Diane Sawyer Is ABC's Last Diva," *New York Observer*.

Peyser and Roberts: "Will viewers accept . . . mascara" and "Couric is cut . . . ever on television" and "We've seen her . . . literally" and "We know her kids . . . gossip magazines": Marc Peyser and Jonnie L. Roberts, "Katie's News," *Newsweek*.

Peyser and Roberts: "Couric cries regularly" and "the girl next door" and "succeed as a network news anchor": Ibid.

Matt Lauer: "Welcome to a very special . . . *Today*" and "Now, after more than fifteen thousand . . . May 31, 2006": *Today*, May 31, 2006, YouTube. Peter Johnson, "Couric's Good Mornings," *USA Today*.

Barbara Walters: "I can't help but contrast . . . would be enormous": Barbara Walters, *Audition*.

Joe Hagan: "a chatty, friendly vibe . . . Katie": Joe Hagan, "Charlie the Conqueror," *New York*.

Source speaking to Nikki Finke: "needed someone . . . hard on him": Nikki Finke, "Update: More Diane Does Mel," Deadline.com, YouTube clips.

Fareed Zakaria: "a vapid emptying out . . . into her head": Fareed Zakaria, "Palin Is Ready? Please," *Newsweek*.

Phoebe Eaton: "peeled . . . like a raw carrot": Phoebe Eaton, "Katie Couric's Primetime," *Harper's Bazaar*.

Sources Particularly Helpful to the Author on Specific Subjects:

On Diane's friendship with Robin Roberts:

Diane Salvatore, "Robin Roberts and Diane Sawyer: Soul Sisters," *Ladies' Home Journal*.

On salary decreases for other CBS correspondents:

Joe Hagan, "Alas, Poor Couric," *New York*.

On CBS Evening News's ratings collapse:

For the figure 5.5 million viewers to 7 million viewers: David Bauder, "Iraq Is Ratings Drag for Katie Couric," *USA Today*.

Among the Many Transcripts and Videos of Katie's and Diane's Interviews Described and Quoted from in This Chapter:

Katie interviewing the Edwardses:

Katie Couric, "John and Elizabeth Edwards Open Up," *60 Minutes*.

Diane interviewing Gibson:

"How Despairing Gibson Found 'The Passion,'" ABCNews.com. "Mel Gibson Says He Feels 'Powerless Over Everything,'" *Good Morning America*, ABCNews.com. "Mel Gibson Addresses Accusations of Anti-Semitism," *Good Morning America*, ABCNews.com. Various YouTube clips of Mel Gibson talking to Diane Sawyer on *Good Morning America* and *Primetime*.

Katie interviewing Ahmadinejad:

Katie Couric, "Ahmadinejad: The Status Quo Cannot Keep," *CBS Evening News,* various YouTube clips.

Katie interviewing Palin:

Interview transcripts from the 2008 campaign, CBSNews.com. Katie Couric, "One-on-One with Sarah Palin," CBSNews.com. Jacques Steinberg, "Couric Rebounds with Web and Palin," *New York Times*.

Articles That Were Particularly Useful for the Sweep of Katie's and Diane's Careers over the Period of This Chapter:

Rebecca Dana, "The ABCs of Diane's Deal," *Daily Beast*.

Rebecca Dana, "Diane Sawyer Is ABC's Last Diva," *New York Observer.*

Kurt Andersen, "Humor Is the New Gravitas," *New York*.

Joe Hagan, "Alas, Poor Couric," *New York*.

Joe Hagan, "Charlie the Conqueror," *New York*.

Alessandra Stanley, "In Iraq, Couric Hones Her Hard-News Image," *New York Times*.

Jacques Steinberg, "Couric Rebounds with Web and Palin," *New York Times*.

Brian Stelter, "Doubts Fade and Couric Is Energized," *New York Times*.

CHAPTER TEN : **Two Out of Three and Then Three Out of Six**

Among the People the Author Interviewed Are:

Jon Banner, Margaret Aro, Andrew Tyndall, Andrew Heyward, Andrew Tkach, Mark Phillips, Kathy O'Hearn, Karim Sadjadpour, Richard Wald, Bella Pollen, Lisa Paulsen, Ron Haviv, and various anonymous sources.

Quotes from the Principal Subjects Obtained from Media Sources:

"When we landed . . . help would arrive" and "It's so hackneyed . . . don't exist in Haiti": Katie Couric, "Haiti: One Year Later," *Huffington Post*.

"My husband . . . my politics": Lee Woodruff, "The Latest News on Diane Sawyer," *Ladies' Home Journal*.

To My Family at CNN . . . to the first Gulf War and never never wav[er] . . . not goodbye, Christiane: Christiane Amanpour, "To My Family at CNN," e-mail.

"into the palace encircled by chaos" and "those rioting thugs . . . on this breaking story" and "an extraordinary experience . . . "'Egyptians fighting Egyptians'": "Diane Sawyer Checks In with Christiane Amanpour in Egypt," ABCNews.com.

"I'm a reporter . . . not an anchorperson": Jon Friedman, "Christiane Amanpour," Market Watch, *Wall Street Journal.*

"It's clearly an appalling . . . nightmare" and "I am grateful . . . much worse": "Christiane Amanpour on Lara Logan Assault," PiersMorgan.Blogs.CNN.com.

"looking every inch . . . he had honed" and "But if you say . . . capturing Benghazi" and "Your own airline pilots . . . defected": Christiane Amanpour, "'My People Love Me,'" ABCNews.com.

"the storm without pity" and "master class in enduring crisis" and "to come together in one body" and "*for three hours*": "Staying Strong in the Face of Tragedy," ABCNews.com.

Quotes from Other Speakers Obtained from Media Sources:

Bill Carter and Brian Stelter: "two of the three . . . female" and "in the past . . . Connie Chung" and "the longtime . . . long-suffering": Bill Carter and Brian Stelter, "At ABC, an Anchor Shift," *New York Times.*

Howard Kurtz: "When Diane Sawyer . . . news anchor" and "her first words . . . President David Westin" and "only after Westin . . . not to retire": Howard Kurtz, "Diane Sawyer to Become ABC's Evening News Anchor," *Washington Post.*

Andrew Tyndall: "No evening newscast . . . with Diane Sawyer" and Her enthusiasm . . . inspirational, not partisan: Ibid.

Kati Marton: "I noticed a tall, blond woman . . . wordless embrace": Kati Marton, *Paris: A Love Story.*

Alessandra Stanley: "panache and a no-nonsense briskness" and "Ms. Amanpour is not . . . those who have": Alessandra Stanley, "A TV Host Challenges a Guest," *New York Times.*

Tom Shales: "The Grand Duchess Amanpour . . . Overseas" and "With pomp . . . relocated to a desk job" and "highly touted global orientation . . . contrived": Tom Shales, "Tom Shales Reviews Christiane Amanpour's Lackluster Debut," *Washington Post.*

Page Six: "The knives are out . . . a 'distant outsider'": "Staff at ABC News' DC Bureau Is Icy," Page Six, *New York Post.*

Jim Newell: "Here's 'America's Girl' . . . *Just don't*": Jim Newell, "Leave Our Katie Couric Alone!," Gawker.

Lara Logan: "Suddenly, before I even . . . from behind" and "I think my shirt . . . different directions": "Lara Logan Breaks Her Silence," *60 Minutes.*

Sources Particularly Helpful in Overview of Diane's Ascent to Anchor Chair:

Alessandra Stanley, "Good Evening, America," *New York Times.*

Alessandra Stanley, "A TV Host Challenges a Guest," *New York Times.*

"Charlie Gibson's Announcement Email," *Huffington Post.*

"Brian Williams: Charlie Gibson 'A Pro, 'Diane Sawyer' Legendary,'" *Huffington Post.*

On ABC News's referencing of miracles, per Tyndall:

"Video Witnesses Claim Miracle Man Saved Car Crash Victim," ABCNews.com.

CHAPTER ELEVEN: **"Any White Male in the Chair . . ."**

Among the People the Author Interviewed Are:

Paul Friedman, Sandy Socolow, Rick Kaplan, Liza McGuirk, Jeff Zucker, Ginny Vicario, and various anonymous sources.

Quotes from the Principal Subjects Obtained from Media Sources:

"I have decided . . . *News*" and "I'm really proud . . . about the future": Alicia Dennis, "Katie Couric: I Am Leaving," *People.*

"I don't understand—why are [the Kardashians] so famous": Danielle Valente. "Kim Kardashian, Katie Couric Dispute Fueled by Magazine Interviews, Hashtags," *Newsday.*

"I can barely contain . . . *no* moral equivalence" and "*Wait just a second*" and "The president . . . go unchecked" and "Fifteen, sixteen . . . Rwanda" *Anderson Cooper 360,* CNN, YouTube clip and transcript of Christiane Amanpour, Charles Blow, Christopher Dickey, and Andrew Sullivan.

"It's not emotion . . . It's not emotion": Ibid.

"I'm still here . . . 'got to do something'": Lee Woodruff, "The Latest News on Diane Sawyer," *Ladies' Home Journal.*

Quotes from Other Speakers Obtained from Media Sources:

Jeff Fager: "best for both parties": Andrea Morabito, "New CBS News Chair," BroadcastingCable.com.

Howard Kurtz: "CBS has asked Katie": Howard Kurtz, "CBS Wants Contract Extension for Katie Couric," *Daily Beast.*

CNN Representative: "We could not be happier . . . colleague and friend": Brian Stelter, "Amanpour to Leave ABC," *New York Times.*

Bill Carter: "scored the best initial rating . . . in 2002" and "Couric has bolted . . . enormous audience": Bill Carter, "Big Ratings for Debut of *Katie,*" *New York Times.*

Darius Rubin: This summer . . . an amazing trip and "I even got in some . . . efforts" and "never scared" and "driver seemed . . . in a movie": Christiane Amanpour, "Retracing Bible's 'Story of a Family,'" ABCNews.com.

New York Daily News: "seriously considering retirement" and "few close friends . . . care of her family": "Diane Sawyer Weighs Stepping Down," *New York Daily News.*

ABC Representative: "That's a bunch. . . . in any way": Ibid.

Bill Carter: "Like Johnny Carson. . . . 'in the best way,'": Bill Carter, "Walters to Announce 2014 Retirement on 'The View,'" *New York Times.*

Brian Stelter: ABC's 6.30 newscast . . . ratings competition and In a twist . . . was at work: Brian Stelter, "ABC News Dethrones NBC," *New York Times.*

Austin Smith: "The show was oversold . . . expectations": Austin Smith, "Couric's ABC Future Is Hazy," Page Six, *New York Post.*

Perez Hilton: "an unmitigated disaster" and "dreadfully boring": Perez Hilton, "Katie Couric's 'Dreadfully Boring,'" PerezHilton.com.

Jennifer Aniston: "Is she a legitimate . . . the *Today* show": Chiderah Monde, "Jennifer Aniston Slams Nudist Rumors, Disses Katie Couric: 'Is She a Legitimate Journalist?'" *New York Daily News.*

Marissa Mayer: "Katie's depth of experience . . . Yahoo Network," Paul Fahri, "Katie Couric Set to Officially Join Yahoo," *Washington Post.*

Andrew Tyndall: "*ABC World News* Is Certifiably Disneyfied" and "a grand plan to homogenize . . . and reality TV": *Tyndall Report,* December 2013.

ABC News rebuttal: "Our mission . . . quantity with quality": Meenal Vamburkar, "ABC News Refutes Report," *Mediaite*.

Alessandra Stanley: "In the era of Diane . . . entrust to a woman": Alessandra Stanley, "In Barbara Walters' Highlight Reel," *New York Times*.

Alessandra Stanley: "As in other fields . . . penthouse office suites": Alessandra Stanley, "A New Anchor Steps In, Skipping Frills and Drama," *New York Times*.

BIBLIOGRAPHY

The following are articles, both online and in print, as well as YouTube clips, books, correspondence, and so forth that were utilized in the writing of this book. Not included are the sources—principally, Web-searchable—of my general research on the multitude of national and international news events mentioned in this book as stories these women covered.

ARTICLES, ONLINE AND IN PRINT

Allen, Jenny. "Taking a Chance on Herself." *Good Housekeeping*, November 2006.

———. "Welcome Back, Katie." *Good Housekeeping*, September 2012.

Allocca, Kevin. "Diane Sawyer Interviews Rihanna." TVNewser, Mediabistro.com, November 2, 2009.

Amanpour, Christiane. "'My People Love Me': Moammar Gadhafi Denies Demonstrations Against Him Anywhere in Libya." Reporter's Notebook, ABCNews.com.

———. "Retracing Bible's 'Story of a Family.'" Reporter's Notebook, ABCNews.com, December 10, 2012.

———. "Revolutionary Journey." Amanpour.Blogs.CNN.com, April 13, 2012.

———. "Sudan's Hellish Humanitarian Crisis." CNN.com, July 26, 2004.

Andersen, Kurt. "Humor Is the New Gravitas." *New York*, September 11, 2006.

Auletta, Ken. "The Dawn Patrol." *New Yorker*, August 8, 2005.

———. "Promise Her the Moon." *New Yorker*, February 14, 1994.

Baker, K. C. "Cancer 'Destroyed My Family.'" *People*, August 27, 2008.

Bankoff, Caroline. "Diane Sawyer Either Has or Has Not Landed the First Gabrielle Giffords Interview." *New York*, September 12, 2011.

Bauder, David. "Iraq Is Ratings Drag for Katie Couric." *USA Today*, September 11, 2007.

———. "Katie Couric Leaving *CBS Evening News* Anchor Chair, According to Network Executive." Associated Press, April 4, 2011.

Bennetts, Leslie. "Woman o' War." *Vanity Fair*, September 1, 1996.

Berkowitz, Elana. "Five Minutes With: Christiane Amanpour." *Nation*, October 30, 2006.

Brenner, Marie. "Marie Colvin's Private War." *Vanity Fair*, August 2012.

"Brian Williams: Charlie Gibson 'A Pro,' Diane Sawyer 'Legendary.'" *Huffington Post*, September 2, 2009.

Buck, Joan Juliet. "Live Mike." *Vanity Fair*, June 1994.

Bumiller, Elisabeth. "What You Don't Know About Katie Couric." *Good Housekeeping*, August 1996.

Burrough, Bryan. "Remembrance of Wings Past." *Vanity Fair*, March 2013.

Carr, David. "An Anchor Lets Down Her Hair." *New York Times*, September 14, 2008.

Carter, Bill. "ABC's Nightly News Scores a Rare Ratings Win over NBC's." *New York Times*, April 15, 2014.

———. "Big Ratings for Debut for *Katie*." Media Decoder, *New York Times*, September 11, 2012.

———. "Katie Couric Signs NBC Contract Said to Be Largest in TV News." *New York Times*, December 20, 2001.

———. "Television: Women Anchors Are on the Rise as Evening Stars." *New York Times*, August 12, 1990.

———. "The 1992 Campaign: Surprise Interview with Bush for *Today*." *New York Times*, October 14, 1992.

———. "Walters to Announce 2014 Retirement on 'The View.'" *New York Times*, May 12, 2013.

Carter, Bill, and Brian Stelter. "At ABC, an Anchor Shift; for TV, an Image Shift." *New York Times*, September 2, 2009.

Celizic, Mike. "News Anchors Differ on War Coverage." MSNBC.com, May 28, 2008.

"Christiane Amanpour on Lara Logan Assault: 'Clearly an Appalling Thing . . . I Think It's Every Woman's Nightmare.'" PiersMorgan.Blogs.CNN.com, June 21, 2011.

Cohen, Mark Francis. "Colleagues Turn Out to Mourn with Couric," Associated Press, January 30, 1998.

———. "Flack Like Me: Jamie Rubin's Ego-System." *Capital Style*, February 2000.

Conant, Jennet. "Don't Call Me Perky." *Redbook*, June 1992.

Couric, Katie. "Faculty Couple Keep Physically, Mentally Fit." *Cavalier Daily*, Fall 1997.

———. "Haiti: One Year Later." *Huffington Post*, January 12, 2011.

———. "One-on-One with Sarah Palin." CBSNews.com, September 24, 2008.

Dana, Rebecca. "Diane Sawyer Is ABC's Last Diva, Ready to Roar." *New York Observer*, November 6, 2006.

———. "The ABCs of Diane's Deal." *Daily Beast*, September 3, 2009.

DeMoraes, Lisa. "ABC News Parts Company with Katie Couric." DeadlineHollywood.com, November 22, 2013.

———. "ABC's World News Tonight; Beats 'NBC Nightly News' in News Demo, with 'Mad Men' Pitching In." DeadlineHollywood.com, April 15, 2014.

Dennis, Alicia. "Katie Couric: I Am Leaving *CBS Evening News*." *People*, April 26, 2011.

DePaulo, Lisa. "Killer Katie." *George*, May 1997.

"Diane Sawyer: Beauty in Coke-Bottle Glasses." ABCnews.com, September 8, 2006.

"Diane Sawyer Checks In with Christiane Amanpour." ABCNews.com, February 3, 2011.

"Diane Sawyer Weighs Stepping Down from ABC News." *New York Daily News*, January 29, 2013.

Dickey, Christopher. "Love and Rockets," review of *The Sand Café* by Neil MacFarquhar. *New York Times Book Review*, May 7, 2006.

DiGiacomo, Frank. "Sob Sister Diane Sawyer." *New York Observer*, May 29, 2000.

Dominus, Susan. "Hey, Katie—How's That New Job?" *Glamour*, December 2006.

DuBrow, Rick. "*Today* Sends Wake-up Call to *GMA*." *Los Angeles Times*, June 2, 1992.

Eaton, Phoebe. "Katie Couric's Primetime." *Harper's Bazaar,* February 2010.

Exley, Frederick. "If Nixon Could Possess the Soul of This Woman, Why the Hell Can't I?" *Esquire,* December 1989.

Fahri, Paul. "Katie Couric Set to Officially Join Yahoo as Global News Anchor." *Washington Post,* November 25, 2013.

Fehrman, Craig. "All the President's Memories." *New York Times,* November 4, 2010.

Fisher, Luchina. "Katie Couric: 'I Wrestled with Bulimia.'" ABCnews.com, September 24, 2013.

Flander, Judy. "The Two Faces of Katie Couric." *American Journalism Review,* May 1992.

Flint, Joe. "Relationship Between CBS and Couric Ending with a Whimper, Not a Bang." Company Town, *Los Angeles Times,* March 26, 2011.

Friedman, Jon. "Brian Williams: A Cronkite for the 21st Century." Market Watch, *Wall Street Journal,* June 2, 2010.

———. "Christiane Amanpour: 'A Reporter at Heart.'" Market Watch, *Wall Street Journal,* February 4, 2011.

Garvey, Marianne, Brian Niemietz, and Lachlan Cartwright. "Katie Couric Isn't Happy About Gossipy New Direction for *Katie,* Say Insiders." *New York Daily News,* July 2, 2013.

Gilatto, Tom. "With Deborah Norville Switched to the Mommy Track, *Today* Has Arrived for New Coanchor Katie Couric." *People,* April 22, 1991.

Gillette, Felix. "Diane Sawyer to Become Next Anchor of ABC's *World News*; Charles Gibson Retiring." *New York Observer,* September 2, 2009.

———. "MSNBC's Dan Abrams' War of Faith Against CNN," *New York Observer,* September 4, 2007.

Gold, Matea. "Katie Couric Shows Her 'Nerd' Side with YouTube Channel." *Los Angeles Times,* June 17, 2008.

———. "When Katie Met Jeff." *Los Angeles Times,* June 20, 2005.

Goldenberg, Suzanne. "'Somehow I Don't Feel It in My Gut.'" *Guardian,* December 1, 2008.

Gordon, Meryl. "Ambassador A-List." *New York,* December 27, 1999.

———. "Duel at Sunrise." *New York,* May 29, 2005.

———. "Is This Man Ready for Primetime?" *New York,* March 1997.

Green, Jesse. "When in Doubt, Seduce: Mike Nichols." *New York,* March 4, 2012.

Greene, Leonard. "Broadcast Blues: Stars of News Turn Out for Cronkite Funeral." *New York Post,* July 24, 2009.

Grover, Ronald, and Andy Fixmer. "CBS, Couric Discuss Pay Cut, Wider Role as CNN Waits." Bloomberg, December 20, 2010.

Guthrie, Marisa. "Disney Names Ben Sherwood as Anne Sweeney's Successor." HollywoodReporter.com, March 24, 2014.

Hagan, Joe. "Alas, Poor Couric, but Pity Her Not." *New York,* July 8, 2007.

———. "Charlie the Conqueror." *New York,* June 11, 2006.

Hall, Jane. "Q&A with Christiane Amanpour: On Life Near Death: In Bosnia for CNN." *Los Angeles Times,* July 14, 1993.

Heffernan, Virginia. "Barbara Walters: The Exit Interview." *New York Times,* September 5, 2004.

Heilpern, John. "Out to Lunch: Onward, Christiane." *Vanity Fair,* August 2012.

Holmes, Sally. "Mimi Gurbst Sounds Terrifying, Awesome." Daily Intelligencer, *New York,* May 17, 2010.

Holson, Laura M. "Sling and Arrows? Nothing New to Him: The Career of Ben Sherwood." *New York Times,* March 11, 2011.

"How Despairing Gibson Found 'The Passion.'" ABCNews.com, February 17, 2004.

Howard, Margo. "*60 Minutes'* Newest Correspondent, Diane Sawyer." *People,* November 5, 1984.

Huff, Richard. "Couric Breaks the News: Katie Calls It Quits as CBS Anchor." *New York Daily News,* April 27, 2011.

Johnson, Peter. "Couric's Good Mornings—And Some Bad Ones, Too." *USA Today,* May 31, 2006.

Johnson, Zach. "Katie Couric: Why I Went Public with My Bulimia." *Us Weekly,* January 22, 2013.

Junod, Tom. "Katie Couric: What I've Learned." *Esquire,* April 26, 2011.

"Katie Couric Collapses in New Cancer Tragedy." *National Enquirer,* October 26, 2001.

"Katie Couric Engaged to John Molner." *People,* September 3, 2013.

Klein, Edward. "NBC's Great Blond Hope." *Vanity Fair,* January 1990.

Kolata, Gina. "Finding a Bad Night's Sleep with Halcion." *New York Times,* January 20, 1992.

Kralev, Nicholas. "You Can't Hurry Love." *Financial Times,* October 23, 1999.

Krever, Mick. "Iran President Rouhani's English-Language Message to the American People." CNN.com, September 24, 2013.

Kurtz, Howard. "CBS Wants Contract Extension for Katie Couric." *Daily Beast,* February 9, 2011.

———. "Diane Sawyer, Anchor with an Edge." *Washington Post,* June 28, 2010.

———. "Diane Sawyer to Become ABC's Evening News Anchor, Filling Charles Gibson's Spot." *Washington Post,* September 3, 2009.

Lemonick, Michael D. "Bioterrorism: The Next Threat?" *Time,* September 24, 2001.

Lovetkin, Stephen. "Does Katie Couric's Move to Yahoo Signal the End of Old Media Dominance?" *Daily Beast,* November 26, 2013.

Lowry, Brian. "The Couric Effect: A Look Back at Katie's Impactful Year." *Variety,* July 30, 2007.

Mangan, Dan, and Dareh Gregorian. "Hasty Nanny's Mud Blitz vs. Mom—Au Pair to Stars Sued for Gossipy Letter Campaign." *New York Post,* September 22, 2005.

"Margaret Moth: Obituary." *Wichita Eagle,* March 22, 2010.

Marton, Kati. "Starting Over." *Vogue,* August 2012.

McFadden, Robert D. "Richard Holbrooke Is Dead at 69; Strong American Voice in Diplomacy and Crisis." *New York Times,* December 14, 2010.

McGrath, Charles. "Mike Nichols, Master of Invisibility." *New York Times,* April 10, 2009.

McNamara, Mary. "ABC News's Diane Sawyer Gamble Pays Off." *Los Angeles Times,* February 5, 2010.

———. "Critic's Notebook: Katie Couric's Intricate TV Dance." *Los Angeles Times,* April 14, 2011.

"Meet Katie Couric's Young New Boyfriend." *People*, April 20, 2007.

"Mel Gibson Addresses Accusations of Anti-Semitism." *Good Morning America*, ABCNews .com, October 13, 2006.

"Mel Gibson Says He Feels 'Powerless over Everything.'" *Good Morning America*, ABCNews.com, October 10, 2006.

Min, Janice. "Disney Shocker: Top Exec Anne Sweeney to Exit to Become TV Director." HollywoodReporter.com, March 11, 2014.

Monde, Chiderah. "Jennifer Aniston Slams Nudist Rumors, Disses Katie Couric: 'Is She a Legitimate Journalist?'" *New York Daily News*, August 1, 2013.

Morehouse, Macon. "Foreign Affair: Christiane Amanpour and James Rubin Find Love on the Run." *People*, March 30, 1998.

Moylan, Brian. "Katie Couric Gives Alessandra Stanley Page from Her Notebook, Tongue Lashing." Gawker, July 25, 2009.

Nagourney, Adam. "Dole Criticizes Role of Press and Foes in Tobacco Debate." *New York Times*, July 3, 1996.

Neuhaus, Cable. "Whatever Katie Wants." *AARP Magazine*, November–December 2005.

Newell, Jim. "Leave Our Katie Couric Alone!" Gawker, February 2, 2011.

Newman, Judith. "Diane Sawyer." *Ladies' Home Journal*, February 2004.

O'Neill, Joseph. "Roth v. Roth v. Roth." *Atlantic*, April 2012.

Orth, Maureen. "The Jackson Jive." *Vanity Fair*, September 1995.

Peyser, Marc, and Jonnie L. Roberts. "Katie's News: Will She Shine at Night . . . And Who Will Watch?" *Newsweek*, April 17, 2006.

Poggi, Jeanine. "*Katie* Couldn't Last but Viewers Still Love Daytime TV." *Ad Age*, December 20, 2013.

Powell, Joanna. "Katie's Haven." *Good Housekeeping*, September 1999.

Ravitz, Jessica. "Fearless to the End: Remembering Margaret Moth." CNN.com, March 21, 2010.

Rich, Frank. "Journal: The Perils of Diane." *New York Times*, February 24, 1994.

Roberts, Roxanne. "Yipes! It's Katie Couric! Don't Call Her Cute or Perky. Just Call Her *Today*'s Hope for Tomorrow." *Washington Post*, May 21, 1991.

Rohde, David. "Jay Monahan Is Dead at 42; Covered Law for NBC News." *New York Times*, January 26, 1998.

Rovzar, Chris. "Diane Sawyer to Replace Charlie Gibson in January." Daily Intelligencer, *New York*, September 2, 2009.

Rush, George, and Joanna Molloy. "Profile in Couric: Bashed but Unbowed." *New York Daily News*, August 1, 2005.

Salvatore, Diane. "Robin Roberts and Diane Sawyer: Soul Sisters." *Ladies' Home Journal*, August 2008.

Schawbel, Dan. "Katie Couric: Women at Work, Social Media, and Her Best Career Advice." *Forbes*, May 8, 2013.

Schneider, Karen S. "Top of the Morning: Fighting to Stay in TV's Breakfast Club, *Today*'s $65 Million Woman, Katie Couric, Still Finds Time for Her Girls, Her Beau—and Good Bargains." *People*, January 14, 2001.

Sessums, Kevin. "Diane Sawyer on President Nixon." *Parade*, February 25, 2010.

Shafer, Jack. "Reassessing Miller: U.S. Intelligence on Iraq's WMD Deserves a

Second Look. So Does the Reporting of the *New York Times*'s Judith Miller." *Slate*, March 2003.

———. "Unsolicited Advice for Diane Sawyer: Why She Should Reject the *ABC World News* Anchor Slot." *Slate*, September 3, 2009.

Shales, Tom. "Tom Shales Reviews Christiane Amanpour's Lackluster Debut on ABC's *This Week*." *Washington Post*, August 2, 2010.

———. "Top of the Morning, Katie!" *Washington Post*, September 10, 1991.

Smith, Austin. "Cold Seat at *This Week*." Page Six, *New York Post*, December 9, 2011.

———. "Couric's ABC Future Is Hazy." Page Six, *New York Post*, June 9, 2013.

———. "Katie's Finale." Page Six, *New York Post*, May 22, 2011.

Smolowe, Jill. "Gone Too Soon: Four Years After Losing Her Husband to Cancer, Katie Couric Mourns Her Sister Emily." *People*, November 5, 2001.

"Staff at ABC News' DC Bureau Is Icy to 'Cold' Christiane Amanpour." Page Six, *New York Post*, October 24, 2010.

Stanley, Alessandra. "A New Anchor Steps In, Skipping Frills and Drama." *New York Times*, June 7, 2011.

———. "A TV Host Challenges a Guest. That's News." *New York Times*, August 1, 2010.

———. "Good Evening, America: Where Katie Couric Had to Put Perky in the Past, Diane Sawyer, Coolly Regal, Is a Born Anchor, Albeit in an Ever Evaporating Sea." *New York Times*, September 6, 2009.

———. "In Barbara Walters' Highlight Reel, TV's Rise and Fade." *New York Times*, May 13, 2013.

———. "In Iraq, Couric Hones Her Hard-News Image." *New York Times*, September 5, 2007.

———. "The TV Watch: Quiet Departure Is Stark Contrast to Heralded Arrival." *New York Times*, May 19, 2011.

———. "*Today* Seeks Yesterday's Glory." *New York Times*, April 25, 2005.

Starr, Michael. "A Great News Day at Last for Sawyer: Gets ABC Anchor as Gibson Quits." *New York Post*, September 3, 2009.

Stasi, Linda. "She Overcame Taint of Nixon to Rise to Top." *New York Post*, September 3, 2009.

"Staying Strong in the Face of Tragedy." ABCNews.com, March 14, 2011.

Steinberg, Jacques. "Couric Rebounds with Web and Palin." *New York Times*, October 11, 2008.

———. "Sawyer Signals Commitment to Morning Show." *New York Times*, January 3, 2007.

Stelter, Brian. "ABC News Dethrones NBC in Crucial Ratings Race." *New York Times*, July 30, 2013.

———. "Amanpour to Leave ABC's *This Week* and Rejoin CNN." Media Decoder, *New York Times*, December 13, 2011.

———. "Doubts Fade and Couric Is Energized." *New York Times*, September 20, 2009.

"Taliban Briefly Detains EU Commissioner, 18 Others." CNN Interactive World News, September 29, 1997.

Traister, Rebecca. "Katie Couric: Reports of Her Demise Were Greatly Exaggerated." *Elle*, March 19, 2009.

Valente, Danielle. "Kim Kardashian, Katie Couric Dispute Fueled by Magazine Interview, Hashtags." *Newsday*, August 19, 2013.

Vamburkar, Meenal. "ABC News Refutes Report That Diane Sawyer 'Seriously Considering' Retiring in 2013." *Mediaite*, January 29, 2013.

Venezia, Todd. "Gibson Furious Sawyer Taking Over." *New York Post*, September 4, 2009.

"Was She Celebrating Early? Twitter A-Buzz That ABC News Anchor Diane Sawyer Was 'Drunk' During Network's Election Coverage." Associated Press, November 7, 2012.

Weber, Bruce. "Home with Katie Couric: A Morning Cup of Regular." *New York Times*, April 9, 1992.

Weller, Sheila. "My Faith Is My Rock," interview with Robin Roberts. *Good Housekeeping*, June 2012.

Wilson, Rita. "Christiane Amanpour's Headline Style." *Harper's Bazaar*, August 2009.

————. "Diane Sawyer: Truth and Beauty." *Harper's Bazaar*, March 12, 2013.

Win, Hanna Ingber. "Christiane Amanpour on Her Genocide Documentary, International Reporting and New Media." *Huffington Post*, December 4, 2008.

Winfrey, Oprah. "Oprah Talks to Christiane Amanpour." *O, The Oprah Magazine*, September 2005.

Woodruff, Lee. "The Latest News on Diane Sawyer." *Ladies' Home Journal*, January 8, 2014.

Wyatt, Edward. "Katherine Anne Couric: Coming Back to Hard News." *New York Times*, April 6, 2006.

"Yushchenko: Live and Carry On. Yushchenko Tells His Incredible Story to CNN's Christiane Amanpour." CBS.com, February 11, 2009.

Zakaria, Fareed. "Palin Is Ready? Please." *Newsweek*, September 28, 2008.

Zoglin, Richard. "Star Power: Diane Sawyer." *Time*, August 7, 1989.

Zoglin, Richard, and William Tynan. "Good Morning, Diane." *Time*, January 18, 1999.

OTHER ONLINE SOURCES

Amanpour, Christiane, "Find the Thing That Ignites Your Passion, Engages Your Mind and Dare to Lead." California Women's Conference 2008 Web site, October 2008.

Amanpour, Christiane, and Ed Bradley. "2000 Murrow Awards Ceremony Acceptance Speech." Radio Television Digital News Association, RTDNA.org, September 13, 2000.

Andreeva, Nellie. "Yahoo Announces Deal with Katie Couric." DeadlineHollywood.com, November 25, 2013.

Ariens, Chris. "Gibson Retires, Sawyer to *World News*: Diane's Statement." TVNewser, Mediabistro.com, September 2, 2009.

————. "Here's the Katie Couric We Haven't Seen in a While." TVNewser, Mediabistro .com, January 24, 2013.

"Christiane Amanpour's Address to University of Michigan Spring Commencement." University of Michigan News Service, April 29, 2006, Bentley.UMich.edu.

Coffee, Patrick. "Katie Couric Scores Manti Te'o Interview (They Share a Publicist, BTW)." PRNewser.com, January 24, 2013.

Ephron, Nora. "Nora Ephron's Commencement Address to Wellesley Class of 1996." *Huffington Post*, June 26, 2012.

Feinberg v. Poznek. Justia US Supreme Court Center, Supreme.Justia.com, July 2006.

Finke, Nikki. "Update: More Diane Does Mel." Deadline.com, October 10, 2006.

"Fitzgerald: A Tribute to Christiane Amanpour," anonymous anti-Amanpour rebuttal. JihadWatch.org, January 19, 2007.

Gibson, Charlie. "Charlie Gibson's Announcement E-mail: 'I Love This Department to the Depths of My Soul.'" *Huffington Post*, September 2, 2009.

Gloria Steinem. GloriaSteinem.com.

Hilton, Perez. "Katie Couric's 'Dreadfully Boring' Show Is a 'Disaster!' ABC Desperate to Replace Her." PerezHilton.com, June 5, 2013.

Jay Monahan Center for Gastrointestinal Health, MonahanCenter.org.

Kennedy, Lesley. "Katie Couric Admits to Bulimia Struggles." More.com.

"Keynote Speaker, Christiane Amanpour: International Center for Journalists Awards Dinner." International Center for Journalists, November 12, 2008, ICFJ.org.

Morabito, Andrea. "New CBS News Chair: 'I Don't Know Whether' Couric Wants to Stay." BroadcastingCable.com, February 8, 2011.

National Colorectal Cancer Research Alliance, Entertainment Industry Foundation, EIFoundation.org.

Numerous blog posts by and biographies about Frank Gannon, NixonLibrary.gov.

Piers Morgan Tonight: "Interview with Christiane Amanpour," June 22, 2011. Transcript.

Stableford, Dylan. "Tenacious D: Why Diane Sawyer Deserves Anchor Slot." Mediabistro .com, September 16, 2009.

Stelter, Brian. "*Today*'s Tom Touchet Is Fired." TVNewser, Mediabistro.com, April 19, 2005.

"Still Dreaming Big: Diane Sawyer Answers Questions About Dreams, Faith and Advice." Guideposts.com, February 17, 2006.

Tresca, Amber J. "Colorectal Screening Gets 'The Katie Couric Effect' as Popular Morning Show Host Gets a Colonoscopy On Air." About.com, November 22, 2012.

Tyndall, Andrew. "Year in Review: 2013: *ABC News* Is Certifiably Disneyfied." TyndallReport.com.

Weprin, Alex. "Andrew Tyndall on Diane Sawyer and the Chilean Miners." Mediabistro .com, October 17, 2010.

———. "Katie Couric: 'Some Said I Lacked "Gravitas," Which I've Since Decided Is Latin for "Testicles."'" TVNewser, Mediabistro.com, May 21, 2012.

White, Deborah. "Profile of Christiane Amanpour, CNN International Correspondent." About.com.

Wilmouth, Brad. "MSNBC's Abrams Hits CNN's Amanpour for Defending Islamic Fundamentalism." NewsBusters.com, August 28, 2007.

BOOKS

Anson, Robert Sam. *Exile: The Unquiet Oblivion of Richard M. Nixon*. New York: Simon & Schuster, 1984.

Auletta, Ken. *Three Blind Mice: How the TV Networks Lost Their Way*. New York: Random House, 1991.

Brinkley, Douglas. *Cronkite*. New York: HarperCollins, 2012.

Couric, Katie, ed. *The Best Advice I Ever Got: Lessons from Extraordinary Lives*. New York: Random House, 2011.

Dean, John. *Blind Ambition.* New York: Simon & Schuster, 1976.

Editors of *Life* magazine, with an introduction by Katie Couric. *Life with Mother.* New York: Little, Brown, 1995.

Fellow, Anthony. *American Media History.* Stamford, CT: Cengage Learning, 2009.

Fensch, Thomas. *Television News Anchors: An Anthology of Profiles of Major Figures and Issues in United States Network Reporting.* Woodlands, TX: New Century Books, 2002.

Gutgold, Nichola D. *Seen and Heard: The Women of Television News.* Plymouth, UK: Lexington Books, 2008.

Haag, Christina. *Come to the Edge: A Memoir.* New York: Spiegel & Grau, 2011.

Hosley, David H., and Gayle K. Yamada. *Hard News: Women in Broadcast Journalism.* Westport, CT: Praeger, 1987.

Leamer, Laurence. *Sons of Camelot.* New York: William Morrow, 2004.

Littell, Robert T. *The Men We Became: My Friendship with John F. Kennedy, Jr.* New York: St. Martin's, 2004.

MacFarquhar, Neil. *The Sand Café: A Novel.* New York: Perseus, 2006.

Marlane, Judith. *Women in Television News Revisited.* Austin: University of Texas Press, 1999.

Marton, Kati. *Paris: A Love Story.* New York: Simon & Schuster, 2012.

Nixon, Richard. *RN: The Memoirs of Richard Nixon.* New York: Grosset & Dunlap, 1978.

Povich, Lynn. *The Good Girls Revolt: How the Women of Newsweek Sued Their Bosses and Changed the Workplace.* New York: PublicAffairs, 2012.

Walters, Barbara. *Audition: A Memoir.* New York: Knopf, 2008.

PERSONAL E-MAILS AND PRIVATE CORRESPONDENCE

Amanpour, Christiane. "To My Family at CNN." E-mail to CNN staff, March 23, 2012.

Sawyer, Diane. "Thanks." E-mail to ABC TV staff, April 17, 2013.

PRESS RELEASES

Numerous press releases from ABC, CBS, NBC, CNN, and other news organizations, including biographies of Diane, Katie, Christiane, and numerous producers and executives.

"UM Study: Katie Couric's Colonoscopy Caused Cross-country Climb in Colon Cancer Checks," University of Michigan, Ann Arbor, July 14, 2013.

TV BROADCASTS, TRANSCRIPTS, AND YOUTUBE CLIPS

"1994—Amanpour Questions Bill Clinton." YouTube, posted by F Fan, April 5, 2012.

"A Tribute to JFK Jr. on the Second Anniversary of His Death," interview with Christiane Amanpour, including transcript from July 15, 1999. *Larry King Weekend*, CNN.com, July 15, 2002. Transcript.

Amanpour, Christiane. "Amanpour: World Fails to Save Africa's AIDS Orphans." CNN. Transcript.

Amanpour, Christiane, and Ed Bradley. "The Best of Intentions: UNICEF and the Government of Bangladesh Put in New Pumps and Wells for the People So They Would

Amanpour, Christiane, and Mike Wallace. "A Million Men, Women and Children: Rwandan Courts Try to Deal with the After-Effects of Genocide." *60 Minutes*, CBS News. Transcript.

———. "For Love and Money: Breaking the Silence That Surrounds Dowry in India." *60 Minutes*, CBS News, October 5, 2003. Transcript.

———. "The Women of Afghanistan: A Look at Changes in the Way Women Are Treated in Post-Taliban Afghanistan." *60 Minutes*, CBS News, October 20, 2002. Transcript.

———. "Weapons of Mass Destruction: Russia's Storehouse of Deadly Biological Weapons." *60 Minutes*, CBS News, May 11, 2003. Transcript.

Amanpour, Christiane, and Morley Safer. "Scars of War: Helping the Child Soldiers of Sierra Leone." *60 Minutes*, CBS News, May 19, 2002. Transcript.

———. "Thou Shalt Not Kill: Children in Uganda Kidnapped by Rebel Forces and Made to Fight and Kill or Face Execution Themselves." *60 Minutes*, CBS News, March 22, 1998. Transcript.

Amanpour, Christiane, and Steve Kroft. "Sleeping Sickness: Dr. Mickey Richer Helps Africans with Fatal Sleeping Sickness for Which Pharmaceutical Companies Have Stopped Making a Cure." *60 Minutes*, CBS News, February 11, 2001. Transcript.

———. "Sunni Triangle: Challenges Facing U.S. Soldiers in Iraq's Sunni Triangle." *60 Minutes*, CBS News, February 8, 2004. Transcript.

———. "Trokosi: Young Girls Sent into Slavery Because of Past Crimes Committed by Family Members Years Ago." *60 Minutes*, CBS News, November 30, 1997. Transcript.

"Billion-Dollar Business: Poverty-Stricken Eastern Europe Making Billions of Dollars by Transporting Women to Work in Western Cities in the Sex Trade." *60 Minutes*, CBS News, June 3, 2001. Transcript.

"Christiane Amanpour: My First Big Break." YouTube, posted by Mediabistro, January 2, 2013. Transcript.

"Columbine Interview: NBC_630." KatieCouric.com, April 22, 1999.

Couric, Katie. "Ahmadinejad: The Status Quo Cannot Keep." *CBS Evening News*, September 23, 2009. Transcript.

———. "Exclusive: John and Elizabeth Edwards Open Up About Cancer, Unconditional About Couple's Decision on Presidential Run," *60 Minutes*, CBS News, March 24, 2007. YouTube and transcript.

———. Interviews with Sarah Palin and John McCain. CBSNews.com. Transcripts.

———. "My Speech to Princeton's Class of 2009." KatieCouric.com, July 31, 2009.

———. "Sharon and Lexie Love and the Dating Violence Epidemic." KatieCouric.com, September 20, 2012.

"Good Morning America, ABC Sept. 11, 2011 8 31 am—9 12 am." YouTube, posted by bydesign001, September 11, 2012. Transcript by Sheila Weller.

"Katie: Talk That Matters." KatieCouric.com.

"Katie Couric Talks About Her New Book, Her New Look, and Life After Tragedy." *Larry King Live*, CNN, December 18, 2000. Transcript.

"Lara Logan Breaks Her Silence." *60 Minutes*, CBS News, May 1, 2011.

Sawyer, Diane, with David Muir. "Video Witnesses Claim Miracle Man Saved Car Crash Victim." ABCNews.com, August 9, 2013.

―――. "Young Guns: A Diane Sawyer Special." *20/20*, ABC.com, January 31, 2014. Video and transcript.

"Today—Katie's 1st Show (4/5/91)." YouTube, posted by NoWayJose90210, July 13, 2012.

"TODAY Katie Couric's Last Show." YouTube, posted by Justin Anderson, November 11, 2013.

"*Today*—September 11, 2001 First 15 Minutes. (7am-7:17am)." YouTube, posted by SuperUnBoxDude, September 11, 2011. Transcript by Sheila Weller.

"Whitney Houston and Diane Sawyer." *Primetime*, December 4, 2002. YouTube clip.

YouTube clip and transcript of Christiane Amanpour, Charles Blow, Christopher Dickey, and Andrew Sullivan on *Anderson Cooper 360*, CNN, September 12, 2013.

YouTube clips of Mel Gibson talking to Diane Sawyer on *Good Morning America* and *Primetime*, 2004 and 2006.

OTHER SOURCES

Author's notes on and tape recordings of the three newscasters' various newscasts over the course of researching and writing this book.

Blue Notes of Wellesley College, *You Ain't Been Blue*. Record album, privately produced, 1966.

"Diane Sawyer." Museum of Broadcast Communications, Chicago.

Rust, David. "Encrypted Diaries of David Rust, Sarajevo, 1992–1993." Provided by David Rust to author.

Web- and otherwise-accessed brief biographies of figures in news, politics, business, communications, and private life.

Yearbook, 1977. New Hall Convent of the Holy Sepulchre. Provided to author.

INDEX

PHOTOGRAPH CREDITS

2/4/15